JOHN CHRYSOSTOM,
HOMILIES ON COLOSSIANS

WRITINGS FROM THE GRECO-ROMAN WORLD

JOHN CHRYSOSTOM, *HOMILIES ON COLOSSIANS*

Introduced, translated, and annotated by

Pauline Allen

For Michael Lattke and Irmtraud Petersson
True readers
True scholars
True friends

Contents

Acknowledgments

I am indebted to Dr. Kosta Simić, Australian Catholic University (Brisbane), for careful work in the preparation of this volume and for keying in Field's text with commendable exactitude. In addition, I am grateful to Professor John T. Fitzgerald, University of Notre Dame (Indiana) and North-West University (Potchefstroom), for his attentive reading of the manuscript and his valuable suggestions for improvement, based on his expertise in the Pauline letters. Grateful thanks are due to Bob Buller, Director of SBL Press, for pairing the Greek and English texts and for managing the production of the volume.

Brisbane, September 2020

Abbreviations

ACT	Ancient Christian Texts
AK	Arbeiten zur Kirchengeschichte
AKT	Arbeiten zur Kirchen- und Theologiegeschichte
b.	born
BBOM	Birmingham Byzantine and Ottoman Monographs
BETL	Bibiotheca Ephemeridum Theologicarum Lovanensium
BHSTF	Bibliotheca Herder: Sección de teologia y filosofía
BK	Bibliothek der Kirchenväter
BSGRT	Bibliotheca Scriptorum Graecorum et Romanorum Teubneriana
ca.	circa (about)
CAEC	Critical Approaches to Early Christianity
CEC	Collection d'Études classiques
CPG	Geerard, Maurits, ed. *Clavis Patrum Graecorum*. 5 vols. Turnhout: Brepols, 1974–1987.
CPL	Dekkers, Eligius, ed. *Clavis Patrum Latinorum*. 3rd ed. Steenbrugge: Petri, 1995.
CSCP	Cornell Studies in Classical Philology
CSEL	Corpus Scriptorum Ecclesiasticorum Latinorum
CurMus	*Current Musicology*
d.	died
ECF	Early Church Fathers
Field	Field, Frederick, ed. *Ioannis Chrysostomi interpretatio omnium epistularum Paulinarum*. 7 vols. Oxford: Parker, 1854–1862.
GBS	Guides to Biblical Scholarship
GCRW	Greek Culture in the Roman World
GR	*Greece and Rome*
Hist.	Herodotus, *Historiae*
Hom. 1 Cor.	John Chrysostom, *Homiliae in epistulam i ad Corinthios*

Hom. Col.	John Chrysostom, *Homiliae in epistulam ad Colossenses*
Hom. Eph.	John Chrysostom, *Homiliae in epistulam ad Ephesios*
Hom. Phil.	John Chrysostom, *Homiliae in epistulam ad Philippenses*
JECS	*Journal of Early Christian Studies*
JSH	*Journal of Sport History*
KTAH	Key Themes in Ancient History
LAHR	Late Antique History and Religion
LXX	Septuagint
*NPNF*¹	Schaff, Philip, and Henry Wace, eds. *A Select Library of Nicene and Post-Nicene Fathers of the Christian Church.* Series 1. 14 vols. Grand Rapids: Eerdmans, 1978–1979.
NT	New Testament
NTAbh	Neutestamentliche Abhandlungen
OCD	Hornblower, Simon, and Antony Spawforth, eds. *Oxford Classical Dictionary.* 3rd ed. Oxford: Oxford University Press, 1996.
OCP	*Orientalia Christiana Periodica*
OCT	Oxford Classical Texts
OECS	Oxford Early Christian Studies
OrChrAn	Orientalia Christiana Analecta
OT	Old Testament
OTRM	Oxford Theology & Religion Monographs
par(s).	parallel(s)
Per.	Plutarch, *Pericles*
PG	Migne, Jacques-Paul, ed. Patrologia graeca. 161 vols. Paris: Migne: 1857–1886.
PGL	Lampe, Geoffrey W. H., ed. *Patristic Greek Lexicon.* Oxford: Clarendon, 1968
PL	Migne, Jacques-Paul, ed. Patrologia Latina. 217 vols. Paris, 1844–1855.
REByz	*Revue des études byzantines*
sc.	*scilicet*, it is permitted to know
SC	Sources chrétiennes
Sir	Sirach or Ecclesiasticus
STAC	Studien und Texte zu Antike und Christentum
s.v.	*sub verbo*, under the word
TCH	The Transformation of the Classical Heritage
ThH	Théologie historique
TL/CSCP	Townsend Lectures/Cornell Studies in Classical Philology

TS	Texts and Studies
UCPCS	University of California Publications in Classical Studies
VC	*Vigiliae Christianae*
Vit. phil.	Diogenes Laertius, *Vitae philosophorum*
WGRW	Writings from the Greco-Roman World
WUNT	Wissenschaftliche Untersuchungen zum Neuen Testament

Introduction

Questions of Dating and Provenance

A native of Syrian Antioch, John Chrysostom received the standard education reserved at this time for young men of some status and probably frequented the lectures of the Sophist Libanius before his baptism.[1] Although he was ordained lector by Bishop Meletius of Antioch in 371, John opted for the ascetic life on the outskirts of Antioch until ill health forced him to return to the city.[2] He was ordained deacon in 381 and priest in 386 (an office he held for twelve years under the episcopate of Meletius's successor, Flavian).[3] During this time John became known for his eloquent preaching (hence his sobriquet *Chrysostom*, or "Golden Mouth"), to the extent that he came to the attention of the imperial court and was chosen as

---

1. Standard works on Chrysostom are Chrysostomus Bauer, *John Chrysostom and His Time*, 2 vols., trans. M. Gonzaga (Westminster, MD: Newman, 1959–1960); Bauer, *Johannes Chrysostomus und seine Zeit*, 2 vols. (Munich: Hueber, 1929–1930); John N. D. Kelly, *Golden Mouth: The Story of John Chrysostom—Ascetic, Preacher, Bishop* (London: Duckworth, 1995); Wendy Mayer and Pauline Allen, *John Chrysostom*, ECF (London: Routledge, 2000). Newer to the field are Wendy Mayer, *The Homilies of St John Chrysostom—Provenance: Reshaping the Foundations*, OrChrAn 273 (Rome: Pontificio Istituto Orientale, 2005); Mayer and Pauline Allen, *The Churches of Syrian Antioch (300–638 CE)*, LAHR (Leuven: Peeters, 2012); Chris L. de Wet, *Preaching Bondage: John Chrysostom and the Discourse of Slavery in Early Christianity* (Oakland: University of California Press, 2015); Wendy Mayer and Pauline Allen, "John Chrysostom," in *The Early Christian World*, 2nd ed., ed. Philip F. Esler (London: Routledge, 2017), 1054–71 (a summary of trends in recent scholarship on Chrysostom); Chris L. de Wet and Wendy Mayer, eds., *Revisioning John Chrysostom: New Approaches, New Perspectives*, CAEC 1 (Leiden: Brill, 2019).
2. On John's ascetic phase, see Kelly, *Golden Mouth*, 14–35; in detail, Martin Illert, *Johannes Chrysostomus und das antiochenisch-syrische Mönchtum: Studien zu Theologie, Rhetorik und Kirchenpolitik im antiochenischen Schrifttum des Johannes Chrysostomus* (Zürich: Pano, 2000).
3. On this period in John's life, see Kelly, *Golden Mouth*, 36–82.

bishop of Constantinople, being consecrated there on February 26, 398.[4] In the capital John preached forcefully against social abuses, such as those of wealth and ostentation, which are vilified also in the homilies to the Colossians, and in favor of the proper observance of the Scriptures, activities that earned him many powerful enemies. As a result, he was deposed by a synod (the so-called Synod of the Oak) in 403[5] but subsequently was allowed to resume his post. However, after riots instigated by his enemies broke out in the following year, John was exiled to Cucusus in Armenia,[6] where he remained for three years before the order came to transfer him to the east coast of the Black Sea. He died en route on September 14, 407. It was not until January 27, 438, that his remains were ceremoniously returned to Constantinople and buried in the Church of the Holy Apostles.[7]

Chrysostom was a highly productive preacher and writer. Apart from his seventy-six homilies on Genesis, an incomplete set on the Psalms, and homilies on several Old Testament themes, there are ninety homilies on Matthew's Gospel, eighty-eight on John's, fifty-five on Acts, and treatments of Romans, Corinthians, Galatians, Ephesians, Philippians, Colossians, Thessalonians, Timothy, Titus, Philemon, and Hebrews. In addition, there are catechetical homilies and homilies on feast days, martyrs' festivals, ethical issues, and occasional themes, as well as treatises on various topics. Over 240 letters survive from his years in exile. Chrysostom's admiration for the apostle Paul is evident from the seven homilies he composed in Paul's honor.[8]

Modern scholarship reckons that Colossians and Ephesians are a development of Paul's legacy by later disciples, and thus Chrysostom's chronology of the Pauline writing in *Homily* 1 is misleading.[9] Hans-Josef Klauck, for example, maintains that the structure of the Pauline text was borrowed

---

4. See Kelly for details of John's elevation and subsequent episcopal ministry in Constantinople (*Golden Mouth*, 104–44).

5. On this synod, see Kelly, *Golden Mouth*, 211–27.

6. Kelly deals with this exile and Chrysostom's correspondence during it (*Golden Mouth*, 259–85).

7. See Kelly on this triumphal return of the relics (*Golden Mouth*, 286–90).

8. *Laudes Pauli* 1–7. See André Piédagnel, ed., *Panégyriques de saint Paul*, SC 300 (Paris: Cerf, 1982); English translation by Margaret M. Mitchell, *The Heavenly Trumpet: John Chrysostom and the Art of Pauline Interpretation* (Louisville: Westminster John Knox, 2002), 440–87.

9. Chrysostom gives a detailed chronology of Paul's letters as he perceived it in *Argumentum epistulae ad Romanos* (CPG 4427): Field, 1:1–6.

from older Pauline letters and probably not written by the apostle or even his secretary.[10]

Chrysostom's surviving homilies on Colossians number twelve.[11] Their dating and provenance have been examined by Wendy Mayer and Pauline Allen,[12] whose findings will be summarized here. The first point to be made is that the many series of Chrysostom's homilies, exegetical and otherwise, must be treated with suspicion with regard to their homogeneity, which means that it is difficult to assign a particular series either to Antioch during John's presbyterate or to Constantinople during his patriarchate. One of the scholarly arguments used in favor of a Constantinopolitan provenance of two homilies on Colossians has been the evidence of so-called episcopal tone, which has been perceived in *Homilies* 7 and 8, the first homily lambasting women's luxurious lifestyles and the second attacking those who have recourse to pagan practices to cure sick children.[13] Allen and Mayer argue that the preacher's apparent authoritarian tone in banning individuals from the church or communal prayer was caused by the belief of Chrysostom and his contemporaries that such statements were the prerogative of both clergy *and* bishops, and that consequently one should not assume that John preached these two homilies while bishop in the eastern capital.[14]

---

10. Hans-Josef Klauck, with the collaboration of Daniel P. Bailey, *Ancient Letters and the New Testament: A Guide to Context and Exegesis* (Waco: Baylor University Press, 2006), 321. Ian J. Elmer asserts that according to recent scholarship both Ephesians and Colossians were developments by later disciples and perhaps originated in Rome (see lit.). See Elmer, "The Pauline Letters as Community Documents," in *Collecting Early Christian Letters: From the Apostle Paul to Late Antiquity*, ed. Bronwen Neil and Pauline Allen (Cambridge: Cambridge University Press, 2015), 41–42, 46. Both these views were earlier advocated by William G. Doty, *Letters in Primitive Christianity*, GBS (Philadelphia: Fortress, 1973).

11.See Field, 5:172–312 (text), 531–54 (notes).

12. Pauline Allen and Wendy Mayer, "Chrysostom and the Preaching of Homilies in Series: A New Approach to the Twelve Homilies *In epistulam ad Colossenses* (CPG 4433)," *OCP* 60 (1994): 21–39. This was followed the next year by the article "Chrysostom and the Preaching of Homilies in Series: A Re-examination of the Fifteen Homilies *In epistulam ad Philippenses* (CPG 4432)," *VC* 49 (1995): 270–89.

13. See, e.g., Max von Bonsdorff, "Zur Predigtätigkeit des Johannes Chrysostomus, biographisch-chronologische Studien über seine Homilienserien zu neutestamentlichen Büchern" (diss., Helsinki, 1922), 82–83.

14. Allen and Mayer, "Chrysostom and the Preaching of Homilies in Series: A New Approach," 26.

Another argument advanced in favor of the homogeneity of the homilies on Colossians also involves *Homily 7*, in there is find a demonstration of the instability and dangers of high office that many scholars see as a reference to the demise of the powerful eunuch Eutropius in the imperial court, therefore indicating a Constantinopolitan provenance for the homily. However, there are instances in Antioch too of highly placed administrative officials being dismissed that could also serve as exempla for the Antiochene presbyter in his preaching.[15]

On the other hand, in *Homily 3* there is clear proof of Chrysostom's status when he delivered this homily, because he speaks on more than on one occasion of himself as bishop, which ties this homily to Constantinople, and since on internal evidence *Homily 2* is connected with *Homily 3*, one must assume that these two homilies were not delivered in Antioch.[16] As a consequence of these findings, one has to treat these homilies on Colossians as an artificial series, delivered in at least two different locations. In the discussion of the pericopes transmitted in the manuscripts, this lack of homogeneity will become even clearer.

Once the provenance of this so-called series on Colossians is called into doubt, it follows that the dates of Chrysostom's various homilies on Paul's letter to the inhabitants of Colossae that are transmitted to us will also be dubious. If one accepts that *Homilies 2* and *3* belong to Constantinople, then they can be dated to between Chrysostom's accession to the patriarchal throne in that city in 398 and his exile in 404. With regard to *Homilies 7* and *8*, which according to our calculations are similarly paired, one could posit that *Homily 7* was delivered in Antioch sometime between January 17, 395, and October 397, and presumably *Homily 8* not long before.[17] The rest of these homilies cannot be dated with any certainty, something that applies also to other so-called series and individual homilies in the Chrysostomic corpus.[18]

To substantiate the doubt regarding the homogeneity of the series, a consideration of the pericopes that are transmitted in the manuscripts

---

15. Allen and Mayer, "Chrysostom and the Preaching of Homilies in Series: A New Approach," 32–34.

16. See Allen and Mayer, "Chrysostom and the Preaching of Homilies in Series: A New Approach," 36–37.

17. See Allen and Mayer, "Chrysostom and the Preaching of Homilies in Series: A New Approach," 35.

18. Discussed in detail in Mayer, *Homilies of St John Chrysostom—Provenance*.

at the beginning of each homily will be helpful. Whereas in the homilies on Philippians it is clear that the exegesis did not cover Paul's letter in its entirety, does not always flow sequentially, and contains overlaps in the treatment of the text,[19] the case of the pericopes given at the beginning of each homily on Colossians is different. In only four homilies, 4, 9, 10, and 11, does the exegesis conform to the stated verses. In *Homily 3*, for example, where Col 1:15–18 is purportedly the subject of the preaching, there is no exegesis of verses 16–17, and the discussion of verse 15 is found in *Homily* 2. Again, while the pericope for *Homily* 5 is given as Col 1:16–28, 2:1 and 2:4–5 are treated. These examples demonstrate that what we have in Chrysostom's homilies on Colossians is far from a seamless exegesis, in itself an argument against the homogeneity of the series, and that we need to be on our guard about the accuracy of the stated pericopes as they have come down to us in the manuscript tradition. It is only fair to point out that this deconstructionist approach to series in Chrysostom's corpus has been challenged by Guillaume Bady on the grounds that the manuscript tradition of homilies (such as those on Colossians) needs to be respected.[20]

OTHER CONSIDERATIONS ABOUT THE *HOMILIES ON COLOSSIANS*

There are five major considerations to take into account in assessing John Chrysostom's homilies on Colossians, namely, his representations of Hellenes, Jews, angels/angel worship, servants/slaves, and children in his preaching.

In this volume the words *pagan* and *Greek* have been avoided in favor of the appellation *Hellenes*, although it must be admitted that none of these terms is totally satisfactory in describing the people whom Chrysostom has in his sights in the homilies on Colossians or elsewhere in his

---

19. See John Chrysostom, *John Chrysostom, Homilies on Paul's Letter to the Philippians*, trans. Pauline Allen, WGRW 16 (Atlanta: Society of Biblical Literature, 2013), xiii–xiv.

20. Guillaume Bady, "La tradition des œuvres de Jean Chrysostome, entre transmission et transformation," *REByz* 68 (2010): 149–63. For Bady's argument, see in more detail Allen, *John Chrysostom, Homilies on Paul's Letter to the Philippians*, xiv–xv. More recently, James Daniel Cook has argued for the integrity of Chrysostom's series on the basis of the use of *lectio continua*, or sequential pericopes, in the text, an argument that is not supported by the present study of the *Homilies on Colossians*. See Cook, *Preaching and Popular Christianity: Reading the Sermons of John Chrysostom*, OTRM (Oxford: Oxford University Press, 2019), esp. 201–10.

works. Isabella Sandwell expresses a preference for the term *Greek* over *pagan*,[21] although, one may note, this is not without its difficulties either, particularly since, according to Raffaella Cribiore, Libanius's *Hellenism*, for example, does not have the same belligerent character as that of the emperor Julian.[22] Another objection is that non-Christians, for instance in Gaul or Italy, cannot be properly designated as Hellenes. The late Robert Markus has already pointed out that "the image of society neatly divided into 'Christian' and 'pagan' is the creation of late fourth-century Christians, and has been too readily taken at face-value by modern historians."[23] This is not to say, however, that Chrysostom's apparent vitriol against Hellenes/pagans was not a useful rhetorical device that he hoped would influence his audiences to stay closer to the Christian path.

Much the same strategy can be observed in Chrysostom's portrayal of Jews in his homilies on Colossians. As Isabella Sandwell reminds us:

> Neither Christian nor Greek nor Jewish identity existed essentially or objectively in Chrysostom's world. Rather, Chrysostom continually had to construct them out of a situation where many practices were shared by people whatever their religious allegiance.[24]

At this stage the late Roman Empire was still pluralistic, and it must not be forgotten that Jews had assisted in the colonization of Antioch toward the end of the third century BCE and were still a prominent part of the Antiochene community in Chrysostom's time, a part that he viewed as a rival to Christianity as Jewish cults grew and Christians were attracted to them.[25]

Chrysostom's *Homilies on Colossians* betray a preoccupation with angels and angel worship that is explained by the persistence of these beliefs in and around Colossae, where the people were heirs to a syncre-

---

21. Isabella Sandwell, *Religious Identity in Late Antiquity: Greeks, Jews and Christians in Antioch*, GRCRW (Cambridge: Cambridge University Press, 2007), 10–17.

22. Raffaella Cribiore, *Libanius the Sophist: Rhetoric, Reality, and Religion in the Fourth Century*, TL/CSCP (Ithaca, NY: Cornell University Press, 2013), 8.

23. Robert A. Markus, *The End of Ancient Christianity* (Cambridge: Cambridge University Press, 1990), 28.

24. Sandwell, *Religious Identity in Late Antiquity*, 5.

25. Robert L. Wilken, *John Chrysostom and the Jews: Rhetoric and Reality in the Late Fourth Century*, TCH 4 (Berkeley: University of California Press, 1983), 17; see further Sandwell, *Religious Identity in Late Antiquity*, 46–47, 143.

tistic tradition that combined elements of Judaism and Hellenism. Thus, for example, at the outset in *Homily* 1 the preacher avers that the populace "used to approach God through angels; they had many Jewish and Hellenic observances. Therefore, he [Paul] is correcting these faults"; in *Homily* 2 he states that "We must be brought to him [God] through the Son, no longer through angels"; and in *Homily* 3 explains that in former times the approach to God was made by angels, whereas Paul demonstrates that subsequently the angels had no power. In this same *Homily* 3 Chrysostom dilates on the enmity between human beings and angels, and in *Homily* 4 explains that "The one who knows what Christ has done has higher thoughts than angels do." The surviving exegetical fragments of Severian of Gabala on Colossians also demonstrate a great concern about the place of angels in Christianity.[26]

Because slaves and servants were part of the makeup of households and societies in antiquity, and given that in his preaching on Paul's letters to the Colossians, as in other homilies, Chrysostom sought to engage his congregations in real-life scenarios, it is not surprising that slaves and servants (some scholars prefer to refer to the latter as "attendants") appear regularly in our texts. The different vocabulary for these members of the household is not well defined either in ancient texts or in modern scholarship, but as a rule of thumb one can posit that δοῦλος or οἰκέτης was used of slaves and διάκονος of a servant or attendant. However, there may be some overlap, as in *Homily* 1 on Colossians, where in Chrysostom's imaginary depiction of two different tables, one for the rich and the other for the poor, those who serve the guests in both cases are διάκονοι.[27]

There are some appealing passages in Chrysostom's homilies on Colossians that portray various aspects of childhood in Christian antiquity, such as the weaning and toilet-training of children, sickness and the use of amulets, early childhood education, and the death of children. In general

---

26. See in detail Clinton E. Arnold, *The Colossian Syncretism: The Interface between Christianity and Folk Belief at Colossae*, WUNT 2/77 (Tübingen: Mohr Siebeck, 1995), esp. 90–102. Severian explains in a fragmentary work that both Hellenes and Jews persuaded the Colossians to worship angels: see Severian of Gabala, *Fragmenta in epistulas s. Pauli* (*CPG* 4219), edited by Karl Staab, in *Pauluskommentare aus der griechischen Kirche aus Katenenhandschriften gesammelt und herausgegeben*, NTAbh 15 (Münster: Verlag der Aschendorffschen Verlagsbuchhandlung, 1933), 315–16.

27. On the difficulties presented by the nomenclature, see de Wet, *Preaching Bondage*, 46–47, 57 n. 30, 95–96, 113 n. 118, 201–2, 229–30 (the last case referring to *Hom. Col.* 1 and those waiting on tables).

Chrysostom's presentations of these themes have received little attention in modern scholarship.[28]

Maurice Wiles maintains that Chrysostom's homilies on Colossians contain "striking exceptions" to the preacher's usual stress on the good life, because there is an emphasis on the fact that the beginning of discipleship, the character of the divine plan, and the mystery are to be found in faith and baptism, apart from virtue and good works.[29]

Since the time of Erasmus Chrysostom's homilies on the Pauline Epistles have been criticized for falling below the standard of other works by the preacher.[30] Wenzel Stoderl, for example, who translated these homilies into German, remarks that the language lacks the final touch, and the structures of the sentences are loose, hasty, not seldom confused and unclear. But he goes on to say that there are passages in which the preacher's brilliance breaks through.[31] These would include the tirades against wealth in *Homilies* 7 and 10, the denunciation of showy and immoral practices

---

28. And this in spite of some major recent edited works, such as those of Cornelia B. Horn and Robert R. Fenix, eds., *Children in Late Ancient Christianity*, Studien und Texte zu Antike und Christentum 58 (Tübingen: Mohr Siebeck, 2009); Judith Evans Grubbs, Tim Parkin, and Roslynne Bell, eds., *The Oxford Handbook of Childhood and Education in the Classical World* (Oxford: Oxford University Press, 2013); Christian Laes and Ville Vuolanto, eds., *Children and Everyday Life in the Roman and Late Antique World* (London: Routledge, 2016). However, Blake Leyerle has made significant contributions to the subject in a number of articles and chapters. See, e.g., her "Appealing to Children," *JECS* 5 (1997): 243–70; "Children and 'the Child' in Early Christianity," in Grubbs, Parkin, and Bell, *Oxford Handbook of Childhood*, 559–79; "'Keep Me, Lord, as the Apple of Your Eyes': An Early Christian Child's Amulet," *JECS* 3 (2013): 73–93.

29. Maurice F. Wiles, *The Divine Apostle: The Interpretation of St Paul's Epistles in the Early Church* (Cambridge: Cambridge University Press, 1967), 24.

30. For a history of the evaluation of the Pauline commentaries, see Blake Goodall, who believes that stenographers are responsible for this uneven quality. See Goodall, *The Homilies of St. John Chrysostom on the Letters of St. Paul to Titus and Philemon: Prolegomena to an Edition*, UCPCS 20 (Berkeley: University of California Press, 1979), 63–66, 78.

31. John Chrysostom, *Des hl. Kirchenlehrers Johannes Chrysostomus, Erzbischofs von Konstantinopel, Kommentar zu den Briefen des hl. Paulus an die Philipper und Kolosser*, trans. Wenzel Stoderl, BK 45 (Munich: Kösel & Pustet, 1924), 3.

at weddings (*Homily* 12), and the vignettes of children being weaned and toilet-trained (*Homily* 4). It may be noted that, like Chrysostom's homilies on Philippians, those on Colossians betray a train of thought that is not always apparent, because it is difficult to discern whether one is dealing with the preacher's own ideas, those of Paul as transmitted by Chrysostom in paraphrase and extrapolation, or objections real or imaginary from the congregation and other groups.

In general, Chrysostom follows the Byzantine text-type[32] in his preaching on Colossians, with some minor variants demanded by the flow of his argument. In these homilies there are several inaccuracies and conflations in the citations of the biblical text, instances where there is inconsistent use of tenses, or Greek that is terse, and some passages which are obscure or nonsensical. All these are indicated in the notes. There may be here inherent inconsistencies in Chrysostom's exegesis of the Pauline text[33] or problems attributable to the manuscript tradition or the work of stenographers.

Like Theodore of Mopsuestia, in elucidating his homilies on Colossians John follows the New Testament text closely, as one would expect from a graduate of the Antiochene biblical tradition. Sometimes because of the lack of personal pronouns in the Greek text it is difficult to discern which person Chrysostom has in mind, and accordingly I have inserted names such as *Paul* and *Christ* to help the reader follow the argument. In keeping with the colloquial style of these homilies, as in the translations of those on Philippians, I have regularly used contractions in English, such as *don't* and *won't*. Verbatim biblical citations in this volume are reproduced in italics (often within quotation marks) to distinguish them from Chrysostom's many paraphrases of scriptural texts. Citations from the Old Testament are generally to the LXX.

CONTENTS OF JOHN CHRYSOSTOM'S *HOMILIES ON COLOSSIANS*

John opens *Homily* 1 by telling his congregation that the letters Paul sent from prison, namely, to the Ephesians, to Philemon, to Timothy (second letter), to the Philippians, and to the Colossians, are holier than his other writings. The preacher accepts that the letter to the Colossians is indeed by

---

32. On which see Bruce M. Metzger, *A Textual Commentary on the Greek New Testament* (London: United Bible Societies, 1971), xx, xxx–xxxi.

33. On which see Margaret M. Mitchell, "A Variable and Many-Sorted Man: John Chrysostom's Treatment of Pauline Inconsistency," *JECS* 6 (1998): 93–111.

Paul, whereas modern scholars generally believe that this letter, together with that to the Ephesians, was the product of the followers of Paul, as discussed in the introduction above (p. 2). Chrysostom gives a short chronology of the letters to the Philippians, to the Romans, and the Colossians, also treated above in the introduction (pp. 2–3). According to Chrysostom's reasoning, at the time of writing to the Colossians Paul had not seen them, nor the Romans, nor the Hebrews.

The argument of this first letter, Chrysostom says, is that, while the Colossians used to approach God through angels and had many Jewish and Hellenic observances, Paul is correcting their faults. The preacher points out that Colossae was a city in Phrygia, close to Laodicea, a fact that was important because of the long-standing practice of angel worship in that region. Mention of the practice recurs not only in this homily but in others to the Colossians. As he continues, Chrysostom follows the Pauline text verse by verse until Colossians 1:8, which contains the phrase "love in the Spirit," prompts him to dwell on different kinds of earthly friendships, which are inferior to spiritual friendships.

As an example of the dichotomy of the two kinds of love, Chrysostom adduces a long comparison of two tables set for a feast. The one is full of the blind, the lame, and the handicapped, and has no silver table settings or cups, no excess of food or drink, but everyone is happy. The other table is populated by well-clad dignitaries and fitted out with expensive utensils, cloths, and food. For his part the preacher declares that he will join the first table, while ostensibly assuming that his listeners will choose the more glamorous group at the other. The description of the contrast continues: freedom of expression at the poor table versus fear and trembling at the rich table, where people do not dare to converse with their well-to-do fellow diners; gladness of heart at the former and lack of honor at the other. The preacher also addresses the cares of the two hosts of the tables, pointing out that the host of the poor table has an easy, impromptu agenda for his guests, whereas the rich host spends days and nights worrying about preparations and discussions with cooks and the like. Then there is the musical entertainment to comment on. The rich table has flutes and harps, while the poor table has only hymns and psalmody. The former, indeed, has flutes playing odes to demons; and then it is but a short step for the preacher to denounce the presence of prostitutes at parties, a theme to which he returns with increased vitriol at the end of *Homily* 12. While the banquet at the rich table ends in debauchery, the participants at the poor table go home afterward in thanksgiving and praise of God. The obvious

text for Chrysostom to quote now in the context of the two tables is Matt 25:36: "*You saw me hungry and you fed me; naked and you clothed me; a stranger and you welcomed me*," which turns the argument back at the end of the homily to authentic friendships and almsgiving.

Homily 2 on Colossians is a long, meandering piece, most of the contents of which have little to do with the stated pericope at the beginning (Col 1:9–10). However, because the role and placement of the pericopes in the transmission of Chrysostom's homilies are uncertain, one should allow the preacher some leeway in his exegesis, which he definitely needs in this homily.

The text skips forward quickly to Col 1:11, then back again to verse 9, on the basis of which the preacher avers that human beings must be brought to God through the Son, not through angels anymore, another reference to angel worship in the region of Colossae, already encountered in *Homily* 1. While dealing with Paul's prayers for his readers and listeners in Col 1:9, Chrysostom embarks on a commendation of the right way of life, a concept that will recur in this homily, particularly in the next section with the quotation from Col 1:11: "*Strengthened with all power.*" Then the exegesis reverts to Col 1:10 (*bearing fruit*), before moving on again to 1:11 (*for all endurance and patience*) and 1:12 (*who has qualified us to share in the inheritance of the saints in light*). Colossians 1:13 prompts the preacher to dwell on the transfer of humankind to the heavenly kingdom, before he decides that the text of Col 1:15 with its statement of *complete redemption* by Christ is leading into difficult christological territory. The remainder of the Pauline text, he promises, will be addressed on the next day. What follows, however, is a statement that the preacher is going to put a stop to the homily after making one point, which is that the congregation should be ever mindful of what they have been delivered from and what they have obtained, namely, the kingdom of heaven. This one point turns into several points, which continue at some length, giving the impression that this part may have belonged to another homily. The argument is that winter, by which Chrysostom means the last judgment, will lead to suffering for those who deserve it, namely, those whom he cannot convince. People in the past who had no examples of salvation to consider and no Scriptures did not believe, and therefore the congregation, who has all these things at their disposal, should honor their baptismal promises, otherwise they are no different from Hellenes. Chrysostom returns to the divinity of Christ, but it is not clear whether he has angel worship or Arianism or both in his sights. The devil, he maintains, persists in persuading us to be ignorant of

God's gift of salvation. The next section of the homily contains advice to the congregation about discussing religion with the Hellenes: the Christian should posit that Christ is God and the child of God, while the gods of the Hellenes are demons. However, advises Chrysostom, it is futile to discuss with the Hellenes if they do not believe in a final judgment, because "none of those who live in virtue disbelieves the doctrine of judgment, whether they are a Hellene or a heretic." Asserting in conclusion that there will certainly be a judgment and a resurrection, the preacher warns his listeners to avoid the devil, who encourages us to neglect virtue and to worship the demons.

In *Homily* 3 Chrysostom resumes his exegesis of Col 1:15 (*He is the image of the invisible God*), which he had embarked on briefly in *Homily* 2 before deferring his argument until this homily. Now, although the theme of angel worship remains in the background, the preacher's target is Arianism, which posits a change in the divinity when Christ became human, thus negating *the image of the invisible God*. If, says Chrysostom, Christ is like an image of a human being, the preacher will avoid such people as being mad. For if Christ is a creature, how is he an image of the Creator? The expression *firstborn of all creation* induces similar people to claim that Christ is created; *firstborn from the dead* (Col 1:18) demonstrates that Christ was the firstfruits of the resurrection.

The next section of the homily combines anti-Arian arguments with the theme of angel worship. Chrysostom maintains that, while the heretics believe that Christ is more recent, because in former times approach to the divinity was made through angels, Paul shows that angels have no power and that Christ antedates them. The preacher asks what Paul of Samosata, a monarchian of the adoptionist type, who was generally agreed by early Christian theologians not to have recognized the full divinity of Christ, would reply at this point. The argument continues with the assertion that the *firstborn* is like a *foundation* (1 Cor 3:10) and that the apostle Paul has eradicated the doctrines of Paul of Samosata. Then the preacher goes further in the Pauline text, namely, to Colossians 1:19–20 (which incidentally goes beyond the verses quoted at the beginning of the homily), drawing the conclusion that whatever belongs to the Father belongs to the Son as well.

From here the exegesis concentrates on *things in heaven* (Col 1:20), which leads the preacher to discourse on how the angels were once at war with human beings, only to appear afterward because a human being had appeared in heaven. However, it seems that some of his congregation run to angels nonetheless. Giving a little ground, Chrysostom concedes that

every believer has an angel and should therefore be sober in their prayers for peace. There follow references to peace in the liturgy, before Chrysostom rails against strife and polemics, again referring to liturgical terminology, which should extinguish enmity among its hearers. He draws his authority from the fact that he has received the throne by succession, from the time that Christ gave him the ministry of reconciliation.

The next section of the homily is important because it puts beyond doubt that John was bishop of Constantinople when he delivered it. His listeners do not despise him but the priesthood itself, and, although he is unworthy, he sits on the first throne and occupies the first office. They are put on notice that, when he issues orders, it is the grace of God that is active in him. A clever argument ensues, in which the preacher plays on the Greek word *presbyter*, with its two meanings of "church elder" and "ambassador." Secular ambassadors enjoy great honor and are sent on from one country to another in safety, whereas Chrysostom's ambassadorial role seems to offend the congregation, and he asks them to listen to the office of bishop rather than to his person.

In *Homily* 4 Chrysostom deals with Col 1:21–22, stating at the outset that Paul "continues to show that Christ has reconciled those even who were unworthy of reconciliation," the theme of reconciliation having already been prominent in *Homilies* 2 and 3. Angels feature again, for, says the preacher, they were incapable of reconciling people who were enemies or to deliver them from the devil. This was to be Christ's work, namely, by his shameful death, which also rendered the believers in the congregation *irreproachable*, if only they would continue in the faith, *stable and steadfast*. The preacher concentrates on Paul's claim that he is a minister and willing to take on Christ's sufferings in order to reconcile people to the Savior. Again, as in *Homily* 3, Chrysostom says that he is Christ's ambassador and that Christ has not suffered everything yet, not being satisfied with death alone. What need, then, of angels, since Paul's ministry is part of the divine plan? Among other things, this plan encompassed the conversion of the gentiles and explains Christ's arrival in our own times, not earlier, for that would have resulted in less respect for him because he would have come after the servants did. An imaginary interlocutor quizzes the preacher about the poor state of contemporary Jews and Hellenes, which Chrysostom attributes to their great stupidity because they do not admit that Christ's arrival and mission were successful. Everyone would say that God is without beginning; then why were human beings not created many years before? But this is not a matter for inquiry, says the preacher, who

next dilates on the various phases of human life. In the phase of child-hood God placed Moses as schoolmaster over the Jews, and bribed them with wealth and luxury, just as Chrysostom's congregation gives cakes and coins to their children to persuade them to attend school. Moses in his turn persuaded God not to renounce the Jews for their wrongdoing. There follow illustrations of how a schoolmaster like Moses educated children, before the preacher moves on to the topic of the Jews in Egypt, who were intransigent. In fact, the behavior of the Jews was that of children, who when being weaned are given all kind of treats but miss the breast, just as the Jews missed the fleshpots of Egypt.

Chrysostom continues with the theme of Moses as the schoolmaster, then father, and pedagogue, including some vignettes from child-rearing, such as toilet-training and the tyranny of childish behavior. All this leads to the conclusion that Christ should not have appeared in those past times, but rather now, when by God's grace there is moderation and virtue every-where. We should not demand an account from God of what he does or scrutinize past events. Here the preacher stops for the moment before offering the doxology.

In *Homily* 5 Chrysostom dwells initially on the mystery of God's provi-dence, which hitherto nobody, including angels and archangels, had known but was hidden in Christ. This is the completion of God's plan, which was discussed in the previous homily, and was manifest to the saints alone. Paul's emphasis, maintains the preacher, is that God's mystery is evident in many peoples, but particularly in the gentiles, who were brought by it from the worship of stones and the earth to the dignity of angels, such that, from being prisoners of the demons, they have progressed to become the body of the Master of the angels and archangels. The gentiles learned that noth-ing was to be worshiped above God, not even angels and archangels, to whom they are now superior. To be noted in this homily is that the stated pericope, namely, Col 1:26–28, on several occasions slides into Col 2, again raising questions about the role of pericopes at the beginning of homilies.

Pursuing his treatment of angels in the previous homilies, Chrysostom argues that if Christ is in the congregation, there is no need to seek angels. The believers will be complete in Christ, not in the law, nor in angels. This is what Paul is striving for, in his great affection for those also in Laodicea (see Col 2:1) and his anxiety, like birth pangs, namely, that the Colossians be encouraged (see Col 2:2) to be *knit together in love*. The following sec-tion deals with the assurance that comes from faith, but it is disjointed, and in the process the text jumps again to Col 2. Steadfastness is the next

virtue to which Chrysostom draws attention, a virtue that demands faith rather than reasoning and is exemplified by the argument that God is not anywhere and yet is everywhere. This leads the preacher to consider the incorporeality of God and by extension how unchangeable the divinity is, an exposition that asks much of the congregation.

Possibly because of the abstract nature of his last musings, Chrysostom then asks the congregation whether they want the homily to go on to discuss more tangible cases, namely, what has in fact happened. Jonah in the belly of the whale is an example of this, as are the cases of Elijah, Enoch, and Noah, who, as forerunners, constitute a ladder to the present reality. Jacob's ladder is another sign. In an argument that does not convince, the preacher links Jacob with the birth of Christ, referring obliquely to Sarah's miraculous conception of Isaac. This, along with other births from barren women, is said to have been a type of God being able to beget alone. Similarly there were many signs of resurrection in the old dispensation, such as Enoch, Elijah, Jonah, Daniel, and Noah, proving that nothing happens without God's providence (a return to the opening of the homily). There were also many indications of baptism in both Testaments, and all these types are to be found in the Scriptures, if only the congregation would train themselves in these matters.

Although Col 2:6–7 is the preacher's starting-point in *Homily* 6, on occasion in this homily he treats later verses in Col 2 as well as verses in Col 3. Walking in Christ, advises the preacher as he echoes Col 2:6, means that this is the way to the Father, not through angels, another instance of the insubordinate place Chrysostom ascribes to angels in these homilies on Paul's behalf (and perhaps on his own as well). Paul's advice that nobody should make a prey of the Colossians through philosophy or deceit is Chrysostom's next discussion point, as he interprets the apostle's words to castigate the (unnamed) non-Christians and then Christians, who do not appreciate the benefits they have received but reverence the elements, such as the sun and the moon. With great appreciation, Chrysostom records Paul's demolition of the observances of the Jews and the Hellenes, as he had already done in *Homily* 5, before embarking on Col 2:9 with its insistence that in Christ the fullness of the deity dwells bodily. This leads the preacher to Col 2:11 and the nature of spiritual circumcision, which of course is baptism. According to Col 2:12, Chrysostom explains, those who are buried in baptism are also raised in Christ, and he proceeds to exegete Col 2:13 and 13–15, with emphasis on the bond that Christ rendered null and void on the cross, thereby destroying both sin and punishment and at

the same time thwarting the devil, who had the bond in his possession. In short, the devil received the death blow from Christ's dead body, which, unlike his resurrection, was witnessed publicly. The crucifixion did not put Christ to shame but was rather an achievement that the angels had been unable to attain, and consequently it initiated a second bond, different from the former. This consideration leads the preacher to part of the baptismal formula: "I renounce Satan and align myself with you, Christ," and the homily continues with references to elements of the baptismal ceremony. Those baptized are in heaven, which is inaccessible to the devil. But, warns Chrysostom, while the benefits of baptism are great, so too are the punishments for reneging on it.

Harking back to Paul's injunctions in Col 2:8 about becoming a prey to ideas and in Col 2:4 about being deluded by beguiling words, in *Homily 7* Chrysostom places the apostle's reproof in Col 2:16–19 concerning food, drink, festivals, and Sabbath days in the context of the recriminations of Jews toward Christians. His injunction to the latter group is that they should not be judged if they have stood above the devil and sin. Some people, he says, believe that we should not be brought into the church by Christ, but by angels, whereas Christ is the head of the church, which will increase if it remains with the head. The preacher next moves to Col 2:20, which concerns dying with Christ to the elements of the world, then to Col 2:21, the exegesis of which Chrysostom maintains makes fun of the Colossians' cowardice and aloofness from important matters. Passing quickly through Col 2:23 and 3:1, Chrysostom argues that the apostle prepares to draw his readers/listeners from enjoyment and leisure, transferring them to heaven itself in order to show that they share with Christ in everything.

The homily continues with the thought that this life is not ours; rather, we are *strangers and sojourners*. Consequently, buying servants, building houses, or preparing costly garments for a corpse is stupid, when burial in Christ in baptism is the one thing to be sought. We were clay before baptism but golden after it. Chrysostom makes much of Paul's comment in 1 Cor 15:47 that *the first human being was dust from earth* in order to lead into his extended argument about the transience of earthly power, honor, and wealth. The one who yesterday was at the forefront of politics has today lost everything, like dust thrown up. Wealth in particular, so goes the argument, brings dishonor, and it is better to die than to be dishonored. An example of dishonor is adduced from the time when the city offended the emperor and was destroyed, although the neighboring city petitioned on their account. As discussed above (p. 4), this passage indicates that the

homily refers to the riots of 387 in Antioch and was delivered in that city possibly between 395 and 397.

Wealth and power, continues the homilist, are shameful and produce arrogance, a disease of the soul, full of lusts and absurdities, such as devising worse things than hippocentaurs, chimeras, serpent-footed monsters, and Scyllas. Not that Chrysostom himself was born into wealth, he hastens to add, but he has heard, for example, of a Persian king who made a tree of gold and a golden sky above it. Such luxury is senseless, although there are people at the moment who in similar vein make silver chamber pots and pitchers and scent bottles, and here Chrysostom singles out women, subsequently accusing their husbands of ministering to their madness and illness. He proceeds to denounce pride, vainglory, and excess. The tirade against women continues—will they next even desire to have hair of gold, like the Persian king with his golden beard?—culminating in the preacher's assertion that he will put up with such monstrous and irrational behavior no longer and will even ban women from the church because the situation makes them is a laughingstock among the Hellenes. The men in the congregation are also included in the opprobrium. An imaginary interlocutor points out that such people, if banned from church, will cross over to other heresies. In conclusion Chrysostom beseeches and entreats his congregation to correct themselves and from their wealth to come to the aid of even one poor person standing around the church.

Ostensibly *Homily* 8 treats Col 3:5–7, but, as will become clear, its compass is broader. Chrysostom begins by admitting that many were offended by the previous homily, a comment that allows us to tie *Homilies* 7 and 8 together, as explained in the introduction to this volume. He explains that he is not to blame for denouncing covetousness, madness, and the weakness for silver, but asks all the same for forgiveness for being forced to speak on such topics. He has spoken not so much for the suffering of the poor as for the sake of his congregation's salvation, for, after all, Paul said that this life is not ours but the one in heaven. This, explains the preacher, is not to discredit the earth but earthly vices, which the congregation lived in formerly. The exegesis then jumps to Col 3:8, followed by 3:9 and 3:10–11, the latter with its baptismal overtones of putting off the old person with its deeds, because the baptized have become like the image of Christ, who created them. With the abolition of the distinction between races, genders, circumcised and uncircumcised, Christ *is everything and in everything.* This thought enables the preacher to move on to Col 2:12–13 and its litany of virtues and to 3:14 with its injunction to *put on love, which is the bond of*

perfection. This means, according to Chrysostom, that it is love that binds all the virtues together; it is a bond that holds fast things that produce perfection.

Colossians 3:15 provides the homilist with the image of God's peace as umpire in life, which for its part sets up the idea of a stadium that the apostle has created. In this stadium the faithful are called to receive the prize, whereas the devil knows that he has no hope of doing so. All this is grounds for thanksgiving, Chrysostom reminds his congregation, before explaining why in Col 3:5 Paul focuses on the powerful, earthly vice of fornication, as he often does elsewhere in his writings. But the apostle has positioned his hearers above earth, near the heavenly throne, before telling them to put to death things of the earth, including fornication and other passions, which render the soul unclean and passible.

Covetousness, which is another component of Paul's litany of vices, is treated next and linked to idolatry. This is followed by a non sequitur that is a praise of thanksgiving, especially in difficult times when the tongue gives thanks to God, as in the case of the mother of a sick child who attains a martyr's crown by giving thanks. This putative mother did not make amulets for her sick child but preferred to see it dead than to commit idolatry by using them. Much of the remainder of the homily deals with the use of amulets to ward off death from children, a practice, says the preacher, that not even a sensible Hellene would countenance. "When," asks the homilist, "will these satanical acts end?" They make Christians a laughingstock to the Hellenes. The bereft parent should not love the dead child more than the Master, for even if it was born in old age and was an only child, it was not more handsome than Isaac or more loving than Moses. If the child has siblings, then the parents should think of Job or Jacob. Chrysostom then adduces several examples from the Old Testament of dead children and how their parents coped with their loss, before encouraging the congregation to think of people worse off than themselves and to be thankful.

The pericope stated at the beginning of *Homily* 9 is Col 3:16–17, and indeed, unlike other homilies on Colossians in this volume, the discourse stays close to these verses. Chrysostom reminds his congregation that he has recently spoken on Paul's exhortations to be thankful, presumably a reference to *Homily* 8, and that the path to thanksgiving is to *let the word of Christ dwell in you richly*. This means careful attention to the Scriptures, which will enable believers to put up with calamities more easily. The preacher points out that the apostle calls virtue wisdom, namely, humility of mind and almsgiving and all such things. Their opposites are sin,

characterized by Scripture as mindlessness and exemplified by people who overlook nakedness and starvation around them. Taking up again the importance of Scripture, Chrysostom explains that nobody can teach his congregation better and that they should at least buy the New Testament, the works of Paul, the Acts of the Apostles, and the Gospels as their constant teachers, because ignorance of Scripture is the cause of all evils—a theme already employed in *Homily* 5 and one that recurs frequently in Chrysostom. The preacher likens himself to a grammarian whose pupils continue to study but in fact learn nothing, just like his congregation, who hear his homilies but learn nothing: this is why his work is so onerous. Whereas Paul directed the Colossians to the Psalms, now the children in Chrysostom's congregation prefer songs and dances of Satan, and nobody seems to know the Psalms any more, although they contain everything for the believer. Further words for parents follow: children should not be allowed to mix with servants, particularly corrupt slaves. The next two sections in the translation embody a pastiche of pious injunctions, most of which are not aimed at the young. It is difficult to imagine a congregation enjoying or even comprehending the sixteen-odd quotations from both Testaments, which ends in the question: "What is the hymn of those above?" The answer, explains the homilist, is first of all the Psalms, then the hymns. But the believer needs to *do everything in word and deed in the name of the Lord Jesus*, which means engaging with the Lord no matter what one is doing—eating, sleeping, traveling, and so on. This will drive out demons and diseases and make matters auspicious. Some Old Testament examples follow to illustrate how God is honored by being called on by name, which translates into calling on and thanking both Father and Son. The closing section of the homily, including some baptismal references, is devoted to the holy name, which fights the demons and their incantations; it also makes both martyrs and confessors.

According to the pericope at the beginning of *Homily* 10, Col 3:18–25 will be treated, a passage in which Paul instructs husbands, wives, children, and slaves about their respective duties. However, Chrysostom slightly exceeds the compass of these verses, progressing to Col 4:3–4 in the course of his exegesis. At the outset Chrysostom speculates why Paul did not give these injunctions everywhere in his letters but only to the Colossians, the Ephesians, Timothy, and Titus, and concludes that in Colossae the church was now well-grounded, and these instructions are a summary of his preaching. He points out that the apostle is advocating reciprocity between husband and wife, although he puts this in terms of the husband's

love and the wife's obedience to him: she is by nature weak and must be submissive, although on the other hand the husband should not play the autocrat in the relationship. In a similar vein, there is subjection and love with regard to children, whereas in the case of slaves it is a question less of love than of an obedience that comes from their nature. However, obedience for all must not be sycophantic but come from *singleness of heart*, and this will free slaves not only from hypocrisy but also from inertia. According to Chrysostom, Paul has in mind Hellene masters of Christian slaves, but whatever the case, the masters should give their slaves *what is just and equal*. In the next part of the homily, Chrysostom claims that Paul has made slavery common, because everyone has a Lord in heaven. The congregation should continue *steadfastly in prayer* (Col 4:2), because the devil knows what a powerful deterrent prayer is. The theme of prayer continues, with the preacher giving the example of a holy man known to him, and how this person prayed. The prayer is given at some length, with the note that the holy man added the prayer of the faithful (the Our Father) to it. Next the preacher moves on to Col 4:3, which speaks about God opening *the door of the word to us*, a word we must speak, as Paul did even in his chains, an incarceration that the preacher goes on to elucidate: this was a punishment that Chrysostom greatly loves to contemplate, because the chains made Paul powerful, as an athlete who, just like the sun, cannot be chained. This is the marvel of the gospel, continues Chrysostom, because those who suffer evil conquer, and the one who does evil comes off worse.

Another marvel is that the first preachers were fishermen and were not as confident as Paul was when he was free as when he was in chains. People were drawn to the apostles even without their performing miracles, for Paul and his followers could not be impeded even in chains but proclaimed all the more. The apostle himself could not be gagged, and his chains should therefore be emulated, particularly, says the preacher, by women who adorn themselves with golden chains. In fact, avers Chrysostom, the sight of Paul in chains would have attracted more spectators than the empress in her finery if they had entered the church together, for the apostle is an angel on earth and his chains are to be desired. Golden chains will bind us hand and foot in the hereafter, so we should put on the apostle's chains and Christ, not gold. What follows is the recommendation that, instead of golden objects, people should adorn themselves with virtues such as almsgiving. Then the preacher introduces the story of Joseph's attempted seduction in Egypt, both woman and man being adorned with jewelry. The woman, like Eve, had no modesty, and the preacher's point is

that putting on fine apparel makes the wearer uglier, just as if one were to put on a pimp's garment on top of royal apparel. It is clear that Chrysostom's invective is still addressed to women, for he warns his listeners to watch out for their small daughters, lest they inherit their mothers' proclivities for ornament and immodesty.

The pericope given at the beginning of *Homily* 11 is Col 4:5–6, but the exegesis ranges beyond these verses. Chrysostom begins by tying Paul's injunction "*Conduct yourselves wisely toward outsiders*" to Christ's sending the disciples *as sheep in the midst of wolves* (Matt 10:16), and it becomes clear as the homily progresses that by "*outsiders*" and "*wolves*" the Hellenes are meant. The congregation is urged to use the short time left to them to give no hold to the outsiders, for the only thing worth fighting for is the gospel, and they should give honor where honor is due, as long as they are not harmed. On the other hand, *gracious* speech, *seasoned with salt*, which the apostle advocates, should not lead to indifference, and one should not discourse in the same way with Hellenes as with Christians.

There follows a catalogue of Paul's coworkers and associates, as tabulated in Col 4:7–11, with words of praise for each of them. The catalogue is interrupted as the preacher returns to Col 4:5 and its advice about proper conduct toward outsiders, pointing out that it is, however, senseless to invent occasions of war and enmity with them that will make it difficult to convert them, because the Hellenes are outside the kingdom and the Father's house. Nor should the gracious speech enjoined by Paul be interpreted as hypocrisy, says Chrysostom, but one should address persons according to their status and not call the Hellenes polluted, although, if questioned, it is permissible to call their doctrine polluted and impious. It is best not to discuss doctrine with them at all until they have become a good friend, and then the discussion should take place gradually.

The catalogue of coworkers and associates comes to an end at this point (although it continues in *Hom. Col.* 12) and is replaced by the preacher's thoughts on the subject of envy. Rather than being envious, it is more commendable to rejoice at the good esteem of another, for the victory is a common one, and while the work may have been another's, still the praise is ours. Even in dealings with outsiders it is a great virtue not to be envious but to make another's good our own. Rejoicing in the success of another pains the devil, whereas if we are downcast at another's success, the devil is pleased. The oratorical prowess of the one person is the joy of another, who in fact has won two crowns, that of joy and of the love that overcomes envy. Furthermore, the one devoid of envy receives a third crown, namely, the

applause of the angels above. Chrysostom argues that the envious person is at war with the church and with the body of Christ and has to be freed from this destructive passion. Envy inflicts wounds on ourselves. In summing up, the preacher asks the congregation to reflect on what he has said: the two crowns belong to those who do not envy.

The pericope stated at the beginning of *Homily* 12 is Col 4:12–13, whereas in fact the exegesis continues to the end of the letter. Chrysostom picks up where he left off in *Homily* 11 with his catalogue of Paul's coworkers and associates, beginning with Epaphras and exegeting the verses concerning this man's virtues and the affection Paul had for him. Next there is an encomium of the physician and evangelist Luke, and of Demas, before the preacher moves on to the apostle's greetings to the community in Laodicea, especially Nymphas[34] and the members of his house church (Col 4:15). That the faithful in Colossae are told to have this letter read in Laodicea (Col 4:16) seems to Chrysostom to indicate that those in Laodicea also needed to know what Paul had written, while the apostle's admonition to Archippus (Col 4:17) is treated by the preacher as a possible reminder to him to be more enthusiastic about his ministry. The letter, like this section, closes with the words *The greeting in my own hand, Paul. Grace be with you. Amen* (Col 4:18), the autograph reminding the readers/listeners of the sincerity and affection on both sides.

Chrysostom now returns to the opening verses of the homily, which deal with the ministerial prowess of Epaphras, before continuing with Paul's message to Archippus via the Colossians, and in particular the apostle's words "*Look out.*" The message to Archippus, says the preacher, means that the apostle subjects the Colossians to himself after they have been committed to God and that if the master is in chains, still grace releases him. Therefore, we should not be worried about suffering for Christ's sake, but remember Paul's chains in all activities: giving to the poor, covetousness, love of luxury, wearing silk, trying to appear beautiful, being angry with slaves. Paul's tears in his imprisonment should be remembered, for like a fountain they watered souls and can quench the fiery weapons of the devil. Nothing is sweeter than these tears, which saw paradise. The topic of tears continues, those not only of Paul but also of Christ.

These tears should be shed for children who have adopted evil ways, for Timothy wept and so did the psalmist David. The congregation should

---

34. On whom see n. 130 below.

follow their example by using tears for the right purpose, namely, weeping over a sinning person, but not, however, over somebody in poverty, in disease, or a corpse, for these persons are not worthy of tears. Like laughter, tears need to be used appropriately, because nothing wipes out sins as tears do.

This consideration leads the preacher to denounce participation in weddings, dances, and satanical bands, in particular the presence of effeminate men and prostitutes at such celebrations. Marriage is a chain, says Chrysostom, harking back to Paul's fetters, while a prostitute is a severing and a dissolving of that chain. However, the preacher does not rule out full tables and special garments at wedding, but stipulates that the tone should be one of modesty, gravity, and orderliness, rather than an occasion on which people frisk like camels and mules. A virgin, warns Chrysostom, should not appear in public at a wedding at all. At the celebration there are two groups of women, the unmarried and the married, but there is no place for prostitutes: the former group demonstrates the kind of young woman they are giving up, and the married women are there to guard her. After all, marriage is not a theater but rather a mystery, a type of the church, and thus Hellenic dances are out of place, while at a Christian wedding there should be silence, decorum, respect, and dignity. The mystery of marriage is that God, having created two from one (in the case of Adam and Eve) now makes the two one, and they are, so to speak, two halves, each incomplete for the procreation of children, but together bringing forth a child, as a kind of bridge.

Chrysostom realizes that many of his listeners are affronted by what he has said, but continues nevertheless with his attempt to shame them for their behavior at weddings. If marriage is a type of the presence of Christ, one should not be drunk at it: sins have become an art form at which the devil is present, making his own contributions. Now the preacher guesses that his congregation are finding him wearisome. However, the point is that if all the unlawful pleasures are banished from the celebration, Christ will be there, and the angels, too.

Nothing is more pleasant than virtue, according to the homilist. Consequently a fitting husband should be sought who will be a protector and not treat his future wife as a slave; he should be poorer rather than well-to-do, and Christ's help should be solicited in the selection process. Then the preparations for the wedding should not entail going around the neighborhood borrowing mirrors and clothing, nor should there be an orchestra present, but Christ should be invited before all the rest, and the poor with

him. Let the bride be clothed with gentleness and modesty, rather than gold finery, for then Christ will be present, whereas Satan attends an intemperate celebration. Chrysostom asks his congregation to stop the evil of weddings forthwith.

Other Ancient Commentaries on Colossians

Before embarking on this part of the introduction to the volume, it is opportune, as was done in the volume on Philippians, to deal briefly with the problematical relationship between commentary and homily. While indeed Chrysostom's series on the letter to the Colossians contains real homilies, the same cannot be said for all commentaries on Scripture, particularly when such works are transmitted in abbreviated form, as is the case with some of the commentaries in the list that follows. It is a particularly difficult task to distinguish between the homily that was prepared beforehand or delivered impromptu in a liturgical context, on the one hand, and on the other hand the "desk homily," written in homiletic form but intended for private study or reading rather than public performance. This problem has been investigated for the homilies of third-century theologian Origen, leading to the conclusion that Origen as a preacher was more restrained, his aim being to keep his entire congregation on the path to perfection, whereas in his commentaries and tractates he leaves no stone unturned in his exegesis, which was probably written for the benefit of the few.[35] Another example of the live homily versus the desk homily is Augustine's *Enarrationes in Psalmos*, transmitting 205 homilies, of which it is estimated only 119 were in fact delivered, while the remaining 86 are supposed to have been dictated by Augustine to a scribe in homiletic form in order to fill the gaps.[36] What one can say about Chrysostom's twelve homilies on Colossians that have come down, even if they do not properly constitute a series, is that together they are the most comprehensive treatment of the Colossians text, like his homilies on Philippians: this can be seen, by con-

---

35. See Éric Junod, "Wodurch unterscheiden sich die Homilien des Origenes von seinen Kommentaren?," in *Predigt in der Alten Kirche*, ed. Ekkehard Mühlenberg and Johannes van Oort (Kampen: Kok Pharos, 1994), 50–81, esp. 77–81.

36. See further Alexandre Olivar, *La predicación cristiana Antigua*, BHSTF 189 (Barcelona: Editorial Herder, 1991), 933; Hildegund Müller and Michael Fiedrowicz, "Enarrationes in psalmos," in *Augustinus-Lexikon*, ed. Cornelius Mayer (Basel: Schwabe, 1996–2002), 2:804–58.

trast, from the fragmentary and abbreviated exegeses of the Colossians text in the rest of Christian antiquity in the following list.

GREEK

+ From Severian of Gabala (d. after 408) there are thirty-one fragments that survive in Greek catenae (*CPG* 4219).[37]

+ A commentary on Paul's letter to the Colossians (*CPG* 3845) was composed by Theodore of Mopsuestia (d. 428) and survives in a Latin translation and Greek fragments.[38]

+ Theodoret, bishop of Cyrrhus, born circa 393, composed a commentary on Colossians as part of his exegesis of the twelve epistles of Paul (*CPG* 6209). The text was edited by Jean-Paul Migne and again by Charles Marriott.[39] It has received an English translation.[40]

+ From sixth-century exegete Oecumenius, better known for his commentary on Revelation, there are eleven fragments (*CPG* 7471) that have come down in catenae.[41]

+ Theophylact, archbishop of Ochrid (b. ca. 1050, d. after 1126), an exegete and epistolographer among his other roles, commented on all Paul's letters.[42] In general he follows Chrysostom's exegesis.

---

37. In Staab, *Pauluskommentare aus der griechischen Kirche*, 314–28.

38. Theodore of Mopsuestia, *Commentarii in epistulas Pauli minores* (*CPG* 3845), ed. Henry B. Swete, in *Theodori episcopi Mopsuesteni in epistolas b. Pauli commentarii* (*The Latin Version with the Greek Fragments*), Galatians-Colossians (CPG 3845) (Cambridge: University Press, 1882), 1:253–310; *Theodore of Mopsuestia: The Commentaries on the Minor Epistles of Paul*, trans. Rowan A. Greer, WGRW 26 (Atlanta: Society of Biblical Literature, 2010), 362–437.

39. PG 82:299–392; Theodoret of Cyrrhus, *Interpretatio in xii epistulas s. Pauli* (*CPG* 6209), ed. Charles Marriott, in *Commentarius in omnes b. Pauli epistolas* (Oxford: Parker, 1870), 2:68–95.

40. Theodoret of Cyrus, *Theodoret of Cyrus: Commentary on the Letters of St. Paul*, trans. Robert Charles Hill (Brookline, MA, Holy Cross Orthodox Press, 2001), 2:84–106. There is little comment on Theodoret's exegesis of Colossians in Jean-Noël Guinot, *L'Exégèse de Théodoret de Cyr*, ThH 100 (Paris: Beauchesne, 1995), although he does argue for more merit and creativity in Theodoret than earlier studies had done.

41. In Staab, *Pauluskommentare aus der griechischen Kirche*, 453–55. See now Oecumenius, *On Revelation*, in *Greek Commentaries on Revelation: Oecumenius and Andrew of Samosata*, trans. William C. Weinrich, ed. Thomas C. Oden, ACT (Downers Grove, IL: IVP Academic, 2011), 1–107.

42. For his commentary on Paul's letter to the Colossians, see Theophylact of

Latin

- ♦ Ambrosiaster, who flourished in Rome in the time of Pope Damasus (366–384), wrote a short commentary on Paul's letter to the Colossians (*CPL* 184).[43]
- ♦ Pelagius (d. 423–429) composed commentaries on all twelve of Paul's epistles (*CPL* 728), but they are really brief explanatory notes.[44]

Translator's Notes

The text of Chrysostom's homilies on Colossians established by Dom Bernard de Montfaucon in his monumental edition of all Chrysostom's works[45] rested on three manuscripts, one of them partial. De Montfaucon's text of Colossians was taken over by Jean-Paul Migne in Patrologia Graeca 62:299–392. De Montfaucon states that he collated a Coislin and a Colbert manuscript, plus another defective witness, which he designates as "Regius."[46] Following the policy established in the series Writings from the Greco-Roman World for volumes presenting Chrysostom's commentaries

---

Ochrid, *Commentarius in epistolam ad Colossenses*, PG 124:1207–78. On Theophylact in general, but particularly as an epistolographer, see Margaret Mullett, *Theophylact of Ochrid: Reading the Letters of a Byzantine Archbishop*, BBOM 2 (Ashgate, UK: Aldershot, 1997).

43. See Ambrosiaster, *Ambrosiastri qui dicitur Commentarius in epistulas Paulinas*, ed. Henricus I. Vogels, CSEL 81 (Vienna: Hoelder–Pichler–Temsky, 1969), 3:167–207. For a new translation of this work, see volume 1 of Theodore S. de Bruyn, Stephen A. Cooper, and David G. Hunter, *Ambrosiaster's Commentary on the Pauline Epistles: Romans*, WGRW 41 (Atlanta: SBL Press, 2017), esp. xxiii–cxiii of their introduction.

44. See Wiles, *Divine Apostle*, 12–13. For the text, see Pelagius, *Expositiones xiii epistularum Pauli*, ed. Alexander Souter, TS (repr., Nendeln, Lichtenstein: Kraus Reprint, 1967), 2:451–73.

45. John Chrysostom, *Sancti patris nostri Ioannis Chrysostomi archiepiscopi Constantinopolitani opera omnia quae extant, uel quae eius nomine circumferentor*, ed. Bernard de Montfaucon (Paris: Gaume Fratres Bibliopolas, 1718–1738), 11:370A–490B (the Colossians text).

46. See John Chrysostom, *In epistulam ad Colossenses homiliae 1–12*, PG 62:177 n. (a). Cf. Field's Monitum to his Philippians edition, 5:ix–x, on the manuscripts used by de Montfaucon, noting that the Coislin ("quisque fuerit") seems to be connected with the recension in Field's own manuscripts C and G, while de Montfaucon rarely uses the Colbert.

on the Pauline Epistles, Frederick Field's text of 1855 has been used for the translation below of Colossians, with the exception of some paragraphing and punctuation, and occasional departures from Field, which are indicated in the footnotes. Field's text itself is based on an edition published in 1529 in Verona, which he was satisfied was the correct text, although it rests on only one manuscript.[47] Until new text editions are made of Chrysostom's works employing modern scientific principles, Field must remain the guiding light, although many questions of a textual nature, especially with regard to the homilies on the Pauline Epistles, have to be regarded as tentative.[48] Apart from the Verona edition, Field seems to have consulted three manuscripts for his text of Colossians, all different from those listed by de Montfaucon and listed by him as follows:

C British Library, Burney 48A, folios 159–196 (early twelfth century)

E Vienna, Theologici 111 (olim Vindobonensis 140), folios 188–223v (fourteenth century)

G Moscow, Synodal Collection greco 100, folios 169–231 (993 CE)

Subsequently Field consulted other witnesses.[49]

The Pinakes search engine of the Institut de Recherche et d'Histoire des Textes/Centre National de la Recherche Scientifique records no fewer than thirty-four manuscripts in which Chrysostom's *Homilies on Colossians* have been transmitted, among which the following older manuscripts need to be taken into consideration for a future edition of this work in order to update Field's text:

- Alexandria, Bibliothêkê tou Patriarcheiou 12, folios 217–315v (tenth century)
- Alexandria, Bibliothêkê tou Patriarcheiou 34, folios 232v–280 (968 CE)
- Oxford, Bodleian Library Auctarium T 3.15 (Misc. 232), folio 105v (tenth century)

---

47. John Chrysostom, *In omnes Pauli epistolas acuratissima vereque aurea et divina interpretatio: Veronae; typis aereis excusum per Stephanum et fratres a Sabio, quarto Kal. Jul. 1529*, 4 tomes in 2 vols., ed. Bernardino Donato (Verona, 1529). See further Goodall, *Homilies of St. John Chrysostom*, 2.

48. See Goodall, *Homilies of St. John Chrysostom*, 1–5.

49. Field, Monitum, 5:x–xi.

- ◆ Oxford, New College 78, folios 1v–82v (eleventh century)
- ◆ Paris, Bibliothèque nationale de France greco 1017, folios 159–84 (tenth century)
- ◆ Vatican, Bibliotheca Apostolica Vaticana, Vaticano greco 1659, folios 241–351v (tenth century)

There is considerable discrepancy between the text of de Montfaucon and that of Field, the latter's edition being in general better but terser, sometimes to the point of incomprehensibility. Further investigation is needed to establish whether there are here different versions, perhaps rough and smooth, as is indeed the case in other works of Chrysostom.[50]

Bolded numbers in square brackets in the following English translation of Chrysostom's homilies on Colossians refer to page numbers in Field's text. I have made grateful use of John Ashworth's translation of 1843, based on the seventeenth-century edition at Eton by Sir Henry Savile with some consultation by Savile of de Montfaucon's edition and the so-called new Paris edition of 1834–1839.[51] Ashworth's translation was revised by John Broadus in 1889 on the basis of Field's edition.[52] The need to update these translations by a modern, idiomatic, twenty-first-century rendering of Chrysostom's work is obvious. There exist a nineteenth-century French translation, based on the text of de Montfaucon, and a twentieth-century German translation based on the Oxford text.[53] *Homilies* 7 and 12 have received more recent English translations.[54]

---

50. See further Bady, "Tradition des œuvres," 155, and the literature cited there.

51. John Chrysostom, *S. Johannis Chrysostomi opera omnia*, vol. 4, ed. Henry Savile (Eton: Norton, 1612).

52. John Chrysostom, *The Homilies of S. John Chrysostom, Archbishop of Constantinople, on the Epistles of St. Paul the Apostle to the Philippians, Colossians, and Thessalonians*, trans. John Ashworth (Oxford: Parker, 1843), 181–334. Rev. ed. by John A. Broadus, NPNF[1] 13:257–321.

53. John Chrysostom, *Œuvres complètes de Saint Jean Chrysostome: Traduction nouvelle*, trans. Abbé J. Bareille (Paris: Vivès, 1873), 10:15–91; Stoderl, *Des hl. Kirchenlehrers Johannes Chrysostomus*, 235–419.

54. *Homily* 7, by Mayer and Allen, *John Chrysostom*, 73–84; *Homily* 12, by Catherine P. Roth and David Anderson, *St John Chrysostom. On Marriage and Family Life* (Crestwood, NY: St Vladimir's Seminary Press, 1986), 73–80.

TEXT, TRANSLATION, AND NOTES

[172] ΤΟΥ ΕΝ ΑΓΙΟΙΣ ΠΑΤΡΟΣ ΗΜΩΝ ΙΩΑΝΝΟΥ ΑΡΧΙΕΠΙΣΚΟΠΟΥ ΚΩΝΣΤΑΝΤΙΝΟΥΠΟΛΕΩΣ ΤΟΥ ΧΡΥΣΟΣΤΟΜΟΥ ΥΠΟΜΝΗΜΑ ΕΙΣ ΤΗΝ ΠΡΟΣ ΚΟΛΟΣΣΑΕΙΣ ΕΠΙΣΤΟΛΗΝ

ΛΟΓΟΣ Α.

Παῦλος ἀπόστολος Ἰησοῦ Χριστοῦ διὰ θελήματος θεοῦ, καὶ Τιμόθεος ὁ ἀδελφός, τοῖς ἐν Κολοσσαῖς ἁγίοις καὶ πιστοῖς ἀδελφοῖς ἐν Χριστῷ, χάρις ὑμῖν καὶ εἰρήνη ἀπὸ θεοῦ πατρὸς ἡμῶν.

Πᾶσαι μὲν ἅγιαι αἱ ἐπιστολαὶ Παύλου, ἔχουσι δέ τι πλέον αἱ δεδεμένου αὐτοῦ πεμπόμεναι, οἵα ἐστὶν ἡ πρὸς Ἐφεσίους, οἵα ἡ πρὸς Φιλήμονα, οἵα ἡ πρὸς Τιμόθεον, οἵα ἡ πρὸς Φιλιππησίους, οἵα αὕτη ἡ παροῦσα· καὶ γὰρ καὶ αὕτη δεσμίου ὄντος ἐπέμπετο, καθὼς γράφων ἔλεγε· "Δι' ὃ καὶ δέδεμαι, ἵνα φανερώσω αὐτό, ὡς δεῖ με λαλῆσαι." Ἀλλ' αὕτη μὲν δοκεῖ τῆς πρὸς Ῥωμαίους ὑστέρα εἶναι. Ἐκείνην μὲν γὰρ οὐδέπω ἰδὼν Ῥωμαίους ἔγραφε, ταύτην δὲ ἤδη τεθεαμένος, καὶ πρὸς τῷ τέλει τοῦ κηρύγματος ὤν. Καὶ δῆλον ἐκεῖθεν. Ἐν γὰρ τῇ ἐπιστολῇ φησι τῇ πρὸς Φιλήμονα, "Τοιοῦτος ὤν, ὡς Παῦλος πρεσβύτης," καὶ ὑπὲρ Ὀνησίμου ἀξιῶν· ἐν ταύτῃ δὲ αὐτὸν πέμπει τὸν Ὀνήσιμον, καθώς φησι, "Σὺν Ὀνησίμῳ τῷ πιστῷ [173] καὶ ἀγαπητῷ ἀδελφῷ," πιστὸν καὶ ἀγαπητὸν καὶ ἀδελφὸν αὐτὸν καλῶν. Διὸ καὶ θαρρούντως λέγει ἐν ταύτῃ τῇ ἐπιστολῇ· "Ἀπὸ τῆς ἐλπίδος τοῦ Εὐαγγελίου, οὗ ἠκούσατε, τοῦ κηρυχθέντος ἐν πάσῃ τῇ κτίσει τῇ ὑπὸ τὸν οὐρανόν." ἤδη γὰρ χρόνον εἶχε τὸ κήρυγμα. Ταύτης οὖν ὑστέραν οἶμαι τὴν πρὸς Τιμόθεον εἶναι, καὶ πρὸς αὐτῇ τῇ τελευτῇ λοιπόν· ἐκεῖ γάρ φησιν, "Ἐγὼ γὰρ ἤδη σπένδομαι." Τῆς μὲν οὖν

[172] OUR FATHER AMONG THE SAINTS, JOHN CHRYSOSTOM,
ARCHBISHOP OF CONSTANTINOPLE,
A COMMENTARY ON THE EPISTLE TO THE COLOSSIANS

HOMILY 1

Paul, an apostle of Jesus Christ by the will of God, and Timothy his brother, to the holy ones and faithful brethren in Christ in Colossae: grace be to you and peace from God our Father [Col 1:1].

All the letters of Paul are holy, but more so those sent while he was in chains,[1] such as that to the Ephesians, that to Philemon, that to Timothy, that to the Philippians, and this present one. Indeed, this one was sent while he was a prisoner, as he says in writing, *"That is indeed why I am in prison, in order to make this clear, as I ought to speak"* [Col 4:4]. But this letter seems to be posterior to that to the Romans.[2] I say this because the letter to the Romans he wrote before seeing them, but this letter when he had already sighted them and was at the end of his preaching. And it's clear from this, for in the letter to Philemon he says, *"Being like Paul the ambassador"* [Phlm 9], and requesting on behalf of Onesimus, but in this letter he sends Onesimus himself, just as he says, *"With Onesimus the faithful* [173] *and beloved brother"* [Col 4:9], calling him a beloved and faithful brother. This is why Paul says encouragingly in the same letter, *"From hope of the gospel that you have heard, preached to every creature under heaven"* [Col 1:23], for it had already been preached for some time.[3] Therefore, I think that the letter to Timothy was written after this one, and at the very end

---

1. The Greek word δεσμός, which occurs frequently in this and the following homilies, is rendered as either "chain" or "bond," according to the context. On Chrysostom's various encomia on Paul's chains, see Mitchell, *Heavenly Trumpet*, 176–85.

2. On Chrysostom's perceptions of the chronology of the Pauline corpus, see p. 2 n. 9 above.

3. Lit. "the preaching already had some time/age."

πρὸς Φιλιππησίους πρεσβυτέρα· ἐκεῖ γὰρ ἦν τότε ἀρχὴν ἔχων τῶν δεσμῶν τῶν ἐν Ῥώμῃ.

Τίνος δὲ ἕνεκεν λέγω πλέον ἔχειν ταύτας τὰς ἐπιστολὰς κατὰ τοῦτο, ὅτι ἐν δεσμοῖς ὢν γράφει; Ὡς ἂν εἰ ἀριστεὺς σφαγὰς μεταξὺ καὶ τρόπαια ἱστὰς ἐπέστελλεν· οὕτω δὴ ἐποίει καὶ αὐτός. Οἶδε γὰρ καὶ αὐτὸς τοῦτο μέγα ὄν· τῷ γὰρ Φιλήμονι γράφων φησὶν, ""Ὃν ἐγέννησα ἐν τοῖς δεσμοῖς μου." Ταῦτα δὲ εἶπεν, ἵνα μὴ ἀσχάλλωμεν πρὸς τὰ δεινά, ἀλλὰ καὶ χαίρωμεν. Ἐνταῦθα ἦν παρὰ τούτοις Φιλήμων· καὶ γὰρ ἐκεῖ γράφων φησί, "Καὶ Ἀρχίππῳ τῷ συστρατιώτῃ ἡμῶν·" καὶ ἐνταῦθα, "Εἴπατε Ἀρχίππῳ." Δοκεῖ μοι οὗτος ἐγκεχειρίσθαι τινὰ τῆς Ἐκκλησίας.

Οὐκ εἶδε δὲ οὔτε τούτους, οὔτε Ῥωμαίους, οὔτε Ἑβραίους, ἡνίκα ἔγραφε πρὸς αὐτούς. Καὶ περὶ μὲν ἐκείνων πολλαχοῦ δηλοῖ, περὶ δὲ τούτων ἄκουε αὐτοῦ λέγοντος, "Καὶ ὅσοι οὐχ ἑωράκασι τὸ πρόσωπόν μου ἐν σαρκί." καὶ πάλιν, "Εἰ καὶ τῇ σαρκὶ ἄπειμι, ἀλλὰ τῷ πνεύματι σὺν ὑμῖν εἰμι." Οὕτως ἤδει μέγα ὂν τὴν παρουσίαν αὐτοῦ πανταχοῦ, καὶ ἀεὶ ἑαυτὸν καὶ ἀπόντα ἐφίστησι· καὶ ὅταν κολάζῃ τὸν πορνεύοντα, ὅρα πῶς ἑαυτὸν ἐφίστησι τῷ δικαστηρίῳ. "Ἐγὼ μὲν γὰρ, φησὶν, ὡς ἀπὼν τῷ σώματι, παρὼν δὲ τῷ πνεύματι, ἤδη κέκρικα ὡς παρών·" καὶ πάλιν, "Ἐλεύσομαι πρὸς ὑμᾶς, καὶ γνώσομαι οὐ τὸν λόγον τῶν πεφυσιωμένων, ἀλλὰ τὴν δύναμιν." καὶ πάλιν, "Μὴ μόνον ἐν τῷ παρεῖναί με πρὸς ὑμᾶς, ἀλλὰ πολλῷ μᾶλλον ἐν τῷ ἀπεῖναί με."

"Παῦλος ἀπόστολος Ἰησοῦ Χριστοῦ διὰ θελήματος θεοῦ." Ἄξιον δὲ καὶ τὴν ὑπόθεσιν εἰπεῖν, ἣν ἐκ τῆς ἐπιστολῆς εὕρ-[174] ομεν. Τίς οὖν ἐστιν αὕτη; Δι᾽ ἀγγέλων προσήγοντο τῷ θεῷ, παρατηρήσεις εἶχον πολλὰς Ἰουδαϊκὰς καὶ Ἑλληνικάς. Ταῦτ᾽ οὖν διορθοῦται. Διὰ τοῦτο καὶ ἀρχόμενός φησι, "διὰ θελή-

of his life, for there he says, *"for I am already being sacrificed"* (2 Tim 4:6). Therefore, this is earlier than the letter to the Philippians, for there at that time was the beginning of his imprisonment[4] in Rome.

But is the reason I say that these letters are more valuable that he is writing in chains? Just as if a champion in the midst of slaughter and trophies wrote his letters, so indeed did he. You see, he himself knew that this was a great thing, for writing to Philemon he says, *"The one whom I have begotten in my chains"* [Phlm 10]. This he said so that we should not be distressed in adversity, but even rejoice. In this passage Philemon was with them,[5] for writing to him there Paul says, *"And to Archippus, our fellow soldier"* [Phlm 2], and in this letter, *"Tell Archippus"* [Col 4:17]. This man seems to me to have been entrusted with some office of the church.

But Paul hadn't seen these people,[6] nor the Romans, nor the Hebrews, when he wrote to them. That this is disclosed regarding the Hebrews he demonstrates in many passages, while, regarding the Colossians, listen to him saying, *"And all those who have not seen my face in the flesh"* [Col 2:1], and again: *"For even if I am absent in the flesh, I am with you in spirit"* [Col 2:5]. So great did he know his presence everywhere to be, and always, even when absent, he establishes himself [as present]. And when he punishes the fornicator, see how he establishes himself on the tribunal: *"For I,"* he says, *"although absent in body, but present in the spirit, have already pronounced judgement as if present"* [1 Cor 5:3]. And again: *"I will come to you ..., and I will find out not the talk of the arrogant but their power"* [1 Cor 4:19].[7] And again: *"Not only when I am present with you, but much more when I am absent"* [Phil 2:12; Gal 4:18].

Paul, the apostle of Jesus Christ by the will of God [Col 1:1]. It's fitting to ask too what we have found the argument of the letter [**174**] to be. What, then, is it? They used to approach God through angels; they had many Jewish and Hellenic observances.[8] Therefore, he is correcting these faults.

---

4. Lit. "at the beginning of his chains."

5. That is, the Colossians.

6. The view of Theodore of Mopsuestia (*Commentarii in epistulas Pauli minores*, ed. Swete, 253) and Theodoret as well (PG 82:592BC).

7. This quotation is slightly shorter than the New Testament text.

8. Angels and angel worship are frequent themes in Chrysostom's homilies on Colossians, because the people of Colossae were heirs to a syncretistic tradition that combined elements of Judaism and paganism (see in detail Arnold, *Colossian Syncretism*). Severian of Gabala explains in a fragmentary work that both Hellenes and

ματος θεοῦ." Ἰδοὺ πάλιν τὸ, διὰ, τέθεικε. "Καὶ Τιμόθεος ὁ ἀδελφός," φησίν. Οὐκοῦν καὶ αὐτὸς ἀπόστολος. Εἰκὸς ἦν καὶ τοῦτον αὐτοῖς γνωρίζεσθαι. "Τοῖς ἐν Κολοσσαῖς ἁγίοις." Ἡ πόλις τῆς Φρυγίας ἦν· καὶ δῆλον ἐκ τοῦ τὴν Λαοδίκειαν πλησίον εἶναι· "Καὶ πιστοῖς ἀδελφοῖς ἐν Χριστῷ." Πόθεν, φησίν, ἅγιος γέγονας, εἰπέ μοι; πόθεν πιστὸς καλῇ; οὐχ ὅτι διὰ τοῦ θανάτου ἡγιάσθης; οὐχ ὅτι εἰς Χριστὸν πιστεύεις; Πόθεν ἀδελφὸς γέγονας; οὐ γὰρ ἐν ἔργῳ, οὐδὲ ἐν λόγῳ, οὐδὲ ἐν κατορθώματι πιστὸς ἐφάνης. Πόθεν τοσαῦτα ἐπιστεύθης, εἰπέ μοι, μυστήρια; οὐ διὰ Χριστόν;

"Χάρις ὑμῖν καὶ εἰρήνη ἀπὸ θεοῦ πατρὸς ἡμῶν." Πόθεν ἡ χάρις ὑμῖν; πόθεν ἡ εἰρήνη; "Ἀπὸ θεοῦ, φησί, Πατρὸς ἡμῶν." Καίτοι ἐν ταύτῃ τὸ τοῦ Χριστοῦ οὐ τίθησιν ὄνομα. Πρὸς τοὺς τὸ πνεῦμα διαβάλλοντας ἐρῶ, πόθεν ὁ θεὸς πατὴρ τῶν δούλων; Ταῦτα τὰ μεγάλα τίς κατώρθωσε; τίς ἅγιόν σε ἐποίησε; τίς πιστόν; τίς υἱὸν τοῦ θεοῦ; Ὁ ποιήσας σε ἀξιόπιστον, αὐτὸς καὶ τοῦ πιστευθῆναί σε ἅπαντα αἴτιος. Πιστοὶ γὰρ οὐ διὰ τὸ πιστεύειν καλούμεθα μόνον, ἀλλὰ καὶ διὰ τὸ πιστευθῆναι παρὰ τοῦ θεοῦ μυστήρια, ἅπερ οὐδὲ ἄγγελοι πρὸ ἡμῶν ᾔδεσαν. Ἀλλ' ἀδιάφορον τῷ Παύλῳ οὕτω ταῦτα τιθέναι.

"Εὐχαριστοῦμεν τῷ θεῷ τῷ πατρὶ τοῦ κυρίου ἡμῶν Ἰησοῦ Χριστοῦ." Ἐμοὶ δοκεῖ πάντα ἐπὶ τὸν πατέρα ἀνατιθέναι, ὥστε μὴ εὐθέως αὐτοῖς προστῆναι τὸν λόγον. "Πάντοτε περὶ ὑμῶν προσευχόμενοι." Οὐ διὰ τῆς εὐχαριστίας μόνον, ἀλλὰ καὶ τῆς διηνεκοῦς εὐχῆς, τὴν ἀγάπην δείκνυσιν, ὅτι καὶ οὓς οὐχ ἑώρα, τούτους εἶχε διὰ παντὸς ἐν ἑαυτῷ. "Ἀκούσαντες τὴν πίστιν ὑμῶν ἐν Χριστῷ Ἰησοῦ." Ἀνωτέρω, "τοῦ κυρίου [175] ἡμῶν," εἰπών, αὐτός ἐστι κύριος, φησίν, οὐχ οἱ δοῦλοι. "Ἰησοῦ Χριστοῦ." Καὶ ταῦτα σύμβολα τῆς εὐεργεσίας· "Αὐτὸς γὰρ, φησί, σώσει τὸν λαὸν αὐτοῦ ἀπὸ τῶν ἁμαρτιῶν αὐτῶν."

Ἀκούσαντες τὴν πίστιν ὑμῶν ἐν Χριστῷ Ἰησοῦ, καὶ τὴν ἀγάπην τὴν εἰς πάντας τοὺς ἁγίους." Ἤδη οἰκειοῦται αὐτούς. Ἐπαφρόδιτός ἐστιν ὁ ταῦτα ἀπαγγέλλων· πέμπει δὲ τὴν ἐπιστολὴν διὰ Τυχικοῦ, ἐκεῖνον παρ' ἑαυτῷ κατασχών. "Καὶ τὴν ἀγάπην, φησί, τὴν εἰς πάντας τοὺς ἁγίους." Οὐκ εἰς τόνδε

This is why he says right at the beginning *"by the will of God."* See, again he has used the word *"by."* *"And Timothy our brother"* [Col 1:1], he says. Naturally, he too was an apostle, and likely also known to them. *"To the holy ones in Colossae"* [Col 1:2]. This was a city in Phrygia, which is obvious from its proximity to Laodicea. *"And to the faithful brethren in Christ."* "How is it," he says, "that you have become a saint—tell me? How is it that you're called faithful? Isn't it because you were sanctified by death?[9] Isn't it because you have faith in Christ? How is it that you've become a brother? I mean that you didn't demonstrate that you were faithful by deed or word or achievement. How is it that you've been entrusted with such great mysteries—tell me? Isn't it because of Christ?"

Grace be to you and peace from God our Father [Col 1:2]. How is it that grace is to you? How is it that peace is? *"From God,"* he says, *"our Father."* Yet in this passage he doesn't mention the name of Christ. To those who malign the Spirit I ask how it is that God is the father of servants. Who wrought these mighty achievements? Who made you a saint? Who [made you] faithful? Who [made you] a son of God? The one who made you worthy of faith is the same one who is responsible for having you entrusted with everything. You see, we are called faithful not only because we have faith but also because of being entrusted by God with mysteries that not even the angels knew before we did. However, it was a matter of indifference to Paul whether to express these matters this way.

We give thanks to God, the Father of our Lord Jesus Christ [Col 1:3]. He seems to me to refer everything to the Father, in order not to impose his words on them immediately. *Praying for you at all times* [Col 1:9]. It isn't only by giving thanks but also by constant prayer that he shows his love, because the ones whom he didn't see, he kept in himself throughout. *Having heard of your faith in Christ Jesus* [Col 1:4]. Above, while saying [**175**] *"of our Lord"* [Col 1:3], he says that he is Lord, not that they're the servants of Jesus Christ. And these expressions are the symbols of his bounty to us, for *"he,"* it means, *"will save his people from their sins"* [Matt 1:21].

Since we heard of your faith in Christ Jesus, and of your love toward all the saints [Col 1:4]. He is already winning them over. It was Epaphroditus who brought this news, but Paul sends the letter through Tychicus, because he kept Epaphroditus with him. *"And the love,"* he says, *"that you*

Jews persuaded the Colossians to worship angels (see Staab, *Pauluskommentare aus der griechischen Kirche*, 315–16).

9. That is, the death of Christ.

καὶ τόνδε· οὐκοῦν καὶ εἰς ἡμᾶς. "Διὰ τὴν ἐλπίδα τὴν ἀποκειμένην ὑμῖν ἐν τοῖς οὐρανοῖς." Τὰ μέλλοντά φησιν ἀγαθά. Τοῦτο πρὸς τοὺς πειρασμούς, ὥστε μὴ ἐνταῦθα ζητεῖν τὴν ἄνεσιν. Ἵνα γὰρ μή τις εἴπη, καὶ τί τὸ κέρδος τῆς ἀγάπης τῆς εἰς τοὺς ἁγίους, κοπτομένων αὐτῶν; χαίρομεν, φησίν, ὅτι μεγάλα ἑαυτοῖς προξενεῖτε ἐν τοῖς οὐρανοῖς. "Διὰ τὴν ἐλπίδα, φησί, τὴν ἀποκειμένην." Τὸ ἀσφαλὲς ἔδειξεν. "Ἣν προηκούσατε ἐν τῷ λόγῳ τῆς ἀληθείας." Ἐνταῦθα πλήττοντος αὐτοὺς ἐστι τὸ ῥῆμα, ὅτι πολὺν χρόνον ἔχοντες μετέστησαν. "Ἣν προηκούσατε, φησίν, ἐν τῷ λόγῳ τῆς ἀληθείας τοῦ εὐαγγελίου." Καὶ ἀλήθειαν μαρτυρεῖ, εἰκότως· ὅτι οὐδὲν ψεῦδος ἐν αὐτῷ.

"Τοῦ εὐαγγελίου." Οὐ λέγει, τοῦ κηρύγματος, ἀλλ᾽ εὐαγγέλιον καλεῖ, συνεχῶς ἀναμιμνήσκων αὐτοὺς τῶν εὐεργεσιῶν τοῦ θεοῦ. Καὶ πρῶτον ἐπαινέσας αὐτούς, οὕτω τούτων ἀναμιμνήσκει. "Τοῦ παρόντος εἰς ὑμᾶς, καθὼς καὶ ἐν παντὶ τῷ κόσμῳ." Ἤδη χαρίζεται αὐτοῖς. "Παρόντος" δὲ μεταφορικῶς εἶπεν· οὐ παρεγένετο, φησί, καὶ ἀπέστη, ἀλλ᾽ ἔμεινε καὶ ἔστιν ἐκεῖ. Εἶτα, ἐπειδὴ μάλιστα οἱ πολλοὶ ἐκ τοῦ κοινωνοὺς ἔχειν πολλοὺς τῶν δογμάτων στηρίζονται, διὰ τοῦτο ἐπήγαγε, "καθὼς καὶ ἐν παντὶ τῷ κόσμῳ." Πανταχοῦ πάρεστι, πανταχοῦ κρατεῖ, πανταχοῦ ἔστηκε. "Καὶ ἔστι καρποφορούμενον, καὶ αὐξανόμενον, καθὼς καὶ ἐν ὑμῖν." Καρποφορούμενον διὰ τὰ ἔργα, αὐξανόμενον τῷ πολλοὺς παραλαμβάνειν, τῷ μᾶλλον στηρίζεσθαι. Καὶ γὰρ ἐν τοῖς φυτοῖς τότε πυκνὰ γίνεται, ὅταν [176] στηριχθῇ τὸ φυτόν. "Καθὼς καὶ ἐν ὑμῖν," φησί. Προκαταλαμβάνει τὸν ἀκροατὴν τοῖς ἐπαίνοις, ὥστε μηδὲ ἄκοντα ἀποστῆναι. "Ἀφ᾽ ἧς ἡμέρας ἠκούσατε." Τὸ θαυμαστόν, ὅτι ταχέως προσήλθετε καὶ ἐπιστεύσατε, καὶ εὐθέως ἐκ προοιμίων ἐπεδείξασθε τοὺς καρπούς. "Ἀφ᾽ ἧς ἡμέρας ἠκούσατε καὶ ἐπέγνωτε τὴν χάριν τοῦ θεοῦ ἐν ἀληθείᾳ." Οὐκ ἐν λόγῳ, φησίν, οὐδὲ ἐν ἀπάτῃ, ἀλλ᾽ ἐν αὐτοῖς τοῖς ἔργοις. Τοῦτο τοίνυν λέγει, "καρποφορούμενον·" ἤτοι τὰ σημεῖα καὶ τὰ θαύματα, ὅτι ἅμα ἐδέξασθε, ἅμα ἔγνωτε τὴν χάριν τοῦ θεοῦ. Τὸ τοίνυν εὐθέως ἐπιδειξάμενον τὴν οἰκείαν δύναμιν νῦν ἀπιστεῖσθαι πῶς οὐ χαλεπόν;

"Καθὼς καὶ ἐμάθετε παρὰ Ἐπαφρᾶ τοῦ ἀγαπητοῦ συνδούλου ἡμῶν." Τοῦτον εἰκὸς ἐκεῖ κεκηρυχέναι· ἐμάθετε τὸ εὐαγγέλιον. Εἶτα τὸ ἀξιόπιστον

have toward all the saints" [Col 1:4], not to this one or that one—of course to us also. *Because of the hope laid up for us in heaven* [Col 1:5]. He means the good things to come. This is with a view to their temptations, so that they don't seek relief here. You see, lest anybody say, "What's the benefit of love for the saints if they themselves are stricken?" he says, "We rejoice that you are procuring great things for yourself in heaven. '*Through the hope*,' he says, '*that is laid up*'" [Col 1:5].[10] He has shown what is safe. *Which you have heard before in the word of the truth* [Col 1:5]. Here the expression is of one chiding them, because having held it [sc. the word of the truth] for a long time, they had changed their minds. "*Which you heard before*," he says, "*in the word of the truth of the gospel.*" And he testified to the truth of the word—rightly so, because there is nothing false in it.

Of the gospel. He doesn't say "of the preaching" but calls it "*the gospel*," reminding them continually of God's benefits, and having first praised them he thus reminds them of these. "*Which has come to you, as indeed it has in the whole world*" [Col 1:6]. Now he humors them. "*Has come*" he said metaphorically; he doesn't say it didn't come and go away, but that it remains and exists there. Then, because most people very strongly confirm the many doctrines that are held in common, he therefore adds, "*as indeed it has in the whole world.*" It is present everywhere, everywhere victorious, everywhere established. "*And it is bearing fruit and growing, just as it is also in you*" [Col 1:6]. It's bearing fruit because of works; it's growing because of admitting many, by becoming firmer. You see, in plants they begin to become dense when [**176**] the plant becomes firm. "*Just as it is also in you*," he says. He overtakes the listener by his praise, so that not even unwillingly does the latter reject it. *Since the day you heard it* [Col 1:6]. What is amazing is that you quickly came to it and believed, and immediately from the very first you showed its fruits. *Since the day you heard it and understood the grace of God in truth* [Col 1:6]. Not in the word, he means, nor in deceit, but in works themselves. This is what he means by *bearing fruit*, or else it is signs and wonders, because the moment you received it you understood the grace of God. Therefore, how isn't it difficult now to disbelieve what immediately gave proof of its own power?

Just as you also learned from Epaphras our beloved fellow servant [Col 1:7]. It's likely that he had preached there: you've learned the preaching.

---

10. Severian of Gabala states explicitly that *the hope that is laid up* has nothing to do with angels but with the parousia (see Staab, *Pauluskommentare aus der griechischen Kirche*, 316).

δεικνὺς τοῦ ἀνδρός, φησί, "τοῦ συνδούλου ἡμῶν. Ὅς ἐστι πιστὸς ὑπὲρ ὑμῶν διάκονος τοῦ Χριστοῦ, ὁ καὶ δηλώσας ἡμῖν τὴν ὑμῶν ἀγάπην ἐν πνεύματι." Μὴ ἀμφιβάλλετε, φησί, περὶ τῆς μελλούσης ἐλπίδος· ὁρᾶτε τὴν οἰκουμένην ἐπιστρέφουσαν. Καὶ τί δεῖ λέγειν τὰ ἐν τοῖς ἄλλοις; τὰ ἐν ὑμῖν αὐτοῖς καὶ χωρὶς τούτων πιστά. "Ἐπέγνωτε γὰρ τὴν χάριν τοῦ Θεοῦ ἐν ἀληθείᾳ." τουτέστιν, ἐν τοῖς ἔργοις. Ὥστε δύο ταῦτα τὰ μέλλοντα βεβαιοῦται, τό τε πάντας πιστεῦσαι, τό τε καὶ ὑμᾶς· καὶ οὐκ ἄλλα μὲν ἐγένετο, ἄλλα δὲ εἶπεν Ἐπαφρᾶς. "Ὅς ἐστι, φησί, πιστός." τουτέστιν, ἀληθής. Πῶς "ὑπὲρ ὑμῶν διάκονος"; Τῷ πρὸς αὐτὸν ἀπελθεῖν. "Ὁ καὶ δηλώσας ἡμῖν, φησί, τὴν ὑμῶν ἀγάπην ἐν πνεύματι·" τουτέστι, τὴν πνευματικὴν τὴν εἰς ἡμᾶς. Εἰ οὗτος τοῦ Χριστοῦ διάκονος, πῶς δι' ἀγγέλων λέγετε προσάγεσθαι; "Ὁ καὶ δηλώσας ἡμῖν, φησί, τὴν ὑμῶν ἀγάπην ἐν πνεύματι."Αὕτη γὰρ θαυμαστὴ καὶ βεβαία ἡ ἀγάπη· ὡς αἵ γε ἄλλαι ὄνομα ἀγάπης ἔχουσι μόνον. Εἰσὶ δέ τινες οὐ τοιαῦται· ἀλλ' οὐ φιλία τοῦτο· διὸ καὶ εὐδιάλυτος γίνεται.

Πολλαὶ προφάσεις εἰσὶν αἱ φιλίας ποιοῦσαι· καὶ τὰς μὲν αἰσχρὰς παρήσομεν· οὐδεὶς γὰρ ἡμῖν ὑπὲρ ἐκείνων ἀντερεῖ, ὡς πονηρῶν οὐσῶν· ἀλλ', εἰ βούλεσθε, τὰς φυσικὰς καὶ τὰς βιωτικὰς εἰς μέσον παραγάγωμεν. Βιωτικαὶ μὲν οὖν εἰσιν αὗται· [177] οἷον εὖ ἔπαθέ τις, ἀπὸ προγόνων ἐκτήσατο φίλον, ἐκοινώνησε τραπέζης ἢ ἀποδημίας, ἢ γείτων ἐστί· καλαὶ καὶ αὗται· ἢ ὁμότεχνος γέγονεν· αὕτη μὲν οὖν οὐκ ἔστιν εἰλικρινής· ἔχει γάρ τινα καὶ ζῆλον καὶ βασκανίαν. Αἱ δὲ φυσικαί, οἷον πατρὸς πρὸς υἱόν, υἱοῦ πρὸς πατέρα, ἀδελφοῦ πρὸς ἀδελφόν, πρὸς ἔκγονον πάππου, μητρὸς πρὸς τέκνα· εἰ δὲ βούλεσθε, καὶ τὴν τῆς γυναικὸς πρὸς ἄνδρα· καὶ γὰρ πᾶσαι αἱ γαμικαί εἰσι βιωτικαὶ καὶ γήϊναι. Αὗται μὲν οὖν ἐκείνων εἶναι δοκοῦσι σφοδρότεραι· δοκοῦσι δέ, εἶπον, διὰ τὸ πολλάκις ὑπ' ἐκείνων ἡττηθῆναι. Καὶ γὰρ φίλοι ἀλλαχοῦ γνησιώτερον ἐφάνησαν ἀδελφῶν διακείμενοι, καὶ υἱῶν πρὸς πατέρας· καὶ ὁ μὲν γεννηθεὶς οὐκ ἐβοήθησεν, ὁ δὲ μὴ γνοὺς αὐτόν, παρέστη καὶ ἐβοήθησεν. Ἡ δὲ πνευματικὴ ἀγάπη πασῶν ἐστιν ἀνωτέρα, καθάπερ τις βασίλισσα τῶν ἰδίων

Then, demonstrating the trustworthiness of the man, he says, "*Our fellow servant.*" "*He is a faithful minister of Christ on your behalf and has shown us your love in the Spirit*" [Col 1:8]. "Don't doubt," he says, "about the hope that is to come: you see that the world is being converted. And why is it necessary to speak about the cases of others? Your own case even without them is [evidence of] faith. For *you understood the grace of God in truth,* that is, in works. So that these two things, the faith of all and of yourselves too, confirm what is to come." Nor was what happened one thing, and what Epaphras said another. "*He is faithful,*" Paul says, which means true. How is he *a minister on your behalf*? Because he had gone to Paul, and, Paul says, "*shown us your love in the Spirit,*" that means the spiritual love toward us. If Epaphras was a minister of Christ, how can you say that you were brought [to God] by angels?[11] "*He showed us your love in the Spirit,*" he says. For this love is amazing and strong, because all other kinds have only the name of love. There are some that aren't of this kind, but this isn't friendship, which is why it's also easily dissolved.

There are many occasions that produce friendships,[12] and we shall pass over the shameful ones, for nobody will speak against me on their behalf, because they are evil friendships. But, if you like, let's adduce publicly natural friendships and those that pertain to life. Well then, the ones pertaining to life are these, [**177**] for instance: someone has experienced a kindness; he has inherited a friend from his ancestors; he has been a table or travel companion; or he is a neighbor (and these are virtuous friendships); or he has been of the same trade, although this is not sincere for it contains both rivalry and envy. But natural friendships are, for instance, that of a father to a son, a son to a father, a brother to a brother, grandfather to a descendant, a mother to her children. If you like, it's also the friendship of the wife to her husband, for all marital friendships pertain to life and are earthly. Now, these appear to be more robust than the former—I have said that they seem to be, because of their being bested often by the former. And, you see, friends have appeared from time to time more genuinely disposed than brothers, and sons toward their fathers; and when the one who has fathered him is not helped, the one who didn't know him has stood by him and helped. But the spiritual love is higher than all, just as

---

11. On angels and angel worship, see n. 8 above.

12. The theme of friendship occurs frequently in classical and late antique writers. See in detail David Konstan, *Friendship in the Classical World*, KTAH (Cambridge: Cambridge University Press, 1997).

κρατοῦσα, καὶ λαμπρὸν ἔχει τὸ σχῆμα. Οὐδὲν γὰρ γήϊον αὐτὴν τίκτει, καθάπερ ἐκείνην, οὐ συνήθεια, οὐκ εὐεργεσία, οὐ φύσις, οὐ χρόνος, ἀλλ᾽ ἄνωθεν
κάτεισιν ἐκ τοῦ οὐρανοῦ. Καὶ τί θαυμάζεις, εἰ εὐεργεσίας οὐ δεῖται πρὸς τὸ
συνεστάναι, ὅπου γε οὐδὲ τῷ κακῶς παθεῖν ἀνατρέπεται;

Ὅτι δὲ αὕτη μείζων ἐκείνης ἐστίν, ἄκουσον Παύλου λέγοντος· "Ηὐχόμην ἀνάθεμα εἶναι αὐτὸς ἐγὼ ἀπὸ τοῦ Χριστοῦ ὑπὲρ τῶν ἀδελφῶν μου."
Τίς ἂν τοῦτο ηὔξατο πατήρ, ὥστε ἐν κακοῖς εἶναι; Καὶ πάλιν, "Τὸ ἀναλῦσαι
καὶ σὺν Χριστῷ εἶναι πολλῷ μᾶλλον κρεῖσσον· τὸ δὲ ἐπιμεῖναι ἐν τῇ σαρκὶ
ἀναγκαιότερον δι᾽ ὑμᾶς." Ποία μήτηρ ταῦτα ἂν ἕλοιτο εἰπεῖν, ὥστε τὰ αὑτῆς
παριδεῖν; Καὶ πάλιν ἄκουε αὐτοῦ λέγοντος· "Ἀπορφανισθέντες γὰρ ἀφ᾽ ὑμῶν
πρὸς καιρὸν ὥρας, προσώπῳ, οὐ καρδίᾳ." Καὶ ἐνταῦθα μὲν ὁ πατὴρ ὑβρισθεὶς ἔλυσε τὴν φιλίαν, ἐκεῖ δὲ οὐκέτι, ἀλλὰ πρὸς τοὺς λιθάζοντας ἀπήει
εὐεργετήσων αὐτούς. Οὐδὲν γάρ, οὐδὲν οὕτως ἰσχυρόν, ὡς ὁ τοῦ πνεύματος
δεσμός. Ὁ μὲν γὰρ διὰ τὸ παθεῖν εὖ φίλος γενόμενος, ἂν μὴ διηνεκῶς τοῦτο
γίνηται, ἔσται ἐχθρός· ὁ ἀπὸ συνηθείας ἀδιάσπαστος ὤν, πάλιν τῆς συνηθείας
διακοπείσης, ἔσβεσε τὴν φιλίαν. Ἡ γυνὴ πάλιν, ἂν μάχη γένηται, ἀφῆκε τὸν
ἄνδρα, καὶ τὸν πόθον ἔλυσεν· ὁ υἱός, ἂν ἐπιπολὺ ζῶντα τὸν πατέρα ἴδῃ, καὶ
βαρύνεται. Ἐπὶ δὲ τοῦ πνεύματος τούτων οὐκ ἔστιν οὐδέν· οὐδενὶ γὰρ τούτων
λύεται, [178] ἐπεὶ μηδὲ ἐκ τούτων συνέστη· οὔτε χρόνος, οὔτε μῆκος ὁδοῦ,
οὔτε τὸ κακῶς παθεῖν, οὔτε τὸ κακῶς ἀκοῦσαι, οὐ θυμός, οὐχ ὕβρις, οὐκ ἄλλο
οὐδὲν ἐπεισέρχεται, οὐδὲ δύναται αὐτὴν διαλῦσαι. Καὶ ἵνα μάθῃς, ἐλιθάζετο
ὁ Μωϋσῆς, καὶ ὑπὲρ αὐτῶν ἠξίου. Τίς ἂν τοῦτο εἰργάσατο πατὴρ ὑπὲρ τοῦ
λιθάσαντος, ἀλλ᾽ οὐχὶ καὶ αὐτὸν ἂν κατέλευσε;

Ταύτας δὴ μεταδιώκωμεν τὰς φιλίας τὰς ἀπὸ τοῦ πνεύματος· ἰσχυραὶ
γάρ εἰσι καὶ δυσδιάλυτοι· μὴ τὰς ἀπὸ τῶν τραπεζῶν· ἐκεῖ γὰρ καὶ κωλυόμεθα
ταύτας εἰσάγειν. Ἄκουε γὰρ τοῦ Χριστοῦ λέγοντος ἐν τῷ εὐαγγελίῳ. "Μὴ
καλέσῃς τοὺς φίλους σου, μηδὲ τοὺς γείτονάς σου, ἐὰν ποιήσῃς δοχήν, ἀλλὰ
τοὺς χωλούς, τοὺς ἀναπήρους." εἰκότως· πολὺς γὰρ ὁ ὑπὲρ τούτων μισθός.
Ἀλλ᾽ οὐ δύνασαι, οὐδὲ ἀνέχῃ μετὰ χωλῶν καὶ τυφλῶν ἑστιᾶσθαι, ἀλλὰ βαρὺ
καὶ φορτικὸν ἡγῇ τοῦτο, καὶ παραιτῇ; Μάλιστα μὲν οὖν οὐκ ἔδει, πλὴν ἀλλ᾽
οὐκ ἔστιν ἀνάγκη· κἂν μὴ συγκαθίσῃς αὐτοὺς μετὰ σοῦ, τὰ ἐδέσματα αὐτοῖς
ἀπόστειλον τὰ ἀπὸ τῆς τραπέζης. Καὶ ὁ φίλους καλῶν, οὐδὲν μέγα ἐποίησεν·
ἀπέλαβε γὰρ ἐνταῦθα τὸν μισθόν· ὁ δὲ ἀνάπηρον καλῶν καὶ πένητα, ἔχει

some empress, ruling her people, also shines in her appearance. For nothing earthly brings her forth, just as no acquaintance, no beneficence, no nature, no time has, but she descends from on high from heaven. And why are you amazed if she doesn't need beneficence to subsist, where she isn't overthrown even by suffering?

That this love is greater than the other, listen to Paul saying: "*I could wish that I myself were accursed from Christ, for the sake of my brothers*" [Rom 9:3]. What father would make this prayer, in order to end up in misery? And again: "*To depart and be with Christ is by far the better; but remaining in the flesh is more necessary because of you*" [Phil 1:23–24]. What mother would choose to speak these words, in order to overlook herself? And again listen to Paul saying: "*For being bereft of you for a short time, in person, not in heart*" [1 Thess 2:17]. And here [in this life] the father, when insulted, lets his love go, there, on the other hand, it goes no further, but he went to those who had stoned him, trying to do them good. You see, nothing, nothing is as powerful as the bond of the Spirit. I mean, the one who has become a friend through experiencing a kindness will be an enemy if this situation is not ongoing; the one who is inseparable through acquaintance, when the acquaintance is broken through, has put a check on the friendship; again, the wife, if there has been a dispute, has left her husband and let affection go; the son, if he sees his father living to a great age, is indeed depressed. But in the case of spiritual love there's none of this, for it's dissolved by none of these things, [**178**] since it isn't composed from them. Not time, not the length of a journey, not experiencing hurt, not being spoken of badly, not anger, not insult, not anything else comes into it, or is able to dissolve it. And so that you may learn this, Moses was stoned [see Exod 17:4], yet prayed for them. What father would have done this on behalf of the one who stoned him, and not stoned him to death?

Let's then pursue those friendships that are from the Spirit, for they're strong and difficult to dissolve: they aren't the ones that arise from tables, for those we are prevented from bringing in there [sc. heaven]. For hear Christ saying in the gospel: "*Don't invite your friends, nor your neighbors, if you are having a reception, but the lame, the crippled*" [Luke 14:12]. Rightly so, for great is the reward for these deeds. But is it that you can't, nor can you bear to feast with the lame and the blind, but you think this is disgusting and burdensome, and you refuse? Most certainly you shouldn't refuse, but it is, however, not necessary. Even if you don't seat them with you, send them food from your table. The one who invites friends has done nothing

τὸν θεὸν ὀφειλέτην. Μὴ τοίνυν ἀσχάλλωμεν, ὅταν μὴ ἐνταῦθα ἀπολάβωμεν, ἀλλ' ὅταν ἀπολάβωμεν· ἐκεῖ γὰρ οὐκέτι ἀποληψόμεθα ὁμοίως. Ἂν ἄνθρωπος ἀποδῷ, θεὸς οὐκ ἀποδίδωσιν· ἂν οὗτος μὴ ἀποδῷ, τότε ἀποδώσει θεός. Μὴ τοίνυν ἐκείνους ζητῶμεν εὐεργετεῖν τοὺς ἀνταποδοῦναι ἡμῖν δυναμένους, μηδὲ ἐπὶ τοιαύταις αὐτοὺς ἐλπίσιν εὐεργετῶμεν· ψυχρὰ αὕτη ἡ διάνοια. Τὸν φίλον ἂν καλέσῃς, μέχρι τῆς ἑσπέρας ἡ χάρις· διὰ τοῦτο τῶν καταβαλλομένων ταχύτερον ἡ τῶν καιρῶν δαπανᾶται φιλία· τὸν μέντοι πένητα καὶ ἀνάπηρον ἂν καλέσῃς, οὐδέποτε ἀπολεῖται ἡ χάρις· τὸν γὰρ πάντοτε μνημονεύοντα θεὸν, καὶ οὐδέποτε ἐπιλανθανόμενον, ἔχεις αὐτὸν ὀφειλέτην. Πόσης δὲ καὶ βλακείας, εἰπέ μοι, τὸ μὴ δύνασθαι πένησι συγκαθέζεσθαι; Τί λέγεις; Ἀκάθαρτός ἐστι, φησὶ, καὶ ῥυπαρός. Καὶ λοῦσον αὐτὸν, καὶ ἀνάγαγε ἐπὶ τράπεζαν τὴν σήν. Ἀλλ' ἱμάτια ἔχει ἐρρυπωμένα; Καὶ ἄμειψον, καὶ δὸς καθαρὰν στολήν. Οὐχ ὁρᾷς τὸ κέρδος ὅσον; Ὁ Χριστὸς δι' αὐτοῦ παρα-[179]γίνεται, καὶ σὺ ὑπὲρ τούτου μικρολογῇ; τὸν βασιλέα καλῶν ἐπὶ τὴν τράπεζαν, ὑπὲρ τούτων δέδοικας;

Ὑποκείσθωσαν τράπεζαι δύο, καὶ ἡ μὲν ἐκ τούτων πεπληρώσθω, καὶ ἐχέτω τυφλοὺς, χωλοὺς, κυλλοὺς, τὴν χεῖρα, τὸ σκέλος πεπηρωμένους, ἀνυποδέτους, ἕνα περικειμένους χιτωνίσκον, καὶ τοῦτον ἐκτετριμμένον· ἡ δὲ ἑτέρα ἐχέτω δυνάστας, στρατηγοὺς, τοπάρχας, ἄρχοντας μεγάλους, ἐνδεδυμένους ἱμάτια πολυτελῆ καὶ ὀθόνας λεπτὰς, ἐζωσμένους ζώνας χρυσᾶς. Πάλιν ἐνταῦθα ἐν τῇ τῶν πενήτων τραπέζῃ μήτε ἄργυρος ἔστω, μήτε οἶνος πολὺς, ἀλλ' ὁ ἀρκῶν καὶ εὐφρᾶναι δυνάμενος· τὰ δὲ ἐκπώματα καὶ τὰ λοιπὰ σκεύη ἀπὸ ὑέλου κατασκευαζέσθω μόνης· ἐκεῖ δὲ ἐν τῇ τῶν πλουσίων τραπέζῃ ἔστω μὲν σκεύη τὰ πάντα ἐξ ἀργύρου καὶ χρυσοῦ, καὶ μηδὲ εἷς φερέτω τὸ ἡμικύκλιον, ἀλλὰ δύο νεανίαι μόλις αὐτὸ κινείτωσαν· καὶ οἱ ἀμφορεῖς κείσθωσαν ἐφεξῆς πολλῷ ἄμεινον τοῦ ἀργύρου ἀπολάμποντες τῷ χρυσῷ· ἔστω δὲ καὶ τὸ ἡμικύκλιον ἀπαλῇ στρωμνῇ πάντοθεν ἐστορεσμένον. Πάλιν ἐνταῦθα μὲν ἔστωσαν διάκονοι πολλοὶ, τῶν κατακειμένων οὐχ ἧττον κεκοσμημένοι τοῖς ἱματίοις, καὶ ἐνδεδυμένοι λαμπρῶς, καὶ ἀναξυρίδας ἔχοντες, καλοὶ μὲν ἰδεῖν, αὐτὸ τῆς ἡλικίας τὸ ἄνθος, σφριγῶντες καὶ εὐσωματοῦντες· ἐκεῖ δὲ δύο μόνοι ἔστωσαν διάκονοι, πάντα τὸν τῦφον τοῦτον πεπατηκότες· καὶ ἔστω τοῖς μὲν τὰ ἐδέσματα πολυτελῆ, τοῖς δὲ τοσαῦτα ὅσα σβέσαι τὸν λιμὸν, καὶ εὐφροσύνης ἐμπλῆσαι. Ἆρα εἶπον ἀρκούντως; καὶ μετὰ ἀκριβείας κατεσκευασμέναι εἰσὶν ἀμφότεραι αἱ τράπεζαι; μή τι ἐνδεῖ; Ἐγὼ μὲν οὐκ οἶμαι· καὶ γὰρ τοὺς κεκλημένους ἐπῆλθον, καὶ τὴν πολυτέλειαν καὶ τῶν σκευῶν καὶ τῶν στρωμάτων καὶ τῶν ἐδεσμάτων· πλὴν ἀλλὰ καὶ εἴ τι παρελίπομεν, ἐπεξαγαγόντες τὸν λόγον εὑρήσομεν.

great, for he has received his reward here, whereas the one who invites the crippled and the poor has God as his debtor. Therefore, let's not be distressed when we don't receive a reward here but when we *do* receive it here, for we shall no longer receive it there in like measure. If a human being pays you, God won't pay; if a human being doesn't pay, then God will pay. Therefore, let's not seek to do good to those who are able to pay us back, nor do good to them out of such expectations. That is a cold thought. If you invite your friend, the good will last until evening; that is because the friendship is used up sooner than the cost and the time. If, however, you invite the poor and the crippled, the friendship will never be abandoned, for God, who always remembers and never forgets—you have him as your debtor. Tell me, how stupid is it not to be able to sit down with the poor? What do you reply? "He's unclean," you say, "and filthy." Well, wash him and bring him to your table. But he's got soiled clothes? Well, change them and give him a clean garment. Don't you see how great the gain is? Christ comes to you through him [179], and do you speak pettily of him? If you invite the emperor to your table, are you afraid of these things?

Let two tables be supposed, and let one be filled with those people and have the blind, the lame, the bent, those stiff in hand and limb, the barefoot, those clad in one short piece of clothing, and that worn out. But let the other have rulers, generals, governors, great leaders, dressed in costly clothes and fine linens, girded with gold belts. Again, there at the table of the poor let there be neither silver nor an abundance of wine, but what is sufficient and can make people happy. Let the drinking cups and other vessels be made only of glass. But there at the table of the rich let all the vessels be of silver and gold, and let not one person be able to lift the semicircular table, but let two young men move it with difficulty; and let the wine jars lie in order, glittering much better than the silver with their gold. Let the semicircular table be spread all over with soft covering. Again, let there be many attendants there, adorned with their cloaks no less that those who are seated, and brilliantly clad, and wearing trousers, handsome to behold, in the very flower of youth, vigorous and well-grown. But there let there be only two servants, who have despised all that vanity. And let there be expensive dishes on the one side, but on the other just as much as to quell hunger and to fill with good cheer. Well, have I said enough? And are both tables set with care for detail? Is there anything missing? I don't think so. You see, I've gone over the guests, and the cost of the utensils, and the cloths, and the dishes. However, if we've passed over something, we shall find out as we continue the argument.

Φέρε οὖν, ἐπειδὴ τὸ πρόσφορον καλῶς ἡμῖν ἀπέλαβε σχῆμα ἑκάστη τράπεζα, ἴδωμεν ποῦ ὑμεῖς κατακλιθήσεσθε. Ἐγὼ μὲν γὰρ ἐπ' [180] ἐκείνην ἄπειμι τὴν τῶν τυφλῶν, τὴν τῶν χωλῶν· ὑμῶν δὲ τάχα οἱ πλείους ταύτην αἱρήσονται, τὴν τῶν στρατηγῶν, τὴν λαμπρὰν καὶ φαιδράν. Ἴδωμεν οὖν ποία πλείονος γέμει τῆς ἡδονῆς· μήπω γὰρ τὰ μέλλοντα ἐξετάσωμεν· ἐν ἐκείνοις μὲν γὰρ αὕτη κρατεῖ ἡ ἐμή. Διὰ τί; Ὅτι αὕτη μὲν ἔχει τὸν Χριστὸν ἀνακείμενον, ἐκείνη δὲ ἀνθρώπους· αὕτη τὸν δεσπότην, ἐκείνη τοὺς δούλους. Ἀλλὰ μήπω ταῦτα, ἀλλ' ἴδωμεν ποία πλείονα ἔχει τὴν ἡδονὴν τὴν ἐν τῷ παρόντι. Καὶ κατὰ τοῦτο μὲν οὖν πλείων αὕτη ἡ ἡδονή· τὸ γὰρ μετὰ βασιλέως ἀναπεσεῖν, πλείονα φέρει τὴν ἡδονὴν τοῦ μετὰ τῶν οἰκετῶν. Ἀλλὰ καὶ τοῦτο ὑπεξέλωμεν, αὐτὸ καθ' ἑαυτὸ τὸ πρᾶγμα ἐξετάσωμεν. Οὐκοῦν ἐγώ, καὶ οἱ σὺν ἐμοὶ ταύτην ἑλόμενοι τὴν τράπεζαν, μετὰ πολλῆς τῆς ἐλευθερίας καὶ τῆς θυμηδίας καὶ ἐροῦμεν ἅπαντα, καὶ ἀκουσόμεθα· ὑμεῖς δὲ τρέμοντες καὶ δεδοικότες, καὶ τοὺς ἀνακειμένους αἰδούμενοι, οὐδὲ ἐκτεῖναι χεῖρα τολμήσετε, καθάπερ εἰς παιδαγωγεῖον, ἀλλ' οὐκ εἰς ἄριστον εἰσελθόντες, καθάπερ δεσπότας δεινοὺς τρέμοντες. Ἀλλ' οὐκ ἐκεῖνοι οὕτως. Ἀλλὰ τὰ τῆς τιμῆς, φησί, μεγάλα. Καὶ μὴν ἐγὼ ἐν πλείονί εἰμι τιμῇ· ὑμῶν μὲν γὰρ ἡ εὐτέλεια μείζων φαίνεται, ὅταν καὶ τῆς αὐτῆς τραπέζης κοινωνοῦντες, δούλων προβάλλησθε ῥήματα.

Καὶ γὰρ ὁ δοῦλος τότε μάλιστα φαίνεται, ὅταν μετὰ τοῦ δεσπότου κατακείμενος ᾖ. Ἐκεῖνος μὲν γὰρ, ἔνθα μὴ προσῆκεν αὐτῷ, γίνεται, οὐ τοσαύτην ἀπὸ τῆς οἰκειώσεως ἔχων σεμνότητα, ὅσην τὴν ταπείνωσιν· σφόδρα γὰρ τότε ταπεινοῦται. Καὶ τὸν δοῦλον ἴδοι τις ἂν λαμπρὸν ὄντα καθ' ἑαυτόν, καὶ τὸν πένητα λαμπρὸν ὄντα καθ' ἑαυτόν, ἢ ὅταν μετὰ πλουσίου βαδίζῃ· τὸ γὰρ ταπεινὸν, ὅταν ἐγγὺς ᾖ τοῦ ὑψηλοῦ, τότε φαίνεται ταπεινόν, καὶ ἡ παράθεσις τὸ ταπεινὸν ταπεινότερον δείκνυσιν, οὐχ ὑψηλότερον. Οὕτω καὶ ὑμᾶς εὐτελεστέρους δείκνυσι τὸ μετ' ἐκείνων ἀνακεῖσθαι, ἀλλ' οὐχ ἡμᾶς. Δύο μὲν οὖν τούτοις πλεονεκτοῦμεν, τῇ τε ἐλευθερίᾳ, καὶ τῇ τιμῇ, ὧν οὐδὲν ἴσον εἰς ἡδονῆς λόγον ἐστί. Βουλήσομαι γὰρ ἂν ἔγωγε ἄρτου μεταλαβεῖν μετ' ἐλευθερίας, ἢ μυρίων ἐδεσμάτων μετὰ δουλείας. "Κρεῖσσον γάρ, φησί, ξενισμὸς λαχάνων πρὸς φιλίαν καὶ χάριν, ἢ βοῦς ἀπὸ φάτνης μετ' ἔχθρας." Ὁ γὰρ ἂν εἴπωσιν ἐκεῖνοι, ἀνάγκη τοὺς παρόντας ἐπαινεῖν, ἢ [181] προσκρούειν,

Now then, since each table has assumed its fitting appearance well, let's see where you will recline.[13] For my part, I'm [**180**] going off to the table of the blind, of the lame, but probably most of you will choose the one of the generals, which is resplendent and joyous. Let's see, then, which of them is more replete with pleasure; for let's not examine yet the things that are to come. Indeed, in the case of these tables, mine is superior. Why? Because it's devoted to Christ, but the other to human beings. One has the Master, the other the slaves. But none of that as yet; let's look at how much more pleasure it affords at present. And in this respect, then, there is more pleasure, for to lie down with the emperor brings more pleasure than lying down with the household menials. But let's withdraw this point too; let's examine the issue itself. So I and those who chose this table with me will speak on all matters with great freedom and gladness of heart, and we shall be heard. But you, trembling and afraid,[14] and in shame at those who recline at table with you, will not dare even to reach out a hand, as if you were entering a school rather than a dinner, as if trembling at dreaded masters. But they don't agree. "But the honor is great," they say. Indeed, I am in greater honor, for your cheapness appears greater, when even while sharing the same table you utter words of slaves.

I mean that a slave most of all appears as such when he reclines with his master, for he is in a place where he shouldn't be, and he draws not so much dignity from the familiarity as he does abasement. You see that at that stage he is seriously abased. And one may see a slave being splendid by himself, and the poor person splendid in himself, or[15] when he is walking with a rich man. For the abased, when close to the lofty, then appears abased, and the juxtaposition demonstrates that the abased is more abased, not loftier. And accordingly, reclining with them demonstrates that you are cheaper, but we are not. Therefore, we have the advantage on two points, both freedom and honor, of which there is no equal in respect to pleasure. You see, I for my part would prefer to partake of bread with freedom than a myriad of meat dishes in servitude. For "*better*," it says, "*is entertainment with herbs in friendship and kindness than a fatted ox with hatred*" [Prov 15:17]. Whatever they may say, it's necessary for those present to approve or [**181**] else give

---

13. Here and in the following passages two different Greek verbs are used for reclining at table, namely, ἀνάκειμαι (lie at table) and κατακλίνω (recline). I have used *recline* for both.

14. See 1 Cor 2:3; 2 Cor 7:15; Eph 6:5; Phil 2:12.

15. One manuscript omits "or."

παρασίτων τάξιν ἀναδεδεγμένους, μᾶλλον δὲ ἐκείνων χείρους ὄντας. Τοῖς μὲν
γὰρ εἰ καὶ μετ' αἰσχύνης καὶ τοῦ ὑβρίζεσθαι, ὅμως μέτεστι παρρησίας· ὑμῖν
δὲ οὐδὲ τούτου. Ἀλλ' ἡ μὲν εὐτέλεια τοσαύτη· δεδοίκατε γὰρ καὶ κατεπτή-
χατε· ἡ δὲ τιμὴ οὐκέτι. Οὐκοῦν πάσης μὲν ἡδονῆς ἀπεστέρηται ἡ τράπεζα
ἐκείνη, πάσης δὲ αὕτη γέμει θυμηδίας.
Ἀλλὰ καὶ αὐτῶν τῶν ἐδεσμάτων τὴν φύσιν ἐξετάσωμεν. Ἐκεῖ μὲν γὰρ
ἀνάγκη καὶ μὴ βουλομένῳ διαρρήγνυσθαι τῷ πολλῷ οἴνῳ, ἐνταῦθα δὲ οὐκ
ἔνι μὴ βουλόμενον ἐσθίειν καὶ πίνειν. Ὥστε ἐκεῖ μὲν τὴν ἐκ τῆς τῶν σιτίων
ποιότητος ἡδονὴν ἥ τε προλαβοῦσα ἀτιμία ἀφαιρεῖται, καὶ ἡ ἐκ τῆς πλησμονῆς ἀηδία. Οὐ γὰρ ἧττον λιμοῦ τὰ σώματα ἡμῖν ἡ πλησμονὴ διαφθείρει καὶ
ὀδυνᾷ, ἀλλὰ καὶ πολλῷ χαλεπώτερον· καὶ ὃν ἂν θέλῃς μοι δοῦναι, εὐκολώτερον αὐτὸν διαρρηγνύω τῇ πλησμονῇ τοῦ λιμοῦ. Οὕτω γὰρ τοῦτο ἐκείνου
φορητότερον, ὅτι λιμὸν μὲν ἄν τις καὶ εἴκοσιν ἡμέρας ἐνέγκοι, πλησμονὴν δὲ
οὐδὲ δύο μόνας· καὶ τούτῳ μὲν προσπαλαίοντες διηνεκῶς οἱ ἐν τοῖς ἀγροῖς,
ἐν ὑγείᾳ εἰσὶ καὶ οὐ δέονται ἰατρῶν· ταύτην δέ, τὴν πλησμονὴν λέγω, οὐκ ἂν
ἐνέγκαιεν μὴ συνεχῶς καλοῦντες ἰατρούς· μᾶλλον δὲ καὶ τὴν ἐκείνων βοήθειαν ἤλεγξε πολλάκις ἡ ταύτης τυραννίς.
Καὶ ἡδονῆς μὲν οὖν ἕνεκεν αὕτη τὰ πρῶτα ἔχει. Εἰ γὰρ ἡ τιμὴ τοῦ ἀτι-
μάζεσθαι ἡδίων, καὶ τὸ ἐν ἐξουσίᾳ εἶναι τοῦ ὑποτάσσεσθαι, καὶ τὸ θαρρεῖν
τοῦ τρέμειν καὶ δεδοικέναι, καὶ τὸ τῶν ἀρκούντων ἀπολαύειν τοῦ πέρα τοῦ
μέτρου εἰς τὸ τῆς τρυφῆς καταποντίζεσθαι κλυδώνιον, βελτίων αὕτη ἐκείνης
ἡ τράπεζα καὶ ἡδονῆς ἕνεκεν. Καὶ τὰ τῆς δαπάνης δὲ ἐνταῦθα βελτίω· ἐκείνη
μὲν γὰρ δαπανηρά, αὕτη δὲ οὐκέτι.
Ἀλλὰ τί; ἆρα τοῖς ἀνακειμένοις μόνον ἡδίων αὕτη ἡ τράπεζα, ἢ καὶ τῷ
καλοῦντι πλείονα αὕτη φέρει τὴν ἡδονὴν ἐκείνης; Τοῦτο γάρ ἐστι τὸ μᾶλλον
ζητούμενον ἡμῖν. Οὐκοῦν ὁ μὲν ἐκείνους καλῶν, πρὸ πλειόνων ἡμερῶν παρα-
σκευάζεται, καὶ πράγματα ἔχειν ἀναγκάζεται καὶ φροντίδας καὶ μερίμνας,
οὔτε τὰς νύκτας καθεύδων, οὔτε τὰς ἡμέρας ἡσυχάζων· ἀλλὰ [182] ἀναπλάτ-
των παρ' ἑαυτῷ πολλά, μαγείροις διαλεγόμενος, ὀψοποιοῖς, τραπεζοποιοῖς.
Εἶτα αὐτῆς τῆς ἡμέρας ἐπιστάσης ἴδοι τις ἂν αὐτὸν μᾶλλον δεδοικότα, ἢ
τοὺς μέλλοντας πυκτεύειν, μή τι παρὰ λόγον γένηται, μὴ βασκανίᾳ βληθῇ,
μὴ κατηγόρους ἐκεῖθεν λάβῃ πολλούς. Οὗτος δὲ πάσης ταύτης ἀπήλλακται

offense, assuming the status of parasites, or rather being worse than they. For parasites, albeit with shame and insult, still have free speech, whereas you don't have even this. But your cheapness is so great (you are afraid and cower), but not so great is your honor. Surely that table is deprived of every pleasure, but this one is replete with gladness of heart.

But let's examine the nature of the dishes themselves. For there [at that table] it's necessary, even for the unwilling, to burst with a large amount of wine, whereas here it isn't possible to eat and drink if one doesn't want to. The upshot is that there the dishonor that precedes detracts from the pleasure of the quality of the food, and the nausea from the surfeit. For no less than hunger does surfeit destroy and cause distress to the body, but even much more seriously; the person you wish to give me I shall make burst more easily by surfeit than by hunger. Thus hunger is more easily borne than surfeit, because someone might endure hunger for twenty days, but surfeit scarcely for only two. And in the country people who are continuously struggling with hunger are in good health and don't need doctors, whereas that thing, I mean surfeit, they can't endure without constantly calling doctors. Yes, rather, its stranglehold has often confounded their attempt to help.

And, then, with respect to pleasure, this table holds pride of place. For if honor is more pleasurable than dishonor, and being in power more than being in subjection, and confidence more than trembling and fear,[16] and enjoying what is sufficient more than to drown beyond measure in the tide of luxury—this table is better than that on the score of pleasure. Indeed, here is better in terms of expense, while the other is expensive—but not so here.

What then? Is it only for those who recline that this table is more pleasurable, or does it confer more pleasure than the other to the person who issues the invitation? This is rather what we are inquiring about. So the one who issues the invitation to them makes preparations for many days beforehand and is forced to have practical matters and worries and concerns, neither sleeping at night nor relaxing during the day. No, [182] imagining to himself many points, conversing with cooks, bakers, table setters. Then, when the very day arrives, one may see him more afraid than those who are going to have a boxing match—afraid lest something may turn out contrary to expectation, lest he be harmed by envy, lest from this event he acquire

---

16. See 1 Cor 2:3; 2 Cor 7:15; Eph 6:5; Phil 2:12.

τῆς φροντίδος καὶ τῶν πραγμάτων, αὐτοσχεδιάζων τὴν τράπεζαν, καὶ οὐ πρὸ πολλῶν ἡμερῶν μεριμνῶν. Καὶ μετὰ δὴ ταῦτα οὗτος μὲν εὐθέως τὴν χάριν ἀπώλεσεν, ἐκεῖνος δὲ ἔχει τὸν θεὸν ὀφειλέτην, καὶ χρησταῖς τρέφεται ταῖς ἐλπίσι, καθ' ἑκάστην ἡμέραν εὐωχούμενος ἀπ' ἐκείνης τῆς τραπέζης. Τὰ μὲν γὰρ σιτία ἀναλίσκεται, ἡ δὲ χάρις οὐκ ἀναλίσκεται, ἀλλὰ καθ' ἑκάστην ἡμέραν μᾶλλον χαίρει καὶ γάννυται ἐκείνων τῶν τὸν πολὺν οἶνον ἐμφορηθέντων. Οὐδὲν γὰρ οὕτω τρέφει τὴν ψυχὴν, ὡς ἐλπὶς ἀγαθὴ καὶ τὸ χρηστὰ προσδοκᾶν.

Ἀλλὰ δὴ τὰ μετὰ ταῦτα ἴδωμεν. Ἐκεῖ μὲν αὐλοὶ καὶ κιθάραι καὶ σύριγγες, ἐνταῦθα δὲ οὐδὲν ἀπηχὲς μέλος· ἀλλὰ τί; ὕμνοι, ψαλμῳδίαι. Ἐκεῖ μὲν οἱ δαίμονες ἀνυμνοῦνται, ἐνταῦθα δὲ ὁ πάντων δεσπότης θεός. Ὁρᾷς πόσης μὲν αὕτη χάριτος, πόσης δὲ ἀγνωμοσύνης ἐκείνη καὶ ἀναισθησίας γέμει; Εἰπὲ γάρ μοι· ὁ θεός σε ἔθρεψεν ἐκ τῶν ἀγαθῶν αὐτοῦ, καὶ δέον αὐτῷ εὐχαριστεῖν μετὰ τὸ τραφῆναι, σὺ δὲ τοὺς δαίμονας ἐπεισάγεις; τὰ γὰρ διὰ τῶν πηκτίδων οὐδὲν ἄλλο ἐστὶν, ἢ τῶν δαιμόνων ᾄσματα. Δέον εἰπεῖν, εὐλογητὸς εἶ, κύριε, ὅτι ἔθρεψάς με ἐκ τῶν ἀγαθῶν σου, σὺ δὲ, καθάπερ τις κύων ἄτιμος, οὐδὲ μέμνησαι, ἀλλὰ τοὺς δαίμονας ἐπεισάγεις; Μᾶλλον δὲ οἱ μὲν κύνες λαβόντες καὶ μὴ λαβόντες σαίνουσι τοὺς οἰκείους, σὺ δὲ οὐδὲ τοῦτο. Ὁ κύων καὶ μὴ λαμβάνων σαίνει τὸν δεσπότην, σὺ δὲ καὶ λαβὼν ὑλακτεῖς κατ' αὐτοῦ. Πάλιν ὁ κύων καὶ εὐεργετούμενος παρὰ τοῦ ἀλλοτρίου, οὐδὲ οὕτω καταλύει τὴν ἔχθραν τὴν πρὸς αὐτὸν, οὐδὲ ἐπισπᾶται πρὸς φιλίαν· σὺ δὲ καὶ μυρία πάσχων κακὰ παρὰ τῶν δαιμόνων, ἐπ' ἄριστα αὐτοὺς εἰσάγεις· ὥστε διπλῇ τοῦ κυνὸς εἶ χείρων. Καλῶς δὲ ἀνεμνήσθην νῦν τῶν κυνῶν πρὸς τοὺς τότε μόνον εὐχαριστοῦντας, ὅταν εὖ πάσχωσιν. Αἰδέσθητε, παρακαλῶ, τοὺς κύνας, οἳ καὶ λιμώττοντες

many accusers. But [the other host] escaped from all this worry and practical matters, setting up the table in an impromptu manner and not being anxious for many days beforehand. And then, indeed, after the event the former host immediately lost the goodwill, whereas the other has God as his debtor and is supported by worthy hopes, being fed sumptuously every day from that table of his. You see, for the former the food is used up, whereas [for the latter] the goodwill isn't used up, but every day he rejoices and is brightened more than those who are filled with an excess of wine. For nothing so nourishes the soul as virtuous hope and the expectation of worthy things.

But now let's look at the things that follow. There [at the other table] are flutes and harps, while here there is no sound of anything unsuitable[17]—only hymns and psalmody. There [at the other table] the demons are praised in song, whereas here it is God, the Master of all. Do you see the extent of the goodwill of this one, and the extent to which the other is full of arrogance and lack of feeling? I mean, tell me, if God has nourished you from his good things, and when you need to thank him after you have been nourished, do you for your part introduce the demons? You see, the songs emanating from the flute are nothing other than odes to the demons. When you should say, "Blessed are you, Lord, because you have nourished me from your good things," like some unworthy dog do you not even remember him, but introduce the demons? No, dogs, whether they receive something or not, fawn upon their owners, but you don't do even that. The dog, even though it receives nothing, fawns upon its master, but you, even when you have received something, bark at him. Again, the dog, even though treated well by someone else, even so does not stop its hatred of them, nor is it attracted to friendship. But you, even though you have suffered myriad evils at the hands of the demons, introduce them to your meals, so in two ways you're worse than the dog. The mention I have just made of the dogs is opportune, with regard to those who only give thanks on the occasion when they receive a benefit. Please be ashamed by

---

17. Instrumental music was much criticized by the fathers, who considered that the instruments were evil in themselves. See James McKinnon, "The Meaning of the Patristic Polemic against Musical Instruments," *CurMus* 1 (1965): 69–82. However, the masses apparently did not agree with the fathers about the evils of music, as can be seen from Chrysostom's tirades here and in *Hom. Col.* 12, where it is a case of music at weddings. See Christopher Page, *The Christian West and Its Singers* (New Haven: Yale University Press, 2010), 32.

σαίνουσι τοὺς δεσπότας· σὺ δὲ ἂν ἀκούσῃς, ὅτι ὁ δαίμων τινὰ ἐθεράπευσεν, ἀφίης εὐθέως τὸν δεσπότην, ὦ κυνῶν ἀλογώτερε.

Ἀλλ᾽ [183] αἱ πόρναι, φησὶν, ἡδονὴν ἔχουσιν ὁρώμεναι. Ποίαν ἡδονήν; ποίαν δὲ οὐκ ἀτιμίαν; Πορνεῖον γέγονέ σου ἡ οἰκία, μανία καὶ οἶστρος· καὶ οὐκ αἰσχύνῃ ταῦτα ἡδονὴν καλῶν; Ἂν μὲν οὖν ἐξῇ χρήσασθαι, πάσης ἡδονῆς μείζων ἡ αἰσχύνη καὶ ἡ ἐκ ταύτης ἀηδία, πορνεῖον τὴν οἰκίαν ποιεῖν, καθάπερ χοίρους ἐγκαλινδουμένους βορβόρῳ. Ἂν δὲ μέχρι τοῦ φανῆναι μόνον, ἰδοὺ πάλιν ὀδύνη μείζων· ἡ γὰρ ὄψις οὐχ ἡδονή, ὅταν ἡ χρῆσις μὴ ᾖ, ἀλλὰ καὶ μείζων ἡ ἐπιθυμία, καὶ σφοδροτέρα ἡ φλόξ.

Ἀλλὰ τὸ τέλος βούλει μαθεῖν; Οἱ μὲν τοῖς μαινομένοις καὶ τοῖς παραπλῆξιν ἐοίκασιν ἀπὸ τῆς τραπέζης ἀνιστάμενοι, θρασεῖς, ὀργίλοι, καταγέλαστοι καὶ τοῖς ἀνδραπόδοις· καὶ οἱ μὲν οἰκέται ἀναχωροῦσι νήφοντες, οὗτοι δὲ μεθύοντες. Ὢ τῆς αἰσχύνης. Ἐκεῖ δὲ τοιοῦτον οὐδὲν, ἀλλ᾽ εὐχαριστίᾳ τὴν τράπεζαν κατακλείσαντες, οὕτως ἀναχωροῦσιν οἴκαδε, ἡδόμενοι καθεύδοντες, ἡδόμενοι ἐγειρόμενοι, πάσης αἰσχύνης ἀπηλλαγμένοι καὶ κατηγορίας.

Εἰ βούλει καὶ αὐτοὺς τοὺς κεκλημένους ἰδεῖν, ὄψει τούτους μὲν τοιούτους ὄντας ἔνδον, ὅπερ οὗτοι ἔξω, τυφλοὺς, ἀναπήρους, χωλούς· καὶ οἷα τούτων τὰ σώματα, τοιαῦται ἐκείνων αἱ ψυχαὶ, ὑδέρῳ καὶ φλεγμονῇ κατεχόμεναι. Τοιοῦτον γὰρ ἡ ἀπόνοια· μετὰ γὰρ τὴν τρυφὴν πήρωσις γίνεται· τοιοῦτον γὰρ ἡ πλησμονὴ καὶ ἡ μέθη, χωλοὺς καὶ κυλλοὺς ποιοῦσα. Καὶ ὄψει καὶ τούτους τοιαύτας ἔχοντας ψυχὰς, οἷα οὗτοι τὰ σώματα, λαμπρὰς, κεκοσμημένας. Οἱ γὰρ ἐν εὐχαριστίᾳ ζῶντες, οἱ τῆς αὐταρκείας μηδὲν πλέον ἐπιζητοῦντες, οἱ φιλοσοφοῦντες οὕτως εἰσὶν ἐν πάσῃ φαιδρότητι.

Ἴδωμεν δὲ καὶ ἐνταῦθα κἀκεῖ τὸ τέλος. Ἐκεῖ μὲν ἡδονὴ ἀκόλαστος, γέλως κεχυμένος, μέθη, εὐτραπελία, αἰσχρολογία· ἐπειδὴ γὰρ αὐτοὶ αἰδοῦνται αἰσχρὰ φθέγγεσθαι, διὰ τῶν πορνῶν τοῦτο γίνεται· ἐνταῦθα δὲ φιλανθρωπία, ἡμερότης. Τῷ μὲν οὖν ἐκείνους καλοῦντι παρέστηκε κενοδοξία ὁπλίζουσα αὐτόν· τῷ δὲ ἐνταῦθα φιλανθρωπία καὶ ἡμερότης. Ἐκείνην [184] μὲν γὰρ τὴν τράπεζαν φιλανθρωπία συνίστησι, ταύτην δὲ κενοδοξία καὶ ὠμότης ἐξ ἀδικίας καὶ πλεονεξίας. Κἀκείνη μὲν καταλήγει εἰς ἅπερ εἶπον, εἰς ἀπόνοιαν,

the dogs, which even when starving fawn upon their masters, whereas you, if you have heard that the demon has cured someone, immediately desert your master—you who are more brutish than dogs.

"But," [183] says [someone], "prostitutes give pleasure when they're looked at." What kind of pleasure? What kind of disgrace are they not? Your house has become a brothel, a madness and a frenzy, and don't you have any shame in calling this pleasure? Then if it's permitted to enjoy them, the shame of that exceeds every pleasure and the disgust that arises from it: to make your house a brothel, just as pigs wallow in mud. But if it goes only as far as their appearance, see again that the pain is greater. For seeing is not pleasure when there is no use permitted, but the desire is all the greater, and the flame more grievous.

But do you want to learn the outcome? When they stand up from the table, they are like madmen and the deranged,[18] overconfident, irascible, derided even by the slaves. And the servants depart soberly, whereas these are drunk. Oh, the shame of it! But at the other table there is nothing of this sort—no, when they have closed down the table with thanksgiving, thus they return to their homes, enjoying sleep, enjoying waking up, free from all shame and blame.

If you want to look at the guests themselves, you'll see that the ones inside are of that kind, as the others are outside—blind, crippled, lame— and like the bodies of the latter, the souls of the former are such, being afflicted by dropsy and inflammation. You see, such is their derangement, for after the wantonness a maiming sets in, such as surfeit and drunkenness, making them lame and crooked. And you'll see too that the other people have souls of the same kind as the bodies of the former ones, bright, adorned. You see, those who live in thanksgiving, who seek nothing more than sufficiency, are thus philosophers who are in all brightness.

But let's see the outcome, both here and there. There there's unbridled pleasure, laughter that pours out, drunkenness, ribaldry, foul language: you see, since they're ashamed to utter filth themselves, this happens through the prostitutes. Here, on the other hand, there's a loving-kindness, gentleness. [184] Next to the host of the former stands vainglory, arming him, whereas next to the other stand loving-kindness and gentleness. For here love of people prepares the table, but the other, vainglory and cruelty born of injustice and greed. And the latter ends in what I have said—in

---

18. Παραπλῆξιν, which seems to be a *hapax legomenon*.

εἰς ἔκστασιν, εἰς μανίαν· τοιαύτη γὰρ ἡ τῆς κενοδοξίας βλάστη· αὕτη δὲ εἰς εὐχαριστίαν καὶ δόξαν θεοῦ. Καὶ ὁ ἔπαινος δὲ ὁ παρὰ ἀνθρώπων ταύτῃ πλείων· ἐκείνῳ μὲν γὰρ καὶ βασκαίνουσι, τοῦτον δὲ ὡς κοινὸν πατέρα πάντες ἔχουσι καὶ οἱ μὴ παθόντες εὖ. Καὶ καθάπερ ἐπὶ τῶν ἠδικημένων καὶ οἱ μηδὲν ἠδικημένοι συναλγοῦσι, καὶ κοινῇ γίνονται πάντες ἐχθροί· οὕτω καὶ ἐπὶ τῶν πασχόντων εὖ καὶ οἱ μὴ παθόντες εὖ, καθάπερ οἱ παθόντες, ἐπαινοῦσι καὶ θαυμάζουσι τὸν πεποιηκότα. Κἀκεῖ μὲν πολὺς ὁ φθόνος, ἐνταῦθα δὲ πολλὴ ἡ κηδεμονία, πολλαὶ παρὰ πάντων εὐχαί.

Καὶ ἐνταῦθα μὲν ταῦτα· ἐκεῖ δὲ, ὅταν ὁ Χριστὸς παραγένηται, οὗτος μὲν στήσεται μετὰ πολλῆς τῆς παρρησίας, καὶ ἀκούσεται ἐπὶ πάσης τῆς οἰκουμένης, "Πεινῶντά με εἶδες, καὶ ἔθρεψας· γυμνὸν, καὶ ἐνέδυσας· ξένον, καὶ συνήγαγες," καὶ ὅσα τοιαῦτα· ἐκεῖνος δὲ τὰ ἐναντία ἀκούσεται, "Πονηρὲ δοῦλε καὶ ὀκνηρέ." καὶ πάλιν, "Οὐαὶ οἱ κατασπαταλῶντες ἐπὶ ταῖς στρωμναῖς αὐτῶν, καὶ οἱ καθεύδοντες ἐπὶ κλινῶν ἐλεφαντίνων, οἱ πίνοντες τὸν διϋλισμένον οἶνον, καὶ τὰ πρῶτα μύρα χριόμενοι· ὡς ἑστῶτα ἐλογίσαντο, καὶ οὐχ ὡς φεύγοντα."

Ταῦτα ἡμῖν οὐχ ἁπλῶς εἴρηται, ἀλλ' ὥστε μεταθεῖναι ὑμῶν τὴν γνώμην, καὶ μηδὲν ὑμᾶς ἀκερδὲς ποιεῖν. Τί οὖν, φησὶν, ὅτι καὶ ταῦτα κἀκεῖνα ποιῶ; Πολὺς οὗτος ὁ λόγος παρὰ πᾶσι. Καὶ ποία ἀνάγκη, εἰπέ μοι, ἐξὸν πάντα χρησίμως ποιεῖν, διαιρεῖν, καὶ τὰ μὲν εἰς οὐδὲν δέον, ἀλλὰ καὶ εἰκῆ ἀναλίσκειν, τὰ δὲ χρησίμως; Εἰπέ μοι, εἰ σπείρων τὰ μὲν εἰς πέτραν ἔρριπτες, τὰ δὲ εἰς γῆν ἀρίστην, ἆρα ἂν ἀπέχρησέ σοι τοῦτο, καὶ εἶπες ἄν· τί γὰρ βλάπτει, ἂν τὰ μὲν εἰκῆ, τὰ δὲ εἰς ἀρίστην ῥίψωμεν γῆν; Διὰ τί γὰρ μὴ πάντα εἰς ἀρίστην; διὰ τί τὸ κέρδος ἐλαττοῖς; Κἂν μὲν συνάγειν δέῃ χρήματα, οὐκ ἐρεῖς τοῦτο, ἀλλὰ πάντοθεν συνάγεις, ἐκεῖ δὲ οὐκέτι· κἂν δανείζειν δέῃ, οὐκ ἐρεῖς, διὰ τί τὰ μὲν τοῖς ἀπόροις, τὰ δὲ τοῖς εὐπόροις δώσομεν, ἀλλὰ πάντα ἐκείνοις· ἐνταῦθα δὲ, ἔνθα το-[185]σοῦτον τὸ κέρδος, οὐ λογίζῃ τοῦτο, καὶ παύσῃ ποτὲ τοῦ εἰκῆ δαπανᾶσθαι καὶ μάτην ἀναλίσκειν;

loss of sense, in derangement, in madness. (You see, such are the offshoots of vainglory.) But this table ends in thanksgiving and praise of God. And the praise too given by people is greater here, for the latter host is even the object of envy, while they all regard the other as a common father, even those who haven't benefited from him. And just as in the case of those who have been wronged, even those who have suffered no wrong feel with them, and all become enemies in common; so too in the case of those who have received benefit, those who have not fared well, like those who have, praise and marvel at the One who has brought this about. And there, there is much envy, while here, there is much solicitude, many prayers from all.

And that is how things are here. But there, when Christ arrives, that host will stand with great confidence and will hear before the whole world: "*You saw me hungry and you fed me; naked and you clothed me; a stranger and you welcomed me*" [Matt 25:36],[19] and similar words. The other host will hear the opposite: "*Wicked and slothful servant*" [Matt 25:26], and again: "*Woe to those who live wantonly on their bedding and sleep on beds of ivory, who drink filtered wine, and anoint themselves with the best unguents. They reckoned that these things were permanent, and not fleeting*" [see Amos 6:4–6].[20]

These things have been said not idly by us, but in order to change your minds and for you to do nothing that is without gain. "What then," says [someone], "when I do both this and the other?" This argument is found a great deal among many. And what kind of necessity, tell me, is there when it's possible to do everything to advantage, to divide it up and spend on what's not needed but is even without purpose, while the other part is spent to advantage? Tell me, if while you're sowing you've thrown some seeds onto rock and others onto the best soil, would this be sufficient for you and would you have said, "What harm is there if we've thrown some without purpose but others onto the best soil?" I mean, why not throw everything onto the best soil? Why are you lessening the gain? And if you have to get money together, you won't say this, but get it together from everywhere, but in the other case you don't do so. And if it's necessary to lend money you don't say: "Why? We shall give some to the needy and some to the well-off," but you give all to the needy. But in this case, where [**185**] the gain is so great, don't you calculate this, and at some time stop laying out money without purpose and spending fruitlessly?

---

19. This is in a different order from the text in Matthew.

20. This is an imperfect rendering of the Septuagint text and the ordering of its argument.

Ἀλλ᾽ ἔχει καὶ τοῦτο κέρδος, φησί. Ποῖον, εἰπέ μοι; Τὰς φιλίας αὔξει. Οὐδὲν ἀνθρώπων ψυχρότερον ἀπὸ τούτων φίλων γινομένων, ἀπὸ τῆς τραπέζης καὶ πλησμονῆς· τῶν παρασίτων αἱ φιλίαι ἐντεῦθεν τίκτονται μόνον.

Μὴ ὑβρίσῃς πρᾶγμα οὕτω θαυμαστὸν, τὴν ἀγάπην, μηδὲ ταύτην αὐτῆς εἶναι ῥίζαν φῇς· ὥσπερ ἂν εἴ τις δένδρου χρυσὸν καὶ λίθους τιμίους φέροντος τὴν ῥίζαν οὐχὶ τοιαύτην ἔλεγεν εἶναι, ἀλλ᾽ ἀπὸ σηπεδόνος τίκτεσθαι. Τοῦτο καὶ σὺ ποιεῖς· κἂν γὰρ τεχθῇ φιλία ἐντεῦθεν, οὐδὲν αὐτῆς ψυχρότερον γένοιτ᾽ ἄν. Ἀλλ᾽ ἐκεῖναι αἱ τράπεζαι φιλίαν ποιοῦσιν, οὐχὶ πρὸς ἀνθρώπους, ἀλλὰ πρὸς τὸν θεόν, καὶ ἐπιτεταμένην, ὅταν ἐπιτεταμέναι γίνωνται. Ὁ μὲν γὰρ τὰ μὲν ἐνταῦθα, τὰ δὲ ἐκεῖ καταναλίσκων, κἂν πολλὰ δῷ, οὐδὲν μέγα πεποίηκεν· ὁ δὲ πάντα ἐνταῦθα ἀναλίσκων, κἂν ὀλίγα δεδωκὼς ᾖ, τὸ πᾶν εἰργάσατο. Τὸ γὰρ ζητούμενον οὐχὶ πολλὰ δοῦναι, ἢ ὀλίγα, ἀλλὰ τῆς οἰκείας δυνάμεως μὴ ἔλαττον. Ἐννοῶμεν τὸν τὰ πέντε τάλαντα, καὶ τὸν τὰ δύο· ἐννοῶμεν τὴν τοὺς δύο ὀβολοὺς καταβαλοῦσαν· ἐννοῶμεν τὴν χήραν τὴν ἐπὶ τοῦ Ἠλία. Οὐκ εἶπεν ἐκείνη ἡ τοὺς δύο ὀβολοὺς καταβαλοῦσα· τί γὰρ βλάπτει, ἂν τὸν μὲν ἕνα ὀβολὸν ἐμαυτῇ κατάσχω, τὸν δὲ ἕνα δῶ; ἀλλ᾽ ὅλον ἔδωκε τὸν βίον· σὺ δὲ ἐν τοσαύτῃ ἀφθονίᾳ ὢν, ἐκείνης φειδωλότερος εἶ. Μὴ τοίνυν ἀμελῶμεν τῆς ἑαυτῶν σωτηρίας, ἀλλ᾽ ἐπιθώμεθα τῇ ἐλεημοσύνῃ. Οὐδὲν γὰρ ταύτης βέλτιον· καὶ δείξει ὁ μέλλων χρόνος· τέως δὲ καὶ ὁ παρὼν ἔδειξεν. Εἰς δόξαν τοίνυν τοῦ θεοῦ ζήσωμεν, καὶ τὰ αὐτῷ δοκοῦντα πράττωμεν, ἵνα καταξιωθῶμεν τῶν ἐπηγγελμένων ἀγαθῶν· ὧν γένοιτο πάντας ἡμᾶς ἐπιτυχεῖν, χάριτι καὶ φιλανθρωπίᾳ τοῦ κυρίου ἡμῶν Ἰησοῦ Χριστοῦ, μεθ᾽ οὗ τῷ πατρὶ ἅμα τῷ ἁγίῳ πνεύματι δόξα, κράτος, τιμή, νῦν καὶ ἀεὶ καὶ εἰς τοὺς αἰῶνας τῶν αἰώνων. Ἀμήν.

"But," says [someone], "this too has its gain." What kind of gain, tell me? "It increases friendships." Nothing is colder than people who become friends from these causes, from the table and surfeit. It's only the friendships of parasites that come about from that source.

Don't insult a thing as wonderful as love, nor say that this is its root, just as if one were to say that a tree bearing gold and precious stones didn't have its root as the same but came about from rottenness. And you too do this, for even if friendship should come about from that source, nothing would be colder than it. But the other tables produce friendship, not toward people but toward God, and it is committed when it happens in a committed way. You see, the one who expends something here and something there, even if they give a great deal, hasn't done anything great, whereas the one who expends everything in this case, even if they have only given a little, has accomplished everything. For what's required is not to give a great deal, or a little, but what isn't less than our own means. Let's think of the person with the five talents, and the one with two [see Matt 25:15]. Let's think of the woman who put in two obols [see Mark 12:42; Luke 21:2–4]. Let's think of the widow at the time of Elijah [see 1 Kgs 17]. The woman who put in two obols didn't say: "What harm is there if I keep back one obol for myself, and give the other?" No, she gave her whole livelihood. But you, who are in such abundance, are more niggardly than she. Therefore, let's not neglect our own salvation but apply ourselves to almsgiving.[21] I mean, there's nothing better than this, and the time to come will show it. Meanwhile the present has also shown it. Let's live therefore for the glory of God, and let's do what pleases him, so that we may be judged worthy of the good things that have been promised. May we all attain these, by the grace and loving-kindness of our Lord Jesus Christ, with whom to the Father, together with the Holy Spirit, be praise, power, honor, now and always, forever and ever. Amen.

---

21. On almsgiving in late antiquity, see Richard Finn, *Almsgiving in the Later Roman Empire: Christian Promotion and Practice 313–450* (Oxford: Oxford University Press, 2008); and Pauline Allen, Bronwen Neil, and Wendy Mayer, *Preaching Poverty in Late Antiquity: Perceptions and Realities*, AKT 28 (Leipzig: Evangelische Verlagsanstalt, 2009).

[186] ΛΟΓΟΣ Β.

Διὰ τοῦτο καὶ ἡμεῖς ἀφ' ἧς ἡμέρας ἠκούσαμεν, οὐ παυόμεθα ὑπὲρ ὑμῶν προσευχόμενοι, καὶ αἰτούμενοι ἵνα πληρωθῆτε τὴν ἐπίγνωσιν τοῦ θελήματος αὐτοῦ ἐν πάσῃ σοφίᾳ καὶ συνέσει πνευματικῇ· περιπατῆσαι ὑμᾶς ἀξίως τοῦ κυρίου εἰς πᾶσαν ἀρέσκειαν, ἐν παντὶ ἔργῳ ἀγαθῷ καρποφοροῦντες, καὶ αὐξανόμενοι ἐν τῇ ἐπιγνώσει τοῦ θεοῦ.

Διὰ τοῦτο, ποῖον; Ἐπειδὴ ἠκούσαμεν τὴν πίστιν ὑμῶν καὶ τὴν ἀγάπην· ἐπειδὴ χρηστὰς ἔχομεν ἐλπίδας, εὐέλπιδές ἐσμεν καὶ περὶ τῶν μελλόντων αἰτεῖν. Καθάπερ γὰρ ἐν τοῖς ἀγῶσιν ἐκείνους μάλιστα διεγείρομεν τοὺς ἐγγὺς ὄντας τῆς νίκης· οὕτω δὴ καὶ ὁ Παῦλος τούτους μάλιστα παρακαλεῖ τοὺς τὸ πλέον κατωρθωκότας.

"Ἀφ' ἧς ἡμέρας ἠκούσαμεν, φησὶν, οὐ παυόμεθα ὑπὲρ ὑμῶν προσευχόμενοι." Οὐ μίαν ἡμέραν ὑπερευχόμεθα, οὐδὲ δύο, οὐδὲ τρεῖς. Ἐνταῦθα καὶ τὴν ἀγάπην δείκνυσι, καὶ ἠρέμα αὐτοὺς αἰνίττεται ὡς οὐδέπω πρὸς τὸ τέλος ἐφθακότας· τὸ γὰρ, "ἵνα πληρωθῆτε," τοῦτο δηλοῦντος ἦν. Καὶ ὅρα μοι τὴν σύνεσιν τοῦ μακαρίου τούτου· οὐδαμοῦ τοῦ παντὸς αὐτοὺς ἀπεστερῆσθαί φησιν, ἀλλὰ λείπειν αὐτούς. Πανταχοῦ τὸ, "ἵνα πληρωθῆτε," τοῦτο δηλοῖ. Καὶ πάλιν, "εἰς πᾶσαν ἀρέσκειαν ἐν παντὶ ἔργῳ ἀγαθῷ·" καὶ πάλιν, "ἐν πάσῃ δυνάμει δυναμούμενοι·" καὶ πάλιν, "εἰς πᾶσαν ὑπομονὴν καὶ μακροθυμίαν." Τὸ γὰρ, "πᾶσαν," ἀεὶ προστιθέναι, μαρτυροῦντός ἐστι καὶ τι τοῖς κατορθοῦσιν, εἰ καὶ μὴ τὸ πᾶν. Καὶ "ἵνα πληρωθῆτε," φησὶν, οὐχ ἵνα λάβητε· ἔλαβον γάρ· ἀλλὰ τὸ λεῖπον ἵνα πληρωθῆτε. Οὕτω καὶ ὁ ἔλεγχος ἀνεπαχθὴς ἐγίνετο, καὶ τὸ ἐγκώμιον οὐκ ἠφίει αὐτοὺς καταπεσεῖν καὶ γενέσθαι ὑπτίους ὁλοσχερὲς γενόμενον. Τί δέ ἐστιν, "ἵνα πληρωθῆτε τὴν ἐπίγνωσιν τοῦ θελήματος αὐτοῦ;" Διὰ τοῦ υἱοῦ προσάγεσθαι ὑμᾶς αὐτῷ, οὐκέτι δι' ἀγγέλων. Ὅτι [187] μὲν οὖν δεῖ προσάγεσθαι, ἔγνωτε· λείπει δὲ ὑμῖν τὸ τοῦτο μαθεῖν, καὶ διὰ τί τὸν υἱὸν ἔπεμψεν. Εἰ γὰρ δι' ἀγγέλων ἔδει σώζεσθαι, οὐκ ἂν αὐτὸν ἔπεμψεν, οὐκ ἂν ἐξέδωκεν. "Ἐν πάσῃ σοφίᾳ, φησὶ, καὶ συνέσει πνευματικῇ." Ἐπειδὴ

For this reason we too, from the day we heard it, do not cease praying for you, and begging so that you be filled with the knowledge of his will in all wisdom and spiritual understanding; that you lead a life worthy of the Lord in all obsequiousness, bearing fruit in every good deed, and increasing in the knowledge of God [Col 1:9–10].

For this reason. What reason? "Because we heard of your faith and love; because we have worthy hopes, we are hopeful of asking for future things also." You see, just as in the games we cheer on especially those who are close to victory, so too then Paul encourages those who have achieved the greater part.

"*From the day we heard it,*" he says, "*we do not cease praying for you.* Not for one day do we pray for you, nor two, nor three." In this passage he both shows his love and intimates gently that they have not yet reached the end. You see, the expression "*so that you be filled*" signified this. And please consider the sagacity of this blessed man: nowhere does he say that they've been cut off from completeness, but that they were wanting. In every way the expression "*so that you be filled*" discloses this. And again, "*in all obsequiousness in every good deed*"; and again: "*strengthened with all power*" [Col 1:11]; and again: "*for all endurance and patience*" [Col 1:11]. You see, always to add the word *all* is of one bearing witness to those who have achieved something, even if not in all things. And "*so that you be filled,*" he says, not "*so that you might receive*" (for they had received), but "*that you be filled*" with regard to what was wanting. Thus both the charge occurred without offense, and the praise didn't cause their spirits to fall and them to be laid low, being complete. But what is the meaning of "*so that you may be filled with the knowledge of his will*"? We must be brought to him through the Son, no longer through angels. Now [187] you have learned that you must be brought to him, but it remains for you to learn this, namely, why he sent the Son. For if we had to be saved through angels, he wouldn't have sent him, he wouldn't have given him up.[22] "*In all wisdom,*" he says, "*and*

---

22. A very explicit statement about the subordinate place of angels in salvation,

γὰρ αὐτοὺς οἱ φιλόσοφοι ἠπάτων, βούλομαι ὑμᾶς ἐν πνευματικῇ, φησὶ, σοφίᾳ εἶναι, μὴ κατὰ τὴν σοφίαν τῶν ἀνθρώπων. Εἰ δὲ ὥστε τὸ θέλημα θεοῦ μαθεῖν πνευματικῆς δεῖ σοφίας, ὥστε τὴν οὐσίαν, τί ἐστιν, εὐχῶν διηνεκῶν.

Καὶ δείκνυσιν ἐνταῦθα τοῦτο, ὅτι ἐξ ἐκείνου ὁ Παῦλος εὔχεται, καὶ οὐδέπω ἤνυσε, καὶ οὐκ ἀπέστη· τὸ γὰρ, "ἀφ' ἧς ἡμέρας ἠκούσαμεν," τοῦτο δηλοῖ. Κατάγνωσιν δὲ αὐτοῖς φέρει, εἰ ἐξ ἐκείνου καὶ εὐχαῖς βοηθούμενοι μὴ ἀνεκτήσαντο ἑαυτούς. "Καὶ αἰτούμενοι," φησὶ, τουτέστι, μετὰ πολλῆς τῆς σπουδῆς· τοῦτο γὰρ δείκνυσιν ὅτι ἔγνωτε, ἀλλὰ δεῖ τι καὶ ἐπιγνῶναι. "Εἰς τὸ περιπατῆσαι ὑμᾶς, φησὶν, ἀξίως τοῦ κυρίου." Ἐνταῦθα περὶ βίου καὶ τῶν ἔργων φησί· καὶ γὰρ καὶ τοῦτο πανταχοῦ ποιεῖ· ἀεὶ τῇ πίστει συζεύγνυσι τὴν πολιτείαν. "Εἰς πᾶσαν ἀρέσκειαν." Πῶς δὲ, "πᾶσαν ἀρέσκειαν;" "Ἐν παντὶ ἔργῳ ἀγαθῷ καρποφοροῦντες, καὶ αὐξανόμενοι ἐν τῇ ἐπιγνώσει τοῦ Θεοῦ." Ὥσπερ, φησὶν, ἀθρόως ὑμῖν ἑαυτὸν ἀπεκάλυψε, καὶ ὥσπερ τηλικαύτην ἐλάβετε γνῶσιν, οὕτω καὶ πολιτείαν ἀξίαν ἐπιδείξασθε τῆς πίστεως· μεγάλης γὰρ αὕτη δεῖται πολιτείας, καὶ πολλῷ μείζονος, ἢ ἡ παλαιά. Ὁ γὰρ τὸν θεὸν εἰδὼς, καὶ τοῦ θεοῦ δοῦλος εἶναι καταξιωθεὶς, μᾶλλον δὲ καὶ υἱὸς, ὅρα ὅσης δεῖται ἀρετῆς.

"Ἐν πάσῃ δυνάμει δυναμούμενοι." Ἐνταῦθα περὶ τῶν πειρασμῶν καὶ τῶν διωγμῶν φησιν· εὐχόμεθα ἵνα πληρωθῆτε [188] δυναμούμενοι, ὥστε μὴ ἀκηδιάσαι, μηδὲ ἀπογνῶναι· "κατὰ τὸ κράτος τῆς δόξης αὐτοῦ." ἀλλ' ἵνα τοιαύτην ἀναλάβητε προθυμίαν, οἵαν πρέπει τῇ ἰσχύϊ τῆς δόξης αὐτοῦ δοῦναι. "Εἰς πᾶσαν ὑπομονὴν καὶ μακροθυμίαν." Ὃ λέγει, τοιοῦτόν ἐστι· συντόμως εὐχόμεθα, φησὶν, ὥστε ἐνάρετον ὑμᾶς βίον σχεῖν καὶ τῆς πολιτείας ἄξιον, καὶ στῆναι βεβαίως, δυναμωθέντας ὡς εἰκὸς ἀπὸ θεοῦ δυναμωθῆναι. Διὰ τοῦτο τέως οὐδέπω ἅπτεται δογμάτων, ἀλλ' ἐν τῷ βίῳ στρέφεται, ἔνθα οὐδὲν εἶχεν ἐγκαλέσαι· καὶ ἐπαινέσας ἐφ' οἷς ἐχρῆν, τότε καθίησιν εἰς κατηγορίαν. Τοῦτο καὶ πανταχοῦ ποιεῖ· ὅταν μέλλῃ τισὶ γράφειν, ἔχων μέν τι ἐγκαλεῖν, ἔχων δὲ καί τι ἐπαινέσαι, πρότερον ἐπαινεῖ, καὶ τότε καθίησιν εἰς

spiritual understanding" [Col 1:9]. You see, the philosophers had deceived them; "I want you," he says, "to be in spiritual wisdom, not according to the wisdom of human beings." But if, in order to learn the will [of God] there needs to be spiritual wisdom, in order to learn the nature of his essence there need to be continual prayers.

And Paul shows in this passage that since the time that he's been praying, and hasn't yet succeeded, he hasn't given up. You see, the expression *"from the day we heard it"* discloses this. But it brings condemnation on them if from that time, even helped by prayers, they haven't repaired themselves. *"And begging,"* he says, with a great deal of enthusiasm, for this, the expression *"you know"* shows. But it's necessary to know something besides. *"For you to lead a life worthy of the Lord,"* he says. In this passage he's speaking about life and its deeds, and indeed this is what he does everywhere: he always associates way of life[23] with faith. *In all obsequiousness.* But how, *in all obsequiousness? In bearing fruit in every good deed, and increasing in the knowledge of God.* "Just as he has revealed himself fully to you," he says, "and just as you have received such great knowledge, so too should you display a way of life worthy of the faith, for this needs an extended way of life, far greater than that of the Old [Testament]." I mean, the one who knows God and has been judged worthy of being his servant—no, even his son—see how much virtue he needs.

Strengthened with all power. In this passage Paul speaks of trials and persecutions. "We pray that you may be filled [**188**] with strength, so that you are not weary, nor despairing. *According to his glorious might* [Col 1:11]." "No, so that you may assume again such eagerness as befits the power of his glory to give." *For all endurance and patience.* What he means is like this. "In short," he says, "we pray that you have a virtuous life, and one worthy of your way of life, and may stand firm, as those should who have been strengthened by God." This is why he doesn't as yet touch on doctrines but turns to life, where he had nothing to charge them with, and having praised them for necessary reasons, he then establishes an accusation. This is what he does everywhere as well: when he's going to write to people, when he has something to complain about but also something to

---

which is stressed by Paul and Chrysostom alike. See Severian of Gabala on this passage, who is also explicit that salvation comes not from angels but from Christ (Staab, *Pauluskommentare aus der griechischen Kirche*, 317).

23. Greek πολιτεία, which has several meanings, including "conversation" and "citizenship." It is mostly translated in this volume as "way of life."

τὰ ἐγκλήματα. Οἰκειοῦται γὰρ πρότερον τὸν ἀκροατὴν, καὶ τὴν κατηγορίαν ἀπαλλάττει πάσης ὑποψίας, καὶ δείκνυσιν ὅτι αὐτὸς μὲν ἐβούλετο διόλου ἐγκωμιάζειν, ὑπὸ δὲ τῆς ἀνάγκης εἰς τούτους ἐμβιβάζεται τοὺς λόγους. Τοῦτο καὶ ἐν τῇ προτέρᾳ πρὸς Κορινθίους ποιεῖ. Ἐπαινέσας γὰρ αὐτοὺς μυρία ὡς ἀγαπῶντας αὐτὸν, καὶ ἀπὸ τοῦ πεπορνευκότος, τότε εἰς κατηγορίαν καθίησιν. Ἐν δὲ τῇ πρὸς Γαλάτας οὐκέτι, ἀλλὰ τοὐναντίον· μᾶλλον δὲ εἴ τις ἐξετάσειε, κἀκείνη ἐξ ἐπαίνου ἡ κατηγορία. Ἐπειδὴ γὰρ αὐτῶν οὐδὲν εἶχε κατόρθωμα τότε εἰπεῖν, καὶ σφοδρὸν τὸ ἔγκλημα ἦν, καὶ πάντες διεφθάρησαν, καὶ φέρειν ἠδύναντο ἰσχυροὶ ὄντες, ἀπὸ κατηγορίας ἄρχεται λέγων, "Θαυμάζω·" ὥστε καὶ τοῦτο ἐγκώμιόν ἐστιν. Ὕστερον δὲ αὐτοὺς ἐπαινεῖ, οὐκ ἐπὶ τοῖς παροῦσιν, ἀλλ' ἐπὶ τοῖς παρελθοῦσι, λέγων, ὅτι "Εἰ δυνατὸν, τοὺς ὀφθαλμοὺς ὑμῶν ἐξορύξαντες ἂν ἐδώκατέ μοι."

"Καρποφοροῦντες," φησί· τοῦτο περὶ ἔργων· "δυναμούμενοι·" περὶ πειρασμῶν. "Εἰς πᾶσαν ὑπομονὴν καὶ μακροθυμίαν·" μακροθυμίαν πρὸς ἀλλήλους, ὑπομονὴν πρὸς τοὺς ἔξω. Μακροθυμεῖ γάρ τις πρὸς ἐκείνους, οὓς δυνατὸν καὶ ἀμύνασθαι, ὑπομένει δὲ οὓς οὐ δύναται ἀμύνασθαι. Διὰ τοῦτο ἐπὶ μὲν θεοῦ οὐδέποτε ὑπομονὴ λέγεται, μακροθυμία δὲ πολλαχοῦ· καθὼς αὐτὸς οὗτος ὁ μακάριός φησι, γράφων ἀλλαχοῦ· "Ἡ τοῦ πλούτου τῆς [189] χρηστότητος αὐτοῦ καὶ τῆς ἀνοχῆς καὶ τῆς μακροθυμίας καταφρονεῖς;" "Εἰς πᾶσαν." Μὴ νῦν μὲν, μετὰ ταῦτα δὲ οὐκέτι. "Ἐν πάσῃ, φησί, σοφίᾳ καὶ συνέσει πνευματικῇ." Ἄλλως γὰρ οὐκ ἔνι τὸ θέλημα αὐτοῦ ἐπιγνῶναι. Καίτοιγε ᾤοντο τὸ θέλημα αὐτοῦ ἔχειν, ἀλλ' οὐ πνευματικὴ ἦν ἡ σοφία. "Εἰς τὸ περιπατῆσαι ὑμᾶς, φησὶν, ἀξίως τοῦ κυρίου." Τοῦτο γὰρ ὁδὸς γίνεται τῆς ἀρίστης πολιτείας. Ὁ γὰρ τοῦ θεοῦ τὴν φιλανθρωπίαν καταμαθών· καταμανθάνει δὲ, ἂν ἴδῃ τὸν υἱὸν ἐκδεδομένον· μείζονα ἕξει προθυμίαν. Καὶ ἄλλως δὲ οὐ τοῦτο εὐχόμεθα μόνον ἵνα μάθητε, ἀλλ' ἵνα καὶ ἐπὶ τῶν ἔργων ἐπιδείκνυσθε· ὁ γὰρ εἰδὼς χωρὶς τοῦ ποιεῖν, καὶ κολάζεσθαι μέλλει. "Εἰς τὸ περιπατῆσαι ὑμᾶς," φησί· τουτέστιν, ἀεὶ· οὐχ ἅπαξ, ἀλλὰ διαπαντός. Ὥσπερ τὸ περιπατεῖν ἀναγκαῖον ἡμῖν, οὕτω καὶ τὸ ὀρθῶς βιοῦν. Καὶ ἀεὶ περίπατον τὸ τοιοῦτον καλεῖ, εἰκότως, δεικνὺς ὅτι οὗτος ἡμῖν ὁ βίος ἐστιν ὁ προκείμενος·

praise, he praises them first and then proceeds to the complaints.[24] You see, first he wins the hearer over, and frees his accusation from all suspicion, and shows that for his part he wanted to extol him throughout, but because of necessity he is led to these words. This is what he does also in the First Letter to the Corinthians, for having praised them myriad times for loving him, from the case of the fornicator [see 1 Cor 5] he then proceeds to accuse them. But in the letter to the Galatians no longer so, but the opposite—no, if one were to look closely, the accusation there comes from praise. For since he had no accomplishments of theirs to speak of on that occasion, and the accusation was serious, and they were all corrupt and capable of bearing it because they were strong, he begins with an accusation, saying, "*I am astonished*" [Gal 1:6], so that this too is praise. But later on he praises them, not for what they are in the present, but for what they had been, saying: "*If possible, you would have plucked out your eyes and given them to me*" [Gal 4:15].

"*Bearing fruit*" [Col 1:10], he says, meaning works; "*strengthened*," meaning trials. *For all endurance and patience*: patience toward each other, endurance toward those outside. For someone shows endurance toward those on whom it is possible to take vengeance, while they are patient toward those on whom they cannot. This is why the word *patience* is never applied to God, while *endurance* is everywhere. As this same blessed man says elsewhere in his writings: "*Or do you despise the riches* [**189**] *of his goodness and his long-suffering and endurance?*" [Rom 2:4]. *For all [endurance and patience]*. Not now, but no longer afterward. "*In all wisdom*," he says, "and *spiritual understanding*" [Col 1:9]. For otherwise it isn't possible to know his will. And yet they thought they understood his will, but the wisdom was not spiritual. "*To lead a life worthy of the Lord*," he says [Col 1:10]. For this is the path of the best way of life. For the one who has learned God's loving-kindness (they learn when they see the Son delivered up) will have greater eagerness. Otherwise we don't make this prayer only that you may learn, but so that you show this forth also in works, for the one who knows without doing is indeed going to be punished. "*For you to lead a life*," Paul says—that means always, not once, but continually. Just as it's necessary for you to lead a life, so too is living rightly. And he always uses the term *lead*, rightly so, showing that this life lies before all

---

24. What follows is part of the classical and late-antique perspective on the art of letter writing, incorporating praise, accusation, and so on. See *Hom. Phil.* 1 and Allen's translation and notes in *John Chrysostom, Homilies on Paul's Letter*, 7.

ἀλλ' οὐχ ὁ κοσμικὸς τοιοῦτος. Καὶ πολὺ δὲ τὸ ἐγκώμιον. "Περιπατῆσαι ὑμᾶς, φησὶν, ἀξίως τοῦ κυρίου," καὶ, "ἐν παντὶ ἔργῳ ἀγαθῷ," ὥστε ἀεὶ ἐπιδιδόναι, καὶ μηδαμοῦ ἵστασθαι· καὶ μεταφορικῶς, "καρποφοροῦντες, καὶ αὐξανόμενοι ἐν τῇ ἐπιγνώσει τοῦ θεοῦ," ἵνα οὕτω δυναμωθῆτε κατὰ τὴν ἰσχὺν τοῦ θεοῦ, ὡς ἀνθρώπῳ δυνατὸν ἦν. "Διὰ τοῦ κράτους αὐτοῦ." Πολλὴ ἡ παραμυθία. Οὐκ εἶπε δύναμιν, ἀλλὰ κράτος, ὅπερ μεῖζόν ἐστι. "Διὰ τοῦ κράτους, φησὶ, τῆς δόξης αὐτοῦ·" ὅτι πανταχοῦ ἡ δόξα αὐτοῦ κρατεῖ. Ἤδη παρεμυθήσατο τοὺς ἐν ὀνείδει ὄντα. Καὶ πάλιν, "περιπατῆσαι ὑμᾶς ἀξίως τοῦ κυρίου." Περὶ τοῦ υἱοῦ τοῦτό φησι, τὸ πανταχοῦ κρατεῖν αὐτὸν, καὶ ἐν οὐρανῷ καὶ ἐν γῇ, ὅτι ἡ δόξα αὐτοῦ πανταχοῦ βασιλεύει.

Οὐχ ἁπλῶς ἐνδυναμοῦσθε, ἀλλ' ὡς εἰκὸς τοὺς οὕτως ἰσχυρῷ δεσπότῃ δουλεύοντας. "Ἐν τῇ ἐπιγνώσει τοῦ θεοῦ." Ἄμα καὶ παράπτεται τῶν τῆς γνώσεως λόγων· τοῦτο γὰρ πεπλανῆσθαί ἐστι, τὸ μὴ εἰδέναι θεὸν, ὡς δεῖ. Ἡ ὥστε ἐπιδοῦναι, φησίν, ἐν τῇ ἐπιγνώσει τοῦ θεοῦ. Εἰ γὰρ ὁ τὸν [190] υἱὸν οὐκ εἰδὼς, οὐδὲ τὸν πατέρα, εἰκότως δεῖ τῆς ἐπιγνώσεως· οὐδὲν γὰρ ὄφελος βίου ταύτης ἄνευ.

"Εἰς πᾶσαν ὑπομονὴν καὶ μακροθυμίαν, φησὶ, μετὰ χαρᾶς εὐχαριστοῦντες τῷ θεῷ." Εἶτα μέλλων αὐτοὺς παρακαλεῖν, οὐ μέμνηται τῶν μελλόντων αὐτοῖς ἀποκεῖσθαι, ἀλλὰ τοῦτο μὲν ᾐνίξατο ἐν τῇ ἀρχῇ εἰπών, "Διὰ τὴν ἐλπίδα τὴν ἀποκειμένην ὑμῖν ἐν τοῖς οὐρανοῖς·" ἐνταῦθα δὲ τῶν ἤδη ὑπαρξάντων μέμνηται· ταῦτα γὰρ ἐκείνων αἴτια. Καὶ πολλαχοῦ τοῦτο ποιεῖ. Τὰ γὰρ ἤδη γεγονότα πλέον πιστοῦται, καὶ μᾶλλον αἱρεῖ τὸν ἀκροατήν. "Μετὰ χαρᾶς, φησὶν, εὐχαριστοῦντες τῷ θεῷ." Ἡ ἀκολουθία αὕτη ἐστίν· οὐ παυόμεθα εὐχόμενοι ὑπὲρ ὑμῶν, καὶ εὐχαριστοῦντες ἐπὶ τοῖς προτέροις. Ὁρᾷς πῶς ἑαυτὸν ἐμβιβάζει εἰς τὸν περὶ τοῦ υἱοῦ λόγον; Εἰ γὰρ εὐχαριστοῦμεν μετὰ χαρᾶς πολλῆς, μεγάλα τὰ λεγόμενα. Ἔστι γὰρ εὐχαριστεῖν διὰ φόβον μόνον, ἔστιν εὐχαριστεῖν καὶ ἐν λύπη ὄντα, οἷον ὁ Ἰὼβ ηὐχαρίστει μὲν, ὀδυνώμενος δέ· καὶ ἔλεγεν, "Ὁ κύριος ἔδωκεν, ὁ κύριος ἀφείλετο." Μὴ γάρ τις λεγέτω, ὅτι οὐκ ἐλύπει αὐτὸν τὰ γενόμενα, οὐδὲ ἀθυμία περιέβαλλε, μηδὲ τὸ μέγα ἐγκώμιον ἀφαιρείσθω τοῦ δικαίου. Ὅταν δὲ τοιαῦτα ᾖ, οὐ διὰ τὸν φόβον, οὐδὲ διὰ δεσποτείαν μόνον, ἀλλὰ καὶ δι' αὐτὴν τὴν τῶν πραγμάτων φύσιν εὐχαριστοῦμεν. "Τῷ ἱκανώσαντι ἡμᾶς εἰς τὴν μερίδα τοῦ κλήρου τῶν ἁγίων ἐν τῷ φωτί." Μέγα ἐφθέγξατο. Τοιαῦτά ἐστι τὰ δεδομένα, φησὶν, ὡς μὴ δοῦναι μόνον, ἀλλὰ καὶ ἰσχυροὺς ποιῆσαι πρὸς τὸ λαβεῖν. Τῷ οὖν εἰπεῖν "τῷ ἱκανώσαντι,"

of us, but such a life is not of this world. And great is the praise. "*For you to lead a life worthy of the Lord*," he says, and "*in every good work*," so that you always advance and nowhere stand still, and metaphorically "*bearing fruit and increasing in the knowledge of God*," so that you may be strengthened according to the power of God such as is possible for a human being. *According to his glorious might*. The consolation is considerable. He didn't say power, but might, which is greater. "*Through the might*," he says, "*of his glory*," because everywhere his glory is mighty. Already he has the one who is in disgrace. And again: "*For you to lead a life worthy of the Lord*." Concerning the Son, he says that he prevails everywhere, both in heaven and on earth, because his glory reigns everywhere.

Paul didn't say "*strengthened*" to no purpose, but as they might be expected to be, in the service of a powerful master. *In the knowledge of God*. And at the same time he touches on the means of knowledge. You see, this is to be in error, not to know God as one ought; or Paul means in order to increase in the knowledge of God. For if the one [**190**] who doesn't know the Son doesn't know the Father either [see Matt 11:27], it's right that there needs to be knowledge: nothing in life is of use without this.

"*For all endurance and patience*," he says, "*with joy, giving thanks to God*" [Col 1:11]. Then, about to exhort them, he doesn't mention what's going to be in store for them, but he did hint at the beginning [of the letter] when he says, "*Because of the hope in store for you in heaven*." But in this passage he mentions things that were already theirs, for these were the causes of the other. And in many places he does this. You see, what has already happened is believed and captures the hearer the more. "*With joy*," he says, "*giving thanks to God*." The sequel is this: we don't stop praying for you and giving thanks for previous benefits. Do you see how he leads himself on to the discussion about the Son? For if we give thanks with great joy, what has been said is huge. You see, it's possible to give thanks only through fear, it's possible to give thanks even when in sorrow: for example, Job gave thanks, but in anguish. And he said, "*The Lord has given, the Lord has taken away*" [Job 1:21]. For nobody should say that the events did not pain Job, nor that they encompassed him with faintheartedness, nor let his great praise be taken away from the righteous man. But when things like this happen, it isn't through fear, nor because he is sole Lord, but also through the very nature of the deeds themselves that we give thanks. *Who has qualified us to share in the inheritance of the saints in light* [Col 1:12]. He has made a significant pronouncement. "The things that have been given," Paul says, "are of the kind that God not only gives but also makes us strong

πολὺ τὸ βάρος ἔδειξεν. Οἷον ἐάν τις εὐτελὴς καὶ βασιλεὺς γένηται, δυνατὸν αὐτῷ ἐπαρχότητα δοῦναι ᾧ βούλεται· καὶ τοσοῦτον δύναται μόνον, τὸ ἀξίωμα δοῦναι, ἀλλ᾿ οὐχὶ καὶ ἐπιτήδειον ποιῆσαι πρὸς τὴν ἀρχήν· πολλάκις δὲ τὸν τοιοῦτον καὶ καταγέλαστον ἡ τιμὴ ποιεῖ· ἐὰν μέντοι καὶ τὸ ἀξίωμα δῷ, καὶ ἐπιτήδειον ποιήσῃ πρὸς τὴν τιμήν, καὶ ἱκανὸν πρὸς τὴν οἰκονομίαν, τότε τιμὴ τὸ πρᾶγμά ἐστι. Τοῦτο οὖν καὶ ἐνταῦθά φησιν, ὅτι οὐ μόνον ἡμῖν ἔδωκε τὴν τιμήν, ἀλλὰ καὶ ἰσχυροὺς πρὸς τὸ λαβεῖν [191] ἐποίησε.

Διπλῆ γὰρ αὕτη τιμὴ τὸ καὶ δοῦναι, καὶ ἐπιτηδείους κατασκευάσαι τῆς δωρεᾶς. Οὐκ εἶπε, δόντι, ἁπλῶς, ἀλλ᾿, "ἱκανώσαντι εἰς τὴν μερίδα τοῦ κλήρου τῶν ἁγίων ἐν τῷ φωτί." τουτέστι τῷ κατατάξαντι ἡμᾶς μετὰ τῶν ἁγίων. Ἀλλ᾿ οὐχ ἁπλῶς εἶπε, κατατάξαντι, ἀλλὰ καὶ τῶν αὐτῶν ἀπολαῦσαι παρεσχηκότι. Ἡ γὰρ μερὶς ἐκεῖνό ἐστιν ὅπερ ἕκαστος λαμβάνει. Ἔστι γὰρ καὶ ἐν τῇ αὐτῇ εἶναι πόλει, καὶ μὴ τῶν αὐτῶν ἀπολαύειν· τὴν δὲ αὐτὴν μερίδα ἔχειν, καὶ μὴ τῶν αὐτῶν ἀπολαύειν, οὐκ ἔστιν. Ἔστιν ἐν τῷ αὐτῷ κλήρῳ εἶναι, καὶ μὴ τὴν αὐτὴν ἔχειν μερίδα· οἷον ἐν τῷ κλήρῳ πάντες ἐσμέν, ἀλλ᾿ οὐ τὴν αὐτὴν ἔχομεν πάντες μερίδα. Ἐνταῦθα δὲ οὐ τοῦτό φησιν, ἀλλὰ καὶ τὴν μερίδα μετὰ τοῦ κλήρου. Διὰ τί κλῆρον καλεῖ; Δεικνὺς ὅτι οὐδεὶς ἀπὸ κατορθωμάτων οἰκείων βασιλείας τυγχάνει· ἀλλ᾿ ὥσπερ ὁ κλῆρος ἐπιτυχίας μᾶλλόν ἐστιν, οὕτω δὴ καὶ ἐνταῦθα. Οὐδεὶς γὰρ τοιαύτην ἐπιδείκνυται πολιτείαν ὥστε βασιλείας ἀξιωθῆναι, ἀλλὰ τῆς αὐτοῦ δωρεᾶς ἐστι τὸ πᾶν. Διὰ τοῦτό φησιν, "Ὅταν πάντα ποιήσητε, λέγετε, ὅτι ἀχρεῖοι δοῦλοί ἐσμεν· ἃ γὰρ ὠφείλομεν ποιῆσαι, πεποιήκαμεν." "Εἰς τὴν μερίδα τοῦ κλήρου τῶν ἁγίων ἐν τῷ φωτί." καὶ τῷ μέλλοντι λέγει, καὶ τῷ παρόντι· τουτέστι, τῇ γνώσει. Δοκεῖ δέ μοι καὶ περὶ τῶν παρόντων, καὶ περὶ τῶν μελλόντων ὁμοῦ λέγειν.

Εἶτα δείκνυσιν ὧν ἠξιώθημεν. Οὐ γὰρ τοῦτο μόνον ἐστὶ τὸ θαυμαστόν, ὅτι βασιλείας ἀξιούμεθα, ἀλλὰ καὶ τίνες ὄντες, δεῖ προστιθέναι· οὐ γάρ ἐστιν ἴσον. Ὅπερ καὶ ἐν τῇ πρὸς Ῥωμαίους ποιεῖ, λέγων· "Μόλις γάρ τις ὑπὲρ τοῦ ἀδίκου ἀποθανεῖται· ὑπὲρ δὲ τοῦ ἀγαθοῦ τάχα τις καὶ τολμᾷ ἀποθανεῖν. " Ὃς ἐρρύσατο ἡμᾶς, φησίν, ἀπὸ τῆς ἐξουσίας τοῦ σκότους." Αὐτοῦ τὸ πᾶν ἐστι, καὶ ταῦτα δοῦναι κἀκεῖνα· οὐδαμοῦ γὰρ ἡμῶν κατόρθωμα. "Ἀπὸ τῆς

to receive." Then by saying *"who has qualified"* he demonstrated that the weight [of the expression] was great. For example, if some lowly person were indeed to become emperor, it's possible for him to assign governorship to whom he wishes; and such is the extent of his power—to give the office—but not also to make the person equipped for the office, and often the honor makes such a person even ridiculous. And so even if he bestows the office and makes the recipient equipped for the honor and qualified for the administrative activity, then the thing is an honor. Therefore Paul says this in this passage too, namely, that he hasn't only given us the honor but has also made us strong enough to receive it [191].

You see, the honor here is twofold, both the giving and the equipping for the gift. Paul didn't say simply "to the giver" but *"who has qualified us to share in the inheritance of the saints in light,"* that is, the one who has appointed us with the saints. No, he didn't simply say "appointed," but also provided us enjoyment of the very same, for the portion is what each receives. You see, it's possible to be in the same city and not enjoy the same [benefits], but to have the same portion and not enjoy the same benefits isn't possible. It's possible to be included in the same inheritance and not to have the same portion; for example, we are all included in the same inheritance, but we don't all receive the same portion. But in this passage he doesn't say so; no, he adds the portion to the inheritance. Why does he call it an inheritance? Showing that none of his own achievements gains the kingdom, but just as the inheritance is rather a case of good luck—so indeed is it in this passage also. You see, nobody demonstrates that such a way of life worthy of the kingdom is earned, but everything is his own gift. This is why he [Christ] says: *"When you do everything, say that we are unprofitable servants; we have only done what was our duty* [Luke 17:10]; *to share in the inheritance of the saints in the light"* [Col 1:12]. And Paul is speaking of what is to come and what is present, that is, *"in knowledge."* He seems to me to be speaking of both present and future things at the same time.

Then he demonstrates what things we have been deemed worthy of. You see, this isn't the only marvelous thing, namely, that we are deemed worthy of the kingdom, but who we are has to be added, for it isn't the same thing. This is what he did in the Epistle to the Romans, when he said, *"For one will hardly die for an unjust person, but for a just person one will dare even to die"* [Rom 5:7]. *"The one who has delivered us,"* he says, *"from the dominion of darkness"* [Col 1:13]. The sum total is from him, both the giving of these things and of those, for nowhere is there any achievement of ours. *"From the dominion of darkness,"* he says, which means error, the

ἐξουσίας τοῦ σκότους," φησί· τουτέστι, τῆς πλάνης, τοῦ διαβόλου τῆς τυραν-
νίδος. Οὐκ [192] εἶπε, σκότους, ἀλλ᾽, "ἐξουσίας·" πολλὴν γὰρ ἡμῶν εἶχε τὴν
ἐξουσίαν, καὶ ἐκράτει ἡμῶν. Χαλεπὸν μὲν γὰρ καὶ τὸ ἁπλῶς εἶναι ὑπὸ τῷ δια-
βόλῳ· τὸ δὲ καὶ μετ᾽ ἐξουσίας, τοῦτο χαλεπώτερον. "Καὶ μετέστησε, φησὶν,
εἰς τὴν βασιλείαν τοῦ υἱοῦ τῆς ἀγάπης αὐτοῦ." Οὐκ ἄρα εἰς τὴν ἀπαλλαγὴν
τοῦ σκότους μόνον ἔδειξεν αὐτοῦ τὴν φιλανθρωπίαν. Μέγα μὲν οὖν καὶ τὸ
τοῦ σκότους ἀπαλλάξαι· τὸ δὲ καὶ εἰς βασιλείαν εἰσαγαγεῖν, πολλῷ μεῖζον.
Ὅρα οὖν πῶς πολύπλοκον γίνεται τὸ δῶρον, ὅτι ἐν τῷ πυθμένι κειμένους
ἀπήλλαξεν ἡμᾶς· δεύτερον, ὅτι οὐκ ἀπήλλαξε μόνον, ἀλλὰ καὶ μετέθηκεν εἰς
βασιλείαν. "Ὃς ἐρρύσατο ἡμᾶς." Οὐκ εἶπεν, ἐξέβαλεν, ἀλλ᾽, "ἐρρύσατο," τὴν
πολλὴν ταλαιπωρίαν δεικνὺς ἡμῶν, καὶ ἐκείνων τὴν αἰχμαλωσίαν. Εἶτα καὶ
τὸ εὔκολον τῆς τοῦ θεοῦ δυνάμεως· "καὶ μετέστησε," φησίν· ὥσπερ ἂν εἴ τις
στρατιώτην ἀπὸ τόπου εἰς τόπον μεταγάγοι. Καὶ οὐκ εἶπε, μετήγαγεν, οὐδὲ
μετέθηκε· τὸ μὲν γὰρ ὅλον τοῦ μεταθέντος ἦν, οὐ τοῦ μετελθόντος· ἀλλά,
"μετέστησεν," εἶπεν, ὥστε καὶ ἡμῶν καὶ αὐτοῦ ἐστιν. "Εἰς τὴν βασιλείαν τοῦ
υἱοῦ τῆς ἀγάπης αὐτοῦ." Οὐχ ἁπλῶς εἶπε, βασιλείαν οὐρανῶν, ἀλλὰ σεμνότερον εἰργάσατο τὸν λόγον, βασιλείαν υἱοῦ εἰπών· τούτου γὰρ οὐδὲν μεῖζον
ἐγκώμιον· ὃ καὶ ἀλλαχοῦ φησιν· "Εἰ ὑπομένομεν, καὶ συμβασιλεύσομεν."
Τῶν αὐτῶν ἠξίωσεν ἡμᾶς, φησί, τῷ υἱῷ· καὶ οὐ τοῦτο μόνον, ἀλλὰ καὶ ἡ
ἐπίτασις, τῷ ἀγαπητῷ. Τοὺς ἐχθροὺς, τοὺς ἐσκοτισμένους, ἀθρόον που αὐτοὺς
μετέστησεν, ἔνθα ὁ υἱός, εἰς τὴν αὐτὴν ἐκείνῳ τιμήν. Καὶ οὐδὲ τούτῳ ἠρκέσθη
μόνῳ, ἵνα δείξῃ μέγα τὸ δῶρον· οὐκ ἠρκέσθη τῷ εἰπεῖν, βασιλείαν, ἀλλὰ καὶ
τοῦ υἱοῦ προσέθηκε· καὶ οὐδὲ τούτῳ, ἀλλὰ καὶ τοῦ ἀγαπητοῦ· καὶ οὐδὲ τούτῳ,
ἀλλὰ καὶ τὸ τῆς φύσεως ἔντιμον. Τί γάρ φησιν; "Ὅς ἐστιν εἰκὼν τοῦ θεοῦ τοῦ
ἀοράτου." Ἀλλ᾽ οὐκ εὐθέως ἐπὶ τοῦτο ἦλθεν, ἀλλὰ παρενέβαλε τὴν εὐεργεσίαν
τὴν εἰς ἡμᾶς. Ἵνα γὰρ μὴ ἀκούων, ὅτι τὸ πᾶν τοῦ πατρὸς ἦν, νομίσῃς τὸν υἱὸν
ἐκτὸς εἶναι, δίδωσι τὸ πᾶν τῷ υἱῷ, καὶ τὸ πᾶν τῷ πατρί. Ἐκεῖνος μὲν γὰρ
[193] μετέθηκεν, ἀλλ᾽ οὗτος τὴν αἰτίαν παρέσχε.

Τί γάρ φησιν; "Ὃς ἐρρύσατο ἡμᾶς ἐκ τῆς ἐξουσίας τοῦ σκότους." Ταὐτὸν
δέ ἐστιν, "Ἐν ᾧ ἔχομεν τὴν ἀπολύτρωσιν, τὴν ἄφεσιν τῶν ἁμαρτημάτων."
Εἰ γὰρ μὴ ἀφείθημεν τῶν ἁμαρτημάτων, οὐκ ἂν μετέστημεν. Ἰδοὺ πάλιν
ἐνταῦθα τὸ, "ἐν ᾧ." Καὶ οὐκ εἶπε λύτρωσιν, ἀλλ᾽, "ἀπολύτρωσιν," ὥστε μηδὲ

tyranny of the devil. [192] He didn't say "from darkness" but "*from the dominion*," for it exercised great dominion over us and was sovereign over us. You see, it's a serious thing to be under the devil at all, but to be so under dominion—that's more serious. "*And he has transferred us*," he says, "*to the kingdom of the Son of his love*" [Col 1:13]. Not only, indeed, did he demonstrate his loving-kindness by delivering it from darkness. While, therefore, it's a great deed to deliver [someone] from darkness, to bring [that person] to the kingdom is much greater. So see how complex the gift is: namely, Christ delivered us who were prostrate in the pit. Second, that he hasn't only delivered us but has also transposed us to the kingdom. *Who has redeemed us* [Col 1:13]. He didn't say "cast us out," but "*he redeemed us*," demonstrating our hardship and their [sc. the devils'] capture [of us]. Then too the ease of God's power: "*and he has transferred*," Paul says, just as of one were to lead a soldier from one place to another. And he didn't say "has conveyed" or "transposed," for so the whole world would belong to the one who transposed, not to the one who went over. No, he said, "*he transferred*," so that it belongs both to us and to him. *To the kingdom of the Son of his love*. He didn't simply say "the kingdom of heaven" but made his argument more solemn by saying "*the kingdom of the Son*," for no praise can be greater than this, as he says also elsewhere: "*If we endure, we shall also reign with him*" [2 Tim 2:12]. God has counted us worthy of the same things as the Son, and not only this but also the intensity, with the beloved [Son]. Those who were enemies, those who were in darkness he has somehow transferred to where the Son is, to the same honor with him. And nor was Paul content with this alone: in order to demonstrate the great gift, he wasn't content with saying "*kingdom*," but he also added "*of the Son*"; and neither was he content with this, but he added also "*beloved*"; nor was he content with this, but he added the dignity of his nature. Well, what does Paul say? "*He is the image of the invisible God*" [Col 1:15]. No, he didn't proceed immediately to this point, but inserted the benefit to us. You see, so that when you hear that everything belonged to the Father, you don't suppose that the Son is excluded, he assigns everything to the Son and everything to the Father. For the Father [193] transferred us, but the Son provided the cause.

What, then, does he say? "*He has saved us from the dominion of darkness*." That means, "*In whom we have complete redemption, the forgiveness of sins*." You see, if we hadn't been forgiven our sins, we wouldn't have been *transferred*. See again in this passage the expression "*in whom*." And he didn't say "redemption" but "*complete redemption*," so that neither shall

ἐκπεσεῖν λοιπόν, μηδὲ γενέσθαι θνητούς. "Ὅς ἐστιν εἰκὼν τοῦ θεοῦ τοῦ ἀοράτου, πρωτότοκος πάσης κτίσεως." Εἰς ζήτημα ἐμπίπτομεν αἱρετικόν· διὸ σήμερον ἀναβαλλομένους αὔριον τοῦτο προθεῖναι δεῖ, ἀκμαζούσαις ὑμῶν ταῖς ἀκοαῖς προσβάλλοντας. Εἰ δὲ δεῖ τι πλέον εἰπεῖν, μεῖζον τοῦ υἱοῦ ἔργον. Πῶς; Ἐκεῖνο μὲν γὰρ ἀδύνατον γίνεται, τὸ ἐν τοῖς ἁμαρτήμασι μένουσι δοῦναι βασιλείαν, τοῦτο δὲ εὐκολώτερον· ὥστε τῇ δωρεᾷ ὡδοποίησε. Τί λέγεις; Τῶν ἁμαρτημάτων σε αὐτὸς ἀφῆκεν; οὐκοῦν καὶ αὐτὸς προσήγαγεν. Ἤδη προκατεβάλετο τοῦ δόγματος τὴν ῥίζαν.

Τέως δὲ ἐκεῖνο εἰπόντας καταπαῦσαι τὸν λόγον ἀνάγκη. Ποῖον δὴ τοῦτο; Ὅτι τοσαύτης ἀπολαύσαντες εὐεργεσίας ἀεὶ ταύτης μεμνῆσθαι ὀφείλομεν, καὶ στρέφειν διαπαντὸς ἐν ἑαυτοῖς τὴν τοῦ θεοῦ δωρεάν, καὶ τίνων ἀπηλλάγημεν, τίνων ἐτύχομεν ἐννοεῖν· καὶ οὕτως ἐσόμεθα εὐχάριστοι, οὕτω τὴν ἀγάπην τὴν πρὸς αὐτὸν ἐπιτενοῦμεν. Τί λέγεις, ἄνθρωπε; εἰς βασιλείαν κέκλησαι, εἰς βασιλείαν υἱοῦ τοῦ θεοῦ, καὶ χάσμης πληροῦσαι, καὶ κνᾶσαι, καὶ ναρκᾷς; Εἰ γὰρ εἰς μυρίους θανάτους πηδῆσαι ἑκάστης τῆς ἡμέρας ἔδει, οὐ πάντα ἐχρῆν ὑπομεῖναι; Ἀλλ' ὑπὲρ μὲν ἀρχῆς πᾶν ὁτιοῦν ποιεῖς, τῆς δὲ βασιλείας μέλλων κοινωνεῖν τῆς τοῦ μονογενοῦς, οὐ καθάλλῃ κατὰ μυρίων ξιφῶν, οὐκ ἐμπηδᾷς εἰς πῦρ; Καὶ οὔπω τοῦτο δεινόν, ἀλλ' ὅτι καὶ [194] μέλλων ἀπιέναι θρηνεῖς, καὶ ἐμφιλοχωρεῖς τοῖς ἐνταῦθα φιλοσώματος ὤν. Τί δὴ τοῦτο; καὶ τὸν θάνατον φρικτὸν πρᾶγμα εἶναι νομίζεις; Ἡ τρυφὴ τούτων αἰτία, ἡ ἄνεσις· ἐπεὶ ὅ γε κατάπικρον βίον ζῶν, καὶ πτερωθῆναι ἔλοιτο ἂν καὶ ἀπαλλαγῆναι ἐντεῦθεν. Νῦν δὲ ταὐτὸν πάσχομεν, οἷον εἰ νεοττοὶ μαλακισθέντες, διαπαντὸς ἐπὶ τῆς καλιᾶς μένειν ἐθέλοντες. Ἀλλ' ὅσῳπερ ἂν μένωσι, τοσούτῳ ἀσθενέστεροι γίνονται. Καλιὰ γὰρ ὁ παρὼν βίος ἐστίν, ἀπὸ καρφῶν καὶ πηλοῦ συγκεκολλημένος. Κἂν τὰς μεγάλας μοι δείξῃς οἰκίας, κἂν αὐτὰ τὰ βασίλεια λάμποντα πολλῷ τῷ χρυσῷ καὶ τοῖς λίθοις, οὐδὲν οἰήσομαι διαφέρειν καλιᾶς χελιδόνων· τοῦ γὰρ χειμῶνος ἐπιστάντος, αὐτόματα πάντα πεσεῖται. Χειμῶνα δὲ τὴν ἡμέραν ἐκείνην λέγω, οὐχὶ πᾶσι χειμῶνα. Ἐπεὶ καὶ ὁ θεὸς

we fall any more, nor become subject to death. We fall into a question of heresy. So we should put this off today and propose it tomorrow,[25] addressing it to you when you're feeling eager. But if one ought to say something more, the work of the Son is the greater. How? You see, it's impossible to give the kingdom to those who remain in their sins, but this is easier, so he prepared the way for the gift. What do you say? He removed you from your sins? Surely then he has brought you forward. Already he has laid in advance the root of his teaching.

At this time it's necessary for us to put a stop to this homily when we have made one point. What kind of point is it? That because we have enjoyed such a great benefit we should be always mindful of it, and continually turn over in our minds the gift of God, and reflect on what we have been delivered from and what we have obtained. And so we shall be thankful, so we shall heighten our love of him. What do you say, sir? You've been called to a kingdom, to a kingdom of the Son of God, and are you full of yawns, and scratching, and torpor? You see, if it were necessary for you to jump into myriad deaths each day, shouldn't you put up with everything? No, for the sake of office you do everything possible, but when you're going to share the kingdom of the Only-Begotten, don't you leap down on myriad swords, don't you jump into the fire? And this isn't the only thing that's strange, but that [**194**] when you're going to depart you mourn and are fond of dwelling with things here, being a lover of the body. What *is* this? Do you regard even death as a terrifying thing? It is luxury that is the cause of these things, ease, since even the one who lives a very bitter life would choose wings and to be released from this life. But now we are experiencing the same thing as chicks that show weakness, wanting to remain always in the nest. But the longer they remain, so much the weaker they become. You see, the present life is a nest cemented together from twigs and mud. And even if you were to show me great houses, even the imperial palace itself, glistening with much gold and precious stones, I shall think them no different from the nests of swallows, for when winter arrives then all will fall down by themselves. By winter I mean that day, not winter for everybody.[26] Because God

---

25. On the duration of preaching in this period, and whether a homily was cut short or extended, see Olivar, *Predicación cristiana antigua*, 670–82. In the present case, although the preacher states that he is postponing his theme for the next day, we note that the homily continues at some length.

26. By "winter" Chrysostom means the last judgment, as becomes clear from what follows.

νύκτα τε ὁμοῦ καὶ ἡμέραν καλεῖ, τὸ μὲν πρὸς τοὺς ἁμαρτωλούς, τὸ δὲ πρὸς τοὺς δικαίους. Οὕτω καὶ ἐγὼ νῦν χειμῶνα αὐτὴν καλῶ. Ἂν ἐν τῷ θέρει μὴ ἐκτραφῶμεν καλῶς, ὥστε δύνασθαι ἵπτασθαι τοῦ χειμῶνος ἐπιστάντος, οὐ λήψονται ἡμᾶς αἱ μητέρες, ἀλλ᾽ ἐάσουσιν ἡμᾶς τῷ λιμῷ διαφθαρῆναι, ἢ τῆς καλιᾶς πεσούσης ἀπολέσθαι. Καθάπερ γὰρ καλιάν, μᾶλλον δὲ καὶ εὐκολώτερον ταύτης, ἅπαντα καθαιρεῖ τότε ὁ θεός, ἀνασκευάζων καὶ μεταρρυθμίζων ἅπαντα. Οἱ δὲ ἄπτηνες καὶ ἀπαντῆσαι αὐτῷ μὴ δυνάμενοι εἰς τὸν ἀέρα, ἀλλ᾽ οὕτω βαναύσως τραφέντες, ὡς μὴ ἔχειν τὸ πτερὸν κοῦφον, πείσονται ταῦτα, ἅπερ εἰκὸς τοὺς οὕτω διακειμένους παθεῖν. Ἡ μὲν οὖν τῶν χελιδόνων νεοττιά, ὅταν καταπέσῃ, ταχέως ἀπόλλυται· ἡμεῖς δὲ οὐκ ἀπολλύμεθα, ἀλλὰ κολαζόμεθα διηνεκῶς. Χειμὼν ἔσται ὁ τότε καιρός, μᾶλλον δὲ χειμῶνος χαλεπώτερος. Οὐ γὰρ χείμαρροι κατασύρονται ὕδατος, ἀλλὰ ποταμοὶ πυρός· οὐ σκότος ἀπὸ νεφῶν γίνεται, ἀλλὰ σκότος ἄλυτον καὶ ἀφεγγές, ὥστε μήτε τὸν οὐρανὸν ἰδεῖν, μήτε τὸν ἀέρα, ἀλλὰ τῶν εἰς γῆν κατωρυγμένων μᾶλλον στενοχωρεῖσθαι.

Πολλάκις [195] ταῦτα λέγομεν, ἀλλ᾽ οὐ πείθομέν τινας. Ἀλλ᾽ οὐδὲν θαυμαστόν, εἴγε ἡμεῖς ἄνθρωποι εὐτελεῖς ταῦτα πάσχομεν ὑπὲρ τοιούτων διαλεγόμενοι, ὅπου γε καὶ οἱ προφῆται ἔπασχον ταῦτα, οὐχ ὑπὲρ τοιούτων μόνον πραγμάτων διαλεγόμενοι, ἀλλὰ καὶ ὑπὲρ πολέμου καὶ αἰχμαλωσίας. Καὶ ὁ Σεδεκίας ὑπὸ τοῦ Ἱερεμίου ἠλέγχετο, καὶ οὐκ ᾐσχύνετο. Διὰ τοῦτο ἔλεγον οἱ προφῆται· "Οὐαὶ οἱ λέγοντες, ἐγγισάτω τὸ τάχος ἃ ποιήσει ὁ θεός, ἵνα ἴδωμεν, καὶ ἐλθέτω ἡ βουλὴ τοῦ ἁγίου Ἰσραήλ, ἵνα γνῶμεν." Μὴ θαυμάζωμεν τοῦτο. Οὐδὲ γὰρ οἱ ἐπὶ τῆς κιβωτοῦ ἐπίστευον, ἀλλ᾽ ἐπίστευσαν ὅτε τῆς πίστεως κέρδος ἦν οὐδέν· οὐδὲ οἱ ἐν Σοδόμοις προσεδόκησαν, ἀλλ᾽ ἐπίστευσαν καὶ αὐτοί, ὅτε οὐδὲν πλέον αὐτοῖς γέγονε. Καὶ τί λέγω τὰ μέλλοντα; τίς ἂν ταῦτα προσεδόκησε τὰ νῦν γινόμενα κατὰ διαφόρους τόπους, τοὺς σεισμούς, τῶν πόλεων τὰς ἀναιρέσεις; Καίτοιγε ταῦτα ἐκείνων πιστότερα, τῆς κιβωτοῦ λέγω.

Πόθεν δῆλον; Ὅτι ἐκεῖνοι μὲν οὐκ εἶχον εἰς ἄλλο παράδειγμα ἰδεῖν, οὐδὲ τῶν γραφῶν ἤκουσαν· ἐνταῦθα δὲ μυρία ὅσα γέγονε, καὶ ἐπὶ τῶν ἐτῶν τῶν

calls it at the same time both night and day, the one regarding the sinners, the other regarding the just. So indeed do I now call this winter. If in the summer we haven't been properly brought up, so as to be able to fly when winter has come, our mothers won't take us but allow us to die of hunger or to perish when the nest falls down. You see, just as at that time God will destroy everything, like a nest, but even more easily than that, dismantling and remodeling everything. But those who can't fly, being unable *to meet him in the air* [1 Thess 4:17], but have been so badly brought up that they don't have a lightness of wing, will suffer those things that it is reasonable for those so disposed to suffer. Now then, the nest of swallows, when it falls down, is quickly destroyed, whereas we're not destroyed but are punished continually. The season on that occasion will be winter, but more severe than winter. For it isn't torrents of water that roll down, but rivers of fire; it isn't darkness arising from clouds, but a darkness ceaseless and dim, so that they can see neither heaven, nor the air, but are more straightened than those buried in the earth.

Often [**195**] we make these statements, but some people we cannot convince. But it's not amazing if we mere human beings experience these things, when we preach on such topics, where the prophets experienced these things too, not only when preaching about such matters but also about war and captivity. And Zedekiah was rebuked by Jeremiah, and was not ashamed [see Jer 21:11; 27:12]. This is why the prophet said, "*Woe to those who say: let God make haste, so that we may see it, and let the counsel of the holy Israel come, so that we may know it*" [Isa 5:18, 19].[27] Let's not be surprised at this. You see, neither did those in the day of the ark believe, but they did believe when their belief was of no gain to them. Nor did the people of Sodom expect [what would happen to them], but they too believed, when nothing more happened to them. And why do I speak about the future? Who would have expected what has happened now in various places—the earthquakes, the destruction of cities?[28] And yet these happenings are easier to believe than those, I mean those in the time of the ark.

From what is this clear? Because the people didn't have any example to consider, nor had they heard the Scriptures. But in our case there are myriad examples that have happened, both in our own and in former years.

---

27. This is not an accurate citation.

28. This is probably a rhetorical ploy rather than a reference to contemporary events.

ἡμετέρων, καὶ ἐπὶ τῶν προτέρων. Ἀλλὰ πόθεν ἡ ἀπιστία τῶν τοιούτων; Ἀπὸ μαλακῆς ψυχῆς· ἔπινον καὶ ἤσθιον, καὶ διὰ τοῦτο οὐκ ἐπίστευον. Ἃ γὰρ βούλεταί τις, ταῦτα καὶ οἴεται, ταῦτα καὶ προσδοκᾷ· οἱ δὲ ἀντιλέγοντες λῆρός εἰσιν.

Ἀλλὰ μὴ πάθωμεν ταὐτόν· οὐ γὰρ κατακλυσμὸς ἔσται λοιπόν, οὐδὲ μέχρι τελευτῆς ἡ κόλασις, ἀλλ᾽ ἀρχὴ τιμωριῶν ὁ θάνατος ἀπιστούντων ὅτι ἐστὶ κρίσις. Καὶ τίς ἐκεῖθεν ἦλθε, φησί, καὶ ταῦτα ἐφθέγξατο; Εἰ μὲν παίζων ταῦτα λέγεις, οὐδὲ οὕτω καλῶς· οὐ γὰρ δεῖ ἐν τοῖς τοιούτοις παίζειν· οὐ γὰρ ἐν παικτοῖς, ἀλλ᾽ ἐπικινδύνως παίζομεν· εἰ δὲ ὄντως οὕτως ἔχων, καὶ οὐκ οἴει εἶναί τι μετὰ ταῦτα, πῶς εἶναι φὴς Χριστιανός; οὐδεὶς γάρ μοι τῶν ἔξω λόγος. Διὰ τί λουτρὸν λαμβάνεις; διὰ τί τῆς ἐκκλησίας ἐπιβαίνεις; μὴ γὰρ ἀρχὰς ὑπισχνούμεθα; πᾶσα ἡμῶν ἐλπὶς ἐν τοῖς μέλλουσι. Τί τοίνυν προσέρχῃ, εἰ οὐ πιστεύεις ταῖς γραφαῖς; Εἰ μὴ πιστεύεις τῷ Χριστῷ, οὐκ ἂν εἴποιμι τὸν τοιοῦτον Χριστιανὸν εἶναι, μὴ γένοιτο, ἀλλὰ καὶ Ἑλλήνων χείρω. Κατὰ τί; Κατὰ τοῦτο, ὅτι τὸν Χριστὸν νομίζων εἶναι θεόν, οὐ πιστεύεις ὡς θεῷ. Ἐκείνη μὲν [196] γὰρ ἀκολουθίας ἔχεται ἡ ἀσέβεια· τὸν γὰρ μὴ νομίζοντα εἶναι θεὸν τὸν Χριστόν, ἀνάγκη μηδὲ πιστεύειν· αὕτη δὲ ἡ ἀσέβεια οὐδὲ ἀκολουθίαν ἔχει, θεὸν ὁμολογεῖν, καὶ μὴ νομίζειν ἀξιόπιστον εἶναι ὑπὲρ ὧν ἔφη. Τῆς μέθης ταῦτα τὰ ῥήματα, τῆς τρυφῆς, τῆς σπατάλης· "Φάγωμεν καὶ πίωμεν· αὔριον γὰρ ἀποθνῄσκομεν." Οὐκ αὔριον, ἀλλ᾽ ὅταν ταῦτα λέγητε, ἤδη τεθνήκατε. Οὐδὲν οὖν τῶν χοίρων διοίσομεν, οὐδὲ τῶν ὄνων, εἰπέ μοι; Εἰ γὰρ μήτε κρίσις ἐστί, μήτε ἀντίδοσις, μήτε δικαστήριον, τίνος ἕνεκεν τοιούτῳ τετιμήμεθα δώρῳ, τῷ λόγῳ, καὶ πάντα ἔχομεν ὑποτεταγμένα; διὰ τί ἡμεῖς μὲν ἄρχομεν, ἐκεῖνα δὲ ἄρχονται; Ὅρα πῶς πάντοθεν ὁ διάβολος ἐπείγεται πεῖσαι ἡμᾶς ἀγνοῆσαι τὴν δωρεὰν τοῦ θεοῦ. Τοὺς δούλους ἀναμίγνυσι τοῖς δεσπόταις· καθάπερ τις ἀνδραποδιστὴς καὶ οἰκέτης ἀγνώμων, τὸν ἐλεύθερον εἰς τὴν αὐτὴν βιάζεται τῷ προσκεκρουκότι καταγαγεῖν εὐτέλειαν. Καὶ δοκεῖ μὲν τὴν κρίσιν ἀναιρεῖν, ἀναιρεῖ δὲ τὸ εἶναι θεόν.

But how did the unbelief of those people come about? From a slack soul: they drank and they ate [see 1 Cor 15:32], and because of this they didn't believe. You see, what somebody wishes for, they both think and expect, while those who contradict them are useless.

But let's not experience the same thing, for after this it won't be a flood, nor punishment till death, but death will be the beginning of the retribution for those who don't believe that there is a judgment. "And who has come from the other side and said so?" says [someone]. If you say these things in jest, not even so is it right, for one ought not to jest in such matters. You see, we do not jest in trifling matters,[29] but to our peril. But if you think things are really so and you don't think that there is anything after this, how do you call yourself a Christian? For I don't take into account those who are outside [the church]. Why do you receive baptism? Why do you go to church? Surely we didn't promise you magistracies? All our hope is in the things to come. Why then do you come, if you don't believe in the Scriptures? If you don't believe in Christ, I wouldn't call somebody like that a Christian—heaven forbid—but worse even than Hellenes. In what respect? In this respect, that when you think that Christ is God, you don't believe in him as in God. [**196**] You see that impiety has consistency, for the one who doesn't think that Christ is God, of necessity won't even believe him: that impiety contains inconsistency. For it's necessary for the one who doesn't think that Christ is God not even to believe. But this impiety doesn't even contain inconsistency—to confess God and not to think that what he said is worthy of belief. These are the words of drunkenness, of luxury, of lewdness. "*Let us eat and drink, for tomorrow we die*" [1 Cor 15:32]. Not tomorrow, but when you say these words you're already dead. Therefore, tell me, shall we be in no way different from pigs, nor asses? For if there's going to be neither judgment, nor retribution, nor a tribunal, on what account have we been honored with such a gift, with reason, and have everything subjected to us? Why do we rule, while those animals are ruled? See how the devil on every side insists on persuading us to be ignorant of God's gift. He mixes slaves with their masters; like some slave dealer and ungrateful servant, he presses the free person to descend to the same base level as the criminal. And the devil seems to be overthrowing the judgment, but he is overthrowing the being of God.

---

29. Παιϰτός, an unusual word, found only in Chrysostom, according to *PGL*, 997 s.v.

Τοιοῦτος γὰρ ἀεὶ ὁ διάβολος, μεθοδείᾳ πάντα, καὶ οὐκ ἐξ εὐθείας προβάλλει, ἵνα φυλαττώμεθα. Εἰ κρίσις οὐκ ἔστιν, οὐκ ἔστι δίκαιος ὁ θεός· κατὰ ἄνθρωπον λέγω· εἰ δίκαιος οὐκ ἔστιν ὁ θεός, οὐδὲ θεὸς ἔστιν· εἰ θεὸς οὐκ ἔστιν, ἁπλῶς ἅπαντα φέρεται, οὐδὲν ἀρετὴ, οὐδὲν κακία. Ἀλλ᾽ οὐδὲν τούτων λέγει φανερῶς. Εἶδες τοῦ σατανικοῦ ἐνθυμήματος τὴν διάνοιαν; πῶς ἐξ ἀνθρώπων ἄλογα βούλεται ποιῆσαι, μᾶλλον δὲ θηρία, μᾶλλον δὲ δαίμονας; Μὴ τοίνυν πειθώμεθα. Ἔστι γὰρ κρίσις, ἄθλιε καὶ ταλαίπωρε. Οἶδα πόθεν ἔρχῃ ἐπὶ τούτους τοὺς λόγους· πολλά σοι ἡμάρτηται, προσκέκρουκας, παρρησίαν οὐκ ἔχεις, οἴει τοῖς σοῖς λόγοις ἀκολουθεῖν καὶ τὴν τῶν πραγμάτων φύσιν. Τέως μὴ ὀδυνήσω, φησὶ, τὴν ψυχὴν τῇ προσδοκίᾳ τῆς γεέννης· κἂν ᾖ γέεννα, πείσω αὐτὴν ὅτι οὐκ ἔστι· τέως ἐνταῦθα τρυφήσω. Διὰ τί προστιθεῖς ἁμαρτήματα ἁμαρτήμασιν; Ἂν ἁμαρτήσας πιστεύσῃς εἶναι γέενναν, ἀπελεύσῃ τῶν ἁμαρτημάτων μόνον τίνων δίκην· ἂν δὲ καὶ τοῦτο προσθῇς τὸ ἀσέβημα, καὶ τῆς ἀσεβείας καὶ τοῦ λογισμοῦ τούτου δώσεις τὴν ἐσχάτην κόλασιν· καὶ ἡ ἐν βραχεῖ γενομένη σοι παραμυθία ψυχρὰ ἔσται σοι [197] διηνεκοῦς κολάσεως ὑπόθεσις. Ἔστω, ἥμαρτες· τί καὶ τοὺς ἄλλους ἁμαρτάνειν προτρέπεις, λέγων μὴ εἶναι γέενναν; τί ἠπάτας τοὺς ἀφελεστέρους; τί τὰς χεῖρας ἐξέλυες τοῦ λαοῦ; Τὸ σὸν μέρος, ἅπαντα ἀνατέτραπται· οὔτε οἱ σπουδαῖοι σπουδαιότεροι ἔσονται, ἀλλὰ ῥάθυμοι· οὔτε οἱ κακοὶ ἀποστήσονται τῆς κακίας. Μὴ γὰρ, ἂν ἑτέρους διαφθείρωμεν, συγγνώμην ἔχομεν τῶν ἁμαρτημάτων; Οὐχ ὁρᾷς τὸν διάβολον πῶς ἐπεχείρησε κατενεγκεῖν τὸν Ἀδάμ; ἆρα τούτῳ συγγνώμη γέγονε; Μείζονος μὲν οὖν κολάσεως ἀφορμή, ἵνα μὴ ὑπὲρ τῶν οἰκείων, ἀλλὰ καὶ ὑπὲρ τῶν ἀλλοτρίων ἁμαρτημάτων κολάζηται. Μὴ νομίζωμεν τοίνυν τὸ ἑτέρους καταστρέφειν εἰς τὴν αὐτὴν ἡμῖν ἀπώλειαν, ἡμερώτερον ἡμῖν τὸ δικαστήριον ἐργάζεσθαι· τοῦτο μὲν οὖν χαλεπώτερον αὐτὸ ποιήσει. Τί ὠθοῦμεν ἑαυτοὺς, καὶ ἀπόλλυμεν; Σατανικὸν τοῦτο ὅλον ἐστίν.

Ἄνθρωπε, ἥμαρτες; Φιλάνθρωπον ἔχεις τὸν δεσπότην· παρακάλει, ἱκέτευε, δάκρυε, στέναζε, καὶ τοὺς ἄλλους φόβει, καὶ ἀξίου μὴ τοῖς αὐτοῖς περιπεσεῖν. Εἴ τις, εἰπέ μοι, ἐν οἰκίᾳ δοῦλος ὢν τῶν προσκεκρουκότων λέγει πρὸς τὸν ἑαυτοῦ παῖδα· τέκνον, ἐγὼ προσέκρουσα τῷ δεσπότῃ, σὺ σπούδασον ἀρέσαι, ἵνα μὴ τὰ αὐτὰ πάθῃς· οὐχ ἕξει τινὰ συγγνώμην, εἰπέ μοι; οὐκ ἐπικλάσει καὶ κατακάμψει τὸν δεσπότην; Ἂν δὲ ταῦτα ἀφεὶς τὰ ῥήματα, λέγῃ ἐκεῖνα, οἷον, ὅτι τὸ κατ᾽ ἀξίαν ἑκάστῳ οὐκ ἀποδώσει, ὅτι ἁπλῶς πάντα

You see, the devil is always like that: he puts forward everything with wiliness, not in a straightforward way, so that we should be on our guard. If there's no judgment, there's no just God (I speak as a human being): if God isn't just, everything proceeds willy-nilly; there's no virtue, no evil. But he doesn't say any of this openly. Have you seen the thrust of Satan's argument? How he wants to make brutes out of human beings, or rather beasts, rather demons? Well then, let's not be persuaded. For there is a judgment, you wretched and miserable person! I know where you come from to these arguments: you've sinned greatly, you're a criminal, you have no confidence, you think that even the nature of things follows your arguments. "Meanwhile," he says, "I won't torment my soul with the expectation of Gehenna, and even if there is a Gehenna I shall persuade it that it doesn't exist. Meanwhile I shall live here in luxury." For what reason do you heap sins on sins? If when you have sinned you believe that Gehenna exists, you'll depart with only the penalty of your sins. But if you add this further impiety, you'll pay the utmost penalty both for the impiety and this thought. And what was a brief and cold comfort will be to you [197] a cause of continuous punishment. Granted, you have sinned. Why do you encourage others too to sin, saying that Gehenna doesn't exist? Why do you deceive the simpler people? Why do you enfeeble the hands of the people? For your part, everything has been turned upside down: neither will the serious become more serious but lazy; nor will the evil ones desist from evil. Surely it's not the case that if we corrupt them we have pardon for our sins. Don't you see how the devil attempted to bring down Adam [see Gen 3]? Then has there been pardon for him? It will be the occasion of greater punishment, so that he can have us chastised not on account of our own sins but also on account of the sins of others. Let's therefore not reckon that to bring down others into the same destruction as ourselves will make the tribunal more lenient to us. Indeed, this will make it worse. Why do we push ourselves onward and perish? This whole business is from Satan.

Sir, have you sinned? You have as your master one who loves human beings. Exhort, beg, weep, groan, and make the others afraid, and pray that they don't fall into the same things. Tell me, if some servant in a house who belongs to offenders says to his own son, "Child, I have offended the master; you must make an effort to please him, lest you experience the same things as I." Tell me, won't he have some pardon? Won't he bend and overcome his master? But if, leaving such words, he were to say the following: for example, that he won't return to each one according to merit, that

ἀνακέχυται, καὶ τὰ καλὰ καὶ τὰ κακά, ὅτι οὐκ ἔστιν εὐχαριστία ἐν τῷ οἴκῳ τούτῳ, τίνα νομίζεις τὸν δεσπότην νοῦν ἔχειν περὶ αὐτοῦ; ἆρα οὐχὶ τῶν οἰκείων ἁμαρτημάτων μείζονα δώσει δίκην; Εἰκότως· ἐκεῖ μὲν γὰρ τὸ πάθος ἀπολογήσεται, εἰ καὶ ἀσθενῶς, ἐνταῦθα δὲ οὐδείς. Εἰ μηδένα τοίνυν ἕτερον, τὸν γοῦν πλούσιον μίμησαι τὸν ἐν τῇ γεέννῃ, τὸν λέγοντα, "Πάτερ Ἀβραὰμ, πέμψον ἐπὶ τοὺς συγγενεῖς μου, ἵνα μὴ ἔλθωσιν εἰς τὸν τόπον τοῦτον," ἐπειδὴ αὐτὸς ἀπελθεῖν οὐκ ἠδύνατο, ὥστε μὴ τοῖς αὐτοῖς ἐκείνους περιπεσεῖν. Ἀποστῶμεν τῶν ῥημάτων τούτων τῶν σατανικῶν.

[198]Τί οὖν, ὅταν Ἕλληνες ἡμᾶς ἐρωτῶσι, φησίν; οὐκ ἐκείνους βούλει θεραπεῦσαι; Ἀλλ᾽ εἰς ἀπορίαν ἐμβαλὼν τὸν Χριστιανὸν προσχήματι τοῦ τὸν Ἕλληνα θεραπεύειν, κυρῶσαι βούλει τὸ δόγμα τὸ σατανικόν. Ἐπειδὴ γὰρ αὐτὸς μόνῃ τῇ ψυχῇ διαλεγόμενος ὑπὲρ τούτων οὐ πείθεις, ἑτέρους θέλεις παράγειν μάρτυρας. Εἰ δὲ Ἕλληνι χρὴ διαλέγεσθαι, οὐκ ἐντεῦθεν ἡ ἀρχὴ τῆς διαλέξεως, ἀλλ᾽ εἰ θεὸς ὁ Χριστός, καὶ θεοῦ παῖς, εἰ δαίμονες οἱ παρ᾽ ἐκείνοις θεοί. Ἐὰν ταῦτα κατασκευασθῇ, πάντα τὰ ἄλλα ἕπεται· πρὶν δὲ τὴν ἀρχὴν θέσθαι, μάταιον περὶ τῆς τελευτῆς διαλέγεσθαι· πρὶν ἢ τὰ πρῶτα στοιχεῖα μαθεῖν, περιττὸν καὶ ἀνόνητον περὶ τὸ τέλος ἔρχεσθαι. Ἀπιστεῖ ὁ Ἕλλην τῇ κρίσει, καὶ αὐτὸς τὸ αὐτό σοι πάσχει· ἐπεὶ ἔχει καὶ αὐτὸς πολλοὺς ὑπὲρ τούτων φιλοσοφήσαντας, εἰ καὶ τὸ σῶμα ἀποσχίσαντες τῆς ψυχῆς τοῦτο εἶπον· ἀλλ᾽ ὅμως δικαστήριον ἐκάθισαν. Καὶ τοσαύτη ἐστὶ τοῦ πράγματος ἡ περιφάνεια, ὡς μηδένα σχεδὸν ἀγνοῆσαι τοῦτο, ἀλλὰ καὶ ποιητάς, καὶ πάντας συμφωνῆσαι ἑαυτοῖς καὶ περὶ δικαστηρίου καὶ περὶ κρίσεως. Ὥστε κἀκεῖνος τοῖς οἰκείοις ἀπιστεῖ πρώτοις, καὶ Ἰουδαῖος ἀμφισβητεῖ περὶ τούτων, καὶ πᾶς ἄνθρωπος.

Τί τοίνυν ἀπατῶμεν ἑαυτούς; Ἰδοὺ ταῦτα λέγεις πρὸς ἐμέ· τί πρὸς τὸν θεὸν ἐρεῖς τὸν πλάσαντα καταμόνας τὰς καρδίας ἡμῶν; τὸν εἰδότα τὰ ἐν τῇ διανοίᾳ πάντα; τὸν ζῶντα καὶ ἐνεργοῦντα καὶ τομώτερον ὑπὲρ πᾶσαν μάχαιραν δίστομον; Εἰπὲ γάρ μοι μετὰ ἀληθείας· σὺ οὐ καταγινώσκεις σαυτοῦ; Καὶ πῶς ἂν ἀπὸ ταὐτομάτου τοσαύτη σοφία γέγονεν, ὥστε αὐτὸν τὸν ἁμαρτάνοντα καταγινώσκειν ἑαυτοῦ; τοῦτο γὰρ μεγάλης σοφίας ἐστί. Σὺ σαυτοῦ καταγινώσκεις· ὁ δὲ τὴν τοιαύτην σοι διδοὺς διάνοιαν πάντα ἁπλῶς ἀφήσει φέρεσθαι; Κανὼν οὖν οὗτος ἔσται καθολικός, καὶ ὅρος· οὐδεὶς τῶν ἐν ἀρετῇ

all these things are simply mixed up together, both the good and the bad, that there is no thanksgiving in this house, what opinion do you think the master has about him? Won't he give a judgment greater than his own sins? Rightly so, for in the former case his feeling will plead for him, although weakly, but in this case nobody will. If therefore there's nobody else, imitate at least that rich man in Gehenna who said, "Father Abraham, send [Lazarus] to my relatives, lest they come to this place" [see Luke 16:27–28], since he couldn't leave himself, so that they shouldn't fall into the same circumstances. Let's stay away from these satanical words.

[198] "What then," Paul asks, "when the Hellenes put questions to us?" Don't you want to cure them? No, by throwing Christians into perplexity by pretending to cure the Hellene, you want to confirm the satanical teaching. For when you dialogue with your soul alone about these matters, you don't persuade [her];[30] you want to introduce other witnesses. But if one should dialogue with the Hellenes, the dialogue shouldn't begin with this, but whether Christ is God, and the child of God, whether their gods are demons. If these points have been prepared, all the rest follow. But before establishing the beginning, it's a waste of time to dialogue about the end, before learning the first principles, superfluous and useless to proceed to the conclusion. The Hellene doesn't believe in the judgment and experiences the same as yourself, since they too have many people who have philosophized about these matters; even if they said this while separating the body from the soul, they nevertheless established a tribunal. And the clarity of the matter is so obvious that hardly anyone is ignorant of it, but both poets and all agree among themselves, both about tribunal and judgment. The upshot is that the Hellene doesn't disbelieve their own authorities, and the Jew has no doubt about these matters, and every human being [is the same].

Why then do we deceive ourselves? Look, you're saying these things to me. What will you say to God, *who fashioned our hearts one by one* [Ps 33:15], who knows everything in our minds [see Ps 94:11], who *is living and active and sharper than any two-edged sword* [Heb 4:12]? Tell me truthfully: Don't you condemn yourself? And how should wisdom so great happen by itself, such that the one who sins condemns themself? For this is a work of mighty wisdom. You condemn yourself. But will the one who paid so much attention to you allow everything to go on aimlessly? This rule, therefore,

---

30. The Greek word for soul, ψυχή, is feminine.

ζώντων διαπιστεῖ τῷ τῆς κρίσεως λόγῳ, κἂν Ἕλλην ᾖ, κἂν αἱρετικός· οὐδεὶς τῶν ἐν κακίᾳ ἀναστρεφομένων πολλῇ, πλὴν ὀλίγων, παραδέχεται τὸν τῆς ἀναστάσεως λόγον. Καὶ τοῦτό φησιν ὁ Ψαλμῳδός· "Ἀνταναιρεῖται τὰ κρίματά σου ἀπὸ προσώπου αὐτοῦ." Διὰ τί; Ὅτι βεβηλοῦνται αἱ ὁδοὶ [199] αὐτοῦ ἐν παντὶ καιρῷ· "Φάγωμεν γάρ, φησί, καὶ πίωμεν· αὔριον γὰρ ἀποθνήσκομεν."

Ὁρᾷς ὅτι ταπεινῶν ἐστι ταῦτα λέγειν; Ἀπὸ τοῦ τρώγειν καὶ πίνειν ταῦτα τὰ ῥήματά ἐστι τὰ ἀνατρεπτικὰ τῆς ἀναστάσεως. Οὐ φέρει γάρ, οὐ φέρει τὸ ἀπὸ τοῦ συνειδότος κριτήριον ἡ ψυχή· καὶ ταὐτὸν γίνεται, οἷον ὁ ἀνδροφόνος πρότερον ὑποθεὶς ἑαυτῷ ὅτι οὐχ ἁλώσεται, οὕτω φονεύει· ἐπεὶ, τοῦ συνειδότος αὐτὸν κρίνοντος, οὐκ ἂν ταχέως ἦλθεν ἐπὶ τὸ τόλμημα. Καὶ οἶδεν οὖν, καὶ ἀγνοεῖν προσποιεῖται, ἵνα μὴ βασανίζηται τῷ συνειδότι καὶ τῷ φόβῳ· ἢ γὰρ ἄν, ἀσθενέστερος γέγονε πρὸς τὴν τόλμαν. Οὕτω δὴ καὶ οἱ ἁμαρτάνοντες, καὶ καθ' ἑκάστην ἐν τοῖς αὐτοῖς κακοῖς κυλινδούμενοι, οὐ θέλουσιν εἰδέναι, καίτοι τοῦ συνειδότος αὐτῶν ἐπιλαμβανομένου.

Ἀλλὰ μὴ ἐκείνοις προσέχωμεν· ἔσται γάρ, ἔσται πάντως κρίσις καὶ ἀνάστασις, καὶ οὐκ ἀφήσει εἰκῆ τοσαῦτα ἔργα ὁ θεός. Διό, παρακαλῶ, τῆς κακίας ἀποσχόμενοι, τῆς ἀρετῆς ἐχώμεθα, ἵνα τὸν ἀληθῆ λόγον παραδεξώμεθα ἐν Χριστῷ Ἰησοῦ τῷ κυρίῳ ἡμῶν. Καίτοι τί εὐκολώτερον, τὸν περὶ ἀναστάσεως δέξασθαι λόγον, ἢ τὸν περὶ εἱμαρμένης; Ἐκεῖνος ἀδικίας γέμει, ἐκεῖνος ἀλογίας, ἐκεῖνος ὠμότητος, ἐκεῖνος ἀπανθρωπίας· οὗτος δικαιοσύνης, τοῦ κατ' ἀξίαν ἀπονεμητικός· καὶ ὅμως αὐτὸν οὐ παραδέχονται. Τὸ δὲ αἴτιον ἡ ἀργία· ἐπεὶ οὐδεὶς νοῦν ἔχων, ἐκεῖνον δέχεται. Καὶ γὰρ καὶ ἐν Ἕλλησιν οἳ τὴν ἡδονὴν ὁριζόμενοι τέλος εἶναι, φασίν, ἐκεῖνοι αὐτὸν ἐδέξαντο· οἱ δὲ τὴν ἀρετὴν ἀγαπήσαντες, οὐκέτι, ἀλλ' ἐξέβαλον ὡς ἄλογον. Εἰ δὲ ἐν Ἕλλησι τοῦτο, πολλῷ μᾶλλον καὶ ἐν τῷ περὶ τῆς ἀναστάσεως λόγῳ οὕτω. Θέα δέ μοι πῶς δύο ἐναντία κατεσκεύασεν ὁ διάβολος· ἵνα γὰρ ἀμελῶμεν ἀρετῆς, καὶ ἵνα θεραπεύωμεν δαίμονας, τὴν ἀνάγκην εἰσήγαγεν, καὶ δι' ἑκατέρων ἀμφότερα ἔπεισε. Τίνα οὖν δυνήσεται λόγον δοῦναι ὁ διαπιστῶν πράγματι οὕτω θαυμαστῷ,

will be general and a fixed boundary. None of those who lives in virtue disbelieves the doctrine of judgment, whether they are a Hellene or a heretic. None of those who conduct themselves with great evil, except for a few, receive the doctrine of the resurrection. And this is what the psalmist says: "*Your judgments are removed before his face*" [Ps 9:26 LXX]. Why? *Because his ways are polluted* [**199**] *at every* opportunity [Ps 9:26 LXX]. For "*let us eat,*" he says, "*and drink, for tomorrow we die*" [1 Cor 15:32].

Do you see that saying these words is the mark of low-lying people? From luxuriating and drinking come these expressions, which are subversive of the resurrection. For the soul doesn't endure, doesn't endure that court that belongs to the conscience. And the same happens, for example, in the case of a murderer who, having first suggested to themselves that they won't be caught, thus continues to murder, since, if conscience had been their judge they wouldn't have proceeded quickly to recklessness. And yet they know, and profess not to know, lest they be tortured by conscience and fear, for certainly in that case they would have been less resolute in the face of recklessness. So too indeed is it that the sinners, who also wallow in their own evil deeds, refuse to admit knowledge of it, yet their conscience pricks them.

But let's not pay attention to those people, for there will be, there will certainly be a judgment and a resurrection, and God won't allow such great works to be in vain. Therefore, please, when we have left off wickedness, let's hold fast to virtue, so that we may inherit the true doctrine in Christ Jesus, our Lord. And yet what is easier to receive, the doctrine of the resurrection or that of fate? The latter is full of injustice, of absurdity, of cruelty, of inhumanity; the former of justice, awarding according to merit—and still people don't inherit it. The fault is laziness, since nobody who has understanding receives the other. Indeed, even among the Hellenes, those who ordained that pleasure was the goal said themselves that they didn't receive it, but those who loved virtue wouldn't receive it but rejected it as absurdity.[31] If this was the case among the Hellenes, much more will it be so in the doctrine of the resurrection. Please see how the devil has set up two opposing entities: for in order for us to neglect virtue, and to worship demons, he introduced this necessity, and persuaded both sides by means of the other. Therefore, what reason will the one be able to give who doesn't

---

31. Here Epicurus (d. 270 BCE) and his followers are meant, together with the opponents he faced during his lifetime and later because of the hedonism he professed, which was supposed to lead to a happy life (see *OCD*, 532–34).

καὶ τοῖς ἐκεῖνα ληροῦσι πειθόμενος; Μὴ τοίνυν μηδὲ αὕτη σε ἡ παραμυθία τρεφέτω, ὡς τεύξῃ συγγνώμης· ἀλλὰ συστρέψαντες ἑαυτούς, διεγείρωμεν πρὸς ἀρετήν, καὶ ζήσωμεν ἀληθῶς τῷ Θεῷ, ἐν Χριστῷ Ἰνσοῦ [200] τῷ κυρίῳ ἡμῶν, μεθ᾽οὗ τῷ πατρὶ ἅμα τῷ ἁγίῳ πνεύματι δόξα, κράτος, τιμή, νῦν καὶ ἀεὶ καὶ εἰς τοὺς αἰῶνας τῶν αἰώνων. Ἀμήν.

believe in a matter so amazing and is persuaded by those who say these things idly? Then don't let this consolation support you either, namely, that you will obtain forgiveness. No, gathering ourselves together, let us stir ourselves to virtue, and let us live truly to God, in Christ Jesus [200] our Lord, with whom to the Father together with the Holy Spirit be glory, might, honor, now and always and forever and ever. Amen.

ΛΟΓΟΣ Γ

Ὅς ἐστιν εἰκὼν τοῦ Θεοῦ τοῦ ἀοράτου, πρωτότοκος πάσης κτίσεως. Ὅτι ἐν αὐτῷ ἐκτίσθη τὰ πάντα, τὰ ἐν τοῖς οὐρανοῖς καὶ τὰ ἐπὶ τῆς γῆς, τὰ ὁρατὰ καὶ τὰ ἀόρατα, εἴτε θρόνοι εἴτε κυριότητες, εἴτε ἀρχαὶ, εἴτε ἐξουσίαι· τὰ πάντα δι᾽ αὐτοῦ, καὶ εἰς αὐτὸν ἔκτισται· καὶ αὐτός ἐστι πρὸ πάντων, καὶ τὰ πάντα ἐν αὐτῷ συνέστηκε. Καὶ αὐτός ἐστιν ἡ κεφαλὴ τοῦ σώματος τῆς ἐκκλησίας.

Τήμερον ἀποδοῦναι ἀναγκαῖον τὸ ὄφλημα, ὅπερ χθὲς ἀνεβαλόμην, ὥστε ἀκμαζούσαις ὑμῶν προσβαλεῖν ταῖς διανοίαις. Περὶ τῆς τοῦ υἱοῦ ἀξίας διαλεγόμενος ὁ Παῦλος ταῦτά φησιν, ὥσπερ καὶ ἀπεδείξαμεν· "Ὅς ἐστιν εἰκὼν τοῦ θεοῦ τοῦ ἀοράτου." Τίνος οὖν βούλει εἰκόνα εἶναι; τοῦ θεοῦ; Οὐκοῦν ἀπαράλλακτος οὗπερ ἂν θῇς. Εἰ μὲν γὰρ ὡς ἀνθρώπου εἰκών, εἰπὲ, καὶ λοιπὸν ὡς μαινομένου ἀποστήσομαι· εἰ δὲ ὡς θεὸς καὶ θεοῦ υἱός, θεοῦ εἰκὼν, τὸ ἀπαράλλακτον δείκνυσι. Διὰ τί μηδαμοῦ μήτε εἰκὼν, μήτε υἱός, ἄγγελος κέκληται, ἀλλ᾽ ἄνθρωπος ἀμφότερα; διὰ τί; Ὅτι ἐκεῖ μὲν τὸ τῆς φύσεως ἀνηγμένον ταχέως ἂν τοὺς πολλοὺς εἰς ταύτην τὴν ἀσέβειαν ἐνέβαλεν· ἐνταῦθα δὲ τὸ εὐτελὲς καὶ ταπεινὸν ἐγγυᾶται τὴν ἀσφάλειαν, καὶ οὐδὲ βουλομένους ἀφίησιν ὑποπτεῦσαί τι τοιοῦτον, καὶ καταγαγεῖν τὸν λόγον κάτω. Διὰ τοῦτο ἔνθα μὲν ἦν πολλὴ ταπεινότης, θαρρούντως ἡ γραφὴ τίθησι τὴν τιμήν· ἔνθα δὲ μείζων ἡ φύσις, οὐκέτι. Ἡ τοῦ ἀοράτου εἰκὼν, καὶ αὐτὴ ἀόρατος, καὶ ὁμοίως ἀόρατος, ἐπεὶ οὐδ᾽ ἂν [201] εἰκὼν εἴη. Τὴν γὰρ εἰκόνα, καθὸ ἐστιν εἰκὼν, καὶ παρ᾽ ἡμῖν ἀπαράλλακτον δεῖ εἶναι, οἷον τῶν χαρακτήρων καὶ τῆς ὁμοιώσεως. Ἀλλ᾽ ἐνταῦθα μὲν οὐδαμῶς τοῦτο δυνατόν· τέχνη γάρ ἐστιν ἀνθρωπίνη ἡ πολλαχοῦ διαπίπτουσα, μᾶλλον δὲ πανταχοῦ, ἐὰν μετὰ ἀκριβείας ζητῇς· ἔνθα δὲ ὁ Θεὸς, οὐδαμοῦ σφάλλεται, οὐδὲ διάπτωσίς τις γίνεται.

He is the image of the invisible God, the firstborn of all creation,
because in him all things were created, those in heaven and those on
earth, the visible and the invisible, whether thrones, or dominions, or
principalities, or powers, all things were created through him and for
him. And he is before all things, and in him all things hold together.
And he is the head of the body of the church [Col 1:15–18].

Today it's necessary to repay the debt that I put off yesterday,[32] in order to address your minds when they're eager. When speaking about the dignity of the Son, Paul said the following, as we have indeed shown: *"He is the image of the invisible God."* Whose image, then, do you want this to be? God's?[33] So, not unchanged from what you would posit. But if he's like an image of a human being, say so, and in future I'll stay away from you as from a mad person; but if he *is* like God and a Son of God, an image of God, it demonstrates lack of change. What's the reason that nowhere has an angel been called either image or Son, but the human being has been called both? What's the reason? Because in the former case the exaltedness of the nature would quickly have thrown many people into this impiety,[34] while in the latter case the paltriness and lowliness are a pledge of security against this, and won't allow even those who want to, to suspect anything of this kind and to bring down the Word. On this account, where the lowliness was great, Scripture boldly expresses the honor, but where the nature is higher, it doesn't. The image of the invisible, even while itself invisible, and similarly invisible, wouldn't [201] be an image. You see, the image, insofar as it's an image, should be unchangeable even among us, like the characteristics of the resemblance. But here indeed among us this is in no way possible, for human art fails utterly in many respects, or rather in all, if you're seeking carefully. But where God is, nowhere does it go wrong, nor does any error occur.

---

32. See the previous homily and the note there on the duration of homilies.

33. After this Field has a different text from that of Savile and several manuscripts.

34. It seems that Chrysostom has Arianism in his sights here, but possibly angel worship is included too.

Εἰ δὲ κτίσμα, πῶς εἰκὼν τοῦ κτίσαντος; οὐδὲ γὰρ ἵππος ἀνθρώπου εἰκών. Εἰ μὴ τὸ ἀπαράλλακτον τοῦ ἀοράτου δηλοῖ ἡ εἰκών, τί κωλύει καὶ ἀγγέλους εἰκόνα εἶναι; καὶ γὰρ καὶ αὐτοὶ ἀόρατοι, ἀλλ᾽ οὐχ ἑαυτοῖς. Ἀλλὰ ψυχὴ ἀόρατος· ἀλλ᾽ ἐπειδὴ ἀόρατος, ἁπλῶς διὰ τοῦτο εἰκών, καὶ μὴ οὕτως, ὥσπερ αὐτός καὶ ἄγγελοι εἰκόνες; "Πρωτότοκος πάσης κτίσεως." Τί οὖν, φησίν; ἰδοὺ ἔκτισται. Πόθεν, εἰπέ μοι; Ἐπειδὴ, "πρωτότοκος," εἶπε. Καὶ μὴν οὐ, πρωτόκτιστος, εἶπεν, ἀλλὰ, "πρωτότοκος." Ἔπειτα πολλὰ εἰκὸς αὐτὸν λέγεσθαι· καὶ γὰρ ἀδελφὸν αὐτὸν δεῖ λέγειν κατὰ πάντα, καὶ τὴν δημιουργίαν ἀφαιρεῖν, καὶ μήτε ἀξιώματι, μήτε ἄλλῳ τινι προέχειν. Τὸ γὰρ, πρωτότοκος, οὐχὶ ἀξίας ἢ τιμῆς, οὐδὲ ἄλλου οὐδενὸς, ἀλλὰ χρόνου μόνον. Τί σημαίνει ὁ πρωτότοκος; Τὸ ἔκτισται, φησί. Καλῶς. Ἐὰν οὖν τοῦτο ᾖ, καὶ ἀδελφὰ ἔχει. Ἄλλως δὲ ὁ πρωτότοκος ὁμοούσιός ἐστιν ὧν ἐστι πρωτότοκος. Οὐκοῦν πάντων ἔσται ὁ υἱὸς πρωτότοκος· πάσης γὰρ εἶπε κτίσεως· οὐκοῦν καὶ [202] λίθων, καὶ ἐμοῦ πρωτότοκός ἐστιν ὁ θεὸς λόγος. Ἄλλως δὲ, εἰπέ μοι, "Πρωτότοκος ἐκ τῶν νεκρῶν," τί δηλοῖ; Οὐχ ὅτι πρῶτος ἀνέστη· οὐ γὰρ εἶπε, νεκρῶν, ἀλλὰ πρωτότοκος ἐκ τῶν νεκρῶν· καὶ οὐκ εἶπεν ὅτι ἀπέθανε πρῶτος, ἀλλ᾽ ὅτι πρωτότοκος ἐκ τῶν νεκρῶν ἀνέστη. Ὥστε οὐδὲν ἕτερον δηλοῖ, ἢ τοῦτο, ὅτι τῆς ἀναστάσεως ἀπαρχὴ γέγονεν. Οὐκοῦν οὐδὲ ἐνταῦθα.

Εἶτα λοιπὸν ἐμβαίνει εἰς τὸ δόγμα αὐτό. Ἵνα γὰρ μὴ νομίσωσι νεώτερον αὐτὸν εἶναι, διὰ τὸ πάλαι μὲν δι᾽ ἀγγέλων προσάγεσθαι, νῦν δὲ δι᾽ αὐτοῦ, δείκνυσι πρῶτον, ὅτι οὐδὲν ἴσχυσαν ἐκεῖνοι· οὐ γὰρ ἂν ἀπὸ σκότους οὗτος ἤγαγε· δεύτερον, ὅτι καὶ πρὸ αὐτῶν ἐστι. Καὶ σημεῖον ποιεῖται τοῦ πρὸ αὐτῶν εἶναι, τὸ δι᾽ αὐτοῦ αὐτοὺς ἐκτίσθαι· ""Ὅτι ἐν αὐτῷ, φησίν, ἐκτίσθη τὰ πάντα."

But if it's a creature, how is it an image of the Creator? For neither is a horse an image of a human being. But if the image discloses the unchangeability of the invisible, what prevents angels too from being his image? I mean, they too are invisible, but not to one another. No, the soul is invisible, but because it's invisible, is it simply on that account an image, even if it isn't in the way that it and the angels are images?

The firstborn of all creation. "What then?" says [someone]. "Look, he's created. How can it be, tell me?" "Because he said *"firstborn."* However, he didn't say "first-created" but *"firstborn."* Then it's very fitting that he be called this. You see, we should call him brother in all respects, and remove the act of creation[35] from him, and have him eminent neither in rank nor in anything else.[36] For the word *firstborn* has nothing of merit or honor or anything else, except of time only. What does *firstborn* signify? "That he is created," someone says. Very well. If therefore this is so, he also has brotherly affinities. Otherwise the *firstborn* is consubstantial with those with whom he is the *firstborn.* Accordingly the Son will be the *firstborn* of all. For Paul said *"of all creation."*[37] Accordingly, [202] God the Word is the *firstborn* of stones and of me. In other words, tell me, what does *"firstborn from the dead"* [Col 1:18] disclose? Not that he was the first to rise up? For Paul didn't say "of the dead" but *"firstborn from the dead."* And he didn't say that he was the first to die, but that he rose as *"firstborn from the dead."* So they disclose nothing else than this, that he was the firstfruits of the resurrection. Surely not even in the present passage.

Then next he proceeds to the doctrine itself. You see, lest they think that Christ is more recent, because of the fact that in former times the approach was made through angels but now through him, Paul demonstrates first that the angels had no power, for he wouldn't have brought them *out of darkness* [Col 1:13]. Second, he demonstrates that Christ is also anterior to them. And he gives a sign that Christ was anterior to them, that they were created through him. *"Because in him,"* Paul says, *"all things*

---

35. Greek δημιουργίαν.

36. Wiles points out that as early as Origen, and indeed in the pre-Nicene period generally, *firstborn* was shorthand for expressing Christ's preexistent and eternal nature (*Divine Apostle*, 78).

37. At this point in Paul's exegesis, Severian of Gabala states that, because all things were created in Christ, we should reject belief in angels and have hope in Christ (see Staab, *Pauluskommentare aus der griechischen Kirche*, 319).

Τί λέγουσιν ἐνταῦθα οἱ Παύλου τοῦ Σαμοσατέως; "Τὰ ἐν τοῖς οὐρανοῖς·" ὅπερ ἀμφισβητούμενον ἦν, πρῶτον τέθεικε· "καὶ τὰ ἐπὶ τῆς γῆς." Εἶτά φησι, "τὰ ὁρατὰ καὶ τὰ ἀόρατα· ἀόρατα, οἷον ψυχὴ, καὶ ὅσα ἐν οὐρανῷ γέγονεν· ὁρατά, οἷον ἄνθρωποι, ἥλιος, πόλος. "Εἴτε θρόνοι." Καὶ τὸ μὲν ὁμολογούμενον ἀφίησι, τὸ δὲ ἀμφιβαλλόμενον τίθησιν. "Εἴτε θρόνοι, εἴτε κυριότητες, εἴτε ἀρχαὶ, εἴτε ἐξουσίαι." Τὸ, εἴτε καὶ εἴτε, τοῦ παντὸς περιληπτικόν ἐστιν· ἀλλὰ ἀπὸ τῶν μειζόνων καὶ τὰ ἐλάττω δεικνύντος ἐστί. Τὸ δὲ πνεῦμα οὐ μετὰ τῶν ἐξουσιῶν. "Τὰ πάντα, φησὶ, δι' αὐτοῦ, καὶ εἰς αὐτὸν ἔκτισται." Ἰδοὺ τὸ, "ἐν αὐτῷ," δι' αὐτοῦ ἐστιν. Εἰπὼν γὰρ, ὅτι "ἐν αὐτῷ," [203] ἐπήγαγε, "δι' αὐτοῦ." Τὸ δὲ, "εἰς αὐτὸν," τί ἐστι; Τουτέστιν, εἰς αὐτὸν κρέμαται ἡ πάντων ὑπόστασις. Οὐ μόνον αὐτὸς αὐτὰ ἐκ τοῦ μὴ ὄντος εἰς τὸ εἶναι παρήγαγεν, ἀλλὰ καὶ αὐτὸς αὐτὰ συγκρατεῖ νῦν· ὥστε ἂν ἀποσπασθῇ τῆς αὐτοῦ προνοίας, ἀπόλωλε καὶ διέφθαρται. Ἀλλ' οὐκ εἶπε, διακρατεῖ, ὅπερ ἦν παχύτερον, ἀλλὰ τὸ λεπτότερον, ὅτι εἰς αὐτὸν κρέμαται. Μόνον γὰρ τὸ πρὸς αὐτὸν νεύειν, ἱκανὸν διακρατῆσαι καὶ συσφίγξαι. Οὕτω καὶ τὸ, πρωτότοκος, ὡς θεμέλιος. Τοῦτο δὲ οὐ τὸ ὁμοούσιον τῶν κτισμάτων, ἀλλὰ τὸ δι' αὐτοῦ πάντα εἶναι, καὶ ἐν αὐτῷ φέρεσθαι δηλοῖ. Ἐπεὶ καὶ Παῦλος ὅταν λέγῃ, "Θεμέλιον τέθεικα," οὐ περὶ τῆς οὐσίας φησίν, ἀλλὰ τῆς ἐνεργείας. Ἵνα γὰρ μὴ νομίσῃς ὑπηρέτην εἶναι αὐτὸν, φησιν, αὐτὸν αὐτὰ διακρατεῖν, ὅπερ οὐχ ἧττον τοῦ ποιῆσαί ἐστι. Καίτοι ἐφ' ἡμῶν καὶ μεῖζον· ἐκεῖνο μὲν γὰρ ἡ τέχνη εἰσάγει, τοῦτο δὲ οὐκέτι, οὐδὲ φθειρόμενον κατέχει.

"Καὶ αὐτός ἐστι πρὸ πάντων," φησί. Τοῦτο θεῷ ἁρμόζον. Ποῦ Παῦλος ὁ Σαμοσατεύς; "Καὶ τὰ πάντα ἐν αὐτῷ συνέστηκε." τουτέστιν, εἰς αὐτὸν ἔκτισται. Συνεχῶς αὐτὰ στρέφει, τῇ συνεχείᾳ τῶν ῥημάτων καθάπερ πυκναῖς τισι πληγαῖς πρόρριζον ἀνασπῶν τὸ δόγμα τὸ ὀλέθριον. Εἰ γὰρ καὶ τοσαῦτα εἴρηται, καὶ μετὰ τοσοῦτον χρόνον ἀνέφυ Παῦλος ὁ Σαμοσατεὺς, πόσῳ μᾶλλον,

were created." What do the followers of Paul of Samosata[38] say at this point? "*Things in heaven,*" which was disputed, first he asserted "*and things on earth.*" Then he says, "*The visible and the invisible*": "*invisible,*" like the soul and whatever has happened in heaven. "*Visible,*" like human beings, the sun, the firmament. *Whether thrones.* And what is agreed on he lets alone, but what is disputed he asserts. *Whether thrones, or dominions, or principalities, or authorities.* The words *whether ... whether* embrace everything, but by means of greater things it demonstrates the lesser. However, the Spirit is not among the *authorities.* "*Everything,*" Paul says, "was *created through him and for him.*" Look at the expression *in him,* through whom everything is. You see, while saying "*in him*" [**203**] he added "*through him.*" What does the expression *in him* mean? That is, the substance of all things hangs on him. Not only did he himself bring them out of nonexistence into existence, but he himself holds them together now, such that if they were separated from his providence, they would be ruined and destroyed. But he didn't say "he continues to hold them together," which was a rougher statement, but the more subtle one, namely, that they hang on him. Only to bend the head to him is enough to hold fast and to bind close. So also *firstborn* is like a *foundation* [1 Cor 3:10], but this doesn't disclose a consubstantiality with created things, but that all things are *through him* and *in him* are borne along. Since when Paul too says, "*I have laid a foundation*" [1 Cor 3:10], he isn't speaking about essence but activity. You see, so that you don't think him to be an underling, he says that he continues these things, which is not less than making them. Indeed, in our case it's even greater, for with regard to the former, art leads us, but not with regard to the latter, nor does it remain in decay.[39]

"*And he is before all things,*" Paul says. This is fitting for God. Where is Paul of Samosata? *And him all things hold together,* which means that they are created into him. Paul deploys these expressions continuously, by means of a continuity of words, as if by his thick and fast blows pulling up by the roots the pernicious doctrine. For if even when such great pronouncements had been made, and after such a long time, Paul of Samosata sprang up, how much more would it have been the case if these pronounce-

---

38. Much reviled in the history of Christology, Paul of Samosata, bishop of Antioch between 260 and 270, supposedly advocated a monarchian or adoptionist Christology, whereby the union between Jesus and the Logos was a moral one.

39. The meaning of this passage is obscure.

εἰ μὴ ταῦτα προείρητο; "Καὶ τὰ πάντα, φησὶν, ἐν αὐτῷ συνέστηκε." Πῶς συνέστηκεν ἐν τῷ οὐκ ὄντι; Ὥστε καὶ τὰ δι᾽ ἀγγέλων αὐτοῦ ἐστι. "Καὶ αὐτός ἐστιν ἡ κεφαλὴ τοῦ σώματος τῆς ἐκκλησίας." Εἶτα εἰπὼν περὶ τῆς ἀξίας, λέγει λοιπὸν καὶ περὶ τῆς φιλανθρωπίας. "Αὐτός ἐστι, φησὶν, ἡ κεφαλὴ τοῦ σώματος τῆς ἐκκλησίας." Καὶ οὐκ εἶπε, τοῦ πληρώματος, αὐτὸ μὲν δηλῶν, θέλων δὲ ἡμῖν οἰκειότερον δεῖξαι αὐτὸν, ὅτι ὁ οὕτως ἄνω καὶ πάντων ἀνώτερος, τοῖς κάτω ἑαυτὸν συνῆψε. Πανταχοῦ γὰρ πρῶτος· ἄνω πρῶτος, ἐν τῇ ἐκκλησίᾳ πρῶτος· κεφαλὴ γάρ ἐστιν· ἐν τῇ ἀναστάσει πρῶτος.

[204] Τουτέστιν, "Ἵνα γένηται αὐτὸς πρωτεύων." Ὥστε καὶ ἐν γενέσει πρῶτος. Καὶ τοῦτό ἐστι μάλιστα τὸ σπουδαζόμενον δεῖξαι τῷ Παύλῳ. Ἂν γὰρ τοῦτο κατασκευασθῇ, ὅτι πρὸ πάντων ἦν τῶν ἀγγέλων, κἀκεῖνο συνεισάγεται, ὅτι τὰ ἐκείνων αὐτὸς ἐποίει ἐπιτάττων. Καὶ τὸ δὴ θαυμαστὸν, ἐν τῇ ὑστέρᾳ γενέσει ἐφιλονείκησε πρῶτον αὐτὸν δεῖξαι. Καίτοιγε ἀλλαχοῦ πρῶτόν φησι τὸν Ἀδὰμ, ὥσπερ οὖν καὶ ἔστιν· ἀλλὰ τὴν ἐκκλησίαν ἔλαβεν ἀντὶ τοῦ παντὸς ἀνθρώπων γένους. Τῆς γὰρ ἐκκλησίας πρῶτός ἐστι, καὶ τῶν μὲν ἀνθρώπων, καθάπερ τῆς κτίσεως, πρῶτος κατὰ σάρκα· καὶ διὰ τοῦτο ἐνταῦθα τὸν πρωτότοκον τίθησι.

Τί ἐστιν ἐνταῦθα ὁ πρωτότοκος; Ὁ πρῶτος κτισθεὶς, ἢ ὁ πρὸ πάντων ἀναστὰς, ὥσπερ καὶ ἐκεῖ, ὁ πρὸ πάντων ὤν. Καὶ ἐνταῦθα μὲν ἀπαρχὴν τέθεικεν εἰπών· "Ὅς ἐστιν ἀπαρχή, πρωτότοκος ἐκ τῶν νεκρῶν, ἵνα γένηται ἐν πᾶσιν αὐτὸς πρωτεύων·" δεικνὺς ὅτι καὶ οἱ ἄλλοι τοιοῦτοι· ἐκεῖ δὲ οὐκ ἀπαρχὴ τῆς κτίσεως. Καὶ ἐκεῖ μὲν, "εἰκὼν τοῦ Θεοῦ τοῦ ἀοράτου," καὶ τότε τὸ, πρωτότοκος.

"Ὅτι ἐν αὐτῷ ηὐδόκησε πᾶν τὸ πλήρωμα κατοικῆσαι, καὶ δι᾽ αὐτοῦ ἀποκαταλλάξαι τὰ πάντα εἰς αὐτόν, εἰρηνοποιήσας διὰ τοῦ αἵματος τοῦ σταυροῦ αὐτοῦ, εἴτε τὰ ἐπὶ τῆς γῆς, εἴτε τὰ ἐν τοῖς οὐρανοῖς." Ὅσα τοῦ πατρός, φησὶ, ταῦτα καὶ τοῦ υἱοῦ, καὶ μετὰ πλείονος σπουδῆς, ὅτι καὶ νεκρὸς γέγονε, καὶ ἥνωσεν ἑαυτὸν ἡμῖν. Ἀπαρχὴν δὲ εἶπε, καθάπερ ἐπὶ καρποῦ τινος. Οὐκ εἶπεν, ἀνάστασις, ἀλλὰ, "ἀπαρχὴ," δεικνὺς ὅτι πάντας ἡμᾶς ἡγίασε, καὶ ὥσπερ θυσίαν προσήνεγκε. Τὸ πλήρωμα οἱ μὲν τῆς θεότητός φασι, καθάπερ ὁ Ἰωάννης ἔλεγεν· "Ἐκ τοῦ πληρώματος αὐτοῦ ἡμεῖς πάντες ἐλάβομεν." Τουτ-[205]έστιν, εἴ τι ἦν ὁ υἱός, ὅλος ὁ υἱὸς ἐκεῖ ᾤκησεν, οὐχὶ ἐνέργειά τις, ἀλλ᾽ οὐσία.

ments had not been made beforehand? "*And in him,*" he says, "*all things hold together.*" How did they *hold together* in one who didn't exist? So that what was done also by angels belongs to him.

And he is the head of the body of the church. Then, having spoken of his dignity, Paul speaks next too about his loving-kindness. "*He is,*" he says, "*the head of the body of the church.*" And he didn't say "*the fullness*" [Col 1:19; 1 Cor 10:26], although he discloses this, but wishing to show that he is quite familiar with us, because the one who was thus above and above all connected himself with those below. For he is first everywhere: first above; in the church first, for he is the head; in the resurrection, first.

[204] For this is the meaning of *so that he might hold the first place* [Col 1:18], such that in that generation too he is first. And this is what Paul is chiefly striving to demonstrate. You see, if this has been established, namely, that Christ was before all the angels, this is introduced as a consequence, namely, that he did their works by commanding them. And what is really wonderful: he takes trouble to show that he is the first in the later generation [see 1 Cor 15:45]. And yet elsewhere he says that Adam is the first [see 1 Cor 15:45], as indeed he is, but Paul has taken the church as the entire human race. You see, Christ is the first of the church and of human beings, just as of creation, the first according to the flesh. And this is why Paul uses the word *firstborn* in this passage.

What is the meaning of *firstborn* in this passage? The one who was created first, or rose before everybody, as in the former passage, he was before everybody. And in this passage Paul uses the word *firstfruits* when he says, "*He is the firstfruits, the firstborn from the dead, so that in everything he might hold the first place,*" showing that the rest too are such as Christ, but in the former passage he is not the firstfruits of creation. And it is there *an image of the invisible God,* and then the word *firstborn.*

Because in him was all the fullness of the Father pleased to dwell, and through him to reconcile everything to himself, making peace through the blood of his cross, whether things on earth or things in heaven [Col 1:19–20]. "Whatever belongs to the Father," he says, "also belongs to the Son [see John 5:17–24], and with more poignancy because he both became a dead man and united himself to us." He said "*firstfruits,*" as if of some fruit. He didn't say "resurrection" but "*firstfruits,*" showing that he has hallowed us all and, as it were, offered a sacrifice. The expression *fullness* some say of the Godhead, just as John said, "*Of his fullness we have all received*" [John 1:16]. [205] So what does this mean? If the Son existed, the Son dwelled there completely, not some activity, but an essence.

Οὐκ ἔχει αἰτίαν εἰπεῖν οὐδεμίαν, ἀλλὰ τὴν θέλησιν τοῦ θεοῦ· τοῦτο γάρ ἐστιν, "ὅτι ἐν αὐτῷ ηὐδόκησε." "Καὶ δι' αὐτοῦ ἀποκαταλλάξαι τὰ πάντα εἰς αὐτόν." Ἵνα μὴ νομίσῃς, ὅτι ὑπηρέτου τάξιν ἀνέλαβεν, "εἰς ἑαυτὸν," φησί. Καὶ μὴν ἀλλαχοῦ φησιν, ὅτι τῷ Θεῷ καταλλάττει, καθάπερ ἐν τῇ πρὸς Κορινθίους ἐπιστολῇ γράφων ἔλεγε. Καὶ καλῶς εἶπε, "δι' αὐτοῦ ἀποκαταλλάξαι." Ἤδη γὰρ ἦσαν κατηλλαγμένοι, ἀλλὰ τελείως, ὥστε μηκέτι ἐχθραίνειν αὐτῷ, φησί. Πῶς; Οὐ γὰρ ἡ καταλλαγὴ ἀπεδίδοτο μόνον, ἀλλὰ καὶ ὁ τρόπος τῆς καταλλαγῆς. "Εἰρηνοποιήσας διὰ τοῦ αἵματος τοῦ σταυροῦ αὐτοῦ." Τὸ μὲν τὴν ἔχθραν δείκνυσι τὸ καταλλάξαι· τὸ δὲ τὸν πόλεμον. "Διὰ τοῦ αἵματος, φησί, τοῦ σταυροῦ αὐτοῦ δι' αὐτοῦ, εἴτε τὰ ἐπὶ τῆς γῆς, εἴτε τὰ ἐπὶ τοῖς οὐρανοῖς." Μέγα μὲν τὸ καταλλάξαι, τὸ δὲ καὶ δι' αὐτοῦ, μεῖζον· καὶ τὸ τούτου μεῖζον, τὸ δι' ἑαυτοῦ πῶς; διὰ τοῦ αἵματος· καὶ οὐχ ἁπλῶς αἵματος, ἀλλὰ τὸ τούτου μεῖζον, διὰ τοῦ σταυροῦ. Ὥστε πέντε ἐστὶ τὰ θαυμαστά, τῷ θεῷ κατήλλαξε, δι' αὐτοῦ, διὰ θανάτου, διὰ σταυροῦ. Βαβαὶ, πῶς ἀνέμιξε πάλιν; Ἵνα γὰρ μὴ νομίσῃς ἓν εἶναι, μηδὲ τὸν σταυρὸν εἶναί τι καθ' ἑαυτό, λέγει, "δι' ἑαυτοῦ." Πῶς οἶδε μέγα τοῦτο ὄν; Ὅτι οὐ ῥήματα εἰπών, ἀλλ' ἑαυτὸν ἐκδοὺς ὑπὲρ τῆς καταλλαγῆς, οὕτως ἅπαντα εἰργάσατο. Τί δέ ἐστι, "τὰ ἐν τοῖς οὐρανοῖς;" Τὰ μὲν γὰρ ἐπὶ τῆς γῆς, εἰκότως· ἔχθρας γὰρ ἐμπέπληστο, καὶ εἰς πολλὰ διῄρητο· καὶ πρὸς ἑαυτὸν ἕκαστος ἡμῶν διεστασίαζε, καὶ πρὸς τοὺς πολλούς· τὰ δὲ ἐν τοῖς οὐρανοῖς πῶς εἰρηνοποίησε; καὶ ἐκεῖ πόλεμος ἦν καὶ μάχη; καὶ πῶς εὐχόμεθα λέγοντες, "Γενηθήτω τὸ θέλημά σου, ὡς ἐν οὐρανῷ, καὶ ἐπὶ τῆς γῆς;" Τί [206] οὖν ἔστιν; Ἀπέσχιστο ἡ γῆ τοῦ οὐρανοῦ, ἐκπεπολεμωμένοι ἦσαν οἱ ἄγγελοι πρὸς τοὺς ἀνθρώπους, τὸν δεσπότην ὁρῶντες τὸν αὐτῶν ὑβριζόμενον. "Ἀνακεφαλαιώσασθαί, φησι, τὰ πάντα ἐν τῷ Χριστῷ, τὰ ἐν τοῖς οὐρανοῖς, καὶ τὰ ἐπὶ τῆς γῆς." Πῶς; Τὰ μὲν ἐν τοῖς οὐρανοῖς οὕτω· μετέστησεν ἐκεῖ τὸν ἄνθρωπον, ἀνήγαγεν αὐτοῖς τὸν ἐχθρόν, τὸν μισούμενον. Οὐ μένοντα ἐπὶ τῆς γῆς ἐποίησεν εἰρηνεύειν, ἀλλ' ἀνήγαγεν αὐτὸν πρὸς αὐτούς, τὸν ἐχθρὸν καὶ πολέμιον. Τοῦτο εἰρήνη βαθεῖα. Ἄγγελοι πάλιν ἐπὶ γῆς ἐφαίνοντο λοιπόν, ἐπειδὴ καὶ ἄνθρωπος ἐν οὐρανῷ ἐφάνη. Δοκεῖ δέ μοι

Paul doesn't have any reason to say this, except the will of God, for this is the meaning of *because it pleased him*. *And through him to reconcile all things to himself*. Lest you think that he took on the rank of a servant, he says "*to himself*." Indeed, he says elsewhere that he reconciles us to God, just as he said when he wrote in the letter to the Corinthians. And he did well to say, "*to be reconciled through him*" [2 Cor 5:18]. You see, they were already reconciled, but he means completely [reconciled], so that they're no longer at enmity with him. How? You see, not only was the reconciliation rendered, but also the manner of the reconciliation. *Having made peace through the blood of his cross*. The expression *reconciled* demonstrates the enmity; the [rest], the war. "*Through the blood of his cross*," he says, "*by himself, whether things on earth or in heaven*." While it's a great thing to reconcile, that this is in fact through himself is greater. And how is this greater, what comes through himself? Through his blood, and not simply his blood but what is greater than this through the cross. The result is that the marvels are five: he reconciled us to God, through him, through death, through the cross.[40] Heavens, how has he combined them? For lest you should think that it's one thing and that the cross is a thing by itself, he says "*through himself*." How did he know that this was a great thing? Because not by speaking words, but by giving himself up on behalf of the resurrection, he thus effected everything.

What's the meaning of *things in heaven*? You see, *things on earth* is reasonable, for those filled with enmity and torn apart in many directions, and each one of us formed into different factions against themselves, and with many people. But how did he make peace *in heaven*? Was war, and battle, there too? And how do we pray when we say, "*Your will be done on earth as it is in heaven*" [Matt 6:10]? What's [**206**] this, then? Earth was divided from heaven, the angels were at war with human beings, seeing their master insulted. "*To unite all things in Christ*," Paul says, "*those in heaven and those on earth*" [Eph 1:10]. How? The things in heaven are like this: he has transferred the human being there, he brought up to them the enemy, the hated one. He didn't cause the things remaining on earth to be at peace, but he brought to them the one who was their enemy and foe. This is a profound peace. Angels again appeared on earth afterward, because indeed a human being had appeared in heaven.[41] It seems to me that Paul

---

40. The marvels as recounted here are only four.
41. A further denunciation of the place of angels in Christian worship.

ἡ ἁρπαγὴ τοῦ Παύλου τούτου τε ἕνεκεν γεγενῆσθαι, καὶ τοῦ δεῖξαι ὅτι καὶ ὁ υἱὸς ἐκεῖ ἀνελήφθη. Ἐν μὲν γὰρ τῇ γῇ διπλῆ ἡ εἰρήνη, καὶ πρὸς τὰ ἐπουράνια, καὶ πρὸς ἑαυτά· ἐν δὲ τοῖς οὐρανοῖς ἁπλῆ. Εἰ γὰρ ἐπὶ ἑνὶ ἁμαρτωλῷ μετανοοῦντι χαίρουσιν οἱ ἄγγελοι, πολλῷ μᾶλλον ἐπὶ τοσούτοις. Ταῦτα πάντα ἡ τοῦ θεοῦ ἰσχὺς κατώρθωσε. Τί οὖν ἀγγέλοις θαρρεῖτε, φησί; Τοσοῦτον γὰρ ἀπέχουσιν ἐκεῖνοι προσάγειν ὑμᾶς, ὅτι καὶ ἐκπεπολεμωμένοι ἦσαν, εἰ μὴ ὁ θεὸς αὐτὸς ὑμᾶς ἐκείνοις κατήλλαξεν.

Τί τοίνυν ἐκείνοις προστρέχετε; Βούλει μαθεῖν τῶν ἀγγέλων τὸ μῖσος ὅσον εἶχον πρὸς ἡμᾶς, καὶ πῶς ἀπεστρέφοντο ἀεί; Εἰς τιμωρίαν ἐπέμποντο ἐπὶ τῶν Ἰσραηλιτῶν, ἐπὶ τοῦ Δαυΐδ, ἐπὶ τῶν Σοδομιτῶν, ἐπὶ τῆς κοιλάδος τοῦ κλαυθμῶνος. Ἀλλ᾽ οὐ νῦν· ἀλλ᾽ ἐξ ἐναντίας, ἐπὶ γῆς ᾖδον σφόδρα χαίροντες· καὶ τούτους κατήγαγε πρὸς αὐτούς, καὶ τοὺς ἀνθρώπους ἀνήγαγεν ἐκεῖ. Καὶ θέα μοι τὸ παράδοξον. Τούτους πρώτους κατήγαγεν ὧδε, καὶ τότε τὸν ἄνθρωπον ἀνήγαγε πρὸς αὐτούς· οὐρανὸς ἡ γῆ γέγονεν, ἐπειδὴ τὰ τῆς γῆς ἔμελλεν οὐρανὸς δέχεσθαι. Διὰ τοῦτο εὐχαριστοῦντες λέγομεν, "Δόξα ἐν ὑψίστοις θεῷ, καὶ ἐπὶ γῆς εἰρήνη, ἐν ἀνθρώποις εὐδοκία." Ἰδού, φησί, καὶ ἄνθρωποι ἐφάνησαν εὐαρεστοῦντες λοιπόν. Τί ἐστιν, εὐδοκία; Καταλλαγή· οὐκέτι μεσότοιχόν ἐστιν ὁ οὐρανός. Τὸ πρῶτον κατὰ ἀριθμὸν ἐθνῶν ἦσαν οἱ ἄγγελοι· νῦν δὲ οὐ κατὰ [207] ἀριθμὸν ἐθνῶν, ἀλλὰ κατὰ ἀριθμὸν πιστῶν. Πόθεν δῆλον; Ἄκουε τοῦ Χριστοῦ λέγοντος· "Ὁρᾶτε μὴ καταφρονήσητε ἑνὸς τῶν μικρῶν τούτων· οἱ γὰρ ἄγγελοι αὐτῶν διαπαντὸς βλέπουσι τὸ πρόσωπον τοῦ Πατρός μου τοῦ ἐν τοῖς οὐρανοῖς." Ἕκαστος γὰρ πιστὸς ἄγγελον ἔχει, ἐπεὶ καὶ ἐξ ἀρχῆς ἕκαστος ἀνὴρ τῶν εὐδοκίμων ἄγγελον εἶχε· καθώς φησιν ὁ Ἰακώβ, "Ὁ ἄγγελος ὁ τρέφων με, καὶ ὁ ῥυόμενός με ἐκ νεότητός μου."

Εἰ τοίνυν ἀγγέλους ἔχομεν, νήφωμεν, καθάπερ παιδαγωγῶν τινων ἡμῖν παρόντων· πάρεστι γὰρ καὶ δαίμων. Διὰ τοῦτο εὐχόμεθα, καὶ λέγομεν αἰτοῦντες τὸν ἄγγελον τῆς εἰρήνης, καὶ πανταχοῦ εἰρήνην αἰτοῦμεν. Οὐδὲν γὰρ ταύτης ἴσον· ἐν ταῖς ἐκκλησίαις εἰρήνην, ἐν ταῖς εὐχαῖς, ἐν ταῖς λιταῖς, ἐν ταῖς προσρήσεσι· καὶ ἅπαξ, καὶ δὶς, καὶ τρὶς, καὶ πολλάκις αὐτὴν δίδωσιν ὁ τῆς ἐκκλησίας προεστώς, εἰρήνη ὑμῖν. Διὰ τί; Ὅτι αὕτη μήτηρ πάντων τῶν

was caught up [see 2 Cor 12:2] on this account and to show that the Son too had been caught up there. You see, on earth the peace was twofold, both toward heavenly things and themselves, but in heaven it was simple. For if the angels rejoice over one sinner who repents [see Luke 15:7, 10], much more will they do so over many. All this God's power has effected. "Then why do you place your confidence in angels?" Paul asks. "For they were so far from bringing you close that they were even at war with you, if God himself hadn't reconciled you with them."

So why do you run to them? Do you want to learn the extent of the hatred that the angels had for us and how averse to us they always were? They were sent to take vengeance in the case of the Israelites, of David, of the people of Sodom, of the valley of weeping.[42] But not now. No, on the contrary, they sang while greatly rejoicing on earth, and Christ led the first ones down to them and led human beings up there. And please see the phenomenon: he brought these first down here, and then he brought up the human being to them; earth became heaven, since heaven was about to receive the things of earth. This is why when we give thanks we say, *"Glory to God in the highest, and peace on earth, goodwill to human beings"* [Luke 2:14 and par.]. "Look," Paul says, "even human beings appeared acceptable to him after that." What is *goodwill*? Reconciliation. No longer is heaven the *dividing wall* [Eph 2:14]. At first the angels existed according to the number of nations, but now they aren't [**207**] according to the number of nations but the number of believers. From what is this clear? Listen to Christ saying, *"See that you don't despise one of these little ones, for their angels continually behold the face of my Father in heaven"* [Matt 18:10]. You see, each believer has an angel, since right from the beginning each man of those of goodwill had an angel, just as Jacob says, *"The angel who nourishes me and saves me from my youth"* [Gen 48:15–16 LXX].

Therefore, if we have angels, let's be sober, as if we're in the presence of some tutors,[43] for a demon is present also. This is why we pray, saying that we beg the angel of peace, and begging for peace everywhere (for nothing is equal to this), peace in the churches, and in prayers, in supplications, in prophecies. And once, and twice, and three times, and often does the one who is first in the church give it—*peace to you* [John 14:27].[44]

---

42. See Gen 19:13; Exod 23:21; 2 Kgdms 24:16.

43. Greek παιδαγωγῶν.

44. On the importance of Chrysostom's evidence for the greeting of peace in the liturgy of his time, see Frans van de Paverd, *Geschichte der Messliturgie in Antio-*

ἀγαθῶν ἐστιν, αὕτη τῆς χαρᾶς ὑπόθεσις. Διὰ τοῦτο καὶ ὁ Χριστὸς εἰσιοῦσιν εἰς τὰς οἰκίας τοῖς ἀποστόλοις τοῦτο λέγειν προσέταξεν εὐθέως, καθάπερ τι σύμβολον τῶν ἀγαθῶν· "Εἰσερχόμενοι γὰρ, φησὶν, εἰς τὰς οἰκίας, λέγετε, εἰρήνη ὑμῖν." Ταύτης γὰρ οὐκ οὔσης, πάντα περιττά. Καὶ ὁ Χριστὸς τοῖς μαθηταῖς ἔλεγεν, "Εἰρήνην ἀφίημι ὑμῖν, εἰρήνην τὴν ἐμὴν δίδωμι ὑμῖν." Αὕτη τῇ ἀγάπῃ προοδοποιεῖ. Καὶ οὐ λέγει ὁ τῆς ἐκκλησίας προεστὼς, εἰρήνη ὑμῖν ἁπλῶς, ἀλλ᾽, εἰρήνη πᾶσι. Τί γὰρ, ἂν μετὰ τοῦδε μὲν εἰρήνην ἔχωμεν, μεθ᾽ ἑτέρου δὲ πόλεμον καὶ μάχην; τί τὸ κέρδος; Οὐδὲ γὰρ ἐν τῷ σώματι, ἂν τὰ μὲν ἡσυχάζῃ τῶν στοιχείων, τὰ δὲ διαστασιάζῃ, δυνατὸν ὑγίειαν συνεστάναι ποτὲ, ἀλλὰ διὰ τῆς ἁπάντων εὐταξίας καὶ συμφωνίας καὶ εἰρήνης· κἂν μὴ πάντα ἡσυχάζῃ, καὶ ἐπὶ τῶν οἰκείων ὅρων μένῃ, πάντα ἀνατραπήσεται. Καὶ ἐν τῇ διανοίᾳ δὲ τῇ ἡμετέρᾳ, ἐὰν μὴ πάντες ἡσυχάζωσιν οἱ λογισμοὶ, εἰρήνη οὐκ ἔσται. Τοσοῦτόν ἐστιν ἀγαθὸν ἡ εἰρήνη, ὡς υἱοὺς θεοῦ καλεῖσθαι τοὺς αὐτῆς ποιητὰς καὶ δημιουργούς· εἰκότως· ἐπεὶ καὶ ὁ υἱὸς τοῦ θεοῦ ἐπὶ τούτῳ ἦλθεν εἰς τὴν γῆν, εἰρηνοποιήσων τὰ ἐν τῇ γῇ, καὶ τὰ ἐν τοῖς οὐρανοῖς. Εἰ δὲ οἱ εἰρηνοποιοὶ υἱοὶ τοῦ θεοῦ, οἱ νεωτεροποιοὶ υἱοὶ διαβόλου.

Τί λέγεις; ἔρεις καὶ [208] μάχας ἐμβάλλεις; Καὶ τίς οὕτως ἄθλιος, φησίν; Εἰσὶ γὰρ πολλοὶ χαίροντες ἐπὶ τοῖς κακοῖς, καὶ τὸ σῶμα τοῦ Χριστοῦ διασπῶντες μᾶλλον, ἢ οἱ στρατιῶται τῇ λόγχῃ διέτεμον, ἢ οἱ Ἰουδαῖοι τοῖς ἥλοις διέκοψαν. Ἐκεῖνο τούτου ἔλαττον τὸ κακόν· ἐκεῖνα διατμηθέντα τὰ μέλη πάλιν συνήφθη· ταῦτα δὲ ἀποσπασθέντα, ἂν ἐνθάδε μὴ συναφθῇ, οὐκέτι συναφθήσεται, ἀλλὰ μένει τοῦ πληρώματος ἔξω. Ὅταν βούλῃ τῷ ἀδελφῷ πολεμῆσαι, ἐννόησον ὅτι τοῖς μέλεσι τοῦ Χριστοῦ πολεμεῖς, καὶ παῦσαι τῆς μανίας. Τί γὰρ, εἰ ἀπερριμμένος ἐστί; τί γὰρ, εἰ εὐτελής; τί γὰρ, εἰ εὐκαταφρόνητος; "Οὕτως οὐκ ἔστι θέλημα, φησὶν, ἔμπροσθεν τοῦ πατρός μου, ἵνα ἀπόληται εἷς τῶν μικρῶν τούτων." καὶ πάλιν· "Οἱ ἄγγελοι αὐτῶν διαπαντὸς βλέπουσι τὸ πρόσωπον τοῦ πατρός μου τοῦ ἐν τοῖς οὐρανοῖς." Ὁ θεὸς δι᾽ αὐτὸν καὶ σὲ καὶ δοῦλος ἐγένετο, καὶ ἐσφάγη· σὺ δὲ οὐδὲν αὐτὸν εἶναι νομίζεις; Οὐκοῦν μάχη

Why? Because peace is the mother of all good things; it's the reason for joy. This is why Christ commanded his apostles when they entered houses to say this immediately: "For as you enter houses," he says, "say 'peace be to you'" [see Matt 10:12–13],[45] like a kind of symbol of good things, for if peace isn't present, everything is redundant. And Christ said to his disciples, "*Peace I leave with you, my peace I give to you*" [John 14:27]. Peace prepares the way for love. And the one who is first in the church doesn't simply say "peace to you" but "peace to all." For what if we have peace with this person but with another we have war and fighting? What's the gain? You see, neither in the body, if some elements are at rest but others are at variance, is it possible for health ever to be sustained, except that when all of them are in good order and harmony and peace, and if all of them aren't at rest and remain in their proper limits, they will all be overturned. Indeed, in our minds, if all our thoughts aren't at rest, there won't be peace. Peace is such a great good that those who make it and work at it are called sons of God [see Matt 5:9; John 11:52], and rightly so, since the Son of God came on earth for this reason, making peace with things on earth and things in heaven. But if those who make peace are sons of God, those who make innovation are sons of the devil.

What do you say? Do you stir up strife [**208**] and polemics? "And who is as wretched as that?" someone asks. You see, there are many who rejoice in evil, and rather tear apart the body of Christ, whether they are soldiers who pierce it through with a lance [see John 19:34] or the Jews who stuck it through with nails [see Matt 27:35 and par].[46] That was a lesser evil than this: those members when cut off were reunited, but when these were torn off, if they aren't brought together there, will never be united again but remain outside the fullness. When you wish to war against your brother, consider that you're warring against the members of Christ and stop your madness. For what if he's an outcast, what if he's low in status? What if he's to be despised? "So," says Christ: "*It is not the will of my father that one of these little ones should perish*" [Matt 18:14], and again: "*Their angels always look at the face of my father in heaven*" [Matt 18:10]. God for his sake even became a servant and was killed, but do you consider him to be nothing?

---

cheia und Konstantinopel gegen Ende des vierten Jahrhunderts: Analyse der Quellen bei Johannes Chrysostomos, OrChrAn 187 (Rome: Pontificium Institutum Orientalium Studiorum, 1970), 82–93.

45. This is an inaccurate conflation of two verses in the Matthean text.
46. The tenses of the verbs here are inconsistent.

καὶ κατὰ τοῦτο τῷ θεῷ, τὰς ἐναντίας αὐτῷ φέρων ψήφους. Ὅταν εἰσέλθῃ ὁ τῆς ἐκκλησίας προεστὼς, εὐθέως λέγει, εἰρήνη πᾶσιν· ὅταν ὁμιλῇ, εἰρήνη πᾶσιν· ὅταν εὐλογῇ, εἰρήνη πᾶσιν· ὅταν ἀσπάζεσθαι κελεύῃ, εἰρήνη πᾶσιν· ὅταν ἡ θυσία τελεσθῇ, εἰρήνη πᾶσι· καὶ μεταξὺ πάλιν, χάρις ὑμῖν καὶ εἰρήνη. Πῶς οὖν οὐκ ἄτοπον, εἰ τοσαυτάκις ἀκούοντες εἰρήνην ἔχειν, ἐκπεπολεμώμεθα πρὸς ἀλλήλους; καὶ λαμβάνοντες καὶ ἀντιδιδόντες, τῷ διδόντι τὴν εἰρήνην πολεμοῦμεν; Λέγεις, καὶ τῷ πνεύματί σου, καὶ διαβάλλεις αὐτὸν ἔξω; Οἴμοι, ὅτι τὰ σεμνὰ τῆς ἐκκλησίας, σχήματα γέγονε πραγμάτων μόνον, οὐκ ἀλήθειά τις· οἴμοι, ὅτι μέχρι ῥημάτων τὰ σύμβολα μένει τοῦ στρατοπέδου τούτου. Ὅθεν καὶ ἀγνοεῖτε διὰ τί λέγεται, εἰρήνη πᾶσιν. Ἀλλ᾿ ἀκούετε τῶν ἑξῆς, τί φησιν ὁ Χριστός. "Εἰς ἣν δ᾿ ἂν πόλιν ἢ κώμην εἰσέλθητε, εἰσερχόμενοι εἰς τὴν οἰκίαν, ἀσπάσασθε αὐτήν· καὶ ἐὰν μὲν ᾖ ἡ οἰκία ἀξία, ἐλθέτω ἡ εἰρήνη ὑμῶν ἐπ᾿ αὐτήν· ἐὰν δὲ μὴ ᾖ ἀξία, ἡ εἰρήνη ὑμῶν πρὸς ὑμᾶς ἀποστραφήτω." Διὰ τοῦτο οὐκ ἴσμεν, ὅτι τύπον ῥημάτων νομίζομεν ταῦτα εἶναι, καὶ οὐ συντιθέμεθα τῷ νῷ. Μὴ γὰρ [209] ἐγὼ δίδωμι τὴν εἰρήνην; Ὁ Χριστὸς, δι᾿ ἡμῶν φθέγγεσθαι καταξιῶν. Εἰ καὶ τὸν ἄλλον ἅπαντα χρόνον κενοὶ τῆς χάριτός ἐσμεν, ἀλλ᾿ οὐ νῦν δι᾿ ὑμᾶς. Εἰ γὰρ εἰς ὄνον ἐνήργησε καὶ εἰς μάντιν ἡ τοῦ θεοῦ χάρις, δι᾿ οἰκονομίαν καὶ τὴν τῶν Ἰσραηλιτῶν ὠφέλειαν, εὔδηλον ὅτι οὐδὲ εἰς ἡμᾶς παραιτήσεται ἐνεργεῖν, ἀλλ᾿ ἀνέξεται καὶ τοῦτο δι᾿ ἡμᾶς.

Μηδεὶς τοίνυν εἴπῃ, ὅτι εὐτελὴς ἐγὼ καὶ ταπεινὸς καὶ οὐδενὸς ἄξιος λόγου, καὶ οὕτω μοι προσεχέτω. Εἰμὶ γὰρ τοιοῦτος· ἀλλ᾿ ἀεὶ ἔθος τῷ θεῷ διὰ τοὺς πολλοὺς καὶ τοῖς τοιούτοις ἐφίστασθαι. Καὶ ἵνα μάθητε, τῷ Κάϊν κατηξίωσε λαλῆσαι διὰ τὸν Ἄβελ, τῷ διαβόλῳ διὰ τὸν Ἰώβ, τῷ Φαραὼ διὰ τὸν Ἰωσήφ, τῷ Ναβουχοδονόσορ διὰ τὸν Δανιήλ, τῷ Βαλτάσαρ διὰ τὸν αὐτόν. Καὶ μάγοι δὲ ἀποκαλύψεως ἔτυχον, καὶ Καϊάφας προεφήτευσε χριστοκτόνος ὢν καὶ ἀνάξιος, διὰ τὸ τῆς ἱερωσύνης ἀξίωμα. Λέγεται καὶ Ἀαρὼν διὰ τοῦτο μὴ λεπρωθῆναι. Διὰ τί γὰρ, εἰπέ μοι, ἀμφοτέρων καταλαλησάντων, ἐκείνη μόνη τὴν δίκην ὑπέμεινε; Μὴ θαυμάσῃς· εἰ γὰρ ἐν τοῖς ἔξωθεν ἀξιώμασι, κἂν μυρία τις κατηγορῆται, οὐ πρότερον εἰς δικαστήριον ἄγεται, ἕως ἂν ἀπόθηται

Surely in this respect you're fighting against God, because you deliver a judgment contrary to his. When the first in the church goes in, he says immediately, "peace to all"; when he preaches he says, "peace to all"; when he blesses, "peace to all"; when he bids us to greet each other, "peace to all"; when the sacrifice is finished, "peace to all"; and in the middle [of the liturgy] again, "grace and peace to you." How then isn't it extraordinary, if hearing so many times that we are to have peace, we're feuding against each other? And receiving peace and reciprocating, we war against the one who gives peace? You say, "And to your spirit," and you slander him outside [the church]. Oh dear! That the hallowed characteristics of the church have become only characteristics of pragmatic actions, not the truth. Oh dear! That the pledges of this army go no further than words. This is why you're ignorant of the reason "peace to all" is said. But listen to what Christ says in what follows: *"And whatever city or village you enter, ... when you come to a house, greet it; and if the house is worthy, let your peace come upon it, but if it is not worthy, let your peace return to you"* [Matt 10:11, 13]. For this reason we're ignorant, because we consider this as a figure of speech and don't perceive it in our minds. You see, I don't **[209]** give [the sign of] peace, do I? It's Christ, deigning to speak through us. But even if at all other times we're devoid of grace, yet we aren't now, for your sakes. For if the grace of God was active in an ass and a diviner [see Num 22] for the sake of a divine dispensation and to help the Israelites, it's very clear that it won't refuse to be active in us but will put up with even this for your sakes.

Let nobody say, then, that I'm mean and lowly and worthy of no consideration, and so pay no attention to me. I mean, I'm like this, but God's custom is to stand by such people for the sake of the many. And so that you may learn this, he judged Cain worthy to speak for Abel's sake [see Gen 4], the devil for Job's [see Job 1], Pharaoh for Joseph's [see Gen 41], Nebuchadnezzar for Daniel's [see Dan 2], Belshazzar for the same [see Dan 5]. And magi hit upon a revelation [see Matt 2:2], and Caiaphas prophesied, although he was a killer of Christ and unworthy, because of the worthiness of the priesthood [see John 11:49]. And it's said that for this reason Aaron didn't become leprous [see Num 12]. For why, tell me, when both had spoken,[47] was she [sc. Miriam] the only one to suffer punishment? Don't be amazed, for if in worldly ranks, even though someone is accused of myriad charges, they aren't brought to the tribunal before they have laid

---

47. I.e., Aaron and Miriam.

τὴν ἀρχήν, ἵνα μὴ ἐκείνη μετ' αὐτοῦ ὑβρίζηται· πολλῷ μᾶλλον ἐπὶ τῆς ἀρχῆς τῆς πνευματικῆς, κἂν ὁστισοῦν ᾖ, ἐνεργεῖ ἡ τοῦ θεοῦ χάρις· ἐπεὶ πάντα ἂν ἀπόλωλεν· ὅταν δὲ αὐτὴν ἀπόθηται, εἴτε ἀπελθών, εἴτε καὶ ἐνταῦθα, τότε δή, τότε χαλεπωτέραν δώσει τὴν δίκην.

Μὴ δὴ νομίζετε παρ' ἡμῶν ταῦτα λέγεσθαι· ἡ τοῦ Θεοῦ χάρις ἐστὶν ἡ καὶ εἰς ἀνάξιον ἐνεργοῦσα, οὐ δι' ἡμᾶς, ἀλλὰ δι' ὑμᾶς. Ἀκούσατε οὖν τί φησιν ὁ Χριστός· "Ἐὰν ᾖ ἡ οἰκία ἀξία, ἐλθέτω ἡ εἰρήνη ὑμῶν ἐπ' αὐτήν." Πῶς δὲ ἀξία γίνεται; "Ἐὰν δέξωνται ὑμᾶς, " φησίν. "Ἐὰν δὲ μὴ δέξωνται ὑμᾶς, μηδὲ ἀκούσωσι τὸν λόγον ὑμῶν, ἀμὴν λέγω ὑμῖν, ἀνεκτότερον ἔσται γῇ Σοδό-μων καὶ Γομόρρας ἐν ἡμέρᾳ κρίσεως, ἢ τῇ πόλει ἐκείνῃ." Τί οὖν ὄφελος, ὅτι δέχεσθε ἡμᾶς, καὶ οὐκ ἀκούετε τῶν παρ' ἡμῶν λεγομένων; τί τὸ κέρδος, ὅτι θεραπεύετε, καὶ οὐ προσέχετε τοῖς λεγομένοις ὑμῖν; Ἐκείνη ἐστὶ τιμὴ ἡμῖν, ἐκείνη θε-[210]ραπεία ἡ θαυμαστή, ἡ καὶ ὑμᾶς ὠφελοῦσα καὶ ἡμᾶς, ἐὰν ἡμῶν ἀκούητε. Ἀκούετε καὶ τοῦ Παύλου λέγοντος, "Οὐκ ᾔδειν, ἀδελ-φοί, ὅτι ἀρχιερεύς ἐστιν." Ἄκουε καὶ τοῦ Χριστοῦ λέγοντος, "Πάντα ὅσα ἂν λέγωσιν ὑμῖν τηρεῖν, τηρεῖτε καὶ ποιεῖτε." Οὐκ ἐμοῦ καταφρονεῖς, ἀλλὰ τῆς ἱερωσύνης· ἂν ἴδῃς ταύτης γυμνόν, τότε καταφρόνει, τότε οὐδὲ ἐγὼ ἀνέχομαι ἐπιτάττειν. Ἕως δ' ἂν ἐπὶ τοῦ θρόνου τούτου καθώμεθα, ἕως ἂν τὴν προε-δρίαν ἔχωμεν, ἔχομεν καὶ τὴν ἀξίαν καὶ τὴν ἰσχύν, εἰ καὶ ἀνάξιοί ἐσμεν. Εἰ ὁ Μωϋσέως θρόνος οὕτως ἦν αἰδέσιμος, ὡς δι' ἐκεῖνον ἀκούεσθαι, πολλῷ μᾶλλον ὁ τοῦ Χριστοῦ θρόνος. Ἐκεῖνον ἡμεῖς διεδεξάμεθα· ἀπὸ τούτου φθεγγόμεθα, ἀφ' οὗ καὶ ὁ Χριστὸς ἔθετο ἐν ἡμῖν τὴν διακονίαν τῆς καταλλαγῆς.

Οἱ πρέσβεις, οἱοίπερ ἂν ὦσι, διὰ τὸ τῆς πρεσβείας ἀξίωμα πολλῆς ἀπο-λαύουσι τῆς τιμῆς. Ὅρα γάρ· εἰς μέσην βαρβάρων ἔρχονται τὴν γῆν μόνοι, μεταξὺ τοσούτων πολεμίων· καὶ ἐπειδὴ μεγάλα ὁ τῆς πρεσβείας ἰσχύει νόμος, πάντες αὐτοὺς τιμῶσι, πάντες εἰς αὐτοὺς ἀποβλέπουσι, πάντες μετὰ ἀσφαλείας ἐκπέμπουσι. Καὶ ἡμεῖς τοίνυν πρεσβείας ἀνεδεξάμεθα λόγον, καὶ ἥκομεν παρὰ τοῦ θεοῦ· τοῦτο γάρ ἐστι τὸ τῆς ἐπισκοπῆς ἀξίωμα. Ἥκομεν πρὸς ὑμᾶς πρεσβεύοντες, ἀξιοῦντες καταλῦσαι τὸν πόλεμον, καὶ λέγομεν ἐπὶ τίσιν· οὐ πόλεις ἐπαγγελλόμενοι δώσειν, οὐδὲ σίτου μέτρα τόσα καὶ τόσα, οὐδὲ

down their office, lest it also be insulted together with them; much more is it the case with the spiritual office, no matter who they are; the grace of God is active in them, since [if not] everything would be lost. But when they have resigned from it, whether after they have gone or are still here, then indeed they will pay a more grievous penalty.

Don't really consider that these words are spoken by us: it's the grace of God that's active even in the unworthy, not through us but through you. Listen, then, to what Christ says: "*If the house is worthy, let your peace come upon it*" [Matt 10:13]. How does it become worthy? "*If they receive you,*" it says [Luke 10:8]. "*But if they don't receive you or listen to your words, ... truly I say to you that it will be more tolerable for the land of Sodom and Gomorrah in the day of judgment than for that city*" [Matt 10:14–15]. What then is the use, in that you receive us and don't listen to what we say? What's the gain, in that you serve us but don't pay attention to what we say? That will be an honor for us, that [**210**] will be an amazing service, useful to both you and us, if you listen to us. Listen to what Paul says too: "*I didn't know, brethren, that he was the high priest*" [Acts 23:5]. Hear also Christ saying, "*Observe everything they tell you, observe and do*" [Matt 23:3]. You're despising not me but the priesthood; when you see me stripped of this, then despise me; then no longer will I continue to issue commands. But as long as we sit on this throne, as long as we have the first place, we have both the dignity and the power, even if we are unworthy. If the throne of Moses was so revered that for its sake they were to be heard, much more is the throne of Christ. That throne we have received through succession, from this we speak, since the time that Christ installed in us the ministry of reconciliation.

Ambassadors,[48] whatever their kind, enjoy great honor because of the dignity of the embassy. For see: they go into the midst of the land of barbarians by themselves, in between so many enemies, and because the law of the embassy has great power, everyone honors them, everyone looks up to them, everyone sends them onward in safety. So we too have received a promise of an embassy, and we have come from God, you see, this is the dignity of the episcopate. We have come to you on an embassy, begging you to stop the war, and we say on what terms, not promising to give cities, nor this or that many measures of grain, nor captives, nor gold, but the

---

48. There is a pun here on the Greek word πρεσβύτερος, which can mean both "ambassador" and "presbyter/priest."

ἀνδράποδα, οὐδὲ χρυσίον, ἀλλὰ βασιλείαν οὐρανῶν, ζωὴν αἰώνιον, συνουσίαν τὴν μετὰ Χριστοῦ, τὰ ἄλλα ἀγαθὰ, ἃ μήτε εἰπεῖν ἡμῖν δυνατὸν, ἕως ἂν ἐν τῇ σαρκὶ ταύτῃ ὦμεν καὶ τῷ παρόντι βίῳ. Πρεσβεύομεν τοίνυν· ἀπολαύειν δὲ βουλόμεθα τιμῆς· οὐ δι' ἡμᾶς, μὴ γένοιτο· ἴσμεν γὰρ αὐτῆς τὸ εὐτελές· ἀλλὰ δι' ὑμᾶς, ἵνα ὑμεῖς μετὰ σπουδῆς τὰ παρ' ἡμῶν ἀκούητε, ἵνα ὑμεῖς ὠφελῆσθε, ἵνα μὴ μετὰ ῥᾳθυμίας ἢ ἀπροσεξίας προσέχητε τοῖς λεγομένοις. Οὐχ ὁρᾶτε τοὺς πρέσβεις πῶς πάντες αὐτοὺς περιέπουσιν; Ἡμεῖς θεοῦ πρέσβεις ἐσμὲν πρὸς ἀνθρώπους. Εἰ δὲ πρόσαντες ὑμῖν τοῦτο, οὐχ ἡμεῖς, ἀλλ' αὕτη ἡ ἐπισκοπή· οὐχὶ ὁ δεῖνα, ἀλλ' ὁ ἐπίσκοπος. Μηδεὶς ἐμοῦ ἀκουέτω, ἀλλὰ τοῦ ἀξιώματος. Πάντα τοίνυν ποιῶμεν κατὰ τὸ τῷ θεῷ δοκοῦν, ἵνα εἰς δόξαν θεοῦ ζήσωμεν, καὶ κατα-[211]ξιωθῶμεν τῶν ἐπηγγελμένων ἀγαθῶν τοῖς ἀγαπῶσιν αὐτὸν, χάριτι καὶ φιλανθρωπίᾳ τοῦ κυρίου ἡμῶν Ἰησοῦ Χριστοῦ, μεθ' οὗ τῷ πατρὶ δόξα, ἅμα τῷ ἁγίῳ πνεύματι, νῦν καὶ ἀεὶ καὶ εἰς τοὺς αἰῶνας τῶν αἰώνων. Ἀμήν.

kingdom of heaven, eternal life, being with Christ, the other good things that we're unable to tell you about, while we're in this flesh and the present life. So we are ambassadors, but we wish to enjoy the honor, not for our own sakes, heaven forbid (you see, we know it's worthless), but for yours, so that you may listen with great enthusiasm to what we say, so that you may be profited, so that you won't listen to what is said with indifference or carelessness. Don't you see how everyone treats them with great care? We are God's ambassadors to human beings, but if this offends you, it isn't we but the episcopate itself; it's not this person, but the bishop. Let nobody listen to me, but to the office. Let's then do everything according to what God sees is best, so that we may live in God's glory and [**211**] be considered worthy of the good things promised to those who love him [see Jas 2:5], in the grace and loving-kindness of our Lord Jesus Christ, with whom be glory to the Father, together with the Holy Spirit, now and always and forever and ever. Amen.

ΛΟΓΟΣ Δ.

Καὶ ὑμᾶς ποτε ἐχθροὺς ὄντας καὶ ἀπηλλοτριωμένους τῇ διανοίᾳ ἐν τοῖς ἔργοις τοῖς πονηροῖς, νυνὶ δὲ ἀποκατήλλαξε τῷ σώματι τῆς σαρκὸς αὐτοῦ διὰ τοῦ θανάτου, παραστῆσαι ὑμᾶς ἁγίους καὶ ἀμώμους καὶ ἀνεγκλήτους κατενώπιον αὐτοῦ.

Ἐνταῦθα λοιπὸν δείκνυσιν, ὅτι καὶ ἀναξίους ὄντας καταλλαγῆς κατήλλαξε. Τὸ μὲν γὰρ εἰπεῖν, ὅτι ὑπὸ τὴν ἐξουσίαν τοῦ σκότους ἦσαν, δείκνυσι τὴν συμφορὰν, ἐν ᾗ ἦσαν. Ἀλλ᾿ ἵνα μὴ ἀκούσας ἐξουσίαν σκότους, ἀνάγκην νομίσῃς εἶναι, ἐπάγει· "Καὶ ὑμᾶς ὄντας ἀπηλλοτριωμένους." ὥστε δοκεῖ μὲν τὸ αὐτὸ λέγειν, οὐκ ἔστι δὲ τὸ αὐτό· οὐ γάρ ἐστιν ἴσον ἀνάγκῃ κακῶς παθόντα, καὶ ἑκόντα τοῦτο ὑπομείναντα ἀπαλλάξαι τῶν δεινῶν. Ἐκεῖνος μὲν γὰρ ἐλεεῖσθαι ἄξιος, οὗτος δὲ μισεῖσθαι. Ἀλλ᾿ ὅμως ὑμᾶς, φησίν, οὐχὶ ἄκοντας οὐδὲ ἀναγκαζομένους, ἀλλ᾿ ἑκόντας καὶ μετὰ τοῦ βούλεσθαι ἀποπηδῶντας αὐτοῦ, καὶ ἀναξίους ὄντας ἀπήλλαξε. Καὶ ἐπειδὴ τῶν ἐν τοῖς οὐρανοῖς ἐμνήσθη, δείκνυσιν ὅτι ἡ ἔχθρα πᾶσα ἐντεῦθεν εἶχε τὴν ἀρχὴν, οὐκ ἐκεῖθεν. Ἐκεῖνοι μὲν γὰρ πάλαι ἐβούλοντο, καὶ ὁ θεός· ὑμεῖς δὲ οὐκ ἠθελήσατε. Καὶ διόλου δείκνυσι τοὺς ἀγγέλους μηδὲν ἰσχύσαντας ἐν τοῖς κάτω χρόνοις, εἴγε ἔμενον ἐχθροί· οὔτε πεῖσαι ἠδύναντο, οὔτε πεισθέντας ἀπαλλάξαι τοῦ διαβόλου. Οὐδὲ γὰρ τὸ πεῖσαι εἶχέ τι κέρδος, τοῦ κατέχοντος μὴ δεθέντος· οὐδὲ τὸ δεθῆναι εἶχέ τι κέρδος, τῶν κατεχομένων μὴ βουλομένων ἐπανελθεῖν· ἀλλ᾿ ἀμφότερα ἔδει· ὧν ἐκεῖνοι μὲν οὐδὲν, ὁ Χριστὸς δὲ ἀμφότερα πεποίηκεν. Ὥστε τοῦ τὸν θάνατον λῦσαι θαυμασιώτερον τὸ πεῖσαι. Ἐκεῖνο μὲν γὰρ ὅλον αὐτοῦ ἦν, καὶ αὐτὸς μόνος κύριος ἦν· τούτου δὲ οὐχὶ αὐτὸς μόνος, ἀλλὰ καὶ ἡμεῖς· εὐκολώτερον δὲ ταῦτα ἀνύομεν, ὧν αὐτοὶ κύριοί ἐσμεν. Ἅτε οὖν καὶ μεῖζον ὂν, ὕστερον αὐτὸ τίθησι. [212] Καὶ οὐχ ἁπλῶς εἶπεν, ἐχθραίνοντας, ἀλλά, "ἀπηλλοτριωμένους," ὃ πολλῆς ἔχθρας ἐστίν· οὐδὲ ἠλλοτριωμένους, ἀλλὰ μηδὲ προσδο-

Homily 4

And you, who were once enemies and alienated in your mind in your evil deeds, he has yet now reconciled to the body of his flesh through his death, in order to present you holy and blameless and irreproachable before him [Col 1:21–22].

In this passage he continues to demonstrate that Christ has reconciled those even who were unworthy of reconciliation. You see, by saying that they were under the *dominion of darkness* [Col 1:13], he demonstrated the misfortune in which they found themselves. But lest on hearing "*dominion of darkness*" you consider that it's necessity, he adds, "*and you who were alienated*," so that he seems to be saying the same thing, but it isn't the same. For it isn't the equivalent to reconcile from evils a person who suffers badly from necessity and the person who willingly endures dire things: the former is worthy of pity, but the latter of hatred. "But nevertheless," he says, "it wasn't unwillingly nor from compulsion, but willingly and with your wish that you leapt away from him, and he reconciled you even though you were unworthy." And since he had mentioned *things in heaven*, he demonstrates that all enmity has its origin from here, not from there. You see, they were willing a long time ago, and so was God, but you didn't want it.

And throughout he demonstrates that the angels had no power in the times afterward, inasmuch as human beings remained enemies; nor were they able to convince them; nor, if they were reconciled, to redeem them from the devil. For neither would reconciling them have had any gain, since the one who held them was bound, nor did binding him have any gain, when those whom he held were unwilling to return. No, both of these were needed, and they did nothing, but Christ did both. The upshot is that reconciling them is more amazing than loosening their bonds. For the former was totally of himself, and he had sole authority, whereas the second possibility was not his sole authority but also ours. But we accomplish those things more easily over which we have authority. Therefore, inasmuch as it's even greater, Paul places it last. [212] And he didn't simply say "were enemies," but "*were alienated*," which denotes great enmity. Nor did he say

κῶντας ἐπανελθεῖν. "Καὶ ἐχθροὺς, φησὶ, τῇ διανοίᾳ." Εἶτα οὐχὶ μέχρι τῆς προαιρέσεως μόνον ἡ ἀλλοτρίωσις, ἀλλὰ τί; "Καὶ ἐν τοῖς ἔργοις τοῖς πονηροῖς." Καὶ ἐχθροὶ ἦτε, φησὶ, καὶ τὰ τῶν ἐχθρῶν ἐπράττετε.

"Νυνὶ δὲ ἀποκατήλλαξεν ἐν τῷ σώματι τῆς σαρκὸς αὐτοῦ διὰ τοῦ θανάτου, παραστῆσαι ὑμᾶς ἁγίους καὶ ἀμώμους καὶ ἀνεγκλήτους κατενώπιον αὐτοῦ." Πάλιν τίθησι καὶ τὸν τρόπον τῆς καταλλαγῆς, ὅτι ἐν τῷ σώματι, οὐχ ἁπλῶς πληγεὶς, οὐδὲ μαστιγωθεὶς, οὐδὲ πραθεὶς, ἀλλὰ καὶ ἀποθανὼν τῷ αἰσχίστῳ θανάτῳ. Πάλιν τοῦ σταυροῦ μέμνηται, καὶ πάλιν ἑτέραν τίθησιν εὐεργεσίαν. Οὐ γὰρ ἀπήλλαξε μόνον, ἀλλὰ καὶ ὅ φησιν ἀνωτέρω, "τῷ ἱκανώσαντι ἡμᾶς," τοῦτο δὲ καὶ ἐνταῦθα αἰνίττεται. "Διὰ τοῦ θανάτου αὐτοῦ, φησὶ, παραστῆσαι ὑμᾶς ἁγίους καὶ ἀμώμους καὶ ἀνεγκλήτους κατενώπιον αὐτοῦ." Οὐ γὰρ δὴ μόνον τῶν ἁμαρτημάτων ἀπήλλαξεν, ἀλλὰ καὶ ἐν τοῖς εὐδοκιμηκόσι κατέστησεν. Οὐ γὰρ ἵνα κακῶν ἀπαλλάξῃ μόνον τοσαῦτα ἔπαθεν, ἀλλ' ἵνα καὶ τῶν πρώτων ἐπιτύχωμεν· ὥσπερ ἂν εἴ τις κατάδικον μὴ μόνον τῆς τιμωρίας ἐλευθερώσοι, ἀλλὰ καὶ εἰς τιμὴν ἀναγάγοι. Καὶ τοῖς οὐδὲν ἡμαρτηκόσιν ἐγκατέταξε· μᾶλλον δὲ οὐ τοῖς μὴ ἡμαρτηκόσι μόνον, ἀλλὰ καὶ τοῖς κατωρθωκόσι τὰ μέγιστα· καὶ τὸ δὴ μέγα, ὅτι ἁγιωσύνην τὴν κατενώπιον αὐτοῦ ἔδωκε, καὶ τὸ ἀνέγκλητον. Ἐπίτασις τοῦ ἀμώμου τὸ ἀνέγκλητον, ὅταν μηδὲ μέχρι καταγνώσεως, μηδὲ μέχρι ἐγκλήματος ᾖ πεπραγμένον ἡμῖν. Ἀλλ' ἐπειδὴ τὸ ὅλον αὐτοῦ τέθεικεν, ὅτι διὰ τοῦ θανάτου [213] ταῦτα κατώρθωσεν, τί οὖν, φησὶ, πρὸς ἡμᾶς; οὐδενὸς χρήζομεν; Διὰ τοῦτο ἐπήγαγεν· "Εἴγε ἐπιμένετε τῇ πίστει τεθεμελιωμένοι καὶ ἑδραῖοι, καὶ μὴ μετακινούμενοι ἀπὸ τῆς ἐλπίδος τοῦ εὐαγγελίου."

Τὴν ῥαθυμίαν αὐτῶν ἐνταῦθα ἐπικόπτει. Καὶ οὐχ ἁπλῶς εἶπεν, "ἐπιμένετε." ἔστι γὰρ ἐπιμένειν σαλευόμενον καὶ διχοστατοῦντα· ἔστιν ἑστάναι περιφερόμενον καὶ μένειν. "Εἴγε ἐπιμένετε, φησὶ, τεθεμελιωμένοι καὶ ἑδραῖοι, καὶ μὴ μετακινούμενοι." Βαβαὶ, ἡλίκῃ κέχρηται τροπῇ· οὐ μόνον μὴ σαλευόμενοι, φησὶν, ἀλλὰ μηδὲ κινούμενοι. Καὶ ὅρα· οὐδὲν φορτικὸν τέως τίθησιν, οὐδὲ ἐπίπονον, ἀλλὰ πίστιν καὶ ἐλπίδα. Τουτέστιν, ἐὰν μένητε πιστεύοντες, ὅτι ἀληθὴς ἡ ἐλπὶς τῶν μελλόντων. Ἐνταῦθα μὲν γὰρ δυνατόν· ἐπὶ δὲ τῆς ἀρετῆς οὐκ ἔνι μὴ μετασαλευθῆναι, κἂν μικρόν· οὕτως οὐκ ἔστιν ἐπαχθής.

"Ἀπὸ τῆς ἐλπίδος, φησὶ, τοῦ εὐαγγελίου, οὗ ἠκούσατε, τοῦ κηρυχθέντος ἐν πάσῃ κτίσει τῇ ὑπὸ τὸν οὐρανόν." Τίς δέ ἐστιν ἡ ἐλπὶς τοῦ εὐαγγελίου,

[just] say "*alienated*," but with no expectation of their return. "And *enemies in your mind*," he says. Then, as their alienation didn't proceed as far as choice only—but what? "*And in evil deeds.*" "And you are enemies," he says, "and you have performed the deeds of enemies."

Yet now he has reconciled in the body of his flesh through death to present you holy and blameless and irreproachable in his sight. Again he lays down the manner of the reconciliation, namely, that it was in the body, not simply by being beaten or scourged, but also by dying a most shameful death. Again he mentions the cross, and again lays down another benefit. You see, he didn't only reconcile, but, as Paul says above, "*he made us sufficient*" [Col 1:12], in fact he alludes to the same point in this passage also. "*Through* his *death*," he says, "*to present you holy and blameless and irreproachable in his sight.*" For indeed, he hasn't only reconciled us from sins but also established us among the approved. You see, it wasn't only to reconcile us from sins that he suffered to such a great extent, but so that we might also obtain the first benefits: it's just as if someone were not only to free a condemned person from punishment, but also to advance them to honor. And he has ranked you with those who have committed no sins—rather, not only with those who haven't committed sins, but even with those who have achieved the greatest righteousness. And what is indeed great is that he has given holiness that is *in his sight* and the state of being *irreproachable. Irreproachable* is an advance on *blameless*, when we have done [nothing] either as far as condemnation is concerned or as far as blame is concerned. But since Paul ascribed the whole thing to him, in saying that by his death [**213**] Christ achieved this, what then does he say to us? "Do we need nothing?" This is why he adds: "*Provided you continue in the faith, stable and steadfast, and not moving away from the hope of the gospel.*"

In this passage he strikes a blow at their indifference. And he didn't simply say "*continue*," for it's possible to continue wavering and vacillating; it's possible also to continue standing while being buffeted. "*Provided you continue*," he says, "*stable and steadfast, and not moving away.*" Wonderful that he uses an extraordinary metaphor: he doesn't say only not tossed about, but not even moved. And see: he lays down so far nothing that is burdensome or tedious, but faith and hope. That is, if you continue believing, that the hope of things to come is true. For indeed this is possible in the here and now, but with regard to virtuous living it isn't possible to be tossed about, even though slightly. Thus it's not grievous.

"*From the hope*," he says, "*of the gospel, which you have heard, which was preached to every creature under heaven.*" But what is the hope of the

ἀλλ' ἢ ὁ Χριστός; αὐτὸς γάρ ἐστιν ἡ εἰρήνη ἡμῶν, καὶ πάντα ταῦτα ὁ ἐργασάμενος. Ὥστε ὁ ἑτέροις ἐπιγράφων, μετακεκίνηται· πάντα γὰρ ἀπώλεσεν, ἐὰν μὴ εἰς τὸν Χριστὸν πιστεύῃ. "Οὗ ἠκούσατε," φησί. Καὶ πάλιν αὐτοὺς φέρει μάρτυρας, εἶτα τὴν οἰκουμένην ἅπασαν. Οὐ λέγει, τοῦ κηρυττομένου, ἀλλ' ἤδη πιστευθέντος καὶ κηρυχθέντος· ὅπερ καὶ ἀρχόμενος ἐποίησεν, ἀπὸ τῆς τῶν πολλῶν μαρτυρίας καὶ τούτους στῆσαι βουλόμενος. "Οὗ ἐγενόμην ἐγὼ Παῦλος διάκονος." Καὶ τοῦτο εἰς τὸ ἀξιόπιστον συντελεῖ. "Ἐγὼ, φησὶ, Παῦλος διάκονος." Μέγα γὰρ αὐτοῦ ἦν τὸ ἀξίωμα λοιπὸν πανταχοῦ ἀδομένου, καὶ τῆς οἰκουμένης ὄντος διδασκάλου.

"Νῦν χαίρω ἐν τοῖς παθήμασί μου ὑπὲρ ὑμῶν, καὶ ἀνταναπληρῶ τὰ ὑστερήματα τῶν θλίψεων τοῦ Χριστοῦ ἐν τῇ σαρκί μου ὑπὲρ τοῦ σώματος αὐτοῦ, ὅ ἐστιν ἡ ἐκκλησία." Καὶ ποία αὕτη ἀκολουθία; Δοκεῖ μὲν ἀπηρτῆσθαι, πολλὴν δὲ ἔχει τὴν ἀκολουθίαν. Καὶ, "διάκονος," φησίν· ἀντὶ τοῦ, οὐδὲν παρ' ἐμαυτοῦ εἰσφέρων, ἀλλὰ τὰ ἑτέρου καταγγέλλων. Οὕτω δὲ πιστεύω, ὅτι καὶ πάσχω ὑπὲρ αὐτοῦ· καὶ οὐ πάσχω μόνον, [214] ἀλλὰ καὶ χαίρω πάσχων, πρὸς τὴν ἐλπίδα τὴν μέλλουσαν ὁρῶν· καὶ πάσχω οὐχ ὑπὲρ ἐμαυτοῦ, ἀλλ' ὑπὲρ ὑμῶν. "Καὶ ἀνταναπληρῶ, φησὶ, τὰ ὑστερήματα τῶν θλίψεων τοῦ Χριστοῦ ἐν τῇ σαρκί μου." Δοκεῖ μὲν μέγα εἶναι ὅπερ ἐφθέγξατο, ἀλλ' οὐκ ἔστιν ἀπονοίας, μὴ γένοιτο, ἀλλὰ καὶ πολλῆς φιλοστοργίας τῆς περὶ τὸν Χριστόν· οὐ γὰρ βούλεται αὐτοῦ εἶναι, ἀλλ' ἐκείνου τὰ πάθη, τούτους οἰκειῶσαι αὐτῷ βουλόμενος. Καὶ ἃ ἐγὼ πάσχω, δι' ἐκεῖνον πάσχω, φησίν· ὥστε μὴ ἐμοὶ χάριν ὁμολογεῖτε, ἀλλ' ἐκείνῳ· αὐτὸς γὰρ πάσχει ταῦτα. Ὥσπερ ἂν εἴ τις πεμφθεὶς πρός τινα, ἕτερον ἀξιώσειε λέγων, παρακαλῶ σε, ὑπὲρ ἐμοῦ ἄπελθε πρὸς τόνδε· εἶτα ἐκεῖνος λέγοι ὅτι διὰ τόνδε ταῦτα ποιῶ. Ὥστε οὐκ ἐπαισχύνεται καὶ ταῦτα αὐτοῦ παθήματα λέγειν. Οὐ γὰρ μόνον ἀπέθανεν ὑπὲρ ἡμῶν, ἀλλὰ καὶ μετὰ τὸ ἀποθανεῖν ἕτοιμός ἐστι θλιβῆναι δι' ὑμᾶς. Ἐφιλονείκησε καὶ ἐβιάσατο δεῖξαι αὐτὸν καὶ νῦν κινδυνεύοντα ὑπὲρ τῆς ἐκκλησίας διὰ τοῦ ἰδίου σώματος, καὶ πρὸς ἐκεῖνο ἀποτείνεται, ὅτι οὐ δι' ἡμῶν προσάγεσθε, ἀλλὰ δι' αὐτοῦ, κἂν ἡμεῖς ταῦτα ποιῶμεν· οὐ γὰρ οἰκεῖον ἔργον ἀνεδεξάμεθα, ἀλλὰ τὸ ἐκείνου. Καὶ ταυτόν ἐστιν, ὥσπερ ἂν εἴ τις τάξις λαχοῦσα στρατηγὸν τὸν ὑπερασπίζοντα

gospel, unless it's Christ? You see, Christ himself is our peace and the one who has accomplished all these things, so that the one who ascribes them to others is moved away, for they've lost everything if they don't believe in Christ. *"Which you have heard,"* Paul says. And again he brings themselves as witnesses, then the whole world. He doesn't say "which is being preached," but "has already been believed and preached." And this he did also at the beginning, wishing from the witness of the many to establish these also. *Of whom I, Paul, have become a minister* [Col 1:6]. This too contributes to make it credible. *"I,"* he says, *"Paul, a minister."* You see, his authority was great, being celebrated afterward everywhere, and he was a teacher of the world.[49]

Now I rejoice in my sufferings for your sake, and complete in my flesh what is missing in the sufferings of Christ, for the sake of his body, which is the church. And what is the connection with this? While it seems to be unattached, it has a very close connection. "And *minister,*" he says, "instead of bringing nothing from myself, but announcing what is from another. So I believe that I suffer for his sake, and I don't just suffer, [214] but even rejoice in suffering, looking toward the hope that is to come, and I suffer not for my own sake but because of you." *"And complete in my body,"* he says, *"what is missing in the sufferings of Christ."* What he's uttered seems indeed to be a great thing, but it doesn't come from arrogance (heaven forbid!) but even from a great affection toward Christ, for he doesn't want the sufferings to be his but Christ's, in his wish to make those persons Christ's own. "And the things I suffer," he says, "I suffer for his sake," such that you don't express your gratitude to me, but to him, for he's the very one who suffers these things. Just as if a person who is sent to somebody should beg the other, saying, "Please, go for my sake to that person," then the other should say, "I'm doing this because of him." The upshot is that Christ isn't ashamed to call these sufferings also his own. You see, he didn't only die for our sakes, but even after his death he's prepared to be afflicted for your sakes. He's keen and makes every effort to demonstrate that even now he's in danger of peril through his own body for the church's sake, and he aims at this point, namely, that we aren't brought to God by us, but by him, even though we do these things, for we haven't undertaken a work of our own but his. And it's the same as if some military squadron appointed its commander to pro-

---

49. On the depiction of Paul as teacher of the world, which is very common in Chrysostom, see Mitchell, *Heavenly Trumpet*, 75 n. 29.

αὐτῆς, καὶ ἐν τῷ πολέμῳ στήκοι, εἶτα ἀπελθόντος ἐκείνου, ὁ ὑποστράτηγος τὰ ἐκείνου τραύματα ἀναδέξοιτο μέχρι τοῦ λυθῆναι τὸν πόλεμον. Εἶτα ὅτι καὶ δι' αὐτὸν ταῦτα ποιεῖ, ἄκουσον. "Ὑπὲρ τοῦ σώματος αὐτοῦ," φησίν· ἢ τοῦτο θέλων εἰπεῖν, ὅτι οὐχ ὑμῖν χαρίζομαι, ἀλλὰ τῷ Χριστῷ· ἃ γὰρ ἐκεῖνον ἔδει παθεῖν, ἐγὼ πάσχω ἀντ' αὐτοῦ. Ὅρα πόσα κατασκευάζει. Δείκνυσι πολὺ τὸ φίλτρον· ὥσπερ ἐν τῇ δευτέρᾳ πρὸς Κορινθίους ἐπιστολῇ γράφων ἔλεγεν; "Ἐν ἡμῖν ἔθετο τὴν διακονίαν τῆς καταλλαγῆς·" καὶ πάλιν, "Ὑπὲρ Χριστοῦ πρεσβεύομεν, ὡς τοῦ θεοῦ παρακαλοῦντος δι' ἡμῶν·" τοῦτο καὶ ἐνταῦθά φησιν, ὑπὲρ αὐτοῦ πάσχω, ἵνα μᾶλλον αὐτοὺς ἐπισπάσηται. Τουτέστιν, εἰ καὶ ὁ ὀφείλων ὑμῖν ἀπῆλθεν, ἀλλ' ἐγὼ ἀποδίδωμι. Διὰ γὰρ τοῦτο καὶ ὑστερήματα εἶπεν, ἵνα δείξῃ ὅτι οὐδὲ τὸ πᾶν ἡγεῖται οὐδέπω πεπονθέναι. Ὑπὲρ ὑμῶν, φησὶ, καὶ μετὰ θάνατον πάσχει, εἴγε ἔτι ἐλλείμματα ἔμεινε. Τοῦτο ἐν τῇ πρὸς Ῥω-[215]μαίους ἑτέρως ποιεῖ λέγων· "Ὡς καὶ ἐντυγχάνει ὑπὲρ ἡμῶν." δεικνὺς ὅτι οὐκ ἠρκέσθη τῷ θανάτῳ μόνον, ἀλλὰ καὶ μετὰ ταῦτα μυρία ποιεῖ.

Οὐ τοίνυν ἑαυτὸν ἐπαίρων ταῦτα λέγει, ἀλλὰ τὸν Χριστὸν δεῖξαι βουλόμενος ἔτι καὶ νῦν ὑπὲρ αὐτῶν φροντίζοντα. Καὶ τὸν λόγον ἀξιόπιστον δείκνυσι τῷ ἐπαγαγεῖν, "ὑπὲρ τοῦ σώματος αὐτοῦ." Ὅτι γὰρ οὕτως ἔχει, καὶ οὐδὲν ἀπεικός, δῆλον ἐκ τοῦ ὑπὲρ τοῦ σώματος αὐτοῦ ταῦτα γενέσθαι. Ὅρα πῶς ἡμᾶς συνῆψεν ἑαυτῷ. Τί τοίνυν ἐπεισάγετε διὰ μέσου ἀγγέλους; "Ἧς ἐγὼ ἐγενόμην, φησὶ, διάκονος." Τί ἑτέρους ἐπεισάγετε ἀγγέλους; ἐγώ εἰμι διάκονος. Εἶτα δείκνυσιν ὅτι οὐδὲν αὐτὸς ἐποίησεν, εἴγε διάκονός ἐστιν. "Ἧς ἐγενόμην ἐγώ, φησὶ, διάκονος κατὰ τὴν οἰκονομίαν τοῦ θεοῦ τὴν δοθεῖσάν μοι εἰς ὑμᾶς πληρῶσαι τὸν λόγον τοῦ θεοῦ." "Οἰκονομίαν." Ἤτοι τοῦτό φησιν, ὅτι οὕτως ἠθέλησεν, αὐτοῦ ἀπελθόντος, ἡμᾶς διαδέξασθαι τὴν οἰκονομίαν, ἵνα μὴ ὡς ἐγκαταλελειμμένοι διάκεισθε· αὐτὸς γάρ ἐστιν ὁ παθὼν, αὐτὸς ὁ πρεσβεύων· ἢ τοῦτό φησιν, ὅτι ἐμὲ τὸν μάλιστα πάντων διώκτην διὰ τοῦτο εἴασε διῶξαι, ἵνα ἀξιόπιστος ὦ κηρύσσων· ἢ οἰκονομίαν φησὶν, ὅτι οὐκ ἔργα ἐζήτησεν, οὐδὲ πράξεις οὐδὲ κατορθώματα, ἀλλὰ πίστιν καὶ βάπτισμα· οὐ

tect it and were to stand in battle, and then when he's left, his subordinate should take over his wounds until the war has finished.

Then, that for his sake he does these things, listen. "On behalf of his body," says Paul, wishing to say, "I gratify not you, but Christ, for the things he had to suffer, I suffer in his stead." See the extent of his preparations. He demonstrates that the charm is great. Just as in his Second Letter to the Corinthians he wrote in these words, "*In us he placed the ministry of reconciliation*" [2 Cor 5:18]. And again: "*We are ambassadors for Christ, God making his appeal through us*" [2 Cor 5:20]. In the same passage he also says this, namely, "*for his sake I suffer*," so that he may all the more draw them to him. That is, "even if your debtor has gone away, yet I shall repay." For this is why he also called this *what is missing*, in order to demonstrate that neither does he think that Christ has suffered everything yet. "For your sakes," Paul says, "he suffers even after his death, in that there still remains what is missing." He does the same thing differently in the Letter [215] to the Romans when he says, "*Who indeed intercedes for our sakes*" [Rom 8:34], demonstrating that Christ wasn't satisfied with his death alone, but even afterward does myriad things.

He doesn't then say this to exalt himself, but wishing to demonstrate that Christ is still even now taking care of them. And Paul demonstrates that what he's said is credible by adding, "*for his body's sake*." You see, that this is how things are and that there's nothing unreasonable in it is clear from the things that are done for his body's sake. See how he has knit us to himself. Why then bring in the angels between? "*Of which I have become a minister*," he says. "Why do you bring in other angels? I'm a minister." Then he demonstrates that he himself has done nothing, although he's a minister. "*Of which I have become a minister*," he says, "*according to the divine plan*[50] *that was given to me, to make the word of God fully known*." "*Plan*." Either he means this, that Christ so willed that after his departure we should succeed to the plan, so that you might not feel so deserted (for he's the one who suffers, who is the ambassador); or he means this, that me who of all people was a persecutor he allowed to persecute, so that by my preaching I might be credible; or by "*plan*" he means that he didn't require deeds, or good works, or accomplishments, but faith and baptism. You see, other-

---

50. Greek οἰκονομία, by which in theological terms is meant God's plan for salvation. See in detail Gerhard Richter, *Oikonomia: Der Gebrauch des Wortes Oikonomia im Neuen Testament, bei den Kirchenvätern und in der theologischen Literatur bis ins 20. Jahrhundert*, AK 90 (Berlin: de Gruyter, 2008).

γὰρ ἂν ἑτέρως ἐδέξασθε τὸν λόγον. "Εἰς ὑμᾶς, φησὶ, πληρῶσαι τὸν λόγον τοῦ Θεοῦ." Περὶ τῶν ἐθνῶν λέγει, δεικνὺς αὐτοὺς ἔτι σαλευομένους τῷ εἰπεῖν, "πληρῶσαι." Τὸ γὰρ ἔθνη ἀπερριμμένα δυνηθῆναι τοσοῦτον ὕψος δογμάτων δέξασθαι, οὐχὶ Παύλου ἦν, ἀλλ' οἰκονομίας τῆς τοῦ θεοῦ· ἐπεὶ ἐγὼ οὐκ ἂν ἴσχυσα, φησί. Δείξας δὴ τὸ μεῖζον, τὰ αὐτοῦ παθήματα τοῦ Χριστοῦ ὄντα, τότε τὸ σαφέστερον ἐπάγει, ὅτι καὶ τοῦτο τοῦ θεοῦ ἐστι, τὸ πληρῶσαι τὸν λόγον εἰς ὑμᾶς. Καὶ δείκνυσιν ἐνταῦθα οὐ φανερῶς, ὅτι καὶ τοῦτο οἰκονομίας, τὸ νῦν λεχθῆναι, ὅτι δύνασθε ἀκούειν, ἀλλ' οὐκ ἀμελείας, ἀλλ' ὥστε δεκτικοὺς γενέσθαι. Ὁ γὰρ θεὸς οὐκ ἀθρόως πάντα ποιεῖ, ἀλλὰ κέχρηται συγκαταβάσει διὰ τὴν πολλὴν αὐτοῦ φιλανθρωπίαν. Καὶ τοῦτο αἴτιον τοῦ νῦν παραγενέσθαι τὸν Χριστὸν, ἀλλὰ μὴ πάλαι. Καὶ δείκνυσιν ἐν τῷ εὐαγγελίῳ, ὅτι διὰ τοῦτο τοὺς δούλους ἀπέστειλε πρώτους, ἵνα [216] μὴ ἐπὶ τὸν φόνον ἔλθωσι τοῦ υἱοῦ. Εἰ γὰρ οὐδὲ μετὰ τοὺς δούλους ἐλθόντα τὸν υἱὸν ᾐδέσθησαν, πολλῷ μᾶλλον πρὸ τούτου· εἰ τῶν ἐλαττόνων οὐκ ἤκουον προσταγμάτων, πῶς τῶν μειζόνων ἤκουσαν ἄν;

Τί οὖν, φησιν; οὐκ εἰσὶν Ἰουδαῖοι καὶ νῦν, καὶ Ἕλληνες ἀτελέστερον διακείμενοι; Τοῦτο λοιπὸν ὑπερβολὴ ῥαθυμίας. Τὸ γὰρ μετὰ τοσοῦτον χρόνον, μετὰ τοσαῦτα διδάγματα ἔτι μένειν ἀτελεῖς, πολλῆς νωθείας ἐστίν. Ὅταν οὖν λέγωσιν Ἕλληνες, διὰ τί νῦν ἦλθεν ὁ Χριστός; μὴ τοῦτο ἀφῶμεν λέγειν αὐτοὺς, ἀλλ', εἰ μὴ κατώρθωσεν, ἐρωτῶμεν. Ὥσπερ γὰρ εἰ καὶ παρὰ τὴν ἀρχὴν ἦλθε καὶ μὴ κατώρθωσεν, οὐκ ἤρκει ἡμῖν πρὸς ἀπολογίαν ὁ καιρός· οὕτως, ἐπειδὴ κατώρθωσεν, οὐκ ἂν εἴημεν δίκαιοι τοῦ καιροῦ τὰς εὐθύνας ὑπέχειν. Οὐδὲ γὰρ ἰατρόν τις τὴν νόσον λύσαντα καὶ ἐπὶ ὑγείαν ἀγαγόντα

wise you wouldn't have received the word. "For you," he says, "*to make the word of God fully known.*" He's speaking of the gentiles, demonstrating that they're still wavering by saying "*fully known.*" You see, for the castaway gentiles to have been able to receive such lofty doctrines didn't come from Paul but from God's plan, "for I didn't have the power," he says. Having demonstrated what is greater, namely, that the sufferings of Christ are his, he then adduces what is more evident, namely, that this too is from God, *to make the word fully known in you.* And in this passage he demonstrates in a way that isn't manifest that this too belongs to the plan: that it's said to you now because you're able to hear it and comes not of neglect but so that you may become recipients of it. You see, God doesn't do everything all of a sudden but uses his accommodation[51] because of his great loving-kindness. And this is the reason for Christ's appearing now but not in former times. And Christ demonstrates in the gospel that for this reason he sent the servants first, so that [216] they might not proceed to kill the Son. For if they didn't respect the Son, even when he came after the servants, much more would they have had no respect for him if he came sooner.[52] If they didn't pay attention to the lesser commandments, how would they have paid attention to the greater ones?

"What, then," says [someone], "aren't there Jews even now, and Hellenes, who are in a pretty poor state?" This is besides an excess of sluggishness. You see, the fact that after such a long time, after such great teachings, they remain in a poor state, comes from great stupidity. Therefore, when the Hellenes say, "Why did Christ come now?" let's not allow them to say this, but let's ask them whether Christ didn't succeed. For just as if he had come at the very start and not succeeded, the chronology wouldn't have been a sufficient excuse for us. So, since he *has* succeeded, we can't be brought to account about chronology. You see, neither does anyone demand from a doctor who has removed the disease and led the patient back to health to

---

51. Greek συγκατάβασις, which admits of various other translations, such as "condescension." It refers to God's graciousness in assuming human form and to the consequent salvation of humankind. On the term, see David Rylaarsdam, *John Chrysostom on Divine Pedagogy: The Coherence of His Theology and Preaching*, OECS (Oxford: Oxford University Press, 2014), esp. 23–30. Rylaarsdam discusses the difficulties of rendering the term into English and prefers "adaptation." See also Margaret M. Mitchell, "Pauline Accommodation and 'Condescension' (συγκατάβασις): 1 Cor 9:19–23 and the History of Influence," in *Paul beyond the Judaism/Hellenism Divide*, ed. Troels Engberg-Pedersen (Louisville: Westminster John Knox, 2001), 197–214.

52. This is an expansion to make the terse Greek intelligible.

ἀπαιτεῖ τῆς ἰατρείας τὰς εὐθύνας, οὐδὲ στρατηγὸν νενικηκότα ἐξετάζει, διὰ τί τῷδε τῷ καιρῷ, καὶ διὰ τί ἐν τῷδε τῷ τόπῳ. Ταῦτα γὰρ, μὴ κατορθώσαντος, ἢν ἐρωτᾶν· κατορθώσαντος δὲ, καὶ ἀποδέχεσθαι. Τίς γὰρ, εἰπέ μοι, ἀξιοπιστότερος, ὁ σὸς λογισμὸς καὶ ἡ συκοφαντία, ἢ ἡ τοῦ πράγματος τελειότης; Ἐνίκησεν, ἢ οὐκ ἐνίκησε; τοῦτο δεῖξον· ἐκράτησεν, ἢ οὐκ ἐκράτησεν; ἐξήγαγεν εἰς τέλος ἅπερ εἶπεν, ἢ οὔ; Αὗταί εἰσιν αἱ εὐθῦναι. Εἰπὲ δή μοι, θεὸν πάντως ὁμολογεῖς εἶναι, εἰ καὶ μὴ Χριστόν. Ἐρωτῶ δή σε· ἄναρχος ὁ θεός; Πάντως ἐρεῖς. Εἰπὲ οὖν μοι, διὰ τί μὴ πρὸ μυρίων ἐτῶν τοὺς ἀνθρώπους ἐποίησε; πλείονα γὰρ ἔμελλον ζήσεσθαι χρόνον. Εἰ γὰρ καλὸν τὸ εἶναι, πολλῷ μᾶλλον τὸ ἐπιπλεῖον εἶναι· νῦν δὲ ἐζημιώθησαν ὃν οὐκ ἐγένοντο χρόνον; Ἀλλ' οὐκ ἐζημιώθησαν· τὸ δὲ πῶς, αὐτὸς οἶδεν ὁ πεποιηκώς. Πάλιν σε ἐρωτῶ, διὰ τί μὴ πάντας ἀθρόον ἐποίησεν, ἀλλ' ἡ μὲν τοῦ δεῖνος ψυχὴ τοῦ πρώτου γενομένου τοσαῦτα ἔτη ἔχει οὖσα, ἡ δὲ ἑτέρα ἠλάττωται ἡ μηδέπω γενομένη; διὰ τί τὸν μὲν πρῶτον, τὸν δὲ ὕστερον ἐποίησεν εἰς τόνδε παραχθῆναι τὸν κόσμον;

Καίτοι ταῦτα ὄντως ζητήσεως ἄξια, ἀλλ' οὐ πολυπραγμοσύνης· τοῦτο γὰρ οὐδὲ ζητήσεως. Ἐγὼ γὰρ ἐρῶ τὴν αἰτίαν [217] ἥνπερ εἶπον. Ὑπόθου γάρ μοι τὴν ἀνθρωπίνην φύσιν ὥσπερ μίαν τινὰ ἡλικίαν, καὶ τοὺς μὲν πρώτους χρόνους μειρακίου τάξιν ἔχειν τὸ γένος τὸ ἡμέτερον, τοὺς δὲ μετ' ἐκεῖνο νεανίσκου, τούτους δὲ τοὺς ἐγγὺς τοῦ γήρως πρεσβύτου. Λοιπὸν ὅταν ἡ ψυχὴ ἀκμάζῃ, τῶν τοῦ σώματος μελῶν χαλασθέντων, καὶ τοῦ πολέμου λυθέντος, τότε ἤχθημεν ἐπὶ τὴν φιλοσοφίαν. Καὶ μὴν τοὐναντίον, φησί· μειράκια ὄντα διδάσκομεν. Ἀλλ' οὐ τὰ μεγάλα δόγματα, ἀλλὰ ῥητορείαν, ἀλλὰ δεινότητα λόγων· ταῦτα μὲν οὖν, ὅταν ἀκμάζων γένηται. Ὅρα καὶ τὸν θεὸν ταῦτα ποιοῦντα ἐπὶ τῶν Ἰουδαίων. Καθάπερ γὰρ παιδίοις τοῖς Ἰουδαίοις γραμματιστὴν τὸν Μωϋσέα οὕτως αὐτοῖς ἐπέστησε, καὶ καθάπερ παιδίοις ταῦτα ἔπραττεν ἐκεῖνος σκιαγραφῶν, καθάπερ ἡμεῖς τὰ στοιχεῖα. "Σκιὰν γὰρ, φησίν, ἔχων ὁ νόμος τῶν μελλόντων ἀγαθῶν, οὐκ αὐτὴν τὴν εἰκόνα τῶν πραγμάτων." Καθάπερ ἡμεῖς τοῖς παιδίοις καὶ πλακοῦντας ὠνούμεθα, καὶ ἀργύρια δίδομεν, ἓν μόνον παρ' αὐτῶν ἀπαιτοῦντες, τὸ τέως βαδίζειν ἐπὶ τὸ διδασκαλεῖον· οὕτω καὶ ὁ θεὸς τότε καὶ πλοῦτον ἔδωκε καὶ τρυφήν, ἓν παρ' αὐτῶν ὠνούμενος μόνον διὰ τῆς πολλῆς συγχωρήσεως, τὸ ἀκούειν Μωϋσέως. Διὰ τοῦτο αὐτοὺς διδασκάλῳ παρέδωκεν, ἵνα μὴ αὐτοῦ καταφρονῶσι, καθάπερ πατρὸς φιλοστόργου. Ὅρα οὖν ὅτι ἐκεῖνον μόνον ἐδεδοίκεσαν. Οὐ γὰρ εἶπον, ποῦ ἐστιν ὁ θεός; ἀλλὰ, ποῦ

give an account of the treatment, nor does anyone examine closely a victorious general: Why at this time and why in this place? For these questions, if he hadn't been successful, it was possible to ask, but when he has been successful they must even be admitted. For who, tell me, is more credible: your reasoning and slander, or the end result of the matter? Was he victorious, or wasn't he victorious? Demonstrate this. Did he prevail, or didn't he prevail? Did he carry out to a conclusion what he said, or not? These are the subject of the accounts. Then please tell me: you confess wholeheartedly that God exists, even though not Christ. I ask you then: "Is God without beginning?" You will assent wholeheartedly. So, tell me, why didn't he create human beings myriad years before? For they would have lived for a longer time. You see, if to be in existence is a good thing, it's much better to exist for a longer time, but as it is, they have been disadvantaged by the time in which they didn't exist. No, they weren't disadvantaged, but how, the one who created them knows. Again I ask you: Why didn't he create everyone at once? But the one whose soul was created first has many years of existence, while the other is deprived because it wasn't yet created. Why did he bring the one first into the world, but the second one afterward?

Further, these matters are really fit subjects for inquiry, but not for meddlesomeness, for this is not for inquiry at all. You see, I'll tell you the reason [**217**] I spoke of. Please suppose human nature as being like one continuous life, and that in the first times our race held the position of boyhood, while those who came next, of manhood, while those near extreme age, of an old man. After that, when the soul is at its prime, when the bodily parts droop, and the war is over, then we are brought to philosophy. "Indeed, the opposite," someone says, "we teach boys when they're young." No, not the important doctrines but rhetoric, and expertise with language, and the other, when they've come into their prime. See that God does this too with the Jews. You see, just as if the Jews had been little children he placed Moses as schoolmaster over them in this way, and like little children he made these representations in a sketchy way, just as we teach the alphabet. "*For since the law had a shadow of the good things to come,*" he says, "*it does not have the image of these realities*" [Heb 10:1]. As we buy cakes for small children and give them coins, asking only one thing from them, that for the time being they go to school, so too God at that time gave the Jews both wealth and luxury, buying only one thing from them through his great concession, namely, that they would listen to Moses. This is why he gave them over to a schoolmaster, so that they might not despise him [sc. God], since he was a loving father. So see that they feared Moses only,

ἐστι Μωϋσῆς; καὶ παρὼν μόνον φοβερὸς ἦν. Ὅτε γοῦν κακῶς ἔπραξαν, ὅρα πῶς αὐτοὺς ἐκόλασεν. Ὁ μὲν γὰρ θεὸς αὐτοὺς ἀποκηρῦξαι ἐβούλετο, αὐτὸς δὲ οὐκ ἀφίησι· μᾶλλον δὲ τὸ ὅλον τοῦ θεοῦ γέγονε, καθάπερ πατρὸς ἀπειλοῦντος, διδασκάλου δὲ παραιτουμένου, καὶ λέγοντος, ὅτι ἐμοὶ συγχώρησον, καὶ ἐκ τοῦ νῦν ἀναδέχομαι. Οὕτως ἐγένετο διδασκαλεῖον ἡ ἔρημος. Καὶ καθάπερ παιδία χρονίσαντα ἐπὶ τῆς διατριβῆς, ἀναχωρῆσαι βούλεται· οὕτω καὶ ἐκεῖνοι τότε συνεχῶς τὴν Αἴγυπτον ἐζήτουν, καὶ ἔκλαιον λέγοντες, "Ἀπολώλαμεν, ἐξανηλώμεθα, παραπολώλαμεν." [218] Καὶ τὴν πινακίδα αὐτῶν συνέτριψεν ὁ Μωϋσῆς, γράψας αὐτοῖς καθάπερ ὀνόματά τινα· ὅπερ καὶ διδάσκαλος ποιήσειεν ἄν, τὴν δέλτον λαβών, καὶ ἰδὼν κακῶς γεγραμμένην, καὶ αὐτὴν ῥίπτει τὴν δέλτον, πολὺν θυμὸν ἐνδείξασθαι βουλόμενος· κἂν κατεάξῃ, ὁ πατὴρ οὐ χολᾷ. Αὐτὸς μὲν γὰρ ἐνέκειτο γράφων· ἐκεῖνοι δὲ οὐχ ὁρῶντες εἰς αὐτόν, ἀλλ᾽ ἑτέρωθι ἐστραμμένοι ἠτάκτουν. Καὶ καθάπερ ἐν τῇ διατριβῇ ἀλλήλους τύπτουσιν, οὕτω καὶ τότε ἀλλήλους τύπτειν ἐκέλευσε καὶ ἀναιρεῖν. Καὶ πάλιν καθάπερ μαθήματα δούς, εἶτα ἀπαιτῶν, καὶ οὐχ εὑρίσκων, ἐκόλαζεν. Οἷον, ποῖα γράμματα τῆς δυνάμεως τοῦ θεοῦ τὰ γνωριστικά; τὰ ἐν Αἰγύπτῳ; Ναί, φησίν· Ἀλλὰ ταῦτα τὰ γράμματα τὰς πληγὰς ἐδήλου, ὅτι τοὺς ἐχθροὺς κολάζει, καὶ διδασκαλεῖον αὐτοῖς ἦν. Τί γὰρ ἦν ἄλλο ἡ κόλασις τῶν ἐχθρῶν, ἀλλ᾽ ἢ ὑμετέρα εὐεργεσία; Ἄλλως δὲ καὶ εὐηργέτει ὑμᾶς· καὶ ταὐτὸν γέγονεν, οἷον ἂν εἴ τις λέγοι μὲν εἰδέναι τὰ στοιχεῖα, σποράδην δὲ ἐρωτώμενος μὴ εὑρίσκοι, καὶ τύπτοιτο. Οὕτω κἀκεῖνοι ἔλεγον μὲν εἰδέναι τοῦ θεοῦ τὴν δύναμιν, σποράδην δὲ ἀπαιτούμενοι τὴν γνῶσιν, αὐτὴν οὐ παρείχοντο· διὸ καὶ ἐτύπτοντο.

Εἶδες ὕδωρ; ὀφείλεις ἀναμνησθῆναι τοῦ ὕδατος τοῦ ἐν Αἰγύπτῳ. Ὁ γὰρ ἀπὸ ὕδατος αἷμα ποιήσας, δυνήσεται καὶ τοῦτο ποιῆσαι· ὥσπερ καὶ ἡμεῖς λέγομεν πολλάκις τοῖς παιδίοις, ὅταν ἴδῃς ἐν τῷ βιβλίῳ τὸ ᾱ στοιχεῖον, ἀναμνήσθητι ὅτι ἐν τῇ πινακίδι αὐτὸ εἶχες. Εἶδες λιμόν; ἀναμνήσθητι ὅτι αὐτὸς ἦν ὁ τὰ γεννήματα ἀπολέσας. Εἶδες πολέμους; ἀναμνήσθητι τοῦ καταποντισμοῦ. Εἶδες ὅτι μεγάλοι οἱ τὴν γῆν οἰκοῦντες; ἀλλ᾽ οὐ τῶν Αἰγυπτίων μείζους·

for they didn't say, "Where is God?" but "Where is Moses?" and his presence alone was fearful. When, then, they did something wrong, see how he punished them. You see, God was intending to renounce them, but Moses didn't allow it. No, the whole thing was from God, like a father threatening, while Moses, being a schoolmaster, was entreating him and saying, "Forgive them for my sake, and I shall take them as my responsibility from now on." And so the wilderness became a school. And just as small children who have been spending much time studying want to leave, so too the Jews at that time were continually seeking Egypt, and saying as they wept, "*We are have perished, we are wholly consumed, we are completely undone*" [Exod 32:11; Num 17:12]. [**218**] And Moses broke their tablet [see Exod 32:19], having written on it, as it were, several words for them, which a schoolmaster would have done on taking the tablet and seeing that it was written badly, and throwing away the tablet itself in his desire to demonstrate fully his great anger; even if he has broken it, the father isn't angry. You see, he was busy writing, while they, not seeing him but distracted in other ways, became unruly. And just as in school the boys strike each other, so too on that occasion God commanded the Jews to strike and kill each other. And again, giving them lessons, as it were, then asking for them and finding that they hadn't learned them, he would punish them. For example, what kind of letters denoted the power of God? Those in Egypt? "Yes," says [someone], "but this alphabet disclosed the plagues [see Exod 8–11], because he punishes his enemies, and for them it was a school." For what else was the punishment of enemies but your benefit? And in other ways too he benefited you. And the same thing happened as if someone were to say that they did know their alphabet but when asked casually can't come up with it and are beaten. So they too said that they knew the power of God, but when asked casually about their knowledge were unable to provide it, and accordingly were also beaten.

Have you seen water? You should be reminded of the water in Egypt.[53] For the one who made blood out of water [see Exod 7:17] will be able to do this too. Just as we often say to little children, "When in a book you see the letter 'A', remember that you had it on your tablet." Have you seen famine? Remember that it was God who destroyed the crops [see Exod 9:18; 10:4]. Have you seen wars? Remember the drowning [see Exod 9]. Have you seen the important people who inhabit the land? No, they aren't more important

---

53. I.e., the Red Sea.

ὁ ἐκ μέσου αὐτῶν σε λαβών, οὐ πολλῷ μᾶλλον ἔξωθεν ὄντα σώσειεν ἄν; Ἀλλ᾽ οὐκ ᾔδεσαν σκορπιστὰ ἐρωτᾶσθαι τὰ στοιχεῖα· διὰ τοῦτο ἐτύπτοντο. Ἔφαγον καὶ ἔπιον, [219] καὶ ἀπελάκτισαν. Ἔδει ἐν τῷ μάννα μὴ ζητεῖν τρυφὴν, τὸ ἀπὸ ταύτης μαθόντας κακόν. Καὶ ταὐτὸν ἐποίουν, οἷον εἰ ἐλεύθερος παῖς εἰς διδασκαλεῖον πεμπόμενος, ἐπιζητοίη τὸ μετὰ τῶν δούλων ἄγεσθαι, καὶ ὑπηρετεῖν αὐτοῖς· οὕτω καὶ οὗτοι Αἴγυπτον ζητοῦντες· καὶ τὴν ἀναγκαίαν καὶ ἐλευθέρῳ πρέπουσαν τροφὴν λαβών, καὶ ἐν τῇ τοῦ πατρὸς τραπέζῃ καθήμενος, τῆς τῶν οἰκετῶν ἀπολαύειν θέλοι τῆς δυσώδους, τῆς ταραχῆς ἐμπεπλησμένης. Καὶ ἔλεγον τῷ Μωϋσῇ, "Ναὶ, κύριε, πάντα ὅσα ἂν εἴπῃς ποιήσομεν, καὶ ἀκουσόμεθα." Καὶ ὅπερ ἐπὶ τῶν σφόδρα ἀνελπίστων παίδων γίνεται, τοῦ πατρὸς αὐτοὺς ἀνελεῖν βουλομένου, ὁ διδάσκαλος παραιτεῖται συνεχῶς, τοῦτο καὶ τότε ἐγίνετο.

Τί δὴ ταῦτα ἡμῖν εἴρηται; Ὅτι παίδων οὐδὲν διαφέρομεν. Βούλει ἀκοῦσαι καὶ τὰ δόγματα αὐτῶν, πῶς παίδων ἐστί; "Ὀφθαλμὸν ἀντὶ ὀφθαλμοῦ, φησὶ, καὶ ὀδόντα ἀντὶ ὀδόντος." Οὐδὲν γὰρ οὕτω πρὸς ἄμυναν ὥρμηται, ὡς παιδικὴ διάνοια. Ἐπειδὴ γὰρ ἀλογίας ἐστὶ τὸ πάθος, πολλὴ δὲ ἡ ἀλογία, καὶ πολλὴ τοῦ λογισμοῦ ἡ ἐρημία ἐν ἐκείνῃ τῇ ἡλικίᾳ, εἰκότως τυραννεῖται ὑπὸ θυμοῦ τὸ παιδίον· καὶ τοσαύτη ἡ τυραννὶς, ὥστε πολλάκις προσπταίσαντας καὶ διαναστάντας, ἢ γόνυ τύπτειν ἀγανακτοῦντας, ἢ τὸ ὑποπόδιον καταστρέφειν, καὶ οὕτως ἀναπαύειν αὐτῶν τὴν ὀδύνην καὶ σβεννύναι τὴν ὀργήν. Τοιοῦτόν τι καὶ ὁ θεὸς ἐποίησεν, ὀφθαλμὸν ἀντὶ ὀφθαλμοῦ διδοὺς ἐκκόπτειν, καὶ ὀδόντα ἀντὶ ὀδόντος, καὶ Αἰγυπτίους ἀναιρῶν καὶ Ἀμαληκίτας τοὺς λελυπηκότας αὐτούς. Καὶ τοιαῦτα ἐπαγγέλλεται· ὥσπερ ἂν εἴποι τις, πάτερ, ὁ δεῖνά με ἐτύπτησεν· εἶτ᾽ ἐρεῖ ὁ πατήρ, κακὸς ἄνθρωπος ὁ δεῖνα, καὶ μισήσωμεν αὐτόν· οὕτω καὶ ὁ θεὸς, "Τοῖς ἐχθραίνουσί σοι, φησὶν, ἐχθρεύσω, καὶ τοὺς μισοῦντάς σε μισήσω." Καὶ πάλιν, ὅτε ὁ [220] Βαλαὰμ ηὔχετο, παιδικὴ ἦν ἡ συγκατάβασις ἡ γεγονυῖα αὐτοῖς. Καθάπερ γὰρ ἐπὶ τῶν παιδίων, ὅταν τι φοβηθέντες τῶν οὐ φοβερῶν, οἷον ἢ ἔριον, ἢ ἄλλο τι τοιοῦτον, ἐξαίφνης φοβοῦνται, ὥστε

than the Egyptians. Won't the one who took you out of the midst of them much more save you when you're out? But they didn't know how to answer questions about the letters out of order, for which they were beaten. They *ate* and drank [**219**] and *kicked* [Deut 32:15]. And in the case of the manna, they shouldn't have sought luxury, since they had learned the evils that came from it. And they acted in the same way as if a freeborn child, sent to school, should wish to consort with servants and to wait on them (in this way too the Jews sought after Egypt); and having received the necessary food, fitting for a freeborn child, and seated at their father's table, wishes to enjoy the malodorous table of the menials, which is full of rowdiness. And the Jews said to Moses, "*Yes, Lord, everything you have said we will do, and be obedient*" [Exod 24:3, 7]. And as happens in the case of extremely hopeless children, while their father wants to kill them, the schoolmaster makes frequent entreaties, this happened at that time too.

Now, why have we said this? Because we're no different from children. Do you want to hear the teachings of the Jews too, in that they are those of children? "*An eye for an eye,*" it says, "*and a tooth for a tooth*" [Lev 24:20; Deut 19:21]. You see, nothing is as vengeful as a childish mind. For since it's a passion of irrationality, and there's a great deal of irrationality, and a great deal of lack of thought processes at that age, it's likely that the small child is tyrannized by anger; and so great is the tyranny that often when the child stumbles and gets up again, either it strikes its knee out of irritation or else overturns the footstool, and in this way will allay the pain and check the rage.[54] Something like this God did too, allowing the Jews to knock out *an eye for an eye*, and *a tooth for a tooth*, and kill the Egyptians and the Amalekites who had caused them grief. And he promises such things, as if someone were to say, "Father, that fellow struck me." Then the father will say, "That person is bad, and let's hate him." And so God said, "*I will be an enemy to your enemies, and I shall hate those who hate you*" [Exod 23:22]. And again, when [**220**] Balaam prayed, the accommodation that happened to the Jews was childish [see Num 24; Deut 23:5].[55] You see, just as in the case of children, when they're afraid of things that aren't fearful, such as wool or something other that's similar, they are immediately afraid; so as

---

54. On Chrysostom's idea of the lack of reason in children, see Leyerle, "Appealing to Children," 259.

55. It is difficult to ascertain the meaning of this reference, even with Deut 23:5 in mind: "Nevertheless the Lord your God would not hearken to Balaam; but the Lord your God returned the curse into a blessing for you, because the Lord your God loved you."

μὴ ἐναπομεῖναι αὐτοῖς τὸν φόβον, ἄγομεν ὑπὸ τὰς ἐκείνων χεῖρας αὐτὸ, καὶ τίτθας ποιοῦμεν ὑποδεικνύειν· οὕτω καὶ ὁ θεὸς ἐποίησεν· ἐπειδὴ φοβερὸς ἦν ὁ μάντις, ἔτρεψεν αὐτοῦ τὸν φόβον εἰς θάρσος. Καὶ καθάπερ τὰ ἀπογαλακτιζόμενα τῶν παιδίων ἐν καλαθίσκοις πάντα ἔχουσιν· οὕτω κἀκείνοις πάντα ἐδίδου, καὶ πολλὴν τὴν τρυφήν. Ἀλλὰ τὸ παιδίον τὴν θηλὴν ἐπιζητεῖ· οὕτω καὶ οὗτοι τὴν Αἴγυπτον, καὶ τὰ ἐκεῖ κρέα.

Ὥστε καὶ διδάσκαλον καὶ τροφέα, καὶ παιδαγωγὸν οὐκ ἄν τις ἁμάρτοι τὸν Μωϋσέα προσειπών, καὶ πολλὴν τὴν σοφίαν τοῦ ἀνδρός. Οὐ γάρ ἐστιν ἴσον ἀνδρῶν ἤδη φιλοσόφων ἡγεῖσθαι, καὶ παίδων ἀλογίστων ἄρχειν. Καὶ, εἰ βούλεσθε καὶ ἕτερον ἀκοῦσαι, καθάπερ ἡ τροφὸς τῷ παιδίῳ λέγει, ὅταν ἀποπατῇς, ἀνάστειλόν σου τὰ ἱμάτια, καὶ μέχρι τοσούτου, ὅταν καθιζάνῃς· οὕτω καὶ ὁ Μωϋσῆς ἐποίει. Πάντα γὰρ τὰ πάθη τυραννεῖ ἐν τοῖς παισίν· οὐδέπω γὰρ ἔχει τὸν ἡνίοχον· κενοδοξία, ἐπιθυμία, ἀλογία, θυμός, βασκανία, καθάπερ ἐν παισὶν, οὕτως ἐκράτει· ἐνέπτυον, ἔτυπτον τὸν Μωϋσέα. Καὶ καθάπερ παιδίον λαμβάνει λίθον, καὶ πάντες βοῶμεν, ὦ μὴ ῥίψῃς· οὕτω κἀκεῖνοι λίθους ἐλάμβανον κατὰ τοῦ πατρὸς, ὁ δὲ ἔφευγε. Καὶ καθάπερ εἰ κόσμον τινὰ ἔχοι πατὴρ, τὸ παιδίον αἰτεῖ παρ' αὐτοῦ φιλόκοσμον ὄν· οὕτω δὴ οἱ περὶ Δαθὰν καὶ Ἀβειρὼν πεποιήκασι τῇ ἱερωσύνῃ ἐπαναστάντες. Καὶ βάσκανοι δὲ μάλιστα πάντων ἦσαν, καὶ μικρόψυχοι, καὶ κατὰ πάντα ἀτελεῖς.

Τότε οὖν ἔδει φανῆναι τὸν Χριστὸν, εἰπέ μοι; τότε τὰ διατάγματα ταῦτα δοῦναι τὰ φιλόσοφα, ὅτε ἐμαίνοντο ὑπὸ τῆς ἐπιθυμίας, ὅτε ἵπποι [221] ἦσαν θηλυμανεῖς, ὅτε χρημάτων δοῦλοι, ὅτε γαστρός; Ἀλλ' ἐξέχεεν ἂν τὰ τῆς φιλοσοφίας διδάγματα ἀνοήτοις οὖσι διαλεγόμενος· καὶ οὔτε ταῦτα, οὔτε ἐκεῖνα ἔμαθον ἄν. Καὶ ὥσπερ ὁ πρὸ τῶν στοιχείων ἀναγινώσκειν διδάσκων, οὐδέποτε οὐδὲ τὰ στοιχεῖα διδάξει, οὕτω δὴ καὶ τότε. Ἀλλ' οὐ νῦν· ἀλλὰ τῇ χάριτι τοῦ θεοῦ πολλὴ ἡ ἐπιείκεια, πολλὴ ἡ ἀρετὴ πανταχοῦ καταπεφύτευται. Εὐχαριστῶμεν οὖν ὑπὲρ πάντων, καὶ μὴ πολυπραγμονῶμεν. Τὸν γὰρ καιρὸν οὐχ ἡμεῖς ἴσμεν, ἀλλ' ὁ τοῦ καιροῦ ποιητὴς, καὶ τῶν αἰώνων δημιουργός.

not to prolong their fear we bring the object into their hands and make the nurses show it to them. This is what God did too: when the prophet was fearful to them, he turned their fear of him into confidence [see Exod 23:23]. And just as small children who are being weaned have all kinds of things in little baskets,[56] so too did he give the Jews all kinds of things, and a great number of treats. But the small child misses the breast; so too did the Jews miss Egypt and the fleshly things there.

So nobody would be wrong in calling Moses schoolmaster [see Exod 16:3], and nourishing father [see Num 11:4, 5], and pedagogue, and the wisdom of the man was great. You see, it isn't the same to guide men nowadays to philosophize and to rule unreasoning children. And if you wish to hear something else as well: just as the nurse says to the small child, "When you relieve yourself, pull up your clothes, and for as long you're sitting, as Moses did too" [see Deut 23:13]. You see, all the passions are tyrannous in children (for as yet they have nothing to bridle them), vainglory, desire, irrationality, anger, envy. Just as in children, so these prevailed in the Jews—they spat upon, they beat Moses. And just as a small child picks up a stone and everyone exclaims, "Oh, don't throw it," so too did the Jews pick up stones against their father, but he fled. And just as if a father were to have some ornament, the small child, being keen on ornaments, asks for it from him, so indeed did the followers of Dathan and Abiram act when they rebelled over the priesthood [see Num 16]. And more than everyone they were jealous and small-minded, and in all respects imperfect.

Therefore, should Christ have appeared at that time, tell me? At that time to have given them the teachings of philosophy, when they were mad with lust, when they were horses [**221**] mad for a mare, when they were the slaves of money, of the belly? No, he would've wasted the teaching of philosophy by speaking to those of no understanding, and they would've learned neither this nor that. And like the person who teaches reading before they have learned the alphabet will never teach even the alphabet, so indeed then also was it so. But not so now; no, by the grace of God a great deal of moderation, a great deal of virtue, has been planted everywhere. Therefore, let's rejoice on all accounts and not be meddlesome. For we don't know the time [see Mark 13:33], but the maker of time and the creator of the universe does.

---

56. On this custom, see Leyerle, who adduces other passages in Chrysostom pertaining to the practice ("Children and 'the Child,'" 561).

Πάντων τοίνυν αὐτῷ παραχωρῶμεν· τοῦτο γάρ ἐστι δοξάζειν τὸν θεὸν, τὸ μὴ ἀπαιτεῖν αὐτὸν εὐθύνας ὧν ποιεῖ. Οὕτω καὶ Ἀβραὰμ δόξαν ἔδωκε τῷ θεῷ, "Καὶ πληροφορηθεὶς, φησὶν, ὅτι ὃ ἐπήγγελται, δυνατός ἐστι καὶ ποιῆσαι." Ἐκεῖνος οὐδὲ τὸ μέλλον ἠρώτησεν· ἡμεῖς δὲ καὶ τῶν παρελθόντων ἐξετάζομεν τὸν λόγον. Ὅρα πόση ἡ ἄνοια, πόση ἡ ἀγνωμοσύνη. Ἀλλὰ παυσώμεθα λοιπόν· οὐδὲν γὰρ ἀπὸ τούτου κέρδος, ἀλλὰ καὶ πολλὴ ἡ βλάβη· καὶ εὐγνωμόνως διατεθῶμεν περὶ τὸν ἡμέτερον δεσπότην, καὶ δόξαν ἀναπέμψωμεν τῷ θεῷ, ἵνα ὑπὲρ ἀπάντων τὴν εὐχαριστίαν ἀναφέροντες, τῆς παρ᾽ αὐτοῦ φιλανθρωπίας ἀξιωθῶμεν, χάριτι καὶ φιλανθρωπίᾳ τοῦ μονογενοῦς αὐτοῦ, μεθ᾽ οὗ τῷ πατρὶ ἅμα τῷ ἁγίῳ πνεύματι δόξα, κράτος, τιμή, νῦν καὶ ἀεὶ καὶ εἰς τοὺς αἰῶνας τῶν αἰώνων. Ἀμήν.

Let's then yield to him on all accounts, for this is to glorify God, not to demand an account of what he does. In this way too Abraham gave glory to God, "*being fully persuaded*," it says, "*that what he promised, he is able also to do*" [Rom 4:21]. Nor did he ask about the future, but we scrutinize the account of even past events. See how great this stupidity is, how great this ingratitude. But let's stop here for the moment, for no gain comes of it, no—even a great deal of harm.[57] And let's be gratefully disposed toward our Master, and let's send up glory to God, so that offering thanksgiving on all accounts, we may be considered worthy of his loving-kindness, by the grace and loving-kindness of his only-begotten Son, with whom to the Father together with the Holy Spirit be glory, power, honor, now and forever and ever. Amen.

---

57. See n. 25 above on the homilist's shortening or lengthening a homily.

ΛΟΓΟΣ Ε.

Τὸ μυστήριον τὸ ἀποκεκρυμμένον ἀπὸ τῶν αἰώνων καὶ ἀπὸ τῶν γενεῶν, νυνὶ δὲ ἐφανερώθη τοῖς ἁγίοις αὐτοῦ, οἷς ἠθέλησεν ὁ Θεὸς γνωρίσαι, τίς ὁ πλοῦτος τῆς δόξης τοῦ μυστηρίου τοῦ ἐν τοῖς ἔθνεσιν, ὅς ἐστι Χριστὸς ἐν ὑμῖν, ἡ ἐλπὶς τῆς δόξης, ὃν ἡμεῖς καταγγέλλομεν, νουθετοῦντες πάντα ἄνθρωπον, καὶ διδάσκοντες πάντα ἄνθρωπον ἐν πάσῃ σοφίᾳ, ἵνα παραστήσωμεν πάντα ἄνθρωπον τέλειον ἐν Χριστῷ Ἰησοῦ.

Εἰπὼν ὧν ἐτύχομεν, καὶ δείξας τοῦ θεοῦ τὴν φιλανθρω-[222]πίαν καὶ τὴν τιμὴν τῷ μεγέθει τῶν δοθέντων, πάλιν ἑτέραν ἐπίτασιν εἰσάγει, ὅτι οὐδὲ πρὸ ἡμῶν τις αὐτὸ ἔμαθεν· ὃ καὶ ἐν τῇ πρὸς Ἐφεσίους ποιεῖ λέγων· Οὔτε ἄγγελοι, οὔτε ἀρχαὶ, οὔτε ἄλλη τις κτιστὴ δύναμις, ἀλλὰ μόνος ὁ τοῦ θεοῦ υἱὸς ᾔδει. Καὶ οὐχ ἁπλῶς κεκρυμμένον εἶπεν, ἀλλ' "ἀποκεκρυμμένον·" καὶ ὅτι εἰ καὶ νῦν γέγονεν, ἀλλὰ παλαιόν ἐστι, καὶ ἄνωθεν ταῦτα ὁ θεὸς ἐβούλετο, καὶ οὕτω διετετύπωτο· διὰ τί δὲ, οὐκέτι λέγει. "Ἀπὸ τῶν αἰώνων," φησίν· ἐξ ἀρχῆς, ὥσπερ γὰρ εἴποι τις. Καὶ μυστήριον εἰκότως καλεῖ, ὃ οὐδεὶς ᾔδει πλὴν ὁ θεός. Καὶ ποῦ κεκρυμμένον; Ἐν τῷ Χριστῷ· ὥσπερ ἐν τῇ πρὸς Ἐφεσίους λέγει· ἢ ὥσπερ ὅταν λέγῃ ὁ προφήτης, "Ἀπὸ τοῦ αἰῶνος, καὶ ἕως τοῦ αἰῶνος σὺ εἶ." "Νυνὶ δὲ ἐφανερώθη, φησί, τοῖς ἁγίοις αὐτοῦ." Ὥστε τῆς οἰκονομίας ἐστὶ τοῦ θεοῦ τὸ ὅλον. "Νυνὶ δὲ, φησίν, ἐφανερώθη." Οὐκ εἶπεν, ἐγένετο, ἀλλ', "ἐφανερώθη τοῖς ἁγίοις αὐτοῦ." Ὥστε καὶ ἔτι νῦν κρύπτεται, εἴγε τοῖς ἁγίοις ἐφανερώθη μόνοις.

Μὴ τοίνυν ὑμᾶς ἀπατάτωσαν ἐκεῖνοι· οὐ γὰρ ἴσασι. Διὰ τί μόνοις; "Οἷς ἠθέλησε," φησίν. Ὅρα πῶς πανταχοῦ ἐπιστομίζει τὰς ἐρωτήσεις αὐτῶν. "Οἷς ἠθέλησεν ὁ θεὸς, φησὶ, γνωρίσαι." Τὸ δὲ θέλειν αὐτοῦ, οὐκ ἄλογον. Χάριτος μᾶλλον ὑπευθύνους ποιῶν, ἢ ἀφιεὶς αὐτοὺς ἐπὶ κατορθώματι μέγα φρονεῖν, εἶπεν, "Οἷς ἠθέλησε γνωρίσαι." "Τίς ὁ πλοῦτος τῆς δόξης τοῦ μυστηρίου τούτου ἐν τοῖς ἔθνεσι." Σεμνῶς εἶπε, καὶ ὄγκον ἐπέθηκεν, ἀπὸ πολλῆς διαθέσεως ἐπιτάσεις ζητῶν ἐπιτάσεων. Καὶ γὰρ καὶ τοῦτο ἐπιτάσεως, τὸ ἀορίστως

The mystery hidden away for ages and generations, but now made manifest to his saints. To them God wished to make known what the wealth of the glory of this mystery is among the gentiles, which is Christ in you, the hope of glory. Him we proclaim, warning every person and teaching every person in all wisdom, so that we may present every person complete in Christ Jesus [Col 1:26–28].

Having said what we have obtained, and demonstrated God's loving-kindness [**222**] and the honor by the greatness of the things given, again Paul introduces another emphasis, namely, that not even before us did anyone know it. This is what he does in the Letter to the Ephesians, when he says that neither angels nor principalities nor any other created power, but only the Son of God, knew [see Eph 3:5, 9–10]. And he didn't simply say "hidden" but *"hidden away,"* and that even if it happened in the present, still it is old, and from the beginning God willed these things, and they were so arranged, but for what reason Paul doesn't yet say. *"For ages,"* he says, as if someone were to say "from the beginning." And with reason does he call it a mystery, which nobody knew except God. And where was it hidden? In Christ, as he says in the Letter to the Ephesians [see Eph 3:9], or as when the prophet said, *"From everlasting to everlasting, you are"* [Ps 90:2 LXX]. *"But now it is made manifest,"* he says, *"to his saints."* The upshot is that this is the whole of God's plan. *"Now,"* he says, *"it is made manifest."* He didn't say, "it's happened," but *"it is manifest to his saints,"* such that it's hidden up to now, in that it's manifest to the saints alone.

Don't, therefore, let them deceive you, for they don't know. Why to them alone? *"To whom he wished,"* says Paul. See how everywhere he puts a muzzle on their questions. *"To whom,"* he says, *"God wished to make known."* But God's will isn't without reason. No, Paul said this making them accountable for grace, or allowing them to have grand thoughts about their achievement, he said, *"What the richness of the glory of this mystery is among the gentiles."* He spoke solemnly and placed importance on it, seeking from great earnestness for emphasis on emphasis. Indeed,

εἰπεῖν, "ὁ πλοῦτος τῆς δόξης τοῦ μυστηρίου τούτου ἐν τοῖς ἔθνεσι." Μάλιστα γὰρ ἐν τοῖς ἔθνεσι φαίνεται, καθὼς καὶ ἀλλαχοῦ φησι, "Τὰ δὲ ἔθνη ὑπὲρ ἐλέους [223] δοξάσαι τὸν θεόν." Φαίνεται μὲν γὰρ καὶ ἐν ἑτέροις, πολλῷ δὲ πλέον ἐν τούτοις ἡ πολλὴ τοῦ μυστηρίου δόξα. Τὸ γὰρ ἀθρόον ἀνθρώπους λίθων ἀναισθητοτέρους εἰς ἀγγέλων ἀγαγεῖν ἀξίωμα ἁπλῶς διὰ ψιλῶν ῥημάτων καὶ πίστεως μόνης, χωρὶς ἐργωδίας πάσης, ὄντως δόξα καὶ πλοῦτος μυστηρίου· ὥσπερ ἂν εἴ τις κύνα λιμῷ καὶ ψώρᾳ διεφθαρμένον, αἰσχρόν τινα καὶ δυσειδῆ καὶ οὐδὲ κινεῖσθαι δυνάμενον, ἀλλ᾽ ἐρριμμένον, ἐξαίφνης καὶ ἄνθρωπον ποιήσειε, καὶ ἐπὶ τοῦ θρόνου δείξειε τοῦ βασιλικοῦ. Τοὺς λίθους προσεκύνουν, καὶ τὴν γῆν· ἔμαθον ὅτι καὶ οὐρανοῦ καὶ ἡλίου ἀμείνους εἰσί, καὶ ὁ κόσμος ἅπας αὐτοῖς δουλεύει· αἰχμάλωτοι καὶ δεσμῶται ἦσαν τοῦ διαβόλου· ἀθρόον γεγόνασιν αὐτοῦ τῆς κεφαλῆς ἐπάνω, καὶ ἐπέταττον αὐτῷ, καὶ ἐμάστιζον αὐτόν· δαιμόνων ὄντες αἰχμάλωτοι καὶ δοῦλοι, τοῦ τῶν ἀγγέλων δεσπότου καὶ τῶν ἀρχαγγέλων γεγόνασι σῶμα· οὐδὲ τί ἐστι θεὸς εἰδότες, γεγόνασιν ἐξαίφνης καὶ σύνθρονοι τοῦ θεοῦ. Βούλει μυρίους ἰδεῖν ἀναβαθμοὺς, οὓς ὑπερεπήδησαν; Ἔδει μαθεῖν πρῶτον, ὅτι οἱ λίθοι οὐ θεοί· δεύτερον, ὅτι οὐ μόνον οὐ θεοί, ἀλλὰ καὶ ἀνθρώπων ἐλάττους· τρίτον, ὅτι καὶ ἀλόγων· τέταρτον, ὅτι καὶ φυτῶν· πέμπτον, ὅτι τὰ ἄκρα συνήγαγον εἰς ταὐτόν, ὅτι οὐ μόνον λίθοι, ἀλλ᾽ οὐδὲ γῆ, οὐδὲ ζῶα, οὐδὲ φυτά, οὐδὲ ἄνθρωπος, οὐδὲ οὐρανός· ἢ ἄνωθεν πάλιν, ὅτι οὐ λίθοι, οὐ ζῶα, οὐ φυτά, οὐ στοιχεῖα, οὐ τὰ ἄνω, οὐ τὰ κάτω, οὐκ ἄνθρωπος, οὐ δαίμονες, οὐκ ἄγγελοι, οὐκ ἀρχάγγελοι, οὐχ ἑτέρα τις τῶν ἄνω δυνάμεων ἐκείνων ὑπὸ τῆς ἀνθρωπίνης φύσεως θεραπεύεσθαι ὀφείλει. Καθάπερ ἀπό τινος βυθοῦ ἀνιμωμένους ἔδει μαθεῖν, ὅτι ὁ πάντων δεσπότης οὗτος θεός ἐστιν, ὅτι θεραπεύειν αὐτὸν μόνον χρή, ὅτι καλὸν ἡ θαυμαστὴ πολιτεία, ὅτι ὁ παρὼν θάνατος οὐ θάνατος, ὅτι ἡ ζωὴ οὐ ζωή, ὅτι τὸ σῶμα ἀνίσταται, ὅτι ἄφθαρτον γίνεται, ὅτι εἰς οὐρανοὺς ἄνεισιν, ὅτι ἀθανασίας ἐπιτυγχάνει, ὅτι μετὰ ἀγγέλων ἕστηκεν, ὅτι μεθίσταται. Ἀλλὰ τοῦτον τὸν ἐκεῖ κάτω, ταῦτα πάντα ὑπερπηδήσαντα, ἄνω ἐκάθισεν ἐπὶ τοῦ θρόνου, τῶν ἀγγέλων καὶ τῶν ἀρχαγγέλων καὶ τῶν θρόνων καὶ τῶν κυριοτήτων ποιήσας κυριώτερον τὸν ὑποκάτω λίθων ὄντα. Ὄντως, "τίς ὁ πλοῦ-[224]τος τῆς δόξης τοῦ μυστηρίου τούτου." Ὥσπερ ἂν εἴ τις μωρόν τινα φιλόσοφον ἐξαίφνης δείξειε· μᾶλλον δὲ ὅσα ἂν εἴποι τις, οὐδὲν ἐρεῖ· καὶ γὰρ καὶ τὰ τοῦ Παύλου ἀόριστά ἐστι. "Τίς ὁ πλοῦτος, φησὶ, τῆς δόξης τοῦ μυστηρίου τούτου ἐν τοῖς ἔθνεσιν, ὅς ἐστι Χριστὸς ἐν ὑμῖν." Πάλιν ἔδει μαθεῖν, ὅτι ὁ πάντων ἀνώτερος, καὶ ὁ ἀγγέλων καὶ

this is also an emphasis, his saying in an undefined way, "*The riches of the glory of this mystery among the gentiles.*" For it's extremely evident that it appeared among the gentiles, as he says elsewhere too: "*That the gentiles* [223] *might glorify God for his mercy*" [Rom 15:9]. You see, the great glory of the mystery is evident even in others, but more in these people. For suddenly to bring people more senseless than stones to the dignity of angels, simply through bare words and faith alone, without any difficulty, is indeed a glory and wealth of mystery, just as if someone were to take a smelly dog, completely consumed by hunger and mange, foul and loathsome, and unable even to move, but cast out, and make it at once a human being and display it on the royal throne. They used to worship stones and the earth: they learned that they are better than heaven and sun and that the whole world serves them; they were prisoners and captives of the devil; suddenly they are above his head and command and scourge him; prisoners and captives of the demons, they have become the body of the Master of the angels and archangels; from not knowing what God is, they have become at once sharers even in God's throne. Do you want to see the myriad steps they jumped over? First, it was necessary for them to learn that stones are not gods; second, that not only are they not gods, but inferior even to human beings; third, even to animals; fourth, even to plants; fifth, that they brought together the extremes into the same thing, not only stones, but not even earth, not even animals, nor plants, nor a human being, nor heaven; or to begin again, that not stones, not animals, not plants, not elements, not things above, not things below, not a human being, not demons, not angels, not archangels, not any other of those powers above, should be worshiped by human nature. Being drawn up, as it were, from some deep place, they had to learn that the Master of all is the one who is God, that it was necessary to worship him alone, that the admirable life is a good thing, that death in the present isn't death, that life isn't life, that the body is raised, that it becomes incorruptible, that it ascends to heaven, that it attains immortality, that it stands with angels, that it's removed from here. But the one who was here below, having jumped over all those steps, he has seated on high on the throne, having made the one who was subordinate to stones higher in dominion than the angels and the archangels and the thrones and the dominions. Truly *what is the riches* [224] *of the glory of this mystery?* Just as if someone were suddenly to show a fool to be some philosopher; no, whatever someone would say, they would say nothing, for even the words of Paul are unlimited. "*What is the riches,*" he says, "*of the glory of this mystery among the gentiles, which is Christ in you.*" Again, they

ἄρχων καὶ τῶν ἄλλων ἁπασῶν δυνάμεων κρατῶν, κατέβη κάτω, καὶ ἄνθρωπος γέγονε, καὶ μυρία ἔπαθε, καὶ ἀνέστη, καὶ ἀνελήφθη. Ταῦτα πάντα μυστηρίου ἦν. Καὶ μετ᾽ ἐγκωμίου τίθησι λέγων, "ὅς ἐστι Χριστὸς ἐν ὑμῖν." Εἰ δὲ ἐν ὑμῖν ἐστι, τί ἀγγέλους ζητεῖτε; "Τοῦ μυστηρίου τούτου." Ἔστι γὰρ καὶ ἄλλο μυστήριον. Ἀλλὰ τοῦτο ὄντως μυστήριον, ὃ οὐδεὶς οἶδεν, ὅ ἐστι θαυμαστὸν, ὃ παρὰ τὴν κοινὴν προσδοκίαν, ὃ ἐκρύπτετο. "Ὅς ἐστι Χριστὸς ἐν ὑμῖν, φησὶν, ἡ ἐλπὶς τῆς δόξης, ὃν ἡμεῖς καταγγέλλομεν," ἄνωθεν αὐτὸν φέροντες· ὃν ἡμεῖς, οὐκ ἄγγελοι· "διδάσκοντες καὶ νουθετοῦντες," οὐκ ἐπιτακτικῶς οὐδὲ μετὰ ἀνάγκης· καὶ γὰρ καὶ τοῦτο τῆς τοῦ θεοῦ φιλανθρωπίας, τὸ μὴ τυραννικῶς προσάγεσθαι. Ἐπειδὴ τὸ, "διδάσκοντες," μέγα ἦν, ἐπήγαγε, "νουθετοῦντες," ὅπερ ἦν μᾶλλον πατρὸς, ἢ διδασκάλου. "Ὃν ἡμεῖς, φησὶ, καταγγέλλομεν, νουθετοῦντες πάντα ἄνθρωπον, καὶ διδάσκοντες πάντα ἄνθρωπον ἐν πάσῃ σοφίᾳ." "Ὥστε σοφίας δεῖ πάσης. Τουτέστι, πάντα ἐν σοφίᾳ λέγοντες. Τὸ γὰρ τὰ τοιαῦτα δυνηθῆναι μαθεῖν, οὐ τῶν τυχόντων ἐστίν. "Ἵνα παραστήσωμεν πάντα ἄνθρωπον τέλειον ἐν Χριστῷ Ἰησοῦ." Τί λέγεις; πάντα ἄνθρωπον; Ναὶ, φησὶ, τοῦτο σπουδάζομεν. Τί γὰρ εἰ μὴ γίνεται τοῦτο; ἔσπευδεν ὁ μακάριος Παῦλος. "Τέλειον." Ἆρα τοῦτο τελειότης, ἐκεῖνο δὲ ἀτελές· ὥστε κἂν μὴ πᾶσάν τις ἔχῃ τὴν σοφίαν, ἀτελής ἐστι. "Τέλειον ἐν Χριστῷ Ἰησοῦ," οὐκ ἐν νόμῳ οὐδὲ ἐν ἀγγέλοις· ἐκεῖνο γὰρ οὐ τέλειον. "Ἐν Χριστῷ," τουτέστιν, ἐν τῇ γνώσει τοῦ Χριστοῦ. Ὁ εἰδὼς τί ἐποίησεν ὁ Χριστὸς, μεῖζον φρονήσει ἀγγέλων.

"Ἐν [225] Χριστῷ Ἰησοῦ· εἰς ὃ καὶ κοπιῶ ἀγωνιζόμενος." Καὶ οὐχ ἁπλῶς σπουδάζω, φησὶν, οὐδὲ ὡς ἔτυχεν, ἀλλὰ, "κοπιῶ ἀγωνιζόμενος," μετὰ πολλῆς τῆς σπουδῆς, μετὰ πολλῆς τῆς ἀγρυπνίας. Εἰ ἐγὼ ὑπὲρ τῶν ὑμετέρων ἀγαθῶν οὕτως ἀγρυπνῶ, πολλῷ μᾶλλον ὑμεῖς ὀφείλετε. Εἶτα πάλιν δεικνὺς θεῖον ὄν, "Κατὰ τὴν ἐνέργειαν αὐτοῦ, φησὶ, τὴν ἐνεργουμένην ἐν ἐμοὶ ἐν δυνάμει." Δείκνυσιν ὅτι τοῦ θεοῦ τοῦτο ἔργον ἐστίν. Ὁ τοίνυν ἰσχυρόν με ποιῶν εἰς τοῦτο, δῆλον ὅτι τοῦτο βούλεται· διὸ καὶ ἀρχόμενός φησι, "διὰ θελήματος θεοῦ." Ὥστε οὐ μόνον μετριάζων αὐτὸ τέθεικεν, ἀλλὰ καὶ ἐπαληθεύων τῷ λόγῳ, καὶ ἀγωνιζόμενος. Τοῦτο εἰπὼν, δείκνυσιν ὅτι πολλοὶ μάχονται πρὸς αὐτόν.

Εἶτα ἡ φιλοστοργία πολλή· "Θέλω γὰρ ὑμᾶς εἰδέναι ἡλίκον ἀγῶνα ἔχω περὶ ὑμῶν, καὶ τῶν ἐν Λαοδικείᾳ." Εἶτα ἵνα μὴ δόξῃ τῆς αὐτῶν ἀσθενείας εἶναι τοῦτο, συνῆψε καὶ ἑτέρους, καὶ οὐδέπω κατέγνω. Ἀλλὰ διὰ τί, "Καὶ ὅσοι οὐχ ἑωράκασι τὸ πρόσωπόν μου ἐν σαρκί," φησί; Θείως δείκνυσιν ἐνταῦθα, ὅτι ἑώρων συνεχῶς ἐν πνεύματι. Μαρτυρεῖ δὲ αὐτοῖς ἀγάπην πολλήν. "Ἵνα

had to learn that the one who is above all, ruling the angels and prevailing over all the other powers, came down below, and was made a human being and suffered myriad things, and rose, and was taken up.

All these things are part of the mystery. And Paul lays this down with a tribute, saying, "*Which is Christ in you.*" But if he's in you, why do you seek angels? *Of this mystery.* You see, there's yet another mystery. But this is really a mystery, which nobody knew, which is wonderful, which exceeds common expectation, which was hidden. "*Which is Christ in you,*" he says, "*the hope of glory, whom we proclaim,*" bringing him from above (we, not angels). *Teaching and warning,* not in a commanding manner, nor with force, for this too is part of God's love of humankind—that they are not brought to him in the manner of a tyrant. Since the word *teaching* was a great thing, Paul added *warning,* which is the word of a father rather than a teacher. "*Whom we proclaim,*" he says, "*warning every person and teaching every person in all wisdom.*" So there is need of all wisdom, that is, saying everything in wisdom. You see, the ability to learn such things is not possible for just anyone. *So that we may present every person complete in Christ Jesus.* Why do you say "*every person*"? "Yes," says Paul, "we're eager for that." What then if this doesn't happen? Blessed Paul was eager. *Complete.* Therefore, this is completeness, that is incomplete. *Complete in Christ Jesus,* not in the law, nor in angels, for that is not completeness. *In Christ,* that is, in the knowledge of Christ. The one who knows what Christ has done has higher thoughts than angels do.

In [225] *Christ Jesus. For this I toil as I strive.* And he didn't say simply, "I'm eager," nor as if it were fortuitous, but, "*I toil as I strive,*" with great eagerness, with great watchfulness. "If I'm so watchful with regard to your good, you should be so much more." Then again, showing that it's from God, "*According to his activity,*" he says, "*which acts with power in me.*" He shows that this is the work of God. "Therefore the one who makes me strong for this clearly wants it." This is why at the beginning he says, "*by the will of God.*" The upshot is that it isn't out of modesty that he expresses this, but also by substantiating the word and striving. In saying this he demonstrates that many are fighting against him.

Then great is his affection. "*I wish you to know the magnitude of the struggle I have for your sakes, and for those in Laodicea*" [Col 2:1]. Then, lest this seem to stem from their own weakness, he joined others with them and so far didn't condemn them. But why does he say, "*And all those who have not seen my face in the flesh*"? He demonstrates in this passage in a divine manner that they saw him constantly in the Spirit. And he bears wit-

παρακληθῶσιν αἱ καρδίαι αὐτῶν, συμβιβασθέντων ἐν ἀγάπῃ, καὶ εἰς πάντα πλοῦτον τῆς πληροφορίας τῆς συνέσεως, εἰς ἐπίγνωσιν τοῦ μυστηρίου τοῦ θεοῦ πατρὸς καὶ τοῦ Χριστοῦ· ἐν ᾧ εἰσι πάντες οἱ θησαυροὶ τῆς σοφίας καὶ τῆς γνώσεως ἀπόκρυφοι."

Ἤδη λοιπὸν σπεύδει καὶ ὠδίνει ἐμβαλεῖν εἰς τὸ δόγμα, οὔτε κατηγορῶν, οὔτε ἀπαλλάττων αὐτοὺς τῆς κατηγορίας. "Ἀγῶνα ἔχω," φησίν· ἵνα τί; Ἵνα συμβιβασθῶσιν. Ὃ λέγει, τοιοῦτόν ἐστιν· ἵνα στῶσι βέβαιοι ἐν τῇ πίστει. Ἀλλ' οὐ τίθησιν οὕτως, ἀλλ' ὑποτέμνεται τὰ τῆς κατηγορίας. Τουτέστιν, ἵνα ἑνωθῶσι μετὰ ἀγάπης, οὐ μετὰ ἀνάγκης, οὐδὲ μετὰ βίας. Ὅπερ γὰρ εἶπον, ἀνεπαχθής ἐστιν ἀεὶ αὐτοῖς ἐπιτρέπων, καὶ διὰ τοῦτό [226] ἀγωνιῶν, ἐπειδὴ μετὰ ἀγάπης, καὶ ἑκόντας βούλομαι. Οὐχ ἁπλῶς τῷ στόματι, οὐδὲ ἁπλῶς τὴν συναγωγὴν βούλομαι γίνεσθαι, ἀλλ' "ἵνα αἱ καρδίαι αὐτῶν παρακληθῶσι."

"Συμβιβασθέντων ἐν ἀγάπῃ εἰς πάντα πλοῦτον τῆς πληροφορίας τῆς συνέσεως." Τουτέστιν, ἵνα ὑπὲρ μηδενὸς ἀμφιβάλλωσιν, ἵνα ὑπὲρ πάντων πεπληροφορημένοι ὦσι. Πληροφορίαν δὲ εἶπον τὴν διὰ πίστεως· ἔστι γὰρ πληροφορία ἡ διὰ λογισμῶν, ἀλλ' οὐδενὸς λόγου ἐκείνη ἀξία. Οἶδα, φησίν, ὅτι πιστεύετε, ἀλλὰ πληροφορηθῆναι ὑμᾶς βούλομαι, οὐκ εἰς τὸν πλοῦτον μόνον, ἀλλ' εἰς πάντα τὸν πλοῦτον, ἵνα καὶ ἐν πᾶσι καὶ ἐπιτεταμένως πεπληροφορημένοι ἦτε. Καὶ θέα τὴν σύνεσιν τοῦ μακαρίου τούτου. Οὐκ εἶπεν, ὅτι κακῶς ποιεῖτε, ὅτι οὐ πεπληροφόρησθε, καὶ κατηγόρησεν· ἀλλ', οὐκ ἴστε πῶς σπουδάζω, ἵνα πληροφορηθῆτε μετὰ συνέσεως, οὐχ ἁπλῶς. Ἐπειδὴ γὰρ εἶπε πίστιν, μὴ νομίσητε, φησίν, ὅτι ἁπλῶς καὶ ἀνονήτως εἶπον, ἀλλὰ μετὰ συνέσεως, μετὰ ἀγάπης. "Εἰς ἐπίγνωσιν τοῦ μυστηρίου τοῦ θεοῦ πατρός, καὶ τοῦ Χριστοῦ." Ὥστε τοῦ θεοῦ τοῦτό ἐστι τὸ μυστήριον, τὸ διὰ τοῦ υἱοῦ προσάγεσθαι. "Καὶ τοῦ Χριστοῦ, ἐν ᾧ εἰσι πάντες οἱ θησαυροὶ τῆς σοφίας καὶ τῆς γνώσεως ἀπόκρυφοι." Εἰ δὲ ἐν αὐτῷ εἰσιν, ἄρα σοφῶς καὶ νῦν ἦλθε. Τίνος οὖν ἕνεκεν ἐγκαλοῦσί τινες τῶν ἀνοήτων; Ὅρα πῶς τοῖς ἁπλουστέροις διαλέγεται· "Ἐν ᾧ εἰσι πάντες οἱ θησαυροί." Αὐτὸς πάντα οἶδεν. "Ἀπόκρυφοι." Μὴ γὰρ δὴ νομίσητε ἤδη τὸ πᾶν ἔχειν· ἀπόκρυφοί εἰσι καὶ ἀπὸ ἀγγέλων, οὐκ ἀφ' ὑμῶν μόνον· ὥστε παρ' αὐτοῦ δεῖ πάντα αἰτεῖν· αὐτὸς δίδωσι σοφίαν καὶ γνῶσιν. Τῷ μὲν οὖν, θησαυροί, εἰπεῖν, τὸ πολὺ δείκνυσι· τῷ δὲ, πάντες, τὸ μηδὲ ἀγνοεῖν· τῷ δὲ, ἀπόκρυφοι, τὸ μόνος εἰδέναι. "Τοῦτο δὲ λέγω, ἵνα μή τις ὑμᾶς παραλογίζηται ἐν πιθανολογίᾳ." Ὁρᾷς ὅτι διὰ τοῦτο εἶπον, φησί, ταῦτα,

ness to their great love: *So that their hearts may be encouraged, being knit together in love, and to have all the riches of the assured understanding, to have the knowledge of the mystery of the Father and of Christ, in whom are hidden all the treasures of wisdom and knowledge* [Col 2:2].

Already for the future he is keen and in pangs,[58] to enter into teaching, neither accusing them nor excusing them from accusation. "*I have a struggle*," he says. For what purpose? So that they may be *knit together*. What he means is like this: that they may stand firm in the faith. But he didn't express it in this way but undercut the accusation. That is, that they may be united with love, not with necessity, nor with force. For, as I have said, Paul was always avoiding offense, and for this reason [**226**] "struggling, since I wish it to be with love, and willingly. I don't simply wish them to come together, nor simply by lip service, but so that *their hearts may be encouraged*."

Being knit together in love, to have all the riches of assured understanding. That is, that they may have doubts about nothing, that they may be assured about all things. But he meant the assurance that comes from faith, for there is an assurance that comes from argument, but that is worth no consideration. "I know," he says, "that you believe, but I want you to be assured, not *to have riches only*, but to have all riches, so that you may be both intense and in all things." And behold the understanding of this blessed man. He didn't say, "You who do evil are not assured," and accuse them, but "you don't know how eager I am for you to be assured, not simply that, but with understanding." You see, since he spoke of faith, "don't consider," he says, "that I meant simply and unintelligently, but with understanding, with love." *To have knowledge of the mystery of God the Father and of Christ.* So that is the mystery of God, which was brought through the Son. *And of Christ in whom all the treasures of wisdom and knowledge are hidden.* But if they are in him, then he came in wisdom and at this time. Therefore, why do some senseless people make objections? "See how he discourses with the simpler people." *In whom are all the treasures.* Christ knows everything. *Hidden.* For don't consider that you have everything: they're hidden even from angels, not only from you, so that you should make all your requests through him. He alone gives wisdom and knowledge. *But I say this so that nobody may delude you with beguiling speech* [Col 2:4]. "Do you see that I've

---

58. The image is from childbirth. See Matt 24:8; Mark 13:8; Rom 8:22; 1 Thess 5:3; Rev 12:2.

ἵνα μὴ παρὰ ἀνθρώπων ζητῆτε. "Παραλογίζηται, φησὶν, ἐν πιθανολογίᾳ." Τί [227] γὰρ, εἰ πιθανῶς λέγει; "Εἰ γὰρ καὶ τῇ σαρκὶ ἄπειμι, ἀλλὰ τῷ πνεύματι σὺν ὑμῖν εἰμι." Τὸ ἀκόλουθον τοῦτο ἦν εἰπεῖν, εἰ γὰρ καὶ τῇ σαρκὶ ἄπειμι, ἀλλ᾽ ὅμως οἶδα τοὺς ἀπατεῶνας· νῦν δὲ εἰς ἐγκώμιον κατέληξε. "Χαίρων καὶ βλέπων ὑμῶν τὴν τάξιν καὶ τὸ στερέωμα τῆς εἰς Χριστὸν πίστεως ὑμῶν." "Τὴν τάξιν, τὴν εὐταξίαν, φησί. "Καὶ τὸ στερέωμα τῆς εἰς Χριστὸν πίστεως." Ταῦτα ἐγκωμίων μᾶλλόν ἐστι. Καὶ οὐκ εἶπε, τὴν πίστιν, ἀλλὰ, "τὸ στερέωμα," καθάπερ πρὸς στρατιώτας εὐτάκτως ἑστῶτας καὶ βεβαίως. Τὸ στερρὸν οὐκ ἀπάτη, οὐ πειρασμὸς διασαλεύει. Οὐ μόνον, φησὶν, οὐ πεπτώκατε, ἀλλ᾽ οὐδὲ τὴν τάξιν ὑμῶν συνέχεέ τις. Ἐπέστησεν ἑαυτὸν αὐτοῖς, ἵνα ὡς παρόντα φοβῶνται· ἡ γὰρ τάξις οὕτω φυλάττεται. Ἀπὸ τοῦ στερεώματος τὸ πεπυκνωμένον· οὕτω γὰρ γίνεται στερέωμα, ὅταν πολλὰ συναγαγὼν συγκολλήσῃς πυκνῶς καὶ ἀδιασπάστως· οὕτω στερέωμα γίνεται, οἷον ἐπὶ τοίχου. Τοῦτο δὲ τῆς ἀγάπης ἔργον ἐστί· τοὺς γὰρ καθ᾽ ἑαυτοὺς ὄντας, ὅταν ἀκριβῶς συγκολλήσῃ καὶ συνάψῃ, στερροὺς ἐργάζεται. Καὶ ἡ πίστις πάλιν τὸ αὐτὸ ποιεῖ, ὅταν μὴ ἀφῇ λογισμοὺς ἐπεισελθεῖν. Ὥσπερ γὰρ οἱ λογισμοὶ διαιροῦσι καὶ σαλεύουσι, οὕτως ἡ πίστις στερεοῖ καὶ παγῆναι ποιεῖ.

Ἐπειδὴ γὰρ μείζονα ἢ κατὰ ἀνθρώπινον λογισμὸν εὐηργέτησεν ἡμᾶς ὁ θεός, εἰκότως τὴν πίστιν ἐπεισήγαγεν. Οὐκ ἔστιν εἶναι στερρὸν τὸν λογισμοὺς ἀπαιτοῦντα. Ἰδοὺ γὰρ τὰ σεμνὰ ἡμῶν πάντα πῶς ἔρημα λογισμῶν, καὶ πίστεως ἔχεται μόνης. Οὐκ ἔστιν οὐδαμοῦ ὁ θεός, καὶ πανταχοῦ ἐστι. Τί τούτου ἀλογώτερον; Ἕκαστον καθ᾽ ἑαυτὸ ἀπορίας γέμει. Οὐ γὰρ δὴ ἐν τόπῳ ἐστὶν, οὐδὲ τόπος ἐστί τις ἐν ᾧ ἐστιν. Οὐκ ἐγένετο, οὐχ ἑαυτὸν ἐποίησεν, οὐκ ἤρξατο τοῦ εἶναι. Ποῖος ταῦτα λογισμὸς καταδέξεται, ἂν μὴ πίστις ᾖ; ἢ οὐχὶ κατάγελως εἶναι δοκεῖ, καὶ αἰνίγματος μᾶλλον οὐκ ἔχει τέλος;

[228] Τὸ μὲν οὖν ἄναρχον αὐτοῦ καὶ ἀγέννητον καὶ ἀπερίγραφον καὶ ἄπειρον, οὕτως ἄπορον· τὸ δὲ ἀσώματον ἴδωμεν, μήποτε λογισμῷ ἐξετάσαι δυνάμεθα. Ἀσώματός ἐστιν ὁ θεός. Τί ἐστιν, ἀσώματος; Ῥῆμα ψιλὸν μόνον· ἡ γὰρ ἔννοια οὐδὲν ἐδέξατο, οὐδὲ ἐνετύπωσεν ἑαυτῇ· κἂν γὰρ ἀνατυπώσῃ, εἰς φύσιν ἔρχεται, καὶ τὰ τοῦ σώματος ποιητικά. Ὥστε λέγει μὲν τὸ στόμα, οὐκ οἶδε δὲ ἡ διάνοια τί λέγει, ἢ ἓν μόνον, ὅτι οὐκ ἔστι σῶμα· τοῦτο μόνον οἶδε. Καὶ τί λέγω ἐπὶ θεοῦ; ἐπὶ γὰρ ψυχῆς τί ἐστι τὸ ἀσώματον, τῆς γενομένης, τῆς ἐγκεκλεισμένης, τῆς περιγραφομένης; εἰπὲ, δεῖξον. Ἀλλ᾽ οὐκ ἂν ἔχοις. Ἀήρ

said these things on this account," he says, "so that you may not seek it from human beings?" "*Delude you*," he says, "*with beguiling speech.*" But what [227] then if anyone speaks persuasively? *For if I am absent in the flesh, I am yet with you in the spirit* [Col 2:5]. The consequence of this was to say, "For even if I am absent in the flesh, yet nevertheless I know the deceivers," but he's ended with praise. *Rejoicing and seeing your order and steadfastness in your faith in Christ* [Col 2:5]. *Your order*: he means "your good order." *And steadfastness of faith in Christ*. This is more than praise. And he didn't say "faith" but "*steadfastness*," as if to soldiers standing in good order and firmly. What is steadfast neither deceit nor trials can shake violently. "Not only," he says, "have you not fallen, but nobody has even destroyed your order." He has set himself over them so that they may fear him as if he were present, for in this way order is preserved. From steadfastness comes protection, for so steadfastness will happen, when having brought many things together you cement them protectively and inseparably. In this way steadfastness happens, as in the case of a wall. But this is a work of love, for when it has closely cemented and knitted together those who were by themselves, it makes them steadfast. And again, faith does the same thing when it doesn't allow reasoning to enter. You see, just as reasoning divides and shakes, so does faith make steadfast and solid.

For since God has bestowed on us benefits greater than human reasoning, fittingly he has introduced faith. You see, it isn't possible for the person who demands reasons to be steadfast. For look at how all our hallowed beliefs are devoid of reasoning and dependent on faith alone. God is not anywhere and is everywhere. What is more unreasonable than this? Each thing by itself is full of difficulty, for he's not in a place, nor is there a place in which he is. He wasn't made, he didn't make himself, he didn't begin to be. What sort of reasoning will accept this, if there's no faith? Doesn't it seem ridiculous and more endless than a riddle?

[228] Then, if he's without beginning, and uncreated, and uncircumscribed, and infinite, there is thus a problem. But let's look at his incorporeality [to see whether] we can ever examine it by reason. God is incorporeal. What does incorporeality mean? It's just a word, for the idea hasn't received anything, nor has it impressed anything on itself. You see, if it hasn't made an impression, it comes down to nature and what constitutes a body. So the mouth speaks, while the understanding doesn't know what it says, except for one thing, that it's not body—that's all it knows. And why am I speaking of God? In the case of the soul, what is incorporeality, when it is created, enclosed, circumscribed? Tell me, demonstrate. But you can't.

ἐστιν; Ἀλλ' ὁ ἀὴρ σῶμα, εἰ καὶ μὴ ναστὸν, καὶ πολλαχόθεν δῆλον ὅτι σῶμά ἐστι χαῦνον. Τὸ πῦρ σῶμά ἐστιν, ἀλλ' ἡ ἐνέργεια τῆς ψυχῆς ἀσώματον. Διὰ τί; Εἰ πανταχοῦ διήκει. Εἰ αὐτὴ σῶμά ἐστιν, ἐν τόπῳ τὸ ἀσώματον· οὐκοῦν περιγράφεται· τὸ δὲ περιγραφόμενον, ἐν σχήματί ἐστι· τὰ δὲ σχήματα ἀπὸ γραμμῆς, αἱ δὲ γραμμαὶ σωμάτων. Πάλιν τὸ ἀσχημάτιστον ποίαν ἔννοιαν ἔχει; Οὐ σχῆμα ἔχει, οὐκ εἶδος, οὐ τύπον. Ὁρᾷς πῶς ἰλιγγιᾷ ἡ διάνοια;

Πάλιν ἄδεκτος ἡ φύσις τῶν κακῶν ἐκείνη; Ἀλλὰ καὶ ἑκών ἐστιν ἀγαθός· οὐκοῦν δεκτική. Ἀλλ' οὐκ ἔστιν εἰπεῖν· μὴ γένοιτο. Πάλιν θέλων εἰς τὸ εἶναι παρήχθη, ἢ μὴ θέλων; Ἀλλ' οὐδὲ τοῦτο ἔστιν εἰπεῖν. Πάλιν περιγράφει τὴν οἰκουμένην, ἢ οὔ; Εἰ μὴ περιγράφει, αὐτὸς περιγράφεται· εἰ δὲ περιγράφει, ἄπειρός ἐστι τῇ φύσει. Πάλιν ἑαυτὸν περιγράφει; Εἰ περιγράφει ἑαυτὸν, ἄρα οὐκ ἄναρχος ἑαυτῷ, ἀλλ' ἡμῖν· οὐκοῦν οὐ φύσει ἄναρχος. Πανταχοῦ τὰ ἐναντία δεῖ δοῦναι.

Ὁρᾷς τὸν ζόφον ὅσος, καὶ ὅτι πανταχοῦ πίστεως δεῖ; Αὕτη ἐστὶν ἡ στερρά. Ἀλλ', εἰ βούλεσθε, ἐπὶ τὰ τούτων ἐλάττω ἔλθωμεν. Ἔχει ἐνέργειαν ἐκείνη ἡ οὐσία. Καὶ τί ἐστιν ἐνέργεια ἐπ' αὐτοῦ; ἆρα κίνησίς τις; Οὐκοῦν οὐκ ἄτρεπτος· τὸ γὰρ κινούμενον οὐκ ἄτρεπτον· ἐξ ἀκινησίας γὰρ κινεῖται. Ἀλλ' ὅμως κινεῖται, καὶ οὐδέποτε ἵσταται. Ποίαν δὲ κίνησιν, εἰπέ μοι; παρὰ γὰρ ἡμῖν ἑπτά τινές εἰσιν, ἢ κάτω, ἢ ἄνω, ἢ ἐντὸς, ἢ ἐκτὸς, ἢ δεξιὰ, ἢ ἀριστερὰ, ἢ κυκλοφορικῶς· ἢ εἰ μὴ τοῦτο, [229] αὔξησις, μείωσις, γένεσις, φθορὰ, ἀλλοίωσις. Ἀλλ' οὐδεμίαν τούτων, ἀλλ' οἵαν ὁ νοῦς κίνησιν κινεῖται; Ἀλλ' οὐδὲ τοῦτο· μὴ γένοιτο· πολλὰ γὰρ καὶ ἀτόπως ὁ νοῦς κινεῖται. Τὸ θέλειν ἐστὶ τὸ ἐνεργεῖν, ἢ οὐχί; Εἰ τὸ θέλειν ἐστὶ τὸ ἐνεργεῖν, πάντας δὲ ἀνθρώπους θέλει ἀγαθοὺς εἶναι καὶ σωθῆναι, πῶς οὐ γίνεται; Ἀλλ' ἕτερον τὸ θέλειν, ἄλλο δὲ τὸ ἐνεργεῖν; Οὐκοῦν οὐκ ἀρκεῖ πρὸς ἐνέργειαν τὸ θέλειν. Πῶς οὖν λέγει ἡ γραφὴ, "Πάντα, ὅσα ἠθέλησεν, ἐποίησε;" καὶ πάλιν ὁ λεπρός φησι τῷ Χριστῷ· "Ἐὰν θέλῃς, δύνασαί με καθαρίσαι;" Εἰ γὰρ ἅμα τῷ θελήματι ἔπεται τοῦτο, τί ἔστιν εἰπεῖν; Βούλεσθε καὶ ἄλλο εἴπω; πῶς ἐξ οὐκ ὄντων τὰ ὄντα γέγονε; πῶς εἰς τὸ μηδὲν ἀναλύεται; τί ἀνώτερον τοῦ οὐρανοῦ; κἀκείνου δὲ πάλιν τί; κἀκείνου τί; καὶ μετ' ἐκεῖνον; καὶ τοῦτο ἐπ' ἄπειρον. Τί κατώτερον τῆς γῆς; θάλαττα· καὶ μετὰ ταύτην τί; καὶ μετ' ἐκείνην πάλιν; Ἀλλ' εἰς τὰ δεξιὰ, εἰς τὰ ἀριστερὰ; οὐχ ἡ αὐτὴ ἀπορία;

Is it air? But air is body, even if it's close pressed, and it's clear on many sides that a body is insubstantial. Fire is a body, but the activity of the soul is without body. Why? If it penetrates everywhere; but if it's body, it's bodiless in place; therefore it is circumscribed. But what is circumscribed has a figure; but figures are linear, while lines belong to bodies. Again, what kind of conception does the figureless have? It doesn't have a figure, or a form, or an outline. Do you see how understanding loses its head?

Again, isn't that nature susceptible to evil? No, God is good of his free will, therefore susceptible. But this is impossible to say—heaven forbid! Again, was he brought into being as he wished, not as he didn't wish? But one may not say this either. Again, does he circumscribe the world, or not? If he doesn't circumscribe it, he is himself circumscribed, but if he does circumscribe it, he is infinite in nature. Again, does he circumscribe himself? If he circumscribes himself, there is therefore no beginning to himself, but to us. Therefore he is not in his nature without beginning. Everywhere it's necessary to concede contradictions.

Do you see how great the darkness is and that everywhere there's a need for faith? That is what's solid. But, if you wish, let's proceed to things of a lesser order than these. That substance possesses an activity. And what in his case is activity? Is it some movement? Then he isn't unchangeable, for what is moved is not unchangeable—you see, from being motionless it moves. But nevertheless God is in motion and never stands still. But what kind of motion, tell me? For among us there are seven kinds: down, up, in, out, right, left, circular; or if not this, [229] increase, decrease, generation, destruction, alteration. No, if none of these, what kind of movement is the mind moved with? No, it's not that either—heaven forbid!—for in many cases the mind is moved even absurdly. Is willing being active, or not? If willing is being active, then God wills all persons to be good and to be saved [see 1 Tim 2:4]. How does it not happen? But is willing one thing, while being active is another? Then willing is not sufficient for activity. Then how can Scripture say, "*He did whatever he willed*" [Ps 115:3]? And again the leper says to Christ, "*If you will it, you can make me clean*" [Matt 8:2]. You see, if this follows the will, what is it possible to say? Do you want me to say something else too? How did things that are come into being from things that are not [see Rom 4:17]? How are they resolved into nothing? What is above heaven? Again, what is above that? And what above that? And beyond that? And so on to infinity. What is below the earth? Sea, and beyond this, what? And again, beyond that, what? No, to the right and to the left, is there not the same difficulty?

Ἀλλὰ ταῦτα μὲν ἀόρατα. Βούλεσθε ἐπὶ τῶν ὁρωμένων ἀγάγω τὸν λόγον; ἐπὶ τῶν ἤδη συμβάντων; Εἰπέ μοι, πῶς τὸ θηρίον τὸν Ἰωνᾶν εἶχεν ἐν τῇ γαστρί, καὶ οὐκ ἀπώλλυτο; οὐχὶ ἄλογόν ἐστιν; οὐχὶ ἁπλῶς κινεῖται; πῶς ἐφείσατο τοῦ δικαίου; πῶς αὐτὸν οὐκ ἀπέπνιξεν ἡ θέρμη; πῶς οὐκ ἔσηψεν; Εἰ γὰρ τὸ ἐν βυθῷ εἶναι μόνον ἄπορον, τὸ καὶ ἐν σπλάγχνοις καὶ τῇ θέρμῃ ἐκείνῃ, πολλῷ μᾶλλον ἀπορώτερον. Εἰ ἐκεῖθεν τὸν ἀέρα ἀναπνέομεν, πῶς ἤρκει δύο ζώοις ἡ ἀναπνοή; πῶς δὲ αὐτὸν καὶ ἤμεσεν ἀσινῆ; πῶς δὲ καὶ ἐφθέγγετο; πῶς δὲ καὶ ἐν ἑαυτῷ ἦν, καὶ προσηύχετο; ἆρα ταῦτα οὐκ ἄπιστα; Ἂν λογισμῷ ἐξετάζωμεν, ἄπιστα· ἂν δὲ πίστει, σφόδρα πιστά.

Εἴπω τι τούτου πλέον; Ὁ σῖτος ἐν τῷ κόλπῳ τῆς γῆς φθείρεται, καὶ ἀνίσταται. Ὅρα τὰ θαύματα ἐναντία, καὶ ἄλληλα νικῶντα· θαυμαστὸν τὸ μὴ σαπῆναι, θαυμαστὸν τὸ σαπέντα ἀναστῆναι. Ποῦ εἰσιν οἱ τὰ τοιαῦτα ληροῦντες, καὶ τῇ ἀνα-[230]στάσει διαπιστοῦντες καὶ λέγοντες, τόδε τὸ ὀστοῦν πῶς τῷδε συγκολλᾶται; καὶ μυθώδη τοιαῦτα εἰσάγοντες; Εἰπέ μοι, πῶς ὁ Ἠλίας ἀνῆλθεν ἐν πυρὸς ἅρματι; Τὸ πῦρ καίειν εἴωθεν, οὐκ ἀνάγειν. Πῶς τοσοῦτον ζῇ χρόνον; ἐν τίνι τόπῳ ἐστί; διὰ τί τοῦτο γέγονε; Ποῦ δὲ Ἐνὼχ μετετέθη; Τροφῆς ἀπολαύει οἵας καὶ ἡμεῖς; καὶ τί τὸ κωλῦον ἐνταῦθα αὐτὸν εἶναι; Ἀλλ᾽ οὐκ ἀπολαύει; καὶ διὰ τί μετετέθη; Ὅρα τὸν θεὸν κατὰ μικρὸν ἡμᾶς παιδαγωγοῦντα. Μετέθηκε τὸν Ἐνώχ· οὐ πάνυ μέγα τοῦτο· ἐπαίδευσεν ἡμᾶς τοῦτο εἰς τὴν ἀναγωγὴν τοῦ Ἠλία. Ἐναπέκλεισε τὸν Νῶε τῇ κιβωτῷ· οὐ πάνυ μέγα οὐδὲ τοῦτο· ἐπαίδευσεν ἡμᾶς τοῦτο εἰς τὴν ἀπόκλεισιν τοῦ προφήτου τὴν ἐν τῷ κήτει. Οὕτω καὶ τὰ παλαιὰ προδρόμων ἐδεήθη καὶ τύπων. Καθάπερ γὰρ ἐπὶ κλίμακος ὁ πρῶτος βαθμὸς παραπέμπει τῷ δευτέρῳ, ἀπὸ δὲ τοῦ πρώτου οὐκ ἔνι ἐπὶ τὸν τέταρτον ἐλθεῖν, καὶ οὗτος ἐκείνῳ, ἵνα ἐκεῖνος τούτῳ γένηται ὁδός· οὐδὲ πρὸ τοῦ πρώτου δυνατὸν ἐπὶ τὸν δεύτερον ἐλθεῖν· οὕτω καὶ ἐνταῦθα.

Καὶ θέα σημεῖα σημείων· καὶ ὄψει τοῦτο ἐπὶ τῆς κλίμακος, ἣν εἶδεν Ἰακώβ. Ἄνω, φησίν, ὁ κύριος ἐπεστήρικτο, κάτω δὲ ἄγγελοι ἀνέβαινον καὶ κατέβαινον." Προεφητεύετο ὅτι υἱὸν ἔχει ὁ πατήρ· ἔδει τοῦτο πιστευθῆναι·

But these things are unseen. Do you want me to take the homily on to what is seen? To what has already happened? Tell me, how did the beast contain Jonah in its belly, without his perishing [see Jonah 1:17]? Isn't it devoid of reason? Aren't his movements random? How did it spare the righteous man? How was it that the heat didn't suffocate him? How was it that it didn't corrupt him? You see, if only to be in the deep is difficult to get out of, being in the stomach and that heat is much more difficult to get out of. If we breathe air from that place, how was it sufficient for two beings to breathe? And how did it even vomit him up unharmed? And how too did he speak? And how too was he self-possessed and prayed? Aren't these things incredible? If we examine them by reason, they are incredible, but if by faith, they are exceedingly credible.

Shall I say more than this? The wheat in the bosom of the earth decays and rises again. Look at the contradictory wonders, surpassing each other. A wonder is not to be corrupted, a wonder is rising again from corruption. Where are those who talk such nonsense, [**230**] not believing the resurrection and asking how this bone would be cemented to that, introducing silly tales like that? Tell me, how did Elijah go up in a fiery chariot [see 2 Kgdms 2:11]? Fire usually burns, not carries up. How is it that he lives such a long time? What place is he in? For what reason did this happen? Where was Enoch translated?[59] Does he enjoy the same food as we do too? And what hinders him from being here? No, doesn't he eat? And for what reason was he translated? See how God schools us little by little. He translated Enoch: that isn't a terrific achievement. This schooled us for the ascent of Elijah. He shut Noah up in the ark [see Gen 7:16]: that isn't a terrific achievement. This schooled us for shutting up the prophet in the whale (see Jonah 1:17). So even the things of old needed forerunners and types. You see, just as on a ladder the first step passes to the second, but from the first it's not possible to get to the fourth, and this one passes on to that, so that that may be the way to the next; nor is it possible to get to the second before the first—so too is it here.

And observe the signs of signs, and you will discern that this is about the ladder that Jacob knew. "Above," it says, "*the Lord stood fast, while underneath the angels were going up and down*" [Gen 28:12–13].[60] It was prophesied that the Father had a Son—this had to be believed. Where do

---

59. See Gen 5:24; Eccl 44:16; Heb 11:5.
60. This is not an accurate rendering of the LXX text.

πόθεν θέλεις αὐτοῦ τὰ σημεῖα δείξω; ἄνωθεν κάτω; κάτωθεν ἄνω; Ὅτι ἀπαθῶς γεννᾷ· διὰ τοῦτο ἐγέννησε πρῶτον στεῖρα. Μᾶλλον δὲ ἀνωτέρω, ἔδει πιστευθῆναι, ὅτι ἐξ αὐτοῦ. Τί οὖν; Τοῦτο γίνεται, ἀμυδρῶς μὲν, ἅτε ἐν τύπῳ καὶ σκιᾷ, πλὴν γίνεται· καὶ προϊὸν σαφέστερόν πως γίνεται. Ἐξ ἀνθρώπου μόνου γυνή, καὶ μένει ἐκεῖνος ὁλόκληρος. Πάλιν τῆς ἐκ παρθένου κυήσεως ἔδει γενέσθαι τι τεκμήριον. Τίκτει στεῖρα οὐχ ἅπαξ, ἀλλὰ καὶ δεύτερον καὶ τρίτον καὶ πολλάκις. Τῆς μὲν οὖν ἐκ παρθένου γεννήσεως τύπος ἡ στεῖρα· καὶ αὕτη παραπέμπει τῇ πίστει τὴν διάνοιαν. Πάλιν τοῦτο τύπος ἐγένετο τοῦ μόνον δύνασθαι γεννῆσαι τὸν θεόν. Εἰ γὰρ κυριώτερον ἄνθρωπος, καὶ χωρὶς τούτου τίκτεται, πολλῷ μᾶλλον ἐκ τοῦ κυριωτέρου γεννᾶται. Ἔστι καὶ ἄλλη γέννησις τῆς ἀληθείας τύπος, ἡ ἡμετέρα ἡ ἐκ πνεύματος. Ταύ- [231]της πάλιν ἡ στεῖρα τύπος, ὅτι οὐκ ἐξ αἱμάτων· αὕτη τῆς ἄνω γεννήσεως. Ἡ μὲν οὖν αὐτῆς τὸ ἀπαθὲς δείκνυσιν, ἡ δὲ τὸ ἐκ μόνου δύνασθαι γεννᾶσθαι.

Ἔστι Χριστὸς ἄνω πάντων κρατῶν· ἔδει πιστευθῆναι τοῦτο. Γίνεται τοῦτο ἐν τῇ γῇ ἐπὶ τοῦ ἀνθρώπου. "Ποιήσωμεν ἄνθρωπον κατ' εἰκόνα καὶ καθ' ὁμοίωσιν ἡμετέραν," ἐπὶ τῆς ἀρχῆς τῶν ἀλόγων πάντων. Οὕτως οὐ διὰ ῥημάτων, ἀλλὰ διὰ πραγμάτων ὑμᾶς ἐπαίδευσε. Τὸ ἀνακεχωρηκὸς τῆς φύσεως ὁ παράδεισος ἐδήλου, καὶ τὸ πάντων εἶναι βελτιῶ τὸν ἄνθρωπον. Ἔμελλεν ἀνίστασθαι ὁ Χριστός· ὅρα λοιπὸν πόσα τεκμήρια· ὁ Ἐνώχ, ὁ Ἠλίας, ὁ Ἰωνᾶς, τὰ ἐν τῇ καμίνῳ, τὸ ἐπὶ τοῦ Νῶε τὸ βάπτισμα, τὰ σπέρματα, τὰ φυτά, ἡ γέννησις ἡ ἡμετέρα, ἡ τῶν ζώων πάντων. Ἐπειδὴ γὰρ ἐν τούτῳ πάντα ἐκινδυνεύετο, τοῦτο μάλιστα πάντων πολλοὺς ἔσχε τοὺς τύπους.

Ὅτι οὐκ ἀπρονόητα τὰ πάντα ἐστὶν, ἀπὸ τῶν παρ' ἡμῖν δυνατὸν στοχάσασθαι· οὐδὲν γὰρ ἀπρονόητον μένει, ἀλλὰ καὶ ἀγέλαι καὶ τὰ ἄλλα πάντα ἀρχῆς δεῖται. Καὶ ὅτι οὐκ αὐτόματα γέγονε τὰ πάντα, δείκνυσιν ἡ γέεννα, ἔδειξε δὲ ὁ κατακλυσμὸς ὁ ἐπὶ Νῶε, τὸ πῦρ, ὁ καταποντισμὸς ὁ τῶν Αἰγυπτίων, τὰ ἐν τῇ ἐρήμῳ. Ἔδει καὶ τοῦ βαπτίσματος πολλὰ προηγήσασθαι, καὶ μυρία ὅσα· οἷον τὰ ἐν τῇ παλαιᾷ, τὰ ἐν τῇ κολυμβήθρᾳ, τὸ τὸν μὴ ὑγιαίνοντα

you wish me to demonstrate signs of this from? From above, from below, upward? He engendered without being passible; on this account the barren woman was the first to give birth [see Gen 21:2]. No, it had to be believed that from on high he gave birth from himself. What then? This happens, but obscurely, as in a type and shadow, but still happens, and as it proceeds it somehow becomes clearer. A woman is formed out of a man alone, and he remains completely whole. Again, it was necessary that there should be some sure sign of a birth from a virgin. The barren woman gives birth not once, but even a second and a third time, and often. Therefore, the sterile woman is a type of the birth from a virgin, and she sends the mind forth in faith. Again, this was a type of God being able to beget alone. For if a human being has more authority, and birth takes place without him, much more does the birth take place from the one who has more authority. There is also another birth, a type of the truth, ours from the Spirit. [231] Again, of this the barren woman is a type, which is not of blood [see John 1:13]: this comes from the birth above. The one shows, therefore, that Christ comes from impassibility, the other that he could be born from God alone.

Christ is above, ruling over everything: it was necessary that this be believed. This happens on earth with respect to a human being. *Let us make a human being in our image and likeness* [Gen 1:26], with dominion over all the animals. Thus he schooled us not through words but through deeds. Paradise demonstrated the separateness of his nature and that the human being was the best thing of all. Christ was going to rise again—observe in the future how many signs there were of this: Enoch, Elijah, Jonah, events in the furnace [see Dan 3:19–23], what happened in Noah's time, baptism, the seeds, the plants, our own birth, that of all the animals. You see, since everything was being ventured on this point, it especially had an abundance of types.

That everything is not without providence we can conjecture from events among ourselves, for nothing remains without providence, no, also herds of animals and everything else that has no dominion. And that everything didn't happen by itself, hell demonstrates, and the flood in Noah's time, the fire [see Gen 19:24–5], the drowning of the Egyptians in the sea [see Exod 14:27–8], the events in the wilderness.[61] It was necessary that many things too should prepare for baptism, and myriad things as well. For example, those in the Old Testament, those in the pool [see John 5:2;

---

61. See Exod 15:17, 19; Num 11:12, 16–17; Josh 3.

καθαίρεσθαι, αὐτὸς ὁ κατακλυσμὸς, καὶ ὅσα ἐν ὕδατι γέγονε τὸ βάπτισμα Ἰωάννου.

Ἔδει πιστευθῆναι ὅτι τὸν υἱὸν αὐτοῦ ἐκδίδωσιν ὁ θεός· προλαβὼν ἐποίησε τοῦτο ἄνθρωπος, Ἀβραὰμ ὁ πατριάρχης. Πάντων οὖν τούτων τύπους, ἂν ἐθέλωμεν, εὑρήσομεν, ἂν ζητῶμεν ἐν τῇ γραφῇ. Ἀλλὰ μὴ ἀποκάμωμεν, ἀλλ' ἐν τούτοις ῥυθμίζωμεν ἑαυτούς· στερρὰν ἔχωμεν τὴν πίστιν, καὶ ἀκρίβειαν πολιτείας ἐπιδειξώμεθα, ἵνα διὰ πάντων εὐχαριστήσαντες τῷ θεῷ, καταξιωθῶμεν τῶν ἐπηγγελμένων ἀγαθῶν τοῖς ἀγαπῶσιν αὐτὸν, χάριτι καὶ φιλανθρωπίᾳ τοῦ κυρίου ἡμῶν Ἰησοῦ Χριστοῦ, μεθ' οὗ τῷ πατρὶ ἅμα [232] τῷ ἁγίῳ πνεύματι δόξα, κράτος, τιμὴ, νῦν καὶ ἀεὶ καὶ εἰς τοὺς αἰῶνας τῶν αἰώνων. Ἀμήν.

9:7], the cleansing of the man who wasn't healthy [see John 9:6], the flood itself [see Gen 6:9–9:17] and what happened in the water, the baptism of John [see John 3:1–17].

It had to be believed that God gives up his Son; a human being did this in anticipation: the patriarch Abraham [see Gen 22]. Therefore, types of all these things, if we want to, we shall find if we search the Scriptures. But let's not become weary but train ourselves in these matters. Let's have a steadfast faith and show forth strictness of life, so that in all things having given thanks to God we may be judged worthy of the good things promised to those who love him, by the grace and loving-kindness of our Lord Jesus Christ, with whom, to the Father, together [**232**] with the Holy Spirit, be glory, power, honor, now and forever and ever. Amen.

ΛΟΓΟΣ Σ.

Ὡς οὖν παρελάβετε τὸν Χριστὸν Ἰησοῦν τὸν κύριον, ἐν αὐτῷ περιπατεῖτε, ἐρριζωμένοι καὶ ἐποικοδομούμενοι ἐν αὐτῷ, καὶ βεβαιούμενοι ἐν τῇ πίστει, καθὼς ἐδιδάχθητε, περισσεύοντες ἐν αὐτῇ ἐν εὐχαριστίᾳ.

Πάλιν αὐτοὺς τῇ οἰκείᾳ προκαταλαμβάνει μαρτυρίᾳ, λέγων, "Ὡς οὖν παρελάβετε." Οὐδὲν ξένον, φησὶν, ἐπεισάγομεν· μηδὲ ὑμεῖς. "Ἐν αὐτῷ περιπατεῖτε·" αὐτὸς γάρ ἐστιν ἡ ὁδὸς ἡ προσάγουσα εἰς τὸν πατέρα· μὴ ἐν τοῖς ἀγγέλοις· οὐ φέρει αὕτη ἡ ὁδὸς ἐκεῖ. "Ἐρριζωμένοι." τουτέστι, πεπηγότες· μὴ ποτὲ μὲν ταύτην, ποτὲ δὲ ἐκείνην, ἀλλ' ἐρριζωμένοι· τὸ δὲ ἐρριζωμένον οὐκ ἄν ποτε μετασταίη. Ὅρα πῶς κυρίας τὰς λέξεις τίθησι. "Καὶ ἐποικοδομούμενοι·" τουτέστι, τῇ διανοίᾳ φθάνοντες εἰς αὐτόν. "Καὶ βεβαιούμενοι ἐν αὐτῷ·" τουτέστι, κατέχοντες αὐτὸν, ὡς ἐπὶ θεμέλιον οἰκοδομούμενοι. Δείκνυσιν αὐτοὺς καταπεσόντας· τὸ γὰρ, "οἰκοδομούμενοι," τοῦτό ἐστιν. Οἰκοδομὴ γάρ ἐστιν ὄντως ἡ πίστις, καὶ δεῖ καὶ τοῦ θεμελίου ἰσχυροῦ, καὶ τῆς οἰκοδομίας ἀσφαλοῦς. Ἄν τε γὰρ μὴ ἐπ' ἀσφαλείᾳ τις οἰκοδομήσῃ, σαλεύεται· ἄν τε ἐπ' ἀσφαλείας, καὶ μὴ ἑστήκῃ, οὐκέτι ἵσταται. "Καθὼς ἐδιδάχθητε." Πάλιν τὸ, "καθὼς·" "Περισσεύοντες, φησὶν, ἐν αὐτῇ ἐν εὐχαριστίᾳ." Τοῦτο γὰρ εὐγνώμονος· οὐ λέγω ἁπλῶς εὐχαριστεῖν, ἀλλὰ μετὰ πολλῆς τῆς περιουσίας, πλέον ἢ ἐμάθετε, εἰ οἷόν τε, μετὰ πολλῆς τῆς φιλοτιμίας.

"Βλέπετε μή τις ὑμᾶς ἔσται ὁ συλαγωγῶν." Ὁρᾷς πῶς ἔδειξε κλέπτην ὄντα, καὶ ἀλλότριον, καὶ ἠρέμα ἐπεισιόντα; ἤδη γὰρ παρέστησεν αὐτὸν εἰσιόντα. "Βλέπετε." Καὶ καλῶς εἶπε, [233] "συλαγωγῶν." Ὥσπερ ἄν τις χῶμα κάτωθεν διορύττων μὴ παρέχῃ αἴσθησιν, τὸ δὲ ὑπονοστῇ· οὕτω καὶ ὑμεῖς βλέπετε· τοῦτο γὰρ ἔργον ἐκείνῳ, τὸ μηδὲ αἴσθησιν παρέχειν. Ὥσπερ ἂν εἴ τις ἀπόλλοι καθ' ἑκάστην ἡμέραν, καὶ ἀκούοι, βλέπετε μή τις ἐστί. Καὶ τὴν ὁδὸν δείκνυσι, διὰ τῆσδε τῆς ὁδοῦ· ὥσπερ ἂν εἰ ἐλέγομεν, διὰ τοῦδε τοῦ δωματίου·

"διὰ τῆς φιλοσοφίας," φησίν. Εἶτα, ἐπειδὴ δοκεῖ σεμνὸν εἶναι τὸ τῆς φιλοσοφίας, προσέθηκε, "καὶ κενῆς ἀπάτης." Ἔστι γὰρ καὶ καλὴ ἀπάτη, οἵαν ἠπατήθησαν πολλοὶ, ἣν οὐδὲ ἀπάτην δεῖ καλεῖν· περὶ ἧς φησιν ὁ Ἰερεμίας· "Ἠπάτησάς με, κύριε, καὶ ἠπατήθην." Ἐγὼ δὲ οὐ πείθομαι· τὸ γὰρ τοιοῦτον

HOMILY 6

*As therefore you received Christ Jesus the Lord, walk in him, rooted
and built up in him, and established in the faith, just as you were
taught, abounding in it with thanksgiving* [Col 2:6–7].

Again, Paul takes hold of them beforehand with their own testimony,
saying, "*As therefore you received.*" "We introduce nothing strange," he
says, "neither do you." "*Walk in him,*" for he is the way that leads to the
Father, don't [walk] in the angels—this way doesn't lead there. *Rooted,* that
is, fixed, not ever going this way, never that, but *rooted.* What is rooted can
never change. See how authoritative the expressions are that he employs.
And built up, that is, in thought anticipating him. *And established in him,*
that is, holding onto him and built as on a foundation. He shows that they
had fallen down, for the word *built* has this meaning. You see, the faith is
truly a building and needs both a strong foundation and secure building.
For if someone doesn't build on a secure foundation, it will shake; also, if
they do build on a secure foundation and it isn't firm, it won't stand. *Just as
you were taught.* Again, the words *just as.* "*Abounding in it with thanksgiving,*" he says, for this belongs to well-disposed persons. "I don't say simply
to give thanks, but to do it with great abundance, more than you learned, if
possible, with much ambition."

See to it that nobody makes a prey of you [Col 2:8]. Do you see how Paul
demonstrates them to be a thief, and an alien, and approaches softly? For
he has already presented them as approaching. *See to it.* And he well said
[**233**] "*makes a prey.*" Just as a person digging a mound from underneath
may offer no perceptible sign, but it settles, so too do we see to it. For this
is his purpose, not to offer a perceptible sign. Just as if someone were to
destroy on a daily basis and to hear, *See to it that there is nobody.* And he
demonstrates the way through that way, as if we said "through that room."

"*Through philosophy*" [Col 2:8], he says. Then, because the word *philosophy* has an appearance of dignity, he added, "*And vain deceit.*" For there
exists also a good deceit, such as many have been deceived by, that shouldn't
be called deceit at all. About that Jeremiah said, "*Lord, you have deceived*

οὐδὲ ἀπάτην δεῖ καλεῖν· ἐπεὶ καὶ τὸν πατέρα ἠπάτησεν ὁ Ἰακὼβ, ἀλλ᾿ οὐκ ἀπάτη, ἀλλ᾿ οἰκονομία ἦν. "Διὰ τῆς φιλοσοφίας, φησὶ, καὶ κενῆς ἀπάτης, κατὰ τὴν παράδοσιν τῶν ἀνθρώπων, κατὰ τὰ στοιχεῖα τοῦ κόσμου, καὶ οὐ κατὰ Χριστόν." Τέως τοῦ ἐλέγχου ἅπτεται τῆς τῶν ἡμερῶν παρατηρήσεως, στοιχεῖα κόσμου ἥλιον καὶ σελήνην λέγων, καθάπερ καὶ ἐν τῇ πρὸς Γαλάτας ἔλεγε· "Πῶς πάλιν ἐπιστρέφετε ἐπὶ τὰ ἀσθενῆ καὶ πτωχὰ στοιχεῖα;" Καὶ οὐκ εἶπεν ἡμερῶν παρατηρήσεις, ἀλλὰ διόλου τοῦ κόσμου τοῦ παρόντος, ἵνα τὸ εὐτελὲς δείξῃ· εἰ γὰρ ὁ κόσμος ὁ παρὼν οὐδὲν, πολλῷ μᾶλλον καὶ τὰ στοιχεῖα. Δείξας πρῶτον ὅσα εὐηργετήθησαν, ὅσα εὖ ἔπαθον, τότε ἐπάγει τὴν κατη-γορίαν, ἵνα μείζονα δείξῃ, καὶ ἕλῃ τοὺς ἀκούοντας. Τοῦτο καὶ οἱ προφῆται ποιοῦσιν ἀεί· πρότερον τὰς εὐεργεσίας δεικνύουσι, καὶ τότε τὴν κατηγορίαν αὔξουσι, καθάπερ ὁ Ἡσαΐας φησίν· "Υἱοὺς ἐγέννησα καὶ ὕψωσα, αὐτοὶ δέ με ἠθέτησαν." καὶ πάλιν, "Λαός μου, τί ἐποίησά σοι, ἢ τί ἐλύπησά σε, ἢ τί παρηνώχλησά σοι;" καὶ ὁ Δαυΐδ, ὡς ὅταν [234] λέγῃ· "Ἐπήκουσά σου ἐν ἀποκρύφῳ καταιγίδος·" καὶ πάλιν, "Ἄνοιξον τὸ στόμα σου, καὶ πληρώσω αὐτό·" καὶ πανταχοῦ οὕτως εὑρήσεις.

Μάλιστα μὲν οὖν οὐδὲ εἴ τι ἔλεγον, πείθεσθαι ἔδει· νῦν δὲ καὶ χωρὶς τῶν εὐεργεσιῶν φεύγειν ἐκεῖνα ἔδει. "Καὶ οὐ κατὰ Χριστὸν," φησί. Μάλιστα μὲν γὰρ, εἰ καὶ οὕτως ἦν ἐξ ἡμισείας, ὥστε δύνασθαι καὶ τούτῳ κἀκείνῳ δουλεύ-ειν, οὐδὲ οὕτως ἔδει· νῦν δὲ οὐκ ἀφίησιν ὑμᾶς εἶναι κατὰ Χριστόν. Ἐκεῖθεν αὐτὰ φέρουσι. Πρότερον διασαλεύσας τὰς Ἑλληνικὰς παρατηρήσεις, τότε καὶ τὰς Ἰουδαϊκὰς ἀναιρεῖ. Καὶ γὰρ Ἕλληνες καὶ Ἰουδαῖοι παρετήρουν πλείονα, ἀλλ᾿ οἱ μὲν ἀπὸ φιλοσοφίας, οἱ δὲ ἀπὸ νόμου. Πρότερον τοίνυν πρόσεισι τούτοις, ἔνθα μείζων ἡ κατηγορία. Πῶς οὐ κατὰ Χριστόν;

"Ὅτι ἐν αὐτῷ κατοικεῖ πᾶν τὸ πλήρωμα τῆς θεότητος σωματικῶς, καὶ ἐστὲ ἐν αὐτῷ πεπληρωμένοι, ὅς ἐστιν ἡ κεφαλὴ πάσης ἀρχῆς καὶ ἐξουσίας." Ὅρα πῶς ἐν τῇ τούτων κατηγορίᾳ ἐκεῖνο διορύττει, πρότερον τιθεὶς τὴν λύσιν, καὶ τότε τὴν ἀντίθεσιν. Ἀνύποπτος γὰρ ἡ τοιαύτη λύσις, καὶ μᾶλλον

me, and I was deceived" [Jer 20:7]. But I'm not convinced, for something
like that shouldn't be called deceit at all, since Jacob also deceived his father,
but it wasn't deceit but an arrangement [see Gen 27:24–5]. "*Through philosophy,*" Paul says, "*and vain deceit, according to human tradition, according
to the elements of the universe, and not according to Christ*" [Col 2:8]. Meanwhile he sets about reproving their observance of particular days, meaning
by elements of the universe the sun and moon, just as he said in the Letter
to the Galatians, "*How can you turn back again to the weak and beggarly
elements?*" [Gal 4:9]. And he didn't say "observances of days," but in general
of the present universe, in order to demonstrate its worthlessness, for if the
present universe is nothing, much more indeed are the elements. Having
first demonstrated how many benefits they had received, how many kind-
nesses, he then brings on the accusation, in order to demonstrate its greater
seriousness and win over his listeners. This the prophets always do too: first
they demonstrate the benefits and then they magnify their accusation, just
as Isaiah said, "*I have begotten sons and exalted them, but they have rejected
me*" [Isa 1:2], and again, "*My people, what have I done to you, or in what
have I grieved you, or in what have I troubled you?*" [Mic 6:3]. And David,
as when [**234**] he says, "*I heard you in the secret place of a squall*" [Ps 81:7];
and again; "*Open your mouth and I will fill it*" [Ps 81:10]. And everywhere
you will find it so.

First and above all, then, one should not be persuaded even if they
say something, but at present even without the benefits one should avoid
those things. "*And not according to Christ,*" Paul says. For first of all, even
if it were possible to do so by halves, so that one could serve both the one
and the other, it should not be like this either. But as it is, he doesn't allow
you to be according to Christ. Those things take you away from him. First,
having shaken violently the observances of the Hellenes, he then destroys
those of the Jews as well. Indeed, the Hellenes and the Jews practiced many
observances, but the former from philosophy, the latter from the law.[62]
First, then, he attacks those where the more serious accusation lay. How
not according to Christ?

*For in him the whole fullness of the deity dwells bodily, and you have
come to fullness in him, who is the head of every rule and authority* [Col 2:9].
See how in his accusation of those people he thrusts through the other,
first by stating the solution, and then the objection. For a solution like that

---

62. See *Hom. Col.* 5 for the same argument.

δέχεται ὁ ἀκροατὴς, ὡς οὐ τοῦτο σπουδάζοντος τοῦ λέγοντος. Ἐκεῖ μὲν γὰρ καὶ φιλονεικεῖ μὴ ἡττηθῆναι, ἐνταῦθα δὲ οὔ. "Ὅτι ἐν αὐτῷ, φησὶ, κατοικεῖ." Τουτέστιν, ὅτι ὁ θεὸς ἐν αὐτῷ οἰκεῖ. Ἀλλ᾽ ἵνα μὴ νομίσῃς αὐτὸν συγκεκλεῖσθαι, ὡς ἐν σώματι, φησί· "πᾶν τὸ πλήρωμα τῆς θεότητος σωματικῶς, καὶ ἐστὲ ἐν αὐτῷ πεπληρωμένοι." Ἄλλοι φασὶν ὅτι τὴν ἐκκλησίαν λέγει πεπληρωμένην ὑπὸ τῆς θεότητος αὐτοῦ, καθὼς ἀλλαχοῦ φησι· "Τοῦ πάντα ἐν πᾶσι πληρουμένου·" τὸ δὲ, σωματικῶς, ἐνταῦθα, ὡς ἐν κεφαλῇ σῶμα. Πῶς οὖν οὐκ ἐπήγαγεν, ἥτις ἐστὶν ἡ ἐκκλησία; Ἡ περὶ τοῦ πατρός τινές φασι λέγειν, ὅτι τῆς θεότητος τὸ πλήρωμα ἐν αὐτῷ οἰκεῖ· πρῶτον μὲν, ὅτι τὸ οἰκεῖν οὐ κυρίως λέγεται ἐπὶ θεοῦ· δεύτερον, ὅτι τὸ πλήρωμα οὐ τὸ δεχόμενόν ἐστι· "Τοῦ γὰρ κυρίου ἡ γῆ, καὶ τὸ πλήρωμα αὐτῆς·" καὶ πάλιν ὁ ἀπόστολος, "Ἄχρις οὗ τὸ πλήρωμα τῶν ἐθνῶν εἰσέλθῃ." Τὸ ὅλον λέγε-[235]ται πλήρωμα. Ἔπειτα τὸ, σωματικῶς, τί ἐβούλετο; Ὡς ἐν κεφαλῇ. Τί δὲ πάλιν τὸ αὐτὸ λέγει, "Καὶ ἐστὲ ἐν αὐτῷ πεπληρωμένοι;" Τί οὖν ἐστιν; Ὅτι οὐδὲν ἔλαττον ἔχετε αὐτοῦ· ὥσπερ ἐν ἐκείνῳ ᾤκησεν, οὕτω καὶ ἐν ὑμῖν. Βιάζεται γὰρ ἀεὶ Παῦλος ἐγγὺς ἡμᾶς ἀγαγεῖν τοῦ Χριστοῦ, ὡς ὅταν λέγῃ· "Συνήγειρε καὶ συνεκάθισεν ἡμᾶς." καὶ, "Εἰ ὑπομένομεν, καὶ συμβασιλεύσομεν·" καὶ, "Πῶς οὐχὶ καὶ σὺν αὐτῷ τὰ πάντα ἡμῖν χαρίσεται;" καὶ συγκληρονόμους καλῶν. Εἶτα περὶ τοῦ ἀξιώματος· "Καὶ αὐτός ἐστιν ἡ κεφαλὴ πάσης ἀρχῆς καὶ ἐξουσίας." Ὁ πάντων ἀνώτερος, ἡ αἰτία, οὐχὶ ὁμοούσιος; Εἶτα τὰ τῆς εὐεργεσίας θαυμαστῶς πως ἐπήγαγε, καὶ πολλῷ τῆς πρὸς Ῥωμαίους θαυμαστότερον. Ἐκεῖ μὲν γάρ φησι, "Περιτομὴ καρδίας ἐν πνεύματι, οὐ γράμματι·" ἐνταῦθα δὲ, "ἐν τῷ Χριστῷ."

"Ἐν ᾧ γὰρ, φησὶ, καὶ περιετμήθητε περιτομῇ ἀχειροποιήτῳ, ἐν τῇ ἀπεκδύσει τοῦ σώματος τῶν ἁμαρτιῶν τῆς σαρκὸς, ἐν τῇ περιτομῇ τοῦ Χριστοῦ." Ὅρα πῶς ἐγγὺς γίνεται τοῦ πράγματος. "Ἐν τῇ ἀπεκδύσει," φησίν· οὐκ εἶπεν, ἐκδύσει. "Τοῦ σώματος τῶν ἁμαρτιῶν·" τὸν παλαιόν φησι βίον. Συνεχῶς ταῦτα στρέφει καὶ διαφόρως, ὥσπερ ἄνω ἔλεγεν· "Ὃς ἐρρύσατο ἡμᾶς ἐκ τῆς ἐξουσίας τοῦ σκότους, καὶ ἀποκατήλλαξεν ἀπηλλοτριωμένους εἰς τὸ εἶναι ἡμᾶς ἁγίους καὶ ἀμώμους." Οὐκέτι, φησὶν, ἐν μαχαίρᾳ ἡ περιτομὴ, ἀλλ᾽ ἐν αὐτῷ τῷ Χριστῷ· οὐ γὰρ χεὶρ ἐπάγει, καθὼς ἐκεῖ, τὴν περιτομὴν ταύτην, ἀλλὰ τὸ πνεῦμα· οὐ μέρος, ἀλλ᾽ ὅλον ἄνθρωπον περιτέμνει. Σῶμα καὶ τοῦτο,

is unsuspected, and the hearer accepts it more because the speaker isn't making it his aim. You see, in that case indeed he would strive not to come second best, but not in this case. "*Because in him*," Paul says, "*it dwells*," that is, God dwells in him. But lest you suppose that Christ is constrained, as if in a body, Paul says, "*The whole fullness of the deity bodily, and you have come to fullness in him.*" Others say that Paul means the church filled by his deity, as he says elsewhere, "*The fullness of him who fulfills in all*" [Eph 1:23], and that the word *bodily* is in this passage, as a body in a head. How then didn't he add "which is the church"? Or some say that it's with reference to the Father that he says that the fullness of the deity dwells in him. The first thing is that "to dwell" can't properly be said about God. The second thing is that *the fullness* isn't what is received: *The earth is the Lord's, and the fullness thereof* [Ps 24:1 LXX]. And again the apostle [says], "*Until the fullness of the gentiles has come in*" [Rom 11:25]. By *fullness* is meant the whole. [235] Then what did the word *bodily* signify? "As in a head." But why does he say the same thing again, "*And you are fulfilled in him*"? What then does it mean? That you have nothing less than he does: just as it dwelled in him, so too in you. For Paul is always forced to bring us near to Christ, as when he says, "*He has raised us together and made us sit together*" [Eph 2:6], and, "*If we suffer, we shall also reign with him*" [2 Tim 2:12], and, "*How will he not also grant us everything with him?*" [Rom 8:32]. And he calls us *fellow heirs*. Then concerning his dignity: and "*He is the head of all rule and authority.*" The one who is above all, the cause, isn't he consubstantial? Then Paul added the benefit in a marvelous way, and far more marvelous than in the Letter to the Romans. For there he said: "*Circumcision of the heart in the spirit, not the letter*" [Rom 2:29], but in this passage *in Christ*.

"*In whom,*" he says, "*you were also circumcised with a circumcision made without hands, by putting off completely the body of the sins*[63] *of the flesh*" [Col 2:11]. He didn't say "put off." *The body of the sins*—he means the old life. Often he returns to this and in different ways, as he said also above: "*Who has delivered us from the dominion of darkness and transferred us, hostile, to be holy and blameless*" [Col 1:13, 21]. "No longer," he means, "is circumcision with a knife, but with Christ himself, for no hand performs this circumcision, like here, but the Spirit itself. It doesn't circumcise a part, but the whole person." It's a body both in this case; it's a body in that, but

---

63. "Of the sins" is a variant of the Byzantine text-type, which explains its elucidation in what follows.

σῶμα κἀκεῖνο· ἀλλὰ τὸ μὲν σαρκί, τὸ δὲ πνευματικῶς περιτέμνεται· ἀλλ' οὐχ ὡς Ἰουδαῖοι· οὐ γὰρ σάρκα, ἀλλὰ ἁμαρτήματα ἀπεξεδύσασθε. Πότε, καὶ ποῦ; Ἐν τῷ βαπτίσματι. Καὶ ὃ καλεῖ περιτομήν, πάλιν τάφον καλεῖ. Ὅρα πῶς πάλιν ἐπὶ τὰ δικαιώματα διαβαίνει. "Τῶν ἁμαρτιῶν, φησὶ, τῶν τῆς σαρκός·" ἅπερ ἐν τῇ σαρκὶ [236] ἔπραξαν. Μεῖζον τῆς περιτομῆς λέγει· οὐ γὰρ ἔρριψαν τὸ περιτμηθέν, ἀλλ' ἀπώλεσαν, ἀλλ' ἔφθειραν.

"Συνταφέντες αὐτῷ, φησὶν, ἐν τῷ βαπτισμῷ, ἐν ᾧ καὶ συνηγέρθητε διὰ τῆς πίστεως τῆς ἐνεργείας τοῦ θεοῦ τοῦ ἐγείραντος αὐτὸν ἐκ νεκρῶν." Ἀλλ' οὐ τάφος μόνον ἐστίν· ὅρα γὰρ τί φησιν· "Ἐν ᾧ καὶ συνηγέρθητε διὰ τῆς πίστεως τῆς ἐνεργείας τοῦ θεοῦ τοῦ ἐγείραντος αὐτὸν ἐκ νεκρῶν." Καλῶς εἶπε, "πίστεως·" πίστεως γὰρ ὅλον ἐστίν. Ἐπιστεύσατε ὅτι δύναται ὁ θεὸς ἐγεῖραι, καὶ οὕτως ἠγέρθητε. Εἶτα καὶ τὸ ἀξιόπιστον, "τοῦ ἐγείραντος αὐτὸν, φησὶν, ἐκ νεκρῶν." Ἤδη δείκνυσι τὴν ἀνάστασιν· "Καὶ ὑμᾶς ποτε ὄντας νεκροὺς τοῖς παραπτώμασι καὶ τῇ ἀκροβυστίᾳ τῆς σαρκὸς ὑμῶν, συνεζωοποίησε σὺν αὐτῷ." Ὑπὸ γὰρ τὴν δίκην ἔκεισθε ἀποθανεῖν. Εἰ δὲ καὶ ἀπεθάνετε, θάνατον χρήσιμον. Ὅρα πῶς πάλιν δείκνυσι τίνων ἦσαν ἄξιοι, δι' ὧν ἐπήγαγε· "Χαρισάμενος ἡμῖν πάντα τὰ παραπτώματα· ἐξαλείψας τὸ καθ' ἡμῶν χειρόγραφον τοῖς δόγμασιν, ὃ ἦν ὑπεναντίον ἡμῖν, καὶ αὐτὸ ἦρκεν ἐκ τοῦ μέσου, προσηλώσας αὐτὸ τῷ σταυρῷ· ἀπεκδυσάμενος τὰς ἀρχὰς καὶ τὰς ἐξουσίας, ἐδειγμάτισεν ἐν παρρησίᾳ, θριαμβεύσας αὐτοὺς ἐν αὐτῷ."

"Χαρισάμενος ἡμῖν, φησὶ, "πάντα τὰ παραπτώματα," ἃ τὴν νεκρότητα ἐποίει. Καὶ τί; ἆρα ἀφῆκε μεῖναι; Οὐχὶ, ἀλλὰ καὶ ἐξήλειψεν, οὐκ ἐχάραξε μόνον, ὥστε μὴ φαίνεσθαι. "Τοῖς δόγμασι," φησί. Ποίοις δόγμασι; Τῇ πίστει· ἀρκεῖ πιστεῦσαι. Οὐχὶ ἔργοις ἔργα, ἀλλὰ πίστει ἔργα παρέθηκε. Καὶ τί μετὰ ταῦτα; Ἐπίτασις τοῦ ἀφιέναι τὸ ἐξαλεῖψαι. Πάλιν, "καὶ αὐτὸ ἦρκε, φησὶν, ἐκ τοῦ μέσου." Καὶ οὐδὲ οὕτως ἐφύλαξεν, ἀλλὰ καὶ διέρρηξεν αὐτὸ, "προσηλώσας τῷ σταυρῷ." "Ἀπεκδυσάμενος τὰς ἀρχὰς καὶ τὰς ἐξουσίας, ἐδειγμάτισεν ἐν παρρησίᾳ, θριαμβεύσας αὐτοὺς ἐν αὐτῷ." Οὐδαμοῦ οὕτω μεγαλοφώνως ἐφθέγξατο.

Ὁρᾷς σπουδὴν τοῦ ἀφανισθῆναι τὸ χειρόγραφον ὅσην ἐποιήσατο; Οἷον, πάντες ἦμεν ὑφ' ἁμαρτίαν καὶ κόλασιν· αὐτὸς [237] κολασθεὶς ἔλυσε καὶ τὴν

in the one it's of the flesh, of the other it's spiritually circumcised, but not like the Jews; for you haven't put off the flesh, but sins. When and where? In baptism. And what he calls circumcision, he again calls baptism. See how again he progresses to righteous acts. "*Of the sins,*" he says, "*of the flesh,*" which are the ones they've committed in the flesh. [**236**] He speaks of something more important than circumcision, for they didn't cast away circumcision, but abolished it—yes, they annihilated it.

"*Buried with him,*" Paul says, "*in baptism, in which you were also raised in him with him, through the faith of the activity of God who raised him from the dead*" [Col 2:12]. No, it's not just burial, for see what he says: "*In whom you were also raised through faith in the activity* of God, *who raised him from the dead.*" Paul did well to say "*faith,*" for faith is everything. You believed that God is capable of raising, and so you were raised. Then there's also the credibility issue: "*Who raised him from the dead,*" he says. Now Paul demonstrates the resurrection: "*And you who once were dead in trespasses and the uncircumcision of your flesh, God has made come alive with him.* For you lay under the judgment of death. But even though you died, it was a profitable death." See how again he demonstrates what they deserved, through what he adds: "*Having forgiven us all our trespasses, having canceled the bond that stood against us with its doctrines, which was against us, he even removed it, nailing it to the cross. Having disarmed the principalities and the powers, he made a demonstration of them publicly, having triumphed over them in him*" [Col 2:13–15].

"*Having forgiven,*" he says, "*all your trespasses,*" those that produce deadness. What then? Did Christ allow them to remain? No, he even wiped them out, not just scratched them, so that they couldn't be seen. "*By the doctrines,*" Paul said. By what kind of doctrines? The faith—it's enough to believe. He hasn't set works against works, but works against faith. And what next? Wiping out is an advance on remission; again Paul says, "*And he removed it publicly.*" And yet not even so did Christ preserve it, but tore it apart, *nailing it to the cross. Having disarmed the principalities and powers, he made a demonstration of them publicly, having triumphed over them in him*. Nowhere has Paul spoken so grandiloquently.[64]

Do you see how great his zeal was to have the bond destroyed? For example, we were all subject to sin and punishment. Christ himself, [**237**]

---

64. On Chrysostom's appreciation of Paul's grandiloquence, see Mitchell, *Heavenly Trumpet,* passim, but esp. 124–26.

ἁμαρτίαν καὶ τὴν κόλασιν· ἐκολάσθη δὲ ἐν τῷ σταυρῷ. Ἐκεῖ οὖν αὐτὸ προσέπειρεν· ὡς ἐξουσίαν ἔχων, λοιπὸν διέρρηξε. Ποῖον χειρόγραφον; "Η τοῦτό φησιν, ὃ ἔλεγον πρὸς τὸν Μωϋσέα, ὅτι "Πάντα ὅσα εἶπεν ὁ θεὸς ποιήσομεν, καὶ ἀκουσόμεθα·" ἢ εἰ μὴ τοῦτο, ὅτι ὀφείλομεν τῷ θεῷ ὑπακοήν· ἢ εἰ μὴ τοῦτο, ὅτι κατεῖχεν ὁ διάβολος, τὸ χειρόγραφον ὃ ἐποίησε πρὸς τὸν Ἀδὰμ ὁ θεός, εἰπών· "'Ηι ἂν ἡμέρᾳ φάγῃς ἀπὸ τοῦ ξύλου, ἀποθανῇ." Κατεῖχεν οὖν τὸ χειρόγραφον τοῦτο ὁ διάβολος. Καὶ οὐκ ἔδωκεν ἡμῖν αὐτὸ ὁ Χριστός, ἀλλ' αὐτὸς αὐτὸ ἔσχισεν, ὅπερ τοῦ μετὰ χαρᾶς ἀφιέντος ἐστίν. "Ἀπεκδυσάμενος τὰς ἀρχὰς καὶ τὰς ἐξουσίας." Τὰς διαβολικὰς δυνάμεις λέγει. Ἐπεὶ οὖν αὐτὰς ἡ ἀνθρωπίνη φύσις ἐνδέδυτο, ἢ ἐπειδὴ αὐτὰς ὥσπερ λαβὴν εἶχον, ἄνθρωπος γενόμενος ἀπεδύσατο τὴν λαβήν. Τί ἐστιν, "ἐδειγμάτισε;" Καὶ καλῶς εἶπεν· οὐδέποτε οὕτως ὁ διάβολος ἠσχημόνησε. Προσδοκῶν γὰρ αὐτὸν ἔχειν, καὶ ὅσους εἶχεν ἀπώλεσε· καὶ τοῦ σώματος προσηλουμένου, οἱ νεκροὶ ἀνίσταντο.

Ἐκεῖ τὴν πληγὴν ἔλαβεν ὁ διάβολος, ὑπὸ σώματος νεκροῦ τὴν καιρίαν λαβών. Καὶ καθάπερ ἀθλητὴς νομίζων τὸν ἀντίπαλον βεβληκέναι, καιρίαν κατέχεται λαβών, οὕτω δὴ καὶ οὗτος. Δείκνυσιν ὅτι τὸ μετὰ παρρησίας ἀποθανεῖν, ἀσχημοσύνη ἐστὶ τοῦ διαβόλου. Πάντα γὰρ ἂν ἐποίησεν ἐκεῖνος, εἴγε ἠδύνατο, ὥστε πεῖσαι τοὺς ἀνθρώπους, ὅτι οὐκ ἀπέθανεν. Ἐπειδὴ γὰρ τῆς μὲν ἀναστάσεως ὁ μετὰ ταῦτα πᾶς καιρὸς τεκμήριον ἦν, τοῦ δὲ θανάτου, εἰ μὴ ἐκεῖνος ἐγένετο, οὐκ ἂν ἐγένετο ἕτερος καιρός, διὰ τοῦτο ἀπέθανε μὲν δημοσίᾳ πάντων ὁρώντων, οὐκ ἀνέστη δὲ δημοσίᾳ, εἰδὼς τὸν μετὰ ταῦτα χρόνον μαρτυρήσοντα τῇ ἀληθείᾳ. Τὸ γὰρ τοῦ κόσμου ὁρῶντος ἄνω ἐν τῷ ξύλῳ τὸν ὄφιν σφαγιασθῆναι, τοῦτό ἐστι [238] τὸ θαυμαστόν. Καὶ τί γὰρ οὐκ ἐποίησεν ὁ διάβολος, ὥστε λαθόντα αὐτὸν ἀποθανεῖν; Ἄκουε τοῦ Πιλάτου λέγοντος· "Ἄρατε αὐτὸν ὑμεῖς, καὶ σταυρώσατε· ἐγὼ γὰρ οὐδεμίαν αἰτίαν ἐν αὐτῷ εὑρίσκω." καὶ μυρία ἀνθισταμένου. Καὶ πάλιν Ἰουδαῖοι ἔλεγον αὐτῷ, "Εἰ υἱὸς εἶ τοῦ θεοῦ, κατάβηθι ἀπὸ τοῦ σταυροῦ." Λοιπὸν οὖν ἐπειδὴ καιρίαν ἔλαβε, καὶ οὐ κατέβη, διὰ τοῦτο καὶ ταφῇ παρεδόθη· ἐπεὶ δυνατὸν ἦν εὐθέως ἀναστῆναι, ἀλλ' ἵνα πιστευθῇ τὸ πρᾶγμα. Καίτοι ἐν μὲν ταῖς ἰδιωτικαῖς τελευταῖς ἔνεστιν ὀλιγοψυχίαν αἰτιάσασθαι· ἐνταῦθα δὲ οὐδὲ τοῦτο. Καὶ γὰρ καὶ οἱ στρατιῶται οὐ κατέαξαν αὐτοῦ τὰ σκέλη, καθάπερ τῶν ἄλλων, ἵνα φανερωθῇ ὅτι τέθνηκε· καὶ φανεροί εἰσιν οἱ τὸ σῶμα θάψαντες. Διὰ τοῦτο καὶ αὐτοὶ σφραγίζονται οἱ Ἰουδαῖοι τὸν λίθον μετὰ τῶν στρατιωτῶν. Τὸ γὰρ μάλιστα πάντων σπουδαζόμενον τοῦτο ἦν, τὸ μὴ συσκιασθῆναι. Καὶ οἱ μάρτυρες, παρὰ

having been punished, did away with both the sin and the punishment, and he was punished on the cross. Then he affixed it there; afterward, having the power, he tore it up. What kind of bond? Either he means what they said to Moses, namely, that *"All that God has said we shall do and obey"* [Exod 24:3]; or if not that, that we owe God obedience; or if not that, that the devil had possession of the bond that God made to Adam, saying, *"On the day that you eat from this tree you will die"* [Gen 2:17]. This bond, then, the devil had in his possession. And Christ didn't give it to us, but he himself tore it apart, which is the action of one who remits joyfully. *Having disarmed the principalities and powers.* He means the powers of the devil, since then human nature was clothed in these, or since they had a kind of hold, when he became a human being he put away that hold. What is the meaning of *he made a demonstration of them*? And he spoke well: never was the devil so disgraced. For while expecting to take possession of Christ, he lost even all those he possessed, and when that body was nailed, the dead arose.

There the devil received the wound, receiving the death blow from a dead body. And just as an athlete, supposing he has disabled his adversary, himself receives from him a death stroke, so indeed it is with Christ. He shows that dying with confidence is a disgrace for the devil. For the devil would have done everything, if he'd been able, to persuade human beings that Christ hadn't died. You see, since all the time after his resurrection was evidence, and of his death there would have been no other time, on that account he died publicly in the sight of all, but he didn't rise publicly, knowing that the time afterward would bear witness to the truth. For while the world was looking on this, that the serpent should be slain up high on the cross [see John 3:14]—this is [**238**] the amazing thing. And what did the devil not do, so that Christ might die in secret? Listen to Pilate saying, *"Take him away and crucify him, for I find no fault in him"* [John 19:6], and he opposed myriad things. And again the Jews said to him, *"If you are the son of God, come down from the cross"* [Matt 27:40]. Then further, when he had received a death blow and he didn't come down, for this reason he was committed to burial, since it was in his power to rise up immediately, but [he did not] so the fact might be believed. And yet in the case of private deaths it's possible to impute them to faintheartedness; here that isn't possible at all. You see, even the soldiers didn't break his legs as they did with the others, in order to make apparent that he was dead. And those who buried the body are known. And on this account too the Jews themselves sealed the stone together with the soldiers. You see, what was most of all attended to was that it not happen in obscurity. And the witnesses to it are

τῶν ἐχθρῶν, παρὰ τῶν Ἰουδαίων. Ἄκουε αὐτῶν λεγόντων τῷ Πιλάτῳ· "Εἶπεν ὁ πλάνος ἐκεῖνος ἔτι ζῶν, μετὰ τρεῖς ἡμέρας ἐγείρομαι. κέλευσον οὖν παρὰ τῶν στρατιωτῶν φυλαχθῆναι τὸν τάφον." κἀκείνων σφραγιζομένων τοῦτο ἐγένετο. Ἄκουε δὲ αὐτῶν τοῦτο καὶ μετὰ ταῦτα λεγόντων τοῖς ἀποστόλοις· "Βούλεσθε ἐπαγαγεῖν ἐφ᾽ ἡμᾶς τὸ αἷμα τοῦ ἀνθρώπου τούτου."

Τὸν τρόπον αὐτοῦ τοῦ σταυροῦ οὐκ ἀφῆκεν αἰσχύνεσθαι. Ἐπειδὴ γὰρ οἱ ἄγγελοι οὐδὲν τοιοῦτον πεπόνθασι, διὰ τοῦτο ὑπὲρ τούτου πάντα ποιεῖ, δεικνὺς ὅτι μέγα κατώρθωσεν ὁ θάνατος. Ὥσπερ μονομαχεῖον γέγονεν. Ἔπληξε τὸν Χριστὸν ὁ θάνατος, ἀλλ᾽ ὁ Χριστὸς πληγεὶς, ὕστερον αὐτὸν ἀνεῖλε· νεκρῷ σώματι κατελύετο ὁ δοκῶν ἀθάνατος εἶναι· καὶ τοῦτο ἡ οἰκουμένη ἑώρα. Καὶ τὸ δὴ θαυμαστόν, οὐκ ἐπέτρεψεν ἑτέρῳ τοῦτο. Ἀλλὰ γέγονεν ἕτερον χειρόγραφον πάλιν, οὐ τοιοῦτον, οἷον τὸ πρότερον.

Ὁρᾶτε οὖν μὴ τούτῳ ἁλῶμεν μετὰ τὸ εἰπεῖν, ἀποτάσσομαι τῷ Σατανᾷ, καὶ συντάσσομαι σοί, Χριστέ. Μᾶλλον δὲ οὐκ ἂν κληθείη τοῦτο χειρόγραφον, ἀλλὰ συνθήκη. Χειρόγραφον γάρ ἐστιν, ὅταν τις ὀφλημάτων ὑπεύθυνος κατέχηται· τοῦτο δὲ συνθήκη ἐστίν· οὐκ ἔχει τιμωρίαν, οὐδὲ λέγει, ἐὰν τόδε, ἢ μὴ τόδε· ὃ τὸ αἷμα τῆς [239] διαθήκης ῥαντίζων Μωϋσῆς εἶπε· τούτῳ, καὶ ὁ θεὸς ζωὴν αἰώνιον ἐπηγγείλατο. Ταῦτα πάντα συνθήκη ἐστίν. Ἐκεῖ δοῦλος πρὸς δεσπότην, ἐνταῦθα φίλος πρὸς φίλον· ἐκεῖ, "Ἧι ἂν ἡμέρα φάγῃ, φησίν, ἀποθανῇ·" εὐθέως ἀπειλή· ἐνταῦθα δὲ οὐδὲν τοιοῦτον. Παραγίνεται ὁ θεός, καὶ ἐνταῦθα γυμνότης, κἀκεῖ γυμνότης· ἀλλ᾽ ἐκεῖ μὲν ἁμαρτήσας ἐγυμνώθη, ἐπειδὴ ἥμαρτεν· ἐνταῦθα δέ, ἵνα ἀπαλλαγῇ, γυμνοῦται. Ἀπεδύσατο τότε τὴν δόξαν, ἣν εἶχεν ἐκεῖνος· ἀποδύεται νῦν τὸν παλαιὸν ἄνθρωπον, καὶ πρὶν ἢ ἐπιβῆναι, οὕτως εὐκόλως ἀποδύεται, ὥσπερ τὰ ἱμάτια. Ἀλείφεται, ὥσπερ οἱ ἀθληταὶ εἰς στάδιον ἐμβησόμενοι. Ἅμα γὰρ τίκτεται, καὶ οὐ καθάπερ ἐκεῖνος ὁ πρῶτος, οὐ κατὰ μικρόν, ἀλλ᾽ εὐθέως· οὐ καθάπερ οἱ ἱερεῖς τὸ παλαιὸν τὴν κεφαλὴν μόνον, μᾶλλον δὲ μειζόνως. Ἐκεῖνος μὲν γὰρ τὴν

from the enemies, from the Jews. Listen to them saying to Pilate: "That deceiver said when he was still alive: '*After three days I shall rise.*' *Therefore command that the grave be guarded* by the soldiers" [Matt 27:63–64]. This was done, after they had sealed it. Listen to them saying this afterward too to the apostles, "*You want to bring this man's blood upon us*" [Acts 5:28].

Christ didn't allow the manner of his crucifixion to be put to shame. You see, since the angels suffered nothing of this kind, on this account he does everything for this, demonstrating that his death was a great achievement: there was, as it were, a single combat. Death wounded Christ, but the wounded Christ afterward killed death. The one who seemed immortal was destroyed by a dead body, and the world saw this. And the really amazing thing is that he didn't entrust this to another. No, there was made again a second bond, not the same as the former.

See to it, therefore, that we aren't caught after having said, "I renounce Satan and align myself with you, Christ."[65] But this should rather not be called a bond but a covenant, for a bond is when one is held accountable for debts, while this is a covenant. It contains no penalty, nor does it say, "if this [be done], or this not." [239] This is what Moses said when he sprinkled the blood of the covenant, and God promised everlasting life [see Exod 24:6, 8]. All this is a covenant. There it was a servant to a master; here it is a friend to a friend. There it says, "*On the day you eat, you will die*" [Gen 2:17]—an immediate threat, while here there is nothing of the kind.[66] God appeared, and there was nakedness [see Gen 2:7], and here too nakedness. But here the one who has sinned is made naked, because they sinned, but here one is made naked in order to be set free.[67] Then that person put off the glory that they had, now they put off the old person [see Eph 4:22; Col 3:9], and before they advance they put [the devil] off as easily as if he were garments.[68] They are anointed with oil, just like athletes advancing into the stadium. You see, they are born at once and not little by little, like the first man, but immediately. [They are anointed] not only on the head, like the priests of old [see Lev 8:23–24], but rather more abundantly. For he [sc. a

---

65. A renunciation that was part of the baptismal liturgy. See John Chrysostom, *Huit catéchèses baptismales inédites*, ed. Antoine Wenger, SC 50 (Paris: Cerf, 1970), 79–80.

66. This is a contrast between Old Testament and New Testament covenants.

67. The preacher contrasts the nakedness of Adam and Eve in the garden of Eden after their transgression with the stripping of baptismal candidates.

68. What follows is a mixture of baptismal imagery and the imagery of wrestling.

κεφαλὴν, τὸ οὖς τὸ δεξιὸν, τὴν χεῖρα, ἵνα καὶ πρὸς ὑπακοὴν καὶ ἔργα ἀγαθὰ αὐτὸν διεγείρῃ· οὗτος δὲ τὸ πᾶν. Οὐ γὰρ διδαχθησόμενος ἔρχεται μόνον, ἀλλὰ καὶ ἀθλήσων καὶ γυμνασθησόμενος. Εἰς ἑτέραν ἀνάγεται κτίσιν. Ὅταν γὰρ ὁμολογῇ εἰς ζωὴν αἰώνιον, ὡμολόγησεν ἑτέραν κτίσιν. Ἔλαβε χοῦν ἀπὸ τῆς γῆς, καὶ ἔπλασε τὸν ἄνθρωπον· λοιπὸν δὲ οὐκέτι χοῦν, ἀλλὰ πνεῦμα ἅγιον· τούτῳ πλάττεται, τούτῳ ῥυθμίζεται, καθάπερ καὶ αὐτὸς ἐν τῇ μήτρᾳ τῆς παρθένου. Οὐκ εἶπεν, ἐν παραδείσῳ, ἀλλ', ἐν οὐρανῷ. Μὴ γὰρ, ἐπειδὴ γῇ ὑπόκειται, νομίσῃς εἶναι ἐν γῇ· μετέστη ἐκεῖ πρὸς τὸν οὐρανόν· ἐκεῖ ταῦτα γίνεται μεταξὺ ἀγγέλων. Ἄνω σου λαμβάνει τὴν ψυχὴν ὁ θεός, μεταρρυθμίζων ἄνω, παρὰ τὸν θρόνον ἱστᾷ σε τὸν βασιλικόν. Πλάττεται ἐν τῷ ὕδατι, λαμβάνει δὲ ἀντίψυχον πνεῦμα. Μετὰ δὲ τὸ πλασθῆναι οὐκ ἄγει πρὸς αὐτὸν θηρία, ἀλλὰ δαίμονας καὶ τὸν ἀρχηγὸν αὐτῶν, καὶ λέγει, "Πατεῖτε ἐπάνω ὄφεων καὶ σκορπίων." Οὐ [240] λέγει, "Ποιήσωμεν ἄνθρωπον κατ' εἰκόνα ἡμετέραν καὶ καθ' ὁμοίωσιν ἡμετέραν," ἀλλὰ τί; Δίδωσιν αὐτοῖς υἱοῖς θεοῦ γενέσθαι· "Ἀλλ' ἐκ θεοῦ, φησιν, ἐγεννήθησαν." Εἶτα ἵνα μὴ τοῦ ὄφεως ἀκούσῃς, εὐθέως διδάσκει λέγειν, ἀποτάσσομαί σοι· ἀντὶ τοῦ, ὅπερ ἂν εἴπῃς, οὐκ ἀκούσομαί σου. Εἶτα ἵνα μὴ δι' ἑτέρων σε ἕλῃ, φησὶ, καὶ τῇ πομπῇ σου καὶ τῇ λατρείᾳ σου, καὶ τοῖς ἀγγέλοις σου. Ἔθετο αὐτὸν οὐκέτι φυλάσσειν τὸν παράδεισον, ἀλλὰ πολιτεύεσθαι ἐν οὐρανῷ. Εὐθέως γὰρ ἀνελθὼν, ταῦτα φθέγγεται τὰ ῥήματα· "Πάτερ ἡμῶν ὁ ἐν τοῖς οὐρανοῖς, γενηθήτω τὸ θέλημά σου, ὡς ἐν οὐρανῷ, καὶ ἐπὶ τῆς γῆς." Οὐκ ἐπ' ὄψιν πίπτει τὸ παιδίον, οὐ ξύλον ὁρᾷς, οὐδὲ πηγὴν, ἀλλ' αὐτὸν εὐθέως περιλαμβάνεις τὸν δεσπότην, ἀνακεράννυσαι τῷ σώματι, ἀναφύρῃ τῷ σώματι τῷ ἄνω κειμένῳ, ἔνθα προσελθεῖν οὐκ ἔνι τῷ διαβόλῳ. Οὐκ ἔστι γυνὴ, ἵνα προσέλθῃ, καὶ ὡς ἀσθενεστέραν ἀπατήσῃ· "Οὐκ ἔστι γὰρ, φησὶ, θῆλυ, οὐδὲ ἄρσεν." Ἂν μὴ σὺ κατέλθῃς πρὸς αὐτὸν, οὐ δυνήσεται ἐπιβῆναι ἔνθα εἶ· ἐν γὰρ τῷ οὐρανῷ εἶ, ὁ δὲ οὐρανὸς ἄβατος τῷ διαβόλῳ. Οὐκ ἔχει ξύλον γνωστὸν καλοῦ καὶ πονηροῦ, ἀλλὰ τὸ ξύλον τῆς ζωῆς μόνον. Οὐκέτι ἀπὸ τῆς πλευρᾶς σου γυνὴ, ἀλλὰ πάντες ἕν ἐσμεν

priest of old] was anointed on the head, the right ear, the hand, in order to excite him to obedience and good works, whereas this one is anointed all over. You see, they come not only to be instructed, but to wrestle and be exercised. They are advanced to another creation. For when they confessed to life everlasting, they confessed a second creation. God took dust from the earth and formed the human being [see Gen 2:7], while now it's no longer dust but the Holy Spirit. Christ was formed by this, harmonized by this, just as he himself was in the womb of the Virgin. He didn't say "in paradise," but "in heaven." But don't consider that, because earth is suggested, it happens on earth: he's translated from here to heaven, from here these things come about in the midst of angels. God takes up your soul above, harmonizing it above, placing you near the royal throne. The person is formed in the water but takes a spirit instead of a soul. And after being formed God doesn't bring beasts to him, but demons and their prince, and says, "*Tread upon serpents and scorpions*" [Luke 10:19]. He doesn't [**239**] say, "*Let us make a human being in our image and likeness*" [Gen 1:26], but what? "*He gave them power to become sons of God, but*," he says, "*they were born, from God.*" Then, so that you don't listen to the serpent, immediately you learn to say, "I renounce you," instead of, "whatever you say, I shall not listen to you." Then, so that he doesn't catch you through others, it is said, "And your pomp, and your worship, and your angels."[69] God established him no longer to guard paradise but to have citizenship in heaven. For immediately on coming up[70] he utters these words, "*Our Father, who are in heaven, may your will be done as it is in heaven, and on earth.*" The child doesn't fall on its face, nor do you see a tree, nor a spring,[71] but immediately you receive the Master himself, you're mingled with his body, you're mixed together with the body that is situated above, where the devil can't approach. No woman is there for him to approach and deceive as being the weaker [see Gen 3:1–7]. "*For*," it says, "*there is no female nor male*" [Gal 3:28]. If you don't go down to him, he'll be unable to go up to where you are. You see, you're in heaven, while heaven is inaccessible for the devil. It had no tree with knowledge of good and evil, but the tree of life only. No longer will a woman be formed from your side [see Gen 2:22], but we are

---

69. Another part of the baptismal liturgy. Wenger believes that the inclusion of angels in this part of the renunciation is typical of the Constantinopolitan liturgy (Chrysostom, *Huit catéchèses baptismales*, 81).

70. That is, coming up from the baptismal font.

71. These phrases do not make sense.

ἀπὸ τῆς πλευρᾶς τοῦ Χριστοῦ. Εἰ γὰρ οἱ ἠλειμμένοι ὑπὸ ἀνθρώπων, οὐδὲν πάσχουσιν ὑπὸ ὄφεων, οὐδὲ σὺ πείσῃ τι, ἕως ἂν ᾖς ἠλειμμένος, ἵνα δυνηθῇς κατέχειν τὸν ὄφιν καὶ ἀποπνίγειν, πατεῖν ἐπάνω ὄφεων καὶ σκορπίων. Ἀλλ' ὥσπερ μεγάλα τὰ δῶρα, οὕτω μεγάλη ἡμῖν καὶ ἡ τιμωρία. Οὐκ ἔνι ἐκπεσόντα τοῦ παραδείσου ἀπέναντι οἰκῆσαι τοῦ παραδείσου, οὐδὲ ἐπανελθεῖν ὅθεν ἐξεπέσομεν. Ἀλλὰ τί μετὰ ταῦτα; Γέεννα, καὶ σκώληξ ἀτελεύτητος. Ἀλλὰ μὴ γένοιτό τινα ἡμῶν ὑπεύθυνον γενέσθαι ταύτῃ τῇ τιμωρίᾳ· ἀλλ' ἐναρέτως ζῶντες σπουδάσωμεν τὰ αὐτῷ δοκοῦντα διαπράττεσθαι. Εὐαρεστήσωμεν τῷ θεῷ, ἵνα δυνηθῶμεν καὶ τῆς κολάσεως ἀπαλλαγῆναι, καὶ τῶν αἰωνίων ἀγαθῶν ἐπιτυχεῖν, ὧν γένοιτο πάντας ἡμᾶς ἀξιωθῆναι, χάριτι καὶ φιλανθρωπίᾳ τοῦ κυρίου ἡμῶν Ἰησοῦ Χριστοῦ, μεθ' οὗ τῷ πατρὶ ἅμα τῷ ἁγίῳ πνεύματι δόξα, κράτος, τιμή, νῦν καὶ ἀεὶ καὶ εἰς τοὺς αἰῶνας τῶν αἰώνων. Ἀμήν.

all from the side of Christ. For if those who have been anointed by human beings suffer nothing from serpents, neither will you suffer anything, as long as you are anointed, so that you may be able to catch the serpent and choke him, and you can *tread upon serpents and scorpions* [Luke 10:19]. But as the gifts are great, so great also is the punishment. It isn't possible for someone who has fallen from paradise to dwell *in front of paradise* [Gen 3:24], nor to ascend from the place we have fallen from. But what after this? Hell and the eternal worm. But God forbid that one of us should be liable to this punishment. No, living virtuously, let us strive to carry out his will throughout. Let us become well-pleasing to God, so that we may be able to escape the punishment and obtain the good things of eternity of that we may all be considered worthy, by the grace and love of humankind of our Lord Jesus Christ, with whom with the Father, together with the Holy Spirit be glory, power, honor, now and forever and ever. Amen.

Μὴ οὖν τις ὑμᾶς κρινέτω ἐν βρώσει ἢ ἐν πόσει, ἢ ἐν μέρει ἑορτῆς ἢ νουμηνίας ἢ σαββάτων, ἅ ἐστι σκιὰ τῶν μελλόντων, τὸ δὲ σῶμα Χριστοῦ. Μηδεὶς ὑμᾶς καταβραβευέτω θέλων ἐν ταπεινοφροσύνῃ καὶ θρησκείᾳ τῶν ἀγγέλων, ἃ μὴ ἑώρακεν ἐμβατεύων, εἰκῇ φυσιούμενος ὑπὸ τοῦ νοὸς τῆς σαρκὸς αὐτοῦ, καὶ οὐ κρατῶν τὴν κεφαλήν, ἐξ οὗ πᾶν τὸ σῶμα διὰ τῶν ἁφῶν καὶ συνδέσμων ἐπιχορηγούμενον καὶ συμβιβαζόμενον, αὔξει τὴν αὔξησιν τοῦ θεοῦ.

Πρῶτον αἰνιγματωδῶς εἰπών, "Βλέπετε μή τις ὑμᾶς ἔσται ὁ συλαγωγῶν κατὰ τὴν παράδοσιν τῶν ἀνθρώπων," καὶ πάλιν ἀνωτέρω, "Τοῦτο δὲ λέγω, ἵνα μή τις ὑμᾶς παραλογίζηται ἐν πιθανολογίᾳ·" καὶ προκαταλαβὼν τὴν ψυχὴν καὶ μεμεριμνημένην ἐργασάμενος, εἶτα παρενθεὶς τὰς εὐεργεσίας, καὶ μειζόνως τοῦτο ποιήσας, τότε ἐπάγει τὸν ἔλεγχον ὕστερον, καί φησι· "Μὴ οὖν τις ὑμᾶς κρινέτω ἐν βρώσει, ἢ ἐν πόσει, ἢ ἐν μέρει ἑορτῆς ἢ νεομηνίας ἢ σαββάτων." Ὁρᾷς πῶς αὐτὰ καθαιρεῖ; Εἰ τοιούτων τετυχήκατε, φησί, τί τοῖς μικροῖς ὑπευθύνους ἑαυτοὺς ποιεῖτε; Καὶ ἐξευτελίζει λέγων, "ἢ ἐν μέρει ἑορτῆς·" οὐ γὰρ δὴ πάντα κατεῖχον τὰ πρότερα. "Ἢ νουμηνίας ἢ σαββάτων." Οὐκ εἶπε, μὴ τοίνυν φυλάττετε, ἀλλά, "μή τις ὑμᾶς κρινέτω." Ἔδειξεν αὐτοὺς παραβαίνοντας καὶ λύοντας, ἐφ' ἑτέρους δὲ τὸ ἔγκλημα ἤνεγκε. Μὴ ἀνέχεσθε τῶν κρινόντων, φησίν. Ἀλλ' οὐδὲ τοῦτο· ἀλλ' ἐκείνοις διαλέγεται, μονονουχὶ ἐπιστομίζων αὐτούς, ὅτι οὐκ ὀφείλετε ἀνακρίνειν. Ἀλλ' οὐκ ἂν τούτων καθήψατο. Οὐκ εἶπεν, ἐν καθαροῖς καὶ ἀκαθάρτοις, οὐδὲ εἶπεν, ἐν σκηνοπηγίαις καὶ ἀζύμοις καὶ πεντηκοστῇ· ἀλλ', "ἐν μέρει ἑορτῆς·" οὐ γὰρ ἐτόλμων τὸ πᾶν φυλάττειν· καὶ εἰ ἐφύλαττον, οὐχ ὥστε ἑορτάζειν. "Ἐν μέρει," φησί· δεικνὺς ὅτι τὸ πλέον λέλυται. Εἰ γὰρ καὶ ἐσαββάτιζον, ἀλλ' οὐκ ἀκριβῶς. "Ἃ ἐστι

Therefore, let nobody pass judgment on you in food or drink, or in respect of a festival, or a new moon, or of the Sabbath days, which are to come, but the body is Christ's. Let nobody disqualify you by insisting on humility and angel worship, intruding on what they have not seen, vainly puffed up by their sensuous mind and not holding fast to the head, from which the whole body, nourished and knit together in joints and ligaments, will grow with a growth that is from God [Col 2:16–19].

First, having said enigmatically, "*See to it that nobody makes a prey of you according to human tradition*" [Col 2:8], and again further back, "*And this I say, lest anybody delude you with beguiling words*" [Col 2:4], and preoccupying their soul and making it anxious, then having inserted the benefits and making much of this, he next adds his reproof last, and says, "*Therefore let nobody pass judgment on you in food or drink, or in respect of a festival, or a new moon, or of Sabbath days.*" Do you see how this puts them down? "If you've obtained such things," he says, "why do you make yourselves accountable for petty matters?" And he disparages them, saying, "*In respect of a festival,*" for indeed they didn't retain all the former injunctions. *Or of Sabbath days.* He didn't say, "Therefore don't observe them," but "*let nobody judge you.*" He demonstrated that they were transgressing and undoing, but he brought this accusation against others. "Don't put up with those who judge you," he says. But that's not it. No, he argues against those persons, almost muzzling them, saying, "You shouldn't judge." But he wouldn't have upbraided them. He didn't say "in clean and unclean," nor did he say "in feasts of tabernacles, and unleavened bread, and Pentecost," but "*in respect of a festival,*" for they didn't dare to observe everything, and if they *did* observe it, in was not in order to celebrate. "*In respect,*" he says, demonstrating that most of it is done away with. For even if they celebrated

---

72. For a previous translation of this homily, see Mayer and Allen, *John Chrysostom*, 73–84.

σκιὰ τῶν μελλόντων." Τῆς καινῆς, φησὶ, διαθήκης. "Τὸ δὲ σῶμα Χριστοῦ."
Οἱ μὲν οὖν οὕτω στίζουσι, "Τὸ δὲ σῶμα, Χριστοῦ· ἡ δὲ ἀλήθεια ἐπὶ Χριστοῦ γέγονεν· οἱ δὲ, "Τὸ σῶμα Χριστοῦ μηδεὶς ὑμᾶς καταβραβευέτω," τουτέστιν, ἐπηρεαζέτω. Καταβρα-[242]βευθῆναί ἐστιν ὅταν παρ' ἑτέρῳ μὲν ἡ
νίκη ᾖ, παρ' ἑτέρῳ δὲ τὸ βραβεῖον, ὅταν ἐπηρεάζῃ νικήσας. Ἄνωθεν ἕστηκας
τοῦ διαβόλου καὶ τῆς ἁμαρτίας· τί πάλιν ὑπάγεις σαυτὸν τῇ ἁμαρτίᾳ; Διὰ
τοῦτο ἔλεγεν, ὅτι "Ὀφειλέτης ἐστὶν ὅλον τὸν νόμον πληρῶσαι." καὶ πάλιν,
"Εὑρέθη Χριστὸς ἁμαρτίας διάκονος·" ὃ ἐν τῇ πρὸς Γαλάτας γράφων ἔλεγεν.
Ὅτε αὐτοὺς ἐνέπλησε θυμοῦ διὰ τοῦ εἰπεῖν, "καταβραβευέτω," τότε ἄρχεται·
"Θέλων, φησὶν, ἐν ταπεινοφροσύνῃ καὶ θρησκείᾳ τῶν ἀγγέλων, ἃ μὴ ἑώρακεν ἐμβατεύων, εἰκῇ φυσιούμενος ὑπὸ τοῦ νοὸς τῆς σαρκὸς αὐτοῦ." Πῶς, "ἐν
ταπεινοφροσύνῃ;" ἢ πῶς, "φυσιούμενος;" Δείκνυσι κενοδοξίας ὂν τὸ πᾶν.
    Τί δὲ ὅλως ἐστὶ τὸ λεγόμενον; Εἰσί τινες οἱ λέγοντες, οὐ δεῖ διὰ τοῦ Χρι-
στοῦ προσάγεσθαι, ἀλλὰ διὰ τῶν ἀγγέλων· ἐκεῖνο μεῖζόν ἐστιν, ἢ καθ' ἡμᾶς.
Διὰ τοῦτο ἄνω καὶ κάτω στρέφει τὰ ὑπὸ τοῦ Χριστοῦ πραχθέντα, διὰ τοῦ
αἵματος τοῦ σταυροῦ αὐτοῦ· διὰ τοῦτο λέγει ὅτι ὑπὲρ ἡμῶν ἔπαθεν, ὅτι ἠγά-
πησεν ἡμᾶς. Καὶ ἐν αὐτῷ δὲ τούτῳ ἐπήροντο πάλιν. Καὶ οὐκ εἶπε προσαγω-
γήν, ἀλλὰ θρησκείαν. "Ἃ μὴ ἑώρακεν ἐμβατεύων." Οὐ γὰρ εἶδεν ἀγγέλους,
καὶ οὕτω διάκειται ὡς ἰδών. Διὰ τοῦτό φησι, "Φυσιούμενος ὑπὸ τοῦ νοὸς τῆς
σαρκὸς αὐτοῦ εἰκῇ," οὐδὲ ἐπί τινι ἀληθεῖ πράγματι. Ἐπὶ τῷ δόγματι πεφύ-
σηται, καὶ προβάλλεται ταπεινοφροσύνης σχῆμα. Ὑπὸ σαρκικῆς διανοίας, οὐ
πνευματικῆς· ἀνθρώπινος ὁ λογισμός. "Καὶ οὐ κρατῶν τὴν κεφαλήν, φησὶν,
ἐξ οὗ πᾶν τὸ σῶμα." Πᾶν τὸ σῶμα ἐκεῖθεν ἔχει τὸ εἶναι, καὶ τὸ καλῶς εἶναι.
Τί τὴν κεφαλὴν ἀφεὶς, ἔχῃ τῶν μελῶν; Ἐὰν ἐκεῖθεν ἐκπέσῃς, ἀπόλωλας. "Ἐξ
οὗ πᾶν τὸ σῶμα." Ὅστις ἂν ᾖ, οὐ τὸ ζῆν, ἀλλὰ καὶ τὸ συντίθεσθαι ἐκεῖθεν
αὐτῷ. Πᾶσα ἡ ἐκκλησία, ἕως ἂν ἔχῃ τὴν κεφαλήν, αὔξει· ἐπεὶ οὐκέτι ἀπονοίας [243] καὶ κενοδοξίας τὸ πάθος, ἀνθρωπίνης ἐννοίας τὸ εὕρεμα. Ἰδοὺ τὸ,
"ἐξ οὗ," ἐπὶ τοῦ υἱοῦ. "Διὰ τῶν ἁφῶν καὶ συνδέσμων, φησὶν, ἐπιχορηγούμενον
καὶ συμβιβαζόμενον, αὔξει τὴν αὔξησιν τοῦ θεοῦ·" τὴν κατὰ θεὸν, φησὶ, τὴν
ἀπὸ τῆς πολιτείας τῆς ἀρίστης.

the Sabbath, they didn't do it correctly. *Which are to come.* He means of the new covenant. *The body is Christ's.* So some people punctuate like this, "*but the body* is *Christ's*," meaning that the truth has come with Christ, but others, "Let nobody judge against you with regard to Christ's body," that is, cheat you of it. [242] The expression "judge against you" means that when you're beaten by another, while the prize is with the other, when though victorious you're cheated. You've stood above the devil and sin: Why do you subject yourself again to sin? This is why Paul said, "*He is a debtor to fulfil the whole law*" [Gal 5:3]; and again, "*Is Christ found to be a minister of sin?*" [Gal 2:17], which he said in writing the Letter to the Galatians. When he had filled them with anger by saying, "*Pass judgment*," then he begins: "Wishing,"[73] he says, "*in humility and angel worship, intruding on what they have not seen, vainly puffed up by their sensuous mind.*" How *in humility*? And how *puffed up*? Paul shows that the whole arose from vainglory.

But what did he say in general terms? There are some who say that we should not be brought in through Christ, but by the angels—that is too great a thing for us. On this account he turns over and over what was done by Christ, through the blood of his cross. On this account he says that Christ suffered for our sake, that he loved us. And in this very thing they are pierced again. And he didn't say "bringing in" but "[*angel*]*worship.*" *Intruding into things they have not seen.* For he didn't see angels but is so affected as if he had. On this account he says, "*Puffed up vainly by their sensuous mind*," and it's not about any true fact. They are puffed up by the doctrine and put forward a show of humility. By their sensuous mind, not a spiritual one: his reasoning is human. And "*not holding fast to the head,*" he says, "*from which is the whole body.*" The whole body has its being from there, and its well-being. Why, letting go of the head, do you cling to the members? If you fall off from the head, you're lost. *From which all the body.* Whoever it may be doesn't have life but also has no connection from there to the head. The whole church, while it clings to the head, will increase, because there is no longer the [243] passion of senselessness and vainglory, the invention of human fantasy. Note the expression *from whom*, meaning the Son. "*Through joints and ligaments,*" Paul says, "*nourished and knit together, will grow with a growth the growth that is from God.*" He means growth according to God that comes from a life of virtue.

---

73. This word appears to be an addition by Chrysostom, a stenographer, or a copyist.

"Εἰ οὖν ἀπεθάνετε σὺν Χριστῷ." Μέσον ἐκεῖνο τίθησι, καὶ τὸ σφοδρότερον ἑκατέρωθεν. "Εἰ ἀπεθάνετε σὺν Χριστῷ ἀπὸ τῶν τοῦ κόσμου στοιχείων, φησὶ, τί ὡς ζῶντες ἐν κόσμῳ δογματίζεσθε;" Οὐκ ἔχει ἀκολουθίαν· ἔδει γὰρ εἰπεῖν, πῶς ὡς ζῶντες ὑπόκεισθε τοῖς στοιχείοις; Ἀλλὰ τοῦτο ἀφεὶς, τί φησι; "Μὴ ἅψῃ, μηδὲ γεύσῃ, μηδὲ θίγῃς· ἅ ἐστι πάντα εἰς φθορὰν τῇ ἀποχρήσει, κατὰ τὰ ἐντάλματα καὶ διδασκαλίας τῶν ἀνθρώπων." Οὐκ ἔστε ἐν τῷ κόσμῳ, φησί· πῶς τοῖς στοιχείοις ὑπόκεισθε; πῶς ταῖς τοῦ κόσμου παρατηρήσεσι; Καὶ ὅρα πῶς αὐτοὺς κωμῳδεῖ, "Μὴ θίγῃς, μὴ ἅψῃ, μὴ γεύσῃ," ὡς δειλοὺς καὶ μεγάλων τινῶν ἀπεχομένους. "Ἅ ἐστι πάντα εἰς φθορὰν τῇ ἀποχρήσει." Καθεῖλε τῶν πολλῶν τὴν φυσίωσιν, καὶ ἐπήγαγε· "Κατὰ τὰ ἐντάλματα καὶ διδασκαλίας τῶν ἀνθρώπων." Τί λέγεις; κἂν τὸν νόμον λέγεις; Λοιπὸν διδασκαλία ἐστὶν ἀνθρώπου μετὰ τὸν καιρόν. Ἢ ὅτι παρεποίουν αὐτὸν, ἢ τὰ τῶν Ἑλλήνων αἰνίττεται. Ὅλον ἀνθρώπινον τὸ δόγμα ἐστὶ, φησίν.

"Ἅτινά ἐστι λόγον μὲν ἔχοντα σοφίας ἐν ἐθελοθρησκείᾳ καὶ ταπεινοφροσύνῃ καὶ ἀφειδίᾳ σώματος, οὐκ ἐν τιμῇ τινι πρὸς πλησμονὴν τῆς σαρκός." Λόγον, φησὶν, οὐ δύναμιν, οὐκ ἀλήθειαν. Ὥστε κἂν λόγον ἔχῃ σοφίας, ἀποστρεφώμεθα. Δοκεῖ γὰρ εὐλαβής τις εἶναι καὶ μέτριος, καὶ τοῦ σώματος καταφρονεῖν. "Οὐκ ἐν τιμῇ τινι πρὸς πλησμονὴν τῆς σαρκός." Ὁ θεὸς γὰρ τιμὴν ἔδωκεν, αὐτοὶ δὲ οὐκ ἐν τιμῇ κέχρηνται. Οὕτως, ὅταν δόγμα ᾖ, οἶδε τιμὴν αὐτὸ καλεῖν. Ἀτιμάζουσι τὴν σάρκα, φησὶν, ἀποστεροῦντες αὐτήν, καὶ τὴν ἐξουσίαν ἀφαιρούμενοι, οὐχ ἑκόντος κρατεῖν συγχωροῦντες· ὁ δὲ [244] θεὸς τὴν σάρκα ἐτίμησεν.

"Εἰ οὖν συνηγέρθητε τῷ Χριστῷ." Συνάγει αὐτούς, ἄνω κατασκευάσας ὅτι ἀπέθανε. Διὰ τοῦτό φησιν, "Εἰ οὖν συνηγέρθητε τῷ Χριστῷ, τὰ ἄνω ζητεῖτε." Οὐκ ἔστιν ἐκεῖ παρατήρησις. "Τὰ ἄνω ζητεῖτε, οὗ ὁ Χριστός ἐστιν ἐν δεξιᾷ τοῦ θεοῦ καθήμενος." Βαβαὶ, ποῦ τὸν νοῦν ἀνήγαγε τὸν ἡμέτερον; πῶς φρονήματος αὐτοὺς ἐπλήρωσε μεγάλου; Οὐκ ἤρκει τὰ ἄνω εἰπεῖν, οὐδὲ, οὗ ὁ Χριστός ἐστιν, ἀλλὰ τί; "Ἐν δεξιᾷ τοῦ θεοῦ καθήμενος." Ἐκεῖθεν λοιπὸν τὴν γῆν ὁρᾶν παρεσκεύαζε.

"Τὰ ἄνω φρονεῖτε, μὴ τὰ ἐπὶ τῆς γῆς. Ἀπεθάνετε γὰρ, καὶ ἡ ζωὴ ὑμῶν κέκρυπται σὺν τῷ Χριστῷ ἐν τῷ θεῷ. Ὅταν ὁ Χριστὸς φανερωθῇ, ἡ ζωὴ ὑμῶν, τότε καὶ ὑμεῖς σὺν αὐτῷ φανερωθήσεσθε ἐν δόξῃ." Οὐκ ἔστιν αὕτη, φησίν, ἡ ζωὴ ἡ ὑμετέρα· ζωὴ ἑτέρα τίς ἐστιν. Ἤδη βιάζεται μεταστῆσαι αὐτούς, καὶ φιλονεικεῖ δεῖξαι καθημένους ἄνω, καὶ νεκροὺς ὄντας, ἐξ ἑκατέ-

If you died with Christ. Paul puts this in the middle, and on either side what is more vehement. *"If you died with Christ to the elements of the world,"* he says, *"why do you live as if you are subject to ordinances in the world?"* This is not the consequence, for what he ought to have said was, "How, while living, are you subject to the elements?" But, letting this pass, what does he say? *"Do not handle, nor taste, nor touch—these things all perish with use, according to the human precepts and commandments."* "You're not in the world," he says. "How are you subject to its elements? How are you subject to the observances of the world?" And see how he makes fun of them: *"Don't handle, nor touch, nor taste,"* as if they were cowardly and keeping aloof from some important matters. *Which all perish with use.* He's put down the puffed-up situation of the many, and added, *"According to the human precepts and commandments."* What do you say? Do you speak even of the law? That is now a human doctrine after time. Or else he means that they had adulterated it, or he was referring obliquely to the Hellenes. "The doctrine is completely human," he says.

These have indeed an appearance of wisdom in promoting rigor of devotion and humility, and of severity to the body, not in some honor to the satisfying of the flesh [Col 1:23]. *"Appearance,"* he says—not power or truth, so that even though it has an appearance of wisdom, we should turn away from it. You see, someone seems to be a religious person and moderate and to have contempt for the body. *Not in some honor to the satisfying of the flesh.* For God has given it honor, but they don't use it with honor. So when it's a doctrine, the person thinks to call it honor. "They dishonor the flesh," they say, "turning away from it, and stripping it of its liberty, not allowing it to rule of its own will. But [**244**] God has honored the flesh."

If, then, you have been raised with Christ [Col 3:1]. Paul draws them together, having established above that Christ died. On this account he says this: *"If, then, you have been raised with Christ, seek the things that are above."* No observances are there. *Seek the things above, where Christ is sitting at the right hand of God.* Wonderful! Where does he lead our minds up to? How has he filled them with great thoughts? It wasn't enough to speak of *the things that are above,* nor where Christ is, but what? *Sitting at the right hand of God.* From that point on he prepared them to observe the earth.

Think on the things that are above, not on things on the earth. For you have died, and your life is hidden with Christ in God. When Christ, who is your life, appears, then you also will appear with him in glory [Col 3:1]. "This isn't your life," he says; "your life is another one." He is now forced to remove them and is keen to show that they are seated above and are dead,

ρων κατασκευάζων μὴ ζητεῖν τὰ ἐνταῦθα. Εἴτε γὰρ νεκροί ἐστε, οὐκ ὀφείλετε ζητεῖν· εἴτε ἄνω ἐστέ, οὐκ ὀφείλετε ζητεῖν. Μὴ φαίνεται ὁ Χριστός; οὐδὲ ἡ ζωὴ ὑμῶν. Ἐν τῷ θεῷ ἄνω ἐστί. Τί οὖν; πότε ζησόμεθα; "Ὅταν ὁ Χριστὸς φανερωθῇ, ἡ ζωὴ ὑμῶν," τότε τὴν δόξαν ζητεῖτε, τότε τὴν ζωὴν, τότε τὴν τρυφήν.

Ταῦτα προκατασκευαστικὰ τοῦ τῆς τρυφῆς αὐτοὺς ἀπαγαγεῖν καὶ τῆς ἀνέσεως. Τοιοῦτον ἔθος αὐτῷ, ἄλλα κατασκευάζοντι εἰς ἄλλα μεταπηδᾶν· οἷον, ὥσπερ περὶ τῶν προλαμβανόντων εἰς τὰ δεῖπνα διαλεγόμενος, ἐνέπεσεν ἀθρόον εἰς τὴν τῶν μυστηρίων παρατήρησιν. Μέγα γὰρ ἔχει ἔλεγχος, ὅταν ἀνυπόπτως γένηται. "Κέκρυπται," φησὶν, ἀφ᾽ ὑμῶν. "Τότε καὶ ὑμεῖς σὺν αὐτῷ φανερωθήσεσθε." Ὥστε νῦν οὐ φαίνεσθε. Ὅρα πῶς αὐτοὺς εἰς αὐτὸν τὸν οὐρανὸν μετέστησεν. Ὅπερ γὰρ ἔφην, ἀεὶ φιλονεικεῖ δεῖξαι τὰ αὐτὰ ἔχοντας ἅπερ καὶ ὁ Χριστός· καὶ διὰ πασῶν αὐτοῦ τῶν ἐπιστολῶν οὗτος ὁ λόγος, ἐν πᾶσι κοινωνοῦντας αὐτῷ δεῖξαι. Διὰ τοῦτο καὶ κεφαλὴν, καὶ σῶμα λέγει, καὶ πάντα ποιεῖ, ἵνα τοῦτο παραστήσῃ.

[245] Εἰ τοίνυν τότε φανερούμεθα, μὴ ἀσχάλλωμεν, ὅταν τιμῆς μὴ ἀπολαύωμεν. Εἰ μὴ ἔστιν αὕτη ἡ ζωὴ ζωή, ἀλλὰ κέκρυπται, ὡς νεκροὶ ζῆν ὀφείλομεν ταύτην τὴν ζωήν. "Τότε καὶ ὑμεῖς, φησὶ, σὺν αὐτῷ φανερωθήσεσθε ἐν δόξῃ." "Ἐν δόξῃ," εἶπεν, οὐχ ἁπλῶς· ἐπεὶ καὶ ὁ μαργαρίτης κέκρυπται, ἕως ἂν ᾖ ἐν τῷ ὀστρέῳ. Ἄν τε οὖν ὑβριζώμεθα, μὴ ἀλγῶμεν, ἄν τε ὁτιοῦν πάσχωμεν. Οὐ γάρ ἐστιν ἡμῶν ζωὴ αὕτη ἡ ζωή· ξένοι καὶ παρεπίδημοί ἐσμεν. "Ἀπεθάνετε γὰρ," φησί. Τίς ἐστιν οὕτως ἀνόητος, ὡς τῷ νεκρῷ σώματι τῷ ταφέντι ἢ οἰκέτας ἀγοράζειν, ἢ οἰκίας οἰκοδομεῖν, ἢ ἱμάτια κατασκευάζειν πολυτελῆ; Οὐδείς. Μὴ τοίνυν μηδὲ ἡμεῖς· ἀλλ᾽ ὥσπερ ἓν μόνον ζητοῦμεν, ὥστε μὴ γεγυμνῶσθαι, οὕτω καὶ ἐνταῦθα ἓν μόνον ζητῶμεν. Ἐτάφη ἡμῶν ὁ πρῶτος ἄνθρωπος· ἐτάφη οὐκ ἐν γῇ, ἀλλ᾽ ἐν ὕδατι, οὐ τοῦ θανάτου αὐτὸν καταλύοντος, ἀλλὰ τοῦ τὸν θάνατον καταλύσαντος θάψαντος αὐτὸν, οὐ φύσεως νόμῳ, ἀλλὰ τῷ τῆς φύσεως ἰσχυροτέρῳ προστάγματι τῆς δεσποτείας. Τὰ μὲν γὰρ ὑπὸ φύσεως γενόμενα κἂν ἀναλύσῃ τις, τὰ δὲ ὑπὸ τοῦ προστάγματος αὐτοῦ, οὐκέτι. Οὐδὲν ταύτης μακαριώτερον τῆς ταφῆς, ἐφ᾽ ᾗ πάντες χαίρουσι, καὶ ἄγγελοι καὶ ἄνθρωποι καὶ ὁ τῶν ἀγγέλων δεσπότης. Ταύτῃ τῇ ταφῇ οὐχ ἱματίων, οὐ λάρνακος, οὐκ ἄλλου τῶν τοιούτων οὐδενὸς χρεία. Βούλει τὸ σύμβολον ἰδεῖν; Δείξω σοι κολυμβήθραν, ἐν ᾗ ὁ μὲν ἐτάφη, ὁ δὲ ἀνέστη. Ἐν τῇ

from both sides establishing that they are not to seek the things which are here. "For whether you're dead, you shouldn't seek them, of whether you're above, you shouldn't seek them. Doesn't Christ appear? Neither does your life. It's in God, above. What then? When shall we live? '*When Christ, who is your life, appears*,' then seek glory, then life, then enjoyment."

This is to prepare the way for drawing them away from enjoyment and leisure. Such is his custom, preparing one position to jump to another. For example, just as when discoursing about those who anticipated the meal, at once he falls on the observance of the mysteries.[74] You see, rebuke has great force when it comes about unexpectedly. "*Hidden*," he says, "from you." *Then you also will appear with him.* The result is that you don't now appear with him. See how he has transferred them to heaven itself. For, as I've said, he's always keen to show that they have the same things as Christ, and through all his letters this is the argument: to show that they share with him in everything. On this account Paul says "head" and "body," and does everything to prove this.

[245] If, therefore, we appear on that occasion, let's not grieve when we don't enjoy honor. If this life isn't life but *hidden*, we should live this life as though dead. "*Then you also will appear with him in glory*," he says. "*In glory*," he says, not without reason, since the pearl too is hidden as long as it's inside the oyster. If therefore we're treated with insult, let's not be pained, whatever we suffer. You see, this life isn't ours: we're strangers and sojourners [see Heb 11:13]. "*For you have died*," he says. Who is so stupid either to buy household servants or to build houses, or prepare costly garments as for a corpse, dead and buried? Nobody. Therefore, you shouldn't either, but just as we seek one thing only, so as not to be made naked, so here too let's seek one thing only. Our first human being is buried, buried not in earth but in water, not because death has destroyed him but buried because of the death destroyer, not by the law of nature but by the governing command that is stronger than nature. You see, even if someone destroys what has been done by nature, what has been done by Christ's order will not be destroyed at all. Nothing is more blessed than this burial, in which everyone rejoices, both angels and human beings, as well as the Master of the angels. At this burial there is no need of garments, or a coffin, or anything else of that kind. Do you want to see the type of this? I shall show you a pool in which one was buried and the other raised [see

---

74. See, e.g., *Hom. 1 Cor.* 27 (Field 2:326–38).

ἐρυθρᾷ θαλάσσῃ κατεποντίσθησαν Αἰγύπτιοι, ἀνῆλθον δὲ Ἰσραηλῖται· εἰς τὸ αὐτὸ πρᾶγμα τὸν μὲν θάπτει, τὸν δὲ γεννᾷ.

Μὴ θαυμάσῃς, εἰ γένεσις καὶ φθορὰ γίνεται ἐν τῷ βαπτίσματι. Ἐπεὶ, εἰπέ μοι, τὸ λύειν τῷ συγκολλᾷν οὐκ ἐναντίον; Παντὶ δῆλον. Τοῦτο τὸ πῦρ ποιεῖ· κηρὸν μὲν γὰρ διαλύει καὶ ἀπόλλυσι, γῆν δὲ μεταλλικὴν συγκολλᾷ καὶ χρυσὸν ἐργάζεται. Οὕτω δὴ καὶ ἐνταῦθα, τὸν κήρινον ἀνδριάντα ἀφανίσασα ἡ τοῦ πυρὸς δύναμις, ἔδειξε χρυσοῦν ἀντ' ἐκείνου. Πήλινοι γὰρ ὄντως ἦμεν πρὸ τοῦ λουτροῦ, χρυσοῖ δὲ μετὰ τοῦτο. Πόθεν δῆλον; Ἄκουσον αὐτοῦ λέγοντος· "Ὁ πρῶτος ἄνθρωπος ἐκ γῆς χοϊκὸς, ὁ δεύ-[246]τερος ἄνθρωπος ὁ κύριος ἐξ οὐρανοῦ." Ἐγὼ μὲν ὅσον πηλίνου πρὸς χρυσὸν τὸ μέσον εἶπον, εὗρον δὲ μείζονα διαφορὰν οὐρανίου καὶ γηΐνου· οὐ τοσοῦτον δὲ πηλίνου καὶ χρυσοῦ τὸ μέσον, ὅσον τῶν γηΐνων καὶ τῶν οὐρανίων. Κήρινοι ἦμεν, καὶ πήλινοι· καὶ γὰρ ἡ τῆς ἐπιθυμίας ἡμᾶς ἔτηξε φλὸξ πολλῷ μᾶλλον ἢ τὸν κηρὸν τὸ πῦρ· καὶ ὁ τυχὼν ἡμᾶς συνέκλα πειρασμὸς πολλῷ μᾶλλον ἢ τοὺς πηλίνους ὁ λίθος. Καὶ, εἰ βούλεσθε, ὑπογράψωμεν τὸν πρότερον βίον, εἰ μὴ πάντα ἦν γῆ καὶ ὕδωρ, καὶ τὸ εὐρίπιστον ἔχων κατὰ τὸν κονιορτόν, τούτου δὲ τὸ ἄστατον καὶ διαρρέον.

Καὶ, εἰ βούλεσθε, μὴ τὰ πρότερα, ἀλλὰ τὰ παρόντα ἐξετάσωμεν, εἰ μὴ κονιορτὸν καὶ ὕδωρ εὑρήσομεν πάντα τὰ ὄντα. Τί γὰρ βούλει εἰπεῖν; τὰς ἀρχὰς καὶ τὰς δυναστείας; τούτου γὰρ δοκεῖ οὐδὲν ζηλωτότερον εἶναι ἐν τῷ παρόντι βίῳ. Ἀλλὰ τὸν κονιορτὸν εὕροι τις ἂν μᾶλλον ἐπὶ τοῦ ἀέρος ἱστάμενον, ἢ ταῦτα, μάλιστα νῦν. Τίνι γὰρ οὐχ ὑπόκειται; Τοῖς ἐρῶσιν αὐτῶν, τοῖς εὐνούχοις, τοῖς τῶν χρημάτων ἕνεκεν ἅπαντα πράττουσι, θυμῷ δήμου, ὀργαῖς τῶν δυνατωτέρων. Ὁ χθὲς ἐπὶ τοῦ βήματος ὑψηλὸς, ὁ κήρυκας ἔχων λαμπρᾷ τῇ φωνῇ βοῶντας, καὶ πολλοὺς τοὺς προτρέχοντας καὶ σοβοῦντας κατὰ τὴν ἀγοράν, σήμερον εὐτελὴς καὶ ταπεινὸς καὶ πάντων ἐκείνων ἔρημος καὶ γυμνός, καθάπερ κονιορτὸς ἀναρριπισθεὶς, καθάπερ ῥεῦμα παρελθόν. Καθάπερ δὲ ἡ κόνις ἀπὸ τῶν ποδῶν ἐγείρεται τῶν ἡμετέρων, οὕτω δὴ καὶ αἱ

John 5]. The Egyptians were drowned in the Red Sea, but the Israelites came up out of it [see Exod 14]: the same act buries the one but gives birth to the other.

Don't be surprised if birth and destruction take place in baptism. Since, tell me, are destroying and cementing not the opposite? It's clear to all. This is the effect of fire, for it dissolves and destroys wax, but cements metallic earth and produces gold. So indeed is it here also, when the force of the fire has caused the wax figure to vanish, it displays a golden figure in its place. You see, we truly were made of clay before the bath,[75] but golden after it. From where is this clear? Listen to Paul saying, *"The first human being was dust from earth,* [**246**] *the second human being is the Lord from heaven"* [1 Cor 15:47].[76] For my part I spoke of a difference as great as that between clay and gold, but I've found a greater difference between heaven and earth: the difference between clay and gold is not as great at that between earthly and heavenly. Waxen we were and made of clay. Indeed, the flame of lust did much more to melt us than the fire did wax, and a chance temptation shattered us much more than a stone does with clay. And, if you like, let's sketch the former life, and see whether everything was earth and water, and full of fluctuation because of the dust, and instability and flowing away.

And, if you like, let's examine neither the former things but those of the present, to see whether we shall find that everything that exists is dust and water. I mean, what will you say about this? Authorities and powers? For nothing in this present life seems more enviable than this. But one might find dust stationary in the air rather than these things, especially now. For to whom are they not subject? To their lovers, the eunuchs, to those who do everything for the sake of money, to the passion of the people, to the whims of the more powerful. The one who was yesterday high on the tribunal, who had heralds crying out in a loud voice, and many running before him and clearing the way before him through the marketplace, is today poor and lowly and bereft and denuded of all this, like dust that has been thrown up, like a stream that has gone by.[77] And just as dust is raised by our feet, so too indeed are the offices also born of those concerned about money,

---

75. That is, the baptismal bath.

76. This citation is according to the Byzantine text-type, followed here and elsewhere by Chrysostom.

77. This passage is discussed in Allen and Mayer as part of their argument for the Antiochene provenance of this homily ("Chrysostom and the Preaching of Homilies in Series: A New Approach," 30–34).

ἀρχαὶ ἀπὸ τούτων τίκτονται τῶν περὶ τὰ χρήματα στρεφομένων, καὶ ποδῶν τάξιν ἐχόντων ἐν παντὶ τῷ βίῳ· καὶ καθάπερ ἡ κόνις, ὅταν μὲν αἴρηται, πολὺ μέρος κατέχει τοῦ ἀέρος, αὐτὴ δέ ἐστιν ὀλίγη, οὕτω καὶ ἡ ἀρχή· καὶ καθάπερ ἡ κόνις τυφλοῖ τοὺς ὀφθαλμοὺς, οὕτω καὶ τῆς ἀρχῆς ὁ τῦφος πηροῖ τοὺς ὀφθαλμοὺς τῆς διανοίας.

Ἀλλὰ τί; βούλει τὸ πολύευκτον πρᾶγμα ἐξετάσωμεν, τὸν πλοῦτον; Φέρε κατὰ μέρος αὐτὸν ἐξετάσωμεν. Ἔχει τρυφὴν, ἔχει τιμὰς, ἔχει τὸ δύνασθαι. Πρῶτον οὖν, εἰ βούλει, τὴν τρυφὴν ἐξετάσωμεν· οὐχὶ κονιορτός ἐστι; [247] μᾶλλον δὲ τούτου ταχύτερον πάρεισι; μέχρι γὰρ τῆς γλώττης ἡ ἡδονὴ τῆς τρυφῆς· ὅταν δὲ ἐμπλησθῇ ἡ γαστήρ, οὐδὲ μέχρι τῆς γλώττης. Ἀλλ᾽ αὐταὶ αἱ τιμαὶ πρᾶγμα ἡδὺ, φησί. Καὶ τί τῆς τιμῆς ἐκείνης ἀηδέστερον, ὅταν διὰ χρείαν γίνηται χρημάτων; Ὅταν μὴ ἐκ προαιρέσεως, μηδὲ ἀπὸ προθυμίας τινός, οὐ σὺ καρποῦσαι τὴν τιμὴν, ἀλλ᾽ ὁ πλοῦτος. Ὥστε μάλιστα πάντων ἄτιμον ποιεῖ τὸν πλουτοῦντα τοῦτο αὐτό. Εἰπὲ γάρ μοι, εἴ σε φίλον ἔχοντα πάντες ἐτίμων, ὡμολόγουν δὲ σὲ μὲν οὐδενὸς ἄξιον εἶναι, ἀναγκάζεσθαι δὲ δι᾽ ἐκεῖνον τιμᾷν, ἢν ὅπως ἄν σε ἑτέρως ἠτίμασαν; Ὥστε ἀτιμίας αἴτιος ὁ πλοῦτος ἡμῖν, αὐτῶν τῶν κεκτημένων τιμιώτερος ὢν, καὶ ἀσθενείας, ἢ δυναστείας τεκμήριον. Πῶς οὖν οὐκ ἄτοπον γῆς καὶ σποδοῦ· τοῦτο γὰρ ὁ χρυσὸς· μὴ νομίζεσθαι ἡμᾶς ἀξίους εἶναι, ἀλλ᾽ ἡμᾶς δι᾽ ἐκεῖνον τιμᾶσθαι; Εἰκότως· ἀλλ᾽ οὐχ ὁ τοῦ πλούτου καταφρονῶν, οὕτω· κρεῖττον γὰρ μὴ τιμᾶσθαι ἢ οὕτω τιμᾶσθαι. Εἰπὲ γάρ μοι, εἴ τις εἶπέ σοι, ὅτι σε οὐδεμιᾶς ἡγοῦμαι ἄξιον τιμῆς, διὰ δὲ τοὺς οἰκέτας σου τιμῶ σε, ἆρα τί ταύτης τῆς ἀτιμίας γένοιτο ἂν χεῖρον; Εἰ δὲ τὸ δι᾽ οἰκέτας τιμᾶσθαι αἰσχρὸν τοὺς τῆς αὐτῆς ψυχῆς ἡμῖν κοινωνοῦντας καὶ φύσεως, πολλῷ μᾶλλον διὰ τούτων, ἅπερ ἐστὶν εὐτελέστερα, τοίχους λέγω οἰκιῶν καὶ αὐλὰς, καὶ σκεύη χρυσᾶ, καὶ ἱμάτια.

Γέλως ὄντως καὶ αἰσχύνη ταῦτα· βέλτιον ἀποθανεῖν, ἢ οὕτω τιμηθῆναι. Εἰπὲ γάρ μοι, εἴ τίς σε κινδυνεύοντα ἐν τῷ τύφῳ τούτῳ εὐτελὴς καὶ κατάπτυστος ἐξελέσθαι ἠθέλησε τοῦ κινδύνου, τί τούτου χεῖρον ἦν; Ὅπερ δὲ περὶ τῆς πόλεως πρὸς ἀλλήλους λέγετε, βούλομαι πρὸς ὑμᾶς εἰπεῖν. Προσέκρουσέ τῳ ποτε κρατοῦντι ἡ πόλις ἡ ἡμετέρα, καὶ πᾶσαν αὐτὴν ἐκέλευσεν ἄρδην ἀπολέσθαι μετὰ ἀνδρῶν καὶ παίδων καὶ οἰκημάτων. Τοιοῦτοι γὰρ οἱ θυμοὶ οἱ

and in all their life have the rank of feet; and just as dust when it is raised contains a very small amount of air, although by itself it is insignificant, so too is it with office. And just as dust blinds the eyes, so too does the pride of power mutilate the eyes of the understanding.

So what? Do you want us to examine the object of many prayers, wealth? Come, let's examine it bit by bit. Therefore, first, if you like, let's examine luxury: Isn't it dust? [247] Yes, but doesn't it rather pass by more quickly than dust? For the pleasure of luxurious living only goes as far as the tongue, but when the belly is filled, it doesn't even go as far as the tongue. "But," [someone] says, "honors of themselves are a matter of pleasure." Yet what is more distasteful than that honor, when it comes about through the need for money? When it's not from free choice nor from some eagerness, you don't harvest the honor, but wealth does. The upshot is that this very thing makes the person of wealth, most of all, dishonored. For, tell me, if everybody honored you because you had a friend but confessed that you were worth nothing, while compelled to honor you on his account, would it have been possible for them to dishonor you in some other way? The upshot is that wealth is the cause of dishonor to us, because it is more honored than its very possessors, and a proof of weakness rather than of dominion. How, then, is it not absurd that we're not reckoned to be worthy of earth and ashes (for that's what gold is) but to be honored for its sake? With good cause. But it's not the case with the person who despises wealth—you see, it's better not to be honored than to be honored in this way. For tell me, if somebody said to you, "I think that you're worthy of no honor, but for your household servants I honor you"—could anything be worse than this dishonor? But if to be honored for the sake of household servants, who share the same soul and nature as we do, is disgraceful, much more is it so to be honored by lesser things, I mean the walls and courtyards of a building, and vessels of gold, and garments.

This is truly a laughing matter and a disgrace: it's better to die than to be honored in this way. For, tell me, if someone lowly and disgusting were to wish to extricate you from your danger when you were endangered by this pride, what could be worse than this? What you say to each other about the city, I want to say to you. One time our city offended the emperor, and he ordered that the city be utterly destroyed, with men and children and houses.[78] (Such are the whims of emperors: they indulge their power

78. This is a reference to the crisis concerning the destruction of the imperial stat-

βασιλικοί· τῇ ἐξουσίᾳ ὅσον ἂν θέλωσι, χαρίζονται· τοσοῦτον ἡ ἐξουσία κακόν. Ἦν οὖν ἐν κινδύνοις τοῖς ἐσχάτοις. Ἡ δὲ γείτων πόλις, αὕτη ἡ ἐπιθαλάσσιος, ἐλθοῦσα παρεκάλεσε τὸν βασιλέα ὑπὲρ ἡμῶν· οἱ δὲ τὴν πόλιν οἰκοῦντες τὴν ἡμετέραν ἔλεγον τοῦτο χεῖρον εἶναι τοῦ κατασκαφῆναι τὴν πόλιν. Οὕτω τοῦ ἀτιμασθῆναι τὸ οὕτω τιμᾶσθαι χεῖρόν ἐστιν. Ὅρα γὰρ πόθεν ἔχει τὴν ῥίζαν ἡ τιμή. Μαγείρων χεῖρες ποιοῦσιν ἡμᾶς τιμᾶσθαι, ὥστε ἐκείνοις ὀφεί-[248]λομεν χάριν ἔχειν· καὶ συβῶται παρέχοντες πλουσίαν τὴν τράπεζαν, καὶ ὑφάνται καὶ ἔριθοι, καὶ οἱ μέταλλα ἐργαζόμενοι, καὶ πλακουντοποιοί, καὶ τραπεζοποιοί.

Τοῦ τοίνυν τούτοις εἰδέναι χάριν τῆς τιμῆς οὐ βέλτιον τὸ μὴ τιμᾶσθαι; Καὶ χωρὶς δὲ τούτου, ὅτι ἀτιμίας γέμει τὸ πλουτεῖν, ἐγὼ σαφῶς ἀποδεῖξαι πειράσομαι. Τὴν ψυχὴν αἰσχρὰν ἐργάζεται· τί δὲ τούτου ἀτιμότερον; Εἰπὲ γάρ μοι, εἰ τὸ σῶμα ὡραῖον ἦν, καὶ πάντας νικῶν τῷ κάλλει, ὁ δὲ πλοῦτος προσελθὼν ἐπηγγέλλετο ποιήσειν αἰσχρόν, καὶ ἀντὶ μὲν ὑγιοῦς νοσῶδες, ἀντὶ δὲ κατεσταλμένου φλεγμαῖνον, καὶ πάντα τὰ μέλη ὑδέρου πληρώσας, ἐξώγκωσε μὲν τὴν ὄψιν, καὶ πάντοθεν ἐποίησεν οἰδαίνειν, ἐξώγκωσε δὲ πόδας, καὶ τῶν δοκῶν ἐποίησε βαρυτέρους, ἐξώγκωσε δὲ γαστέρα, καὶ παντὸς πίθου μείζονα εἰργάσατο, καὶ μετὰ τοῦτο οὐδὲ τοῖς βουλομένοις θεραπεύειν ἐπηγγέλλετο συγχωρήσειν· τοῦτο γὰρ ἡ ἐξουσία· ἀλλὰ τοσαύτην δώσειν ἐλευθερίαν, ὥστε ἄν τις προσίῃ ἀπάγων τῶν βλαπτόντων κολάσειν αὐτόν· ἆρα, εἰπέ μοι, τὸ πλουτεῖν, ὅταν τὴν ψυχὴν ταῦτα ἐργάζηται, πῶς ἂν εἴη καλόν;

Ἀλλ' ἡ ἐξουσία αὐτῆς τῆς νόσου χαλεπωτέρα· τὸ γὰρ νοσοῦντα μηδὲ νόμοις ἰατρῶν πείθεσθαι, τοῦ νοσεῖν χαλεπώτερον· ὅπερ ὁ πλοῦτος ἔχει, πανταχόθεν φλεγμαίνειν ποιῶν τὴν ψυχήν, καὶ τοὺς ἰατροὺς προσιέναι κωλύων. Ὥστε διὰ τὴν ἐξουσίαν μὴ μακαρίζωμεν τούτους, ἀλλ' ἐλεῶμεν. Οὐδὲ γὰρ ὑδερικὸν ἰδὼν κατακείμενον, καὶ μηδένα κωλύοντα ἐμφορεῖσθαι πομάτων, ὅσωνπερ ἤθελε, καὶ κρεῶν τῶν βλαπτόντων, ἐμακάρισα ἂν αὐτὸν διὰ τὴν ἐξουσίαν. Οὐ γὰρ πανταχοῦ ἡ ἐξουσία καλόν, ὥσπερ οὖν οὐδὲ αἱ

as much as they choose, so great an evil is power.) The city was then in extreme danger. But the neighboring city, which is on the coast,[79] went and petitioned the emperor on our account, while those who inhabit our city said that this was worse than the complete destruction of the city. To be so honored is worse than so to be dishonored. For see from where honor has its root. The hands of cooks cause us to be honored, so that to them [248] we should be grateful, and the swineherds for providing us with a rich table, and weavers, and spinners, and metalworkers, and confectioners, and table setters.

Isn't it, then, better not to be honored than to be beholden to these people for honor? And apart from this consideration, I for my part shall try to prove clearly that being wealthy is full of dishonor: it works at making the soul shameful—what is more dishonorable than this? For tell me: if the body is handsome and outdoes all in beauty, while wealth on approaching it promised to make it ugly, and instead of healthy, diseased, instead of cool, inflamed, and having filled every limb with dropsy, bloated its face and distended it all over; bloated the feet and made them heavier than logs, and bloated the belly and make it larger than any wine jar, and after that promised not even to permit the people who wished to cure him (for this is what power is), but would give him so much liberty as to punish any person who approached them to withdraw them from what was harmful—then tell me, how could wealth be a good thing, when it works these effects on the soul?

But power is more serious than the disease itself. You see, for the diseased person not to be obedient at all to the physician's orders is more serious than being diseased, which is the case with wealth because it creates inflammation everywhere in the soul and prevents physicians from coming near it. So let's not congratulate these people because of their power, but pity them. For neither if I saw somebody laid low with dropsy and nobody preventing them from taking their fill of liquids, as much as they wished, and foods that are harmful, would I congratulate them because of their power. You see, power isn't a good thing in all cases, just then as offices

---

ues in Antioch in 387. See further Allen and Mayer, "Chrysostom and the Preaching of Homilies in Series: A New Approach," 34–35, and the introduction to this volume. For a study of Chrysostom's homilies on the event, see Frans van de Paverd, *St John Chrysostom, the Homilies on the Statues: An Introduction*, OrChrAn 239 (Rome: Pontificio Istituto Orientale, 1991).

79. Namely, Seleucia Pieria.

τιμαί· καὶ γὰρ καὶ αὗται φρονήματος πληροῦσι πολλοῦ. Εἰ δὲ τὸ σῶμα οὐκ ἂν εἵλου μετὰ πλούτου ταύτην δέξασθαι τὴν νόσον, πῶς τὴν ψυχὴν περιορᾷς, καὶ οὐχὶ τοῦτο μόνον, ἀλλὰ καὶ ἑτέραν κόλασιν δεχομένην; Καὶ γὰρ πυρετοῖς πάντοθεν φλέγεται καὶ φλεγμοναῖς, καὶ τὸν πυρετὸν ἐκεῖνον οὐδεὶς σβέσαι δύναται· οὐ γὰρ ἀφίησιν ὁ πλοῦτος, ἅπερ ἐστὶν ἐλαττώματα, ταῦτα πείσας εἶναι πλεονεκτήματα· οἷον, τὸ μηδενὸς ἀνέχεσθαι, καὶ ἐξουσίᾳ πάντα ποιεῖν. Οὐ γὰρ εὑρήσει τις [249] ἄλλην ψυχὴν τοσούτων γέμουσαν ἐπιθυμιῶν καὶ οὕτως ἀτόπων, ὡς τὰς τῶν βουλομένων πλουτεῖν. Πόσας γὰρ ληρωδίας οὐχ ὑπογράφουσιν ἑαυτοῖς; Μᾶλλον τῶν τοὺς ἱπποκενταύρους ἀναπλαττόντων, καὶ τὰς χιμαίρας καὶ τοὺς δρακοντόποδας καὶ τὰς σκύλλας καὶ τὰ τέρατα, ἴδοι τις ἂν αὐτοὺς ἀναπλάττοντας. Κἂν θέλῃ τις αὐτῶν μίαν ἐπιθυμίαν ἀναπλάσαι, οὐδὲν οὔτε σκύλλα οὔτε χίμαιρα, οὔτε ἱπποκένταυρος φανήσονται πρὸς τὴν τερατωδίαν ἐκείνην, ἀλλ᾽ εὑρήσεις πάντα ὁμοῦ ἔχουσαν τὰ θηρία.

Καὶ τάχα μέ τις οἰήσεται ἐν πλούτῳ γεγενῆσθαι πολλῷ οὕτως ἐπαληθεύοντα τοῖς γινομένοις. Λέγεταί τις· πρότερον γὰρ ἀπὸ τῶν παρὰ τοῖς Ἕλλησιν ᾀδομένων τὸν λόγον πιστώσομαι· λέγεταί τις παρ᾽ αὐτοῖς βασιλεὺς τοσοῦτον ἐνυβρίσαι τῇ τρυφῇ, ὥστε πλάτανον ποιῆσαι χρυσῆν, καὶ οὐρανὸν ἄνωθεν, καὶ οὕτω καθίσαι, καὶ ταῦτα ἐπιστρατεύων ἀνθρώποις πολεμεῖν μεμαθηκόσιν. Ἄρα οὐχ ἱπποκενταύρων αὕτη ἡ ἐπιθυμία; ἄρα οὐ σκύλλης; Ἕτερος πάλιν εἰς βοῦν ξύλινον ἐνέβαλλε τοὺς ἀνθρώπους. Ἄρα οὐ σκύλλα τοῦτο; Τέως δὲ τῶν πρότερον ἐξ ἀνδρὸς γυναῖκα ἐποίησε τὸν βασιλέα, τὸν στρατιώτην ἀπὸ γυναικός, τί εἴπω; θηρίον ἄλογον, καὶ ἔτι τούτου χεῖρον. Τὰ γὰρ θηρία ἄν τε ὑπὸ δένδρον ᾖ, ἀνέχονται τῆς φύσεως, καὶ πλέον οὐδὲν ἐπιζητοῦσιν· οὗτος δὲ καὶ τῶν θηρίων τὴν φύσιν ὑπερηκόντισεν.

Ἄρα τί γένοιτ᾽ ἂν τῶν πλουτούντων ἀνοητότερον; Τοῦτο δὲ ἀπὸ τῆς πλεονεξίας τῶν ἐπιθυμιῶν γίνεται. Ἄρα οὐχὶ πολλοὶ θαυμάζουσιν αὐτόν; Τοιγάρτοι τοῦ γέλωτος κοινωνοῦσιν αὐτῷ. Τοῦτο οὐ τὸν πλοῦτον ἐδείκνυ, ἀλλὰ

aren't either, for these too fill a person with great arrogance. But if you choose that the body should receive this disease together with wealth, how is it that you overlook the soul, when it contracts not only this disease but also another punishment? For it's on fire all over with burning fevers and inflammations, and nobody can put out that fire. You see, wealth won't allow this, being convinced that those things are gains that are losses, for example, not putting up with anybody and doing everything with power. For nobody will find [249] another soul so full of lusts and so absurd as theirs who desire wealth. For how many silly things do they not sketch for themselves? One may see those people devising more than those who devise hippocentaurs, and chimeras, and serpent-footed monsters, and Scyllas, and monsters.[80] And if you wanted to devise a lust of theirs, neither Scylla, nor chimera, nor a hippocentaur would appear anything compared with that prodigy, but you will find it to contain every wild beast at once.

And perhaps someone will think that I was born into great wealth, since I verify what results from it. Someone is reported (you see, I shall first confirm what I've said from the fables of the Hellenes)—it's reported that a certain king became so insolent from luxury as to make a plane tree of gold, and a sky above it, and so sat there, and did this while invading a people skilled in warfare.[81] Wasn't this lust from the hippocentaureans? Wasn't it from Scylla? Again, another used to throw people into a wooden bull.[82] Wasn't this Scylla? Besides, it made the first king a woman from a man.[83] What shall I say about a soldier made from a woman?[84] A brute beast, and even worse than this. For if the beasts are under a tree, they bear with nature and seek nothing further, but that man overshot the nature even of beasts.

What, then, could be more senseless than the wealthy? This is born of the greediness of their lusts. Surely there aren't many who admire this person? So then they share in their derision. That demonstrated not their

---

80. Hippocentaurs are more usually centaurs, human above and horse below (see further *OCD*, 308–9). On chimeras, see *OCD*, 322. On Scyllas, see *OCD*, 1374.

81. According to Herodotus, the rich Lydian Pythius gifted the Persian king Darius with a golden plane tree and a golden wine plant (*Hist.* 7.27). The preacher knew his classical literature.

82. This is either a reference to the legendary Daedalus, who had his wives shut up in a wooden bull, or else to Phalaris of Agrigentum (sixth century BCE), although in his case the bull was not wooden but brazen (see *OCD*, 1153).

83. That is, wealth made the man effeminate.

84. The same king appears to be meant.

τὴν ἄνοιαν. Πόσῳ τῆς χρυσῆς ἐκείνης πλατάνου ἢ τῆς γῆς βελτίων; τὰ γὰρ κατὰ φύσιν τῶν παρὰ φύσιν ἡδίω. Τί δέ σοι ὁ χρυσοῦς οὐρανὸς ἐβούλετο, ἀνόητε; Ὁρᾷς πῶς μαινομένους ποιεῖ ὁ πλοῦτος ὁ πολύς; πῶς ἐφλέγμαινεν; Οἶμαι αὐτὸν καὶ τὴν θάλατταν ἀγνοεῖν, καὶ τάχα βαδίζειν βούλεσθαι ἐπ' αὐτῆς. Ἆρα οὐ χίμαιρα ταῦτα; ἆρα οὐχ ἱπποκένταυρος; Ἀλλ' εἰσὶ καὶ νῦν τινες οἳ οὐδὲ ἐκείνου ἀποδέουσιν, ἀλλὰ πολλῷ ἀνοητότεροι τυγχάνουσιν ὄντες. Τί γὰρ, εἰπέ μοι, τῆς χρυσῆς πλατάνου διαφέρουσι κατὰ ἄνοιαν οἱ [250] κεράμια ποιοῦντες ἀργυρᾶ, καὶ χύτρας καὶ ἀλάβαστρα; Τί δὲ αἱ γυναῖκες· αἰσχύνομαι μὲν οὖν, πλὴν ἀναγκαῖον εἰπεῖν· ἀμίδας ἀργυρᾶς ποιοῦσαι; Ὑμᾶς αἰσχύνεσθαι τὰς ταῦτα ποιούσας ἔδει. Τοῦ Χριστοῦ λιμώττοντος, σὺ οὕτω τρυφᾷς; μᾶλλον δὲ ἀνοηταίνεις; Ποίαν αὗται κόλασιν οὐ τίσουσιν; Ἔτι οὖν ἐρωτᾷς, διὰ τί λησταὶ, διὰ τί ἀνδροφόνοι, διὰ τί τὰ κακά, οὕτως ὑμᾶς τοῦ διαβόλου παρασύραντος; Τὸ μὲν γὰρ πινάκια ἔχειν ἀργυρᾶ, οὐδὲ τοῦτο μὲν κατὰ φιλόσοφον ψυχὴν, ἀλλὰ τρυφῆς τὸ πᾶν· τὸ δὲ καὶ σκεύη ἀκάθαρτα ποιεῖν ἐξ ἀργύρου, ἆρα τρυφῆς; ἀλλ' οὐκ ἂν εἴποιμι τρυφῆς, ἀλλ' ἀνοίας· ἀλλ' οὐδὲ τοῦτο, ἀλλὰ μανίας, μᾶλλον δὲ καὶ μανίας χεῖρον.

Οἶδα ὅτι πολλοί με κωμῳδοῦσιν ἐπὶ τούτῳ, ἀλλ' οὐκ ἐπιστρέφομαι· μόνον γενέσθω τι πλέον. Ὄντως ἀνοήτους ποιεῖ τὸ πλουτεῖν καὶ μαινομένους. Εἰ τοσαύτη ἦν ἡ περιουσία, ἐβουλήθησαν ἂν καὶ τὴν γῆν εἶναι χρυσῆν, καὶ τοίχους χρυσοῦς, τάχα καὶ τὸν οὐρανὸν καὶ τὸν ἀέρα ἀπὸ χρυσοῦ. Τίς ἡ μανία, τίς ἡ παρανομία; τίς ὁ πυρετός; Ἕτερος τῷ κρυμῷ διαφθείρεται ὁ κατ' εἰκόνα θεοῦ, σὺ δὲ τοιαῦτα κατασκευάζεις; Ὦ τοῦ τύφου· τί ἂν πλέον μαινόμενος ἐποίησε; τὰ ἀποπατήματα οὕτω τιμᾷς, ὥστε ἀργύρῳ ὑποδέχεσθαι; Οἶδα ὅτι

wealth but their senselessness. How much better than that golden plane tree is the one that comes from earth? You see, the natural is more pleasing than the unnatural. But what was the meaning of your gold heaven, senseless man? Do you see how wealth that is excessive produces mad people? How it inflames them? I suppose that he doesn't know the sea and will possibly want to walk on it.[85] Aren't these things a hippocentaur? But even now there are some who fall nothing short of him but happen to be much more senseless. For tell me, how do **[250]** those who make silver chamber pots and pitchers and scent bottles differ from the golden plane tree in senselessness? But what about the women? I'm really ashamed, but it's necessary to say this. Do they make silver chamber pots? You're the ones who should be ashamed that they make these things. Christ is famished and you're in such luxury? Rather, are you playing the senseless one? What punishment will these women not pay for? Then do you still ask why there are robbers, why there are murderers, why there is evil, when the devil is perverting you in this way? You see, to possess silver dishes is not even in keeping with a soul devoted to wisdom,[86] but is entire luxury. But is making unclean vessels then luxury? No, I wouldn't say luxury, but senselessness; no, not even that, but madness, worse than even madness.

I know that many people ridicule me on this point, but I don't pay attention—may something more only result from it. Truly, wealth makes people senseless and mad. If excess were so great they would have wished that the earth too was of gold, and walls of gold, perhaps heaven too and the air of gold. What madness is this, what the transgression of decency? What is the fever? Another person, made in the image of God, perishes of cold, and do you arrange things like these? Oh, the pride! What more would a mad person have done? What more would a madman have done? Do you honor your excrements so as to receive them in silver?[87] I know

---

85. See Herodotus, referring to the Persian king Xerxes, a rather fanciful interpretation of the text (*Hist.* 7.35).

86. That is, φιλοσοφία. On this term as a Christian, and more specifically a monastic way of life, see Anne-Marie Malingrey, *Philosophia: Études d'un groupe de mots dans la littérature grecque des Présocratiques au IVe siècle après J.C.* (Paris: Éditions Klincksieck, 1961).

87. On Chrysostom's tirades against wealth and ostentation, see Margaret M. Mitchell, "Silver Chamber Pots and Other Goods Which Are Not Good: John Chrysostom's Discourse against Wealth and Possessions," in *Having Property and Possession in Religious and Social Life*, ed. William Schweiker and Charles T. Mathewes (Grand Rapids: Eerdmans, 2004), 88–121.

ναρκᾶτε ἀκούοντες, ἀλλ' αἱ ποιοῦσαι ναρκᾶν ὀφείλουσι, καὶ οἱ τοῖς τοιούτοις νοσήμασιν ἄνδρες ὑπηρετούμενοι· ἀκολασία γάρ ἐστι καὶ ὠμότης καὶ
ἀπανθρωπία καὶ θηριωδία καὶ ἀσέλγεια τοῦτο. Ποία σκύλλα, ποία χίμαιρα,
ποῖος δράκων, μᾶλλον δὲ ποῖος δαίμων, ποῖος διάβολος ταῦτα ἂν ἐποίησε; Τί
τοῦ Χριστοῦ ὄφελος; τί δὲ τῆς πίστεως, ὅταν ἀνθρώπων ἀνέχηταί τις Ἑλλήνων, μᾶλλον δὲ οὐχ Ἑλλήνων, ἀλλὰ δαιμόνων; Εἰ χρυσῷ καὶ μαργαρίταις
τὴν κεφαλὴν κοσμεῖν οὐ δεῖ, ὁ τῷ ἀργύρῳ εἰς οὕτως ἀκάθαρτον ὑπηρεσίαν
κεχρημένος, ποίας συγγνώμης τεύξεται; Οὐκ ἀρκεῖ τὰ λοιπά, καίτοιγε οὐδὲ
ἐκεῖνα ἀνεκτά, καθέδραι καὶ ὑποπόδια ἐξ ἀργύρου πάντα; καίτοι καὶ ταῦτα
ἀνοίας. Ἀλλὰ πανταχοῦ ὁ τῦφος ὁ περισσός, πανταχοῦ ἡ κενοδοξία· οὐδαμοῦ
τῆς χρείας, ἀλλὰ πανταχοῦ τῶν περιττῶν.

Ἐγὼ δέδοικα μὴ ὑπὸ τῆς μανίας ταύτης προβαῖνον τὸ γυναικεῖον γένος
τεράτων ἀναλάβῃ μορφήν· εἰκὸς γὰρ αὐτὰς ἐπιθυμῆσαι καὶ τρίχας ἔχειν
χρυσᾶς. Ἦ ὁμολογήσατε ὅτι [251] ἐπάθετέ τι πρὸς τὸ λεχθὲν καὶ διανέστητε
καὶ εἰς ἐπιθυμίαν ἐνεπέσετε, καὶ εἰ μή γε ἡ αἰσχύνη κατεῖχεν, οὐκ ἂν παρητή-
σασθε. Εἰ γὰρ καὶ τὰ τούτων ἀτοπώτερα τολμᾶτε, πολλῷ μᾶλλον ταῦτα οἶμαι
αὐτὰς ἐπιθυμῆσαι, καὶ τὰ χείλη, καὶ τὰς ὀφρῦς, καὶ πάντα χρυσὸν κατατη-
κούσας οὕτω περιχρίειν. Εἰ δὲ ἀπιστεῖτε, καὶ νομίζετε γελῶντά με λέγειν,
ἐγὼ διηγήσομαι ὅπερ ἤκουσα, μᾶλλον δὲ καὶ ἔστι νῦν. Ὁ τῶν Περσῶν βασιλεὺς χρυσοῦν ἔχει τὸ γένειον, τῶν περὶ ταῦτα δεινῶν, καθάπερ τῇ κρόκῃ,
οὕτω καὶ ταῖς ἐκείνου θριξὶν ἐνελισσόντων τὰ πέταλα τοῦ χρυσοῦ· καὶ ἀνά-
κειται καθάπερ τέρας.

Δόξα σοι, Χριστέ, πόσων ἐνέπλησας ἀγαθῶν ἡμᾶς; πῶς ἡμᾶς ὑγιαίνειν
παρεσκεύασας; πόσης τερατωδίας, πόσης ἀλογίας ἡμᾶς ἀπήλλαξας; Ἰδοὺ προ-
λέγω· οὐκέτι παραινῶ, ἀλλ' ἐπιτάττω καὶ παραγγέλλω· ὁ βουλόμενος ἀκουέτω, ὁ δὲ μὴ βουλόμενος ἀπειθείτω· ὅτι ἂν ἐπιμένητε ταῦτα ποιοῦσαι, οὐκ
ἀνέξομαι, οὐδὲ δέξομαι ὑμᾶς, οὐδὲ ἀφήσω τῶν οὐδὸν ὑπερβῆναι τοῦτον. Τί
γάρ μοι δεῖ πλήθους νοσούντων; τί δέ, εἰ παιδοτριβῶν ὑμᾶς οὐ κωλύω τὰ
περιττά; Καίτοιγε ὁ Παῦλος ἐκώλυσε, καὶ χρυσὸν καὶ μαργαρίτας. Γελώμεθα
παρὰ τῶν Ἑλλήνων, μῦθος εἶναι δοκεῖ τὰ ἡμέτερα.

that you become numb hearing this, but the women who do such things should become numb, and the men who minister to such illnesses. You see, this is intemperance and savagery and inhumanity and beastliness and wantonness. What Scylla, what chimera, what dragon, or rather what demon, what devil would have done this? What is the benefit of Christ? What of the faith, when one has to put up with people being Hellenes—no, not Hellenes, but demons? If it isn't appropriate to adorn the head with gold and pearls [see 1 Tim 2:9], what kind of pardon shall the one who uses silver for a service so unclean meet with? Isn't the rest enough, even though those things are not bearable, chairs and stools, all made of silver? Yet even these come from senselessness. But everywhere there is excessive pride, everywhere vainglory. Nowhere is there use but everywhere excess.

For my part I am afraid lest under this madness the female race should go on to assume a monstrous form, for it's likely that they will even desire to have hair of gold. Otherwise admit that [**251**] you didn't feel anything about what I said, and that you weren't excited, and fell into a lust, and if shame hadn't held you back, you wouldn't have refused. You see, if even more absurd things than this are dared, much more, I think, will you lust after these things,[88] and lips, and eyebrows, and to melt down everything into gold so as to overlay it. But if you don't believe me and consider that I'm speaking in jest, I shall relate what I have heard, or rather what the case is now. The Persian king has a golden beard: those who are adept in these things, like the nap[89] to wind gold leaf through his hair, and it is set up [as a statue], like a marvel.

Glory to you, Christ—with how many good things have you filled us? How have you brought about our health? From what great monstrousness, from what great irrationality have you freed us? Look, I caution, I advise no longer, but I command and order—let the one who wishes to, listen, and the one who doesn't wish, be disobedient: that if the women continue to do this, I shall not put up with it, nor shall I receive you, nor permit you to cross this threshold. For what need do I have of a crowd of diseased people? And what, if I educate you, I prevent excesses? And yet Paul didn't stand in the way of both gold and pearls. We are a laughingstock among the Hellenes; our beliefs seem to be a fable.

---

88. That is, golden hair.

89. The image is from weaving. The reference to a Persian king seems to be a contemporary one in the preacher's eyes.

Καὶ τοῖς ἀνδράσι παραινῶ ταῦτα· εἰς διδασκαλεῖον παραγίνῃ, παιδευόμενος φιλοσοφίαν πνευματικήν· περίελε τὸν τῦφον ἐκεῖνον. Τοῦτο καὶ ἀνδράσι παραινῶ καὶ γυναιξί· κἂν ἑτέρως τις ποιῇ, λοιπὸν οὐκ ἀνέχομαι. Δώδεκα ἦσαν οἱ μαθηταί, καὶ ἄκουσον τί φησιν ὁ Χριστὸς πρὸς αὐτούς· "Μὴ καὶ ὑμεῖς θέλετε ὑπάγειν;" Ἂν γὰρ διόλου κολακεύωμεν, πότε ἀνακτησόμεθα; πότε ὠφελήσομεν; Ἀλλ' εἰσί, φησίν, αἱρέσεις ἕτεραι, καὶ μετατίθενται. Ψυχρὸς οὗτος ὁ λόγος. "Κρεῖσσον εἷς ποιῶν τὸ θέλημα κυρίου, ἢ μυρίοι παράνομοι." Ἐπεὶ καὶ σὺ τί βούλει, εἰπέ μοι; μυρίους δραπέτας ἔχειν καὶ κλέπτας οἰκέτας, ἢ ἕνα εὔνουν; Ἰδοὺ παραινῶ καὶ παρεγγυῶ καὶ τὸν καλλωπισμὸν τὸν περὶ τὴν ὄψιν, [252] καὶ τὰ σκεύη τὰ τοιαῦτα συντρίβειν, καὶ πένησι διδόναι, καὶ μὴ οὕτω μεμηνέναι.

Ὁ βουλόμενος ἀποπηδάτω, ὁ βουλόμενος ἐγκαλείτω· οὐκ ἀνέχομαι οὐδενός. Ὅταν μέλλω κρίνεσθαι ἐπὶ τοῦ βήματος τοῦ Χριστοῦ, μακρὰν ὑμεῖς ἑστήκατε, καὶ ἡ παρ' ὑμῶν χάρις, ἐμοῦ τὰς εὐθύνας παρέχοντος. Ταῦτα τὰ ῥήματα τὰ πάντα διέφθειρεν· ἵνα μὴ ἀπέλθῃ, φησί, καὶ μετατεθῇ πρὸς ἑτέραν αἵρεσιν· ἀσθενής ἐστι, συγκατάβηθι. Μέχρι τίνος; μέχρι πότε; ἅπαξ, καὶ δίς, καὶ τρίς, μὴ διαπαντός.

Ἰδοὺ παρεγγυῶ πάλιν, καὶ διαμαρτύρομαι κατὰ τὸν μακάριον Παῦλον, "Ὅτι ἂν ἔλθω εἰς τὸ πάλιν, οὐ φείσομαι." Ὅταν δὲ κατορθώσητε, τότε εἴσεσθε ὅσον τὸ κέρδος, ὅση ἡ ὠφέλεια. Ναί, παρακαλῶ καὶ ἀντιβολῶ, καὶ τῶν γονάτων οὐκ ἂν παραιτησαίμην ἅψασθαι, καὶ ἱκετηρίαν θεῖναι ὑπὲρ τούτου. Τίς ἡ βλακεία; τίς ἡ τρυφή; τίς ἡ ὕβρις; οὐ τρυφὴ τοῦτο, ἀλλ' ὕβρις· τίς ἡ ἄνοια; τίς ἡ μανία; Πένητες τοσοῦτοι τὴν ἐκκλησίαν περιεστήκασι, καὶ τέκνα ἔχουσα τοσαῦτα ἡ ἐκκλησία, οὕτω πλουτοῦντα, οὐδὲ ἑνὶ πένητι ἐπαμῦναι δύναται· ἀλλ' ὁ μὲν πεινᾷ, ὁ δὲ μεθύει· ὁ μὲν καὶ ἐν ἀργύρῳ ἀποπατεῖ, ὁ δὲ οὐδὲ ἄρτου μετέχει. Τίς ἡ μανία; τίς ἡ θηριωδία ἡ τοσαύτη; Γένοιτο μὴ ἐλθεῖν ἡμᾶς εἰς τὴν πεῖραν τοῦ ἐπεξελθεῖν τοῖς ἀπειθοῦσι, μηδὲ εἰς ἀγανάκτησιν τοῦ ταῦτα ἐπιτρέψαι, ἀλλ' ἑκόντας καὶ ἀνεχομένους ταῦτα πάντα περιστῆναι· ἵνα εἰς δόξαν τοῦ θεοῦ ζήσωμεν, καὶ τῆς ἐκεῖ κολάσεως ἀπαλλαγῶμεν, καὶ τῶν ἐπηγγελμένων ἀγαθῶν τοῖς ἀγαπῶσιν αὐτὸν ἐπιτύχωμεν, χάριτι καὶ

And to the men I give this advice: Have you come to school to be educated in spiritual philosophy? Strip off that pride. This is my advice to both men and women, and if somebody acts differently, in future I shall not put up with it. The disciples were twelve, and listen to what Christ said to them: "*Do you also wish to go away?*" [John 6:67]. You see, if we flatter you continually, when shall we get you back? When shall we help you? "But," says [someone], "there are other heresies, and people cross over."[90] That argument is cold. *Better is one who does the will of the Lord, than thousands of transgressors* [Sir 16:3]. And what do you too want, tell me? To have thousands of household servants who were runaways and slaves, or one who favors you? Look, I advise and charge you to destroy the facial ornament [252] and such vessels, and to give to the poor, and not be so mad.

Let the person who wishes jump away, the one who wishes to accuse me. I shall not put up with it in anyone. When I am going to be judged at Christ's tribunal, you stand at a distance, and your favor [counts for nothing] when I am rendering my account. "These words have ruined everything. Let him leave and go over to another heresy," [someone] says. "He is weak, give in to him." Until what point? Till when? Once and twice and three times, not perpetually.

Look, I charge you again and protest after the pattern of blessed Paul: "*that if I come again, I shall not spare* [you]" [2 Cor 13:2]. But when you have corrected yourselves, then you'll know how great the gain is, how great the advantage. Yes, I entreat and beseech you, and I wouldn't refuse to clasp your knees and to enter a supplication on behalf of this. What softness is it? What luxury? What wantonness? This isn't luxury but wantonness. What senselessness? What madness? So many poor people stand around the church, and although the church has so many children, so wealthy, it's unable to come to the aid of even one poor person. But *one is hungry, the other is drunk* [1 Cor 11:21]; one relieves themselves even into silver, the other doesn't even partake of bread. What madness? What brutishness as great as this? May it not happen that we ever come to the proof of prosecuting the disobedient, nor to the indignation of allowing these things, but that willingly and patiently you shun all these practices, so that we may live in God's glory and be freed from punishment in that place, and may obtain the good things promised to those who love him, by the grace and loving-

---

90. Given the various sects (rather than heresies) in Antioch at the time, it is not surprising that an imaginary person points to the fluidity of religious alliances and the convenience of changing them.

φιλανθρωπίᾳ τοῦ κυρίου ἡμῶν Ἰησοῦ Χριστοῦ, μεθ' οὗ τῷ πατρὶ ἅμα τῷ ἁγίῳ πνεύματι δόξα, κράτος, τιμὴ εἰς τοὺς αἰῶνας τῶν αἰώνων. Ἀμήν.

kindness of our Lord Jesus Christ, with whom to the Father together with the Holy Spirit be glory, power, honor, forever and ever. Amen.

ΛΟΓΟΣ Η.

Νεκρώσατε τὰ μέλη ὑμῶν τὰ ἐπὶ τῆς γῆς, πορνείαν, ἀκαθαρσίαν, πάθος, ἐπιθυμίαν κακὴν, καὶ τὴν πλεονεξίαν, ἥτις ἐστὶν εἰδωλολατρεία, δι' ἃ ἔρχεται ἡ ὀργὴ τοῦ θεοῦ ἐπὶ τοὺς [253]υἱοὺς τῆς ἀπειθείας, ἐν οἷς καὶ ὑμεῖς περιεπατήσατέ ποτε, ὅτε ἐζῆτε ἐν αὐτοῖς.

Οἶδα πολλοὺς ἀπεχθανομένους ἐν τῇ πρὸ ταύτης διαλέξει· ἀλλὰ τί πάθω; ἠκούσατε τί ἐπέταξεν ὁ δεσπότης. Μὴ γὰρ ἐγὼ αἴτιος; Τί ποιήσω; Οὐχ ὁρᾶτε τοὺς ἀπαιτοῦντας, ὅταν ἀγνωμονῶσιν οἱ ὑπεύθυνοι, πῶς κλοιὰ περίκεινται; Ἠκούσατε τί σήμερον ὁ Παῦλος ἐβόα; "Νεκρώσατε, φησὶ, τὰ μέλη ὑμῶν τὰ ἐπὶ τῆς γῆς, πορνείαν, ἀκαθαρσίαν, πάθος, ἐπιθυμίαν κακὴν, καὶ τὴν πλεονεξίαν, ἥτις ἐστὶν εἰδωλολατρεία." Τί τῆς τοιαύτης πλεονεξίας χεῖρον; Πάσης ἐπιθυμίας αὔτης χείρων. Τοῦτο βαρύτερον οὖπερ ἔλεγον, ἡ μανία καὶ ἡ βλακεία ἡ περὶ ἄργυρον. "Καὶ τὴν πλεονεξίαν, φησὶν, ἥτις ἐστὶν εἰδωλολατρεία·" Ὁρᾶτε ποῦ τὸ κακὸν τελευτᾷ; Μὴ δὴ δυσχεράνητε· οὐ γὰρ ἑκὼν οὐδὲ ἁπλῶς ἐχθροὺς ἔχειν θέλω, ἀλλ' ἐβουλόμην ὑμᾶς εἰς τοῦτο ἀρετῆς ἥκειν, ὡς ἐμὲ παρ' ὑμῶν ἀκούειν τὰ δέοντα. Ὥστε οὐκ αὐθεντίας ἐστὶν, οὐδὲ ἀξιώματος, ἀλλ' ὀδύνης καὶ ἀλγηδόνος. Σύγγνωτέ μοι, σύγγνωτε· οὐ θέλω ἀσχημονεῖν ὑπὲρ τοιούτων διαλεγόμενος, ἀλλ' ἀναγκάζομαι.

Οὐχ ὑπὲρ τῆς τῶν πενήτων ὀδύνης ταῦτα λέγω, ἀλλ' ὑπὲρ τῆς ὑμετέρας σωτηρίας. Ἀπολοῦνται γὰρ, ἀπολοῦνται οἱ μὴ θρέψαντες τὸν Χριστόν. Τί γὰρ, εἰ τρέφεις πένητα; ἀλλ' ἕως ἂν οὕτω σπαταλᾷς καὶ οὕτω τρυφᾷς, πάντα περιττά. Οὐ γὰρ τὸ δοῦναι ζητεῖται πολλὰ, ἀλλὰ τὸ μὴ ἔλαττον τῆς οἰκείας οὐσίας· τοῦτο γὰρ παίζοντός ἐστι. "Νεκρώσατε οὖν τὰ μέλη ὑμῶν, φησὶ, τὰ ἐπὶ τῆς γῆς." Τί λέγεις; οὐ σὺ εἶπας, ὅτι ἐτάφητε; ὅτι συνετάφητε; ὅτι περιετμήθητε; ὅτι ἀπεξεδυσάμεθα τὸ σῶμα τῶν ἁμαρτιῶν τῆς σαρκός; πῶς

Put to death your members that are on earth: fornication, impurity, passion, evil lust, and covetousness, which is idolatry, through which is coming God's wrath on the [253] sons of disobedience. You too walked in these at one time, when you lived in them [Col 3:5–7].

I know that many were offended by the discourse before this, but what is to become of me? Did you hear what the Master commanded? Surely I'm not to blame? What shall I do? Don't you observe that when creditors treat debtors unfairly, they put collars on them?[91] Did you hear what Paul proclaimed today?[92] "*Put to death your members that are on earth,*" he says: "*fornication, impurity, passion, evil lust, and covetousness, which is idolatry.*" What is worse than covetousness of this kind? It's worse than every passion. This is more grievous than what I was speaking about—the madness, and the weakness about silver. "*And covetousness,*" says Paul, "*which is idolatry.*" Do you see how evil ends? Now, don't be annoyed, for not willingly do I want to have enemies, not even openly, but I wanted you to attain such virtue so that I might hear what I wanted from you. The upshot is that it's not due to authority, nor status, but to pain and sorrow. Forgive me, forgive! I don't want to behave disgracefully by speaking on such subjects, but I'm forced to.

It's not for the sake of the suffering of the poor that I say these things, but for the sake of your salvation. You see, they will perish, they will perish who have not nourished Christ. So what, if you nourish a poor person? No, as long as you live so riotously and in such luxury, everything is in vain. For what is required is not giving much, but not too little of your own property: this is joking. *Put to death your members that are on earth.* What do you say? Wasn't it you who said: "*You are buried*"? "*You are buried together*"? "*You are circumcised*"? "*You have divested the body of the sins of the flesh*"

---

91. This appears to be referring to the practices of tax collectors with regard to those recalcitrants who were in the government's debt.

92. This is an indication that Col 3:5–7 formed part of the liturgical readings of the day.

οὖν πάλιν λέγεις, "νεκρώσατε;" Μὴ παίζῃς; ὡς ὄντων αὐτῶν ἐν ἡμῖν οὕτω διαλέγῃ; Οὐκ ἔστιν ἐναντιολογία· ἀλλ' ὥσπερ εἴ τις ἐρρυπωμένον ἀνδριάντα ἀποσμήξας, μᾶλλον δὲ ἀναχαλκεύσας, καὶ λαμπρὸν δείξας ἄνωθεν, λέγοι μὲν ὅτι κατεπόθη ὁ ἰὸς καὶ ἀπώλετο, παραινοῖ δὲ πάλιν σπουδάζειν ἀποτίθεσθαι τὸν ἰόν, οὐκ ἐναντιολογεῖ· οὐ γὰρ ὃν ἀπέσμηξεν ἰόν, ἀλλὰ τὸν ἐπιγι-[254] νόμενον μετὰ ταῦτα παραινεῖ ἀποθέσθαι· οὕτως οὐ τὴν προτέραν νέκρωσιν λέγει, οὐδὲ τὰς πορνείας ἐκείνας, ἀλλὰ τὰς ἐπιγινομένας ὕστερον.

Εἶπεν ὅτι οὐκ ἔστιν ἡμῶν ἡ ζωὴ αὕτη, ἀλλ' ἑτέρα ἡ ἐν οὐρανοῖς. Εἰπὲ δή μοι· ἐπειδὴ εἶπε, "Νεκρώσατε ὑμῶν τὰ μέλη τὰ ἐπὶ τῆς γῆς," οὐκοῦν καὶ ἡ γῆ διαβέβληται; ἢ τὰ ἐπὶ γῆς αὐτὰ καλεῖ τὰ ἁμαρτήματα; "Πορνείαν, ἀκαθαρσίαν," φησί. Παρῆκε τὰ πράγματα, ἃ οὐδὲ εἰπεῖν καλόν, καὶ διὰ τῆς ἀκαθαρσίας ἅπαντα ἐνέφηνε. "Πάθος, φησὶν, ἐπιθυμίαν κακήν." Ἰδοὺ γενικῶς τὸ πᾶν εἶπε· πάντα γὰρ ἐπιθυμία κακή, βασκανία, ὀργή, λύπη. "Καὶ τὴν πλεονεξίαν, φησὶν, ἥτις ἐστὶν εἰδωλολατρεία· διὰ ταῦτα γὰρ ἔρχεται ἡ ὀργὴ τοῦ θεοῦ ἐπὶ τοὺς υἱοὺς τῆς ἀπειθείας." Διὰ πολλῶν ἀπήγαγεν αὐτούς· διὰ τῶν εὐεργεσιῶν τῶν ὑπαρξασῶν, διὰ τῶν μελλόντων ἐξ ὧν ἀπηλλάγημεν κακῶν, τίνες ὄντες, καὶ διὰ τί. Καὶ ὅλα ἐκεῖνα, οἷον, τίνες ἦμεν καὶ ἐν τίσιν, καὶ ὅτι ἀπηλλάγημεν αὐτῶν, πῶς καὶ τίνι τρόπῳ, καὶ ἐπὶ τίσι, ταῦτα ἱκανὰ ἀποστρέ-ψαι· ἀλλὰ πάντων σφοδρότερον τοῦτο, ἀηδὲς μὲν εἰπεῖν, οὐ μὴν ἀνωφελές, ἀλλὰ καὶ ὠφέλιμον· "Δι' ἃ ἔρχεται, φησὶν, ἡ ὀργὴ τοῦ θεοῦ ἐπὶ τοὺς υἱοὺς τῆς ἀπειθείας." Οὐκ εἶπεν, ἐφ' ὑμᾶς, ἀλλ', "ἐπὶ τοὺς υἱοὺς τῆς ἀπειθείας." "Ἐν οἷς καὶ ὑμεῖς περιεπατήσατέ ποτε, ὅτε ἐζῆτε ἐν αὐτοῖς." Ἐντρεπτικῶς, "ὅτε ἐζῆτε, φησὶν, ἐν αὐτοῖς," καὶ μετ' ἐγκωμίων, ὡς νῦν οὐ ζώντων· τότε ἐξῆν. "Νυνὶ δὲ ἀπόθεσθε καὶ ὑμεῖς τὰ πάντα." Καὶ καθολικῶς ἀεὶ λέγει, καὶ ἰδικῶς· ταῦτα δέ ἐστι διαθέσεως. "Ὀργήν, θυμόν, κακίαν βλασφημίαν, αἰσχρολογίαν ἐκ τοῦ στόματος ὑμῶν. Μὴ ψεύδεσθε εἰς ἀλλήλους." "Αἰσχρολογίαν, φησὶν, ἐκ τοῦ στόματος ὑμῶν," ἐμφαντικῶς, ὅτι αὐτὸ ῥυποῖ.

"Ἀπεκδυσάμενοι τὸν παλαιὸν ἄνθρωπον σὺν ταῖς πράξεσιν αὐτοῦ, καὶ [255] ἐνδυσάμενοι τὸν νέον τὸν ἀνακαινούμενον εἰς ἐπίγνωσιν κατ' εἰκόνα τοῦ κτίσαντος αὐτόν." Ἄξιον ἐνταῦθα ζητῆσαι, τί δήποτε μέλη καὶ ἄνθρωπον καὶ σῶμα καλεῖ τὸν διεφθαρμένον βίον, καὶ τὸν ἐνάρετον πάλιν τὸ αὐτό. Καὶ εἰ ὁ ἄνθρωπός εἰσιν αἱ ἁμαρτίαι, πῶς φησι, "σὺν ταῖς πράξεσιν αὐτοῦ;" Ἅπαξ γὰρ εἶπε παλαιὸν ἄνθρωπον, δείξας ὅτι οὐ τοῦτό ἐστιν ἄνθρωπος, ἀλλ' ἐκεῖνο, Τῆς οὐσίας ἡ προαίρεσις κυριωτέρα, καὶ τοῦτο μᾶλλον ἄνθρωπος, ἢ ἐκεῖνο. Οὐ γὰρ ἡ οὐσία ἐμβάλλει εἰς γέενναν, οὐδὲ εἰς βασιλείαν εἰσάγει, ἀλλ' αὐτοὶ οἱ ἄνθρωποι· καὶ οὐδένα οὔτε φιλοῦμεν, οὔτε μισοῦμεν ᾗ ἄνθρωπος, ἀλλ' ᾗ τοιόσδε ᾗ ἄνθρωπος. Εἰ τοίνυν ἡ μὲν οὐσία τὸ σῶμά ἐστιν, αὕτη δὲ ἀνυπεύ-θυνος ἐν ἑκατέροις, πῶς αὐτὸ κακὸν εἶναί φησι; Τί δέ φησι, "σὺν ταῖς πρά-ξεσι;" Τὴν προαίρεσιν μετὰ τῶν ἔργων. Παλαιὸν δὲ αὐτὸν καλεῖ, τὸ αἰσχρὸν

[Col 2:11–12]? How, then, can you say, "*put to death*"? Aren't you joking? Do you discourse in such a way as if these things are in us? There is no contradiction, but just as if someone had scraped clean a statue that was filthy, or rather recast it, and displayed it gleaming afresh, but should say that the rust was eaten away and destroyed, should yet recommend diligence in getting rid of the rust, doesn't contradict themselves. You see, it's not the rust that they scraped off but what **[254]** grows afterward that they recommend should be cleared away. So it's not the former death that Paul speaks of, nor of those occasions of fornication, but what happens afterward.

Paul said that this life is not ours, but the other one in heaven. Then tell me: since he said, "*Put to death your members that are on earth*," surely the earth too is discredited? Or does he call the things of earth sins? "*Fornication, impurity*," he says. He has passed over the fact that it isn't good even to speak about, and by *impurity* he has expressed everything. "*Passion*," he says, "*evil lust*." Look, he's expressed the whole matter generically, for envy, anger, sorrow are all *evil lust*. "*And covetousness*," he says, "*which is idolatry. On account of these the wrath of God is coming upon the sons of disobedience.*" By many means he withdrew them: by the benefits already existing, by the evils to come from which we have been freed—what they are and for what reason. And those entire considerations, for example, who we are and in what circumstances, and that we were freed from them, how and in what manner, and on what terms. These were enough to turn them away, but of all, this was the most powerful, unpleasant indeed to speak of, not, however, unprofitable, but even of profit. *On account of these the wrath of God is coming upon the sons of disobedience.* He didn't say, "upon you," but "*upon the sons of disobedience.*" *You too walked in these at one time, when you lived in them.* Shaming them: "*When you lived in them*," he says, and praising them because they don't live [like that] now. Then it was possible for them to do so. He always speaks both generally and particularly, but that is from his disposition. *Anger, wrath, malice, slander, foul talk from your mouth. Don't lie to one another* [Col 3:9]. "*Foul talk*," he says, "*from your mouth*" [Col 3:8], clearly saying that this pollutes.

You have put off the old person with its deeds, and **[255]** *put on the new, which is being renewed in knowledge after the image of the one who created it* [Col 3:10–11]. It's worth inquiring at this point what on earth the reason is for Paul to call the corrupt life *members* and *human being* and *body*, and again the virtuous life the same thing. And if the *human being* means sins, how is it that he says "*with its deeds*"? You see, he said once "*the old person*," demonstrating that this is not a human being, but that is. Free choice governs

αὐτοῦ βουλόμενος δεῖξαι καὶ τὸ δυσειδὲς καὶ τὸ ἠσθενηκός· καὶ νέον, ἀντὶ τοῦ, μὴ προσδοκήσητε, φησὶν, ὅτι καὶ οὗτος τὸ αὐτὸ πείσεται, ἀλλὰ τοὐναντίον· ὅσῳ γὰρ ἂν προΐῃ, οὐ πρὸς γῆρας ἐπείγεται, ἀλλὰ πρὸς νεότητα μείζονα τῆς προτέρας. Ὅταν γὰρ πλείονα λάβῃ τὴν γνῶσιν, καὶ μειζόνων ἀξιοῦται, καὶ μᾶλλον ἀκμάζει, μᾶλλον ἰσχύει, οὐκ ἀπὸ τῆς νεότητος μόνον, ἀλλὰ καὶ τοῦ εἴδους πρὸς ὅ ἐστιν. Ἰδοὺ κτίσις ἡ ἀρίστη πολιτεία λέγεται. Κατ᾽ εἰκόνα Χριστοῦ· τοῦτο γάρ ἐστι, "κατ᾽ εἰκόνα τοῦ κτίσαντος αὐτόν·" ἐπεὶ καὶ ὁ Χριστὸς οὐ πρὸς γῆρας ἐτελεύτησεν, ἀλλ᾽ οὕτως ἦν καλὸς, ὡς μηδὲ ἔστιν εἰπεῖν.

"Ὅπου οὐκ ἔνι Ἕλλην καὶ Ἰουδαῖος, περιτομὴ καὶ ἀκροβυστία, βάρβαρος, Σκύθης, δοῦλος, ἐλεύθερος, ἀλλὰ τὰ πάντα, καὶ ἐν πᾶσι Χριστός." Ἰδοὺ τρίτον ἐγκώμιον τοῦ ἀνδρὸς τούτου, ὅταν μήτε ἔθνους, μήτε ἀξιώματος, μήτε προγόνων διαφορὰ ἐπεισέρχηται, ὅταν ἔχῃ τῶν ἔξωθεν μηδὲν, μηδὲ δέηται τούτων· τοιαῦτα γὰρ πάντα τὰ ἔξωθεν. "Περιτομὴ καὶ ἀκροβυστία· δοῦλος, ἐλεύθερος, Ἕλλην," τουτέστι, προσήλυτος· "καὶ Ἰουδαῖος," ἐκ προγόνων. Ἂν τοῦτον ἔχῃς μόνον, τῶν αὐτῶν ἐπιτεύξῃ τοῖς ἄλλοις τοῖς ἔχουσιν.

[256] "Ἀλλὰ τὰ πάντα, καὶ ἐν πᾶσι, φησὶν, Χριστός." πάντα ὑμῖν ὁ Χριστὸς ἔσται, καὶ ἀξίωμα καὶ γένος, καὶ ἐν πᾶσιν ὑμῖν αὐτός. Ἢ ἕτερόν φησιν, ὅτι πάντες Χριστὸς εἷς ἐγένεσθε, σῶμα αὐτοῦ ὄντες. "Ἐνδύσασθε οὖν, ὡς ἐκλεκτοὶ τοῦ θεοῦ, ἅγιοι καὶ ἠγαπημένοι." Τὸ εὔκολον δείκνυσι τῆς ἀρετῆς, καὶ ὥστε καὶ διηνεκῶς αὐτὴν ἔχειν, καὶ ὥστε ὡς μεγίστῳ κόσμῳ κεχρῆσθαι. Καὶ μετ᾽ ἐγκωμίου ἡ παραίνεσις· τότε γὰρ μάλιστα ἰσχύει. Ἐγένοντο γὰρ ἅγιοι, ἀλλ᾽ οὐκ ἐκλεκτοί· νυνὶ δὲ καὶ ἐκλεκτοὶ καὶ ἅγιοι καὶ ἠγαπημένοι. "Σπλάγχνα οἰκτιρμοῦ." Οὐκ εἶπεν ἔλεον, ἀλλ᾽ ἐμφαντικώτερον διὰ τῶν δύο. Καὶ οὐκ εἶπεν, ὅτι ὡς ἀδελφοῖς, ἀλλ᾽ ὡς παισὶ πατέρες. Μὴ γάρ μοι εἴπῃς, ὅτι ἥμαρτε· διὰ τοῦτο εἶπε σπλάγχνα. Καὶ οὐκ εἶπεν, οἰκτιρμὸν, ἵνα μὴ ἐκείνους ἐξευτελίσῃ, ἀλλὰ, "σπλάγχνα οἰκτιρμοῦ." "Χρηστότητα, ταπεινοφροσύνην, πραότητα, μακροθυμίαν· ἀνεχόμενοι ἀλλήλων, καὶ χαριζόμενοι ἑαυτοῖς, ἐάν τις πρός τινα ἔχῃ μομφήν· καθὼς καὶ ὁ Χριστὸς ἐχαρίσατο ὑμῖν, οὕτω καὶ ὑμεῖς."

substance, and this rather than the human being, then the other. You see, it's not their substance that throws them into hell, nor leads them on to the kingdom, but people themselves. And we neither love nor hate a human being, but whether it is such or such a human being. If therefore substance is the body, but in both cases can't be accountable, how does Paul say that it's evil? But what does he say: *"with his deeds"*? He means the free choice with the deeds. And he calls it *old* because he wants to demonstrate his ugliness and disfigurement and imbecility; and *new*, instead of "don't expect," he says, "that it will be with this one the same as the other, but the opposite, for as much as he advances, he doesn't rush on to old age but to a youthfulness greater than before." You see, when he's received the fuller knowledge and is judged worthy of greater things and is more mature, with more strength, not only from youthfulness but also from that likeness from which he is. Look, the best life is called the civic life. For this is after the image of Christ, *after the image of him who created him* [Col 3:10], since Christ too ended his life not in old age but was so beautiful as is not even possible to tell.

Where there is neither Hellene nor Jew, circumcision and uncircumcised, barbarian, Scythian, slave, free, but Christ is everything and in everything [Col 3:11]. Look, this is the third encomium of this man, since no difference either of race, or rank, or ancestry comes into it, since he has nothing of external things, nor need of them. You see, such things are all external. *Circumcision and uncircumcision, slave, free, Hellene* (that is, proselyte) *and Jew* from his ancestors. If you have only this man, you will obtain the same things with the others who have him.

[**256**] *"But Christ,"* Paul says, *"is everything and in everything."* Christ will be everything to you, both rank and descent, and himself everything to you in all. Or he means something else, namely, that "you have become one Christ, being his body." *Put on, therefore, as God's elect, holy and beloved* [Col 3:12]. He shows the easiness of virtue, both so that they may possess it continually and use it as the greatest ornament. And with the exhortation comes praise, for then its force is greatest. You see, before they were holy but not elect, but now they are *elect*, and *holy and beloved. Bowels of compassion.* He didn't say "mercy," but with greater emphasis used the two words. And he didn't say it was toward brothers, but as fathers toward children. Don't tell me that he sinned, which is why he said *"bowels."* And he didn't say "compassion," so that he didn't greatly disparage them, but *"bowels of compassion." Kindness, lowliness, meekness, patience, forbearing each other and, if one has a complaint against someone, forgiving each other, as Christ forgave so too must you forgive* [Col 3:12–13].

Πάλιν κατ᾽ εἶδος λέγει, καὶ ἀεὶ αὐτὸ ποιεῖ· ἀπὸ χρηστότητος γὰρ ταπεινοφροσύνη, καὶ ἀπὸ ταύτης μακροθυμία. "Ἀνεχόμενοι, φησὶν, ἀλλήλων,"
τουτέστι, παραπεμπόμενοι. Καὶ ὅρα πῶς αὐτὸ οὐδὲν ἔδειξε, μομφὴν καλέ-
σας, καὶ εἰπών, "καθὼς καὶ ὁ Χριστὸς ἐχαρίσατο ὑμῖν." Μέγα τὸ ὑπόδειγμα·
ὅπερ ἀεὶ ποιεῖ, ἀπὸ τοῦ Χριστοῦ προτρέπων αὐτούς. Μομφήν φησι. Ἐκεῖ μὲν
μικρὸν αὐτὸ ἔδειξεν· ὅτε δὲ τὸ ὑπόδειγμα παρήγαγεν, ἔπεισεν ὅτι κἂν μεγάλα
ἔχωμεν ἐγκαλεῖν, δεῖ χαρίζεσθαι. Τὸ γὰρ, "καθὼς ὁ Χριστὸς," τοῦτο σημαί-
νει· καὶ οὐ τοῦτο μόνον, ἀλλ᾽ ὅτι καὶ ἐξ ὅλης καρδίας· καὶ οὐ τοῦτο μόνον,
ἀλλ᾽ ὅτι καὶ φιλεῖν δεῖ. Ὁ γὰρ Χριστὸς εἰσαχθεὶς εἰς τὸ μέσον, πάντα εἰσάγει
ταῦτα· καὶ ὅτι κἂν μεγάλα ᾖ, κἂν μὴ προηδικηκότες τύχωμεν, κἂν ἡμεῖς μὲν
μεγάλοι, ἐκεῖνοι δὲ μικροὶ, κἂν μέλλωσιν ὑβρίζειν ἡμᾶς καὶ μετὰ ταῦτα, καὶ
ὅτι τὴν ψυχὴν δεῖ ὑπὲρ αὐτῶν θεῖναι· τὸ γὰρ, καθὼς, ταῦτα ἀπαιτεῖ· καὶ ὅτι
οὐδὲ μέχρι θανάτου μόνον στῆναι δεῖ, ἀλλ᾽, εἰ δυνατὸν, καὶ μετὰ ταῦτα.

"Ἐπὶ πᾶσι δὲ τούτοις τὴν ἀγάπην, ἥτις ἐστὶ σύνδεσμος τῆς τελειότητος."
[257] Ὁρᾷς ὅτι τοῦτο λέγει; Ἐπειδὴ γὰρ ἔνι χαριζόμενον μὴ φιλεῖν, ναὶ,
φησὶ, καὶ φιλεῖν, καὶ ὁδὸν δείκνυσι, δι᾽ ἧς δυνατὸν χαρίζεσθαι. Ἔστι γὰρ καὶ
χρηστὸν εἶναί τινα, καὶ πρᾶον καὶ ταπεινόφρονα καὶ μακρόθυμον, καὶ μὴ
ποθεῖν. Διὸ ἀρχόμενος εἶπε, "σπλάγχνα οἰκτιρμοῦ," καὶ ἀγάπην, καὶ ἔλεον.
"Ἐπὶ πᾶσι δὲ τούτοις τὴν ἀγάπην, ἥτις ἐστὶ σύνδεσμος τῆς τελειότητος." Ὃ
δὲ θέλει εἰπεῖν, τοῦτό ἐστιν· ὅτι οὐδὲν ἐκείνων ὄφελος· διαλύεται γὰρ πάντα
ἐκεῖνα, ἂν μὴ μετὰ ἀγάπης γίνηται. Πάντα ἐκεῖνα αὕτη συσφίγγει· ὅπερ ἂν
εἴπῃς ἀγαθὸν, ταύτης ἀπούσης, οὐδέν ἐστιν, ἀλλὰ διαρρεῖ. Καὶ ὃν τρόπον ἐπὶ
πλοίου, κἂν μεγάλα ᾖ τὰ σκεύη, τὰ δὲ ὑποζώματα μὴ ᾖ, οὐδὲν ὄφελος· καὶ
ἐπὶ οἰκίας, ἐὰν μὴ ὦσιν αἱ ἱμαντώσεις· καὶ ἐπὶ σώματος, κἂν μεγάλα ᾖ τὰ
ὀστᾶ, οἱ σύνδεσμοι ἐὰν μὴ ὦσιν, οὐδὲν ὄφελος. Οἷα γὰρ ἐάν τις ἔχῃ κατορθώματα, πάντα φροῦδα, ἀγάπης μὴ οὔσης. Οὐκ εἶπεν, ὅτι κορυφή ἐστιν, ἀλλ᾽
ὃ μεῖζόν ἐστι, σύνδεσμος· ἀναγκαιότερον τοῦτο, ἢ ἐκεῖνο. Κορυφὴ μὲν γὰρ
ἐπίτασις τελειότητος, σύνδεσμος δὲ συγκράτησις τῶν τὴν τελειότητα ποιούντων, ὡσανεὶ ἡ ῥίζα.

"Καὶ ἡ εἰρήνη τοῦ θεοῦ βραβευέτω ἐν ταῖς καρδίαις ὑμῶν, εἰς ἣν καὶ ἐκλήθητε ἐν σώματι ἑνί· καὶ εὐχάριστοι γίνεσθε." Ἡ εἰρήνη τοῦ θεοῦ, ἡ πεπηγυῖα
καὶ βεβαία αὕτη ἐστίν. Ἂν μὲν δι᾽ ἄνθρωπον ἔχῃς εἰρήνην, ταχέως διαλύεται·
ἐὰν δὲ διὰ τὸν θεὸν, οὐκέτι. Καίτοι τὸ καθολικὸν εἶπε τὴν ἀγάπην, ἀλλὰ πάλιν
ἐπὶ τὸ ἰδικὸν ἔρχεται. Ἔστι γὰρ καὶ ἄμετρος ἀγάπη, οἷον, ὅταν ἀπὸ πολλῆς

Again Paul speaks generically, and he always does this. You see, from kindness comes lowliness, and from this, forbearance. "*Forbearing each other*," he says, which means passing things over. And see how he showed this was nothing, calling it a "*complaint*," and saying, "*As Christ too forgave you*." It's a great example, which is what he always does: he exhorts them after Christ. Paul calls it a "*complaint*." In that passage he showed it to be a petty thing, but when he set before us the example, he convinced us that even if we have serious charges to bring, we must forgive. For the expression "*as Christ*" signifies this, and not only this but that they must do it with their whole heart. For Christ being brought into their midst introduces all these things, both that even if the matter is serious, even if we don't happen to be the first to do a further wrong, even if we're important but they are little people, even if they're going to insult us also afterward, and that we must lay down our lives for them (for the expression "*as*" demands this), and that not even until death must we only not stop, but, if possible, even after that.

And above all these things put on love, which is the bond of perfection [Col 3:14]. [**257**] Do you see that he said this? You see, since it's possible for the one who forgives not to love, yes, he says, and to love, and he shows the way through which it is possible to forgive. For it's possible for someone to be kind and meek and humble-minded and forbearing, and not to crave loving. This is why he said at the beginning "*bowels of mercy*," and love and pity. *And above all these things put on love, which is the bond of perfection.* Now what he wants to say this: there's no use in those things, for they all fall apart unless they come about with love. It's love that binds them all together: whatever good word you may say, if love is absent, it's nothing, but it flows away. And similar to a ship, even if its rigging is powerful but the braces aren't there, it's of no use; and in a house, if there are no timbers; and with a body, though the bones are large, if there are no ligaments, it's of no use. For whatever good deeds someone has, they have all fled, because love is absent. Paul didn't say the "summit," but what is greater, the *bond*— this is more necessary than the other. For "summit" is indeed an intensity of perfection, but *bond* is the holding fast of things that produce perfection, the root, as it were.

And may the peace of God be umpire in your hearts, to which indeed you were called in one body, and be thankful [Col 3:15]. *The peace of God*, which is fixed and steadfast. If on account of a human being you have peace, it is quickly dissolved, but if on account of God, never. Although Paul had spoken of love universally, now, however, he comes to the particular. You

τις ἀγάπης ἐγκαλῇ εἰκῇ, καὶ μάχας ἔχῃ καὶ ἀποστρέφηται. Οὔ, φησίν, οὐ τοῦτο βούλομαι· μὴ ὑπερσυντελικῶς, ἀλλ᾿ ὡς ἐποίησεν εἰρήνην πρὸς ὑμᾶς ὁ θεός, οὕτω καὶ ὑμεῖς ποιεῖτε. Πῶς ἐποίησεν; Αὐτὸς θελήσας, οὐ παρ᾿ ἡμῶν τι λαβών. Τί ἐστιν, "Ἡ εἰρήνη τοῦ θεοῦ βραβευέτω ἐν ταῖς καρδίαις ὑμῶν;" Ἐὰν μάχωνται λογισμοὶ δύο, μὴ στήσῃς τὸν θυμόν, μὴ στήσῃς τὴν ἐπήρειαν κατέχουσαν τὸ βραβεῖον, ἀλλὰ τὴν εἰρήνην. Οἷον, ἔστω τις ὑβρισθεὶς ἀδίκως· ἀπὸ τῆς ὕβρεως ἐτέχθησαν δύο λογισμοί, ὁ μὲν κελεύων ἀμύνασθαι, ὁ [258] δὲ ἐνεγκεῖν, καὶ παλαίουσιν ἀλλήλοις. Ἐὰν ἡ εἰρήνη τοῦ θεοῦ ἑστήκῃ μέση βραβεύουσα, τῷ κελεύοντι φέρειν δίδωσι τὸ βραβεῖον, καὶ καταισχύνει ἐκεῖνον. Πῶς; Πείθουσα ὅτι ὁ θεὸς εἰρήνη ἐστίν, ὅτι εἰρήνευσεν ἡμῖν. Οὐχ ἁπλῶς δείκνυσι πολὺν τὸν ἀγῶνα τοῦ πράγματος. Μὴ θυμός, φησί, βραβευέτω, μὴ φιλονεικία, μὴ ἀνθρωπίνη εἰρήνη· ἡ γὰρ ἀνθρωπίνη εἰρήνη ἐκ τοῦ ἀμύνασθαι γίνεται, ἐκ τοῦ μηδὲν πάσχειν δεινόν. Ἀλλ᾿ οὐ ταύτην βούλομαι, φησίν, ἀλλ᾿ ἐκείνην, ἣν καὶ ἀφῆκεν αὐτός.

Στάδιον ἔνδον ἐποίησεν ἐν τοῖς λογισμοῖς, καὶ ἀγῶνα καὶ ἄθλησιν καὶ βραβευτήν. Εἶτα πάλιν προτροπή· "εἰς ἣν ἐκλήθητε," φησί· τουτέστιν, ἐφ᾿ ᾗ ἐκλήθητε. Ἀνέμνησεν ὅσων ἀγαθῶν αἰτία ἡ εἰρήνη. Διὰ ταύτην σε ἐκάλεσεν, ἐπὶ ταύτῃ ἐκάλεσεν, ὥστε ἀξιόπιστον ἀναδέξασθαι τὸ βραβεῖον. Διὰ τί γὰρ ἓν σῶμα ἐποίησεν; οὐχ ἵνα αὕτη κρατῇ; οὐχ ἵνα ἀφορμὴν ἔχωμεν τοῦ εἰρηνεύειν; Διὰ τί πάντες ἓν σῶμά ἐσμεν; πῶς δὲ ἓν σῶμά ἐσμεν; Διὰ τὴν εἰρήνην σῶμα ἕν ἐσμεν, καὶ διὰ τὸ σῶμα ἓν εἶναι, εἰρηνεύομεν. Διὰ τί δὲ οὐκ εἶπεν, ἡ εἰρήνη τοῦ θεοῦ νικάτω, ἀλλά, "βραβευέτω;" Ἀξιοπιστοτέραν αὐτὴν ἐποίησε. Τὸν πονηρὸν λογισμὸν οὐκ ἀφῆκεν αὐτῇ προσπαλαίειν, ἀλλὰ κατώτερον ἑστάναι. Καὶ τὸ τοῦ βραβείου ὄνομα ἐπῆρε τὸν ἀκροατήν· ἂν γὰρ δῷ βραβεῖον τῷ ἀγαθῷ λογισμῷ, ὅσα ἂν ἀναισχυντῇ ἐκεῖνος, οὐδὲν ὄφελος λοιπόν. Ἄλλως δὲ ἐκεῖνος εἰδώς, ὅτι ὅσα ἂν ἐργάσηται, οὐ λήψεται τὸ βραβεῖον· ὅσα ἂν πνεύσῃ, καὶ ἐπιχειρήσῃ σφοδρότερον προσβαλεῖν· ἅτε ἀνόνητα πονῶν ἀποστήσεται. Καὶ καλῶς προσέθηκε, "καὶ εὐχάριστοι γίνεσθε." Τοῦτο γάρ ἐστιν εὐχάριστον εἶναι, καὶ σφόδρα ἐντρεπτικῶς, τὸ ὁμοίως κεχρῆσθαι τοῖς ὁμοδούλοις, ὥσπερ αὐτῷ ὁ θεός, τὸ εἴκειν τῷ δεσπότῃ, τὸ πείθεσθαι, τὸ ὑπὲρ πάντων χάριν ὁμολογεῖν, κἂν ὑβρίσῃ τις, κἂν πλήξῃ. Οὐ γὰρ δὴ ὁ τῷ θεῷ χάριν ὁμολογῶν, ὑπὲρ ὧν ἔπαθε, τὸν ποιήσαντα ἀμυνεῖται· ὡς ὅ γε ἀμυ-

see, there is a love too that is immoderate, for example, when out of much love someone makes accusations without reason, and has fighting on their hands and is put to flight. "No," Paul says, "it's not this that I want, but as God made peace with you in a manner that exceeds the moderate, so you make it." How did God make peace? Of his own will, not receiving anything from you. What's the meaning of *may the peace of God be umpire in your hearts*? If two thoughts are in conflict, don't set up spite to take the prize, but peace. For example, suppose that a person has been insulted unjustly; from the insult are born two thoughts, one ordering them to revenge, the [**258**] other to put up with it. And these two thoughts wrestle with each other. If God's peace stands in the middle as umpire, it gives the prize to the one who orders endurance and puts the other to shame. How? By persuading them that God is peace, that he has made peace with us. It's not simply that he demonstrates the great struggle in the matter. "Don't let anger umpire," he says, "nor contentiousness, not human peace, for human peace comes from avenging, of suffering nothing terrible. No, it isn't this peace that I want," he says, "but the other, which Christ himself left."

Paul has created a stadium in this, in the thoughts, and contest and wrestling and umpire. Then again an exhortation: "*Into which you have been called*," he says, which means "for which you were called." He reminded them of how many good things peace is responsible for. For this reason Christ called you, for he called you to receive the worthy prize. For why did he make us one body? Wasn't it so that peace should umpire? Wasn't it so that we might have an opportunity of being at peace? For what reason are we all one body? How are we one body? Through peace we are one body, and through being one body we are at peace. But why didn't he say, "Let God's peace be victorious," but "*let it be umpire*"? He made peace more credible. He didn't allow the evil thought to wrestle with it, but to stand below. And the very name *prize* elated the listener, for peace would have awarded the prize to the good thought; no matter how shamefully the other behaved, it's no use after that. And besides, the other was aware that no matter what deeds he might perform, he wouldn't take the prize. No matter how he might puff and attempt to attack more violently, seeing that he labors in vain he'll desist. And Paul added properly, "*And be thankful*" [Col 3:15]. For this is to be thankful, and he spoke putting them to great shame, to deal with fellow servants in the same way as God does with him, to submit to the Master, to obey, to confess his gratitude for all things, even if one were to insult him, or beat him. You see, confessing his thanks to God for what he's suffered, he won't avenge himself on the one who's done

νόμενος οὐχ ὁμολογεῖ χάριν. Ἀλλὰ μὴ κατ᾽ ἐκεῖνον τὸν τὰ ἑκατὸν δηνάρια γενώμεθα, ἵνα μὴ ἀκούσωμεν, "Πονηρὲ δοῦλε·" οὐδὲν γὰρ τῆς ἀχαριστίας ταύτης χεῖρον. Ὥστε ἀχάριστοι οἱ ἀμυνόμενοι.

[259] Διὰ τί δὲ ἐπὶ τὴν πορνείαν πρώτην ἦλθεν; εἰπὼν γάρ, "Νεκρώσατε ὑμῶν τὰ μέλη τὰ ἐπὶ τῆς γῆς," εὐθύς φησι, "πορνείαν," καὶ τοῦτο σχεδὸν πανταχοῦ ποιεῖ. Ὅτι μάλιστα τοῦτο κρατεῖ τὸ πάθος· καὶ γὰρ καὶ ἐν τῇ πρὸς Θεσσαλονικεῖς γράφων, τοῦτο ἐποίησε. Καὶ τί θαυμαστόν; ὅπου γε καὶ Τιμοθέῳ φησί, "Σεαυτὸν ἁγνὸν τήρει·" καὶ πάλιν ἀλλαχοῦ, "Εἰρήνην διώκετε μετὰ πάντων, καὶ τὸν ἁγιασμόν, οὗ χωρὶς οὐδεὶς ὄψεται τὸν κύριον." "Νεκρώσατε, φησί, τὰ μέλη ὑμῶν." Τὸ νεκρὸν ἴστε οἷόν ἐστι, μισητόν, βδελυκτόν, διαρρέον. Ἂν νεκρώσῃς, οὐ μένει νεκρόν, ἀλλὰ φθείρεται εὐθέως, καθάπερ τὸ σῶμα. Σβέσον οὖν τὴν θερμότητα, καὶ οὐδὲν νεκρὸν μένει. Δείκνυσιν αὐτὸν τοῦτο ἐργαζόμενον, ὅπερ ὁ Χριστὸς ἐπὶ τοῦ λουτροῦ. Διὰ τοῦτο καὶ μέλη καλεῖ· καθάπερ ἀριστέα τινὰ εἰσάγων, καὶ εἰς μείζονα ἄγων ἔμφασιν. Καὶ καλῶς εἶπε, "τὰ ἐπὶ τῆς γῆς·" ἐνταῦθα γὰρ μένει, καὶ ἐνταῦθα φθείρεται, πολλῷ μᾶλλον τῶν μελῶν τούτων. Ὥστε οὐχ οὕτω τὸ σῶμά ἐστιν ἀπὸ γῆς, ὡς ἡ ἁμαρτία γηΐνη· τοῦτο μὲν γὰρ καὶ καλὸν φαίνεταί ποτε, ἐκεῖνα δὲ οὐδέ-ποτε. Καὶ πάντων τῶν ἐπὶ γῆς ἐπιθυμεῖ ταῦτα τὰ μέλη. Ἂν ὀφθαλμὸς ᾖ τοιοῦτος, οὐχ ὁρᾷ τὰ ἐν οὐρανοῖς· ἂν ἀκοή, ἂν χείρ, ἂν ὁτιοῦν εἴπῃς μέλος. Ὀφθαλμὸς σώματα ὁρᾷ καὶ κάλλη καὶ χρήματα, ταῦτα τὰ ἀπὸ γῆς, τούτοις τέρπεται· ἡ ἀκοὴ μέλει μαλθακῷ, κιθάρᾳ καὶ σύριγγι καὶ αἰσχρολογίᾳ· ταῦτα δὲ περὶ γῆν. Ἐπειδὴ οὖν ἔστησεν αὐτοὺς ἄνω παρὰ τὸν θρόνον, τότε φησί, "Νεκρώσατε τὰ μέλη ὑμῶν τὰ ἐπὶ τῆς γῆς." Οὐ γὰρ ἔνι στῆναι ἄνω μετὰ τούτων τῶν μελῶν· οὐκ ἔνι γὰρ ἐκεῖ, εἰς ὃ ἐνεργεῖν δεῖ. Καὶ οὗτος ὁ πηλὸς χείρων ἐκείνου. Ἐκεῖνος μὲν γὰρ ὁ πηλὸς γίνεται χρυσός· "Δεῖ γάρ, φησί, τὸ φθαρτὸν τοῦτο ἐνδύσασθαι ἀφθαρσίαν·" οὗτος δὲ ὁ πηλὸς οὐκέτι ἀνα-χωνευθῆναι δύναται. Ὥστε ταῦτα μᾶλλον ἐπὶ τῆς γῆς, ἢ ἐκεῖνα. Διὰ τοῦτο οὐκ εἶπεν, ἀπὸ γῆς, ἀλλά, "τὰ ἐπὶ τῆς γῆς·" ἔνι γὰρ ταῦτα μὴ εἶναι ἐπὶ γῆς.

him wrong, since the one who takes revenge doesn't confess thanks. But let's not become like that person with the hundred denarii, so that we don't hear, "*Wicked servant*" [Matt 18:32], for nothing is worse than this ingratitude. So those who take revenge are ungrateful.

[259] But why did he come first to fornication? For having said, "*Put to death your members that are on earth*," immediately he says "*fornication*," and he does this almost everywhere. Because this passion has the greatest power, indeed also in writing to the Thessalonians he did this [see 1 Thess 4:3]. And what's surprising? Since also in writing to Timothy he says, "*Keep yourself pure*" [1 Tim 5:22], and again elsewhere, "*Strive for peace with everyone and for the holiness without which nobody will see the Lord*" [Heb 12:14]. "*Put to death your members*," he says. You know what kind of thing the corpse is, hated, disgusting, wasted. If you put something to death it doesn't stay dead but is corrupted immediately, like the body. Therefore, extinguish the heat, and nothing that's dead remains. He demonstrates that he was working on what Christ did in baptism. This why he calls them "*members*," as though introducing some champion and leading his discourse to greater emphasis. And he did well to say "*which are on earth*," for here they remain, and there they are corrupted, much more than these, our members. So that not really is the body of earth, as sin is earthly, for the former appears even beautiful sometimes, while the latter never do. And those members lust after everything that's on earth. If the eye is such that it doesn't observe things in heaven, if an ear, hand, if you mention any member whatsoever. The eye observes bodies, and beauty and wealth, things from earth—with these it is delighted: the ear with a gentle sound, a harp and pipe and filthy language. But these are things that are on earth.

Since, then, Paul has placed his hearers above, near the throne, he then says, "*Put to death your members that are on earth*." You see, it's not possible to stand above with those members, for there's nothing there that they should produce. And this clay is worse than that, for that clay indeed becomes gold. "*For this corruptible thing*," he says, "*must put on incorruption*" [1 Cor 15:53], but that clay can't be fashioned again. So these members are on earth, rather than those. This is why he didn't say "of earth," but "*that are on earth*." You see that it's possible that these things[93] aren't on earth, for it isn't necessary for them to be on earth, while those have no

---

93. Presumably sinful passions are meant.

Ταῦτα μὲν γὰρ ἀνάγκη ἐπὶ γῆς εἶναι, ἐκεῖνα δὲ οὐκέτι ἀνάγκη. Ὅταν γὰρ ἀκοὴ μηδὲν ἀκούῃ τῶν ἐνταῦθα, ἀλλὰ τῶν ἐν οὐρανοῖς [260] λαλουμένων, ὅταν ὀφθαλμὸς μηδὲν ὁρᾷ τῶν ἐνταῦθα, ἀλλὰ τῶν ἄνω, οὐκ ἐπὶ γῆς ἐστιν· ὅταν τὸ στόμα μηδὲν φθέγγηται τῶν ἐνταῦθα, οὐκ ἐπὶ γῆς ἐστιν· ὅταν ἡ χεὶρ μηδὲν πράττῃ τῶν πονηρῶν, οὐκ ἔστι τῶν ἐπὶ γῆς, ἀλλὰ τῶν ἐν τοῖς οὐρανοῖς.

Τοῦτο καὶ ὁ Χριστός φησιν, "Ἐὰν ὁ ὀφθαλμός σου ὁ δεξιὸς σκανδαλίζῃ σε," τουτέστιν, ἐὰν ἀκολάστως ὁρᾷς, "ἔκκοψον αὐτόν·" τουτέστι, τὸν λογισμὸν τὸν πονηρόν. Ἐμοὶ δὲ δοκεῖ πορνείαν, ἀκαθαρσίαν, πάθος, ἐπιθυμίαν, ταὐτὸ λέγειν, τὴν πορνείαν, διὰ πάντων τούτων ἀπάγων ἡμᾶς τοῦ πράγματος. Πάθος γὰρ ὄντως τοῦτό ἐστι· καὶ καθάπερ τὸ σῶμα πάσχει, ἢ πυρέττει ἢ τραυματίζεται, οὕτω καὶ τοῦτο. Καὶ οὐκ εἶπεν, ἐπίσχετε, ἀλλὰ, "νεκρώσατε," ὥστε μηδὲ ἀναστῆναι λοιπόν· καὶ, "ἀπόθεσθε." Τὸ νεκρούμενον ἀποτιθέμεθα· οἷον, τύλοι ἂν ὦσιν ἐν τῷ σώματι, τὸ σῶμα νεκρόν ἐστι, καὶ ἀποτιθέμεθα αὐτό. Ἀλλὰ ἐὰν μὲν ζῶν κόψῃς, ἀλγηδόνα παρέχει· ἂν δὲ νενεκρωμένον, οὐδὲ αἰσθανόμεθα. Οὕτω δὴ καὶ ἐπὶ τῶν παθῶν· ἀκάθαρτον ποιεῖ τὴν ψυχήν, παθητὴν ποιεῖ τὴν ψυχὴν τὴν ἀθάνατον.

Πῶς εἰδωλολατρεία εἴρηται ἡ πλεονεξία, πολλάκις εἰρήκαμεν. Τὰ τυραννοῦντα γὰρ μάλιστα τὸ τῶν ἀνθρώπων γένος, ταῦτά ἐστι, πλεονεξία, καὶ ἀκολασία καὶ ἐπιθυμία κακή. "Δι᾽ ἃ ἔρχεται, φησίν, ἡ ὀργὴ τοῦ θεοῦ ἐπὶ τοὺς υἱοὺς τῆς ἀπειθείας." Υἱοὺς ἀπειθείας λέγει, ἀποστερῶν αὐτοὺς συγγνώμης, καὶ δεικνὺς ὅτι παρὰ τὸ μὴ πεισθῆναι ἐν τούτοις εἰσίν. "Ἐν οἷς καὶ ὑμεῖς, φησὶ, περιεπατήσατέ ποτε," καὶ ἐπείσθητε. Δείκνυσιν αὐτοὺς ἔτι ἐν αὐτοῖς, καὶ ἐγκωμιάζει λέγων· "Νυνὶ δὲ καὶ ὑμεῖς ἀπόθεσθε τὰ πάντα, ὀργήν, θυμόν, κακίαν, βλασφημίαν, αἰσχρολογίαν." Ἀλλ᾽ ἐφ᾽ ἑτέρους προάγει τὸν λόγον. Πάθους καὶ βλασφημίας τὰς λοιδορίας λέγει, καθάπερ ἀπὸ τοῦ θυμοῦ τὴν πονηρίαν λέγει. Ἀλλαχοῦ δὲ ἐντρεπτικῶς, "Ὅτι ἀλλήλων ἐσμὲν μέλη." Ὥσπερ δημιουργοὺς αὐτοὺς κατασκευάζει τῶν ἀνθρώπων, τὸν μὲν ῥιπτούντων, τὸν δὲ δεχομένων. Εἶπεν [261] αὐτοῦ τὰ μέλη, ἐνταῦθα ὅλον φησίν. Εἶπεν αὐτοῦ τὴν καρδίαν, τὸν θυμόν, τὸ στόμα, τὴν βλασφημίαν, τοὺς ὀφθαλμούς, τὴν πορνείαν, τὴν πλεονεξίαν, χεῖρας καὶ πόδας, ψεῦδος, τὴν διάνοιαν αὐτήν, καὶ τὸν νοῦν τὸν παλαιόν. Μίαν ἔχει μορφὴν βασιλικὴν τὴν τοῦ Χριστοῦ. Ἐδόκουν μοι ἐξ ἐθνῶν εἶναι μᾶλλον οὗτοι. Καθάπερ γὰρ ἡ γῆ ψάμμος οὖσα, κἂν ἡ μὲν μείζων, ἡ δὲ ἐλάττων ᾖ, τὴν οἰκείαν ἀπώλεσε πρότερον μορφήν, ὕστερον δὲ χρυσῆ γίνεται· καὶ καθάπερ τὰ ἔρια, οἷα ἂν ᾖ, ἑτέραν δέχεται ὄψιν, καὶ τὴν προτέραν ἔκρυψεν· οὕτω δὴ καὶ ὁ πιστός. "Ἀνεχόμενοι, φησὶν, ἀλλήλων." Ἔδειξε τὸ δίκαιον· ἀνέχῃ ἐκείνου, καὶ ἐκεῖνός

necessity. I mean, when the ear hears nothing of what is here but what is spoken of in heaven; [260] when the eye sees nothing of what's here, but what's above, it's not on earth; when the mouth utters none of the things here, it's not on earth; when the hand does nothing wrong, it's not of things on earth but of those in heaven.

This is what Christ says too: "*If your right eye offends you* (that is, if you are looking unchastely), *cut it out*" [Matt 5:29] (that is, your evil thought). Paul seems to me to say that *fornication, impurity, passion, evil lust, and covetousness* are the same, namely, are fornication, Paul leading us away from that matter through all those words. For this is really passion, and just as the body suffers either fever or wounds, so too is it with this. And he didn't say "restrain," but "*put to death*," so that they never rise again, and "*divest yourself.*" What is dead we divest ourselves of: for example, if there are calluses in the body, the body is dead, and we divest ourselves of it. But if you cut into what's living, it produces pain, but if into what's dead, we don't even feel it. So indeed is it with the passions: they make the soul unclean, they make the soul, which is immortal, passible.

How covetousness idolatry is said to be, we have often spoken about. You see, the things that most of all tyrannize the human race are these: *covetousness, impurity,* and *evil lust.* "*Because of these,*" Paul says, "*God's wrath is coming upon the sons of disobedience.*" He calls them *the sons of disobedience,* depriving them of an excuse and demonstrating that because they weren't obedient they were in these straits. "*In which you also,*" he says, "*walked at one time*" and obeyed. He points to those who are still in those straits and praises them with the words, "*But now you too must divest yourselves of all of them: anger, wrath, malice, slander, foul talk.*" But he's directing the discourse to others. He calls passions and slander abuse, just as he calls wickedness wrath. And elsewhere, to shame them [he says], "*because we are members of each other*" [Eph 4:25]. He prepares them to be, so to speak, the craftsman of human beings, throwing away this one, receiving that. He said [261] they were his *members*; in this passage he says "*all*": he spoke of the heart (wrath), the mouth (slander), the eyes (fornication), the hands and feet (covetousness), lying (the thought itself and the old mind). One royal form it [sc. the new person] has, namely, that of Christ. Those people seemed to me rather to be from the gentiles. For just as the earth being sand, even though greater, while the other is inferior, has lost its first form, later it becomes gold. And just as wool, whatever kind it is, takes on a different appearance and hides the former one. So indeed is it with the faithful. "*Forbearing,*" he says, "*one another.*" He demonstrated what is just: you for-

σου· ὅπερ ἐν τῇ πρὸς Γαλάτας φησίν, "Ἀλλήλων τὰ βάρη βαστάζετε." "Καὶ εὐχάριστοι, φησί, γίνεσθε." Μάλιστα γὰρ τοῦτο πανταχοῦ ζητεῖ, τὸ κεφάλαιον τῶν ἀγαθῶν.

Εὐχαριστῶμεν τοίνυν ἐν πᾶσιν, ὅπερ ἂν γένηται· τοῦτο γὰρ εὐχαριστία. Τὸ μὲν γὰρ ἐν τῇ εὐπραγίᾳ τοῦτο ποιεῖν, οὐ μέγα· αὐτὴ γὰρ τῶν πραγμάτων ἡ φύσις ἐπὶ τοῦτο ὠθεῖ· ὅταν δὲ ἐν τοῖς ἐσχάτοις ὄντες εὐχαριστῶμεν, τότε ἐστὶ θαυμαστόν. Ὅταν γὰρ ἐφ' οἷς ἕτεροι βλασφημοῦσι καὶ ἀποδυσπετοῦσιν, ἡμεῖς εὐχαριστῶμεν, ὅρα πόση ἡ φιλοσοφία. Πρῶτον, τὸν θεὸν ηὔφρανας· δεύτερον, τὸν διάβολον κατήσχυνας· τρίτον, καὶ τὸ γενόμενον οὐδὲν ἀπέφηνας· ὁμοῦ γὰρ σύ τε εὐχαριστεῖς, καὶ ὁ θεὸς τὴν ὀδύνην ὑποτέμνεται, καὶ ὁ διάβολος ἀφίσταται. Ἂν μὲν γὰρ ἀποδυσπετήσῃς, ἅτε ἀνύσας ὅπερ ἤθελεν, ἐφέστηκε, καὶ ὁ θεὸς ἅτε βλασφημηθεὶς, ἐγκαταλιμπάνει, καὶ ἐπιτείνεται τὸ δεινόν· ἐὰν δὲ εὐχαριστήσῃς, ἅτε μηδὲν ὠφελῶν, ἀφίσταται, καὶ ὁ θεὸς ἅτε τιμηθεὶς, ἀντιτιμᾷ μειζόνως· καὶ οὐκ ἔστιν ἄνθρωπον εὐχαριστοῦντα ἐπὶ τοῖς κακοῖς αἰσθέσθαι τῶν [262] κακῶν. Χαίρει γὰρ ἡ ψυχὴ ἅτε κατορθοῦσα, εὐθέως φαιδρὸν τὸ συνειδὸς, γάννυται τοῖς ἐγκωμίοις τοῖς ἑαυτῆς· τὴν δὲ φαιδρὰν οὐκ ἔνι σκυθρωπὴν εἶναι. Ἐκεῖ δὲ μετὰ τῆς συμφορᾶς καὶ τὸ συνειδὸς ἐπίκειται μαστίζον· ἐνταῦθα δὲ στεφανοῖ καὶ ἀνακηρύττει.

Οὐδὲν τῆς γλώττης ἐκείνης ἁγιώτερον τῆς ἐν τοῖς κακοῖς εὐχαριστούσης τῷ θεῷ· ὄντως τῆς τῶν μαρτύρων οὐδὲν ἀποδεῖ· ὁμοίως καὶ αὕτη κἀκεῖνος στεφανοῦται. Καὶ γὰρ καὶ ταύτῃ ἐφέστηκε δήμιος ἀναγκάζων ἀρνήσασθαι τὸν θεὸν διὰ τῆς βλασφημίας, ἐφέστηκεν ὁ διάβολος δημίοις λογισμοῖς καταξαίνων, ἀθυμίαις σκοτῶν. Ἂν τοίνυν ἐνέγκῃ τὰς ἀλγηδόνας, καὶ εὐχαριστήσῃ, μαρτυρίου στέφανον ἔλαχεν. Οἷον, τὸ παιδίον νοσεῖ, καὶ εὐχαριστεῖ τῷ θεῷ; Τοῦτο αὐτῇ στέφανος. Πόσης βασάνου οὐ χείρων ἡ ἀθυμία; ἀλλ' οὐκ ἀναγκάζει ῥῆμα ἐκβαλεῖν πικρόν. Ἀποθνήσκει· πάλιν ηὐχαρίστησε; Γέγονε θυγάτηρ τοῦ Ἀβραάμ. Εἰ γὰρ μὴ τῇ ἰδίᾳ ἔσφαξε χειρί, ἀλλ' ἐπὶ τῇ θυσίᾳ ἥσθη, ὅπερ ἴσον ἐστίν· οὐκ ἠγανάκτησε λαμβανομένου τοῦ δώρου.

Πάλιν ἐνόσησεν· οὐκ ἐποίησε περίαπτα; Μαρτύριον αὐτῇ λογίζεται· κατέθυσε γὰρ τὸν υἱὸν τῇ γνώμῃ. Τί γὰρ, εἰ καὶ μηδὲν ὠφελεῖ ἐκεῖνα, ἀλλ'

bear him, and he you, which Paul wrote in the Letter to the Galatians: "*Bear one another's burdens*" [Gal 6:2]. "*And be thankful*," he says. You see, this is what he seeks everywhere: the crown of good things.

Let's give thanks, therefore, in all things, whatever happens, for this is thanksgiving. You see, to do this in prosperity is no great thing, for the very nature of the circumstances impels one to do it. But when we give thanks in very bad situations, then it's admirable. For when in circumstances others slander and despair, we give thanks—observe how great this philosophy is. First, you have delighted God; second, you have shamed the devil; third, you have made what has happened appear to be nothing, for all at once you have given thanks, and God has cut short the pain, and the devil departs. You see, if you're despairing, since you accede to his wish he takes his stand close by, and God, since he has been slandered, abandons you and increases your plight. But if you give thanks, since he has made no profit, he departs, and God, since he is honored, pays you back with greater honor. And it's not possible for a human being, giving thanks for their evils, to be sensible [262] of them. For their soul rejoices since it's doing right; immediately their conscience is bright, it's gladdened by its own praise, but it's not possible for a bright soul to be cast down. But in the other case, together with their misfortune, their conscience sets upon them with a lash, whereas in this case she crowns and proclaims them.

Nothing is holier than that tongue that in evils gives thanks to God. Truly in no respect does it fall short of that of the martyrs—both are crowned in the same way, both it and they. Indeed, over the tongue stands the executioner, darkening it with episodes of faintheartedness. If, therefore, someone bears their sufferings and gives thanks, they have gained a crown of martyrdom. For example, the child is sick and the mother gives thanks to God? This is a crown for her. What torture is so bad that faintheartedness isn't worse? Still it didn't force her to utter a bitter word. The child dies; does she give thanks again? She has become a daughter of Abraham [see Gen 22:1–12]. For if she didn't sacrifice it with her own hand, still she was pleased with the sacrifice, which is the same: she felt no indignation when the gift was taken away.

Again, has her child been sick? Didn't the mother make amulets?[94] Martyrdom is attributed to her, for she sacrificed her child with her deter-

---

94. On amulets here and in other passages in Chrysostom, see Andreas Heiser, *Die Paulusinszenierung des Johannes Chrysostomus Epitheta und ihre Vorgeschichte*, STAC 70 (Tübingen: Mohr Siebeck, 2012), 531 n. 19; also Leyerle, "Keep Me, Lord," 73–93

ἀπάτης ἐστὶ καὶ χλεύης; ἀλλ᾽ ὅμως ἦσαν οἱ πείθοντες ὅτι ὠφελεῖ· καὶ εἵλετο μᾶλλον νεκρὸν τὸ παιδίον ἰδεῖν, ἢ εἰδωλολατρείας ἀνασχέσθαι. Ὥσπερ οὖν αὕτη μάρτυς, ἄν τε ἐφ᾽ ἑαυτῆς, ἄν τε ἐπὶ τοῦ παιδὸς ἐργάζηται τοῦτο, ἄν τε ἐπὶ τοῦ ἀνδρὸς, ἢ ἑτέρου τινὸς τῶν φιλτάτων· οὕτως ἡ ἑτέρα εἰδωλολάτρις. Δῆλον γὰρ ὅτι ἔθυσεν ἂν, εἰ ἦν θῦσαι· μᾶλλον δὲ ἤδη ἐποίησε τὸ τῆς θυσίας. Τὰ γὰρ περίαπτα, κἂν μυρία φιλοσοφῶσιν οἱ ἐκ τούτων χρηματιζόμενοι, λέγοντες ὅτι τὸν θεὸν καλοῦμεν, καὶ οὐδὲν πλέον ποιοῦμεν, καὶ ὅσα τοιαῦτα, καὶ Χριστιανή ἐστι, φησίν, ἡ γραῦς καὶ πιστὴ, εἰδωλολατρεία τὸ πρᾶγμά ἐστι. Πιστὴ εἶ; σφράγισον· εἰπέ, τοῦτο ἔχω τὸ ὅπλον μόνον, τοῦτο τὸ φάρμακον· ἄλλο δὲ οὐκ οἶδα. Εἰπέ μοι, ἐὰν προσελθὼν ἰατρὸς, καὶ τὰ τῆς ἰατρικῆς φάρμακα ἀφεὶς, ἐπάδῃ, τοῦτον ἰατρὸν ἐροῦμεν; Οὐδαμῶς· τὰ γὰρ τῆς ἰατρικῆς οὐχ ὁρῶμεν φάρμακα. Οὕτως οὐδὲ ἐνταῦθα τὰ τοῦ [263] Χριστιανισμοῦ.

Ἕτεραι δὲ πάλιν ποταμῶν ὀνόματα περιάπτουσι, καὶ μυρία τοιαῦτα τολμῶσιν. Ἰδοὺ λέγω, καὶ προλέγω πᾶσιν ὑμῖν, ὅτι ἐάν τις ἁλῷ, οὐ φείσομαι πάλιν, ἄν τε περίαπτον, ἄν τε ἐπῳδὴν, ἄν τε ἄλλο τι τῆς τέχνης τῆς τοιαύτης ποιῇ. Τί οὖν, ἀποθάνῃ, φησὶ, τὸ παιδίον; Ἂν οὕτω ζήσῃ, τότε ἀπέθανεν· ἂν δὲ ἄνευ ἐκείνων ἀποθάνῃ, τότε ἔζησε. Νῦν δὲ ἂν μὲν πόρναις ἴδῃς προσέχοντα, εὔχῃ κατορυγῆναι, καὶ λέγεις, τί γὰρ ὄφελος τοῦ ζῆν; ὑπὲρ δὲ σωτηρίας ὁρῶσα κινδυνεύοντα, βούλει ζῶντα ὁρᾶν; Οὐκ ἤκουσας τοῦ Χριστοῦ λέγοντος, ὅτι "Ὁ ἀπολέσας τὴν ψυχὴν αὐτοῦ, εὑρήσει αὐτήν· ὁ δὲ εὑρών, ἀπολέσει αὐτήν·" πιστεύεις τοῖς εἰρημένοις, ἢ μῦθοί σοι δοκοῦσιν εἶναι; Εἰπὲ δή μοι, ἐὰν εἴπῃ τις, ὅτι ἀπάγαγε εἰς εἰδωλεῖον, καὶ ζήσεται, ἀνέξῃ; Οὔ, φησί. Διὰ τί; Ὅτι εἰδωλολατρεῖν ἀναγκάζει· ἐνταῦθα δὲ οὐκ ἔστιν εἰδωλολατρεία, ἀλλ᾽ ἁπλῶς

mination. For what is it, when those things don't help, but a cheat and a mockery? Still there were those who persuaded her that they were helpful, and she chose rather to see her child dead than to put up with idolatry. Since therefore, she's a martyr, whether in her own case or in her child's that she did this, or in her husband's case or that of any other of her nearest and dearest. So is that other one an idolator. You see, she would have sacrificed if it had been possible for her to sacrifice. No, she has already performed the act of sacrifice. For even if those who make money from amulets rationalize a thousand times, saying, "We call upon God, and do nothing more," and words like these, and they say, "The old woman is a Christian and a believer," the matter is idolatry. Are you a believer? Sign yourself with the cross; say, "This I have for my only weapon, this for my remedy. I don't know another." Tell me, if a physician comes and neglects the remedies of the physician's work, do we call that person a physician? In no way, for we don't see the medicinal remedies. So neither in this case do we see those [**263**] of Christianity.

But other women again tie on their children the names of rivers[95] and have the effrontery to do myriad like things. Look, I say, and I forewarn you all, that if one is them is caught I shall not spare them again, and whether they have made an amulet, or an incantation, or any other thing of this kind of art. "What then," says [somebody], "is the child dying?" If it has lived in this way, then it has died; if it has died without these means, then it has lived. But now, if you see them attaching themselves to prostitutes, you pray that they will be buried, and you say, "What's the use of their living?" but when you see them in danger of his salvation, do you want to see them live? Didn't you hear Christ saying, "*The one who loses their soul will find it, but the one who finds it will lose it*" [Matt 16:25]? Do you believe these sayings, or do they seem to you like fables? Do tell me: if someone says, "Take her away to an idol, and he will live," will you go along with it? "No," she says. Why? "Because he urges me on to idolatry, but here there's

---

(on a possible fifth-century amulet); Reidar Aasgaard, "Uncovering Children's Culture in Late Antiquity: The Testimony of the Infancy Gospel of Thomas," in *Children in Late Ancient Christianity*, ed. Cornelia B. Horn and Robert R. Phenix, STAC 58 (Tübingen: Mohr Siebeck, 2009), 1–28, esp. 9; Inta Ivanovska, "Baptized Infants and Pagan Rituals: Cyprian versus Augustine," in Horn and Phenix, *Children in Late Ancient Christianity*, 63–65, on amulets and charms.

95. Leyerle believes that the preacher has the fertility of the Nile River in mind ("Appealing to Children," 249–50).

ἐπῳδὴ, φησίν. Αὕτη γὰρ ἡ σατανικὴ ἔννοια, αὕτη ἡ μεθοδεία ἡ διαβολικὴ, συγκαλύπτειν τὴν πλάνην, καὶ ἐν μέλιτι τὸ δηλητήριον διδόναι φάρμακον. Ἐπειδὴ οἶδεν ἐκεῖσε οὐ πείθων, ταύτην ἐβάδισε τὴν ὁδὸν, εἰς ῥάμματα καὶ γραώδεις μύθους· καὶ ὁ μὲν σταυρὸς ἠτίμωται, τὰ δὲ ῥάμματα προτετίμηται· ὁ Χριστὸς ἐκβέβληται, καὶ εἰσάγεται μεθύουσα γραῦς καὶ ληροῦσα· τὸ μυστήριον πεπάτηται τὸ ἡμέτερον, καὶ ἡ πλάνη χορεύει τοῦ διαβόλου.

Τίνος οὖν ἕνεκεν οὐκ ἐλέγχει, φησὶν, ὁ θεός τὴν ἀπὸ τῶν τοιούτων βοήθειαν; Πολλαχοῦ ἤλεγξε, καὶ οὐκ ἔπεισέ σε· λοιπὸν ἀφίησι τῇ πλάνῃ· "Παρέδωκε γὰρ αὐτοὺς, φησὶν, ὁ θεὸς εἰς ἀδόκιμον νοῦν." Ταῦτα δὲ οὐδ' ἂν Ἕλλην νοῦν ἔχων ἀνέχοιτο. Λέγεταί τις δημαγωγός ποτε ἐν Ἀθήναις ταῦτα περιτεθῆναι· εἶτα φιλόσοφός τις ἐκείνου διδάσκαλος ἰδὼν, ἐπετίμησεν, ἐμέμψατο, ἔδακεν, ἐκωμῴδησεν. Οὕτω γὰρ ἀθλίως διακείμεθα, ὡς καὶ τούτοις πιστεύειν.

Καὶ διὰ τί μὴ εἰσὶ νῦν οἱ ἀνιστῶντες, φησὶ, νεκροὺς καὶ ἰάσεις ἐπιτελοῦντες; Διὰ τί μὴ εἰσὶ νῦν οἱ ἀνιστῶντες, φησὶ, νεκροὺς καὶ ἰάσεις ἐπιτελοῦντες; Διὰ τί γὰρ οὖν λέγω, διὰ τί μὴ εἰσὶ νῦν οἱ τῆς παρούσης καταφρονοῦντες ζωῆς; ἐπὶ μισθῷ δουλεύομεν τῷ θεῷ· Ὅτε ἀσθενέστερον διέκειτο ἡ φύσις ἡ ἀνθρωπίνη, ὅτε [264] φυτευθῆναι τὴν πίστιν ἔδει, ἦσαν καὶ τοιοῦτοι πολλοί· νῦν δὲ οὐ βούλεται ἡμᾶς τούτων ἠρτῆσθαι τῶν σημείων, ἀλλ' ἑτοίμους εἶναι πρὸς θάνατον. Τί τοίνυν τῆς παρούσης ἔχῃ ζωῆς; τί τὰ μέλλοντα οὐχ ὁρᾷς; καὶ ὑπὲρ μὲν ταύτης καὶ εἰδωλολατρεῖν ἀνέχῃ, ὑπὲρ δὲ ἐκείνης οὔτε ἀθυμίας κατασχεῖν; Διὰ ταῦτα οὐκ εἰσὶ νῦν τοιοῦτοι, ὅτι ἄτιμος ἡμῖν ἐφάνη ἐκείνη ἡ ζωὴ, εἴγε ὑπὲρ μὲν ἐκείνης οὐδὲν πράττομεν, ὑπὲρ δὲ ταύτης οὐδὲν παραιτούμεθα ὑπομένειν. Τί δὲ καὶ ὁ ἄλλος γέλως, σποδὸς καὶ ἀσβόλη καὶ ἅλες; καὶ

no idolatry, no, simply incantation," she says. You see, this is the device of Satan, this is the diabolical craft of concealing the deceit, and to administer the deadly drug in honey. When he understood that in this way he wasn't persuasive, he embarked on that road, toward charms and old wives' fables. And the cross is dishonored and the spells preferred above it. Christ is cast out, and a drunken and silly old woman is introduced.[96] That mystery of ours is trampled on, and the deceit of the devil is that he dances.

"Why doesn't God reprove this," [someone] asks, "who has reproved the aid from such sources?" He has reproved on many counts and has not persuaded you; for the rest he leaves you to your own error. "*God gave them over to a base mind and improper conduct*," Paul says [Rom 1:28]. These things not even a Hellene with understanding would put up with. It's said that some leader of the people once in Athens hung these things around himself, and then a philosopher who was his instructor, on seeing this, censured him, blamed, bit into him, ridiculed him.[97] You see, we're in such a pitiable situation that we believe even these things.

"Why now," asks [someone], "aren't there people who raise the dead and perform cures?" You see, why don't I then say, "Why aren't there now people who have a contempt for the present life?" Do we serve God for a wage? When human nature was weaker, when [264] the faith had to be planted, there were indeed many people like this, but now God doesn't want us to depend on these signs but to be ready for death. So why do you hang on to the present life? Why don't you look at the future? And on behalf of this life you uphold even idolatry, while on behalf of that other life don't you even restrain despondency? For these reasons such people don't exist now, namely, because that life has appeared without honor to us, seeing that we do nothing on behalf of that life, but on behalf of this one there's nothing we refuse to undergo. And why too that other farce: ashes,

---

96. The commonplace of a drunken, silly old woman is discussed by John T. Fitzgerald, "Paul, Wine in the Ancient Mediterranean World, and the Problem of Intoxication," in *Paul's Graeco-Roman Context*, ed. Cilliers Breytenbach, BETL 277 (Leuven: Peeters, 2015), 351–52. Fitzgerald argues that Titus 2:3–5 is behind this representation of drunken women.

97. The reference is to Pericles (see Plutarch, *Per.* 38). However, ancient writers such as Theophrastus and, after him, Plutarch generally depict Pericles in a glowing light, so either Chrysostom knows a different tradition or else he has deliberately altered it for his own ends.

πάλιν τὸ γραΐδιον εἰς τὸ μέσον. Γέλως ὄντως, καὶ αἰσχύνη. Καὶ ὀφθαλμὸς, φησὶν, ἥρπασε τὸ παιδίον.

Μέχρι τίνος ταῦτα τὰ σατανικά; πῶς οὐ γελάσονται Ἕλληνες; πῶς οὐ χλευάσουσιν, ὅταν αὐτοῖς λέγωμεν, μεγάλη ἡ δύναμις τοῦ σταυροῦ; πῶς πεισθήσονται, ὅταν ὁρῶσι τούτων δεομένους, ὧν αὐτοὶ καταγελῶσι; Διὰ ταῦτα ὁ θεὸς ἰατροὺς ἔδωκε καὶ φάρμακα; Τί οὖν, ἂν μὴ θεραπεύωσιν ἐκεῖνοι, ἀλλὰ ἀπέρχηται τὸ παιδίον; Ποῦ ἄπεισιν, εἰπέ μοι, ἄθλιε καὶ ταλαίπωρε; πρὸς τοὺς δαίμονας ἄπεισι; πρός τινα τύραννον ἄπεισιν; οὐχὶ πρὸς τὸν οὐρανὸν ἄπεισιν; οὐχὶ πρὸς τὸν οἰκεῖον ἄπεισι δεσπότην; Τί οὖν ἀλγεῖς; τί κλαίεις; τί πενθεῖς; τί τοῦ δεσπότου σου πλέον τὸ παιδίον φιλεῖς; οὐχὶ δι' ἐκεῖνον ἔχεις καὶ τοῦτο; διὰ τί ἀχάριστος εἶ, τὸ δῶρον τοῦ δωρησαμένου πλέον ἀγαπᾷς; Ἀλλ' ἀσθενής εἰμι, φησὶ, καὶ οὐ φέρω, καὶ τὰ σπλάγνα ταράττεται. Ἀλλ' ἀντίστησον τοῦ θεοῦ τὸν φόβον. Εἰ γὰρ ἐν τοῖς σωματικοῖς κακοῖς τὸ μεῖζον τὸ ἔλαττον κρύπτει, πολλῷ μᾶλλον ἐν τῇ ψυχῇ φόβος φόβον ἔλυσε, καὶ λύπη λύπην. Καλὸν ἦν τὸ παιδίον; Ἀλλ' οἷον ἂν ᾖ, οὐκ ἔστιν ὡραιότερον τοῦ Ἰσαάκ. Μονογενὴς ἦν; Κἀκεῖνος. Ἐν γήρᾳ σοι γέγονε; Κἀκεῖνος. Ἀλλ' ἀστεῖόν ἐστιν; Ἀλλ' οἷον ἂν ᾖ ἀστεῖον, οὐκ ἔστιν ὡραιότερον τοῦ Μωϋσέως, ὃς καὶ βαρβαρικὴν ὄψιν ἐπεσπάσατο πρὸς πόθον, καὶ ταῦτα ἐν ἐκείνῳ τῆς ἡλικίας τῷ καιρῷ, ἔνθα οὐδέπω φαίνεται ἡ ὥρα· ἀλλ' ὅμως τὸ φιληθὲν τοῦτο ἔρριπτον εἰς ποταμὸν οἱ γονεῖς. Σὺ μὲν καὶ ὁρᾷς κείμενον, καὶ ταφῇ παραδίδως, καὶ εἰς τὸ σῆμα ἄπει· [265] ἐκεῖνοι δὲ οὐδὲ ᾔδεσαν πότερον ἰχθύσιν ἔσται βορὰ, πότερον κυσὶ, πότερον ἑτέρῳ θηρίῳ τῶν κατὰ τὴν θάλατταν βοσκομένων· καὶ ταῦτα ἐποίουν, οὐδέπω περὶ βασιλείας οὐδὲν εἰδότες, οὐδὲ ἀναστάσεως.

Ἀλλ' οὐκ ἔστι μονογενές, ἀλλὰ μετὰ πολλοὺς καὶ αὐτὸ ἀπῆλθεν; Ἀλλ' οὐχ οὕτως ὡς ἐπὶ τοῦ Ἰὼβ ἀθρόως ἡ συμφορά, καὶ σκυθρωποτέρα· οὐ στέγης κατενεχθείσης, οὐκ ἀριστώντων μεταξὺ, οὐ τῶν συμφορῶν προαγγελθεισῶν.

soot, and salt?[98] And again the old woman is brought in. Truly a farce and a shame. And [someone] says, "An eye has captured the child."

When will these satanical acts end? How will the Hellenes not laugh? How won't they scoff when we tell them that the power of the cross is great? How will they be persuaded when they see us in need of those things that themselves are ridiculous? Was it because of this that God gave us physicians and medicines? What then? Will they cure him, but the child passes away? Tell me, you wretched and miserable person, where does it go to? Does it go to the demons? To what tyrant does it go? Won't it go to heaven? Won't it go to its own Master? So why do you grieve? Why weep? Why mourn? Why love the child more than your Master? Isn't it because of God that you even have the child? Why are you ungrateful, loving the gift more than the giver? "But I'm weak," she says, "and can't bear it, and my innards are in turmoil." Well, make a stand against the fear of God. You see, if in the case of bodily evils the greater hides the less, much rather would fear in the soul have destroyed fear, and grief, grief. Was the child beautiful? But be it as it may, it wasn't more handsome than Isaac [see Gen 21–22]. Was it an only child? So too was Isaac. Was it born in your old age? So too was Isaac. Was it charming? But be that as it may, it wasn't more charming than Moses, who attracted even the gaze of barbarians to a love of him [see Exod 2:5–10], and this too that time of his life when beauty is not yet disclosed. Yet this loving thing his parents threw into a river. You indeed must see the child laid out and committed to the grave, and go off to its monument. [265] But they didn't even know whether Moses would be food for fish, dogs, other beasts that prey at sea. And this they did, knowing as yet nothing of the kingdom nor of the resurrection.

But let's suppose that it isn't an only child; no, after many others this one too departed?[99] But your calamity isn't as sudden as Job's, which was sadder. It isn't the roof falling in, it isn't in the middle of their feasting, it isn't after news of other calamities [see Job 1:18].[100] But was the child

---

98. These are some of the trappings of grief. See bibliography on grief and mourning in n. 101 below.

99. See Leyerle for other references in Chrysostom on losing a child ("Appealing to Children," 248).

100. The figure of Job was popular in Judaism and early Christianity. On the long-suffering man as a spiritual athlete, see Michael B. Poliakoff, "Jacob, Job, and Other Wrestlers: Reception of Greek Athletics by Jews and Christians in Antiquity," *JSH* 11 (1984): 48–65. On Job as exemplary regarding the education of children and the

Ἀλλ' ἐφιλεῖτο παρὰ σοῦ; Ἀλλ' οὐχὶ μᾶλλον τοῦ Ἰωσὴφ τοῦ θηριοβρώτου γενο-
μένου· ἀλλ' ὅμως ἔνεγκε τὴν συμφοράν, καὶ τὴν μετ' ἐκείνην, καὶ τὴν μετὰ
ταύτην ὁ πατήρ. Ἔκλαυσεν, ἀλλ' οὐκ ἠσέβησεν· ἐπένθησεν, ἀλλ' οὐκ ἀπεδυ-
σπέτησεν, ἀλλὰ μέχρι τούτων ἔστη τῶν ῥημάτων, λέγων· "Ἰωσὴφ οὐκ ἔστι,
Συμεὼν οὐκ ἔστι, καὶ τὸν Βενιαμὶμ λήψεσθε; ἐπ' ἐμὲ ἐγένετο ταῦτα πάντα."
Ὁρᾷς πῶς ἐκεῖνον λιμοῦ τυραννὶς ἔπεισε καταφρονῆσαι τῶν παίδων; παρὰ δὲ
σοὶ οὐκ ἰσχύει ὁ τοῦ θεοῦ φόβος ὅσον ὁ λιμός;

Κλαῦσον, οὐ κωλύω, ἀλλὰ μηδὲν βλάσφημον μήτε εἴπῃς, μήτε πράξῃς.
Οἷος ἐὰν ᾖ ὁ παῖς, οὐκ ἔστι κατὰ τὸν Ἄβελ· ἀλλ' οὐδὲν τοιοῦτον εἶπεν ὁ Ἀδάμ·
καίτοι χαλεπὴ ἐκείνη ἡ συμφορά, τὸ τὸν ἀδελφὸν ἀνῃρηκέναι. Ἀλλὰ γὰρ
καὶ ἀδελφοκτόνων ἄλλων εὐκαίρως ἀνεμνήσθην· οἷον ὅτε Ἀβεσσαλὼμ τὸν
Ἀμνὼν ἀνεῖλε τὸν πρωτότοκον, καὶ Δαυῒδ ὁ βασιλεὺς ἠγάπα τὸ παιδίον, καὶ
ἐν σάκκῳ μὲν ἐκάθητο καὶ σποδῷ, οὔτε δὲ μάντεις ἤγαγεν, οὔτε ἐπαοιδούς,
καίτοι ἦσαν τότε· καὶ δηλοῖ ὁ Σαούλ· ἀλλὰ τὸν θεὸν ἱκέτευε. Τοῦτο καὶ σὺ
ποίει· ὅπερ ὁ δίκαιος ἐποίησε, ποίησον καὶ σύ· τὰ αὐτὰ εἰπὲ ῥήματα, ὅταν
ἀποθάνῃ τὸ παιδίον. "Ἐγὼ μὲν ἀπελεύσομαι πρὸς αὐτό, αὐτὸ δὲ οὐχ ἥξει
πρός με." Τοῦτο φιλοσοφίας, τοῦτο φιλοστοργίας. Ὡς ἂν φιλῇς τὸ παιδίον,
οὐ φιλήσεις τοσοῦτον ὅσον ἐκεῖνος τότε. Τῷ μακαρίῳ ἐκείνῳ ἤκμαζεν ὁ περὶ
τὴν μητέρα πόθος, εἰ καὶ ἐκ μοιχείων ἦν· ἴστε δὲ ὅτι κοινωνεῖ τὰ τικτόμενα
τοῦ φίλτρου τῶν τικτόντων· καὶ τοσοῦτος ὁ ἔρως ἦν, ὡς καὶ κατήγορον αὐτῷ
ὂν [266] βούλεσθαι ζῆν· ἀλλ' ὅμως ηὐχαρίστησε τῷ θεῷ. Τί οἴει πάσχειν τὴν

cherished by you? No, not more so than Joseph, who became the prey of beasts [see Gen 37:33]. But still he [Jacob] bore the calamity and the one after that, and his father the one after that: he wept, but didn't commit impiety; he mourned, but he was not downcast but left it at these words, saying: "*Joseph does not exist, Simeon does not exist, and will you take Benjamin away? All these things are against me*" [Gen 42:36]. Do you see how the tyranny of famine convinced him to take no care of his children? And doesn't the fear of God prevail with you as much as famine?

Weep—I don't forbid it, but don't utter or perform a blasphemy.[101] Be your child as it may, it isn't like Abel, and Adam didn't say anything like this, although that calamity was a serious one, namely, the killing of the brother [see Gen 4:2–8]. Yes, you see, I'm reminded of others who have killed their brothers, for example, when Absalom killed Amnon the first-born [see 2 Kgdms 13], and King David loved his small child and didn't sit in sackcloth and ashes [see 2 Kgdms 13], nor did he bring in prophets or enchanters (although they were there at that time), as Saul demonstrates [see 1 Kgdms 28:3–25]. No, he made supplication to God. And you do the same: do what the just man did. Say the same words when your small child is dead: "*I shall go to it, but it will not come to me*" [2 Kdgms 12:23]. This is the stuff of philosophy, this is of affection. However much you love your little child, you won't love it as much as David did then. Even though it was born of adultery, the love of its mother was at a high pitch with that blessed man, and you know that the offspring share the love of the parents. And so great was his love that, even though it would be his accuser, [**266**] he wished it to live, but still he gave thanks to God. What do you think

---

appropriate grief over the death of a child, see Douglas Finn, "Job as Exemplary Father according to John Chrysostom," *JECS* 26 (2018): 275–305.

101. On mourning in general in antiquity, see Margaret Alexiou, *The Ritual Lament in Greek Tradition* (Cambridge: Cambridge University Press, 1974), esp. 24–35 on the Greek fathers' condemnation of funeral rituals. For the topic of the death of children in classical antiquity, see Mark Golden, "Did the Ancients Care When Their Children Died?," *GR*, 2/35 (October 1988): 152–63. On the presentation of death in Chrysostom's works, see François-Xavier Druet, *Langage, images et visages de la mort chez Jean Chrysostome*, CEC 3 (Namur: Société des Études classiques/Presses universitaires, 1990); Jaclyn L. Maxwell, *Christianization and Communication in Late Antiquity: John Chrysostom and His Congregation in Antioch* (Cambridge: Cambridge University Press, 2006), 159; Éric Rebillard, *The Care of the Dead in Late Antiquity*, trans. Elizabeth Trapnell Rawlings and Jeanine Routier-Pucci, CSCP 59 (Ithaca, NY: Cornell University Press, 2009), 132–33 (on appropriate mourning practices).

Ῥεβέκκαν, ὅτε ἀδελφὸς ἠπείλει τῷ Ἰακώβ; καὶ οὐκ ἐλύπησε τὸν ἄνδρα, ἀλλ᾽ ἐκέλευσεν ἀποπέμψαι.

Ἐννόησον τὰ τούτων χείρω, ὅταν τι δεινὸν πάθῃς, καὶ ἱκανὴν ἕξεις παραμυθίαν· καὶ λογίζου, τί δὲ, εἰ ἐν πολέμῳ τεθνήκει; τί δὲ, εἰ ἐν πυρί; Καὶ ὧν ἐὰν πάθωμεν, τὰ δεινότερα ἐννοῶμεν, καὶ ἕξομεν ἀρκοῦσαν παραμυθίαν· καὶ τοὺς τὰ δεινότερα πεπονθότας ἀεὶ περισκοπῶμεν, καὶ εἰ αὐτοὶ βαρύτερα ἐπάθομέν ποτε. Οὕτω καὶ Παῦλος προτρέπει, ὡς ὅταν λέγῃ· "Οὔπω μέχρις αἵματος ἀντικατέστητε πρὸς τὴν ἁμαρτίαν ἀνταγωνιζόμενοι," καὶ πάλιν, "Πειρασμὸς ὑμᾶς οὐκ εἴληφεν, εἰ μὴ ἀνθρώπινος."

Ὧν οὖν ἂν πάθωμεν, τὰ χείρω περισκοπῶμεν, εὑρήσομεν γάρ, καὶ οὕτως ἐσόμεθα εὐχάριστοι. Πρὸ δὲ πάντων εὐχαριστῶμεν ἐπὶ πᾶσι διηνεκῶς· οὕτω γὰρ καὶ ταῦτα παύσεται, καὶ ἡμεῖς εἰς δόξαν θεοῦ ζήσομεν, καὶ τῶν ἐπηγγελμένων ἀγαθῶν ἐπιτευξόμεθα· ὧν γένοιτο πάντας ἡμᾶς ἐπιτυχεῖν, χάριτι καὶ φιλανθρωπίᾳ τοῦ κυρίου ἡμῶν Ἰησοῦ Χριστοῦ, μεθ᾽ οὗ τῷ πατρὶ ἅμα τῷ ἁγίῳ πνεύματι δόξα, κράτος, τιμὴ, νῦν καὶ ἀεὶ καὶ εἰς τοὺς αἰῶνας τῶν αἰώνων. Ἀμήν.

Rebecca suffered when her brother threatened Jacob? She didn't grieve for her husband but ordered him to send the boy away [see Gen 27:41–45].

Imagine what is worse than these circumstances when you suffer something bad, and you'll have sufficient consolation, and consider: What if he'd died in battle? What if in fire? And whatever our sufferings, let's contemplate things more fearful, and we shall have sufficient comfort, and let's always look around for those who have suffered terrible things, and if we ourselves have ever suffered more grievous things. So too does Paul exhort us, as when he says, *"In your struggle against sin, you have not yet resisted to the point of shedding blood"* [Heb 12:4], and again, *"No temptation has overtaken you that is not human"* [1 Cor 10:13].

Therefore, whatever we suffer, let's look around for worse things, for we shall find them, and so we'll be thankful. But above all let's give thanks continually for everything, for thus both these sufferings will be eased and we shall live to God's glory and attain the promised good things. May we all attain these, through the grace and loving-kindness of our Lord Jesus Christ, with whom to the Father together with the Holy Spirit be glory, power, honor, now and always and forever and ever. Amen.

ΛΟΓΟΣ Θ

Ὁ λόγος τοῦ Χριστοῦ ἐνοικείτω ἐν ὑμῖν πλουσίως, ἐν πάσῃ σοφίᾳ διδάσκοντες καὶ νουθετοῦντες ἑαυτοὺς ψαλμοῖς καὶ ὕμνοις καὶ ᾠδαῖς πνευματικαῖς, ἐν χάριτι ᾄδοντες ἐν ταῖς καρδίαις ὑμῶν τῷ θεῷ. Καὶ πᾶν ὅ τι ἂν ποιῆτε ἐν λόγῳ, ἢ ἐν ἔργῳ, πάντα ἐν ὀνόματι τοῦ κυρίου Ἰησοῦ, εὐχαριστοῦντες τῷ θεῷ καὶ πατρὶ δι' αὐτοῦ.

Παραινέσας εὐχαρίστους εἶναι, καὶ τὴν ὁδὸν δείκνυσι, ταύτην ἣν πρῴην ἡμεῖς διελέχθημεν πρὸς ὑμᾶς. Τί λέγων; "Ὁ λόγος τοῦ Χριστοῦ ἐνοικείτω ἐν ὑμῖν πλουσίως." Μᾶλλον δὲ οὐ ταύτην μόνον, ἀλλὰ καὶ ἑτέραν. Ἐγὼ μὲν γὰρ εἶπον, ὅτι δεῖ τοὺς τὰ δεινότερα πεπονθότας ἀναλέγειν, καὶ τοὺς τὰ χαλεπώτερα ὧν ἐπάθομεν ὑπομείναντας ἀναλογίζεσθαι, καὶ εὐχαριστεῖν ὑπὲρ τοῦ μὴ συμβῆναι ἐκεῖνα· αὐτὸς δὲ τί φη-[267]σιν; "Ὁ λόγος τοῦ Χριστοῦ ἐνοικείτω ἐν ὑμῖν·" τουτέστιν, ἡ διδασκαλία, τὰ δόγματα, ἡ παραίνεσις, ἐν αἷς οὐδὲν τὴν παροῦσαν ζωὴν εἶναί φησιν, οὐδὲ τὰ ταύτης ἀγαθά. Ἐὰν ταῦτα εἰδῶμεν, οὐδενὶ τῶν δυσχερῶν εἴξομεν. "Ἐνοικείτω, φησίν, ἐν ὑμῖν πλουσίως," μὴ ἁπλῶς, ἀλλὰ μετὰ πολλῆς τῆς περιουσίας. Ἀκούσατε ὅσοι ἐστὲ κοσμικοί, καὶ γυναικὸς καὶ παίδων προΐστασθε, πῶς καὶ ὑμῖν ἐπιτρέπει μάλιστα τὰς γραφὰς ἀναγινώσκειν· καὶ οὐχ ἁπλῶς οὐδὲ ὡς ἔτυχεν, ἀλλὰ μετὰ πολλῆς τῆς σπουδῆς. Ὥσπερ γὰρ ὁ πλούσιος ἐν χρήμασι ζημίαν καὶ καταδίκην ἐνεγκεῖν δύναται, οὕτως ὁ πλουτῶν ἐν δόγμασι φιλοσοφίας, οὐχὶ πενίαν μόνον, ἀλλὰ καὶ πάσας τὰς συμφορὰς εὐκόλως οἴσει, καὶ ἐκείνου εὐκολώτερον. Ἐκεῖ μὲν γὰρ ἐν τῇ διαλύσει τῆς ζημίας ἀνάγκη τὸν ὄντα πλούσιον ἐλαττοῦσθαι καὶ ἐλέγχεσθαι· κἂν πολλάκις τοῦτο πάθῃ, οὐκέτι δυνήσεται ἐνεγκεῖν· ἐνταῦθα δὲ οὐχ οὕτως· οὐδὲ γὰρ δαπανῶμεν τοὺς ὑγιεῖς λογισμούς, ὅταν ἐνεγκεῖν τι δέῃ τῶν ἀβουλήτων, ἀλλὰ μένουσι διαπαντός. Καὶ ὅρα τὴν σύνεσιν τοῦ μακαρίου τούτου. Οὐκ εἶπεν, ὁ λόγος τοῦ Χριστοῦ ἐν ὑμῖν ἔστω, ἁπλῶς, ἀλλὰ τί; "ἐνοικείτω," καί, "πλουσίως."

HOMILY 9

Let the word of Christ dwell in you richly, as in all wisdom you teach and admonish each other with psalms and hymns and spiritual songs, singing with grace in your hearts to God. And whatever you do, in word or deed, do everything in the name of the Lord Jesus, giving thanks to God the Father through him [Col 3:16–17].

Having exhorted them to be thankful, he also shows the way, which we have recently discoursed on to you.[102] What does Paul say? *"Let the word of Christ dwell in you richly."* Or rather, it isn't this way alone, but also another. For I indeed said that we should reckon up those who have suffered things more terrible, and calculate those who have undergone sufferings more grievous, and give thanks that those things haven't happened.[103] But what [**267**] does Paul say? *"Let the word of Christ dwell in you richly,"* that is, the teaching, the doctrines, the exhortation, in which he says the present life is nothing, nor yet its good things. If we look at these things, we'll give in to no hardships. *"Let it dwell in you richly,"* he says, not simply *dwell,* but with great abundance. Listen, those of you who are in the world and have charge of a wife and children, how Paul entrusts you too especially to read the Scriptures, and not to do it haphazardly, but with great earnestness. You see, just as the person rich in money can bear a fine and damages, so too the one who is wealthy in the doctrines of philosophy will put up easily not only with poverty but with all calamities, more easily even than the other. For the rich person, in discharging the fine, of necessity will be impoverished and put to shame, and even if they should often suffer in that way, they will be unable to put up with it, but in this case it's not like that. You see, neither do we waste our healthy thoughts when we have to bear what we don't want, but they remain through everything. And see the wisdom of this blessed man: he didn't simply say, *"Let the word of Christ* be in you," but what? *"Dwell in you,"* and *"richly."*

---

102. A reference to the previous homily.
103. Another reference to the previous homily.

"Ἐν πάσῃ σοφίᾳ διδάσκοντες καὶ νουθετοῦντες ἑαυτούς." "Ἐν πάσῃ," φησί. Τὴν ἀρετήν φησι σοφίαν· καὶ ἡ ταπεινοφροσύνη σοφία ἐστί, καὶ ἡ ἐλεημοσύνη, καὶ ὅσα τοιαῦτα, σοφία ἐστίν· ὥσπερ οὖν τἀναντία, ἄνοια· καὶ γὰρ ὠμότης ἐξ ἀνοίας. Ὅθεν πολλαχοῦ τὴν πᾶσαν ἁμαρτίαν ἀφροσύνην καλεῖ. "Εἶπε, φησὶν, ἄφρων ἐν καρδίᾳ αὐτοῦ, οὐκ ἔστι θεός·" καὶ πάλιν, "Προσώζεσαν καὶ ἐσάπησαν οἱ μώλωπές μου ἀπὸ προσώπου τῆς ἀφροσύνης μου." Τί γὰρ ἀνοητότερον, εἰπέ μοι, τοῦ τὰ μὲν ἱμάτια τὰ ἑαυτοῦ περιβαλλομένου, τοὺς δὲ ἀδελφοὺς τοὺς αὐτοῦ γυμνοὺς περιορῶντος; τοῦ κύνας μὲν τρέφοντος, τὴν δὲ εἰκόνα τοῦ θεοῦ περιορῶντος ἐν λιμῷ; τοῦ πεπεισμένου ἁπλῶς, ὅτι οὐδὲν τὰ ἀνθρώπινα πράγματα, καὶ ὥσπερ ἀθανάτοις αὐτοῖς προστετηκότος; Ὥσπερ οὖν οὐδὲν τοῦ τοιούτου ἀνοητότερον, οὕτως [268] οὐδὲν σοφώτερον τοῦ τὴν ἀρετὴν κατορθοῦντος. Ὅρα γὰρ, πάσσοφός ἐστι, φησί· μεταδίδωσι τῶν ὄντων, ἐλεήμων, φιλάνθρωπος· ἐπέγνω τὴν φύσιν, ὅτι κοινή· ἐπέγνω τῶν χρημάτων τὴν χρῆσιν, ὅτι οὐδενὸς ἀξία λόγου· ὅτι τῶν σωμάτων τῶν οἰκείων φείδεσθαι μᾶλλον, ἢ τῶν χρημάτων δεῖ. Ὁ δόξης καταφρονῶν πάσσοφός ἐστιν· οἶδε γὰρ τὰ ἀνθρώπινα πράγματα· τῶν θείων καὶ ἀνθρωπίνων πραγμάτων γνῶσις ἡ φιλοσοφία. Οὐκοῦν οἶδε μὲν ποῖα θεῖα, ποῖα δὲ ἀνθρώπινα, καὶ τῶν μὲν ἀπέχεται, ταῦτα δὲ ἐργάζεται· οἶδε δὲ καὶ εὐχαριστεῖν τῷ θεῷ ἐν πᾶσιν· οὐδὲν εἶναι νομίζει τὸν παρόντα βίον· διὰ τοῦτο οὐδὲ ἥδεται τοῖς χρηστοῖς, οὔτε λυπεῖται τοῖς ἐναντίοις.

Μὴ δὴ περιμείνῃς ἕτερον διδάσκαλον· ἔχεις τὰ λόγια τοῦ θεοῦ· οὐδείς σε οὕτω διδάσκει ὡς ἐκεῖνα. Οὗτος μὲν γὰρ πολλὰ καὶ διὰ κενοδοξίαν καὶ διὰ βασκανίαν διαφθονεῖται πολλάκις. Ἀκούσατε, παρακαλῶ, πάντες οἱ βιωτικοὶ, καὶ κτᾶσθε βιβλία φάρμακα τῆς ψυχῆς. Εἰ μηδὲν ἕτερον βούλεσθε, τὴν γοῦν καινὴν κτήσασθε, τὸν ἀπόστολον, τὰς Πράξεις, τὰ εὐαγγέλια, διδασκάλους διηνεκεῖς. Ἂν λύπη συμβῇ, ὥσπερ εἰς ἀποθήκην φαρμάκων ἔγκυψον· λάβε παραμυθίαν ἐκεῖθεν τοῦ δεινοῦ, ἂν ζημία, ἂν θάνατος, ἂν ἀποβολὴ οἰκείων· μᾶλλον δὲ μὴ ἔγκυπτε, ἀλλὰ ἀνάλαβε πάντα, ἔχε ἐπὶ τῆς διανοίας.

Τοῦτο πάντων αἴτιον τῶν κακῶν, τὸ μὴ εἰδέναι τὰς γραφάς. Χωρὶς ὅπλων εἰς πόλεμον βαδίζομεν· καὶ πῶς ἔδει σωθῆναι; Ἀγαπητὸν μετὰ τούτων

In all wisdom, teaching and admonishing each other. "*In all,*" he says. He calls virtue wisdom; and wisdom is humility of mind and almsgiving, and all such things are wisdom, just as then the opposites are folly, for cruelty too comes from folly. Hence in many places [Scripture] calls all sin mindlessness. "*The senseless one,*" it says, "*has spoken in their heart: there is no God*" [Ps 14:1], and again: "*My wounds grow foul and fester because of the face of my mindlessness*" [Ps 37:5 LXX]. For what is more unintelligent, tell me, than one who wraps themselves about in their garments but overlooks their naked brothers? Who feeds dogs while overlooking the image of God that is starving? Who is simply convinced that human affairs are nothing and clings to them as it they were immortal? Therefore, just as nothing is more unintelligent that this person, so [268] nothing is wiser than the person who achieves virtue. For see: does somebody say, "How is the person all-wise?" They share their belongings, they are merciful, a lover of humankind. They have realized that their nature is common with them; they have realized the use of wealth, namely, that it's worth no consideration, that one should spare the bodies that are kin, rather than wealth. They are an all-wise person who despises glory, for they know human affairs: the knowledge of divine and human affairs is philosophy. Therefore, they know what kinds of things are divine, and what human, and they keep away from the latter, whereas on the other they bestow their pains, but give thanks to God in everything: they consider the present life as nothing. On this account they neither delight in prosperity, nor are cast down by its opposite.

Don't wait for another teacher: you have the oracles of God. Nobody can teach you as they can. You see, that teacher often is greatly envied because of their vainglory and their envy. Listen, please, you who are of the world, and buy books that are medicine for the soul. If you don't want anything else, at least buy the New Testament, the apostle,[104] the Acts of the Apostles, the Gospels, as your constant teachers. If grief befalls you, study them like a medicine chest. Take consolation from there for your trouble, whether it is a penalty, or death, or the loss of relatives. No, don't study them but take them all on board, keep them in your mind.

This is the cause of all evils—not knowing the Scriptures.[105] We're going into war unarmed, and how should we be safe? It's desirable to be

---

104. That is, the Pauline writings.
105. The same argument occurs in *Hom. Col.* 5 above and often in Chrysostom's writings.

σωθῆναι, μήτι γε χωρὶς τούτων. Μὴ τὰ πάντα ἐφ' ἡμᾶς ῥίπτετε· πρόβατά ἐστε, ἀλλ' οὐκ ἄλογα, ἀλλὰ λογικά· πολλὰ καὶ ὑμῖν ὁ Παῦλος ἐπιτρέπει. Οἱ διδασκόμενοι οὐ διαπαντὸς ἐπὶ τὸ μαθεῖν διατρίβουσιν, ἐπεὶ οὐ διδάσκονται· ἂν ἀεὶ μανθάνῃς, οὐδέποτε μαθήσῃ. Μὴ οὕτως ἔρχου, ὡς ἀεὶ μαθησόμενος· ἐπεὶ οὐδέποτε εἴσῃ, ἀλλὰ καὶ ὡς ἀπομαθησόμενος, καὶ διδάξων ἕτερον. Ἐν ταῖς τέχναις οὐχὶ ὡρισμένους καιροὺς παραμένουσιν ἅπαντες, ἐν τοῖς μαθήμασι, καὶ ἐν πάσαις ἁπλῶς ταῖς τέχναις; Οὕτως ἅπαντες ὁρί-[269]ζομεν φανερὸν καιρόν· ἂν δὲ ἀεὶ μανθάνητε, τεκμήριόν ἐστι τοῦ μηδὲν μαθεῖν.

Τοῦτο τὸ ὄνειδος τοῖς Ἰουδαίοις ὁ θεὸς εἶπεν· "Αἰρόμενοι ἐκ κοιλίας, καὶ παιδευόμενοι ἕως γήρως." Εἰ μὴ ἀεὶ τοῦτο προσεδοκᾶτε, οὐκ ἂν οὕτως εἰς τοὐπίσω πάντα ἀπῄει. Εἰ ἐνῆν τοὺς μὲν εἶναι μεμαθηκότας, τοὺς δὲ μέλλοντας, προέκοψεν ἂν τὸ ἔργον ἡμῖν· παρεχωρήσατε ἂν ἑτέροις, καὶ συναντελάβεσθε καὶ ἡμῖν. Εἰπέ μοι, εἰ πρὸς γραμματιστὴν τινες ἀπίοιεν, εἶτα μένοιεν ἀεὶ τὰ στοιχεῖα μανθάνοντες, οὐ πολὺν τῷ διδασκάλῳ πόνον παρέξουσι; Μέχρι τίνος ὑμῖν περὶ βίου διαλεγόμεθα; Ἐπὶ τῶν ἀποστόλων οὕτως οὐκ ἦν, ἀλλὰ συνεχῶς μετεπήδων, τοὺς πρότερον μανθάνοντας διδασκάλους καθιστῶντες ἑτέρων τινῶν μαθητευομένων. Οὕτως ἠδυνήθησαν τὴν οἰκουμένην περιελθεῖν, τῷ μὴ προσδεμεῖσθαι τόπῳ ἑνί. Πόσης οἴεσθε διδασκαλίας δεῖσθαι τοὺς ὑμετέρους ἀδελφοὺς τοὺς ἐπὶ τῶν ἀγρῶν, καὶ τοὺς ἐκείνων διδασκάλους; Ἀλλ' ὑμεῖς με κατέχετε προσηλώσαντες. Πρὶν ἢ γὰρ τὴν κεφαλὴν καλῶς διατεθῆναι, περιττὸν ἐπὶ τὸ λοιπὸν σῶμα ἰέναι. Πάντα ἡμῖν ἐπιρρίπτετε. Ὑμᾶς ἐχρῆν παρ' ἡμῶν μανθάνειν μόνον· τὰς δὲ γυναῖκας παρ' ὑμῶν, τὰ παιδία παρ' ὑμῶν· ἀλλὰ πάντα ἡμῖν καταλιμπάνετε· διὰ τοῦτο πολὺς ὁ κόπος.

"Διδάσκοντες, φησὶ, καὶ νουθετοῦντες ἑαυτοὺς ψαλμοῖς καὶ ὕμνοις καὶ ᾠδαῖς πνευματικαῖς." Ὅρα καὶ τὸ ἀνεπαχθὲς τοῦ Παύλου. Ἐπειδὴ ἡ ἀνάγνωσις ἔχει πόνον, καὶ πολὺ τὸ φορτικόν, οὐκ ἐφ' ἱστορίας ἤγαγεν, ἀλλ' ἐπὶ ψαλμούς, ἵνα ὁμοῦ καὶ τέρπῃς τὴν ψυχὴν ᾄδων, καὶ ὑποκλέπτῃς τὸν πόνον. "Ὕμνοις, φησὶ, καὶ ᾠδαῖς πνευματικαῖς." Νῦν δὲ σατανικὰς μὲν ᾠδὰς καὶ ὀρχήσεις ἐροῦσιν οἱ παῖδες οἱ ὑμέτεροι, καθάπερ οἱ μάγειροι καὶ οἱ ὀψῶναι καὶ οἱ χορευταί· ψαλμὸν δὲ οὐδεὶς οὐδένα οἶδεν, ἀλλὰ καὶ αἰσχύνη τὸ πρᾶγμα δοκεῖ εἶναι καὶ χλευασία καὶ γέλως. Ἐκεῖθεν ἅπαντα τὰ κακὰ σῴζεται. Ἐν οἵᾳ γὰρ ἂν ἑστήκῃ γῇ τὸ φυτόν, τοιοῦτον φέρει τὸν καρπόν· ἂν ἐν ἀμμώδει καὶ ἁλμυρᾷ, τοιοῦτον· ἂν ἐν γλυκείᾳ καὶ λιπαρᾷ, πάλιν ὅμοιον. Οὕτω πηγή

safe with them, let alone without them. Don't throw everything at us: you are sheep, although not without reason, but rational; Paul entrusts much to you also. Those people who are being instructed don't continue learning forever, since they aren't instructed: if you're always being instructed, you'll never learn. Don't come so that you are always learning, since you will never know, but so as to finish learning and instruct others. In the trades, doesn't everyone continue for set times, in learning and, in short, in all trades? Thus we all [269] determine a fixed deadline: if you're always learning, it's a proof that you've learned nothing.

This is the reproach which God addressed to the Jews: "*Borne from the belly, and educated until old age*" [Isa 46:3–4 LXX]. If you haven't always been expecting this, everything wouldn't have gone backward in this way. If it had been possible for some to have learned, and others to begin, our work would have been in advance: you would have given way to others and helped us as well. Tell me, if some were to go off to a grammarian, then continue always learning their letters, wouldn't they give their teacher a lot of trouble? How long shall I have to discourse to you about life? In the times of the apostles it wasn't like this, but they continually changed places, appointing those who had learned first as teachers of the others who were learning. In this way they went around the world, not being bound to one place. How much instruction do you think your brothers in the country need, and their teachers? But you hold me nailed here. You see, before the head is set right, it's superfluous to proceed to the rest of the body. You throw everything at us. You should just learn from us, and your wives and children from you. No—you leave everything to us. This is why my work is too much.

"*Teaching,*" he says, "*and admonishing each other with psalms and hymns and spiritual songs.*" See also Paul's leniency. Since reading entails work and its burden is great, he didn't lead them to narratives, but to the Psalms, so that at the same time you might refresh your soul by singing and beguile the work. "*With psalms,*" he says, "*and spiritual songs.*" But now your children choose[106] songs and dances of Satan, like cooks and caterers and musicians; no, nobody knows any psalms; no, it seems a thing both to be ashamed of and a mockery and a joke. There all the evils are stored up. You see, whatever soil the plant stands in, such is the fruit it bears: if it's in a sandy and salty soil, it's of that nature; if it's in a sweet and rich one, again

---

106. This is a departure from Field's text, which would have us translate "utter."

τις ἐστὶ τὰ διδάγματα. Δίδαξον [270] αὐτὸν ᾄδειν ψαλμοὺς ἐκείνους τοὺς φιλοσοφίας γέμοντας, οἷον περὶ σωφροσύνης εὐθέως, μᾶλλον δὲ πρὸ πάντων περὶ τοῦ μὴ συνεῖναι πονηροῖς, εὐθέως ἀπ' αὐτῆς τῆς ἀρχῆς τοῦ βιβλίου· διὰ γὰρ τοῦτο καὶ ἐντεῦθεν ἤρξατο ὁ προφήτης λέγων· "Μακάριος ἀνὴρ ὃς οὐκ ἐπορεύθη ἐν βουλῇ ἀσεβῶν·" καὶ πάλιν, "Οὐκ ἐκάθισα μετὰ συνεδρίου ματαιότητος·" καὶ πάλιν, "Ἐξουδένωται ἐνώπιον αὐτοῦ πονηρευόμενος, τοὺς δὲ φοβουμένους τὸν κύριον δοξάζει"· περὶ τοῦ συνεῖναι ἀγαθοῖς· καὶ ταῦτα εὑρήσεις ἐκεῖ πολλά· περὶ τοῦ γαστρὸς κατέχειν, περὶ τοῦ χειρὸς κατέχειν, περὶ τοῦ ἀκολασίας, περὶ τοῦ μὴ πλεονεκτεῖν· ὅτι οὐδὲν τὰ χρήματα, οὐδὲ ἡ δόξα, καὶ ὅσα τοιαῦτα.

Ὅταν τούτοις ἐκ παιδὸς ἐνάξῃς αὐτόν, κατὰ μικρὸν καὶ ἐπὶ τὰ ὑψηλότερα ἄξεις. Οἱ ψαλμοὶ πάντα ἔχουσιν, οἱ δὲ ὕμνοι πάλιν οὐδὲν ἀνθρώπινον· ὅταν ἐν τοῖς ψαλμοῖς μάθῃ, τότε καὶ ὕμνους εἴσεται, ἅτε θειότερον πρᾶγμα. Αἱ γὰρ ἄνω δυνάμεις ὑμνοῦσιν, οὐ ψάλλουσιν· "Οὐ γὰρ ὡραῖος ὕμνος ἐν στόματι, φησίν, ἁμαρτωλοῦ·" καὶ πάλιν, "Οἱ ὀφθαλμοί μου ἐπὶ τοὺς πιστοὺς τῆς γῆς, τοῦ συγκαθῆσθαι αὐτοὺς μετ' ἐμοῦ·" καὶ πάλιν, "Οὐ κατῴκει ἐν μέσῳ τῆς οἰκίας μου ποιῶν ὑπερηφανίαν·" καὶ πάλιν, "Πορευόμενος ἐν ὁδῷ ἀμώμῳ, οὗτός μοι ἐλειτούργει."

Ὥστε μὴ μόνον φίλοις, ἀλλὰ μηδὲ οἰκέταις ἀναμιγνύναι ἑαυτοὺς ἀσφαλίζεσθε. Τὰ γὰρ μυρία κακὰ τοῖς ἐλευθέροις, ὅταν δούλους αὐτοῖς ἐπιστήσωμεν διεφθαρμένους. Εἰ γὰρ πατρὸς ἀπολαύοντες καὶ φιλοστοργίας καὶ φιλοσοφίας τοσαύτης, μόλις διασῴζονται· ὅταν αὐτοὺς ἐκδῶμεν τῇ ἀφειδείᾳ τῶν οἰκετῶν, καθάπερ ἐχθροῖς αὐτοῖς κέχρηνται, νομίζοντες αὐτοῖς τὴν δεσποτείαν εἶναι ἡμερωτέραν, ἂν μωροὺς αὐτοὺς ἀπεργάσωνται καὶ φαύλους καὶ οὐδενὸς λόγου ἀξίους.

Πρὸ τῶν ἄλλων οὖν ἁπάντων ταῦτα σπουδάζωμεν. "Ἠγάπησα, φησί, τοὺς ἀγαπῶντας τὸν νόμον σου." Τοῦτον οὖν καὶ ἡμεῖς ζηλώσωμεν, καὶ τούτους ἀγαπῶμεν. Ἵνα δὲ πάλιν σωφρονῶσιν οἱ παῖδες, ἀκουέτωσαν τοῦ προ-

it is similar. So instruction is a kind of fountain. Teach [**270**] this person to sing those songs that are full of wisdom,[107] for example those immediately concerning chastity, or rather, before all, those concerning not consorting with the wicked, immediately with the very beginning of the book. For on this account the prophet began from here, saying, "*Blessed is the man who does not walk in the counsel of the wicked*" [Ps 1:1], and again, "*I have not sat in the council of those who labor in vain*" [Ps 26:4]. And again, "*In his eyes a wrongdoer is set at naught, but he honors those who fear the Lord*" [Ps 15:4]. [He talks] about consorting with good people (and you will find these subjects there in abundance), about controlling the belly, about controlling the hands, about flattery, about not being greedy, that money is nothing, nor is glory, and many subjects like these.

When in these matters you've led them on from childhood, little by little you'll lead them on to loftier things. The Psalms contain everything, while the hymns contain nothing human. When they have learned from the Psalms, they will then know hymns also, as a more divine thing. You see, the Powers above sing hymns, not the Psalms. "*For a hymn*," it says, "*is not graceful in the mouth of a sinner*" [Sir 15:9], and again, "*My eyes look on the faithful of the land, that they sit together with me*" [Ps 101:6], and again, "*The one who practices arrogance does not dwell within my house*" [Ps 101:7], and again, "*The one who walks in a blameless way, he shall minister to me*" [Ps 101:6].

So you must guard them[108] from mixing not only with friends but not even with servants. You see, the evils done to the freeborn are myriad, when we place over them corrupt slaves. For if, when enjoying a father's great affection and wisdom, they can with difficulty be kept safe throughout; when we give them into the merciless charge of servants, they use them like enemies, thinking that they'll be milder masters to them, if they've made them foolish and common and worthy of no account.

Therefore, above everything else, let's be diligent about these matters. "I have loved," it says, "those who love your law" [see Ps 118:97].[109] Therefore, let's too emulate this person and love them. Again in order for the

---

107. Lit. "philosophy."
108. That is, children.
109. This is not an exact citation.

φήτου λέγοντος, [271] "Ὅτι αἱ ψύαι μου ἐπλήσθησαν ἐμπαιγμάτων·" καὶ πάλιν ἀκουέτωσαν αὐτοῦ λέγοντος, "Ἐξολοθρεύσας πάντα τὸν πορνεύοντα ἀπὸ σοῦ." Καὶ ὅτι δεῖ γαστρὸς κατέχειν, ἀκουέτωσαν πάλιν· "Καὶ ἀπέκτεινε, φησὶν, ἐν τοῖς πλείοσιν αὐτῶν, ἔτι τῆς βρώσεως οὔσης ἐν τῷ στόματι αὐτῶν." Καὶ ὅτι δεῖ δώρων κρατεῖν · "Πλοῦτος ἐὰν ῥέῃ, μὴ προστίθεσθε καρδίαν·" καὶ δόξης κρατεῖν · "Οὐδὲ συγκαταβήσεται αὐτῷ ἡ δόξα αὐτοῦ." τοὺς πονηροὺς μὴ ζηλοῦν· "Μὴ παραζήλου ἐν πονηρευομένοις·" τὰς δυναστείας ἡγεῖσθαι οὐδέν· "Εἶδον τὸν ἀσεβῆ ὑπερυψούμενον καὶ ἐπαιρόμενον ὡς τὰς κέδρους τοῦ Λιβάνου, καὶ παρῆλθον, καὶ ἰδοὺ οὐκ ἦν·" μηδὲν τὰ παρόντα ἡγεῖσθαι· "Ἐμακάρισαν τὸν λαὸν, ᾧ ταῦτά ἐστι· μακάριος ὁ λαὸς, οὗ κύριος ὁ θεὸς βοηθὸς αὐτοῦ." ὅτι οὐχ ἁπλῶς ἁμαρτάνομεν, ἀλλ᾽ ἔστιν ἀνταπόδοσις· "Ὅτι σὺ ἀποδώσεις, φησὶν, ἑκάστῳ κατὰ τὰ ἔργα αὐτοῦ."

διὰ τί δὲ οὐ καθ᾽ ἡμέραν ἀποδίδωσιν· "Ὁ θεὸς κριτὴς, φησὶν, δίκαιος καὶ ἰσχυρὸς καὶ μακρόθυμος." ὅτι ταπεινοφροσύνη καλόν. "Κύριε, φησὶν, οὐχ ὑψώθη ἡ καρδία μου." ὅτι ὑπερηφανία κακόν· "Διὰ τοῦτο, φησὶν, ἐκράτησεν αὐτοὺς ἡ ὑπερηφανία εἰς τέλος·" καὶ πάλιν, "Κύριος ὑπερηφάνοις ἀντιτάσσεται." καὶ πάλιν, "Ἐξελεύσεται ὡς ἐκ στέατος ἡ ἀδικία αὐτῶν." ὅτι ἐλεημοσύνη καλόν· "Ἐσκόρπισεν, ἔδωκε τοῖς πένησιν· ἡ δικαιοσύνη αὐτοῦ μένει εἰς τὸν αἰῶνα." ὅτι τὸ ἐλεεῖν ἐπαινετόν· "Χρηστὸς ἀνὴρ ὁ οἰκτείρων, καὶ κιχρῶν." Καὶ πολλὰ τούτων [272] πλείονα εὑρήσεις ἐκεῖ ἐμφιλόσοφα δόγματα· οἷον ὅτι κακῶς λέγειν οὐ δεῖ· "Τὸν καταλαλοῦντα, φησὶ, λάθρα τὸν πλησίον αὐτοῦ, τοῦτον ἐξεδίωκον."

Τίς ὁ ὕμνος τῶν ἄνω; ἴσασιν οἱ πιστοί· τί λέγει τὰ Χερουβὶμ ἄνω; Τί ἔλεγον οἱ ἄγγελοι; "Δόξα ἐν ὑψίστοις θεῷ." Διὰ τοῦτο μετὰ τὰς ψαλμῳδίας ὕμνοι, ἅτε τελειότερόν τι πρᾶγμα· "Ψαλμοῖς, φησὶν, ὕμνοις, ᾠδαῖς πνευματικαῖς ἐν τῇ χάριτι ᾄδοντες ἐν ταῖς καρδίαις ὑμῶν τῷ θεῷ." Ἢ τοῦτό φησιν, ὅτι διὰ χάριν ἡμῖν ταῦτα ἔδωκεν ὁ θεὸς, ἢ ταῖς ἐν τῇ χάριτι ᾠδαῖς, ἢ νουθετοῦντες ἑαυτοὺς καὶ διδάσκοντες ἐν χάριτι, ἢ ὅτι ἐν χάριτι εἶχον ταῦτα τὰ χαρίσματα, ἢ ἐπεξήγησίς ἐστιν· ἀπὸ τῆς χάριτος τοῦ πνεύματος, φησίν. "Ἄιδοντες ἐν ταῖς καρδίαις ὑμῶν τῷ θεῷ." Μὴ ἁπλῶς, φησὶ, τῷ στόματι, ἀλλὰ μετὰ προσοχῆς. Τοῦτο γάρ ἐστι τῷ θεῷ ᾄδειν, ἐκεῖνο δὲ τῷ ἀέρι· διαχεῖται γὰρ ἁπλῶς ἡ φωνή. Μὴ πρὸς ἐπίδειξιν, φησίν. Κἂν ἐν ἀγορᾷ ᾖς, δύνασαι συστρέψαι σαυτὸν καὶ

young to be chaste, let them listen to the prophet saying, [271] *"Because my loins are filled with delusions"* [Ps 38:7], and again listen to him saying, *"You have utterly destroyed those who are unfaithful to you"* [Ps 73:27]. And as to the fact that one should control the belly, let them hear again, *"And he slew,"* it says, *"the strongest of them, while the meat was still in their mouths"* [Ps 77:30, 31 LXX]. And that one ought to resist bribes: *"If wealth flows, do not set your heart on it"* [Ps 62:10], and to resist glory: *"Nor will his glory go down together with him"* [Ps 49:17]. And not to envy the wicked: *"Do not be envious of the workers of wickedness"* [Ps 37:1]. To count power as nothing: *"I saw the ungodly one in a very high place and lifted up like the cedars of Lebanon, and I passed by, and, look, he was not there"* [Ps 37:35]. And to take no thought of the present things. *They called the people blessed, to whom these things happen. Blessed are the people whose helper is the Lord their God* [Ps 144:16 LXX]. That we don't sin without cause but that there is retribution: *"Because you will render to each one,"* it says, *'according to their works"* [Ps 62:12].

But why doesn't he render to them on a daily basis? *"God is a just judge,"* it says, *"and strong and longsuffering"* [Ps 7:11]. That humility is good, it says: *"Lord, my heart is not lifted up"* [Ps 131:1]. That pride is evil: *"Therefore,"* it says, *"pride is their necklace"* [Ps 73:6]. And again: *"The Lord resists the proud"* [Jas 4:6; 1 Pet 5:5], and again: *"Their injustice will exude as fat"* [Ps 72:7 LXX]. That almsgiving is good: *"He has distributed freely; he has given to the poor. His righteousness endures forever"* [Ps 112:9]. That to pity is praiseworthy: *"It is a good man who takes pity and lends"* [Ps 112:5]. And you'll find that there are many [272] more teachings than these there, full of philosophy: for example, that one shouldn't speak ill: *"The one who slanders their neighbor secretly, I chased away"* [Ps 100:5].

What is the hymn of those above? The believers know. What do the cherubim say above? What did the angels say? *"Glory to God in the highest"* [Luke 2:14]. For this reason, after the psalmody the hymns, which are a thing of more perfection. *"With psalms,"* he says, *"with hymns, with spiritual songs, with grace singing in your hearts to God."* Paul means either this: that God has given these things to us through grace; or with songs in grace; or admonishing and teaching each other in grace; or that they had these gifts in grace; or it is an additional explanation: he means from the grace of the Spirit. *Singing in your hearts to God.* "Not just with your mouth," he says, "but with attention." You see, this is to *sing to God*, while the other is to the air, for the voice is just scattered. "Not for display," he means. Even if you're in the marketplace, you can collect yourself and sing to God, while

ᾄδειν τῷ θεῷ, μηδενὸς ἀκούοντος· ἐπεὶ καὶ Μωϋσῆς οὕτως ηὔχετο, καὶ ἠκούσθη· φησὶ γάρ· "Τί βοᾷς πρός με;" καίτοιγε οὐδὲν εἶπεν, ἀλλ᾽ ἐβόα κατὰ διάνοιαν· διὸ καὶ ὁ θεὸς ἤκουσε μόνος· μετὰ καρδίας συντετριμμένης. Οὐ κεκώλυται γὰρ καὶ περιπατοῦντα εὔχεσθαι κατὰ καρδίαν, καὶ ἄνω εἶναι.

"Καὶ πᾶν ὅ τι ἂν ποιῆτε, φησὶν, ἐν λόγῳ, ἢ ἐν ἔργῳ, πάντα ἐν ὀνόματι τοῦ κυρίου Ἰησοῦ, εὐχαριστοῦντες τῷ θεῷ καὶ πατρὶ δι᾽ αὐτοῦ." Ἐὰν γὰρ οὕτω ποιῶμεν, οὐδὲν ἔσται μιαρὸν, οὐδὲ ἀκάθαρτον, ἔνθα ἂν ὁ Χριστὸς καλῆται. Ἐὰν ἐσθίῃς, ἐὰν πίνῃς, ἐὰν γαμῇς, ἐὰν ἀποδημῇς, πάντα ἐν ὀνόματι τοῦ θεοῦ πρᾶττε· τουτέστιν, αὐτὸν καλῶν βοηθόν· ἐπὶ πάντων πρότερον αὐτῷ εὐχόμενος, ἅπτου τῶν πραγμάτων. Βούλει τι φθέγξασθαι; τοῦτο πρόταττε. Διὰ τοῦτο καὶ ἡμεῖς [273] τῶν ἐπιστολῶν προτάσσομεν τὸ ὄνομα κυρίου. Ἔνθα ἂν ᾖ τὸ ὄνομα θεοῦ, πάντα αἴσια. Εἰ γὰρ ὑπάτων ὀνόματα ἀσφαλῆ τὰ γραμματεῖα ποιεῖ, πολλῷ μᾶλλον τοῦ Χριστοῦ τὸ ὄνομα. Ἢ τοῦτό φησι, κατὰ θεὸν πάντα καὶ λέγετε, καὶ πράττετε· μὴ τοὺς ἀγγέλους ἐπεισάγετε. Ἐσθίεις; εὐχαρίστησον τῷ θεῷ, καὶ μέλλων, καὶ μετὰ ταῦτα. Καθεύδεις; εὐχαρίστησον τῷ θεῷ, καὶ μέλλων, καὶ μετὰ ταῦτα. Εἰς ἀγορὰν ἐμβάλλεις; ταὐτὸν ποίει. Μηδὲν κοσμικὸν, μηδὲν βιωτικόν· πάντα ἐν ὀνόματι κυρίου ποίει, καὶ πάντα σοι εὐοδωθήσεται. Ὅπου ἂν ἐπιτεθῇ τὸ ὄνομα, πάντα αἴσια. Εἰ δαίμονας ἐκβάλλει, εἰ νόσους ἀπελαύνει, πολλῷ μᾶλλον εὐκολίαν πραγμάτων ποιεῖ.

Καὶ τί ἐστι ποιῆσαι ἐν λόγῳ, ἢ ἐν ἔργῳ; Ἢ ἀξιοῦντα, ἢ ὁτιοῦν ποιοῦντα. Ἄκουσον πῶς ὁ Ἀβραὰμ ἐν ὀνόματι θεοῦ τὸν οἰκέτην ἀπέστειλεν, ὁ Δαυῒδ ἐν ὀνόματι θεοῦ τὸν Γολιὰθ καθεῖλε. Θαυμαστὸν τὸ ὄνομα αὐτοῦ καὶ μέγα. Πάλιν ὁ Ἰακὼβ τοὺς υἱοὺς πέμπων, φησίν· "Ὁ δὲ θεός μου δῴη ὑμῖν χάριν ἐνώπιον τοῦ ἀνθρώπου." Ὁ γὰρ τοῦτο ποιῶν, ἔχει σύμμαχον τὸν θεὸν, οὗ χωρὶς οὐδὲν ἐτόλμησε ποιῆσαι. Ἄτε οὖν τιμηθεὶς τῷ κληθῆναι, ἀντιτιμήσει τῷ ἐξευμαρίσαι τὰ πράγματα. Κάλει τὸν υἱὸν, εὐχαρίστει τῷ πατρί. Καὶ γὰρ τοῦ υἱοῦ καλουμένου ὁ πατὴρ καλεῖται, καὶ αὐτοῦ εὐχαριστουμένου ὁ υἱὸς εὐχαριστήθη.

Ταῦτα μανθάνωμεν μὴ μέχρι ῥημάτων, ἀλλὰ καὶ διὰ τῶν ἔργων πληροῦν. Οὐδὲν τοῦ ὀνόματος τούτου ἴσον· τοῦτο πανταχοῦ θαυμάσιον. "Μύρον, φησὶν,

nobody hears, since Moses too prayed in this way and was heard, for God said, "*Why do you cry out to me?*" [Exod 14:15], yet Moses said nothing but cried out in his mind, which is why only God heard: with a contrite heart. For one isn't prevented from praying in one's heart, even while walking, and to be above.[110]

"*And whatever you do,*" Paul says, "*in word or in deed, do everything in the name of the Lord Jesus, giving thanks to God and to the Father through him.*" If we behave like this, there will be nothing polluted, or unclean, wherever Christ is called on. If you eat, if you drink, if you marry, if you travel, do everything in God's name, that is, calling on him as a helper, in everything first praying to him, engage in your business. Do you want to say something? Put this at the forefront. This is why we too [**273**] put the Lord's name at the forefront of our letters. Wherever the word of God is, all is auspicious. For if the names of consuls authenticate documents,[111] much more will the name of Christ. Or Paul means this: both do and say everything according to God—don't bring in the angels. Are you eating? Give thanks to God both before and afterward. Are you sleeping? Give thanks to God both before and afterward. Are you rushing into the marketplace? Do the same—nothing worldly, nothing of this life. Do everything in the Lord's name, and all prosperity will be yours. Wherever the name is placed, everything is auspicious. If it casts out demons, if it drives away diseases, much more will it make matters auspicious.

And what is to *do in word, or in deed*? Either requesting or doing anything at all. Listen to how Abraham sent his servant in the name of God [see Gen 24:1–9]; David, in the name of God, slew Goliath [see 1 Kgdms 17:45–51]. Marvelous is his name, and great. Again Jacob, on sending his sons, said, "*May my God give you favor in the* sight *of the person*" [Gen 43:14 LXX]. For the one who does this has God as an ally, without whom they dared to do nothing. Inasmuch, therefore, as God is honored by being called on, he will in turn honor them by making their business easy. Call on the Son, give thanks to the Father. You see, when the Son is called on, the Father is called on, and when the Father is thanked, the Son is thanked.

These things let's learn, not as far as words but also fulfilling them by deeds. Nothing is the equal of this name—it is marvelous everywhere.

---

110. That is, in heaven.

111. A reference to the fact that in the Roman Empire legal documents were dated according to the year of a consul's tenure of office.

ἐκκενωθὲν ὄνομά σου." Ὁ τοῦτο εἰπὼν εὐθέως εὐωδίας ἐνεπλήσθη. "Οὐδεὶς δύναται εἰπεῖν κύριον Ἰησοῦν, φησὶν, εἰ μὴ ἐν πνεύματι ἁγίῳ." Τοῦτο τὸ ὄνομα τοσαῦτα ἐργάζεται. Ἐὰν εἴπῃς, ἐν ὀνόματι πατρὸς καὶ υἱοῦ καὶ ἁγίου πνεύματος, μετὰ πίστεως, πάντα ἤνυσας. Ὅρα πόσα ἐποίησας· ἐδημιούργη-σας ἄνθρωπον, καὶ τὰ ἄλλα πάντα τὰ ἀπὸ τοῦ βαπτίσματος εἰργάσω. Οὕτω ταῖς νόσοις ἐπιτασσόμενον φοβερὸν τὸ ὄνομα. Διὰ ταῦτα ὁ διάβολος τὰ τῶν ἀγγέλων ἐπεισήγαγε, βασκαίνων ἡμῖν τῆς τιμῆς. Τῶν δαιμόνων τοιαῦται αἱ ἐπῳδαί. Κἂν ἄγγελος ᾖ, [274] κἂν ἀρχάγγελος, κἂν τὰ Χερουβὶμ, μὴ ἀνέχου· ἐπεὶ οὐδὲ αὗται αἱ δυνάμεις καταδέξονται, ἀλλὰ καὶ ἀποσείσονται, ὅταν ἴδωσι τὸν δεσπότην ἀτιμαζόμενον. Ἐγώ σε ἐτίμησα, φησὶ, καὶ εἶπον· ἐμὲ κάλει· καὶ σὺ ἀτιμάζεις αὐτόν; Ἂν ταύτην ᾄδῃς τὴν ἐπῳδὴν μετὰ πίστεως, καὶ νόσους καὶ δαίμονας ἀπελάσεις· κἂν μὴ ἀπελάσῃς τὴν νόσον, οὐ παρὰ ἀσθένειαν, ἀλλὰ παρὰ τὸ συμφέρον. "Κατὰ τὴν μεγαλωσύνην σου, φησὶν, οὕτω καὶ ἡ αἴνεσίς σου." Διὰ τοῦ ὀνόματος τούτου ἡ οἰκουμένη ἐπεστράφη, ἡ τυραννὶς ἐλύθη, ὁ διάβολος ἐπατήθη, οἱ οὐρανοὶ ἀνεῴχθησαν. Ἡμεῖς ἀνεγεννήθημεν διὰ τοῦ ὀνόματος τούτου. Ἐὰν τοῦτο ἔχωμεν, λάμπομεν. Τοῦτο καὶ μάρτυρας ποιεῖ, καὶ ὁμολογητάς· τοῦτο κατέχωμεν ἀντὶ μεγάλου δώρου, ἵνα ἐν δόξῃ ζήσωμεν, καὶ εὐαρεστήσωμεν τῷ θεῷ, καὶ καταξιωθῶμεν τῶν ἐπηγγελμέ-νων ἀγαθῶν τοῖς ἀγαπῶσιν αὐτὸν, χάριτι καὶ φιλανθρωπίᾳ τοῦ κυρίου ἡμῶν Ἰησοῦ Χριστοῦ, μεθ' οὗ τῷ πατρὶ ἅμα τῷ ἁγίῳ πνεύματι δόξα, κράτος, τιμὴ, νῦν καὶ ἀεὶ καὶ εἰς τοὺς αἰῶνας τῶν αἰώνων. Ἀμήν.

"*Your name,*" it says, "*is ointment poured forth*" [Song 1:3]. The one who says this is immediately filled with fragrance. "*Nobody,*" it says, "*can call Jesus Lord, unless by the Holy Spirit*" [1 Cor 12:3]. This name works such great things. If you say "in the name of the Father and the Son and the Holy Spirit" with faith, you have accomplished everything. See how much you've done: you've created a human being and worked all the rest that comes from baptism. So when used in commanding diseases, the name is fearful. This is why the devil introduced the things[112] of the angels, envying us the honor. Such incantations are from the demons. Even if it's an angel, [274] even if an archangel, even if cherubim, don't allow it, since neither will these Powers accept it, but will even shake it off, when they see that the master is dishonored. "I have honored you," he says, "and have said 'call upon me,' and do you dishonor him? If you sing this incantation with faith, you'll drive out both diseases and demons; even if you haven't driven disease out, it's not from lack of power but because it is beneficial." "*According to your greatness,*" it says, "*so also is your praise*" [Ps 48:10 LXX]. Through this name the world has been converted, tyranny dissolved, the devil trampled on, the heavens opened. We have been born again through this name. If we have it, we are radiant. This makes both martyrs and confessors; let's hold onto this as a great gift, so that we may live in glory and be well-pleasing to God and be counted worthy of the good things promised to those who love him, by the grace and loving-kindness of our Lord Jesus Christ, with whom, to the Father together with the Holy Spirit, be glory, power, honor, now and forever and ever. Amen.

---

112. This must refer to the power the angels acquired from their worshipers.

ΛΟΓΟΣ Ι.

Αἱ γυναῖκες, ὑποτάσσεσθε τοῖς ἀνδράσιν, ὡς ἀνῆκεν ἐν κυρίῳ. Οἱ ἄνδρες, ἀγαπᾶτε τὰς γυναῖκας, καὶ μὴ πικραίνεσθε πρὸς αὐτάς. Τὰ τέκνα, ὑπακούετε τοῖς γονεῦσι κατὰ πάντα· τοῦτο γάρ ἐστιν εὐάρεστον ἐν κυρίῳ. Οἱ πατέρες, μὴ ἐρεθίζετε τὰ τέκνα ὑμῶν, ἵνα μὴ ἀθυμῶσιν. Οἱ δοῦλοι, ὑπακούετε κατὰ πάντα τοῖς κατὰ σάρκα κυρίοις, μὴ κατ᾽ ὀφθαλμοδουλείαν, ὡς ἀνθρωπάρεσκοι, ἀλλ᾽ ἐν ἁπλότητι καρδίας, φοβούμενοι τὸν θεόν. Πᾶν ὅτι ἂν ποιῆτε, ἐκ ψυχῆς ἐργάζεσθε, ὡς τῷ κυρίῳ, καὶ οὐκ ἀνθρώποις, εἰδότες ὅτι παρὰ κυρίου λήψεσθε τὴν ἀνταπόδοσιν τῆς κληρονομίας· τῷ γὰρ κυρίῳ Χριστῷ δουλεύετε. Ὁ δὲ ἀδικῶν, κομιεῖται ὃ ἠδίκησε, καὶ οὐκ ἔστι προσωποληψία παρὰ τῷ θεῷ. Οἱ [275] κύριοι, τὸ δίκαιον καὶ τὴν ἰσότητα τοῖς δούλοις παρέχετε, εἰδότες ὅτι καὶ ὑμεῖς ἔχετε κύριον ἐν οὐρανοῖς.

Διὰ τί μὴ πανταχοῦ καὶ ἐν πάσαις ταῖς ἐπιστολαῖς ταῦτα ἐπιτάττει, ἀλλ᾽ ἐνταῦθα, καὶ τῇ πρὸς Ἐφεσίους, καὶ τῇ πρὸς Τιμόθεον, καὶ τῇ πρὸς Τίτον; Ὅτι εἰκὸς ἐν ταύταις ταῖς πόλεσιν εἶναι τὰς διχοστασίας· ἢ εἰκὸς τὰ ἄλλα αὐταῖς κατωρθῶσθαι, ὥστε δεῖν περὶ τούτων αὐτοὺς ἀκούειν. Μᾶλλον δὲ ἃ πρὸς τούτους λέγει, πρὸς πάντας λέγει. Πολλὴν δὲ ἐμφέρειαν ἔχει αὕτη ἡ ἐπιστολὴ τῇ πρὸς Ἐφεσίους καὶ ἐν τούτοις. Ἢ ὅτι ἀνδράσι λοιπὸν εἰρηνεύουσιν, οὓς ἐχρῆν περὶ δογμάτων μανθάνειν ὑψηλῶν ἔτι ἐλλειπόντων αὐτοῖς, οὐκ ἐχρῆν περὶ τούτων γράφειν· ἢ παρακληθέντας ἐπὶ τοῖς πειρασμοῖς περιττὸν περὶ τούτων ἀκούειν. Ὥστε στοχάζομαι ἐνταῦθα λοιπὸν ἑδραίαν εἶναι τὴν ἐκκλησίαν, καὶ πρὸς τῷ τέλει ταῦτα λέγεσθαι.

"Αἱ γυναῖκες, ὑποτάσσεσθε τοῖς ἀνδράσιν, ὡς ἀνῆκεν ἐν κυρίῳ·" ἀντὶ τοῦ, ὑποτάσσεσθε διὰ τὸν θεόν· ἐπειδὴ τοῦτο ὑμᾶς κοσμεῖ, φησὶν, οὐκ ἐκείνους. Οὐ γὰρ δεσποτικὴν ὑποταγὴν, οὐδὲ τὴν ἀπὸ φύσεως μόνον, ἀλλὰ τὴν διὰ θεόν φημι. "Οἱ ἄνδρες, ἀγαπᾶτε τὰς γυναῖκας, καὶ μὴ πικραίνεσθε πρὸς αὐτάς." Ὅρα πῶς πάλιν τὸ κατάλληλον παρήνεσε. Καθάπερ ἐκεῖ φόβον καὶ

Wives, be subject to your husbands, as is fitting in the Lord. Husbands, love your wives, and don't be harsh with them. Children, obey your parents in all things, for this is well-pleasing in the Lord. Fathers, don't provoke your children, lest they be discouraged. Slaves, obey in everything those who are your lords in the flesh, not with eye-service, nor being sycophantic, but with singleness of heart, fearing God. Whatever you do, work from your spirit as serving the Lord and not human beings, knowing that you will receive from the Lord the recompense of your inheritance, for you serve the Lord Christ. But the wrongdoer will be paid back for the wrongs they have committed, and there is no respect of persons with God. [275] Lords, give your slaves what is just and equal, in the knowledge that you too have a master in heaven [Col 3:18–25].

Why doesn't he give these commands everywhere in all his letters, but in this place, and in the Letter to the Ephesians, and the one to Timothy, and the one to Titus?[113] Because probably there were disagreements in these cities, or probably they were correct in other respects, so that they had to hear about them. No, what he says to them, he says to all. This letter is very similar to that to the Ephesians, also in these matters. Or because the men were making their peace for the future, those who had to be taught lofty doctrines as yet lacking to them, he didn't have to write on these matters. Or else it was superfluous for those who had been comforted in their trials to hear these subjects. The upshot is that I guess in this place the church was now well-grounded and that these matters are said in conclusion.

Wives, be subject to your husbands, as is fitting in the Lord, instead of being subject for God's sake, "since this is your adornment," he says, "not them. For I don't mean that subjection due to a master, nor that which is only of nature, but for God's sake. *Men, love your wives, and don't be harsh with them.*" See how again he has enjoined reciprocity. As he posits fear

---

113. For a commentary on this passage, see Mitchell, *Heavenly Trumpet*, 391 n. 40.

ἀγάπην τίθησιν, οὕτω καὶ ἐνταῦθα· ἔστι γὰρ καὶ ἀγαπῶντα πικραίνεσθαι. Ὁ οὖν φησι, τοῦτό ἐστι· μὴ μάχεσθε· οὐδὲν γὰρ οὕτως τῆς μάχης ταύτης πικρότερον, ὅταν παρὰ ἀνδρὸς πρὸς γυναῖκα γίνηται. Αἱ γὰρ πρὸς τὰ φιλούμενα πρόσωπα γινόμεναι μάχαι, αὗται πικραί. Καὶ δείκνυσιν ὅτι ἀπὸ πολλῆς πικρίας τοῦτο γίνεται, ὅταν πρὸς τὸ μέλος αὐτοῦ, φησὶ, τὶς διαστασιάζῃ. Τὸ μὲν οὖν ἀγαπᾶν τῶν ἀνδρῶν ἐστι, τὸ δὲ εἴκειν ἐκείνων. Ἐὰν οὖν ἕκαστος τὸ ἑαυτοῦ εἰσενέγκῃ, ἔστηκε πάντα βέβαια. Ἀπὸ μὲν τοῦ ἀγαπᾶσθαι γίνεται καὶ ἡ γυνὴ φιλική· ἀπὸ δὲ τοῦ ὑποτάσσεσθαι ὁ ἀνὴρ ἐπιεικής. Ὅρα δὲ ὅτι καὶ ἐν τῇ φύσει οὕτω κατεσκεύασται, ὥστε τὸν μὲν φιλεῖν, τὴν δὲ ὑπακούειν. Ὅταν γὰρ ὁ ἄρχων τὸ ἀρχόμενον φιλῇ, τότε τὰ πάντα συνέστηκεν. Οὐχ οὕτως [276] ἡ παρὰ τοῦ ἀρχομένου ἀγάπη, ὡς ἡ παρὰ τοῦ ἄρχοντος ζητεῖται πρὸς τὸ ἀρχόμενον· παρ' ἐκείνου γὰρ ἡ ὑπακοή. Τὸ γὰρ ἐν ὥρᾳ εἶναι τὴν γυναῖκα, τοῦτον δὲ ἐν ἐπιθυμίᾳ, οὐδὲν ἄλλο δείκνυσιν, ἀλλ' ἢ ὅτι διὰ τὴν ἀγάπην οὕτω γεγένηται. Μὴ τοίνυν, ἐπειδὴ ὑποτέτακται ἡ γυνή, αὐθέντει· μηδὲ σὺ, ἐπειδὴ ἀγαπᾷ ὁ ἀνήρ, φυσιοῦ. Μήτε ἡ τοῦ ἀνδρὸς φιλία τὴν γυναῖκα ἐπαιρέτω, μήτε ἡ τῆς γυναικὸς ὑποταγὴ φυσάτω τὸν ἄνδρα. Διὰ τοῦτό σοι ὑπέταξεν αὐτὴν, ἵνα μᾶλλον φιλῆται· διὰ τοῦτό σε φιλεῖσθαι ἐποίησεν, ὦ γύναι, ἵνα εὐκόλως φέρῃς τὸ ὑποτετάχθαι. Μὴ φοβοῦ ὑποτασσομένη· τῷ γὰρ φιλοῦντι ὑποταγῆναι, οὐδεμίαν ἔχει δυσκολίαν. Μὴ φοβοῦ ἐρῶν· ἔχεις γὰρ αὐτὴν εἴκουσαν. Οὐκ ἂν ἄλλως οὖν ἐγένετο σύνδεσμος. Ἀναγκαίαν τοίνυν ἔχεις ἀπὸ τῆς φύσεως τὴν ἀρχήν, ἔχε καὶ τὸν δεσμὸν τὸν ἀπὸ τῆς ἀγάπης· τὴν γὰρ ἀσθενεστέραν ἀνεκτὴν εἴασε.

"Τὰ τέκνα, ὑπακούετε τοῖς γονεῦσι κατὰ πάντα· τοῦτο γάρ ἐστιν εὐάρεστον ἐν κυρίῳ." Πάλιν τὸ, "ἐν κυρίῳ," τέθεικε, καὶ νόμους τιθεὶς ὑπακοῆς, καὶ ἐντρέπων, καὶ καταβάλλων. "Τοῦτο γὰρ, φησὶν, ἐστὶν εὐάρεστον τῷ κυρίῳ." Ὅρα πῶς οὐκ ἀπὸ τῆς φύσεως μόνης, ἀλλὰ πρὸ ταύτης ἀπὸ τῶν τῷ θεῷ δοκούντων βούλεται ἡμᾶς ἅπαντα πράττειν, ἵνα καὶ μισθὸν ἔχωμεν. "Οἱ πατέρες, μὴ ἐρεθίζετε τὰ τέκνα ὑμῶν, ἵνα μὴ ἀθυμῶσιν." Ἰδοὺ πάλιν καὶ ἐνταῦθα ὑποταγὴ καὶ φίλτρον. Καὶ οὐκ εἶπεν, ἀγαπᾶτε τὰ τέκνα· περιττὸν γὰρ ἦν· αὐτὴ γὰρ ἡ φύσις καταναγκάζει· ἀλλ' ὅπερ ἔδει διώρθωσε, τὸ καὶ τὸ φίλτρον ἐνταῦθα εἶναι σφοδρότερον, ἐπειδὴ καὶ ἡ ὑπακοὴ μείζων. Οὐδαμοῦ γὰρ τίθησιν ὑπόδειγμα τὸ τοῦ ἀνδρὸς καὶ τὸ τῆς γυναικός· ἀλλὰ τί; Ἄκουε τοῦ προφήτου λέγοντος· "Καθὼς οἰκτείρει πατὴρ υἱοὺς, ᾠκτείρησε κύριος

and love in that passage, so does he also here, for it is possible even for one who loves to be harsh. What he says, therefore, is this: don't fight, for nothing is more bitter than this battle, when it occurs from the husband to the wife. I mean, the battles that occur between loved persons, these are bitter. And Paul shows that it arises from great bitterness, when he says someone is at variance with their own member. Therefore, loving is the part of the husbands, but yielding that of the wives. If, then, each one makes their own contribution, everything stands on a firm footing. For from being loved, the wife also becomes affectionate, while from her submissiveness, the husband becomes gentle. See how also in nature it's been arranged like this, namely, that the one should love, the other obey. For when the governing party loves the governed, then everything stands fast. [**276**] Love from the governed isn't as much sought as that from the governing party toward the governed, for from the other obedience is due. You see, the fact that the woman is in the prime of life and he is in a state of desire demonstrates nothing other than that it has come about in this way. Don't, therefore, when your wife is subject to you, act the autocrat; nor do you, because your husband loves you, put on airs. Let neither the husband's love elate the wife, nor her subordination cause the husband to put on airs. It's for this reason that God subjected her to you, so that she may be loved the more; it's for this reason that he made you to be loved, wife, so that you may bear your subjection easily. Don't fear being a subject, for subjection to one who loves you isn't at all difficult. Don't be afraid to love, for you have her in submission. In no other way, then, could there have been a bond. Therefore, you have your governance from nature; maintain also the bond that comes from love, for this allows the weaker to endure.

Children, obey your parents in all things, for this is well-pleasing in the Lord. Again Paul has put "*in the Lord*" and laying down the laws of obedience, both shaming them and bringing them down. "*For this,*" he says, "*is well-pleasing in the Lord.*" See how he wants us to do everything not from nature alone, but before this from what is pleasing to God, so that we may also have a reward. "*Fathers, don't provoke your children, lest they be discouraged.*" Look how again in this passage there is subjection and affection. And he didn't say "love your children," for that was superfluous. You see, nature herself is constrained, but what needed correction he corrected, that the affection in this case should be more intense, because the obedience also is greater. For nowhere is laid down an example of the relationship between husband and wife—no, what? Listen to the prophet saying, "*As a father pities his sons, the Lord pitied those who feared him*" [Ps 103:13].

τοὺς φοβουμένους αὐτόν." Καὶ πάλιν ὁ Χριστός φησι· "Τίς ἐστιν ἐξ ὑμῶν ἄνθρωπος, ὃν ἐὰν αἰτήσῃ ὁ υἱὸς ἄρτον, μὴ λίθον ἐπιδώσει αὐτῷ; καὶ ἐὰν ἰχθὺν αἰτήσῃ, μὴ ὄφιν ἐπιδώσει αὐτῷ; " "Οἱ πατέρες, μὴ ἐρεθίζετε τὰ τέκνα ὑμῶν, ἵνα μὴ ἀθυμῶσιν." Ὃ μάλιστα αὐτοὺς ᾔδει δυνατὸν δακεῖν, τοῦτο τέθεικε, καὶ φιλικώτερον εἶπεν ἐπιτάττων αὐτοῖς, καὶ οὐδαμοῦ τὸν θεὸν τίθησιν· ἐπέκλασε γὰρ τοὺς γονέας, καὶ κατέκαμ-[277]ψεν αὐτῶν τὰ σπλάγχνα. Τουτέστι, μὴ φιλονεικοτέρους αὐτοὺς ποιεῖτε· ἔστιν ὅπου καὶ συγχωρεῖν ὀφείλετε.

Εἶτα ἐπὶ τρίτην ἦλθεν ἀρχήν. Ἐνταῦθα ἔστι μέν τι καὶ φίλτρον, ἀλλ᾽ οὐκέτι φυσικόν, καθάπερ ἄνω, ἀλλὰ συνηθείας, καὶ ἀπ᾽ αὐτῆς τῆς ἀρχῆς, καὶ ἀπὸ τῶν ἔργων. Ἐπεὶ οὖν ἐνταῦθα τὸ μὲν τοῦ φίλτρου ὑποτέτμηται, τὸ δὲ τῆς ὑπακοῆς ἐπιτέταται, τούτῳ ἐνδιατρίβει, βουλόμενος, ὅπερ οἱ πρῶτοι ἔχουσιν ἀπὸ τῆς φύσεως, τοῦτο δοῦναι τούτοις ἀπὸ τῆς ὑπακοῆς. Ὥστε οὐχ ὑπὲρ τῶν δεσποτῶν τοῖς οἰκέταις μόνοις διαλέγεται, ἀλλὰ καὶ ὑπὲρ αὐτῶν, ἵνα ποθεινοὺς ἑαυτοὺς ἐργάζωνται τοῖς δεσπόταις. Ἀλλ᾽ οὐ τίθησι τοῦτο φανερῶς· ἢ γὰρ ἂν ὑπτίους αὐτοὺς ἐποίησεν. "Οἱ δοῦλοι, φησίν, ὑπακούετε κατὰ πάντα τοῖς κατὰ σάρκα κυρίοις."

Καὶ ὅρα πῶς ἀεὶ τὰ ὀνόματα τίθησι, γυναῖκες, τὰ τέκνα, οἱ δοῦλοι. Εὐθέως δικαίωμα τοῦ ὑπακούειν. Ἀλλ᾽ ἵνα μὴ ἀλγήσῃ, ἐπήγαγε, "τοῖς κατὰ σάρκα κυρίοις." Τὸ κρεῖττόν σου ἡ ψυχὴ ἠλευθέρωται, φησί· πρόσκαιρος ἡ δουλεία. Ἐκεῖνο τοίνυν ὑπόταξον, ἵνα μηκέτι ἀνάγκης ᾖ ἡ δουλεία. "Μὴ ἐν ὀφθαλμοδουλείαις, ὡς ἀνθρωπάρεσκοι." Ποίησον, φησί, τὴν ἀπὸ τοῦ νόμου δουλείαν ἀπὸ τοῦ φόβου γίνεσθαι τοῦ Χριστοῦ. Κἂν γὰρ μὴ ὁρῶντος ἐκείνου πράττῃς τὰ δέοντα καὶ τὰ πρὸς τιμὴν τοῦ δεσπότου, δῆλον ὅτι διὰ τὸν ἀκοίμητον ὀφθαλμὸν ποιεῖς. "Μὴ κατ᾽ ὀφθαλμοδουλείαν, φησίν, ὡς ἀνθρωπάρεσκοι." Ὥστε ὑμεῖς τὴν βλάβην ὑποστήσεσθε. Ἄκουε γὰρ τοῦ προφήτου λέγοντος· "Διεσκόρπισεν ὁ θεὸς ὀστᾶ ἀνθρωπαρέσκων." Ὅρα τοίνυν πῶς αὐτῶν φείδεται, καὶ αὐτοὺς ῥυθμίζει. "Ἀλλ᾽ ἐν ἁπλότητι, φησί, καρδίας, φοβούμενοι τὸν θεόν." Ἐκεῖνο γὰρ οὐχ ἁπλότης, ἀλλ᾽ ὑπόκρισις, ἕτερον ἔχειν καὶ ἕτερον ποιεῖν· ἄλλον μὲν παρόντος φαίνεσθαι τοῦ δεσπότου, ἄλλον δὲ ἀπόντος. Οὐκοῦν οὐχ ἁπλῶς εἶπεν, "ἐν ἁπλότητι καρδίας," ἀλλά, "φοβούμενοι τὸν θεόν." Τοῦτο γάρ ἐστι φοβεῖσθαι τὸν θεόν, ὅταν μηδενὸς ὁρῶντος, μηδὲν πράττωμεν πονηρόν· ἂν δὲ πράττωμεν, οὐχὶ τὸν θεόν, ἀλλὰ τοὺς ἀνθρώπους φοβούμεθα. Ὁρᾷς ὅτι ἐκείνους ῥυθμίζει;

"Πᾶν ὅτι ἂν ποιῆτε, [278] φησίν, ἐκ ψυχῆς ἐργάζεσθε, ὡς τῷ κυρίῳ, καὶ οὐκ ἀνθρώποις." Οὐ μόνον ὑποκρίσεως, ἀλλὰ καὶ ἀργίας αὐτοὺς ἀπηλλάχθαι βούλεται. Ἐλευθέρους αὐτοὺς ἐποίησεν ἀντὶ δούλων, ὅταν μὴ δέωνται τῆς

Again Christ says, "*What one of you, if your son asks for bread, will give him a stone? Or if he asks for a fish, will give him a serpent?* [Matt 7:9]. *Fathers, don't provoke your children, lest they be discouraged.*"

Paul set down what he knew had the greatest power to sting them, and while giving them orders he spoke more like a friend and nowhere mentions God, for he would overcome the parents and prostrate [277] their inner feelings. That means, "Don't make them more contentious; there are occasions when you should even give way." Then he comes to the third kind of authority. There is here also a certain affection, but not from nature, as above, but from habit, and from the authority itself and from the works done. Since, therefore, in this case, what pertains to affection is narrowed, while what pertains to obedience is extended, he discourses on this, wanting to give them from their obedience what the first ones have from nature. So that he discourses not only with the servants on behalf of their masters, but also on their own behalf, so that they may make themselves desirable to their masters. But he doesn't set this down openly, for he would have made them supine. "*Slaves,*" he says, "*obey in everything those who are your lords in the flesh.*"

And see how he always sets down the names: women, the children, the slaves. Immediately this is a just claim on their obedience. But so that you shouldn't be pained, he added, "*Your lords according to the flesh.*" He says, "Your better part, the soul, has been freed. Your service is temporary. Therefore, be subject to this, so that your service is no longer a restraint. *Not with eye-service, nor being sycophantic.*" "Make your service," he says, "that is from the law be from the fear of Christ. For if when your master isn't looking you do your duty and what is for his honor, it's clear that you're acting because of the sleepless eye." "*Not with eye-service,*" he says, "*as being sycophantic,*" as if "you will sustain the damage." For listen to the prophet saying, "*God has scattered the bones of the sycophants*" [Ps 54:5 LXX]. See then how Paul spares them and brings them to order. "*But in singleness of heart,*" he says, "*fearing God.*" For that is not singleness, but hypocrisy, to hold one thing and do another; to appear one person when the owner is present, but another when they are absent. Thus he didn't simply say "*in singleness of heart,*" but "*fearing God.*" For this is to fear God, when nobody is watching we do nothing evil, but if we do, we fear not God but human beings. Do you see how he brings them into order?

"*Whatever you do,*" [278] he says, "*work heartily, as for the Lord, and not for human beings.*" He wants to free them not only from hypocrisy but also from inertia. He made them free instead of slaves, when they didn't

τῶν δεσποτῶν ἐπιστασίας· τὸ γὰρ, "ἐκ ψυχῆς," τοῦτό ἐστι, τὸ μετ᾽ εὐνοίας, μὴ μετὰ δουλικῆς ἀνάγκης, ἀλλὰ μετ᾽ ἐλευθερίας καὶ προαιρέσεως. Καὶ τίς ὁ μισθός; "Εἰδότες, φησὶν, ὅτι ἀπὸ κυρίου λήψεσθε τὴν ἀνταπόδοσιν τῆς κληρονομίας ὑμῶν· τῷ γὰρ κυρίῳ Χριστῷ δουλεύετε." Καὶ γὰρ παρ᾽ αὐτοῦ δῆλον ὅτι λήψεσθε τὸν μισθόν. Καὶ ὅτι τῷ κυρίῳ δουλεύετε, δῆλον ἐκ τούτου. "Ὁ δὲ ἀδικῶν, φησὶ, κομίσεται ὃ ἠδίκησεν."

Ἐνταῦθα βεβαιοῖ τὸν πρότερον λόγον. Ἵνα γὰρ μὴ δόξῃ κολακείας εἶναι τὰ ῥήματα, λήψεται, φησὶν, ὃ ἠδίκησε· τουτέστι, καὶ τιμωρίαν δίδωσιν· "Οὐ γὰρ ἔστι προσωποληψία παρὰ τῷ Θεῷ." Τί γὰρ, εἰ δοῦλος εἶ; οὐκ αἰσχύνη. Καὶ μὴν τοῦτο πρὸς τοὺς δεσπότας ἔδει εἰπεῖν, ὥσπερ καὶ ἐν τῇ πρὸς Ἐφεσίους. Ἀλλ᾽ ἐνταῦθά μοι δοκεῖ τοὺς Ἕλληνας αἰνίττεσθαι δεσπότας. Τί γὰρ, εἰ ἐκεῖνος μὲν Ἕλλην, σὺ δὲ Χριστιανός; Οὐ τὰ πρόσωπα, ἀλλὰ τὰ πράγματα ἐξετάζεται· ὥστε καὶ οὕτω μετ᾽ εὐνοίας, καὶ ἐκ ψυχῆς δεῖ δουλεύειν. "Οἱ κύριοι, τὸ δίκαιον καὶ τὴν ἰσότητα τοῖς δούλοις παρέχεσθε."

Τί δέ ἐστι τὸ δίκαιον; τί δέ ἐστιν ἰσότης; Πάντων ἐν ἀφθονίᾳ καθιστᾶν, καὶ μὴ ἐᾶν ἑτέρων δεῖσθαι, ἀλλὰ ἀμείβεσθαι αὐτοὺς τῶν πόνων. Μὴ γὰρ, ἐπειδὴ εἶπον, ὅτι παρὰ θεοῦ ἔχουσι τὸν μισθὸν, διὰ τοῦτο σὺ ἀποστερήσῃς. Ἑτέρωθι δέ φησιν, "Ἀνιέντες τὴν ἀπειλὴν," ἡμερωτέρους ἐργάσασθαι βουλόμενος· τέλειοι γὰρ ἦσαν ἐκεῖνοι. Τουτέστιν, "Ἐν ᾧ μέτρῳ μετρεῖτε, ἀντιμετρηθήσεται ὑμῖν." Καὶ τὸ, "οὐκ ἔστι προσωποληψία," πρὸς τούτους εἴρηται· κεῖται δὲ ἐπ᾽ ἐκείνων, ἵνα οὗτοι δέξωνται. Ὅταν γὰρ ἑτέρῳ ἁρμόζον πρὸς ἕτερον εἴπωμεν, οὐκ ἐκεῖνον τοσοῦτον, ὅσον τὸν ὑπεύθυνον κατωρθώσαμεν. Καὶ ὑμεῖς μετ᾽ ἐκείνων, φησίν. Ἐνταῦθα κοινὴν ἐποίησε τὴν δουλείαν· "Εἰδότες γὰρ, φησὶν, ὅτι καὶ ὑμεῖς ἔχετε κύριον ἐν οὐρανοῖς.

[279] Τῇ προσευχῇ προσκαρτερεῖτε, γρηγοροῦντες ἐν αὐτῇ ἐν εὐχαριστίᾳ." Ἐπειδὴ γὰρ τὸ καρτερεῖν ἐν ταῖς εὐχαῖς ῥαθυμεῖν πολλάκις ποιεῖ, διὰ

need the oversight of their master. You see, the expression *heartily* means this: with goodwill, not with servile necessity, but with freedom and choice. And what's the reward? *"Knowing,"* he says, *"that from the Lord you will receive your inheritance, for you serve Christ the Lord."* Surely it's clear that you'll receive the reward from him. And that you serve the Lord is clear from this. *"But the one who has done wrong,"* Paul says, *"will be paid back for their wrongdoing."*

In this passage he confirms his previous statement. You see, in order for his words not to appear those of flattery, he says, *"will be paid back for their wrongdoing,"* that is, and will receive punishment also, for *there is no partiality with God.* So what if you're a slave?[114] Don't be ashamed. And indeed, he should have said this to the masters, as he did in the Letter to the Ephesians. But in this passage he seems to me to be hinting at Hellene masters. "So what if that fellow is a Hellene and you're a Christian? It isn't the persons but the actions that are examined, so that even in this case you should serve with goodwill and heartily." *Lords, give your slaves what is just and equal.*

What's justice? What's equality? To put them in abundance of everything and not allow them to stand in need of others, but to recompense them for their labors. "For because I've said that they'll receive their reward from God, don't deprive them on that account." Elsewhere he says, *"forbearing threatening"* [Eph 6:9], wanting to make them gentler, for they were perfect people. This means, *"With what measure you measure, it will be measured back to you"* [Matt 7:2]. And the expression *"there is no partiality"* is spoken to those people,[115] but underlying it it's about the others, so that they may receive them. For when we've said to one person what is applicable to another, we haven't corrected them so much as the one who is responsible. "You too, along with them," Paul says. In this passage he has made the servitude common, saying, *"For you know that you also have a lord in heaven."*

[279] *Continue steadfastly in prayer, being watchful in it in thanksgiving:* that means sober, not roaming around. For the devil knows, he knows what

---

114. This apostrophe of a slave could be a rhetorical ploy, but equally it could address slaves in the congregation, because we know that they usually accompanied their owners to church (see Mayer and Allen, *John Chrysostom*, 35). De Wet also draws attention to Chrysostom's *Hom. Eph.* 22 (Field 4:336–37), where the preacher complains that churchgoers often neglect to bring their slaves to church, meaning that he expected them to be present (*Preaching Bondage*, 9 n. 21).

115. That is, the masters.

τοῦτό φησι· "γρηγοροῦντες," τουτέστι, νήφοντες, μὴ ῥεμβόμενοι. Οἶδε γὰρ, οἶδεν ὁ διάβολος ὅσον ἀγαθὸν εὐχή· διὸ βαρὺς ἔγκειται. Οἶδε δὲ καὶ Παῦλος πῶς ἀκηδιῶσι πολλοὶ εὐχόμενοι· διό φησι, "προσκαρτερεῖτε τῇ προσευχῇ," ὡς περί τινος ἐπιπόνου. "Γρηγοροῦντες ἐν αὐτῇ ἐν εὐχαριστίᾳ." Τοῦτο γὰρ, φησὶν, ἔργον ὑμῶν ἔστω, ἐν ταῖς εὐχαῖς εὐχαριστεῖν, καὶ ὑπὲρ τῶν φανερῶν καὶ ὑπὲρ τῶν ἀφανῶν, καὶ ὑπὲρ ὧν ἑκόντας καὶ ὑπὲρ ὧν ἄκοντας ἐποίησεν εὖ, καὶ ὑπὲρ βασιλείας καὶ ὑπὲρ γεέννης, καὶ ὑπὲρ θλίψεως καὶ ὑπὲρ ἀνέσεως. Οὕτω γὰρ ἔθος τοῖς ἁγίοις εὔχεσθαι, καὶ ὑπὲρ τῶν κοινῶν εὐεργεσιῶν εὐχαριστεῖν.

Οἶδα ἐγώ τινα ἅγιον ἄνδρα οὕτως εὐχόμενον. Οὐδὲν πρὸ τούτου τοῦ ῥήματος ἔλεγεν, ἀλλ᾽ ὅτι, Εὐχαριστοῦμεν ὑπὲρ πασῶν τῶν εὐεργεσιῶν σου τῶν ἐκ πρώτης ἡμέρας μέχρι τῆς παρούσης εἰς ἡμᾶς τοὺς ἀναξίους γενομένων· ὑπὲρ ὧν ἴσμεν καὶ οὐκ ἴσμεν, ὑπὲρ τῶν φανερῶν, ὑπὲρ τῶν ἀφανῶν, τῶν ἐν ἔργῳ γενομένων, τῶν ἐν λόγῳ, τῶν ἑκοντί, τῶν ἀκοντί, πασῶν τῶν εἰς τοὺς ἀναξίους ἡμᾶς γεγενημένων· ὑπὲρ θλίψεων, ὑπὲρ ἀνέσεων, ὑπὲρ τῆς γεέννης, ὑπὲρ τῆς κολάσεως, ὑπὲρ βασιλείας τῶν οὐρανῶν. Παρακαλοῦμεν φυλάξαι σε τὴν ψυχὴν ἡμῶν ἁγίαν, καθαρὰν συνείδησιν ἔχουσαν, τέλος ἄξιον τῆς φιλανθρωπίας σου. Ὁ ἀγαπήσας ἡμᾶς ὥστε τὸν μονογενῆ σου δοῦναι ὑπὲρ ἡμῶν, καταξίωσον ἀξίους γενέσθαι τῆς σῆς ἀγάπης· δὸς ἐν τῷ λόγῳ σου σοφίαν, καὶ ἐν τῷ φόβῳ σου. Μονογενὲς Χριστέ, ἔμπνευσον ἰσχὺν τὴν παρὰ σοῦ. Ὁ τὸν μονογενῆ δοὺς ὑπὲρ ἡμῶν, καὶ τὸ πνεῦμά σου τὸ ἅγιον ἐξαποστείλας εἰς ἄφεσιν τῶν ἡμετέρων ἁμαρτιῶν, εἴ τι ἑκόντες ἢ ἄκοντες ἡμάρτομεν, συγχώρησον, καὶ μὴ λογίσῃ. Μνήσθητι πάντων τῶν ἐπικαλουμένων τὸ ὄνομά σου ἐν ἀληθείᾳ· μνήσθητι πάντων τῶν εὖ καὶ τἀναντία ἡμῖν θελόντων· πάντες γὰρ ἄνθρωποί ἐσμεν. Εἶτα ἐπιθεὶς τὴν εὐχὴν τῶν πιστῶν, ἐνταῦθα ἐπαύετο, ὡς κορωνίδα τινὰ καὶ σύνδεσμον ὑπὲρ πάντων τὴν εὐχὴν ποιησάμενος. Πολλὰ γὰρ ἡμᾶς ὁ θεὸς καὶ ἄκοντας εὖ ποιεῖ· πολλὰ γὰρ καὶ οὐκ εἰδότας, [280] καὶ πλείονα. Ὅταν γὰρ τἀναντία εὐχώμεθα, αὐτὸς δὲ τἀναντία ποιῇ, δῆλον ὅτι καὶ οὐκ εἰδότας εὖ ποιεῖ. "Προσευχόμενοι ἅμα καὶ περὶ ἡμῶν."

Ὅρα τὴν ταπεινοφροσύνην· μετ᾽ ἐκείνους ἑαυτὸν τίθησιν. "Ἵνα ὁ θεὸς ἀνοίξῃ ἡμῖν θύραν τοῦ λόγου, λαλῆσαι τὸ μυστήριον τοῦ Χριστοῦ." Εἴσοδόν φησι καὶ παρρησίαν. Βαβαί, ὁ ἀθλητὴς ὁ τοσοῦτος οὐκ εἶπεν, ἵνα ἀπαλλαγῶ τῶν δεσμῶν, ἀλλὰ δέσμιος ὢν ἑτέρους παρεκάλει, καὶ παρεκάλει ἐπὶ

a great good prayer is, so he presses heavily. And Paul also knew how many are heedless when in prayer, so he says, "*Continue steadfastly in prayer,*" as if it were something laborious. *Being watchful in it in thanksgiving.* "For let this be your work," he says, to give thanks in your prayers both for the visible and the invisible, and for his benefits to the willing and the unwilling, and for the kingdom and for Gehenna, and for tribulation and for relief. For it's the custom of the saint to pray in this way and to give thanks for the common benefits.

I know a certain holy man who prays in this way.[116] He said nothing before this prayer[117] but, "We give you thanks for all your benefits toward us the unworthy from the first day until the present, for what we know and what we don't, for the visible, for the invisible, for those in deed, those in word, those with our will, those against our will, for all that has come to us in our unworthiness; for tribulations, for relief, for Gehenna, for punishment, for the kingdom of heaven. We beg you to keep our soul holy, having a pure conscience, an end worthy of your loving-kindness. You who loved us so that you gave your only-begotten Son for our sake, grant us to become worthy of your love; give us wisdom in your word and in fear of you. Only-begotten Christ, inspire the strength that comes from you. You who gave the only-begotten for our sakes and sent your Holy Spirit for the remission of our sins, if we have sinned in any way, willingly or unwillingly, pardon us and don't hold to account. Remember that all call on your name in truth; remember all those who wish us well, and the contrary, for we're all human beings." Then, adding the prayer of the faithful,[118] he stopped at that point, as a certain completion and making the prayer a binding together of all. For God bestows many benefits even against our will; many [280] even greater also without our knowledge. For when we pray for one thing and he does the opposite, it's clear that he benefits us even without our knowledge. *Praying at the same time for us too.*

See his humility—he places himself after them. *So that God may open the door of the word to us, to speak of the mystery of Christ.* He means an entrance and frankness of speech. Wonderful! An athlete of such stature didn't say, "that I may be freed from my chains," but being in chains he exhorted others, and exhorted them for a great matter, so that he might

---

116. This is evidence of Chrysostom's well-known monastic connections, on which see Illert, *Johannes Chrysostomus und das antiochenisch-syrische Mönchtum.*

117. Lit. "this word."

118. This is the Our Father.

πράγματι μεγάλῳ, ἵνα παρρησίαν λάβῃ. Τὰ δύο μεγάλα, καὶ ἡ ποιότης τοῦ προσώπου, καὶ ἡ τοῦ πράγματος. Βαβαί, ὅσον τὸ ἀξίωμα. "Τὸ μυστήριον, φησὶ, τοῦ Χριστοῦ." Δείκνυσιν ὅτι οὐδὲν αὐτῷ τούτου ποθεινότερον, τοῦ λαλῆσαι. "Δι' ὃ καὶ δέδεμαι, ἵνα φανερώσω αὐτὸ, ὡς δεῖ με λαλῆσαι." Μετὰ πολλῆς, φησὶ, τῆς παρρησίας, καὶ μηδὲν ὑποστειλάμενον. Τὰ δεσμὰ φανεροῖ αὐτὸν, οὐ συσκιάζει. Μετὰ πολλῆς, φησὶ, τῆς παρρησίας. Εἰπέ μοι, σὺ δέδεσαι, καὶ ἄλλους παρακαλεῖς; Ναί· μείζονά μοι παρρησίαν δίδωσι τὰ δεσμά· ἀλλὰ δέομαι τῆς τοῦ θεοῦ ῥοπῆς· ἤκουσα γὰρ τοῦ Χριστοῦ λέγοντος· "Ὅταν παραδιδῶσιν ὑμᾶς, μὴ μεριμνήσετε πῶς ἢ τί λαλήσητε." Καὶ ὅρα πῶς μεταφορικῶς εἶπεν· "Ἵνα ὁ θεὸς ἀνοίξῃ ἡμῖν θύραν τοῦ λόγου." Ὅρα πῶς ἄτυφός ἐστιν· ἐν τοῖς δεσμοῖς ὢν πῶς φθέγγεται. Τουτέστιν, ἵνα μαλάξῃ τὰς καρδίας αὐτῶν. Ἀλλ' οὐκ εἶπεν οὕτως, ἀλλ' ἵνα ἡμῖν παρρησίαν δῷ, ταπεινοφρονῶν οὕτως εἴρηκε, καὶ τοῦτο ὅπερ εἶχεν, ἀξιοῖ λαβεῖν. Δείκνυσιν ἐν ταύτῃ τῇ ἐπιστολῇ διὰ τί τότε οὐκ ἦλθεν ὁ Χριστός, τῷ σκιὰν ἐκεῖνα καλέσαι· "Τὸ δὲ σῶμα, φησὶ, Χριστοῦ." Ὥστε ἔδει ἐν τῇ σκιᾷ ἐθισθῆναι. Ἅμα καὶ τῆς ἀγάπης τῆς εἰς αὐτοὺς τεκμήριον ἐμφαίνει μέγιστον· ἵνα ὑμεῖς, φησὶν, ἀκούσητε, ἐγὼ δέδεμαι.

Πάλιν τὸν δεσμὸν εἰς μέσον τίθησιν, οὗ σφόδρα ἐρῶ, ὃς [281] διανίστησί μου τὴν καρδίαν, καὶ ἀεὶ εἰς ἐπιθυμίαν ἄγει τοῦ τὸν Παῦλον δεδεμένον ἰδεῖν, καὶ ἐν δεσμοῖς γράφοντα, καὶ κηρύττοντα, καὶ βαπτίζοντα, καὶ κατηχοῦντα. Ὑπὲρ τῶν ἐκκλησιῶν τῶν ἁπανταχοῦ ἀνεφέρετο αὐτῷ δεδεμένῳ· μυρία ᾠκοδόμει δεδεμένος· τότε εὔλυτος μᾶλλον ἦν. Ἄκουε γὰρ αὐτοῦ λέγοντος· "Ὥστε τοὺς πλείονας τῶν ἀδελφῶν πεποιθότας τοῖς δεσμοῖς μου περισσοτέρως τολμᾶν ἀφόβως τὸν λόγον λαλεῖν." Καὶ αὐτὸς δὲ πάλιν τοῦτο ὁμολογεῖ λέγων· "Ὅταν γὰρ ἀσθενῶ, τότε δυνατός εἰμι." Διὰ τοῦτο καὶ ἔλεγεν· "Ἀλλ' ὁ λόγος τοῦ θεοῦ οὐ δέδεται." Ἐδεσμεῖτο μετὰ κακούργων, μετὰ τῶν δεσμωτῶν, μετὰ ἀνδροφόνων· ὁ τῆς οἰκουμένης διδάσκαλος, ὁ εἰς τρίτον ἀνελθὼν οὐρανὸν, ὁ τὰ ἄρρητα ῥήματα ἀκούσας, ἐδέδετο. Ἀλλὰ τότε ταχύτερος ὁ δρόμος ἦν. Ὁ δεθεὶς ἐλέλυτο, καὶ ὁ μὴ δεδεμένος ἐδέδετο. Οὗτος μὲν γὰρ ὅπερ ἤθελεν, ἔπραττεν· ἐκεῖνος δὲ αὐτὸν οὐκ ἐκώλυεν, οὐδὲ τὴν ἰδίαν ἐπλήρου πρόθεσιν.

Τί ποιεῖς, ὦ ἀνόητε; μὴ γὰρ σωματικός ἐστι δρομεύς; μὴ γὰρ ἐν σταδίῳ τῷ παρ' ἡμῖν ἀγωνίζεται; Ἐν οὐρανῷ πολιτεύεται· τὸν ἐν οὐρανῷ τρέχοντα δῆσαι τὰ ἐπὶ γῆς οὐ δύναται, οὐδὲ κατασχεῖν. Οὐχ ὁρᾷς τουτονὶ τὸν ἥλιον; περίβαλε δεσμὰ ταῖς ἀκτῖσι, στῆσον τοῦ δρόμου· ἀλλ' οὐ δυνήσῃ. Οὐκοῦν

gain frankness of speech. Both the two are great, both the quality of the person and of the matter. Wonderful! How great is the dignity! *"The mystery,"* he says, *"of Christ."* He demonstrates that nothing was more desirable to him than this, namely, to speak. *For which I am also in chains, so that I may make it clear, as I ought to speak.* He means with great freedom of speech and holding back nothing. His chains display, not obscure, him. With much freedom of speech, he means. "Tell me, are you in chains and exhorting others?" "Yes, the chains give me greater freedom of speech; but I beg God's influence, for I've heard the voice of Christ saying: *'When they deliver you up, don't be anxious how you are to speak'"* [Matt 10:19]. And see how he's expressed himself metaphorically: *"So that God may open the door of the word to us"* (see how unassuming he is; how he speaks while in his chains). This means, in order to soften their hearts. But he didn't speak like this, but "so that I may give you frankness of speech"; he spoke this way out of humility, and what he had, he asks to receive. He demonstrates in this letter why Christ didn't come at that time, calling those former things shadows. *"But the body,"* he says, *"is Christ's."* So it was necessary for them to get used to the shadow. At the same time he also exhibits the greatest proof of the love he bears them: "In order that you may hear," he says, "that *I am in chains."*

Again he sets the chains in public view, which I so greatly love, which [281] rouses my heart, and draws me to long to see Paul in chains, and writing in his chains, and preaching, and baptizing, and catechizing. While he was in his chains, he was referred by the churches everywhere; in chains he built up in myriad ways: at that time he was rather unimpeded. For listen to him saying, *"So that most of the brethren have been made confident because of my chains, to dare more boldly to speak the word without fear"* [Phil 1:14]. And again he makes this same avowal himself, saying, *"When I am weak, then I am strong"* [2 Cor 12:10]. This is why he also said, *"But the word of God is not bound"* [2 Tim 2:9]. He was bound by villainous people, by prisoners, by murderers, he the teacher of the world, he who had ascended to the third heaven [see 2 Cor 12:2], had *heard things that cannot be told* [2 Cor 12:4], was bound. But then his race was swifter. The one who was bound was released, and the one who was unbound was bound. For indeed Paul did what he wanted, while the other didn't prevent him, nor fulfill his own purpose.

What are you doing, you senseless one? Surely Paul wasn't a runner in the flesh? Surely he wasn't competing in our stadium? His *way of life is in heaven* [Phil 3:20]; the one who runs in heaven, things on earth can't

οὐδὲ Παῦλον· καὶ πολλῷ μᾶλλον τούτῳ, ἢ ἐκείνῳ· πλείονος γὰρ οὗτος, ἢ ἐκεῖνος ἀπήλαυσε προνοίας, ἅτε φῶς φέρων οὐ τοιοῦτον ἡμῖν, ἀλλὰ τὸ ἀληθινὸν βαστάζων.

Ποῦ νῦν εἰσιν οἱ μηδὲν βουλόμενοι διὰ τὸν Χριστὸν πάσχειν; τί δὲ λέγω πάσχειν, ὅπου γε οὐδὲ χρήματα βούλονται προέσθαι; Ἐδέσμει καὶ Παῦλός ποτε, καὶ ἐνέβαλλεν εἰς δεσμωτήριον· ἀλλ' ἐπειδὴ τοῦ Χριστοῦ γέγονε δοῦλος, οὐ τῷ ποιεῖν λοιπόν, ἀλλὰ τῷ πάσχειν σεμνύνεται. Καὶ τοῦτο δὲ τοῦ κηρύγματος θαῦμα, ὅταν διὰ τῶν πασχόντων αὐτῶν, ἀλλ' οὐ τῶν ποιούντων κακῶς, οὕτως ἐγείρηται καὶ αὔξηται. Ποῦ τις εἶδεν ἀγῶνας τοιούτους; ὁ πάσχων κακῶς, νικᾷ· καὶ ὁ ποιῶν κακῶς, ἡττᾶται· οὗτος ἐκείνου λαμπρότερος. Διὰ δεσμῶν τὸ κήρυγμα εἰσῆλθεν. Οὐκ αἰσχύνομαι, ἀλλὰ καὶ σεμνύνομαι, καὶ τὸν ἐσταυρωμένον κηρύττων, φησίν. Ἐννόησον γάρ μοι· ἡ [282] οἰκουμένη πᾶσα τοὺς λελυμένους ἀφεῖσα, τοῖς δεδεμένοις προσῄει· τοὺς δεσμοῦντας ἀποστρεφομένη, τοὺς τὴν ἄλυσιν περικειμένους τιμᾷ· τοὺς σταυρώσαντας μισήσασα, τὸν ἐσταυρωμένον προσκυνεῖ.

Οὐκ ἔστι μόνον θαυμαστόν, ὅτι ἁλιεῖς, ὅτι ἰδιῶται ἦσαν οἱ κήρυκες, ἀλλ' ὅτι καὶ ἕτερα κωλύματα, φύσει κωλύματα ἦσαν, καὶ πλείων γέγονεν ἡ ἐπίδοσις. Οὐ μόνον οὐδὲν ἐκώλυσεν ἡ ἰδιωτεία, ἀλλὰ καὶ αὐτὸ τοῦτο φανερωθῆναι ἐποίησε τὸ κήρυγμα. Ἄκουε γὰρ τοῦ Λουκᾶ λέγοντος· "Καὶ καταλαβόμενοι, φησίν, ὅτι ἄνθρωποι ἀγράμματοί εἰσι καὶ ἰδιῶται, ἐθαύμαζον." Οὐ μόνον οὐδὲν ἐκώλυεν ὁ δεσμός, ἀλλὰ καὶ αὐτὸ τοῦτο ἐποίησεν αὐτοὺς θαρσαλεωτέρους. Οὐχ οὕτως ἐθάρρουν οἱ μαθηταὶ, λελυμένου τοῦ Παύλου, ὡς δεδεμένου· "Περισσοτέρως γὰρ, φησὶ, τολμᾶν ἀφόβως τὸν λόγον τοῦ θεοῦ λαλεῖν." Ποῦ οἱ ἀντεροῦντες, ὅτι οὐ θεῖον τὸ κήρυγμα; Ἡ ἰδιωτεία οὐκ ἦν ἱκανὴ ποιῆσαι καταγνωσθῆναι αὐτούς; οὐκοῦν ἔδει κἀνταῦθα φοβῆσαι αὐτούς; Ἴστε γὰρ ὅτι δύο πάθεσι τούτοις τὸ πλῆθος κατέχεται, κενοδοξίᾳ καὶ δειλίᾳ. Ἡ ἰδιωτεία οὐκ ἠφίει ἐπαισχύνεσθαι; οἱ κίνδυνοι εἰς δειλίαν ἐμβαλεῖν ὤφειλον.

bind or hold. Don't you see this sun?[119] Put bonds around its beams, stay its course—no, you can't. Then you can't do it with Paul either. And much more this one than that, for Paul enjoyed more of providence than the other, inasmuch as he brings us not light of this kind but bears the true light.

Where now are those who don't want to suffer anything for Christ's sake? But why do I say "suffer," when they don't even want to give up their wealth? In the past Paul both bound and cast into prison, but since he became a slave of Christ he glories no more in doing but in suffering. And this is the wonder of the proclamation, when it is thus raised up and increased through the sufferers themselves, but not by the wrongdoers. Where has anybody seen such contests as this? The one who suffers evils conquers, and the one who does evil comes off worse. The former is brighter than the other. Through bonds the proclamation entered. "*I am not ashamed*" [Rom 1:16], he says—"no, I even glory, and preach the crucified one" [see 1 Cor 1:23]. Please consider: the [282] whole world left those who were freed and went over to those who were bound; turning away from the imprisoners, it honors those with chains around them; hating the crucifers, it worships the crucified one.

Not the only marvel is that the preachers were fishermen and ignorant, but that there were other hindrances too, which were hindrances by nature, and the increase was more abundant. Not only was their ignorance no hindrance, but even it itself caused the proclamation to be made plain. For listen to Luke saying: "*And perceiving*," it says, "*that they were uneducated and ignorant, they marveled*" [Acts 4:13]. Not only were the bonds no hindrance at all, but this very thing made them even more confident. The disciples were not as confident when Paul was free as when he was bound. "For," he says, "*they are much bolder to speak the word of God without fear*" [Phil 2:14]. Where are those who deny that the proclamation was not divine? Wasn't their ignorance enough to ensure that they were condemned? Surely in this case too it would suffice to frighten them. For you know that by these two passions many are possessed, namely, vainglory and cowardice. If their ignorance didn't permit them to be ashamed? The dangers were liable to throw them into fear.

---

119. On the comparisons between the sun and Paul in Chrysostom, see Mitchell, *Heavenly Trumpet*, 81.

Ἀλλὰ θαύματα, φησὶν, ἐποίουν. Πιστεύετε οὖν ὅτι ἐποίουν θαύματα. Ἀλλ' οὐκ ἐποίουν; Τοῦτο μεῖζον θαῦμα τοῦ ποιεῖν, εἰ χωρὶς θαυμάτων προσήγοντο. Ἐδέθη καὶ Σωκράτης παρ' Ἕλλησι· τί οὖν; οὐκ εὐθέως ἔφυγον εἰς Μέγαρα οἱ μαθηταί; Πάνυ γε, οὐ γάρ; τοὺς περὶ ἀθανασίας ἐδέξαντο λόγους. Ἀλλ' ὅρα ἐνταῦθα· ἐδέθη Παῦλος, καὶ μᾶλλον ἐθάρρουν οἱ μαθηταί· εἰκότως· ἑώρων γὰρ οὐκ ἐμποδιζόμενον τὸ κήρυγμα. Μὴ γὰρ γλῶτταν δύνασαι δῆσαι; ταύτῃ μάλιστα τρέχει. Ὥσπερ γὰρ δρομέως ἂν μὴ δήσῃς τοὺς πόδας, οὐκ ἐκώλυσας τοῦ δρόμου· οὕτω καὶ εὐαγγελιστοῦ ἐὰν μὴ δήσῃς τὴν γλῶτταν, οὐκ ἐκώλυσας τοῦ δρόμου. Καὶ ὥσπερ ἐκεῖνος, ἐὰν δήσῃς τὴν ὀσφὺν, μᾶλλον τρέχει καὶ διαβαστάζεται, οὕτω καὶ οὗτος μᾶλλον κηρύττει, καὶ μετὰ πλείονος τῆς παρρησίας.

Δειλιᾷ ὁ δέσμιος, ὅταν δεσμὸς ᾖ μόνον· ὁ δὲ τοῦ θανάτου καταφρονῶν, πῶς ἂν ἐδέθη; Ταυτὸν ἐποίουν, οἷον ἂν [283] εἰ τὴν σκιὰν ἐδέσμουν Παύλου, καὶ τὸ στόμα αὐτῆς ἐνέφραττον. Σκιομαχία γὰρ ἦν· τοῖς τε γὰρ οἰκείοις ποθεινότερος μᾶλλον ἦν, τοῖς τε ἐχθροῖς αἰδεσιμώτερος, ἅτε ἀνδρείας φέρων ἔπαθον τὸν δεσμόν. Καὶ στέφανος δεσμεῖ κεφαλήν, ἀλλ' οὐκ αἰσχύνει, ἀλλὰ καὶ λαμπὰν ποιεῖ. Ἄκοντες ἐστεφάνουν αὐτὸν τῇ ἁλύσει. Εἰπὲ γάρ μοι, σίδηρον εἶχε δεῖσαι ὁ τῶν ἀδαμαντίνων τοῦ θανάτου κατατολμῶν πυλῶν;

Ἔλθωμεν εἰς ζῆλον, ἀγαπητοὶ, τῶν δεσμῶν τούτων. Ὅσαι γυναῖκες χρυσία περίκεισθε, τὰ Παύλου δεσμὰ ποθήσατε. Οὐχ οὕτως ὑμῖν περὶ τὸν τράχηλον τὸ περιδέρραιον ἀπολάμπει, ὡς ἐκείνου περὶ τὴν ψυχὴν ὁ τῶν σιδηρῶν δεσμῶν ἔστιλβε κόσμος. Εἴ τις ἐκεῖνα ποθεῖ, ταῦτα μισείτω. Τίς γὰρ κοινωνία βλακείᾳ πρὸς ἀνδρείαν; καλλωπισμῷ σωματικῷ πρὸς φιλοσοφίαν; Ἐκεῖνα τὰ δεσμὰ ἄγγελοι αἰδοῦνται, τούτων καὶ καταπαίζουσιν· ἐκεῖνα τὰ δεσμὰ πρὸς τὸν οὐρανὸν ἀπὸ τῆς γῆς ἕλκειν εἴωθε, ταῦτα τὰ δεσμὰ ἀπὸ τοῦ οὐρανοῦ κατάγει. Ὄντως γὰρ ταῦτα δεσμὰ, οὐκ ἐκεῖνα· ἐκεῖνα κόσμος, ταῦτα δεσμά· ταῦτα μετὰ τοῦ σώματος καὶ τὴν ψυχὴν θλίβει, ἐκεῖνα μετὰ τοῦ σώματος καὶ τὴν ψυχὴν κοσμεῖ.

Βούλει μαθεῖν ὅτι ἐκεῖνα κόσμος ἐστίν; Εἰπέ μοι, τίς μᾶλλον ἐπεσπάσατο τοὺς ὁρῶντας, σὺ, ἢ Παῦλος; Καὶ τί λέγω, σύ; αὐτὴ ἡ βασιλὶς ἡ πάντα χρυσὸν περικειμένη, οὐκ ἂν μᾶλλον ἐπεσπάσατο τοὺς ὁρῶντας· ἀλλ' εἰ συνέβη καὶ Παῦλον κατὰ τὸν αὐτὸν καιρὸν δεδεμένον, καὶ τὴν βασιλίδα εἰς τὴν ἐκκλησίαν εἰσελθεῖν, πάντες ἂν ἀπ' ἐκείνης ἐπὶ τοῦτον μετήγαγον τοὺς ὀφθαλμούς·

"But," he says, "they performed miracles." So you believe that they performed miracles. But didn't they? This is a greater miracle than performing them if people were drawn to them without miracles. Socrates too among the Hellenes was bound. So what? Didn't his disciples flee immediately to Megara? Yes, of course—they didn't accept his teachings about immortality.[120] But see this passage: Paul was bound and his disciples became more confident, with reason, for they saw that the proclamation was not impeded. Surely you can't put the tongue in bonds? With it especially he runs. You see, just as if you haven't bound the feet of a runner, so too, if you haven't bound the tongue of an evangelist, you won't hinder his running. And as the former, if you've bound his loins, runs on and is sustained, so too the latter proclaims the more, and with greater frankness of speech.

The prisoner is in fear when there are only chains, but how can the one who despises death be chained? They did as if [**283**] they had chained Paul's shadow and had gagged its mouth. For it was fighting with shadows: you see, he was both more desired by his friends and more revered by his enemies, inasmuch as he bore the prize for courage in his chains. A crown binds the head, but doesn't disgrace it—no, it makes it indeed brilliant. Against their will they bound him with his chain. Tell me, was it possible for the one who braved the adamantine gates of death to fear a sword?

Let's go on, beloved, to emulate these chains. All you women who adorn yourselves with gold, long for the chains of Paul. The collar around your necks is not as resplendent as the iron chain, the adornment around his soul, glistened. If somebody wants these things, let them despise them. For what does softness have in common with courage? Bodily finery with philosophy? Those chains the angels revere, these they even mock; those chains are accustomed to draw up to heaven from the earth, those chains lead from heaven to earth. For truly those are chains, not these; these are an adornment, those are chains; those afflict the body together with the soul, these also adorn the soul together with the body.

Do you want to know that those are an ornament? Tell me, who would have attracted the spectators more, you or Paul? And why do I say "you"? The empress herself, who is all bedecked with gold, wouldn't have attracted spectators more. But if had happened that both Paul in his chains and the empress had entered the church at the same time, all would have shifted

---

120. Socrates was convicted of impiety and died in 399, and in the following year his disciples, including Plato, fled to Megara (see Diogenes Laertius, *Vit. phil.* 3.6).

καὶ εἰκότως. Τὸ γὰρ ὁρᾶν ἄνδρα τῆς φύσεως τῆς ἀνθρωπίνης μείζονα, καὶ οὐδὲν ἔχοντα ἀνθρώπινον, ἀλλ᾽ ἄγγελον ἐπὶ γῆς, θαυμασιώτερον τοῦ ὁρᾶν γυναῖκα κεκαλλωπισμένην. Ταῦτα μὲν γὰρ καὶ ἐν θεάτροις, καὶ ἐν πομπαῖς, καὶ ἐν βαλανείοις, καὶ πολλαχοῦ ἔστιν ἰδεῖν· ἄνθρωπον δὲ δεσμὰ περικείμενον, καὶ νομίζοντα τὸν μέγιστον κόσμον ἔχειν, καὶ οὐκ εἴκοντα τοῖς δεσμοῖς, οὐκ ἔστι γῆς θέαμα ἰδεῖν τὸν ὁρῶντα, ἀλλ᾽ οὐρανῶν ἄξιον τὸ θέαμα. Ἡ ταῦτα περικειμένη ψυχὴ περισκοπεῖ, τίς εἶδε, τίς οὐκ εἶδε, τύφου πεπλήρωται, [284] φροντίσι κατέχεται, μυρίοις ἑτέροις δέδεται πάθεσιν· ὁ δὲ ἐκεῖνα περικείμενος, ἄτυφος· ἡ ψυχὴ γαυροῦται, πάσης ἀπήλλακται φροντίδος, γεγηθυῖα, πρὸς τὸν οὐρανὸν βλέπουσα, ἐπτερωμένη. Εἴ τίς μοι Παῦλον ἐδίδου ἀπὸ τοῦ οὐρανοῦ διακύπτοντα ἰδεῖν καὶ φωνὴν ἀφιέντα, ἢ ἐκ τοῦ δεσμωτηρίου, ἐκ τοῦ δεσμωτηρίου ἂν εἱλόμην· οἱ γὰρ ἐκ τοῦ οὐρανοῦ πρὸς αὐτὸν ἔρχονται, ὅταν εἰς τὸ δεσμωτήριον ᾖ. Ὁ σύνδεσμος τοῦ κηρύγματος τὰ δεσμὰ Παύλου, ὁ θεμέλιος ἡ ἄλυσις ἐκείνη. Ἐκεῖνα τὰ δεσμὰ ποθήσωμεν.

Καὶ πῶς, φησίν, ἔνι; Ἐὰν ταῦτα συντρίψωμεν καὶ διακλάσωμεν. Οὐδὲν ἡμῖν ἀπὸ τούτων ὄφελος τῶν δεσμῶν, ἀλλὰ καὶ βλάβη. Δεσμώτας ἡμᾶς ἐκεῖ δείξει ταῦτα, τὰ δὲ Παύλου δεσμὰ λύσει ἐκεῖνα τὰ δεσμά· ἡ τούτοις ἐνταῦθα δεδεμένη καὶ τοῖς ἀθανάτοις ἐκεῖ δεσμοῖς δεθήσεται χεῖρας καὶ πόδας· ἡ τοῖς Παύλου δεθεῖσα ἕξει καθάπερ κόσμον περικείμενον αὐτῇ τότε. Λῦσον καὶ σαυτὴν τοῦ δεσμοῦ, καὶ τὸν πένητα τοῦ λιμοῦ. Τί τῶν ἁμαρτημάτων τὰς σειρὰς ἐπισφίγγεις; Πῶς; φησίν. Ὅταν σὺ μὲν χρυσοφορῇς, ἕτερος δὲ ἀπόλλυται· ὅταν σὺ μὲν ἵνα δόξης τύχῃς τῆς κενῆς, τοσοῦτον λαμβάνῃς χρυσίον, ἕτερος δὲ μηδὲ φαγεῖν ἔχῃ, οὐχὶ τὰς ἁμαρτίας ἐπέσφιγξας; Περίθου τὸν Χριστὸν, καὶ μὴ τὸν χρυσόν. Ἔνθα μαμμωνᾶς, ἐκεῖ Χριστὸς οὐκ ἔστιν· ἔνθα Χριστός, ἐκεῖ μαμμωνᾶς οὐκ ἔστιν. Οὐ βούλει τὸν βασιλέα αὐτὸν περικεῖσθαι τῶν πάντων; Εἴ τις σοι τὴν ἁλουργίδα καὶ τὸ διάδημα ἔδωκεν, οὐκ ἂν ἐδέξω ἀντὶ παντὸς τοῦ χρυσίου; Ἐγώ σοι οὐ τὸν κόσμον δίδωμι τὸν βασιλικὸν, ἀλλ᾽ αὐτὸν περιθέσθαι τὸν βασιλέα παρέχω. Καὶ πῶς ἄν τις περικέοιτο τὸν Χριστὸν, φησίν; Ἄκουσον τοῦ Παύλου λέγοντος· "Ὅσοι εἰς Χριστὸν ἐβαπτίσθητε, Χριστὸν ἐνεδύσασθε." ἄκουσον τῆς παραινέσεως τῆς ἀποστολικῆς·

their gaze from her to him, and with good reason. You see, to observe a man greater in nature than a human being and having no human attributes, but an angel on earth, is more marvelous than observing a woman decked with finery. For indeed one may see both in theaters, in processions, in the baths, and in many places, but who sees a person surrounded by chains, and deeming themselves to have the greatest ornament, and not submitting to their chains, doesn't see a vision of earth but the vision worthy of heaven? The soul that is adorned with these things[121] looks around: Who has seen? Who not seen?—is filled with pride, [284] is possessed with anxious thought, is bound with myriad other passions, while the one who is surrounded by those bonds is without pride. This soul exults, is freed from every anxious thought, is joyous, looking at heaven, has wings. If someone were to give me the choice of seeing Paul stooping down from heaven and uttering voice or out of prison, I would choose the prison, for those from heaven come to him when he is in the prison [see Acts 23:9–11]. Paul's chains were a banding together of the proclamation, that chain was its foundation. May we desire those chains.

"And how," says someone, "is this possible, if we break up and smash these things?"[122] There's no profit to us from these chains, but even harm. These will show us as prisoners there,[123] but Paul's will loosen those chains; the woman who is bound with these chains here will also be bound there, hand and foot, with everlasting chains; the woman who has been bound with Paul's chains will have them at that time as an ornament about her. Release both yourself from this bond and the poor person from hunger. Why do you tighten the cords of your sins? "How?" someone asks. When you wear gold while the other person is perishing; when, to achieve vainglory, you take so much gold while the other person doesn't even have the wherewithal to eat, haven't you intensified your sins? Put on Christ and not gold. Where there is Mammon, there Christ is not; where there is Christ, there Mammon is not. Don't you want to put on the king of all? If someone had offered you the purple and the diadem, wouldn't you have taken them instead of all the gold? I give you not the royal adornment but offer to put on the king himself. "And how can someone put on Christ?" someone asks. Listen to Paul as he says, "*All you who have been baptized in Christ have put on Christ*" [Gal 3:27]. Listen to the apostolic teaching: "*Make no*

---

121. That is, finery.
122. That is, finery.
123. That is, in heaven.

"Τῆς σαρκὸς, φησὶ, πρόνοιαν μὴ ποιεῖσθε εἰς ἐπιθυμίαν." Οὕτω τις ἐνδύεται τὸν Χριστὸν, μὴ προνοῶν τῆς σαρκὸς εἰς ἐπιθυμίας. Ἂν τὸν Χριστὸν ἐνδύσῃ, καὶ δαίμονές σε φοβηθήσονται· ἂν δὲ τὸν χρυσὸν, καὶ ἄνθρωποι καταγελάσονται· ἐὰν ἐνδύσῃ τὸν Χριστὸν, καὶ ἄνθρωποί σε αἰδεσθήσονται.

Βούλει φαίνεσθαι καλὴ καὶ εὐπρεπής; ἀρκέ-[285]σθητι τῇ πλάσει τοῦ δημιουργοῦ. Τί τὰ χρυσία ἐπεισάγεις, ὡς διορθωσομένη τοῦ θεοῦ τὸ πλάσμα; Θέλεις εὐπρεπὴς φαίνεσθαι; περιβαλοῦ ἐλεημοσύνην, περιβαλοῦ φιλανθρωπίαν, περιβαλοῦ σωφροσύνην, ἀτυφίαν· ταῦτα πάντα χρυσοῦ τιμιώτερα· ταῦτα καὶ τὴν ὡραίαν εὐπρεπεστέραν ποιεῖ· ταῦτα καὶ τὴν οὐκ εὔμορφον εὔμορφον ἐργάζεται. Ὅταν γάρ τις μετ᾽ εὐνοίας ὄψιν ὁρᾷ, ἀπὸ ἀγάπης φέρει τὰς ψήφους· τὴν δὲ πονηρὰν οὐ δύναταί τις οὐδὲ καλὴν οὖσαν, καλὴν εἰπεῖν· πεπληγμένη γὰρ ἡ διάνοια οὐ φέρει τὴν ψῆφον ὀρθήν.

Ἐκοσμήθη ποτὲ ἡ Αἰγυπτία, ἐκοσμήθη καὶ ὁ Ἰωσήφ· τίς οὖν ἦν ὁ ὡραιότερος; οὐ λέγω ὅτε ἐν τοῖς βασιλείοις ἦν ἐκείνη, οὗτος δὲ ἐν τῷ δεσμωτηρίῳ. Γυμνὸς ἦν οὗτος, ἀλλ᾽ ἐνεδέδυτο τῆς σωφροσύνης τὰ ἱμάτια· ἐνδεδυμένη ἦν ἐκείνη, ἀλλὰ γυμνῆς αἰσχροτέρα· σωφροσύνην γὰρ οὐκ εἶχεν. Ὅταν σφοδρῶς κοσμήσῃ, ὦ γύναι, τότε τῆς γυμνῆς αἰσχροτέρα γέγονας· ἀπεδύσω γὰρ τὴν εὐκοσμίαν. Ἦν καὶ ἡ Εὔα γυμνή· ἀλλ᾽ ὅτε ἐνεδύσατο, τότε ἦν αἰσχροτέρα· ὅτε μὲν γὰρ ἦν γυμνή, κεκόσμητο τῇ δόξῃ τοῦ θεοῦ· ὅτε δὲ τὸ τῆς ἁμαρτίας ἱμάτιον ἐνεδύσατο, τότε ἦν αἰσχρά. Καὶ σὺ τῆς φιλοκοσμίας ἐνδυομένη τὸ ἱμάτιον, τότε αἰσχροτέρα φαίνῃ. Ὅτι γὰρ ἡ πολυτέλεια οὐκ ἀρκεῖ δεῖξαι εὔμορφον, ἀλλ᾽ ἔστι καὶ ἐνδεδυμένην τῆς γυμνῆς μᾶλλον ἀσχημονεῖν, εἰπὲ δή μοι· εἴ ποτε αὐλητοῦ, ἢ χοραύλου σκεύη ἐνεδύσω, ἆρα οὐκ ἦν ἀσχημοσύνη; Καίτοιγε χρυσᾶ εἰσι τὰ ἱμάτιά· ἀλλὰ διὰ τοῦτο ἀσχημοσύνη, ὅτι χρυσᾶ. Ἡ γὰρ πολυτέλεια τοῖς ἐπὶ σκηνῆς ἁρμόζει, τοῖς τραγῳδοῖς, τοῖς ὑποκριταῖς, τοῖς μίμοις, τοῖς ὀρχησταῖς, τοῖς πρὸς τὰ θηρία μαχομένοις· γυναικὶ δὲ πιστῇ ἕτερα δίδοται ἱμάτια παρὰ τοῦ θεοῦ, αὐτὸς ὁ μονογενὴς τοῦ θεοῦ παῖς. "Ὅσοι, φησὶν, εἰς Χριστὸν ἐβαπτίσθητε, Χριστὸν ἐνεδύσασθε." Εἰπέ μοι, εἴ τίς σοι βασιλικὸν ἔδωκεν ἱμάτιον, σὺ δὲ ἐπάνω ἐκείνου τὸ τοῦ λωτοῦ λαβοῦσα περιέθου, ἆρα οὐκ ἂν μετὰ τοῦ ἀσχημονεῖν καὶ ἐκολάσθης; τὸν τοῦ οὐρανοῦ δεσπό-[286]την καὶ τῶν ἀγγέλων ἐνεδύσω, καὶ περὶ τὴν γῆν ἔτι στρέφῃ; Ταῦτά μοι εἴρηται, ὅτι μέγα μὲν καὶ καθ᾽ ἑαυτὸ κακὸν ἡ φιλοκοσμία, κἂν μηδὲν ἦν ἕτερον ἐντεῦθεν τικτόμενον, ἀλλ᾽ ἐξῆν ἀκινδύνως ἔχειν· εἰς γὰρ κενοδοξίαν ἀλείφει, καὶ τῦφον· νῦν δὲ καὶ ἕτερα πολλὰ τίκτεται ἐκ τοῦ καλλωπισμοῦ, ὑποψίαι πονηραὶ, δαπάναι ἄκαιροι, βλασφημίαι, πλεονεξιῶν ὑποθέσεις. Τί γὰρ καλλωπίζῃ, εἰπέ μοι; ἵνα ἀρέσῃς τῷ ἀνδρί; Οὐκοῦν ἐπὶ τῆς οἰκίας τοῦτο ποίει· ἐνταῦθα δὲ τοὐναντίον γίνεται. Εἰ γὰρ τῷ οἰκείῳ ἀρέσαι θέλεις ἀνδρὶ, τοῖς ἄλλοις μὴ ἄρεσκε· εἰ δὲ τοῖς ἄλλοις ἀρέσκεις, οὐ δυνήσῃ ἀρέσαι τῷ ἰδίῳ. Ὥστε πάντα ἀποτίθεσθαι τὸν κόσμον ἔδει εἰς ἀγορὰν ἐμβάλλουσαν, εἰς ἐκκλησίαν

provision for the flesh to gratify its desire" [Rom 13:14]. In this way does one put on Christ, not providing for the *desires of the flesh*. If you've put on Christ, even the demons will fear you, but if you've put on gold, even human beings will deride you; if you've put on Christ, human beings too will revere you.

Do you want to appear beautiful and good-looking? [**285**] Be content with the fashioning of the creator. Why do you introduce golden objects, as if to put right God's creation? Do you want to appear good-looking? Put on almsgiving, put on love of humankind, put on modesty, humility. All these things are more valuable than gold; these things render even the ugly more good-looking; these things make even the ill-formed well-formed. You see, when someone observes a face with goodwill, they give their judgment from love, whereas they can't call an evil woman, even a beautiful one, beautiful, for the mind when it's wounded can't deliver the right judgment.

In olden times the Egyptian woman was adorned, and Joseph was also adorned [see Gen 39:6]. So which of them was the fairer? I say not when she was in the palace and he was in the prison. Joseph was naked, but he was clad in the garments of modesty, while she was clad, but uglier than if she'd been naked. You see, she had no modesty. When you've adorned yourself excessively, woman, then you've become uglier than a naked woman, for you've taken off your decency. Eve too was naked [see Gen 2:25], but when she had clothed herself, then she was uglier, for when she was naked, she was adorned with God's glory, but when she was clad in the garment of sin, then she was ugly. And you, when you have put on the garment of finery, then you appear uglier. You see, because the costliness isn't sufficient to demonstrate a good-looking person, but it's possible for even one dressed up to disgrace themselves more than a naked woman, so tell me: If you have even put on the costume of a piper or a flute player, wouldn't that have been a disgrace? Still, the garments are golden, but for that reason they are a disgrace, because they are golden. You see, the costliness suits those on the stage, the tragedians, the players, the mimes, the dancers, the gladiators, but to a woman who is a believer other garments have been given by God, the only-begotten Son of God. "*All you,*" he says, "*who have been baptized into Christ have put on Christ*" [Gal 3:27]. Tell me, if someone gave you a royal garment, but you took a pimp's[124] garment and put it on over

---

124. The meaning of this word is not clear, but Chrysostom uses it in this sense in *Hom. Eph.* 13 (Field 4:240); see *PGL*, 818 s.v. λῶταξ.

προϊοῦσαν. Ἄλλως δὲ, μὴ ἀπὸ τούτων ἄρεσκε τῷ ἀνδρὶ, ἀφ' ὧν καὶ αἱ πόρναι, ἀλλ' ἀπὸ τούτων μᾶλλον, ἀφ' οὗ αἱ γυναῖκες αἱ ἐλεύθεραι. Τίνι γὰρ, εἰπέ μοι, διέστηκε γυνὴ πόρνης; Ὅτι ἡ μὲν πρὸς ἓν μόνον ὁρᾷ, ὅπως τῷ κάλλει τοῦ σώματος ἐφελκύσηται τὸν ἐρώμενον· αὕτη δὲ καὶ οἰκίας προΐσταται, καὶ τέκνων κοινωνεῖ, καὶ τῶν ἄλλων ἁπάντων. Θυγάτριον ἔχεις; ὅρα μὴ διαδέξηται τὴν βλάβην· φιλεῖ γάρ πως πρὸς τὰς ἀνατροφὰς τὰ ἤθη ῥυθμίζεσθαι, καὶ μιμεῖσθαι τὰ τῶν μητέρων ἤθη. Ἔσο ὑπόδειγμα τῇ θυγατρὶ σωφροσύνης, κόσμησαι τὸν κόσμον ἐκεῖνον, καὶ ὅρα πῶς τούτου καταφρονήσεις. Ὄντως γὰρ ἐκεῖνα κόσμος ἐστὶ, ταῦτα δὲ ἀκοσμία. Ἀρκεῖ τὰ εἰρημένα. Ὁ δὲ θεὸς ὁ τὸν κόσμον ποιήσας, καὶ δοὺς ἡμῖν τὸν τῆς ψυχῆς κόσμον, κοσμήσειεν ἡμᾶς, καὶ τῇ αὐτοῦ δόξῃ ἀμφιάσειεν· ἵνα πάντες ἐν ἀγαθοῖς ἔργοις διαλάμποντες, καὶ εἰς δόξαν αὐτοῦ ζῶντες, δόξαν ἀναπέμψωμεν τῷ πατρὶ καὶ τῷ υἱῷ καὶ τῷ ἁγίῳ πνεύματι, νῦν καὶ ἀεὶ καὶ εἰς τοὺς αἰῶνας τῶν αἰώνων. Ἀμήν.

the top of it, apart from the disgraceful behavior, wouldn't you have been punished? [**286**] You've put on the Lord of heaven and of the angels, and are you still turning yourself inside out about earth?

I've spoken about these topics because love of ornament is of itself a great evil, even if nothing else were produced from it, but it were possible to hold onto it without danger (for it stimulates vainglory and pride), but now also many other evils are produced from finery: nasty suspicions, unseasonable expenses, occasions of rapacity. I mean, why do you beautify yourself, tell me? To please your husband? So do it at home, but here the opposite is the case. For if you wish to please your own husband, don't please others. But if you please others, you won't be able to please your own. The upshot is that you should put away every adornment when you go to the marketplace, when you proceed to the church. Besides, don't please your husband by these means, which the prostitutes use, but rather by these means, which free wives use. For, tell me, in what respect does a wife differ from a prostitute? In that the one looks to one thing only, namely, that by the beauty of her body she may attract the one she desires, whereas the other both rules over the house, and shares the children, and all other things.

Do you have a small daughter? Look out lest she inherit the mischief, for they love to form their natures according to their nurses and to imitate their mothers' natures. Be an example to your daughter of modesty, adorn yourself with that ornament, and see that you despise the other, for really that is in truth an ornament, but the other a disfigurement. Enough has been said. May God who made the world and has given us the ornament of soul adorn us and clothe us with his glory, so that every one of us, shining brightly in good works and living to his glory, may send up glory to the Father and the Son and the Holy Spirit now and forever and ever. Amen.

ΛΟΓΟΣ ΙΑ.

Ἐν σοφίᾳ περιπατεῖτε πρὸς τοὺς ἔξω, τὸν καιρὸν ἐξαγορα-[287] ζόμενοι. Ὁ λόγος ὑμῶν πάντοτε ἐν χάριτι, ἅλατι ἠρτυμένος, εἰδέναι πῶς δεῖ ὑμᾶς ἑνὶ ἑκάστῳ ἀποκρίνεσθαι.

Ὅπερ ὁ Χριστὸς πρὸς τοὺς μαθητὰς ἔλεγε, τοῦτο καὶ νῦν Παῦλος παραινεῖ. Τί δὲ ὁ Χριστὸς ἔλεγεν; "Ἰδοὺ ἐγὼ ἀποστέλλω ὑμᾶς ὡς πρόβατα ἐν μέσῳ λύκων· γίνεσθε οὖν φρόνιμοι ὡς οἱ ὄφεις, καὶ ἀκέραιοι ὡς αἱ περιστεραί." Τουτέστι, φυλακτικοὶ γίνεσθε, μηδεμίαν αὐτοῖς λαβὴν διδόντες καθ' ὑμῶν. Διὰ γὰρ τοῦτο πρόσκειται, "πρὸς τοὺς ἔξω," ἵνα μάθωμεν, ὅτι πρὸς τὰ μέλη τὰ οἰκεῖα οὐ τοσαύτης ἡμῖν δεῖ ἀσφαλείας, ὅσης πρὸς τοὺς ἔξω. Ἔνθα μὲν γὰρ ἀδελφοὶ, εἰσὶ καὶ συγγνῶμαι πολλαὶ καὶ ἀγάπαι. Δεῖ μὲν οὖν καὶ ἐνταῦθα ἀσφάλειαν εἶναι, πολλῷ δὲ πλέον ἔξω· οὐ γάρ ἐστιν ἴσον μεταξὺ ἐχθρῶν καὶ πολεμίων εἶναι, καὶ φίλων.

Εἶτ' ἐπειδὴ ἐφόβησεν, ὅρα πῶς πάλιν θαρρύνει. "Τὸν καιρὸν, φησὶν, ἐξαγοραζόμενοι." τουτέστι, βραχὺς ὁ παρὼν καιρός. Ταῦτα δὲ ἔλεγεν, οὐ ποικίλους εἶναι βουλόμενος, οὐδὲ ὑποκριτάς· τοῦτο γὰρ οὐ σοφίας, ἀλλὰ ἀνοίας· ἀλλὰ τί; Ἐν οἷς μὴ βλάπτουσι, φησὶ, μηδεμίαν αὐτοῖς δίδοτε λαβήν· ὃ καὶ πρὸς Ῥωμαίους γράφων φησίν· "Ἀπόδοτε πᾶσι τὰς ὀφειλὰς, τῷ τὸν φόρον, τὸν φόρον· τῷ τὸ τέλος, τὸ τέλος· τῷ τὴν τιμὴν, τὴν τιμήν." Διὰ τὸ κήρυγμα μόνον ἔστω σοι πόλεμος, φησί· μηδεμίαν ἑτέραν ὁ πόλεμος οὗτος ἀρχὴν λαμβανέτω. Εἰ γὰρ μέλλοιεν ἡμῖν καὶ δι' ἕτερα ἀπεχθάνεσθαι, οὔτε μισθὸς ἡμῖν ἔσται, καὶ αὐτοὶ χείρους ἔσονται, καὶ δόξουσιν ἡμῖν δίκαια ἐγκαλεῖν· οἷον τὰ τελέσματα ἂν μὴ καταβάλλωμεν, τὰς τιμὰς τὰς προσηκούσας ἐὰν μὴ ἀποδιδῶμεν, ἂν μὴ ὦμεν ταπεινοί. Οὐχ ὁρᾷς Παῦλον, ἔνθα μηδὲν ἔβλαπτε τὸ κήρυγμα, πῶς ἐστι καθυφιείς; Ἄκουε γὰρ αὐτοῦ λέγοντος πρὸς τὸν Ἀγρίππαν· "Μακάριον ἐμαυτὸν ἥγημαι ἐπὶ σοῦ μέλλων ἀπολογεῖσθαι σήμερον, μάλιστα γνώστην σε ὄντα τῶν κατὰ Ἰουδαίους ἐθῶν τε καὶ ζητημάτων." Εἰ δὲ ἐνόμιζε δεῖν ὑβρίζειν τὸν ἄρχοντα, πάντα ἂν ἀνέτρεψεν. Ἄκουε δὲ καὶ τῶν περὶ τὸν μακάριον Πέτρον, πῶς ἐπιεικῶς ἀποκρίνονται τοῖς Ἰουδαίοις λέγοντες· "Πειθαρχεῖν δεῖ θεῷ μᾶλλον, ἢ [288] ἀνθρώποις." Καίτοιγε ἄνθρωποι

Conduct yourselves wisely toward outsiders, making the most of the time. [**287**] *Let your speech always be gracious, seasoned with salt, so that you may know how you ought to answer everyone* [Col 4:5–6].

What Christ said to his disciples is what also Paul now advises. And what did Christ say? *"Look, I send you out as sheep in the midst of wolves, to be therefore wise as serpents and as innocent as doves"* [Matt 10:16]. This means: be on your guard, giving them no hold on you. For therefore is added *"toward outsiders,"* so that we may learn that against our own members we don't need as much caution as against outsiders. For where brethren are, there too are many acts of forgiveness and love. Therefore, there's need of caution even there, but much more outside, for it's not the same to be among enemies and foes and among friends.

Then, because he had put fear into them, see how again he encourages them. *"Making the most of the time,"* he says, which means the present time is short. He made these statements not wanting them to be wily or hypocrites, for this doesn't pertain to wisdom but to senselessness. So what? "In matters where they don't harm you," he says, "give them no hold," which he also says in writing to the Romans: *"Pay all your dues, to whom they are due, respect to those to whom it is due, honor to whom it is due"* [Rom 13:7]. "On account of the gospel alone there is war," he says; "let the war have no other origin. For if they were going to become our foes also for other reasons, there'll be no reward for us, and they'll become worse and will seem to have just complaints against us. For example, if we don't pay the tribute, if we don't render the honors that are due, if we aren't humble." Don't you see how submissive Paul is, where he didn't harm the gospel? Listen to him saying to Agrippa, *"I think myself happy to be going to make my defense today before you, because you are especially familiar with all customs and controversies among the Jews"* [Acts 26:2–3]. But if he thought that he had to insult the ruler, he would've spoiled everything. Listen to those around the blessed Peter, how gently they answer the Jews, saying, *"We must obey God rather* [**288**] *than human beings"* [Acts 5:29]. And yet human beings who

τῆς ἑαυτῶν ψυχῆς ἀπεγνωκότες, καὶ ὑβρίζειν καὶ πᾶν ὁτιοῦν ποιεῖν ἐδύναντο· ἀλλὰ διὰ τοῦτο ἀπέγνωσαν τῆς ψυχῆς, ἵνα μὴ κενοδοξῶσι· κενοδοξίας γὰρ τοῦτό ἐστιν· ἀλλ' ἵνα κηρύσσωσι, καὶ ἵνα μετὰ παρρησίας πάντα φθέγγωνται· ἐκεῖνο δὲ ἀμετρίας ἐστίν.

"Ὁ λόγος ὑμῶν πάντοτε ἐν χάριτι, ἅλατι ἠρτυμένος·" τουτέστι, μὴ εἰς ἀδιαφορίαν τὸ χαρίεν ἐκπίπτειν. Ἔνι γὰρ καὶ χαριεντίζεσθαι, ἔνι καὶ μετὰ τῆς προσηκούσης κοσμιότητος. "Εἰδέναι πῶς δεῖ ὑμᾶς ἑνὶ ἑκάστῳ ἀποκρίνεσθαι." Ὥστε οὐχ ὁμοίως πᾶσι διαλέγεσθαι χρή, Ἕλλησι λέγω καὶ ἀδελφοῖς. Οὐδαμῶς· ἐπεὶ τοῦτο τῆς ἐσχάτης ἀνοίας ἐστί.

"Τὰ κατ' ἐμὲ πάντα γνωρίσει ὑμῖν Τυχικὸς ὁ ἀγαπητὸς ἀδελφὸς, καὶ πιστὸς διάκονος, καὶ σύνδουλος ἐν κυρίῳ." Βαβαὶ, ὅση σοφία Παύλου; πῶς οὐ πάντα ἐντίθησιν εἰς τὰς ἐπιστολάς, ἀλλὰ τὰ ἀναγκαῖα καὶ τὰ κατεπείγοντα; πρῶτον μὲν, οὐ βουλόμενος αὐτὰς εἰς μῆκος ἐκτείνειν· δεύτερον δὲ, καὶ τὸν ἀπερχόμενον αἰδεσιμώτερον ποιῶν, ἵνα ἔχῃ τι καὶ διηγεῖσθαι· τρίτον, δεικνὺς πῶς πρὸς αὐτὸν διάκειται· οὐ γὰρ ἂν αὐτῷ ταῦτα ἐνεχείρισεν. Ἔπειτα, ἥν ἃ οὐκ ἔδει διὰ γραμμάτων δηλωθῆναι. "Ὁ ἀγαπητὸς, φησὶν, ἀδελφός." Εἰ ἀγαπητὸς, πάντα οἶδε, καὶ οὐδὲν αὐτὸν ἔκρυπτε. "Καὶ πιστὸς διάκονος, καὶ σύνδουλος ἐν κυρίῳ." Εἰ πιστὸς, οὐδὲν ψεύσεται· εἰ σύνδουλος, κεκοινώνηκε τῶν πειρασμῶν· ὥστε πάντοθεν τὸ ἀξιόπιστον συνήγαγεν.

"Ὃν ἔπεμψα πρὸς ὑμᾶς εἰς αὐτὸ τοῦτο." Ἐνταῦθα τὴν ἀγάπην δείκνυσι τὴν πολλὴν, εἴγε διὰ τοῦτο αὐτὸν ἀπέσταλκε, καὶ τῆς ἀποδημίας αἰτία αὕτη γέγονεν· ὃ καὶ Θεσσαλονικεῦσι γράφων ἔλεγε, "Διὸ μηκέτι στέγοντες ηὐδοκήσαμεν καταλειφθῆναι ἐν Ἀθήναις μόνοι, καὶ ἐπέμψαμεν Τιμόθεον τὸν ἀδελφὸν ἡμῶν." Καὶ Ἐφεσίοις δὲ αὐτὸν τοῦτον πέμπει, καὶ ὑπὲρ τῆς αὐτῆς αἰτίας· "Ἵνα γνῷ, φησὶ, τὰ περὶ ὑμῶν, καὶ παρακαλέσῃ τὰς καρδίας ὑμῶν." Ὅρα τί φησιν· οὐχ ἵνα ὑμεῖς τὰ ἐμὰ μάθητε, ἀλλ' ἵνα ἐγὼ τὰ ὑμέτερα· οὕτως οὐδαμοῦ τὸ αὐτοῦ τίθησι. Δείκνυσιν αὐτοὺς καὶ ἐν πειρασμοῖς ὄντας τῷ εἰπεῖν, "ἵνα παρακαλέσῃ τὰς καρδίας ὑμῶν."

had renounced their souls could have insulted and done anything whatsoever, but on this account they renounced their souls, lest they became vainglorious (for that was vainglory). No, so that they might preach and so that they might express everything with frankness. That other approach smacks of a want of moderation.

Let your speech always be gracious, seasoned with salt: that means, don't let this graciousness lapse into indifference. You see, it's possible to be agreeable; it's also possible to be so with appropriate decorum. *To know how you ought to answer everyone.* So one shouldn't engage in conversation in the same way, I mean with Hellenes and brothers. In no way, since this is the extreme of senselessness.

Tychicus will tell you all about my affairs; he is a beloved brother and faithful minister and fellow servant in the Lord. Isn't it wonderful, how great Paul's wisdom is? How is it that he didn't put everything in his letters, but what was necessary and urgent? First, not wanting to draw them out; second, to make the messenger more respected, so that he had also something to relate;[125] third, demonstrating his affection toward him; for [otherwise] he wouldn't have entrusted these communications to him. Then there were things that shouldn't have been declared in writing. "*The beloved brother,*" he says. If he's beloved, he knows everything, and Paul concealed nothing from him. *And faithful minister and fellow servant in the Lord.* If he's *faithful*, he won't tell any lies; if he's a fellow servant, he's shared his trials, so that he's brought together from all sides the reason for trustworthiness.

Whom I have sent to you for this purpose. In this passage Paul demonstrates his great love, seeing that he sent him *for this purpose* and this was the cause of his journey. And writing to the Thessalonians he said, "*Therefore, we could bear it no longer; we thought it good to be left in Athens alone and sent Timothy, our brother*" [1 Thess 3:1–2]. And to the Ephesians he sends this very same person and for the same cause. "*So that you may know,*" he says, "*about how I am and comfort your hearts*" [Eph 6:22]. See what he says: not "so you may learn how I am, but so that I may learn how you are." So nowhere does he state what is his own. He demonstrates that they were in trials too, by saying, "*comfort your hearts.*"

---

125. On the role of the letter bearer in late antiquity, who often conveyed verbal as well as written messages, see Pauline Allen and Bronwen Neil, *Greek and Latin Letters: The Christianisation of a Literary Form* (Cambridge: Cambridge University Press, 2020).

"Σὺν Ὀνησίμῳ τῷ ἀγαπητῷ [289] καὶ πιστῷ ἀδελφῷ, ὅς ἐστιν ἐξ ὑμῶν· πάντα ὑμῖν γνωριοῦσι τὰ ὧδε." Ὀνήσιμος οὗτός ἐστι, περὶ οὗ γράφων τῷ Φιλήμονι ἔλεγεν· "Ὃν ἐβουλόμην πρὸς ἐμαυτὸν κατέχειν, ἵνα ὑπὲρ σοῦ μοι διακονῇ ἐν τοῖς δεσμοῖς τοῦ εὐαγγελίου· χωρὶς δὲ τῆς σῆς γνώμης οὐδὲν ἠθέλησα ποιῆσαι." Καὶ τὸ ἐγκώμιον δὲ προστίθησι τῆς πόλεως, ἵνα καὶ ἐγκαλλωπίζωνται, μὴ μόνον οὐκ ἐπαισχύνωνται. "Ὅς ἐστι, φησὶν, ἐξ ὑμῶν· πάντα ὑμῖν γνωριοῦσι τὰ ὧδε.

Ἀσπάζεται ὑμᾶς Ἀρίσταρχος ὁ συναιχμάλωτός μου." Οὐδὲν τούτου τοῦ ἐγκωμίου μεῖζον. Οὗτός ἐστιν ὁ ἀπὸ Ἱεροσολύμων ἀναχθεὶς μετ᾽ αὐτοῦ. Μεῖζον εἶπε τῶν προφητῶν οὗτος· ἐκεῖνοι μὲν γὰρ ξένους καὶ παρεπιδήμους ἑαυτοὺς καλοῦσιν, οὗτος δὲ καὶ αἰχμάλωτον. Καθάπερ αἰχμάλωτος, οὕτως ἤγετο καὶ ἐφέρετο, καὶ πᾶσιν εἰς τὸ κακῶς πάσχειν προὔκειτο, μᾶλλον δὲ καὶ ἐκείνων χεῖρον. Ἐκείνους μὲν γὰρ, ἐπειδὰν λάβωσιν οἱ πολέμιοι, ἐν πολλῇ θεραπείᾳ λοιπὸν ἔχουσιν, ἅτε ὡς οἰκείων κτημάτων ἐπιμελούμενοι· τοῦτον δὲ ὡς ἐχθρὸν καὶ πολέμιον πάντες ἦγον καὶ ἔφερον, δέροντες, μαστίζοντες, ὑβρίζοντες, συκοφαντοῦντες. Τοῦτο καὶ ἐκείνοις παράκλησις ἦν, ὅταν γὰρ καὶ ὁ διδάσκαλος ἐν τοῖς τοιούτοις ᾖ.

"Καὶ Μάρκος ὁ ἀνεψιὸς Βαρνάβα." Καὶ τοῦτον ἐνεκωμίασε τέως ἀπὸ τῆς συγγενείας· μέγας γὰρ ἦν ἀνὴρ ὁ Βαρνάβας. "Περὶ οὗ ἐλάβετε ἐντολάς· ἐὰν ἔλθῃ πρὸς ὑμᾶς, δέξασθε αὐτόν;" Τί γάρ; οὐκ ἐδέχοντο; Ναί· ἀλλὰ μετὰ πολλῆς τῆς σπουδῆς, φησί· καὶ τοῦτο τὸν ἄνδρα δείκνυσι μέγαν. Πόθεν τὰς ἐντολὰς ἔλαβον, οὐ λέγει. "Καὶ Ἰησοῦς ὁ λεγόμενος Ἰοῦστος." Ἴσως Κορίνθιος ἦν οὗτος. Εἶτα πᾶσι τὸ ἐγκώμιον κοινὸν ἀποδίδωσιν, εἰπὼν τὸ ἰδιάζον ἑκάστου· "Οἱ ὄντες ἐκ περιτομῆς· οὗτοι μόνοι συνεργοὶ εἰς τὴν βασιλείαν τοῦ θεοῦ, οἵτινες ἐγενήθησάν μοι παρηγορία." Ἐπειδὴ εἶπε, "συναιχμάλωτος," ἵνα μὴ συγκατενέγκῃ τὴν ψυχὴν τῶν ἀκουόντων, ὅρα πῶς τοῦτο τίθησι, καὶ διανίστησιν αὐτούς· "Συνεργοὶ, φησὶν, εἰς τὴν βασιλείαν τοῦ θεοῦ." Ὥστε τῶν πειρασμῶν κοινωνοῦντες, τῆς βασιλείας [290] κοινωνοῦσιν. "Οἵτινες ἐγενήθησάν μοι παρηγορία." Δείκνυσιν αὐτοὺς μεγάλους, εἴγε Παύλῳ παρηγορία γεγένηνται.

Ἀλλ᾽ ἴδωμεν τὴν σύνεσιν Παύλου. "Ἐν σοφίᾳ, φησὶ, περιπατεῖτε πρὸς τοὺς ἔξω, τὸν καιρὸν ἐξαγοραζόμενοι." Τουτέστιν, οὐκ ἔστιν ὑμέτερος ὁ καιρὸς, ἀλλ᾽ ἐκείνων ἐστί· μὴ τοίνυν βούλεσθε αὐθεντεῖν, ἀλλ᾽ ἐξαγοράζετε τὸν καιρόν. Καὶ οὐκ εἶπεν ἁπλῶς, ἀγοράζετε, ἀλλ᾽, "ἐξαγοράζετε," ὑμέτερον

With Onesimus, the beloved **[289]** *and faithful brother, who is from among you. They will acquaint you with everything from here.* Onesimus is the one about whom, in writing to Philemon, Paul said, *"I would have wanted to keep him with me, in order for him to serve me on your behalf during my imprisonment for the gospel, but without your consent I wished to do nothing"* [Phlm 13, 14]. And he adds too the praise of their city, so that they may also pride themselves, not only be ashamed. *"Who is from among you,"* he says. *"They will acquaint you with everything from here."*

Aristarchus, my fellow prisoner, greets you. Nothing surpasses this praise. He is the one who was brought up from Jerusalem with Paul [see Acts 27:2]. This man said greater things than the prophets, for they call themselves strangers and foreigners, but he calls himself a prisoner. Just like a prisoner he was thus dragged up and down and lay exposed to all those intent on doing him harm—no, even worse than the prisoners. You see, in fact when enemies capture prisoners they take great care of them afterward, inasmuch as they are looking after their own property, whereas Paul, as if a foe and an enemy, they all dragged up and down, beating, scourging, insulting, and maligning him. This too was a consolation to those [to whom he wrote], when even the master is in such a situation.

And Marcus, the cousin of Barnabas. And this man too Paul has praised for a time from his relationship, for Barnabas was a great man. *From him you have received instructions. If he comes to you, receive him.* Why? Wouldn't they have received him? Yes, but he means "with great speed," and this demonstrates that the man is great. Where they received these instructions from, Paul doesn't say.

And Jesus, who is called Justus. That man was probably a Corinthian. Then Paul bestows a common praise on all, having spoken that of each one in particular. *"Those who are of the circumcision, these ones are the only ones of my coworkers for the kingdom of God, who have been a comfort to me."* Then he said *"fellow prisoner,"* in order not to depress the souls of his hearers; see how he expresses this and rouses them. *"My coworkers,"* he says, *"for the kingdom of God."* So that being partakers of the trials, **[290]** they are also partakers of the kingdom. *Who have been a comfort to me.* He demonstrates that they are great persons, seeing that to Paul they have been a comfort.

But let's look at Paul's sagacity. *"Conduct yourselves wisely toward out-siders,"* he says, *"making the most of the time."* That means: the time is not yours but theirs. Then don't want to have your own way, but make the most of the time. And he didn't just say "buy" but *"make the most of the time,"*

αὐτὸν ποιοῦντες ἑτέρως. Ἀνοίας γὰρ περιττῆς, πολέμων καὶ ἀπεχθείας προφάσεις ἐπινοεῖν. Πρὸς γὰρ τῷ κινδύνους περιττοὺς ὑπομένειν καὶ κέρδος οὐκ
ἔχοντας, καὶ ἑτέρα γίνεται βλάβη, τὸ τοὺς Ἕλληνας μὴ προσιέναι ἡμῖν. Ἐν
γὰρ τοῖς ἀδελφοῖς ὅταν ᾖς, εἰκότως θαρρεῖς· ἔξω δὲ οὐχ οὕτω χρή.

Ὁρᾷς πῶς πανταχοῦ τοὺς ἔξω, τοὺς Ἕλληνας λέγει; Διὰ τοῦτο καὶ
Τιμοθέῳ γράφων ἔλεγε· "Δεῖ δὲ αὐτὸν καὶ μαρτυρίαν καλὴν ἔχειν ἀπὸ τῶν
ἔξωθεν." καὶ πάλιν, "Τί γάρ μοι καὶ τοὺς ἔξω κρίνειν;" "Ἐν σοφίᾳ, φησὶ,
περιπατεῖτε πρὸς τοὺς ἔξω." Ἔξω γάρ εἰσι, κἂν τὸν αὐτὸν κόσμον οἰκῶσιν
ἡμῖν, τῆς βασιλείας ὄντες ἔξω καὶ τοῦ οἰκίσκου τοῦ πατρικοῦ. Ἅμα καὶ παρα-
μυθεῖται αὐτούς, ἔξω ἐκείνους καλῶν· ὅπερ ἔλεγεν ἀνωτέρω, ὅτι "Ἡ ζωὴ
ὑμῶν κέκρυπται σὺν τῷ Χριστῷ ἐν τῷ Θεῷ."

Τότε, φησὶ, δόξαν ζητεῖτε, τότε τιμάς, τότε τὰ ἄλλα πάντα· νῦν δὲ μὴ,
ἀλλ' ἐκείνοις παρέχετε. Εἶτα, ἵνα μὴ νομίσῃς χρήματα λέγειν αὐτὸν, ἐπάγει·
"Ὁ λόγος ὑμῶν πάντοτε ἐν χάριτι, ἅλατι ἠρτυμένος, εἰδέναι ὑμᾶς πῶς δεῖ
ἑνὶ ἑκάστῳ ἀποκρίνεσθαι." Ἵνα μὴ ὑποκρίσεως γέμῃ· τοῦτο γὰρ οὐ χάρις,
οὐδὲ ἅλατι ἤρτυται. Οἷον, ἐὰν δέῃ θεραπεῦσαι ἀκινδύνως, μὴ παραιτήσῃ· ἂν
καιρὸς ᾖ προσηνῶς διαλεχθῆναι, μὴ νομίσῃς τὸ πρᾶγμα κολακείαν· πάντα
ποίει τὰ εἰς τιμὴν ἀνήκοντα, ἄνευ τοῦ βλάπτεσθαι τὴν εὐσέβειαν. Οὐχ ὁρᾷς
πῶς Δανιὴλ ἄνθρωπον ἀσεβῆ θεραπεύει; οὐχ ὁρᾷς τοὺς τρεῖς παῖδας, πῶς
μετὰ σοφίας προσεφέροντο, καὶ ἀνδρείαν δεικνύντες, καὶ παρρησίαν, καὶ
οὐδὲν θρασὺ οὐδὲ ἐπαχθές; τοῦτο γὰρ οὐκέτι παρρησίας, ἀλλὰ κενοδοξίας.
"Εἰδέναι, φησὶ, πῶς δεῖ ὑμᾶς ἑνὶ ἑκάστῳ ἀποκρίνεσθαι." Ἑτέρως γὰρ τῷ
ἄρχοντι, ἄλλως τῷ ἀρχομένῳ· ἄλλως τῷ πλουτοῦντι, ἄλλως τῷ πέ-[291]νητι.
Διὰ τί; Ὅτι αἱ τῶν πλουτούντων καὶ ἀρχόντων ψυχαὶ ἀσθενέστεραι τυγχάνουσιν οὖσαι, μᾶλλον φλεγμαίνουσαι, μᾶλλον διαρρέουσαι· ὥστε ἐκεῖ συγκα-
ταβατικὸν εἶναι δεῖ· αἱ τῶν πενήτων καὶ ἀρχομένων, στερρότεραι καὶ συνε-
τώτεραι· ὥστε ἐνταῦθα καὶ παρρησίᾳ μείζονι κεχρῆσθαι, πρὸς ἓν ὁρῶντα, τὴν
οἰκοδομήν. Μὴ ἐπειδὴ ὁ μὲν πλούσιος, ὁ δὲ πένης, ὁ μὲν πλέον τιμάσθω, ὁ δὲ
ἔλαττον· ἀλλὰ διὰ τὴν ἀσθένειαν ὁ μὲν διαβασταζέσθω, ὁ δὲ μὴ οὕτως. Οἷον,
αἰτίας οὐκ οὔσης, μὴ κάλει τὸν Ἕλληνα μιαρὸν, μηδὲ ἔσο ὑβριστής· ἀλλ' ἂν
μὲν ἐρωτηθῇς περὶ τοῦ δόγματος, ἀπόκριναι ὅτι μιαρὸν καὶ ἀσεβές· οὐδενὸς
δὲ ἐρωτῶντος οὐδὲ ἀναγκάζοντος λέγειν, οὐ προσήκει ἁπλῶς ἀπέχθειαν ἀνα-

making the time yours in different way. You see, it smacks of excessive senselessness to invent occasions of war and enmity. For on top of undergoing excessive dangers and not having gain, there is also this harm, namely, that the Hellenes won't come over to us. You see, when you're among the brethren, you're bold with reason, but when among outsiders you shouldn't be like that.

Do you see how everywhere he speaks of the outsiders, the Hellenes? This is why in writing to Timothy he said, "*He must be well thought of by outsiders*" [1 Tim 3:7]. And again: "*For what have I to do with judging outsiders?*" [1 Cor 5:12]. "*Conduct yourselves wisely toward outsiders,*" he says. "For they are outsiders, even if they dwell in the same world with us, being outside the kingdom and the Father's house." And he comforts them, at the same time calling the others outsiders, which he said above: "*Your life is hidden with Christ in God.*"

"Then," he says, "seek glory, then honors, then all the rest, but not now, but surrender them to the outsiders." After that, so you don't think he's talking about money, he adds, "*Let your speech always be gracious, seasoned with salt, so that you may know how you ought to answer everyone.*" So not full of hypocrisy, for this is not *gracious*, nor *seasoned with salt*. For example, if it's necessary to pay court without danger, don't refuse; if the occasion requires that you discourse civilly, don't consider the business flattery; do everything that pertains to honor without injuring piety. Don't you observe how Daniel pays court to a pious person? Don't you observe how wisely the three children conducted themselves, and demonstrated bravery, and frankness of speech, and nothing rash or annoying [see Dan 3:16–18]? For this is no longer frankness of speech, but vainglory. "*Know how you ought to answer everyone,*" Paul says. You see, the ruler should be answered in one way, the ruled in another, the rich in another, [**291**] the poor in another. Why? Because the souls of the rich and those who rule are weaker and more inflammable and fluctuating, so that there it's necessary to be condescending; the souls of the poor and the ruled are stronger and more intelligent, so that in that case one should use greater frankness of speech, looking to one thing, their edification. It is not because one is rich and the other poor, the former is to be honored more, the other less, but because of their weakness let the former be supported, the latter not so. For example, when there is no cause for it, don't call the Hellene polluted, or be insulting, but if you are asked concerning their doctrine, answer that it is polluted and impious. But when nobody asks you or forces you to speak, it isn't becoming simply to promise enmity, for what kind of necessity is there

δέχεσθαι· ποία γὰρ ἀνάγκη περιττὰς ἔχθρας κατασκευάζειν; Πάλιν, ἄν τινα κατηχῇς, λέγε ἐξ ὑποθέσεως ὑποκειμένης· ἐπεὶ σίγα.

Ἐὰν ᾖ ἅλατι ἠρτυμένος ὁ λόγος, κἂν εἰς διαρρέουσαν ἐμπέσῃ ψυχήν, ἐπισφίγξει τὴν χαύνην· κἂν εἰς τραχεῖαν, λεανεῖ τὸ σκληρόν, ἐπίχαρις ὤν. Μήτε φορτικὸς ἔστω, μήτε πάλιν χαῦνος, ἀλλὰ καὶ τὸ στῦφον ἐχέτω, καὶ τὸ μεθ' ἡδονῆς. Ἄν τε γὰρ ἀμέτρως ἐπιστύψῃ, μᾶλλον ἔβλαψεν ἢ ὠφέλησεν· ἐὰν δὲ ἀμέτρως χαριεντίσηται, μᾶλλον ἐλύπησεν ἢ ὤνησεν· ὥστε πανταχοῦ μέτρα δεῖ εἶναι. Μήτε κατηφὴς ἔσο καὶ σκυθρωπός· ἀηδὲς γάρ· μήτε διακεχυμένος· εὐκαταφρόνητον γὰρ καὶ πεπατημένον· ἀλλ' ἑκατέρου τὴν ἀρετὴν λαβών, τὴν κακίαν διάφυγε, καθάπερ ἡ μέλιττα τοῦ μὲν τὸ φαιδρόν, τοῦ δὲ τὸ σεμνόν. Εἰ γὰρ ἰατρὸς οὐχ ὁμοίως πᾶσι χρήσεται τοῖς σώμασι, πολλῷ μᾶλλον διδάσκαλος. Καίτοι μᾶλλον ἂν τὰ σώματα ἀκατάλληλα φάρμακα ἐνέγκοι, ἢ ψυχὴ λόγον. Οἷον, πρόσεισιν Ἕλλην, καὶ γίνεταί σοι φίλος; μηδὲν αὐτῷ περὶ τούτου διαλεχθῇς, ἕως ἂν γένηται πάνυ φίλος· καὶ ὅταν γένηται, ἠρέμα.

Ὅρα γὰρ καὶ ὁ Παῦλος ἡνίκα εἰς τὰς Ἀθήνας παρεγένετο, πῶς αὐτοῖς διελέγετο. Οὐκ εἶπεν, ὦ μιαροὶ καὶ παμμίαροι, ἀλλὰ τί; "Ἄνδρες Ἀθηναῖοι, κατὰ πάντα ὡς δεισιδαιμονεστέρους ὑμᾶς θεωρῶ." Πάλιν ὅτε ὑβρίσαι ἐχρῆν, οὐ παρῃτήσατο· ἀλλὰ μετὰ πολλῆς τῆς σφοδρότητος ἔλεγε τῷ Ἐλύμᾳ, "Ὦ πλήρης παντὸς δόλου καὶ πάσης ῥᾳδιουργίας, υἱὲ διαβόλου, ἐχθρὲ πάσης δικαιοσύνης." Ὥσπερ γὰρ ἐκείνους ὑβρίσαι ἀνοίας [292] ἦν, οὕτω τοῦτον μὴ ὑβρίσαι μαλακίας ἦν. Πάλιν, εἰσήχθης πρὸς ἄρχοντα διὰ πρᾶγμα; τὰς προσηκούσας ἀπόνεμε τιμάς.

"Πάντα ὑμῖν, φησί, γνωριοῦσι τὰ ὧδε." Διὰ τί μὴ συνῆλθες, φησί; Τί δέ ἐστι, "πάντα ὑμῖν γνωριοῦσι;" Τουτέστι, τὰ δεσμά, καὶ τὰ ἄλλα πάντα τὰ κατέχοντά με. Οὐκ ἂν οὖν ὁ προσευχόμενος αὐτοὺς ἰδεῖν, ὁ καὶ ἑτέρους ἀποστέλλων, αὐτὸς ὑστέρησα, μὴ μεγάλης ἀνάγκης με κατεχούσης. Καὶ μὴν τοῦτο οὐκ ἦν ἐγκαλούντων. Καὶ μὴν σφόδρα ἐγκαλούντων. Τὸ γὰρ μαθεῖν ὅτι καὶ πειρασμοῖς περιέπεσε καὶ ἤνεγκε γενναίως, τοῦτο πιστουμένου ἦν τὸ πρᾶγμα, καὶ ἀνορθοῦντος τὰς ἐκείνων ψυχάς.

"Σὺν Ὀνησίμῳ, φησί, τῷ ἀγαπητῷ καὶ πιστῷ ἀδελφῷ." Ἀδελφὸν τὸν δοῦλον ὁ Παῦλός φησιν, εἰκότως· ὅπου γε καὶ ἑαυτὸν δοῦλον ὀνομάζει τῶν

to build superfluous enmities? Again, if you're instructing anybody, speak on the subject before you, then be silent.

If the speech is *seasoned with salt*, even if it falls into a soul that fluctuates, it will bind its looseness; if into a soul that's rough, it will smooth its stiffness, being agreeable. Let it be neither vulgar, nor again stiff, but let it have both sternness and with it pleasure. You see, if one were to be immoderately stern, they would harm more than help. But if they are immoderately charming, they give more pain than pleasure, so that everywhere there should be moderation. Don't be downcast either and sour-faced, for that is offensive; don't be relaxed either, for that's easy to despise and trample underfoot. No, as the bee, gathering the virtue of each, the cheerfulness of the one, the gravity of the other, avoid the defect. For if a physician doesn't deal with bodies in the same way, even less should a teacher. Yet bodies will bear conflicting drugs better than a soul, language. For example, a Hellene comes to you, and do they become your friend? Don't discuss this subject with them at all, until they have become a good friend, and when they have, do it gradually.

See too how Paul conversed with them when he arrived in Athens. He didn't say, "O polluted and all-polluted," but what? "*Men of Athens, I perceive that in all ways you are too superstitious*" [Acts 17:22]. Again, when it was necessary to be insulting, he didn't resile, but with great vehemency he said to Elymas, "*O you who are full of all deceit and all mischief, son of the devil, enemy of all righteousness*" [Acts 13:10]. For just as to have insulted them would have been a sign of senselessness, [**292**] so not to have insulted this one would have been a sign of softness. Again, are you brought to a ruler on a matter of business? Render to him the honors that are due.

"*They will acquaint you,*" he says, "*with everything from here.*" Does he mean, "Why didn't you come?"[126] What's the meaning of *they will acquaint you*? That is, "my chains and everything else that restrains me. I, then, who pray to see them, who also sent others, should not have stayed behind myself unless a dire necessity restrained me." And yet this is not the language of accusation, indeed of vehement accusation. For learning that he had both fallen into trials and was bearing them nobly is the deed of one who was confirming the fact and lifting up their souls.

"*With Onesimus,*" he says, "*the beloved and faithful brother.*" Paul calls the servant "*brother,*" with reason, seeing that he speaks of himself as a ser-

---

126. Some manuscripts read "why didn't I come."

πιστῶν. Κατενέγκωμεν πάντες τὸν τῦφον, πατήσωμεν τὴν ἀλαζονείαν. Δοῦλον ἑαυτὸν ὀνομάζει Παῦλος, ὁ τῆς οἰκουμένης ἀντάξιος καὶ μυρίων οὐρανῶν, καὶ σὺ μέγα φρονεῖς; ὁ πάντα ἄγων καὶ φέρων ὡς ἤθελεν, ὁ τὰ πρωτεῖα ἔχων ἐν τῇ βασιλείᾳ τῶν οὐρανῶν, ὁ ἐστεφανωμένος, ὁ εἰς τρίτον ἀνελθὼν οὐρανὸν, τοὺς δούλους ἀδελφοὺς καλεῖ, καὶ συνδούλους. Ποῦ ἡ μανία; ποῦ ἡ ἀλαζονεία; Οὕτως ἀξιόπιστος γέγονεν ὁ Ὀνήσιμος, ὥστε καὶ τοιαῦτα πιστεύεσθαι.

"Καὶ Μάρκος, φησὶν, ὁ ἀνεψιὸς Βαρνάβα, περὶ οὗ ἐλάβετε ἐντολάς· δέξασθε αὐτόν." Ἴσως παρὰ Βαρνάβα ἐντολὰς ἔλαβον. "Οἱ ὄντες ἐκ περιτομῆς." Καταστέλλει τῶν Ἰουδαίων τὸ φύσημα, ἐπαίρει τούτων τὰς ψυχὰς, ὅτι ὀλίγοι μὲν ἐκ περιτομῆς, οἱ δὲ πλείους ἐκ τῶν ἐθνῶν. "Οἵτινες ἐγενήθησάν μοι, φησὶ, παρηγορία." Δείκνυσιν ἑαυτὸν ἐν πειρασμοῖς ὄντα μεγάλοις. Ὥστε οὐδὲ τοῦτο μικρόν, ὅταν τοὺς ἁγίους παρακαλῶμεν καὶ παρουσίᾳ καὶ λόγῳ καὶ προσεδρείᾳ, ὅταν συγκακουχώμεθα· "Τοῖς δεσμίοις γὰρ, φησὶν, ὡς συνδεδεμένοι·" ὅταν τὰ ἐκείνων ἡμέτερα ποιῶμεν πάθη, καὶ ἐν τοῖς στεφάνοις κοινωνήσομεν.

Οὐχ εἱλκύσθης εἰς τὸ στάδιον; οὐ καθῆκας εἰς τὸν [293] ἀγῶνα; ἄλλος ἀπεδύσατο; ἄλλος παλαίει; Ἀλλ’ ἐὰν θέλῃς, κοινωνήσεις καὶ σύ· ἄλειψον ἐκεῖνον, γενοῦ αὐτοῦ φιλητὴς καὶ σπουδαστής, ἔξωθεν ἐπιβόα μεγάλα, διέγειρε τὴν δύναμιν, ἀνακτῶ τὴν ψυχήν. Ταῦτα ἐπὶ τῶν ἄλλων ἁπάντων γίνεσθαι ἀκόλουθον. Παῦλος γὰρ οὐκ ἐδεῖτο, ἀλλ’ ἐκείνους ἐπαίρων ἔλεγε ταῦτα. Σὺ τοίνυν ἐπὶ τῶν ἄλλων ἁπάντων τοὺς βουλομένους κακίζειν ἐπιστόμιζε, κατασκεύαζε αὐτῷ ἐραστάς, ὑπόδειξαι ἐξιόντα μετὰ πολλῆς τῆς θεραπείας· οὕτω κοινωνήσεις τῶν στεφάνων, οὕτω τῆς δόξης. Κἂν μηδὲν ἕτερον ποιήσῃς, ἡσθῇς δὲ ἐπὶ τοῖς γενομένοις, καὶ οὕτως ἐκοινώνησας οὐχ ὡς ἔτυχεν· εἰσήνεγκας γὰρ ἀγάπην, τὸ πάντων κεφάλαιον τῶν ἀγαθῶν.

Εἰ γὰρ οἱ κλαίοντες δοκοῦσι τοῦ πένθους κοινωνεῖν, καὶ μεγάλα χαρίζονται τοῖς πενθοῦσι, καὶ τὸ πολὺ τῆς ὀδύνης ἀναιροῦσι, πολλῷ μᾶλλον καὶ οἱ χαίροντες μείζονα ποιοῦσι τὴν ἡδονήν. Ὅσον γὰρ κακὸν τὸ μὴ ἔχειν τοὺς συλλυπουμένους, ἄκουε τοῦ προφήτου λέγοντος· "Καὶ ὑπέμεινα συλλυπούμενον, καὶ οὐχ ὑπῆρξε." Διὰ τοῦτο καὶ Παῦλός φησι· "Χαίρειν μετὰ χαιρό-

vant of the faithful [see 2 Cor 4:5]. Let's all bring down our pride, let's trample our arrogance underfoot. Paul speaks of himself as a servant, he who is worth the world and myriad heavens—and do you have lofty thoughts? The one who takes and bears everything as he wished, the one who has the first place in the kingdom of heaven, the one who was crowned, the one who ascended *into the third heaven* [2 Cor 12:2], calls servants *brothers* and *fellow servants*. Where's your madness? Where's your arrogance? So trustworthy was Onesimus as to be entrusted even with such things as these.

"*And Marcus*," he says, "*the cousin of Barnabas. From him you have received instructions. If he comes to you, receive him.*" Perhaps they had received instructions from Barnabas. *Who are of the circumcision.* He represents the swelling pride of the Jews, he inspires the souls of these people,[127] because few of them were of the circumcision, while the greater number came from the gentiles. "*Who have been*," he says, "*a comfort to me.*" He demonstrates that he himself is in the midst of great trials. So this isn't a small thing either, when we comfort the saints by presence, and deeds, and attendance, when we suffer adversity with them ("*for*," he says, "*as bound with those in bonds*"); when we make their sufferings our own, we shall also share in their crowns.

Haven't you been dragged into the stadium?[128] Haven't you gone down to [293] the contest? Is it another one who has stripped off? Another who wrestles? But if you wish, you too can share. Anoint him, become his follower and fan, from outside the contest shout loudly, stir up his strength, refresh his spirit. It follows that the same things should be done in all other cases. You see, Paul wasn't in need, but spoke in order to stimulate them. You, then, with all the others muzzle those who want to abuse him, arrange adherents for him, receive him with great attention as he exits: in this way you will share in the crowns, in this way in the glory. Even if you do nothing else, but rejoice in what is done, in this way too you've shared not accidentally, for you've contributed love, the sum total of all good things.

For if those who weep seem to share in the grief, and gratify greatly the ones in sorrow, and remove the worst of their pain, much more do those who rejoice make their pleasure greater. For how great an evil it is not to have companions in sorrow, listen to the prophet saying, "*And I waited patiently for someone to lament with me, and there was none*" [Ps

---

127. The Colossians are meant.

128. In what follows the masculine pronoun of the Greek has been retained, since in antiquity women did not compete in the games.

ντων, καὶ κλαίειν μετὰ κλαιόντων." Αὔξησον τὴν ἡδονήν· ἂν ἴδῃς τὸν ἀδελφὸν εὐδοκιμοῦντα, μὴ εἴπῃς· ἐκείνου ἡ εὐδοκίμησις, ἐγὼ τίνος ἕνεκεν χαίρω;
οὐκ ἀδελφοῦ ταῦτα τὰ ῥήματα, ἀλλὰ πολεμίου. Ἂν θέλῃς, οὐκ ἐκείνου ἐστὶν,
ἀλλὰ σοῦ· σὺ κύριος ποιῆσαι αὐτὴν μείζονα, ἂν μὴ κατηφῇς, ἀλλ' ἡσθῇς, ἂν
φαιδρὸς γένῃ, ἂν γεγανωμένος. Καὶ ὅτι οὕτως ἔχει, ἐκεῖθεν δῆλον· οἱ φθονοῦντες οὐκ ἐκείνοις φθονοῦσι μόνοις τοῖς εὐδοκιμοῦσιν, ἀλλὰ καὶ τοῖς ταῖς ἐκείνων εὐδοκιμήσεσι χαίρουσιν· οὕτως ἴσασιν ὅτι καὶ οὗτοι ἐν τῇ εὐδοκιμήσει
εἰσὶ, καὶ οὗτοι μάλιστά εἰσιν οἱ σεμνυνόμενοι. Ἐκεῖνος μὲν γὰρ καὶ ἐρυθριᾷ
σφόδρα ἐγκωμιαζόμενος· οὗτος δὲ μετὰ πολλῆς τῆς ἡδονῆς ἐγκαλλωπίζεται.
Οὐχ ὁρᾶτε ἐπὶ τῶν ἀθλητῶν πῶς ὁ μὲν στεφανοῦται, ὁ δὲ οὐ στεφανοῦται;
ἡ δὲ ὀδύνη καὶ χαρὰ τῶν ἐραστῶν ἐστι καὶ τῶν μισούντων· ἐκεῖνοι πηδῶσιν,
ἐκεῖνοι σκιρτῶσιν.

Ὅρα πόσον ἐστὶ τὸ μὴ φθονεῖν· ἑτέρου ὁ πόνος, καὶ σοῦ ἡ ἡδονή· ἕτερος
τὸν στέφανον περίκειται, καὶ σὺ σκιρτᾷς, σὺ ἐγκαλλωπίζῃ. Εἰπὲ γάρ μοι,
ἄλλος νενίκηκε, [294] σὺ τί πηδᾷς; Ἀλλ' ἴσασι κἀκεῖνοι καλῶς, ὅτι κοινὸν τὸ
γενόμενον. Διὰ τοῦτο τούτῳ μὲν οὐκ ἐγκαλοῦσιν οἱ φθονοῦντες, πειρῶνται
δὲ καταβάλλειν τὴν νίκην· καὶ ἀκούεις ῥήματα τοιαῦτα λεγόντων αὐτῶν,
ἐξήλειψά σε, καὶ, κατέβαλόν σε· καίτοιγε ἑτέρου τὸ ἔργον, ἀλλὰ τὸ ἐγκώμιον
σόν. Εἰ δὲ ἐν τοῖς ἔξωθεν τοσοῦτον ἀγαθὸν τὸ μὴ φθονεῖν, ἀλλ' οἰκειοῦσθαι τὰ
ἑτέρου ἀγαθὰ, πολλῷ μᾶλλον ἐπὶ τῇ νίκῃ τοῦ διαβόλου τῇ καθ' ἡμῶν πλέον
πνεῖ, δηλονότι ὡς πλέον ἡδομένων. Καίτοιγε μιαρὸς ὢν καὶ πικρὸς, οἶδεν
ἀκριβῶς ὅτι μεγάλη αὕτη ἡ ἡδονή. Θέλεις αὐτὸν λυπῆσαι; ἥσθητι καὶ χάρηθι.
Θέλεις αὐτὸν εὐφρᾶναι; σκυθρωπὸς γενοῦ· τὴν ἐκ τῆς νίκης τοῦ ἀδελφοῦ
γενομένην αὐτῷ λύπην ἐπικουφίζεις διὰ τῆς σῆς ἀθυμίας· μετ' ἐκείνου ἵστα-
σαι ἀποσχισθεὶς τοῦ ἀδελφοῦ· μεῖζον ἢ ἐκεῖνος ποιεῖς κακόν. Οὐ γάρ ἐστιν
ἴσον ἐχθρὸν ὄντα τὰ τῶν ἐχθρῶν ποιεῖν, καὶ φίλον ὄντα μετὰ τῶν ἐχθρῶν
ἵστασθαι· οὗτος τῶν ἐχθρῶν μιαρώτερος. Εἰ εὐδοκίμησεν ὁ ἀδελφὸς, ἢ λέγων,
ἢ ἐπιδεικνύμενος, ἢ κατορθῶν, γενοῦ κοινωνὸς τῆς εὐδοκιμήσεως, δεῖξον ὅτι
μέλος ἐστὶ σόν.

Καὶ πῶς, φησίν; ἐγὼ γὰρ οὐκ εὐδοκιμῶ. Μὴ φθέγξῃ ποτὲ τὸ ῥῆμα τοῦτο·
σύνελε τὰ χείλη. Εἴγε πλησίον μου ἧς ὁ ταῦτα λέγων, ἐπέθηκα ἂν καὶ τὴν
χεῖρα τοῖς χείλεσι, μὴ ἀκούσῃ ὁ ἐχθρός. Πολλάκις πρὸς ἀλλήλους ἔχθρας
ἔχομεν, καὶ τοῖς ἐχθροῖς οὐκ ἐπιδεικνύμεθα· τῷ διαβόλῳ οὖν ἐπιδείκνυσαι

69:20]. This is why Paul too says, "*Rejoice with those who rejoice, and weep with those who weep*" [Rom 12:15]. Increase their pleasure. If you see your brother enjoying good esteem, don't say, "The good esteem is his; why should I rejoice on account of it?" These words are not those of a brother but of an enemy. If you wish, it's not his, but yours. You have the power of making it greater, if you're not downcast, but pleased, if you're cheerful, if you're joyous. And that this is a fact is clear from this: those who envy don't envy only those in good esteem but also the ones who rejoice at their good esteem, so they know that these are also in good esteem, and that these are the ones who particularly glory in it. For the other blushes when praised exceedingly, but this one with great pleasure prides themselves on it. Don't you observe how with athletes one is crowned, the other is not crowned? But the pain and the joy is among the adherents and those who hate, these are the ones who leap for joy, these are the ones who spring.

See how great a thing it is not to envy. The work is another's, the pleasure is yours; another wears the crown, and you spring, you glory in it. For tell me, another person has won [**294**]—why are you leaping for joy? But they also know well that what's been done is common. This is why the envious ones don't charge them with this but try to overthrow the victory. And you hear them saying words such as these: "I wiped you out" and "I beat you down." Although the work was another's, still the praise is yours. But if in cases with outsiders it's such a great good not to be envious but to make another's good one's own, much more in the case of the victory over the devil, in which he breathes more vehemently against us, evidently because we're more pleased. Although he is foul and wicked, he knows exactly that this pleasure is great. Do you wish to grieve him? Be glad and rejoice. Do you wish to please him? Be downcast. The pain he has from your brother's victory you soothe by your sadness; you stand with the devil, separated from your brother; you work greater evil than he. You see, it isn't the same for one who's an enemy to do the deeds of enemies and for a friend to stand with enemies. That one is fouler than the enemies. If your brother has enjoyed good esteem, by either speaking or by brilliance of achievement, become a sharer in his good esteem, demonstrate that he is your member.

"And how?" asks [someone]. "You see the good esteem isn't mine." Don't ever use this expression. Button your lips. If you who said that were near me, I would have put my hand on your lips, lest the enemy hear you. Often we have enmities with one another, and we don't display them to the enemies. Therefore, do you display them to the devil? Don't say the

σύ; Μὴ εἴπῃς τοῦτο, μὴ ἐννοήσῃς· ἀλλὰ καὶ τοὐναντίον, μέλος ἐστὶν ἐμόν· εἰς τὸ σῶμα διαβαίνει ἡ δόξα. Τί οὖν, φησὶν, ὅτι οἱ ἔξωθεν οὐχ οὕτω διάκεινται; Ὅτι σὺ αἴτιος· ὅταν ἴδωσί σε ἀλλοτριούμενον αὐτοῦ τὴν ἡδονήν, καὶ αὐτοὶ ἀλλοτριοῦνται· ὡς ἂν ἴδωσί σε οἰκειούμενον, οὐ τολμῶσιν· ἀλλ᾽ ὁμοίως εἶ καὶ σὺ λαμπρός.

Οὐκ εὐδοκίμησας λέγων, ἀλλ᾽ εὐδοκίμησας συνηδόμενος μειζόνως, ἢ ἐκεῖνος. Εἰ γὰρ ἡ ἀγάπη μέγα καὶ πάντων κεφάλαιον, σὺ τὸν ἐκ ταύτης ἔλαβες στέφανον· ἐκεῖνος τὸν ἐκ τῆς ῥητορείας, σὺ τὸν ἐκ τοῦ σφόδρα φιλεῖν· ἐκεῖνος ἐπεδείξατο ῥημάτων ἰσχὺν, σὺ διὰ τῶν ἔργων τὸν φθόνον κατέβαλες, ἐπάτησας τὴν βασκανίαν. Ὥστε εἰκότως ἂν μᾶλλον ἐκείνου στεφανωθείης· λαμπρότερος ὁ σὸς ἀγών. Οὐκ ἐπάτησας μόνον τὴν βασκανίαν, ἀλλὰ καὶ ἕτερόν τι πεποίηκας. Ἐκεῖνος ἕνα ἔχει [295] στέφανον μόνον, σὺ δὲ δύο, καὶ τοὺς δύο τοῦ ἑνὸς λαμπροτέρους. Ποίους τούτους; Ἕνα μὲν ὂν ἀνείλου κατὰ τοῦ φθόνου, δεύτερον δὲ ὂν ἀνεδήσω ἐκ τῆς ἀγάπης. Οὐ γὰρ τοῦ καθαρὸν εἶναι φθόνου τεκμήριον μόνον τὸ συνήδεσθαι, ἀλλὰ καὶ τοῦ ἀγάπην ἔχειν ἐρριζωμένην. Ἐκείνῳ πολλάκις καὶ ἀνθρώπινόν τι διενοχλεῖ πάθος, οἷον ἡ κενοδοξία· σὺ δὲ παντὸς εἶ πάθους καθαρός· οὐ γὰρ δὴ κενοδοξῶν χαίρεις ἐπὶ τοῖς ἑτέρου καλοῖς. Ὤρθωσε τὴν ἐκκλησίαν, εἰπέ μοι; ηὔξησε τὸν σύλλογον; ἐπαίνεσον πάλιν· ἔχεις διπλοῦς τοὺς στεφάνους· τὸν φθόνον κατέβαλες, τὴν ἀγάπην ἀνεδήσω. Ναί, δέομαι καὶ ἀντιβολῶ. Βούλει καὶ τρίτον ἀκοῦσαι στέφανον; τοῦτον οἱ κάτω κροτοῦσιν ἄνθρωποι, σὲ οἱ ἄνω ἄγγελοι. Οὐ γάρ ἐστιν ἴσον εὐέπειαν ἐπιδείκνυσθαι, καὶ παθῶν κρατεῖν. Οὗτος ὁ ἔπαινος πρόσκαιρος, ἐκεῖνος αἰώνιος· οὗτος ἐξ ἀνθρώπων, ἐκεῖνος ἐκ θεοῦ· οὗτος φαίνεται ἐστεφανωμένος, σὺ δὲ ἐν τῷ κρυπτῷ στεφανοῦσαι, ὅπου ὁ πατήρ σου ὁρᾷ. Εἰ τὸ σῶμα ἀποσχίσαντα τὴν ἑκάστου ψυχὴν ἦν ἰδεῖν, ἔδειξα ἄν σοι τοῦτον ἐκείνου σεμνότερον, μᾶλλον ἀποστίλβοντα.

Πατήσωμεν τὰ κέντρα τῆς βασκανίας, ἑαυτοὺς ὠφελοῦμεν, ἀγαπητοί, αὐτοὶ ἀναδησόμεθα τὸν στέφανον. Ὁ βασκαίνων, τῷ θεῷ μάχεται, οὐκ ἐκείνῳ· ὅταν γὰρ ἴδῃ χάριν ἔχοντα, καὶ ἀλγῇ, καὶ βούληται καθαιρεῖσθαι τὴν ἐκκλησίαν, οὐκ ἐκείνῳ μάχεται, ἀλλὰ τῷ θεῷ. Εἰπὲ γάρ μοι, εἴ τις κόρην ἐκαλλώπιζε βασιλέως, καὶ εὐδοκίμει καλλωπίζων αὐτὴν καὶ σεμνὴν ἐργαζόμενος, ἕτερος δέ τις ἐβούλετο ταύτην ἀσχημονῆσαι, καὶ μὴ δυνηθῆναι καλλωπίσαι, τίνι ἂν ἐπεβούλευσε, τούτῳ, ἢ ἐκείνῃ καὶ τῷ ταύτης πατρί; Οὕτω καὶ νῦν

following: "Don't think like that," but the very opposite: "He's a member of mine; the glory passes onto the body." "So how is it," asks one, "that the outsiders don't think like that?" Because you're to blame: when they see you appropriating his pleasure, they too appropriate it; if they see you making it your own, they wouldn't dare to do so, but you too would be equally illustrious.

You haven't achieved good esteem by oratory, but by sharing in his joy you have achieved more than he. For if it's a great thing and the sum of everything, you've received the crown this gives: he for oratory, you for your strong love; he displayed force of words, you by deeds have brought down envy, you've trodden evil under foot. So it's reasonable for you to be crowned more than he—your contest is more brilliant. You haven't only trodden evil underfoot but you've done something else besides. He has one crown [295] only, while you have two, and both more brilliant than his one. What are these? The one that you won against envy, the second that you are crowned with love. For it's not only your being cleansed from envy that is a proof of sharing his joy, but also of being rooted in love. Often he's annoyed by some human passion, for example vainglory, but you're cleansed from all passion, for it's not from vainglory that you rejoice at another's good things. Has he put the church to rights, tell me? Has he increased the congregation? Praise him; again you have a double crown: you have brought down envy, you are crowned with love. Yes, I implore and beseech you. Do you want to hear about a third crown too? This person human beings below applaud; you, the angels above. You see, it isn't the same thing to display eloquence and to conquer passions. This praise is temporary, the other is eternal; this is from human beings, that is from God; this person is crowned openly, while you are crowned in secret, where your Father observes. If it were possible to tear off the body and see the soul of each, I would have demonstrated that this one is more dignified than the other, more resplendent.

Let's tread underfoot the goads of envy: we advantage ourselves, beloved, we shall put on the crown ourselves. The one who is envious fights with God, not with themselves. For when they see that the person possesses grace, and is grieved, and wants to pull down the church, they aren't fighting with themselves but with God. Tell me, if someone were to adorn an emperor's daughter, and by adorning and gracing her gain good esteem, while another wished they could make her unseemly and was unable to adorn her, against whom would they have been plotting mischief—against the other? Or against her and her father? So even now you, the envious

σὺ ὁ βασκαίνων μάχῃ τῇ ἐκκλησίᾳ, τῷ θεῷ πολεμεῖς. Ἐπειδὴ γὰρ τῇ εὐδοκιμήσει τοῦ ἀδελφοῦ συμπέπλεκται καὶ ἡ τῆς ἐκκλησίας ὠφέλεια, ἀνάγκη,
ταύτης καταλυομένης, κἀκείνην καταλύεσθαι· ὥστε καὶ κατὰ τοῦτο, ἔργον
σατανικὸν ποιεῖς, ἐπιβουλεύων τῷ σώματι τοῦ Χριστοῦ. Πρὸς τοῦτον ἀλγεῖς;
κακῶς μέν, τὸν οὐδὲν ἠδικηκότα, πολλῷ δὲ μᾶλλον πρὸς τὸν Χριστόν. Τί σε
ἠδίκησεν, ὅτι οὐκ ἀφίης τὸ σῶμα αὐτοῦ καλλωπισθῆναι τῷ κάλλει; ὅτι οὐκ
ἀφίης τὴν νύμφην [296] κοσμηθῆναι; Θέα δέ μοι τὴν τιμωρίαν, ὅση· τοὺς
ἐχθροὺς εὐφραίνεις τοὺς σούς, καὶ αὐτὸν ἐκεῖνον τὸ εὐδοκιμοῦντα, ὃν βούλει
λυπῆσαι φθονῶν, μᾶλλον αὐτὸν εὐφραίνεις, μᾶλλον δεικνύεις, ὅτι εὐδοκίμησε
βασκαίνων· οὐ γὰρ ἂν ἐβάσκηνας· μᾶλλον δεικνύεις ὅτι τιμωρῇ. Αἰσχύνομαι
μὲν οὖν ἀπὸ τούτων προτρέπων·

πλὴν ἀλλ᾽ ἐπειδὴ οὕτως ἀσθενῶς διακείμεθα, καὶ ἀπὸ τούτων παιδευθέ-
ντες τοῦ ὀλεθρίου τούτου πάθους ἀπαλλαγῶμεν. Ἀλγεῖς ὅτι εὐδοκίμησε; τί
οὖν τὴν εὐδοκίμησιν αὐτοῦ ἐπαίρεις φθονῶν; Βούλει αὐτὸν τιμωρήσασθαι; τί
οὖν δεικνύεις ὅτι ἀλγεῖς; τί τιμωρίαν σαυτὸν ἀπαιτεῖς ἔμπροσθεν τούτου, ὃν
βούλει μὴ εὐδοκιμεῖν; Διπλῆ λοιπὸν ἔσται ἡ ἡδονὴ τούτῳ, καὶ σοὶ ἡ τιμωρία, οὐ μόνον ὅτι μέγαν δεικνύεις αὐτόν, ἀλλ᾽ ὅτι καὶ ἑτέραν αὐτῷ ἐντίκτεις
ἡδονὴν τιμωρούμενος σαυτόν· καὶ πάλιν ὑπὲρ ὧν ἀλγεῖς, ἐκεῖνος ἥδεται, σοῦ
φθονοῦντος. Ὅρα πῶς πληγὰς χαλεπὰς ἑαυτοῖς διδόαμεν, καὶ οὐκ αἰσθανόμεθα. Ἐχθρός ἐστι; Καίτοιγε διὰ τί ἐχθρός; τί ἠδίκησεν; ἀλλ᾽ ὅμως τὸν ἐχθρὸν
λαμπρότερον ποιοῦμεν, καὶ ἡμᾶς αὐτοὺς πλέον κολάζομεν. Τούτῳ πάλιν ἑαυτοὺς τιμωρούμεθα, ἂν αἰσθώμεθα ὅτι ἔγνω ἐκεῖνος. Ἴσως μὲν γὰρ ἐκεῖνος οὐχ
ἥδεται· ἡμεῖς δὲ νομίζοντες ὅτι ἥδεται, πάλιν διὰ τοῦτο ἀλγοῦμεν. Οὐκοῦν
παῦσαι φθονῶν· τί τραύματα ἑαυτῷ παρέχεις;

Ταῦτα ἐννοήσωμεν, ἀγαπητοί, τοὺς στεφάνους τοὺς διπλοῦς τῶν μὴ φθο-
νούντων, τοὺς ἐπαίνους τοὺς παρὰ ἀνθρώπων, τοὺς παρὰ θεοῦ, τὰ κακὰ τὰ
ἀπὸ τῆς βασκανίας· καὶ οὕτω δυνησόμεθα σβέσαι τὸ θηρίον, καὶ εὐδοκιμῆ-
σαι ἔμπροσθεν τοῦ θεοῦ, καὶ τῶν αὐτῶν τυχεῖν τοῖς εὐδοκιμοῦσι. Τευξόμεθα
γὰρ ἴσως· κἂν μὴ τύχωμεν δέ, διὰ τὸ συμφέρον· καὶ οὕτω δυνησόμεθα εἰς
δόξαν θεοῦ ζήσαντες, τῶν ἐπηγγελμένων ἀγαθῶν τοῖς ἀγαπῶσιν αὐτὸν τυχεῖν,
χάριτι καὶ φιλανθρωπίᾳ τοῦ κυρίου ἡμῶν Ἰησοῦ Χριστοῦ, μεθ᾽ οὗ τῷ πατρὶ
ἅμα τῷ ἁγίῳ πνεύματι δόξα, κράτος, τιμή, νῦν καὶ ἀεὶ καὶ εἰς τοὺς αἰῶνας
τῶν αἰώνων. Ἀμήν.

person, are fighting against the church, you are at war with God. You see, since into the good esteem of your brother the advantage of the church is also interwoven, of necessity, if one be destroyed the other will be too. So, according to this, you're performing satanical work, plotting mischief against the body of Christ. Are you pained at that person? They wronged you in no way, but much more Christ. In what has Christ wronged you, that you won't permit his body to be adorned with beauty? That you won't permit his bride [296] to be decorated? Please consider how severe the punishment is. You gladden your enemies, and the one who is in good esteem, who in your envy you want to pain, you are rather gladdening, because through your envy he is in good esteem, for otherwise you wouldn't have envied him. Therefore, you demonstrate that you are being punished.

Indeed, I'm ashamed to exhort you from these motives, except that since our weakness is such, let's be instructed also from these and free ourselves from this destructive passion. Does it pain you that he's in good esteem? So why do you excite his good esteem by envying? Do you want to punish him? Why then do you do you demonstrate that you're in pain? Why punish yourself in front of him, the one whom you didn't want to hold in good esteem? After that, his pleasure will be double, also your punishment, not only because you demonstrate that he's great, but because you engender in him another pleasure by punishing yourself. And again, for what reasons are you pained: he's pleased while you're envious. See how we deal ourselves heavy blows and don't feel it. Is he an enemy? And yet why is he an enemy? What did he do wrong? Still, however, we make our enemy the more illustrious and punish ourselves the more. And by this we punish ourselves, if we have discovered that he knows it. For perhaps he isn't pleased, but we, thinking that he is pleased, again on this account are pained. So stop envying. Why inflict wounds on yourself?

Let's reflect on these matters, beloved: the two crowns belonging to those who don't envy, the praises from human beings, those from God, the evils that come from envy. And so shall we be able to quell the savage beast and be in good esteem before God, and obtain the same things as those of good esteem. For perhaps we shall obtain them, and even if we don't, it's through what is fitting. And so we shall be able, if we have lived to the glory of God, to attain the good things promised to those who love him, through the love and loving-kindness of our Lord Jesus Christ, with whom to the Father together with the Holy Spirit be glory, power, honor, now and forever and ever. Amen.

Ἀσπάζεται ὑμᾶς Ἐπαφρᾶς ὁ ἐξ ὑμῶν δοῦλος Χριστοῦ, πάντοτε ἀγωνιζόμενος ὑπὲρ ὑμῶν ἐν ταῖς προσευχαῖς, ἵνα στῆτε τέλειοι καὶ πεπληρωμένοι ἐν παντὶ θελήματι τοῦ θεοῦ. Μαρτυρῶ γὰρ αὐτῷ, ὅτι ἔχει ζῆλον πολὺν ὑπὲρ ὑμῶν, καὶ τῶν ἐν Λαοδικείᾳ, καὶ τῶν ἐν Ἱεραπόλει.

Καὶ ἀρχόμενος τῆς ἐπιστολῆς, συνέστησε τὸν ἄνδρα ἀπὸ ἀγάπης· ἀγάπην δὲ δείκνυσι καὶ τὸ ἐγκωμιάζειν· ὅπερ ἐξ ἀρχῆς εἶπεν, "Ὁ δηλώσας ἡμῖν, φησί, τὴν ὑμῶν ἀγάπην ἐν πνεύματι." Ἀγάπην δείκνυσι καὶ ποιεῖ φιλεῖσθαι, καὶ τὸ ὑπερεύχεσθαι. Συνίστησι δὲ αὐτόν, ἀνοίγων θύραν τῷ λόγῳ αὐτοῦ· τὸ γὰρ αἰδέσιμον εἶναι τὸν διδάσκαλον, μαθητῶν ὠφέλεια· καὶ πάλιν τῷ εἰπεῖν, "ἐξ ὑμῶν," ἵνα καὶ σεμνύνωνται ἐπὶ τῷ ἀνδρὶ, ἅτε τοιούτους φέροντες ἄνδρας. "Καὶ πάντοτε, φησίν, ἀγωνιζόμενος ὑπὲρ ὑμῶν ἐν ταῖς προσευχαῖς." Οὐχ ἁπλῶς εἶπεν, εὐχόμενος, ἀλλ᾽, "ἀγωνιζόμενος," τρέμων καὶ δεδοικώς. "Μαρτυρῶ γὰρ αὐτῷ, φησίν, ὅτι ἔχει ζῆλον πολὺν ὑπὲρ ὑμῶν." Ἀξιόπιστος μάρτυς. "Ὅτι ἔχει, φησί, ζῆλον πολὺν ὑπὲρ ὑμῶν·" τουτέστιν, ὅτι σφόδρα ὑμᾶς ἀγαπᾷ, καὶ ἐκκαίεται τῷ περὶ ὑμᾶς φίλτρῳ. "Καὶ τῶν ἐν Λαοδικείᾳ, φησί, καὶ τῶν ἐν Ἱεραπόλει." Κἀκείνοις αὐτὸν συνίστησιν. Ἀλλὰ πόθεν τοῦτο ἔμελλον εἰδέναι; Μάλιστα μὲν οὖν ἤκουσαν ἄν· πλὴν καὶ τῆς ἐπιστολῆς ἀναγινωσκομένης, ἐμάνθανον. "Ποιήσατε γὰρ, φησίν, ἵνα καὶ ἐν τῇ Λαοδικέων ἐκκλησίᾳ ἀναγνωσθῇ." "Ἵνα στῆτε, φησί, τέλειοι." Ἅμα καὶ κατηγορεῖ αὐτῶν, καὶ ἀνεπαχθῶς παραινεῖ καὶ συμβουλεύει. Ἔνι γὰρ καὶ τέλειον εἶναι, καὶ μὴ ἑστάναι, ὡς ἐάν τις πάντα μὲν εἰδῇ, σαλεύηται δὲ ἔτι· ἔνι καὶ μὴ τέλειον εἶναι, καὶ ἑστάναι, ὡς ἐάν τις μέρος μὲν εἰδῇ, ἑστήκῃ δὲ βεβαίως. Ἀλλ᾽ οὗτος ἀμφότερα εὔχεται, "ἵνα στῆτε, φησί, τέλειοι." Ὅρα ποῦ πάλιν [298] αὐτοὺς ὑπέμνησε τοῦ περὶ τῶν ἀγγέλων λόγου, καὶ περὶ τοῦ βίου. "Καὶ πεπληρωμένοι, φησίν, ἐν παντὶ θελήματι τοῦ θεοῦ." Οὐ γὰρ ἁπλῶς ἀρκεῖ τὸ

[297] *Epaphras, who is one of yourselves, a servant of Christ, greets you, always fighting for you in prayer, so that you may stand complete and fully assured in all the will of God. For I bear him witness, that he has a great zeal for you and for those in Laodicea and in Hierapolis* [Col 4:12–13].

Also in the beginning of the letter he commended the man from his love; also the praise demonstrates love, which he said in the beginning: "*Who also declared to us,*" he says, "*your love in the spirit*" [Col 1:8]. He demonstrates love and brings about affection and makes intercession. Paul commends him, opening a door to what he says, for reverence for the teacher is the disciples' advantage. And so again by saying "*of yourselves*" in order that they might be exalted concerning the man, as they produce such men. "*And always,*" he says, "*fighting for you in prayer.*" He didn't just say "praying," but "*fighting,*" trembling and fearful. "*For I bear him witness,*" he says, "*that he has a great zeal for you.*" Paul is a trustworthy witness. "*That he has a great zeal for you,*" he says, that is, "that he loves you exceedingly and burns with affection for you." "*And for those in Laodicea,*" he says, "*and for those in Hierapolis.*" He commends him to those also. But from what source were they going to know this? Most certainly they would have heard, except that they would learn it when the letter was read. "*For,*" he says, "*have it read also in church of Laodicea.*" "*So that you may stand complete,*" he says. At one and the same time he both accuses them and without offense gives them advice and counsel. You see, it's possible both to be complete and not to stand, as if one were to know all but still waver; it's possible both not to be complete and to stand, as if one were to know [only] a part, but stand firm. But this man prays for both: "*so that you may stand firm,*" he says. See how again [298] he's reminded them about what he said of the angels, and of life. "*And fully assured,*" he says, "*in all the will of God.*" You see, it's not

---

129. For a previous English translation of this homily, see *St John Chrysostom: On Marriage and Family Life,* trans. Roth and Anderson, 73–80.

θέλημα ποιεῖν. Ὁ πεπληρωμένος οὐκ ἀφίησιν ἄλλο θέλημα εἶναι ἐν αὐτῷ, ἐπεὶ οὐ πεπληροφόρηται. "Μαρτυρῶ γὰρ αὐτῷ, φησὶν, ὅτι ἔχει ζῆλον πολύν." Καὶ ζῆλον, καὶ πολύν· ἀμφότερα ἐπιτάσεως· ὥσπερ καὶ αὐτός φησι Κορινθίοις γράφων, "Ζηλῶ γὰρ ὑμᾶς θεοῦ ζήλῳ." "Ἀσπάζεται ὑμᾶς Λουκᾶς ὁ ἰατρὸς ὁ ἀγαπητός." Οὗτός ἐστιν ὁ εὐαγγελιστής. Οὐ τοῦτον δὲ ταπεινῶν, ὕστερον τίθησιν, ἀλλ' ἐκεῖνον ἐπαίρει τὸν Ἐπαφρόδιτον. Εἰκὸς εἶναι καὶ ἄλλους καλουμένους τῷ ὀνόματι τούτῳ. "Καὶ Δημᾶς," φησίν. Εἰπὼν δὲ, "Ἀσπάζεται ὑμᾶς Λουκᾶς ὁ ἰατρὸς," προσέθηκεν, "ὁ ἀγαπητός." Ἐγκώμιον καὶ τοῦτο οὐ μικρὸν, ἀλλὰ καὶ σφόδρα μέγα, τὸ Παύλου εἶναι ἀγαπητόν.

"Ἀσπάσασθε τοὺς ἐν Λαοδικείᾳ ἀδελφοὺς, καὶ Νυμφᾶν, καὶ τὴν κατ' οἶκον αὐτοῦ ἐκκλησίαν." Ὅρα πῶς αὐτοὺς συγκολλᾷ καὶ συνάπτει πρὸς ἑαυτούς, οὐ τῷ ἀσπάσασθαι μόνον, ἀλλὰ καὶ τῷ τὰς ἐπιστολὰς ἀντιδοῦναι. Εἶτα πάλιν χαρίζεται, κατ' ἰδίαν αὐτὸν προσαγορεύων. Ποιεῖ δὲ τοῦτο οὐχ ἁπλῶς, ἀλλὰ καὶ τοὺς ἄλλους εἰς τὸν αὐτὸν ἄγων ζῆλον. Οὐδὲ γὰρ μικρόν ἐστιν, ὅταν μὴ μετὰ τῶν λοιπῶν ἀριθμῆται. Ὅρα γοῦν πῶς δείκνυσι μέγαν τὸν ἄνδρα, εἴγε ἡ οἰκία αὐτοῦ ἐκκλησία ἦν.

"Καὶ ὅταν ἀναγνωσθῇ παρ' ὑμῖν ἡ ἐπιστολὴ, ποιήσατε ἵνα καὶ ἐν τῇ Λαοδικέων ἐκκλησίᾳ ἀναγνωσθῇ." Ἐμοὶ δοκεῖ εἶναί τινα τῶν γραφέντων ἐκεῖ, ἃ καὶ τούτους ἐχρῆν ἀκοῦσαι. Καὶ τούτοις μείζων ἦν ἡ ὠφέλεια, ὅταν ἑτέρων ἐγκαλουμένων, τὰ οἰκεῖα ἁμαρτήματα ἐπιγινώσκωσι. "Καὶ τὴν ἐκ Λαοδικείας, ἵνα καὶ ὑμεῖς ἀναγνῶτε." Τινὲς λέγουσιν, ὅτι οὐχὶ τὴν Παύλου πρὸς αὐτοὺς ἀπεσταλμένην, ἀλλὰ τὴν παρ' αὐτῶν Παύλῳ· οὐ γὰρ εἶπε, τὴν πρὸς Λαοδικέας, ἀλλὰ, τὴν ἐκ Λαοδικείας, φησὶ, γραφεῖσαν. "Καὶ εἴπατε Ἀρχίππῳ· βλέπε τὴν διακονίαν, ἣν παρέλαβες ἐν κυρίῳ, ἵνα αὐτὴν πληροῖς." Τίνος ἕνεκεν οὐ γράφει πρὸς αὐτόν; Ἴσως οὐκ ἐδεῖτο, ἀλλὰ ψιλῆς [299] μόνης ὑπομνήσεως, ὥστε σπουδαιότερος εἶναι.

enough just to do his will. The one who is *fully assured* doesn't allow any other will to be in themselves, since they are *fully assured*. "*For I bear him witness,*" he says, "*that he has a great zeal for you.*" Both *zeal,* and *great;* both are intense, as Paul himself says when writing to the Corinthians: "*I feel a divine jealousy for you*" [2 Cor 11:2].

Luke, the beloved physician, greets you. This is the evangelist. It's not to belittle him that Paul places him afterward, but he is elevating the other, Epaphroditus. It's probable that there were also others called by this name. "*And Demas.*" After saying, "*Luke, the physician, greets you,*" he adds "*beloved.*" And this is no small praise, but even exceedingly great, to be beloved of Paul.

Greet the brothers in Laodicea, and Nymphas, and the church in his[130] *house* [Col 4:15]. See how he binds them together and joins them with each other, not only by greeting but also by exchanging letters. Then again he pays him a compliment, addressing him individually. He doesn't do this without a reason, but drawing the others toward his zeal. You see, it isn't a small thing either when one isn't numbered with the rest. See anyway how he demonstrates that the man is great, inasmuch as his house was a church.

And when this letter has been read among you, have it read also in the church of Laodicea [Col 4:16]. It seems to me that there are some things written there that those people too needed to hear. And they had the greater advantage over the former people, when they recognized their own sins from the accusations brought against others. *And see that you read also the letter from Laodicea* [Col 4:17]. Some say that this isn't the one Paul sent to them but theirs to Paul.[131] For he didn't say "the one to the Laodiceans" but he says, "*the one* written *from Laodicea. And say to Archippus: 'See to it that you fulfill the ministry that you have received in the Lord'*" [Col 4:17]. For what reason doesn't Paul write to him? Perhaps Archippus didn't need it but only a bare [299] reminder, so as to be more enthusiastic.

---

130. Manuscripts of Col 4:15 differ on the question of whether the name and subsequent pronoun are masculine (Nymphas) or feminine (Nympha). Whereas most modern editions and translations of the New Testament think that the author of Colossians is referring to "Nympha and the church in her house," Chrysostom's text refers to "Nymphas and the church in his house." See Rom 16:7, where both Junias (masculine) and Junia (feminine) are possible, but Junia is far more likely.

131. Theodoret maintains that some commentators believed that Paul had written to Laodicea as well and immediately devised a fictitious letter (PG 82:625C–628A).

"Ὁ ἀσπασμὸς τῇ ἐμῇ χειρὶ Παύλου." Τοῦτο γνησιότητος καὶ φιλίας τεκμήριον, τὸ καὶ τὰ γράμματα ὁρᾷν, καὶ πάσχειν τι πρὸς ταῦτα. "Μνημονεύετέ μου τῶν δεσμῶν." Βαβαί, πόση παράκλησις; Τοῦτο γὰρ ἱκανὸν εἰς πάντα αὐτοὺς προτρέψαι, καὶ γενναιοτέρους ποιῆσαι πρὸς τοὺς ἀγῶνας· οὐ μόνον δὲ γενναιοτέρους, ἀλλὰ καὶ οἰκειοτέρους αὐτοὺς ἐποίει. "Ἡ χάρις μεθ' ὑμῶν. Ἀμήν."

Μέγα ἐγκώμιον, καὶ μεῖζον ἢ τῶν ἄλλων ἁπάντων, τὸ λέγειν περὶ τοῦ Ἐπαφρᾶ, "Ὁ ἐξ ὑμῶν δοῦλος Χριστοῦ." Καὶ διάκονον αὐτὸν ὑπὲρ αὐτῶν φησιν, ὥσπερ καὶ ἑαυτὸν τῆς ἐκκλησίας λέγει διάκονον, ὡς ὅταν λέγῃ· "Ἧς ἐγενόμην ἐγὼ Παῦλος διάκονος." Εἰς τὸ αὐτὸ ἀξίωμα ἀναφέρει τὸν ἄνδρα, καὶ σύνδουλον ἀνωτέρω καλεῖ, καὶ ἐνταῦθα δοῦλον. "Ὁ ἐξ ὑμῶν," φησίν· ὡς πρὸς μητέρα διαλεγόμενος, καὶ λέγων, ὁ ἐκ τῆς γαστρὸς τῆς σῆς. Ἀλλὰ τοῦτο φθόνον ἂν ἔτεκε τὸ ἐγκώμιον. Διὰ τοῦτο οὐκ ἀπὸ τούτων αὐτὸν συνίστησι μόνον, ἀλλὰ καὶ ἐκ τῶν πρὸς αὐτούς· καὶ ἐκεῖ φθόνον λύει, καὶ ἐνταῦθα. "Πάντοτε, φησίν, ἀγωνιζόμενος ὑπὲρ ὑμῶν·" οὐ νῦν μόνον παρ' ἡμῖν, ὥστε ἐπιδείξασθαι, οὐδὲ παρ' ὑμῖν μόνον, ὥστε ὑμῖν ἐπιδείξασθαι. Μεγάλην προθυμίαν ἔδειξε τῷ εἰπεῖν, "ἀγωνιζόμενος." Εἶτα, ἵνα μὴ δόξῃ κολακεύειν αὐτούς, ἐπήγαγεν, ὅτι "ζῆλον ἔχει πολὺν ὑπὲρ ὑμῶν, καὶ τῶν ἐν Λαοδικείᾳ, καὶ τῶν ἐν Ἱεραπόλει." Καὶ τὸ, "ἵνα στῆτε τέλειοι," καὶ τοῦτο οὐ κολακείας, ἀλλ' αἰδεσίμου διδασκάλου. Καὶ πεπληρωμένοι, φησί, καὶ τέλειοι. Τὸ μὲν ἔδωκε, τὸ δὲ εἶπεν ὑστερεῖν. Καὶ οὐκ εἶπεν, ἵνα μὴ σαλεύησθε, ἀλλ', "ἵνα στῆτε." Τὸ μέντοι παρὰ πολλῶν ἀσπάζεσθαι αὐτούς, ἀνακτᾶται αὐτούς, ὅταν μὴ μόνον οἱ οἰκεῖοι ἐξ αὐτῶν, ἀλλὰ καὶ ἕτεροι αὐτῶν μνημονεύωσι.

"Καὶ εἴπατε Ἀρχίππῳ· βλέπε τὴν διακονίαν, ἣν παρέλαβες ἐν κυρίῳ." Μάλιστα αὐτοὺς αὐτῷ ὑποτάττει. Οὐκέτι γὰρ ἂν ἔχοιεν ἐγκαλεῖν ἐκείνῳ ἐπιτιμῶντι αὐτούς, ὅταν αὐτοὶ ὦσιν ἀναδεδεγμένοι τὸ πᾶν· ἐπεὶ οὐκ ἔχει λόγον τοῖς μαθηταῖς περὶ τοῦ διδασκάλου λέγειν. Ἀλλ' ἐπιστομίζων αὐτούς, ταῦτα γράφει. "Εἴπατε, φησίν, Ἀρχίππῳ· βλέπε." Φοβοῦντός ἐστι τοῦτο τὸ ῥῆμα πανταχοῦ, ὡς ὅταν [300] λέγῃ, "Βλέπετε τοὺς κύνας·" "Βλέπετε

The greeting in my own hand, Paul [Col 4:18].[132] This is a proof of their sincerity and affection, their seeing his writing and feeling some emotion about it. *Remember my chains.* Wonderful! How great is the consolation? You see, this is enough to urge them on in all things and to make them nobler in their trials, but he made them not only nobler but also more familiar. *Grace be with you. Amen.*

It's great praise and greater than all the rest, his saying about Epaphras, "*Who is one of yourselves, a servant of Christ.*" And he calls him a minister for them, just as he says he himself is a minister of the church, as when he says, "*Of which I, Paul, became a minister*" [Col 1:23]. He elevates the man to the same rank and calls him above a *fellow servant,* and here a *servant.* "*Who is one of yourselves,*" he says, as if speaking to a mother, and saying, "who is from your womb." But this praise might have engendered envy. This is why Paul commends him not only from these things, but also from what had regard to themselves: both in the former place and here he breaks up envy. "*Always fighting for you,*" he says, not only now, in our midst, to make a display, nor only in your midst, to make a display before you. By saying "*fighting*" he demonstrated great earnestness. Then, lest he seem to be flattering them, he added, "*That he has great zeal for you and for those in Laodicea and those in Hierapolis.*" And the words "*So that you may stand complete*" are also not of flattery but of a revered master. And he says "*fully assured*" and "*complete.*" The one he granted them, the other he said was lacking. And he didn't say "so that you may not be shaken" but "*so that you may stand.*" However, their being greeted by many is refreshing to them, seeing that not only the friends among them but also others remember them.

And say to Archippus: "*Look out that you fulfill the ministry that you have received in the Lord*" [Col 4:17]. In particular Paul subjects them to himself entirely. You see, no longer could they complain about him for rebuking them, when they themselves had taken it all upon them, since it isn't possible to talk to the disciples about the master. But muzzling them, he writes this: "*Say to Archippus,*" he says, "*look out.*" This expression is used everywhere of fear, as when [**300**] he says, "*Look out for the dogs*" [Phil 3:2];

---

132. Like Chrysostom, Photius of Constantinople interprets these words as a sign of Paul's affection for the Colossians (fragment in Staab, *Pauluskommentare aus der griechischen Kirche,* 633). In classical and Christian antiquity the signature, or autograph, in the writer's own hand, even if the writer had dictated the letter, was valued as a sign of authenticity and intimacy (see Allen and Neil, *Greek and Latin Letters*).

μή τις ὑμᾶς ἔσται ὁ συλαγωγῶν·" "Βλέπετε μή πως ἡ ἐξουσία ὑμῶν αὕτη πρόσκομμα γένηται τοῖς ἀσθενοῦσι." Καὶ πανταχοῦ οὕτω φησὶν ὅταν φοβῇ. "Βλέπε, φησὶ, τὴν διακονίαν, ἣν παρέλαβες ἐν κυρίῳ, ἵνα αὐτὴν πληροῖς." Οὐδὲ ἀφίησιν αὐτὸν κύριον εἶναι, καθάπερ αὐτὸς ἔλεγεν· "Εἰ γὰρ ἑκὼν τοῦτο πράσσω, μισθὸν ἔχω· εἰ δὲ ἄκων, οἰκονομίαν πεπίστευμαι." "'Ἵνα αὐτὴν πληροῖς·" διηνεκῶς κεχρημένος σπουδῇ. "'Ἣν παρέλαβες ἐν κυρίῳ, ἵνα αὐτὴν πληροῖς." Πάλιν τὸ, ἐν, διὰ κυρίου, ἐστίν· αὐτός σοι ἔδωκε, φησὶν, οὐχ ἡμεῖς. Κἀκείνους ὑποτάττει αὐτῷ, ὅταν δεικνύῃ παρὰ θεοῦ αὐτὸν ἐγκεχειρισμένον· "Μνημονεύετέ μου τῶν δεσμῶν. Ἡ χάρις μεθ' ὑμῶν. Ἀμήν." Τὸν φόβον ἔλυσεν. Εἰ γὰρ ὁ διδάσκαλος ἐν δεσμοῖς, ἀλλ' ἡ χάρις αὐτὸν λύει. Καὶ τοῦτο τῆς χάριτος τὸ συγχωρεῖν αὐτὸν δεθῆναι· ἄκουε γὰρ τοῦ Λουκᾶ λέγοντος, ὅτι "'Ὑπέστρεφον οἱ ἀπόστολοι ἀπὸ προσώπου τοῦ συνεδρίου χαίροντες ὅτι κατηξιώθησαν ὑπὲρ τοῦ ὀνόματος αὐτοῦ ἀτιμασθῆναι." Καταξιωθῆναι γὰρ ὄντως ἐστὶ, καὶ τὸ ἀτιμασθῆναι καὶ τὸ δεθῆναι. Εἰ γὰρ ἐρώμενόν τις ἔχων, κέρδος ἡγεῖται τὸ δι' ἐκεῖνόν τι παθεῖν, πολλῷ μᾶλλον τὸ διὰ τὸν Χριστόν.

Μὴ τοίνυν ἀσχάλλωμεν περὶ τὰς θλίψεις διὰ Χριστόν, ἀλλὰ μνημονεύωμεν τῶν δεσμῶν Παύλου καὶ ἡμεῖς, καὶ τοῦτο ἔστω ἡμῖν προτροπή· οἷον, παραινεῖς τισι πένησι δοῦναι διὰ Χριστόν; ἀνάμνησον αὐτοὺς τῶν Παύλου δεσμῶν, καὶ σαυτὸν κἀκείνους ταλάνισον, εἰ ἐκεῖνος μὲν καὶ τὸ σῶμα ἐξέδωκε δεσμοῖς δι' αὐτὸν, σὺ δὲ οὐδὲ τροφῆς μεταδίδως. Ἐπήρθης ἐπὶ κατορθώμασι; μνημόνευσον τῶν Παύλου δεσμῶν, ὅτι οὐδὲν τοιοῦτον ἔπαθες, καὶ οὐκέτι ἐπαρθήσῃ. Ἐπεθύμησας τῶν τοῦ πλησίον; μνημόνευσον τῶν Παύλου δεσμῶν, καὶ ὄψει πῶς ἄτο-[301]πον ἐκεῖνον μὲν ἐν κινδύνοις εἶναι, σὲ δὲ τρυφᾶν. Ἐπεθύμησας πάλιν τρυφῆς; ἐν νῷ λάβε τὸ δεσμωτήριον Παύλου· ἐκείνου μαθητὴς εἶ, ἐκείνου συστρατιώτης· πῶς ἔχει λόγον, τὸν μὲν συστρατιώτην ἐν δεσμοῖς εἶναι, σὲ δὲ ἐν τρυφῇ; Ἐν θλίψει γέγονας, ἐνόμισας ἐγκαταλελεῖφθαι; ἄκουε τῶν Παύλου δεσμῶν, καὶ ὄψει ὅτι τὸ ἐν θλίψει εἶναι οὐκ ἐγκαταλείψεώς ἐστι τεκμήριον. Θέλεις σηρικὰ φορεῖν ἱμάτια; μνημόνευε τῶν Παύλου δεσμῶν, καὶ ταῦτά σοι φανεῖται τῶν ῥακίων τῆς ἀποκαθημένης ἀτιμότερα τῶν βεβορβορωμένων. Θέλεις χρυσία περιθέσθαι; ἐν νῷ λάβε τὰ Παύλου δεσμὰ, καὶ σχοίνου παλαιᾶς οὐδὲν ἄμεινόν σοι δόξει ταῦτα διακεῖσθαι. Θέλεις διαθεῖναι τὰς τρίχας, καὶ καλὴ φαίνεσθαι; ἐννόησον τὸν αὐχμὸν τοῦ Παύλου τὸν ἐν τῷ δεσμωτηρίῳ, καὶ ἐκκαήσῃ πρὸς ἐκεῖνο τὸ κάλλος, καὶ τοῦτο ἐσχάτην ἡγήσῃ δυσείδειαν, καὶ στενάξεις πικρὸν ἐπιθυμοῦσα ἐκείνων τῶν δεσμῶν.

"*Look out that nobody makes a prey of you*" [Col 2:8]; "*Look out lest somehow this liberty of yours become a stumbling block for the weak*" [1 Cor 8:9].
And he speaks like that everywhere when he's instilling fear. "*Look out for
the ministry,*" he says, "*that you have received in the Lord, that you fulfill it.*"
He doesn't even allow him authority, as he said himself: "*For if I do this of
my own will, I have a reward, but if not of my own will, I am entrusted with
a commission*" [1 Cor 9:17]. *That you fulfill it*, continually using diligence.
That you have received in the Lord, so that you fulfill it. Again the word
"*in*" means *in the Lord.* "He gave it to you," he says, "not we." He subjects
them totally to himself, when he demonstrates that they had been committed by God. *Remember my chains. Grace be with you. Amen.* He has
broken up their fear. You see, if the master is in chains, still grace releases
him. This too is from grace, allowing him to be chained. For listen to Luke
saying, "The apostles *left the presence of the council, rejoicing that they were
counted worthy to suffer dishonor for his name*" [Acts 5:41]. For both to be
dishonored and to be put in chains is truly to be *counted worthy.* You see, if
someone who has a loved one reckons it again to suffer something for their
sake, much more is it to suffer for Christ's sake.

Let's not be distressed, then, about the tribulations for Christ's sake,
but let's remember too Paul's chains, and let this be an exhortation to us.
For example: Do you advise people to give to the poor for Christ's sake?
Remind them of Paul's chains and bemoan your own misery and theirs,
if Paul indeed gave up his body to chains for Christ's sake, but you won't
give even some of your food. Are you elated because of your good deeds?
Remember Paul's chains, that you have suffered nothing of that sort, and
you'll be elated no longer. Do you desire something of your neighbor's?
Remember Paul's chains, and you'll see how [**301**] unnatural it is for him
to be in perils and you in luxury. Again, do you desire luxury? In your
mind picture Paul's prison: you are his disciple, his fellow soldier. How
is it reasonable that your fellow soldier is in chains, and you're in luxury?
Have you come into tribulation, have you reckoned that you're forsaken?
Listen to Paul's chains and you'll see that to be in tribulation is no proof
of being forsaken. Do you wish to wear silk? Remember Paul's chains, and
these things will appear to you to be more worthless than the filthy rags of
a menstruating woman. Do you wish to adorn yourself with gold? In your
mind picture Paul's chains, and these things will seem to you no better than
a withered bulrush. Do you wish to arrange your hair and appear beautiful? Imagine Paul's squalor in the prison and you'll burn for that beauty
and hold this to be the extreme of ugliness, and you'll groan bitterly as you

Θέλεις ἐπιτρίμματα καὶ ὑπογραφὰς ἑαυτῇ περιθεῖναι, καὶ ὅσα τοιαῦτα; ἐννόησον τὰ ἐκείνου δάκρυα· τριετίαν, νύκτα καὶ ἡμέραν οὐκ ἐπαύετο δακρύων.
Τούτῳ τῷ κόσμῳ καλλώπιζε τὴν παρειάν· ταῦτα τὰ δάκρυα λαμπρὰν αὐτὴν
ἐργάζεται. Οὐ λέγω ἵνα ὑπὲρ τῶν ἄλλων δακρύῃς· βούλομαι μὲν γὰρ καὶ
τοῦτο, ἀλλ᾽ ἀνώτερόν σού ἐστι τοῦτο· ἀλλ᾽ ὑπὲρ τῶν σῶν ἁμαρτημάτων τοῦτο
παραινῶ ποιεῖν. Ἐκέλευσας δεσμευθῆναι παῖδα, καὶ ὠργίσθης καὶ παρωξύν-
θης; μνημόνευε τῶν Παύλου δεσμῶν, καὶ εὐθέως παύσεις τὴν ὀργήν· ἀναμνήσθητι ὅτι τῶν δεδεμένων ἡμεῖς, ἀλλ᾽ οὐ τῶν δεόντων, τῶν συντετριμμένων τὴν
καρδίαν, οὐ τῶν συντριβόντων. Διεχύθης, καὶ ἀνεκάγχασας μέγα; ἔννοιαν
λάβε τῶν ἐκείνου ὀδυρμῶν, καὶ στενάξεις· πολλῷ σε λαμπροτέραν τὰ δάκρυα
ταῦτα δείκνυσιν. Εἶδες τρυφῶντας καὶ ὀρχουμένους; μνημόνευσον αὐτοῦ τῶν
δακρύων. Ποία πηγὴ τοσαῦτα ἀνέβλυσε νάματα, ὡς οἱ ὀφθαλμοὶ ἐκεῖνοι τὰ
δάκρυα; Μνημονεύετέ μου, φησί, τῶν δακρύων, ὥσπερ τῶν [302] δεσμῶν
ἐνταῦθα. Καὶ εἰκότως ἐκείνοις ταῦτα εἶπεν, ἡνίκα ἀπὸ τῆς Ἐφέσου αὐτοὺς
μετεστείλατο εἰς τὴν Μίλητον· διδασκάλοις γὰρ ἔλεγεν· ὥστε ἐκείνους μὲν
καὶ τὸ συναλγεῖν ἀπαιτεῖ, τούτους δὲ τὸ κινδυνεύειν μόνον.

Ποίαν βούλει παραβαλεῖν πηγὴν τοῖς δάκρυσι τούτοις; τὴν ἐν τῷ παραδείσῳ, τὴν ποτίζουσαν τὴν γῆν ἅπασαν; Ἀλλ᾽ οὐδὲν ἴσον ἐρεῖς· αὕτη γὰρ ἡ
τῶν δακρύων πηγὴ ψυχὰς ἐπότιζεν, οὐ γῆν. Εἴ τις ἡμῖν δεδακρυμένον ἔδειξε
Παῦλον καὶ στενάζοντα, οὐ πολλῷ ἦν βέλτιον ἰδεῖν, ἢ μυρίους χοροὺς φαιδρῶς
ἐστεφανωμένους; Οὐ λέγω περὶ ὑμῶν· ἀλλ᾽ εἴ τις ἀπὸ τοῦ θεάτρου καὶ τῆς
σκηνῆς ἀποσπάσας τινὰ τῶν ἀκολάστων ἐκκαιόμενον καὶ βακχευόμενον τῷ
τῶν σωμάτων ἔρωτι, ἐδείκνυ κόρην παρθένον ἐν αὐτῷ τῆς ἡλικίας τῷ ἄνθει τά
τε ἄλλα νικῶσαν τὰς ὁμήλικας, καὶ τῇ ὄψει ὑπὲρ τὰ λοιπὰ μέλη, ὀφθαλμὸν
ἔχουσαν μαλακὸν καὶ ἁπαλόν, ἐγκαθήμενον ἠρέμα, περιστρεφόμενον ἠρέμα,
ὑγρόν, ἥμερον, γαληνὸν μειδιῶντα, καὶ πολλῇ μὲν περιεσταλμένον τῇ αἰδοῖ,
πολλῇ δὲ τῇ χάριτι, βλεφάρισι κυαναῖς κάτωθεν καὶ ἄνωθεν ἐστεφανωμένην,
τὴν κόρην ἔμψυχον, ὡς εἰπεῖν, ἔχουσαν, λάμπον τὸ μέτωπον, κάτωθεν πάλιν
τὴν παρειὰν εἰς ἀκριβῆ ἐρυθρότητα ἀφικνουμένην, μαρμάρου δίκην λείαν
ὑποκειμένην, ὁμαλήν· εἶτά μοι ἔδειξε Παῦλον δακρύοντα, ταύτην ἂν ἀφεὶς
ἐπεπήδησα τῇ τούτου θέα· κάλλος γὰρ ἀπέλαμπεν ἀπὸ τούτων τῶν ὀφθαλμῶν πνευματικόν. Ἐκεῖνο μὲν γὰρ ποιεῖ ἐξίστασθαι νέων ψυχάς, ἐκκαίει καὶ

long for those chains. Do you wish to apply cosmetics[133] or pigments to yourself, and all such things? Imagine his tears: over three years, night and day, he didn't stop weeping [see Acts 20:31]. With this adornment beautify your cheek: these tears make it bright. I don't say that you should weep for others (you see, I want this indeed to be so, but this is too lofty for you)—no, I advise you to do this for you own sins. Have you ordered a slave to be put in chains, and were you angry and exasperated? Remember Paul's chains, and you'll stop your anger immediately. Remind yourself that we belong to those who are bound, but not to those who bind, to the bruised of heart, not to the bruisers. Have you broken down and burst into violent laughter? Imagine Paul's lamentations and you'll groan; these tears will demonstrate that you're brighter by far. Have you seen people reveling and dancing? Remember his tears.[134] What fountain has gushed forth such great streams as those eyes did tears? "Remember my tears," he says, "as if [**302**] they were chains here." And with reason he said this to them, when he sent for them from Ephesus to Miletus [see Acts 20:15–17], for he was speaking to teachers. So he demands that those should suffer together, while these should only encounter danger.

What kind of fountain do you want to compare to these tears? The one in paradise, which waters the whole earth [see Gen 2:6]? No, you'll mention nothing like it, for the fountain of tears watered souls, not earth. If someone were to show us Paul in tears and groaning, wouldn't that be better to see than myriad dance groups splendidly crowned? I'm not speaking about you, but if somebody who had dragged away from the theater and the stage a person from among the licentiousness ones, burning and carousing with carnal love, showed them a young girl in the very flower of her youth, both in other respects surpassing those of the same age and in her face more than the rest of her body, one who possessed a tender and soft eye that is quietly steady, quietly turning, moist, mild, calmly smiling, and arrayed in much modesty, in much grace, fringed with dark eyelashes both on the top and the bottom, having a spirited pupil, so to speak, a radiant forehead, underneath again the cheek that achieves exact blush, lying smooth as marble, even. Then show me Paul weeping; leaving that girl, I would have leapt away at the sight of him, for the other one makes the souls of youths amazed, burns and inflames them, but this, on the contrary,

---

133. Greek ἐπιτρίμματα, an unusual word (see *PGL*, 538 s.v.).

134. On the subject of Paul's tears in Chrysostom's work, see the extensive discussion in Mitchell, *Heavenly Trumpet*, 186–90.

φλέγει· τοῦτο δὲ τοὐναντίον καταστέλλει. Τοῦτο τοὺς ὀφθαλμοὺς ὡραιοτέ-
ρους τοὺς τῆς ψυχῆς ἐργάζεται, κατασπᾷ γαστέρα, φιλοσοφίας ἐμπίπλησι,
συμπαθείας πολλῆς, καὶ ἀδαμαντίνην μαλάξαι δύναται ψυχήν. Τούτοις ἄρδε-
ται ἡ ἐκκλησία, τούτοις ψυχαὶ φυτεύονται τοῖς δάκρυσι· κἂν πῦρ ᾖ, ταῦτα τὰ
δάκρυα σβέσαι δύναται, καὶ αἰσθητὸν καὶ σωματικόν· ταῦτα τὰ δάκρυα τὰ
βέλη τοῦ πονηροῦ τὰ πεπυρωμένα σβέννυσι.

Μνημονεύωμεν τοίνυν τῶν δακρύων αὐτοῦ, καὶ πάντων καταγελασόμεθα
τῶν παρόντων. Ταῦτα ἐμακάριζεν ὁ Χριστὸς τὰ δάκρυα, λέγων· "Μακάριοι
[303] οἱ πενθοῦντες," καὶ, "Μακάριοι οἱ κλαίοντες, ὅτι αὐτοὶ γελάσονται."
Τοιαῦτα καὶ Ἡσαΐας, καὶ Ἱερεμίας ἠφίει δάκρυα· καὶ ὁ μὲν ἔλεγεν, "Ἄφετέ
με, πικρῶς κλαύσομαι·" ὁ δὲ ἔλεγε, "Τίς δώσει τῇ κεφαλῇ μου ὕδωρ, καὶ τοῖς
ὀφθαλμοῖς μου πηγὰς δακρύων;" ὡς οὐκ ἀρκούσης τῆς φυσικῆς.

Οὐδὲν τῶν δακρύων τούτων ἥδιον· παντὸς γέλωτος ταῦτα ἡδύτερα.
Ἴσασιν οἱ πενθοῦντες, πόσην ἔχει τὸ πρᾶγμα παραμυθίαν. Μὴ ἀπευκτὸν αὐτὸ
εἶναι νομίζωμεν, ἀλλὰ καὶ σφόδρα εὐκτόν, οὐχ ὥστε ἑτέρους ἁμαρτάνειν, ἀλλ'
ὥστε ἁμαρτανόντων αὐτῶν ἡμᾶς κατακλᾶσθαι. Τούτων μνημονεύωμεν τῶν
δακρύων, τούτων τῶν δεσμῶν. Ἄρα καὶ ἐπὶ τὰ δεσμὰ δάκρυα κατέβαινεν·
οὐκ ἠφίει δὲ αὐτὸν τῆς ἀπὸ τῶν δεσμῶν ἡδονῆς αἰσθάνεσθαι τῶν ἀπολλυμέ-
νων ὁ θάνατος, τῶν δεσμούντων. Καὶ γὰρ καὶ ὑπὲρ ἐκείνων ἤλγει· μαθητὴς
γὰρ ἦν ἐκείνου τοῦ δακρύοντος τοὺς ἱερέας τῶν Ἰουδαίων, οὐχ ὅτι αὐτὸν ἔμελλον σταυροῦν, ἀλλ' ὅτι αὐτοὶ ἀπώλλυντο. Καὶ οὐκ αὐτὸς μόνος αὐτὸ ποιεῖ,
ἀλλὰ καὶ τοὺς ἄλλους οὕτω παρακαλεῖ, λέγων· "Μὴ κλαίετε ἐπ' ἐμέ, θυγατέ-
ρες Ἱερουσαλήμ." Εἶδον τὸν παράδεισον οὗτοι οἱ ὀφθαλμοί, εἶδον τὸν τρίτον
οὐρανόν· ἀλλ' οὐ μακαρίζω αὐτοὺς τῆς θέας ταύτης ἕνεκεν οὕτως, ὡς τῶν
δακρύων ἐκείνων, δι' ὧν εἶδον τὸν Χριστόν. Μακάριον μὲν ὄντως τοῦτο· καὶ
γὰρ καὶ αὐτὸς ἐπ' αὐτῷ σεμνύνεται λέγων· "Οὐχὶ Ἰησοῦν Χριστὸν τὸν κύριον
ἡμῶν ἑώρακα;"

ἀλλὰ μακαριώτερον τὸ δακρῦσαι οὕτως. Ἐκείνου πολλοὶ κεκοινωνή-
κασι τοῦ θεάματος, καὶ τοὺς μὴ κοινωνήσαντας μακαρίζει Χριστός, λέγων·
"Μακάριοι οἱ μὴ ἰδόντες, καὶ πιστεύσαντες·" τούτου δὲ οὐ πολλοὶ ἐπέτυχον.
Εἰ γὰρ τὸ μένειν διὰ Χριστὸν ἐνταῦθα τοῦ ἀναλῦσαι πρὸς αὐτὸν ἀναγκαιότερον διὰ τὴν σωτηρίαν τῶν ἄλλων, ἄρα καὶ τοῦ ἰδεῖν αὐτὸν τὸ δι' αὐτοὺς

subdues them. This one renders the eyes of the soul more beautiful; they curb their belly, are filled with love of wisdom, with great compassion, and are capable of softening steel. With these tears the church is irrigated, with these souls are planted: even if there's fire, these tears are capable of extinguishing it, fire both sensible and material; these tears quench the fiery weapons of the evil one.

Therefore, let's remember his tears, and we shall laugh to scorn all present things. These are the tears Christ called blessed, when he said, "*Blessed are those who mourn*" [Matt 5:4], and, "*Blessed* [**303**] *are those who weep, because they will laugh*" [Luke 6:21]. Similar tears both Isaiah and Jeremiah wept; and the former said, "*Leave me alone, I shall weep bitterly*" [Isa 22:4], while the latter said, "*Who will give my head water, and my eyes fountains of tears?*" [Jer 9:1], as if the natural fountain were not sufficient.

Nothing is sweeter than these tears—they are sweeter than any laughter. Those who mourn know how great a consolation they possess. Let's not reckon this to be abominable,[135] but indeed to be prayed for very much, not so that others may sin, but so that, when they sin, we may be heartbroken for them. Let's remember these tears, these chains. Surely also on those chains tears descended, but the death of the perishing, of those bound, didn't allow him to feel the pleasure of the bonds. And indeed, for their sake he grieved, for he was the disciple of that one who had shed tears over the priests of the Jews, not because they were going to crucify him but because they themselves were perishing. And he doesn't do this by himself alone, but he exhorts others too in this way, saying, "*Don't weep for me, daughters of Jerusalem*" [Luke 23:29]. These eyes saw paradise, they saw the *third heaven* [2 Cor 12:2], but I don't call them so blessed because of this sight as because of those tears, through which they saw Christ. Blessed indeed was that sight, for he himself even glories in it, saying, "*Haven't I seen Jesus Christ our Lord?*" [1 Cor 9:1]—but more blessed to weep like that.

In that sight many have been partakers, and those who haven't been partakers Christ still calls blessed: "*Blessed are those who have not seen and have believed*" [John 20:29]. But not many have attained this. For if to stay here for Christ's sake were more necessary than to depart to him, on account of the salvation of others [see Phil 1:23–24], surely to groan

---

135. Greek ἀπευκτός, an unusual word, followed in the next phrase by its opposite, εὐκτός, a play on words that cannot be rendered into English.

στενάξαι ἀναγκαιότερον. Εἰ γὰρ τοῦ σὺν αὐτῷ εἶναι τὸ δι' αὐτὸν εἰς γέενναν εἶναι ποθεινότερον, καὶ τοῦ συνεῖναι αὐτῷ τὸ χωρίζεσθαι αὐτοῦ δι' αὐτὸν ποθεινότερον· τοῦτο γάρ ἐστιν ὅπερ ἔλεγεν· "Ηὐχόμην ἀνάθεμα εἶναι αὐτὸς ἐγὼ ἀπὸ Χριστοῦ." [304] πολλῷ μᾶλλον καὶ τὸ δακρύειν δι' αὐτόν. "Οὐκ ἐπαυσάμην, φησὶ, μετὰ δακρύων νουθετῶν ἕνα ἕκαστον." Διὰ τί; Οὐχὶ τοὺς κινδύνους δεδοικώς· ἀλλ' ὥσπερ ἄν τις ἀσθενοῦντι παρακαθήμενος, καὶ μὴ εἰδὼς τὸ τέλος, δακρύοι διὰ πόθον, δεδοικὼς μὴ ἐκπέσῃ τῆς ζωῆς· οὕτω καὶ αὐτός, ὅταν εἶδεν ἀσθενοῦντα, καὶ ἐπιπλῆξαι οὐκ ἴσχυσεν, ἐδάκρυε λοιπόν. Τοῦτο καὶ ὁ Χριστὸς ἐποίησεν, ἵνα κἂν τὰ δάκρυα αἰδεσθῶσιν· οἷον, ἡμάρτανέ τις; ἐπετίμα· κατέπτυεν αὐτοῦ ὁ ἐπιτιμώμενος, καὶ ἀπεπήδα; ἐδάκρυεν, ἵνα κἂν οὕτως ἐπισπάσηται.

Τούτων μνημονεύωμεν τῶν δακρύων· οὕτω τὰς θυγατέρας ἀνατρέφωμεν τὰς ἑαυτῶν, οὕτω τοὺς παῖδας, δακρύοντες ὅταν ἴδωμεν ἐν κακοῖς ὄντας. Ὅσαι ἐρᾶσθαι βούλονται, μνημονευέτωσαν τῶν δακρύων Παύλου, καὶ στεναζέτωσαν· ὅσαι μακαρίζεσθε, ὅσαι ἐν θαλάμοις ἐστέ, ὅσαι ἐν ἡδονῇ, τούτων μνημονεύετε· ὅσοι ἐν πένθει, ἀλλάττεσθε δάκρυα δακρύων. Οὐ τοὺς τεθνεῶτας ἐκεῖνος ἐπένθει, ἀλλὰ τοὺς ἀπολλυμένους καὶ ζῶντας. Εἴπω καὶ ἕτερα δάκρυα; Καὶ Τιμόθεος ἔκλαιε· μαθητὴς γὰρ ἦν τούτου· διὸ καὶ γράφων αὐτῷ ἔλεγε· "Μεμνημένος σου τῶν δακρύων, ἵνα χαρᾶς πληρωθῶ." Πολλοὶ καὶ ἐξ ἡδονῆς ὀδύρονται. Οὕτω καὶ ἡδονῆς ἐστι τὸ πρᾶγμα, καὶ μάλιστα ἐπιτεταμένης· οὕτως οὐ φορτικὰ τὰ δάκρυα, ἀλλὰ καὶ ἐκείνων πολλῷ βελτίονα τὰ ἐξ ὀδύνης τοιαύτης τῶν δι' ἡδονὴν κοσμικήν. Ἄκουε τοῦ προφήτου λέγοντος· "Ἤκουσε κύριος τῆς φωνῆς τοῦ κλαυθμοῦ μου, ἤκουσε τῆς φωνῆς τῆς δεήσεως μου." Ποῦ γὰρ οὐ χρήσιμον τὸ δάκρυον; ἐν εὐχαῖς, ἐν παραινέσεσιν; Ἡμεῖς αὐτὰ διαβάλλομεν, οὐκ εἰς ἃ δέδοται κεχρημένοι. Ὅταν ἀδελφὸν παρακαλῶμεν ἁμαρτάνοντα, κλαίειν δεῖ πενθοῦντα καὶ στενάζοντα· ὅταν παραινῶμέν τινι, ὁ δὲ μὴ προσέχῃ, ἀλλ' ἀπολλύηται, κλαίειν δεῖ. Ταῦτα φιλοσοφίας τὰ δάκρυα· ὅταν μέντοι πένης τις γένηται, ὅταν ἐν νόσῳ ᾖ σωματικῇ, ὅταν ἀποθάνῃ, οὐκέτι· ταῦτα γὰρ οὐ δακρύων ἄξια.

Ὥσπερ οὖν καὶ τὸν γέλωτα διαβάλλομεν, ἀκαίρως αὐτῷ κεχρημένοι, οὕτω καὶ τὰ δάκρυα, ἀκαίρως αὐτὰ μεταχειρίζοντες. Ἡ γὰρ ἑκάστου ἀρετὴ τότε φαίνεται, ὅταν πρὸς τὸ ἐπιτήδειον [305] ἔργον ἄγηται· ὅταν δὲ πρὸς τὸ

for the sake of others is more necessary than even to see him. For if to be in Gehenna for his sake is more desirable than to be with him, and to be separated from him for his sake is more desirable than to be with him (for this is what Paul said: *"I could wish that I myself were accursed from Christ"* [Rom 9:3]), [**304**] much more is weeping for his sake. *"I didn't stop admonishing every single one,"* he says, *"with tears"* [Acts 20:31]. Why? Not fearing the dangers—no, but as if one sitting by the side of a sick person, and not knowing the outcome, should weep for affection, fearing that they would lose their life, so too did Paul, when he saw a sick person and couldn't chastise them, then wept. This Christ did too, so that they might respect his tears. For example, did someone sin? Did he rebuke them; did the one rebuked spit at him and jump away? Christ wept, so that he might win them even so.

Remember these tears: in this way let's bring up our own daughters, in this way our sons, weeping when we see them in evil. Let as many women who want to be loved remember Paul's tears and groan; as many of you women who are counted blessed, as many of you as are in bridal chambers, as many as are in pleasure, remember these tears; as many of you who are in mourning, exchange tears for tears. Paul mourned not for the dead, but for those who were perishing while still alive. Shall I speak of other tears? Timothy wept too, for he was this man's disciple. This is why when writing to him he said, *"As I remember your tears, so that I may be filled with joy"* [2 Tim 1:4]. Many lament even from pleasure. So it's a thing that comes also from pleasure, and of the utmost intensity. Thus the tears aren't difficult to bear, but are even far better than those that come from so such pain because of worldly pleasure. Listen to the prophet saying, *"The Lord has heard the voice of my weeping, he has heard the voice of my supplication"* [Ps 6:8, 9]. For where are tears not useful? In prayers? In admonitions? We give them a bad name by using them not for what they are given to us. When we entreat a sinning brother we should wail, grieving and groaning; when we exhort somebody but they don't pay attention but continue to perish, we should wail. These are the tears of the love of wisdom. When, however, somebody is in poverty, when they are in bodily disease, when they are dead, this is no longer [required]. You see, these things aren't worthy of tears.

Just as therefore we give a bad name also to laughter when we use it at an inappropriate time, so too do we for tears, by dealing with it at an inappropriate time. For the virtue of each thing appears then, when it is brought to fitting work, [**305**] but when to one that is alien to it, it's no longer so. For

ἀλλότριον, οὐκέτι. Οἷον, ὁ οἶνος πρὸς εὐφροσύνην δέδοται, ἀλλ' οὐ πρὸς μέθην·
ὁ ἄρτος πρὸς τροφὴν, ἡ μίξις πρὸς παιδοποιΐαν. Ὥσπερ οὖν ταῦτα διαβέβληται, οὕτω καὶ τὰ δάκρυα. Ἐπεὶ κείσθω νόμος, ἐν εὐχαῖς μόναις καὶ παραινέ-
σεσι κεχρῆσθαι τούτοις· καὶ ὅρα πῶς καὶ ποθεινὸν ἔσται τὸ πρᾶγμα. Οὐδὲν
οὕτως ἀποσμήχει τὰ ἁμαρτήματα, ὡς δάκρυα. Καὶ ὄψιν ὡραίαν δείκνυσι καὶ
ταύτην τὴν σωματικήν· πρὸς ἔλεον γὰρ ἐπισπᾶται τὸν ὁρῶντα, σεμνὴν ποιεῖ
ἡμῖν αὐτήν. Οὐδὲν ἥδιον ὀφθαλμῶν δεδακρυμένων. Τὸ γὰρ εὐγενέστερον ἐν
ἡμῖν μέλος καὶ ὡραιότερον καὶ τῆς ψυχῆς τοῦτό ἐστιν. Ἅτε οὖν ὡς αὐτὴν τὴν
ψυχὴν ὁρῶντες ἀποδυρομένην, οὕτω καμπτόμεθα.

Ταῦτα ἡμῖν οὐχ ἁπλῶς εἴρηται, ἀλλ' ὥστε ὑμᾶς μὴ γάμοις, μὴ ὀρχήμασι,
μὴ χοροῖς παραγίνεσθαι σατανικοῖς. Ὅρα γὰρ τί εὗρεν ὁ διάβολος. Ἐπειδὴ
τῆς σκηνῆς καὶ τῶν ἀσέμνων τῶν ἐκεῖ ἡ φύσις αὐτὴ τὰς γυναῖκας ἀπήγαγεν,
εἰς τὴν γυναικωνῖτιν εἰσήγαγε τὰ τοῦ θεάτρου, μαλακοὺς λέγω καὶ πόρνας.
Ταύτην τὴν λύμην ὁ τῶν γάμων ἐπεισήγαγε νόμος· μᾶλλον δὲ οὐχ ὁ τοῦ
γάμου, μὴ γένοιτο, ἀλλὰ τῆς ἡμετέρας βλακείας. Τί ποιεῖς, ἄνθρωπε; οὐκ
οἶδας τί πράττεις; Γυναῖκα ἄγῃ ἐπὶ σωφροσύνῃ καὶ παιδοποιΐᾳ· τί οὖν αἱ
πόρναι βούλονται; Ἵνα ἡ εὐφροσύνη, φησί, γένηται μείζων. Καὶ μὴν ταῦτα
οὐκ εὐφροσύνης, ἀλλὰ ἀφροσύνης. Ὑβρίζεις τὴν νύμφην, ὑβρίζεις τὰς κεκλη-
μένας. Εἰ γὰρ τοιούτοις τέρπονται, ὕβρις τὸ πρᾶγμα. Εἰ τὸ γυναῖκας πόρνας
ὁρᾶν ἀσχημονούσας φέρει τινὰ φιλοτιμίαν, διὰ τί μὴ καὶ τὴν νύμφην ἕλκεις,
ἵνα κἀκείνη θεωρῇ; Πάντως ἄσχημον καὶ αἰσχρὸν, μαλακοὺς ἄνδρας καὶ
ὀρχουμένους, καὶ πᾶσαν τὴν πομπὴν τὴν σατανικὴν ἐπεισάγειν τῇ οἰκίᾳ.

"Μνημονεύετέ μου, φησὶ, τῶν δεσμῶν." Δεσμός ἐστιν ὁ γάμος, δεσμὸς
ὡρισμένος παρὰ θεοῦ· λύσις ἡ πόρνη καὶ διάλυσις. Ἔξεστιν ἑτέροις φαιδρύ-
νειν τὸν γάμον, οἷον τραπέζαις πληθούσαις, ἱματίοις· οὐ περικόπτω ταῦτα, ἵνα
μὴ δόξω σφόδρα εἶναι ἄγριος· καίτοι ἤρκεσε τῇ Ῥεβέκκᾳ θέριστρον μόνον·
ἀλλ' οὐ περικόπτω. Ἔξεστιν ἱματίοις φαιδρύνεσθαι, ἔξεστι παρου-[**306**]

example, wine is given for cheerfulness, but not for drunkenness; bread for sustenance, sexual intercourse for the procreation of children. Therefore, just as these things have been given a bad name, so too have tears. Let there be a law laid down that they be only used in prayers and exhortations, and see how they'll become even a desirable thing. Nothing so wipes out sins as tears do. And tears demonstrate that even this bodily countenance is beautiful, for they win the observer to pity, they make it respected in our eyes. Nothing is sweeter than tearful eyes, for this is the nobler member we have and the more beautiful, and belongs to the soul. So inasmuch as we see the soul itself lamenting, to that extent we're bowed down.

I didn't say these things to you without a reason, but so that you may not participate in weddings, or dances, or satanical bands.[136] For see what the devil has invented. Since nature herself has removed women from the stage and the disgraceful things there,[137] the devil has introduced into the women's chamber the things of the theater, I mean effeminate fellows and prostitutes. This pestilence the custom of marriages had introduced—no, not the custom of marriage (heaven forbid!), but of our own stupidity. What are you doing, you human being? Don't you know what you're doing? Do you marry a wife for chastity and to have children? What then is the meaning of these prostitutes? "So that there may be more rejoicing," says somebody. Indeed, this is not part of rejoicing, but of madness. You insult your wife, you insult the women who are invited. For if they're delighted by such things, the thing's an insult. If to see female prostitutes acting indecorously confers some distinction, why don't you drag the bride there so that she too may look on? It's completely indecorous and disgraceful to bring into one's house effeminate men and dancers, and the complete satanic pomp.

"*Remember*," he says, "*my chains*." Marriage is a chain, a chain ordained by God; a prostitute is a severing and a dissolving. It's permitted to embellish marriage with other things, for example with full tables, garments. I don't cut off these things, lest I seem to be excessively harsh, yet Rebecca was content with only a veil [see Gen 24:65]. No—I don't cut them off. It's possible to be splendid in garments, it's possible with the presence [**306**] of

---

136. On this and other tirades against wedding celebrations in Chrysostom's works, see Blake Leyerle, *Theatrical Shows and Ascetic Lives: John Chrysostom's Attack on Spiritual Marriage* (Berkeley: University of California Press, 2001), esp. 70–71.

137. It is generally assumed that in classical and Christianity antiquity women did not perform on the stage but that on occasion they would have been part of the audience.

σίαις αἰδεσίμων ἀνδρῶν, αἰδεσίμων γυναικῶν. Τί τὰ ἐπιχάρματα ἐκεῖνα, τί τὰ τέρατα ἐπεισάγεις; Εἰπὲ ἃ ἀκούεις παρ' αὐτῶν. Ἀλλ' ἐρυθριᾷς εἰπεῖν; Σὺ ἐρυθριᾷς, κἀκείνους ἀναγκάζεις ποιεῖν; Εἰ καλὸν, διὰ τί μὴ καὶ αὐτὸς ποιεῖς; εἰ δὲ αἰσχρὸν, διὰ τί ἕτερον ἀναγκάζεις; Πάντα σωφροσύνης ἐμπεπλῆσθαι δεῖ, πάντα σεμνότητος, πάντα κοσμιότητος· τοὐναντίον δὲ ὁρῶ, σκιρτῶντας ὡς αἱ κάμηλοι, ὡς αἱ ἡμίονοι. Τῇ παρθένῳ θάλαμος ἐπιτήδειον μόνον. Ἀλλὰ πενιχρά ἐστι, φησίν. Ἐπειδὴ πενιχρά ἐστι, καὶ κόσμιος ὀφείλει εἶναι· ἐχέτω τὸν τρόπον ἀντὶ πλούτου. Οὐκ ἔχει προῖκα ἐπιδοῦναι; τί αὐτὴν καὶ ἑτέρως εὐκαταφρόνητον ποιεῖς ἀπὸ τῆς ἀναστροφῆς; Ἐπαινῶ ὅτι παρθένοι παραγίνονται τὴν ὁμήλικα τιμῶσαι, παραγίνονται γυναῖκες τὴν εἰς αὐτὰς καταχθεῖσαν τιμῶσαι· καλῶς τοῦτο ὥρισται. Δύο γάρ εἰσιν οὗτοι χοροί, ὁ τῶν παρθένων, καὶ ὁ τῶν γεγαμημένων· αὗται παραδιδόασιν, ἐκεῖναι δέχονται· ἡ νύμφη μεταξὺ τούτων ἐστὶν, οὔτε παρθένος, οὔτε γυνή· ἐκεῖθεν μὲν γὰρ ἐξέρχεται, ταύτης δὲ ἐπιβαίνει τῆς συμμορίας. Αἱ δὲ πόρναι, διὰ τί; Δέον αὐτὰς ἐγκαλύπτεσθαι ὅταν γάμος ᾖ, δέον αὐτὰς κατορύττεσθαι· φθορὰ γὰρ γάμου πορνεία· ἡμεῖς δὲ ἄγομεν αὐτὰς εἰς γάμους. Καὶ ὅταν μέν τι ποιῆτε, καὶ μέχρι ῥήματος οἰωνίζεσθε τὰ ἐναντία· οἷον, ὅταν σπείρῃς, ὅταν ἀπαντλῇς τῶν ὑποληνίων τὸν οἶνον, τὰ ὀξίνην σημαίνοντα οὐδ' ἂν ἀποκρίνοιο· ἐνταῦθα δὲ σωφροσύνης γινομένης, ἐπεισάγετε τὴν ὀξίνην; τοῦτο γὰρ ἡ πόρνη. Ὅταν μύρον κατασκευάζητε, οὐδὲν δυσῶδες ἀφίετε πλησιάζειν. Μύρον ἐστὶν ὁ γάμος· τί τοίνυν τὴν τοῦ βορβόρου δυσωδίαν ἐπεισάγεις τῇ τοῦ μύρου κατασκευῇ; Τί λέγεις; ὀρχεῖται ἡ παρθένος, καὶ οὐκ αἰσχύνεται τὴν ὁμήλικα; Ταύτης γὰρ σεμνοτέραν αὐτὴν εἶναι δεῖ· ἐξ ἀγκάλης γε, οὐκ ἐκ παλαίστρας ἐξῆλθε. Φαίνεσθαι γὰρ ὅλως ἐν γάμοις τὴν παρθένον οὐ δεῖ.

Οὐχ ὁρᾷς ἐν τοῖς βασιλείοις, ὅτι οἱ μὲν τετιμημένοι ἔνδον περὶ τὸν βασιλέα εἰσὶν, οἱ δὲ ἄτιμοι ἔξω; Καὶ σὺ ἔνδον ἔσο περὶ τὴν νύμφην. Ἀλλὰ ἁγνὸς μένε ἐπὶ τῆς οἰκίας· μὴ ἐκπόμπευε τὴν παρθε-[307]νίαν. Παρέστηκεν ἑκάτερος ὁ χορὸς, ὁ μὲν οἵαν διδόασι δεικνὺς, ὁ δὲ ἵνα ταύτην φυλάττωσι· τί

revered men, of revered women. Why do you introduce those instances of malignant joy, why those monsters? Say what you hear from them. No— are you embarrassed to tell? Are you embarrassed, and force them to do it? If it's a good thing, why don't you do it yourself as well? But if it's shameful, why do you force another? Everything should be full of chastity, everything of gravity, everything of orderliness; but see the opposite, people frisking like camels, like mules. For the virgin, her chamber is the only fitting place. "But," says somebody, "she's poor." Since she's poor, she should be modest also: let her have her character instead of wealth. Doesn't she have a dowry to contribute? Why do you make her contemptible on other grounds too because of her mode of life? I praise the fact that virgins attend to do honor to their contemporary, that women attend to do honor to the woman who has joined their ranks. This has been rightly ordained. For there are two bands, one of virgins and one of the married; the former are giving her up, the latter are receiving her. The bride is between them, neither virgin nor wife, for she's coming forth from there and entering into the company of these. But why prostitutes? They should hide their faces when there's a marriage, they should be buried (for prostitution is the corruption of marriage), but we bring them into our weddings. And when you are engaged in something, you regard what is contrary to it, right down to the letter, as a bad omen. For example, when you're sowing, when you're drawing off the wine from the vats, you wouldn't, if asked, indicate a sign of vinegar. But in this case, where it is a question of chastity, do you introduce vinegar? For that's what a prostitute is. When you're preparing sweet ointment, you don't permit anything malodorous to come near. Marriage is a sweet ointment. Why then do you introduce the malodor of the mire into the preparation of the sweet ointment? What's your reply? The virgin dances and isn't ashamed before her contemporaries? You see, she should be more respectful than the other, in that at least she has come out of an arm,[138] not of the wrestling school. For a virgin should not appear in public at weddings at all.

Don't you see how in the imperial quarters the honored ones are inside around the emperor, while those without honor are outside? And you should be inside about the bride. But remain in the house in chastity—don't put your virginity [**307**] on show. Each company is standing by, the one demonstrating the kind of woman they are giving up, the other in

---

138. That is, of a nurse or mother.

καταισχύνεις τὴν παρθενίαν; Εἰ γὰρ σὺ τοιαύτη, τοιαῦτα καὶ περὶ ἐκείνης ὁ νυμφίος ὑποπτεύσει· εἰ σὺ ἐρᾶσθαι θέλεις, παντοπώλιδος καὶ λαχανοπώλιδος καὶ δημιουργοῦ ταῦτα. Οὐκ ἔστι ταῦτα αἰσχύνη; Αἰσχύνη ἐστὶ τὸ ἀσχημονεῖν, κἂν βασιλέως θυγάτηρ ᾖ. Μὴ γὰρ ἡ πενία κωλύει; μὴ γὰρ τὸ ἐπιτήδευμα; Κἂν δούλη τις ᾖ παρθένος, ἐν σωφροσύνῃ μενέτω· "Ἐν γὰρ Χριστῷ Ἰησοῦ οὔτε δοῦλος, οὔτε ἐλεύθερος."

Μὴ γὰρ θέατρόν ἐστιν ὁ γάμος; Μυστήριόν ἐστι, καὶ τύπος μεγάλου πράγματος· κἂν αὐτὸ μὴ αἰδῇ, αἰδέσθητι οὗ τύπος ἐστί. "Τὸ μυστήριον τοῦτο, φησὶ, μέγα ἐστίν· ἐγὼ δὲ λέγω εἰς Χριστὸν, καὶ εἰς τὴν ἐκκλησίαν." Τῆς ἐκκλησίας τύπος ἐστὶ καὶ τοῦ Χριστοῦ, καὶ πόρνας εἰσάγεις; Ἂν τοίνυν, φησὶ, μήτε παρθένοι ὀρχῶνται, μήτε γεγαμημέναι, τίς ὀρχήσεται; Μηδείς· ποία γὰρ ὀρχήσεως ἀνάγκη; Ἐν τοῖς τῶν Ἑλλήνων μυστηρίοις αἱ ὀρχήσεις, ἐν δὲ τοῖς ἡμετέροις σιγὴ καὶ εὐκοσμία, αἰδὼς καὶ καταστολή. Μυστήριον τελεῖται μέγα· ἔξω αἱ πόρναι, ἔξω οἱ βέβηλοι. Πῶς μυστήριόν ἐστι; Συνέρχονται, καὶ ποιοῦσιν οἱ δύο ἕνα. Διὰ τί, ὅτε μὲν εἰσῄει, οὐκ ὄρχησις, οὐ κύμβαλα, ἀλλὰ πολλὴ σιγή, πολλὴ ἡσυχία· ὅταν δὲ συνίωσιν, οὐκ εἰκόνα ἄψυχον, οὐδὲ εἰκόνα τινὸς τῶν ἐπὶ γῆς, ἀλλ' αὐτοῦ ποιοῦντες τοῦ θεοῦ, καὶ καθ' ὁμοίωσιν, τοσοῦτον ἐπεισάγεις θόρυβον, καὶ ταράττεις τοὺς ὄντας, καὶ αἰσχύνεις τὴν ψυχήν, καὶ θορυβεῖς; Ἔρχονται ἓν σῶμα γενησόμενοι. Ἰδοὺ πάλιν ἀγάπης μυστήριον. Ἂν οἱ δύο μὴ γένωνται ἕν, οὐκ ἐργάζονται πολλούς, ἕως ἂν δύο μένωσιν· ὅταν δὲ εἰς ἑνότητα ἔλθωσι, τότε ἐργάζονται. Τί μανθάνομεν ἀπὸ τούτου; Ὅτι πολλὴ τῆς ἑνώσεως ἡ ἰσχύς. Τὸ εὐμήχανον τοῦ θεοῦ τὸν ἕνα εἰς δύο διεῖλε παρὰ τὴν ἀρχήν, καὶ θέλων δεῖξαι ὅτι μετὰ τὸ διαιρεθῆναι καὶ εἷς μένει, οὐκ ἀφῆκεν ἕνα ἀρκεῖν πρὸς τὴν γέννησιν. Οὐ γάρ ἐστιν εἷς ὁ οὐδέπω, ἀλλ' ἥμισυ τοῦ ἑνός· καὶ δῆλον, ὅτι οὐ παιδοποιεῖ, καθάπερ καὶ πρότερον. Εἶδες τοῦ γάμου τὸ μυστήριον; Ἐποίησεν ἐξ ἑνὸς ἕνα, καὶ πάλιν τοὺς δύο τούτους ἕνα ποιήσας οὕτω ποιεῖ ἕνα· ὥστε καὶ νῦν ἐξ ἑνὸς τίκτεται ἄνθρωπος. Γυνὴ γὰρ καὶ ἀνὴρ οὐκ εἰσὶν ἄνθρωποι δύο, ἀλλ' ἄνθρωπος εἷς· [308] καὶ παρὸν καὶ πολλαχόθεν αὐτὸ πιστώσασθαι, οἷον ἀπὸ τοῦ Ἰακώβου, ἀπὸ τῆς Μαρίας τῆς

order to guard her. Why do you disgrace virginity? You see, if you are one of this type, the bridegroom will expect her also to be. If you wish to fall in love, this pertains to saleswomen and greengrocers and craftspeople. Isn't this a disgrace? Disgrace is a shame even when it's the emperor's daughter. For does her poverty stand in the way? Surely not her habits? Even if a virgin is a slave, let her remain in chastity. *For in Christ Jesus there is neither slave nor free* [Gal 3:28].

Surely marriage isn't a theater? It's a mystery and a type of a mighty thing: even if you don't respect it, respect the type it stands for. "*This mystery*," Paul says, "*is great, I mean Christ and the church*" [Eph 5:32]. Is it a type of the church and of Christ, and are you introducing prostitutes into it? "If then," says someone, "neither virgins nor married women dance, who will dance?" Nobody, for what kind of need is there of dancing? In the Hellenic mysteries there are dances, but in ours there are silence and decorum, respect and dignity. A great mystery is being celebrated: get rid of the prostitutes, get rid of the profane people. How is it a mystery? They come together, and the two make one. Why is it, when at the entrance there is no dancing, no cymbals, but great silence, great stillness? But when they come together, making not an image without soul, nor yet an image of anything on earth, but of God himself, and in his likeness [see Gen 1:27], you introduce such a great uproar, and disturb those present, and shame the soul, and cause uproar? They come, about to be made one body. Look again at a mystery of love! If the two don't become one, they won't effect many,[139] as long as they remain two, but when they enter into oneness, then they effect many. What do we learn from this? That the power of the union is great. God's ingenuity divided the one into two at the beginning [see Gen 2:22–24], and wishing to demonstrate that after the separation still it remained one, he didn't permit the one to be sufficient for procreation. You see, the one person is no longer one, but half of one, and it's clear that they didn't produce children, as was also the case before.[140] Have you seen the mystery of marriage? God made one from one, and again, having made these two, he makes one in such a way that now too a human being is produced from one. You see, wife and husband are not two human beings, but one human being. [**308**] And it's possible to confirm this from other sources as well, for example, from Jacob [see Gen 28–29], from Mary the

---

139. That is, children.

140. This curious passage, if the text is true, seems to suggest that, before Adam and Eve, the male partner was unable to produce children.

μητρὸς τοῦ Χριστοῦ, ἀπὸ τοῦ λέγειν· "Ἄρσεν καὶ θῆλυ ἐποίησεν αὐτούς." Εἰ ὁ μὲν κεφαλὴ, ἡ δὲ σῶμα, πῶς δύο; Διὰ τοῦτο ἡ μὲν μαθητοῦ, ὁ δὲ διδασκάλου τάξιν ἐπέχει· ὁ μὲν ἄρχοντος, ἡ δὲ ἀρχομένης. Καὶ ἀπ' αὐτῆς δὲ τῆς τοῦ σώματος διαπλάσεως ἴδοι τις ἂν, ὅτι ἕν εἰσιν ἀπὸ γὰρ τῆς πλευρᾶς γέγονε, καὶ ὥσπερ ἡμίτομα δύο.

Διὰ τοῦτο καὶ βοηθὸν καλεῖ, ἵνα δείξῃ ὅτι ἕν εἰσι· διὰ τοῦτο καὶ πατρὸς καὶ μητρὸς προτιμᾷ τὴν συνοίκησιν, ἵνα δείξῃ ὅτι ἕν εἰσι. Καὶ ὁ πατὴρ ὁμοίως χαίρει καὶ θυγατρὸς καὶ υἱοῦ γαμούντων, ὡς πρὸς οἰκεῖον μέλος ἐπειγομένου τοῦ σώματος· καὶ τοσαύτη δαπάνη γίνεται καὶ χρημάτων ἐλάττωσις, καὶ ὅμως οὐκ ἀνέχεται ἄγαμον περιορᾶν. Ὥσπερ γὰρ ἀπεσχισμένης αὐτῇ τῆς σαρκὸς, ἀτελὴς πρὸς παιδοποιΐαν ἑκάτερος, ἀτελής ἐστι πρὸς βίου σύστασιν τοῦ παρόντος ἑκάτερος. Διὰ τοῦτο καὶ ὁ προφήτης φησίν, "Ὑπόλειμμα πνεύματός σου." Πῶς δὲ καὶ γίνονται εἰς σάρκα μίαν; Καθάπερ χρυσοῦ τὸ καθαρώτατον ἂν ἀφέλῃς καὶ ἑτέρῳ ἀναμίξῃς χρυσῷ, οὕτω δὴ καὶ ἐνταῦθα, τὸ πιότατον καθάπερ τῆς ἡδονῆς χωνευούσης ἡ γυνὴ δεχομένη τρέφει καὶ θάλπει, καὶ τὰ παρ' ἑαυτῆς συνεισενεγκαμένη ἄνδρα ἀποδίδωσι. Καὶ γέφυρά τίς ἐστι τὸ παιδίον. Ὥστε οἱ τρεῖς σὰρξ γίνονται μία, τοῦ παιδὸς ἑκατέρωθεν ἑκατέρους συνάπτοντος. Ὥσπερ γὰρ εἰ δύο πόλεων οὐσῶν, καὶ ποταμοῦ διόλου διαιροῦντος, μία γίνεται πόλις, γεφύρας ἑκατέρωθεν ἁπτομένης· οὕτως ἐστὶν ἐνταῦθα, καὶ πλέον, ὅταν αὐτὴ γὰρ ἡ γέφυρα ἐκ τῆς ἑκατέρων οὐσίας ᾖ ἐπὶ τῷ λόγῳ τούτῳ· ὡς τὸ σῶμα καὶ κεφαλὴ ἓν σῶμα· τῷ γὰρ τραχήλῳ διαιρεῖται· ἀλλ' οὐ διαιροῦνται μᾶλλον, ἢ συνάπτονται· μέσος γὰρ ὢν ἑκατέρους συνάγει. Καὶ ταὐτὸν γίνεται, ὥσπερ ἂν εἰ χορὸς διεσπασμένος τὸ μὲν ἓν αὐτοῦ μέρος ἐντεῦθεν λαβὼν, τὸ δὲ ἕτερον ἐκ τῆς δεξιᾶς, ἕνα ποιήσειεν· ἢ ὥσπερ οἱ συνεσταλ-[309]μένοι ὦσιν οὗτοι, καὶ τὰς χεῖρας ἐκτείνοντες ἓν γίνονται· αἱ γὰρ χεῖρες ἐκταθεῖσαι, οὐκ ἀφιᾶσιν εἶναι δύο. Διὰ τοῦτο γοῦν καὶ ἀκριβῶς εἶπεν, οὐκ, ἔσονται μία σάρξ, ἀλλ', "εἰς σάρκα μίαν," τὴν τοῦ παιδὸς συναπτόμενοι. Τί οὖν, ὅταν παιδίον μὴ ᾖ, οὐκ ἔσονται δύο; Ἡ μίξις γὰρ τοῦτο ἐργάζεται, ἀνέχεε καὶ ἀνέμιξεν ἀμφοτέρων τὰ σώματα. Καὶ ὥσπερ εἰ εἰς ἔλαιον μύρον ἐμβαλὼν, τὸ πᾶν ἐποίησεν ἕν, οὕτω δὴ καὶ ἐνταῦθα.

Οἶδα ὅτι πολλοὶ αἰσχύνονται τοῖς λεγομένοις· καὶ τούτου αἴτιον, ὧν εἶπον ἡ ἀσέλγεια καὶ ἡ ἀκολασία. Τὸ οὕτω τοὺς γάμους γίνεσθαι, τὸ παραφθείρεσθαι, τὸ πρᾶγμα διέβαλεν· ἐπεὶ "Τίμιος ὁ γάμος, καὶ ἡ κοίτη ἀμίαντος." Τί

mother of Christ, from the saying, "*He made them male and female*" [Gen 1:27]. If he is the head, and she the body, how are they two? For this reason she holds the rank of disciple, while he that of master; he that of a ruler, she that of one ruled. And from the very fashioning of her body one can see that they are one, for she came from his side [see Gen 2:22–24] and they are, so to speak, two halves.

This is the reason that God calls her a "*helper*" [Gen 2:18], in order to demonstrate that they are one. On this account he privileges their cohabitation above father and mother [see Gen 2:24], in order to demonstrate that they are one. And similarly the father rejoices when both a daughter and a son marry, as if the body were keen to join a member of its own; and although such great expense and cost are incurred, he can't bear to see her unmarried. You see, just as if her own flesh were severed from her, each of them is incomplete for the procreation of children, each one is incomplete regarding the constitution of this present life. This is why the prophet too says, "*The residue of your spirit*" [Mal 2:15]. And how do they become one flesh? Just as if you would remove the purest part of gold and mix it with other gold, so indeed here also just as the wife receives the richest part of it infused by pleasure, nourishes it and cherishes it, and contributing her own share gives back a man. And the child is a sort of bridge. The upshot is that the three become one flesh, the child connecting on either side each to the other. For just as if two cities, separated completely by a river, become one city when a bridge joins both, so it is in this case, and more so, when the bridge itself is formed by the substance of each by this argument, so the body and head are one body. For they're divided by the neck but aren't divided more than separated—you see, the middle brings both together. And the same thing happens just as if a chorus that has been severed should, by taking part of it and the other from the right, makes one. Or as these, when, coming together, [**309**] holding out their hand, become one. You see, the extended hands don't admit of their being two. This is anyway why God said accurately not "they will be one flesh," but "*into one flesh*" [Gen 2:24], namely, that of the child by whom they are connected. Well then, when there's no child, won't they be two? You see, their intercourse has this effect: it has diffused and commingled the bodies of both. And just as one who has cast ointment into oil has made the whole one, so indeed is it in this case too.

I know that many are ashamed at what is said, and the cause of this is your lasciviousness and intemperance, of which I have spoken. The fact that marriages take place in this way, the depravity, has thrown the thing

αἰσχύνῃ τῷ τιμίῳ; τί ἐρυθριᾷς ἐπὶ τῷ ἀμιάντῳ; Ταῦτα αἱρετικῶν ἐστι, ταῦτα τῶν τὰς πόρνας ἐπεισαγόντων. Διὰ τοῦτο αὐτὸν ἐκκαθαίρεσθαι βούλομαι, ὥστε ἐπὶ τὴν οἰκείαν εὐγένειαν ἀναγαγεῖν, ὥστε τῶν αἱρετικῶν ἐμφράξαι τὰ στόματα. Ὕβρισται τὸ τοῦ θεοῦ δῶρον, ἡ ῥίζα τῆς ἡμετέρας γενέσεως· πολλὴ γὰρ περὶ τὴν ῥίζαν ἡ κόπρος καὶ ὁ βόρβορος. Τοῦτον οὖν ἐκκαθάρωμεν τῷ λόγῳ. Ἀνέχεσθε τοίνυν μικρὸν, ἐπεὶ καὶ ὁ βόρβορον κατέχων δυσωδίας ἀνέχεται. Βούλομαι δεῖξαι ὅτι οὐ χρὴ ἐπὶ τούτοις αἰσχύνεσθαι, ἀλλὰ τούτοις οἷς ποιεῖτε· σὺ δὲ ἐπ᾽ ἐκείνοις αἰσχύνεσθαι ἀφεὶς, τούτοις αἰσχύνῃ· οὐκοῦν τοῦ θεοῦ καταγινώσκεις τοῦ οὕτω θεσπίσαντος.

Εἴπω πῶς καὶ μυστήριον τῆς ἐκκλησίας ἐστίν; Ὥσπερ ὁ Χριστὸς ἦλθε πρὸς τὴν ἐκκλησίαν, ὥσπερ ἐξ αὐτοῦ γέγονε, καὶ αὐτῇ συνῆλθε συνουσίᾳ πνευματικῇ· "Ἡρμοσάμην γὰρ ὑμᾶς, φησὶν, ἑνὶ ἀνδρὶ παρθένον ἁγνήν." Ὅτι δὲ ἐξ αὐτοῦ ἐσμεν, "Ἐκ τῶν μελῶν αὐτοῦ, καὶ ἐκ τῆς σαρκὸς αὐτοῦ," φησί. Ταῦτα δὴ πάντα ἐννοοῦντες, μὴ αἰσχύνωμεν τὸ τηλικοῦτον μυστήριον. Τύπος τῆς τοῦ Χριστοῦ παρουσίας ἐστὶν ὁ γάμος, σὺ δὲ μεθύεις; [310] Εἰπέ μοι, εἰ εἰκόνα εἶδες τοῦ βασιλέως, ἆρα ἂν αὐτὴν ᾔσχυνας; Οὐδαμῶς.

Δοκεῖ μὲν οὖν ἀδιάφορον εἶναι πρᾶγμα τὰ περὶ τὸν γάμον γινόμενα, ἔστι δὲ μεγάλων αἴτια κακῶν. Πάντα παρανομίας γέμει. "Αἰσχρότης καὶ μωρολογία καὶ εὐτραπελία μὴ ἐκπορευέσθω, φησίν, ἐκ τοῦ στόματος ὑμῶν·" πάντα δὲ ἐκεῖνα, αἰσχρότης καὶ μωρολογία καὶ εὐτραπελία, οὐχ ἁπλῶς, ἀλλὰ μετὰ ἐπιτάσεως. Τέχνη γὰρ τὸ πρᾶγμά ἐστι, καὶ ἐγκώμια μεγάλα τοῖς αὐτὴν μετιοῦσι· τὰ ἁμαρτήματα τέχνη γέγονεν. Οὐχ ἁπλῶς αὐτὰ μετερχόμεθα, ἀλλὰ μετὰ σπουδῆς, μετὰ ἐπιστήμης· καὶ στρατηγεῖ λοιπὸν ὁ διάβολος τῶν αὐτοῦ ταγμάτων. Ὅπου γὰρ μέθη, ἀκολασία· ὅπου αἰσχρολογία, ὁ διάβολος πάρεστι τὰ παρ᾽ ἑαυτοῦ εἰσφέρων. Τούτοις ἑστιώμενος, εἰπέ μοι, μυστήριον Χριστοῦ τελεῖς, καὶ τὸν διάβολον καλεῖς;

Τάχα με φορτικὸν εἶναι νομίζετε. Καὶ γὰρ καὶ τοῦτο τῆς διαστροφῆς τῆς πολλῆς, ὅτι καὶ ὁ ἐπιτιμῶν γέλωτα ὀφλισκάνει ὡς αὐστηρός. Οὐκ ἀκούετε Παύλου λέγοντος, "Πᾶν ὅ τι ἂν ποιῆτε, εἴτε ἐσθίετε, εἴτε πίνετε, εἴτε τι ποιεῖτε, πάντα εἰς δόξαν θεοῦ ποιεῖτε;" ὑμεῖς δὲ εἰς δυσφημίαν καὶ ἀδοξίαν.

into disrepute, because *marriage is honorable and the bed undefiled* [Heb 13:4]. Why are you ashamed by the honor? Why do you blush at the undefiled? This is the stuff of heretics, this is of those who introduce prostitutes. For this reason I want to have it thoroughly purified, so as to bring it back again to its inherent nobleness, so as to muzzle the mouths of the heretics. God's gift is insulted, the root of our generation, for around the root there is much dung and filth. Therefore, let's purify it thoroughly by our homily. So bear up for a little while, since the filth too has to bear up because it contains malodors. I want to demonstrate that you shouldn't be ashamed at these things but at those that you do, but you, by passing over the shame at the former, are ashamed at the latter. Surely then you condemn God, who has thus decreed.

Shall I say how marriage is also a mystery of the church? Just as Christ came to the church, just as he was made of her and conversed with her by spiritual intercourse, *"for,"* Paul says, *"I betrothed you as a pure virgin to one husband"* [2 Cor 11:2]. That we are of Christ, he says, *"from his members and of his flesh"* [Eph 5:30]. Thinking then on all these things, let's not be ashamed of such a great mystery. Marriage is a type of the presence of Christ, and are you drunk at it? [**310**] Tell me, if you saw an image of the emperor, would you dishonor it? Not at all.

Now, the practices at weddings seem to be a matter of indifference, but they are the causes of great evils. Everything is full of lawlessness. "Let *filthiness and foolish talking and frivolity* not proceed from your mouth," it says [Eph 5:4].[141] All these things, filthiness, foolish talking, and frivolity, and not simply these, but with aggravation, for the matter has become an art form and there is high praise for those who pursue it. Sins have become an art form. We don't pursue them in a random way, but with enthusiasm, with study, and from there on the devil takes command of his forces. You see, where there is drunkenness, there is intemperance; where there is foolish talking, there the devil is present, making his own contributions. With these entertainments, tell me, do you celebrate the mystery of Christ and invite the devil?

Perhaps you reckon me to be wearisome. Indeed, this too is the stuff of extreme perversion, namely, that the one who rebukes you incurs your ridicule as if you were austere. Don't you hear Paul saying, *"Whatever you do, whether you eat or drink, or whatever you do, do everything for the*

---

141. This is not an exact quotation.

Οὐκ ἀκούετε τοῦ προφήτου λέγοντος, "Δουλεύσατε τῷ Κυρίῳ ἐν φόβῳ, καὶ ἀγαλλιᾶσθε αὐτῷ ἐν τρόμῳ;" Ὑμεῖς δὲ διαχεῖσθε. Μὴ γὰρ οὐκ ἔστι καὶ ἤδεσθαι, καὶ μετὰ ἀσφαλείας; Βούλει μελῶν ἀκοῦσαι καλῶν; Μάλιστα μὲν οὐδὲ ἔδει· πλὴν συγκαταβαίνω, εἰ βούλει· μὴ τῶν σατανικῶν ἀκούσῃς, ἀλλὰ τῶν πνευματικῶν. Βούλει χορεύοντας ἰδεῖν; ὅρα τῶν ἀγγέλων τὸν χορόν. Καὶ πῶς δυνατὸν, φησὶν, ἰδεῖν; Ἐὰν ταῦτα ἀπελάσῃς, ἐλεύσεται καὶ ὁ Χριστὸς εἰς τούτους τοὺς γάμους· τοῦ δὲ Χριστοῦ παρόντος, καὶ ὁ τῶν ἀγγέλων πάρεστι χορός. Ἂν θέλῃς, καὶ νῦν θαύματα ἐργάσεται, καθάπερ καὶ τότε· ποιήσει καὶ νῦν τὸ ὕδωρ οἶνον, καὶ πολλῷ θαυμασιώτερον· τὴν διάχυσιν ἐπιστρέψει, τὴν διαρρέουσαν καὶ ψυχρὰν ἐπιθυμίαν, καὶ ἐπὶ τὴν πνευματικὴν μεταστήσει. Τοῦτό ἐστιν ἐξ ὕδατος οἶνον ποιῆσαι. Ἔνθα αὐληταὶ, οὐδαμοῦ ὁ Χριστός· ἀλλὰ κἂν εἰσέλθῃ, τὸ πρῶτον ἐκβάλλει τούτους, καὶ τότε θαυματουργεῖ. Τί τῆς σατανικῆς [311] πομπῆς ἀηδέστερον, ἔνθα ἄναρθρα πάντα, ἔνθα πάντα ἄσημα; ἂν δέ τι καὶ ἔναρθρον, πάλιν πάντα αἰσχρὰ, πάντα ἀηδῆ.

Οὐδὲν τῆς ἀρετῆς ἥδιον, οὐδὲν κοσμιότητος γλυκύτερον, οὐδὲν σεμνότητος ποθεινότερον. Ποιείτω τις γάμους, οἵους ἐγὼ λέγω, καὶ ὄψεται τὴν ἡδονήν· ποίους δὲ γάμους, προσέχετε. Πρῶτον μὲν ἄνδρα ζήτει τῇ παρθένῳ ὄντως ἄνδρα καὶ προστάτην, ὡς σώματι μέλλων ἐπιθήσειν κεφαλὴν, ὡς οὐκ ἀνδράποδον, ἀλλὰ θυγατέρα αὐτῷ μέλλων παραδώσειν. Μὴ χρήματα ζήτει, μὴ γένους λαμπρότητα, μὴ πατρίδος μέγεθος, πάντα ταῦτα περιττὰ, ἀλλὰ ψυχῆς εὐλάβειαν, ἐπιείκειαν, τὴν ἀληθῆ σύνεσιν, τοῦ θεοῦ τὸν φόβον, εἰ βούλει μεθ' ἡδονῆς τὸ θυγάτριον ζῆν. Πλουσιώτερον γὰρ ζητοῦσα, οὐ μόνον αὐτὴν οὐκ ὠφελήσεις, ἀλλὰ καὶ βλάψεις, δούλην ἀντ' ἐλευθέρας ποιοῦσα. Οὐ τοσαύτην γὰρ ἀπὸ τῶν χρυσίων καρπώσεται τὴν ἡδονήν, ὅσην ἀπὸ τοῦ δουλεύειν τὴν ἀηδίαν. Ἀλλὰ μὴ ζήτει ταῦτα, ἀλλὰ μάλιστα μὲν ὁμότιμον· εἰ δὲ

glory of God" [1 Cor 10:31]? But you do it to ill-report and dishonor. Don't you hear the prophet saying, "*Serve the Lord with fear, and rejoice in him with trembling*" [Ps 2:11]?[142] But you're dissipated. Surely it's possible both to have pleasure and to do it with safety? Do you want to hear beautiful songs? Best of all, you shouldn't. Still, I give in, if you want: don't hear satanic songs but spiritual ones. Do you want to see choirs of dancers? See the choir of angels. "And how is it possible," someone asks, "to see them?" If you drive away these things, even Christ will come to these weddings, and if Christ is present the choir of angels is present too. If you wish, he will now also work miracles, as he did too then [see John 2]. Now also he'll make water into wine, and in a much more miraculous way. He'll convert this dissipation, this unstable and cold desire, and change it into the spiritual. This is to make wine out of water. Where there are flutes, Christ is nowhere, but even if he were to enter, he first casts those people out and then performs miracles. What is more disagreeable than this satanic [**311**] pomp? Where everything is inarticulate, where everything is unintelligible? And if in fact there is something articulate, again everything is shameful, everything disagreeable.

Nothing is more pleasant than virtue, nothing sweeter than orderliness, nothing more longed for than dignity. Let anybody celebrate weddings, such as I speak of, and they will see the pleasure, but what kinds of weddings, take heed. First seek a husband for the virgin, who will be truly a husband and protector, as if you were going to place a head on a body, as if not going to hand over a slave, but a daughter to him. Don't seek money, or splendor of family, or greatness of country (all these things are peripheral), but piety of soul, gentleness, the true understanding, the fear of God, if you want your little daughter to live with pleasure. You see, if she seeks[143] a wealthier husband, not only will you not benefit her but you'll also cause harm, making her a slave instead of a free woman. For the pleasure she will reap from the pieces of gold won't be as great as the disagreeable situation that comes from being a slave. No, don't seek these things, but seek

---

142. Of course the psalmist David was not a prophet. In calling him so, Chrysostom is likely to have been influenced by Acts 2, where Pss 16:8–11 (Acts 2:25–28), 16:10 (Acts 2:31), and 100:1 (Acts 2:34–35) are quoted and attributed to David and where David himself is called a prophet. I am indebted to John Fitzgerald for this insight.

143. If the text is correct, suddenly the young woman is in command of the situation.

μὴ δυνατὸν, πενέστερον μᾶλλον, ἢ εὐπορώτερον, εἴγε μὴ ἀποδόσθαι δεσπότῃ, ἀλλ' ἐκδοῦναι ἀνδρὶ βούλει τὴν θυγατέρα. Ὅταν ἀκριβῶς ἐξετάσῃς τἀνδρὸς τὴν ἀρετὴν, καὶ μέλλῃς ἐκδιδόναι, παρακάλεσον τὸν Χριστὸν παραγενέσθαι· οὐ γὰρ ἐπαισχυνθήσεται· μυστήριόν ἐστι τῆς αὐτοῦ παρουσίας. Μάλιστα μὲν οὖν καὶ τότε παρακάλει, ὥστε μνηστῆρα τοιοῦτον δοῦναι. Μὴ γένῃ τοῦ παιδὸς τοῦ Ἀβραὰμ χείρων, ὃς εἰς τοσαύτην ἀποδημίαν πεμπόμενος, ᾔδει ἔνθα χρὴ καταφυγεῖν· διὸ καὶ πάντων ἐπέτυχεν. Ὅταν περιεργάζῃ καὶ ζητῇς τὸν ἄνδρα, εὔχου· εἰπὲ τῷ θεῷ, ὃν ἂν σὺ θέλῃς οἰκονόμησον· ἐγχείρισον αὐτῷ τὸ πρᾶγμα, καὶ τιμηθεὶς ταύτῃ παρὰ σοῦ τῇ τιμῇ ἀμείψεταί σε. Δύο δὴ ποιεῖν χρὴ, αὐτῷ τε ἐγχειρίζειν, καὶ τοιοῦτον ζητεῖν, οἷον αὐτὸς βούληται κόσμιον.

Ὅταν οὖν τοὺς γάμους ποιῇς, μὴ περιέλθῃς οἰκίας, κάτοπτρα καὶ ἱμάτια χρωμένη· οὐ γὰρ πρὸς ἐπίδειξιν τὸ πρᾶγμά ἐστιν, οὐδὲ εἰς πομπὴν εἰσάγεις τὸ θυγάτριον· ἀλλὰ φαιδρύνουσα τὴν οἰκίαν τοῖς ἐνοῦσι, κάλει γείτονας καὶ φίλους καὶ συγγενεῖς. Ὅσους ἂν οἶδας ἐπιεικεῖς, τούτους κάλει, καὶ τοῖς οὖσιν ἐπαρκεῖσθαι παραίνει. Μηδεὶς τῶν ἀπὸ τῆς ὀρχήστρας παρέστω· ἐκεῖ γὰρ δαπάνη περιττὴ καὶ ἄσχημος· κάλεσον τὸν Χριστὸν πρὸ τῶν ἄλλων ἁπάν-
[312]των. Οἶδας διὰ τίνος αὐτὸν καλέσεις; "Ὃς ἂν ποιήσῃ, φησὶν, ἑνὶ τούτων τῶν ἐλαχίστων, ἐμοὶ ἐποίησε." Μὴ νομίσῃς τὸ πρᾶγμα δυσάρεστον εἶναι, τὸ πένητας καλεῖν διὰ τὸν Χριστόν· δυσάρεστόν ἐστι πόρνας καλεῖν. Τὸ γὰρ πένητας καλεῖν, τοῦτο ἀφορμὴ πλούτου, ἐκεῖνο δὲ ἀνατροπῆς. Κόσμει τὴν νύμφην μὴ τούτοις τοῖς κοσμίοις τοῖς ἀπὸ τοῦ χρυσοῦ, ἀλλ' ἐπιεικείᾳ καὶ αἰδοῖ καὶ τοῖς συνήθεσιν ἱματίοις, ἀντὶ παντὸς κόσμου χρυσοῦ καὶ ἐμπλεγμάτων τὸ ἐρυθριᾶν, τὸ αἰσχύνεσθαι περιθεῖσα, καὶ τὸ μὴ ζητεῖν ἐκεῖνα. Μηδεὶς ἔστω θόρυβος, μηδεμία ταραχή· καλείσθω ὁ νυμφίος, δεχέσθω τὴν παρθένον. Τὰ ἄριστα καὶ τὰ δεῖπνα μὴ μέθης ἔστω πλήρη, ἀλλὰ πλησμονῆς μεθ' ἡδονῆς. Ὅρα πόσα ἐκ τούτου καλὰ, ὅταν ἴδωμεν τὰ ἐκείνων· ἐκ δὲ τῶν νῦν γινομένων γάμων, εἴγε γάμους, ἀλλὰ μὴ πομπὰς αὐτὰ δεῖ καλεῖν, ὅσα τὰ κακά. Διελύθησαν αἱ παστάδες, καὶ εὐθέως μέριμνα καὶ φόβος, μή τι παραπέσῃ τῶν κεχρημένων, καὶ διαδέχεται τὴν ἡδονὴν ἀθυμία ἄφορητος. Ἀλλ' αὕτη μὲν τῆς κηδεστρίας ἡ ἀγωνία· μᾶλλον δὲ οὐδὲ αὕτη ἀπήλλακται ἡ νύμφη· τὰ γοῦν μετὰ ταῦτα αὐτῆς τῆς νύμφης ἐστὶν ἅπαντα. Τὸ γὰρ ὁρᾶν καταλυόμενα ἅπαντα, ἀθυμίας ὑπόθεσις, τὸ ὁρᾶν ἔρημον τὴν οἰκίαν.

especially one of equal condition. But if this is impossible, you want rather a poorer man than one well-to-do, at least not giving her away to a master but giving your daughter to a husband. When you have closely examined the virtue of the man and are going to give her to him, beg Christ to be present, for he won't be ashamed: it is a mystery of his presence. Especially then even in the first instance beg him to provide such a suitor. Don't be inferior to the servant of Abraham [see Gen 24:10–41] who, when sent abroad on such a great mission, knew where he had to find recourse; accordingly, indeed, he obtained everything. When you are laboring and seeking a husband, pray: say to God "whomsoever you wish to provide." Put the matter into his hands, and he, being honored, will requite you with honor. Two things in fact it's necessary to do: to put the matter into his hands and to seek such an orderly person as he wishes.

When, then, you're preparing a wedding, don't go around from house to house, borrowing mirrors and garments, for the matter is not one of display, nor are you leading your little daughter into a procession—no, but making your house resplendent with what is in it, invite neighbors, and friends, and relatives. Invite all those you know to be of good character and advise them to be content with what there is. Let nobody from the orchestra be present, for the expense is superfluous and unbecoming. Invite Christ before all the rest. [312] Do you know the way to invite him? "The one who has done this to one of these least," he says, "has done it to me" [see Matt 25:45]. Don't reckon it to be an annoying thing to invite the poor for Christ's sake—to invite prostitutes is not pleasing. You see, to invite the poor is a means of wealth, but the other of ruin. Adorn the bride not with those ornaments that are made from gold, but with gentleness and modesty and the customary garments, instead of all golden ornament and braiding, arraying her in blushes, shamefaced, and not seeking those things. Let there be no uproar, no confusion; let the bridegroom be called, let him receive the virgin. Let the dinners and suppers not be full of drunkenness but of surfeit with pleasure. See how much good will come from this, when we observe those of the others. But from the marriages taking place now, if they *are* marriages (but one shouldn't call them processions), how many are the evils! The bridal chambers are broken up, and immediately there is worry and fear lest anything that has been borrowed be lost, and an intolerable melancholy takes the place of pleasure. But this distress belongs to the mother-in-law; no, rather the bride herself is not even free. At least everything after that belongs to the bride herself. For to see everything broken up is reason for sadness, to see the house empty.

Ἐκεῖ ὁ Χριστός, ἐνταῦθα ὁ Σατανᾶς· ἐκεῖ ἄδεια, ἐνταῦθα φροντίς· ἐκεῖ ἡδονὴ, ἐνταῦθα λύπη· ἐκεῖ δαπάνη, ἐνταῦθα οὐδὲν τοιοῦτον· ἐκεῖ ἀσχημοσύνη, ἐνταῦθα εὐκοσμία· ἐκεῖ φθόνος, ἐνταῦθα ἀφθονία· ἐκεῖ μέθη, ἐνταῦθα νῆψις, ἐνταῦθα σωτηρία, ἐνταῦθα σωφροσύνη. Ταῦτα δὴ πάντα ἐννοοῦντες, στήσωμεν τὸ κακὸν μέχρι τούτου, ἵνα ἀρέσωμεν τῷ θεῷ, καὶ τῶν ἐπηγγελμένων ἀγαθῶν τοῖς ἀγαπῶσιν αὐτὸν ἐπιτυχεῖν καταξιωθῶμεν, χάριτι καὶ φιλανθρωπίᾳ τοῦ κυρίου ἡμῶν Ἰησοῦ Χριστοῦ, μεθ' οὗ τῷ πατρὶ ἅμα τῷ ἁγίῳ πνεύματι δόξα, κράτος, τιμὴ, νῦν καὶ ἀεὶ καὶ εἰς τοὺς αἰῶνας τῶν αἰώνων. Ἀμήν.

There is Christ, here is Satan; there is cheerfulness, here worry; there is pleasure, here grief; here expense, there nothing of the kind; here is inde-corum, there modesty; here is envy, there no envy; here is drunkenness, there sobriety; here is salvation, here is chastity. Indeed, bearing in mind all these things, let's stop the evil forthwith, so that we may please God, and be counted worthy to obtain the good things promised to those who love him, by grace and loving-kindness of our Lord Jesus Christ, with whom to the Father, together with the Holy Spirit be glory, power, honor, now and forever and ever. Amen.

Bibliography

Texts and Translations

John Chrysostom

Des hl. Kirchenlehrers Johannes Chrysostomus, Erzbischofs von Konstantinopel, Kommentar zu den Briefen des hl. Paulus an die Philipper und Kolosser. Translated by Wenzel Stoderl. BK 45. Munich: Kösel & Pustet, 1924.

The Homilies of S. John Chrysostom, Archbishop of Constantinople, on the Epistles of St. Paul the Apostle to the Philippians, Colossians, and Thessalonians. Translated by John Ashworth. Oxford: Parker, 1843.

The Homilies of S. John Chrysostom, Archbishop of Constantinople, on the Epistles of St. Paul the Apostle to the Philippians, Colossians, and Thessalonians. Rev. ed. Translated by John A. Broadus. NPNF¹ 13:257–321.

Homily 12. Pages 73–80 in *St John Chrysostom: On Marriage and Family Life.* Translated by Catherine P. Roth and David Anderson. Crestwood, NY: St Vladimir's Seminary Press, 1986.

Huit catéchèses baptismales inédites. Edited by Antoine Wenger. SC 50. Paris: Cerf, 1970.

In epistulam ad Colossenses homiliae 1–12. PG 62:299–392.

In omnes Pauli epistolas acuratissima vereque aurea et divina interpretatio: Veronae; typis aereis excusum per Stephanum et fratres a Sabio, quarto Kal. Jul. 1529. 4 tomes in 2 vols. Edited by Bernardino Donato. Verona, 1529.

John Chrysostom, Homilies on Paul's Letter to the Philippians. Translated by Pauline Allen. WGRW 16. Atlanta: Society of Biblical Literature, 2013.

Œuvres complètes de Saint Jean Chrysostome: Traduction nouvelle. Vol. 10. Translated by Abbé J. Bareille. Paris: Vivès, 1873.

S. Johannis Chrysostomi opera omnia. Vol. 4. Edited by Henry Savile. Eton: Norton, 1612.

Sancti patris nostri Ioannis Chrysostomi archiepiscopi Constantinopolitani opera omnia quae extant, uel quae eius nomine circumferentur. Edited by Bernard de Montfaucon. 13 vols. Paris: Gaume Fratres Bibliopolas, 1718–1738.

ADDITIONAL AUTHORS AND TEXTS

Ambrosiaster. *Ambrosiaster's Commentary on the Pauline Epistles: Romans*. Translated by Theodore S. De Bruyn, Stephen A. Cooper, and David G. Hunter. WGRW 41. Atlanta: SBL Press, 2017.

———. *Ambrosiastri qui dicitur Commentarius in epistulas Paulinas*. Edited by Henricus I. Vogels. 3 vols. CSEL 81. Vienna: Hoelder–Pichler–Temsky, 1966–1969.

Oecumenius. *On Revelation*. Pages 1–107 in *Greek Commentaries on Revelation: Oecumenius and Andrew of Samosata*. Translated by William C. Weinrich. Edited by Thomas C. Oden. ACT. Downers Grove, IL: IVP Academic, 2011.

Pelagius. *Expositiones xiii epistularum Pauli*. 2 vols. Edited by Alexander Souter. TS. Repr., Nendeln, Lichtenstein: Kraus Reprint, 1967.

Severian of Gabala. *Fragmenta in epistulas s. Pauli*. Edited by Karl Staab. Pages 314–28 in *Pauluskommentare aus der griechischen Kirche aus Katenenhandschriften gesammelt und herausgegeben*. NTAbh 15. Münster: Verlag der Aschendorffschen Verlagsbuchhandlung, 1933.

Theodore of Mopsuestia. *Commentarii in epistulas Pauli minores*. Edited by Henry B. Swete. Pages 253–310 in *Theodori episcopi Mopsuesteni in epistolas b. Pauli commentarii* (*The Latin Version with the Greek Fragments*), *Galatians–Colossians*. Vol. 1. Cambridge: Cambridge University Press, 1882.

———. *Theodore of Mopsuestia: The Commentaries on the Minor Epistles of Paul*. Translated by Rowan A. Greer. WGRW 26. Atlanta: Society of Biblical Literature, 2010.

Theodoret of Cyrrhus. *Interpretatio in xii epistulas s. Pauli*. Edited by Charles Marriott. Pages 68–95 in vol. 2 of *Commentarius in omnes b. Pauli epistolas*. Oxford: Parker, 1870.

———. *Interpretatio in xii epistulas s. Pauli*. PG 82:36–877.

———. *Theodoret of Cyrus: Commentary on the Letters of St. Paul*. Vol. 2. Translated by Robert Charles Hill. Brookline, MA: Holy Cross Orthodox Press, 2001.

Theophylact of Ochrid. *Commentarius in epistolam ad Colossenses.* PG 124:1207–78.

Secondary Works

Aasgaard, Reidar. "Uncovering Children's Culture in Late Antiquity: The Testimony of the Infancy Gospel of Thomas." Pages 1–28 in *Children in Late Ancient Christianity.* Edited by Cornelia B. Horn and Robert R. Phenix. STAC 58. Tübingen: Mohr Siebeck, 2009.

Alexiou, Margaret. *The Ritual Lament in Greek Tradition.* Cambridge: Cambridge University Press, 1974.

Allen, Pauline, and Wendy Mayer. "Chrysostom and the Preaching of Homilies in Series: A New Approach to the Twelve Homilies *In epistulam ad Colossenses* (CPG 4433)." *OCP* 60 (1994): 21–39.

———. "Chrysostom and the Preaching of Homilies in Series: A Re-examination of the Fifteen Homilies *In epistulam ad Philippenses* (CPG 4432)." *VC* 49 (1995): 270–89.

Allen, Pauline, and Bronwen Neil. *Greek and Latin Letters: The Christianisation of a Literary Form.* Cambridge: Cambridge University Press, 2020.

Allen, Pauline, Bronwen Neil, and Wendy Mayer. *Preaching Poverty in Late Antiquity: Perceptions and Realities.* AKT 28. Leipzig: Evangelische Verlagsanstalt, 2009.

Arnold, Clinton E. *The Colossian Syncretism: The Interface between Christianity and Folk Belief at Colossae.* WUNT 2/77. Tübingen: Mohr Siebeck, 1995.

Bady, Guillaume. "La tradition des œuvres de Jean Chrysostome, entre transmission et transformation." *REByz* 68 (2010): 149–63.

Bauer, Chrysostomus. *Johannes Chrysostomus und seine Zeit.* 2 vols. Munich: Hueber, 1929–1930.

———. *John Chrysostom and His Time.* 2 vols. Translated by M. Gonzaga. Westminster, MD: Newman, 1959–1960.

Bonsdorff, Max von. "Zur Predigtätigkeit des Johannes Chrysostomus, biographisch-chronologische Studien über seine Homilienserien zu neutestamentlichen Büchern." Diss., Helsinki, 1922.

Cook, James Daniel. *Preaching and Popular Christianity: Reading the Sermons of John Chrysostom.* OTRM. Oxford: Oxford University Press, 2019.

Cribiore, Raffaella. *Libanius the Sophist: Rhetoric, Reality, and Religion in the Fourth Century.* TL/CSCP. Ithaca, NY: Cornell University Press, 2013.

Doty, William G. *Letters in Primitive Christianity.* GBS. Philadelphia: Fortress, 1973.

Druet, François-Xavier. *Langage, images et visages de la mort chez Jean Chrysostome.* CEC 3. Namur: Société des Études classiques/Presses universitaires, 1990.

Elmer, Ian J. "The Pauline Letters as Community Documents." Pages 37–53 in *Collecting Early Christian Letters: From the Apostle Paul to Late Antiquity.* Edited by Bronwen Neil and Pauline Allen. Cambridge: Cambridge University Press, 2015.

Finn, Douglas. "Job as Exemplary Father according to John Chrysostom." *JECS* 26 (2018): 275–305.

Finn, Richard. *Almsgiving in the Later Roman Empire: Christian Promotion and Practice 313–450.* Oxford: Oxford University Press, 2008.

Fitzgerald, John T. "Paul, Wine in the Ancient Mediterranean World, and the Problem of Intoxication." Pages 331–56 in *Paul's Graeco-Roman Context.* Edited by Cilliers Breytenbach. BETL 277. Leuven: Peeters, 2015.

Golden, Mark. "Did the Ancients Care When Their Children Died?" *GR* 2/35 (1988): 152–63.

Goodall, Blake. *The Homilies of St. John Chrysostom on the Letters of St. Paul to Titus and Philemon: Prolegomena to an Edition.* UCPCS 20. Berkeley: University of California Press, 1979.

Grubbs, Judith Evans, Tim Parkin, and Roslynne Bell, eds. *The Oxford Handbook of Childhood and Education in the Classical World.* Oxford: Oxford University Press, 2013.

Guinot, Jean-Noël. *L'Exégèse de Théodoret de Cyr.* ThH 100. Paris: Beauchesne, 1995.

Heiser, Andreas. *Die Paulusinszenierung des Johannes Chrysostomus Epitheta und ihre Vorgeschichte.* STAC 70. Tübingen: Mohr Siebeck, 2012.

Horn, Cornelia B., and Robert R. Phenix, eds. *Children in Late Ancient Christianity.* STAC 58. Tübingen: Mohr Siebeck, 2009.

Illert, Martin. *Johannes Chrysostomus und das antiochenisch-syrische Mönchtum: Studien zur Theologie, Rhetorik und Kirchenpolitik im antiochenischen Schrifttum des Johannes Chrysostomus.* Zürich: Pano, 2000.

Ivanovska, Inta. "Baptized Infants and Pagan Rituals: Cyprian versus Augustine." Pages 45–71 in *Children in Late Ancient Christianity.*

Edited by Cornelia B. Horn and Robert R. Phenix. STAC 58. Tübingen: Mohr Siebeck, 2009.

Junod, Éric. "Wodurch unterscheiden sich die Homilien des Origenes von seinen Kommentaren?" Pages 50–81 in *Predigt in der Alten Kirche*. Edited by Ekkehard Mühlenberg and Johannes van Oort. Kampen: Kok Pharos, 1994.

Kelly, John N. D. *Golden Mouth: The Story of John Chrysostom—Ascetic, Preacher, Bishop*. London: Duckworth, 1995.

Klauck, Hans-Josef, with the collaboration of Daniel P. Bailey. *Ancient Letters and the New Testament: A Guide to Context and Exegesis*. Waco: Baylor University Press, 2006.

Konstan, David. *Friendship in the Classical World*. KTAH. Cambridge: Cambridge University Press, 1997.

Laes, Christian, and Ville Vuolanto, eds. *Children and Everyday Life in the Roman and Late Antique World*. London: Routledge, 2016.

Leyerle, Blake. "Appealing to Children." *JECS* 5 (1997): 243–70.

———. "Children and 'the Child' in Early Christianity." Pages 559–79 in *The Oxford Handbook of Childhood and Education in the Classical World*. Edited by Judith Evans Grubbs, Tim Parkin, and Roslynne Bell. Oxford: Oxford University Press, 2013.

———. "'Keep Me, Lord, as the Apple of Your Eyes': An Early Christian Child's Amulet." *JECS* 3 (2013): 73–93.

———. *Theatrical Shows and Ascetic Lives: John Chrysostom's Attack on Spiritual Marriage*. Berkeley: University of California Press, 2001.

Malingrey, Anne-Marie. *Philosophia: Études d'un groupe de mots dans la littérature grecque des Présocratiques au IVe siècle après J.C.* Paris: Éditions Klincksieck, 1961.

Markus, Robert A. *The End of Ancient Christianity*. Cambridge: Cambridge University Press, 1990.

Maxwell, Jaclyn L. *Christianization and Communication in Late Antiquity: John Chrysostom and His Congregation in Antioch*. Cambridge: Cambridge University Press, 2006.

Mayer, Wendy. *The Homilies of St John Chrysostom—Provenance: Reshaping the Foundations*. OrChrAn 273. Rome: Pontificio Istituto Orientale, 2005.

Mayer, Wendy, and Pauline Allen. *The Churches of Syrian Antioch (300–638 CE)*. LAHR. Leuven: Peeters, 2012.

———. *John Chrysostom*. ECF. London: Routledge, 2000.

————. "John Chrysostom." Pages 1054–71 in *The Early Christian World*. 2nd ed. Edited by Philip F. Esler. London: Routledge, 2017.

McKinnon, James. "The Meaning of the Patristic Polemic against Musical Instruments." *CurMus*1 (1965): 69–82.

Metzger, Bruce M. *A Textual Commentary on the Greek New Testament*. London: United Bible Societies, 1971.

Mitchell, Margaret M. *The Heavenly Trumpet: John Chrysostom and the Art of Pauline Interpretation*. Louisville: Westminster John Knox, 2002.

————. "Pauline Accommodation and 'Condescension' (συγκατάβασις): 1 Cor 9:19–23 and the History of Influence." Pages 197–214 in *Paul beyond the Judaism/Hellenism Divide*. Edited by Troels Engberg-Pedersen. Louisville: Westminster John Knox, 2001.

————. "Silver Chamber Pots and Other Goods Which Are Not Good: John Chrysostom's Discourse against Wealth and Possessions." Pages 88–121 in *Having Property and Possession in Religious and Social Life*. Edited by William Schweiker and Charles T. Mathewes. Grand Rapids: Eerdmans, 2004.

————. "A Variable and Many-Sorted Man: John Chrysostom's Treatment of Pauline Inconsistency." *JECS* 6 (1998): 93–111.

Müller, Hildegund, and Michael Fiedrowicz. "Enarrationes in psalmos." Pages 804–58 in *Augustinus-Lexikon*. Vol. 2. Edited by Cornelius Mayer. Basel: Schwabe, 1996–2002.

Mullett, Margaret. *Theophylact of Ochrid: Reading the Letters of a Byzantine Archbishop*. BBOM 2. Ashgate, UK: Aldershot, 1997.

Olivar, Alexandre. *La predicación cristiana antigua*. BHSTF 189. Barcelona: Editorial Herder, 1991.

Page, Christopher. *The Christian West and Its Singers*. New Haven: Yale University Press, 2010.

Paverd, Frans van de. *Geschichte der Messliturgie in Antiocheia und Konstantinopel gegen Ende des vierten Jahrhunderts: Analyse der Quellen bei Johannes Chrysostomos*. OrChrAn 187. Rome: Pontificium Institutum Orientalium Studiorum, 1970.

————. *St John Chrysostom, the Homilies on the Statues: An Introduction*. OrChrAn 239. Rome: Pontificio Istituto Orientale, 1991.

Piédagnel, André, ed. *Panégyriques de saint Paul*. SC 300. Paris: Cerf, 1982.

Poliakoff, Michael B. "Jacob, Job, and Other Wrestlers: Reception of Greek Athletics by Jews and Christians in Antiquity." *JSH* 11 (1984): 48–65.

Rebillard, Éric. *The Care of the Dead in Late Antiquity.* Translated by Elizabeth Trapnell Rawlings and Jeanine Routier-Pucci. CSCP 59. Ithaca, NY: Cornell University Press, 2009.

Richter, Gerhard. *Oikonomia: Der Gebrauch des Wortes Oikonomia im Neuen Testament, bei den Kirchenvätern und in der theologischen Literatur bis ins 20. Jahrhundert.* AK 90. Berlin: de Gruyter, 2008.

Rylaarsdam, David. *John Chrysostom on Divine Pedagogy: The Coherence of His Theology and Preaching.* OECS. Oxford: Oxford University Press, 2014.

Sandwell, Isabella. *Religious Identity in Late Antiquity: Greeks, Jews and Christians in Antioch.* GCRW. Cambridge: Cambridge University Press, 2007.

Wet, Chris L. de. *Preaching Bondage: John Chrysostom and the Discourse of Slavery in Early Christianity.* Oakland: University of California Press, 2015.

Wet, Chris L. de, and Wendy Mayer, eds. *Revisioning John Chrysostom: New Approaches, New Perspectives.* CAEC 1. Leiden: Brill, 2019.

Wiles, Maurice F. *The Divine Apostle: The Interpretation of St Paul's Epistles in the Early Church.* Cambridge: Cambridge University Press, 1967.

Wilken, Robert W. *John Chrysostom and the Jews: Rhetoric and Reality in the Late Fourth Century.* TCH 4. Berkeley: University of California Press, 1983.

Index of Biblical Works

GENERAL INDEX

CPSIA information can be obtained
at www.ICGtesting.com
Printed in the USA
FSHW011253051021
85191FS